Critical Acclaim for

WITH GOD ON OUR SIDE

"This book will show the skeptical how simple hometown revivals mushroom into massive movements, how grass-roots organizations grow into influential institutions, and how religious conservatism blossomed from not one but several roots in American history . . . This volume is essential reading for scholars and voters who want to view religious conservatism for what it is."
—HOUSTON CHRONICLE

"Martin astutely examines the personalities, organizations, and galvanizing events that have energized this potent voting bloc."
—BOOKLIST

"*With God on Our Side* is a model of conscientious scholarship and readability—and an invaluable resource for all concerned with religion and public life."
—DETROIT NEWS

"Martin leaves one with heightened concern for the future of religious tolerance in America . . . Both reformers and religious conservatives should find in this penetrating narrative some incentive to work to maintain 'the pluralism that has served us so well.' "
—KIRKUS REVIEWS

"A tour de force of journalistic balance and historical depth."
—PUBLISHERS WEEKLY

"Regardless of how one feels about fundamentalism and the fundamentalists, whether one is with them or against them—and fundamentalists don't allow any middle ground—this is an important book, mostly fair, engaging, and eye-opening. Think of it . . . as part of the story of our times, a window to look in upon ourselves."
—AMERICAN WAY

ALSO BY WILLIAM MARTIN

These Were God's People: A Layman's Bible History

Christians in Conflict

A Prophet with Honor: The Billy Graham Story

My Prostate and Me: Dealing with Prostate Cancer

WITH GOD
ON
OUR SIDE

THE RISE OF THE
RELIGIOUS RIGHT IN AMERICA

William Martin

BROADWAY BOOKS *New York*

To the sons, daughter, and spouses
of our traditional family
Rex and Mary, Jeff and Suzanne, Dale and Rupert

A hardcover edition of this book was published in 1996 by Broadway Books. First trade paperback edition published 1997. Revised trade paperback edition published 2005.

PRINTED IN THE UNITED STATES OF AMERICA

BROADWAY BOOKS and its logo, a letter B bisected on the diagonal, are trademarks of Random House, Inc.

Visit our Web site at www.broadwaybooks.com

Book design by Julie Duquet

The Library of Congress has cataloged the hardcover edition as follows:
Martin, William C. (William Curtis), 1937–
With God on our side : the rise of the religious right in
America / William Martin. — 1st ed.
p.   cm.
Includes bibliographical references and index.
1. Evangelism—United States—Controversial literature.
2. Fundamentalism—Controversial literature.
3. Conservatism—United States—Controversial literature.
4. Christianity and politics. I. Title.
BR1642.U5M37   1996
261.8—dc20   96-2919
                                                       CIP

ISBN 0-7679-2257-3

1 3 5 7 9 10 8 6 4 2

CONTENTS

AUTHOR'S NOTE *vii*

INTRODUCTION: A Righteous Empire *1*

1 Billy Graham—Geared to the Times *25*

2 Warfare of the Spirit *47*

3 A Man on Horseback *74*

4 The Battle of Anaheim *100*

5 Culture War *117*

6 Born Again *144*

7 We—Some of Us—Are Family *168*

8 Moral Majority *191*

9 Prophets and Advisers *221*

10 The Untouchables *238*

11 The Invisible Army *258*

12 Christian Coalition *299*

13 And Who Shall Lead Them? *329*

EPILOGUE: Up Against the Wall *371*

AFTERWORD: A Permanent Fixture on the American
Political Landscape *387*

ENDNOTES *394*

INDEX *415*

AUTHOR'S NOTE

This book is the companion volume to a PBS television documentary series of the same name. Since anyone who sees the series will recognize immediately that the book is neither a script nor transcript of the program, it may be helpful to explain the relationship between them.

The documentary project was conceived by Calvin Skaggs, President of Lumiere Productions, and David Van Taylor. Because of my research and writing about evangelical and fundamentalist Christians, religious broadcasting, and the participation of religious conservatives in the political arena, I was invited to write the companion volume. In general, the book tracks the documentary series' story of the rise of the Religious Right, though almost always at greater length. In most cases, the words of interviewees are presented more fully in the book than in the series. Conversely, the extensive archival footage taken from film and television news clips and from productions of various religious, political, and educational organizations are almost always more vivid than can easily be communicated by the written word. It is probably most accurate to think of the book and the television series as two different, but closely coordinated and complementary, products based on the same body of material.

Lumiere Productions is headquartered in New York. I wrote the book at our home in Wimberley, Texas, during an eighteen-month leave from the Department of Sociology at Rice University in Houston. Though I met with the Lumiere team on several occasions and communicated regularly and extensively by telephone and fax, the predominant mode of our interaction, including transfer of interview transcripts, research notes, and manuscript, has been via the Internet. This has seemed particularly appropriate, both because the Net was originally established as a means of facilitating collaboration among scholars in far-flung locations, and also because the objects of our study have proven themselves to be masters of the technology of data management and communication. I was given the opportunity to respond to "rough cuts" of the various episodes of the series, and members of the Lumiere staff reviewed drafts of my chapters for accuracy, emphasis, and tone. To what I believe is our shared great pleasure, substantial disagreement was virtually nonexistent.

As I trust viewers and readers will quickly discern, neither the documentary nor this book takes an adversarial approach. Our mutual aim has been to represent, as accurately and fairly as we are able, the views and statements of those who have graciously agreed to cooperate in this project. They may, of course, be surprised at our interpretation or at the way their words appear and sound in a larger context. We do not claim infallible insight, but we fully trust that none will feel they have been misquoted or had their statements inappropriately applied. Some expressed just such a fear in the course of the interviews. A small number, most notably Dr. James Dobson and Bill Bright, declined to participate in the project, for fear of having their words misrepresented or misconstrued. We regret that decision, because we feel it is a loss to the historical record.

We have chosen, in the title of the documentary series and this book, to speak of the movement we describe as the Religious Right. It is not a perfect term, since its use by the movement's detractors has created, at least in the perception of some, a negative connotation. After much deliberation, we have used it as the term with the widest recognition in the general population. In the early years of the movement, its own members used the term to speak of themselves, as a way of distinguishing themselves slightly from their ideological forebears, the self-described New Right. In recent years, as the movement has gained detractors and the term therefore has become less neutral in connotation in some quarters, members of the movement have preferred to call themselves religious or Christian conservatives, or simply the "pro-family" movement. I use all of these terms in the book, following a general policy of calling people what they prefer to be called. But since they are religious, and since their political views do, in fact, nestle safely on the right side of the political spectrum in this country, I find no serious fault with the term, nor mean to use it in any sense other than a descriptive one.

Perhaps the most distinctive characteristic of this project has been the obtaining of more than a hundred extensive interviews with people who have been major participants in the various stories we tell.

A careful listener and reader may occasionally detect slight differences between an interviewee's words as presented in the films and the book. Two factors account for almost all such minor differences. First, it seemed both unnecessary and unwise to include most instances of "uh," "um," and "you know," as well as the false starts, back-pedaling, and retakes that are part of most human conversation. A verbatim transcript of what one may regard as a polished discourse can be humiliating when reproduced faithfully in print. Similarly, I have chosen not to reproduce occasional mispronunciations, and when the intended word was quite obvious, I have as a matter of courtesy used it rather than reproduce the mispronounced or malappropriate word, and highlight it with a condescending [sic].

A second factor stems from the nature of the interview process itself. Interviewees routinely participated in lengthy telephone pre-interview, as a way to determine what they knew and were willing to talk about on camera. During the filmed interviews themselves, they were often asked to restate a comment just made, to emphasize a given point or to render an observation more concisely, to heighten its chance of being used in the documentary. Since, unless explicitly noted, all these comments were on the record, I felt free to draw upon the alternative versions occasionally, although in no instance have I used a quotation whose meaning is inconsistent with an ostensibly parallel version, if indeed such examples exist in the materials.

Because such a large portion of the book is based on original interviews, most conducted by the Lumiere production staff, but some by me, in connection with my earlier book, *A Prophet with Honor: The Billy Graham Story,* I have elected not to provide footnotes for material taken from these interviews. On rare occasions, when an interviewee may have a valuable comment to make on a given situation, but is not really a part of the story or has not yet been introduced to the reader, he or she is identified simply as, for example, "a knowledgeable observer" or "a moderate Republican." In such cases, a footnote provides the identity of the speaker. In all other cases, unless a footnote specifically indicates otherwise, all statements by characters in the story are taken from interviews with those individuals. A listing of interviewees is provided at the beginning of the footnotes section.

FAR MORE THAN any research project in which I have ever participated, this has truly been a collaborative process, in which all participants have shared their talents, resources, and insights. I have used my own files and drawn upon years of acquaintance with the people and organizations I discuss, and, with the exception of minor editorial emendations, have written all the words. But this book would not have come into being, at least not for several years, without the enormous and deeply appreciated contribution of the Lumiere staff, whom I now regard as valued colleagues. It is customary in forewords to absolve one's colleagues of all mistakes that might appear in the final product. To do that in this case might be presumptuous, since Lumiere researchers provided me with such mountains of materials, often including their own condensations of books, articles, and pre-interview conversations. We have checked and rechecked each other's assertions of fact so many times and so thoroughly, however, that I trust the number of errors has been greatly reduced, rather than multiplied, by the number of participants.

I gratefully acknowledge my debt to Cal Skaggs, executive producer of the documentary series, for having entrusted me with the task of writing the book, for offering his constant support and counsel, and, not least, for his warm friendship. Cal, series producer David Van Taylor, and producers Jerret Engle and Bennett Singer were invaluable in helping me understand the contours of the individual series episodes for which they had primary responsibility. In addition, Bennett Singer provided sustained and often truly remarkable assistance in his role as coordinator of publications, making sure that I received research materials in a timely fashion, obtaining answers to hundreds of research questions, seeing to it that drafts of chapters were read and returned quickly, and that the finished product made it to the publisher in good order. Associate producers LaShaune Fitch, Brad Lichtenstein, and Ali Pomeroy did massive amounts of background research, responded quickly to my requests for additional materials, and offered helpful feedback on early drafts of the manuscript. Associate producer Lynn Mirabito assisted in research and response to queries, supervised interns, and handled much of the work involved in getting permission to use copyrighted materials. The assembling of archival footage for the television series, another marvelous resource, was directed by Lewanne Jones. Assistant editors Gretchen Schwartz and Jason Boughton provided me with transcripts of all interviews and with rough cuts of various episodes. Jason Bowen, Lina Cheung, and Claudia Gorelick performed additional library research. And, performing a critical role at the end of the process, David Deschamps displayed astonishing competence, thoroughness, and tenacity in checking the accuracy of every assertion of fact and every footnote reference.

The Lumiere team and I were greatly assisted by advice and feedback from a distinguished advisory group that included Chip Berlet, Research Fellow at Political Research Associates of Cambridge, Massachusetts; Michael Cromartie, Senior Fellow at the Ethics and Public Policy Center in Washington; distinguished journalist Frances FitzGerald; John Green, Director of the Ray C. Bliss Institute of Applied Politics at the University of Akron; anthropologist Susan Harding, of the University of California at Santa Cruz; historian George Marsden of the University of Notre Dame; and historian Leo Ribuffo of George Washington University.

At Rice University, Scott Ruthfield regularly retrieved, read, summarized, or sent materials from the library. Former students Peggy Dun Haney and Andrea Johnson assisted with additional research and transcribing of dictated research notes. Their assistance was made possible by a grant from the Center for the Study of Institutions and Values, affiliated with the James A. Baker III Institute for Public Policy at Rice University. Rita Loucks, departmental coordinator for the Department of Sociology, handled printing and periodic storage of back-up versions of the manuscript and, more importantly, served as a lifeline to the department and the university. And, of course, I sincerely appreciate the encouragement of my chairman, Chandler Davidson, and the administration of Rice University for granting me the leave of absence that made it possible for me to write the book.

I am, as always, deeply grateful to my literary agent, Gerard McCauley, who learned of the television project and arranged my introduction to Cal Skaggs and who, with Cal's agent, Virginia Barber, handled the contact with Broadway Books, a division of Bantam Doubleday Dell Publishing Group, Inc. My association with Broadway Books has been a complete delight. My editors John Sterling and Victoria Andros have been encouraging, trusting, and patient, even when we got within hours of deadlines that I came to believe truly were final. Because the work was done under stringent time pressures, in order to have the book ready when the television series aired, their unflagging support, even when tinged with justified anxiety, was truly a blessing. I also owe a debt to Nancy Peske, who copyedited the manuscript until the day before her wedding, and to Rebecca Holland, who oversaw production of the book, a task made more difficult by my using up every possible moment of time allotted for unforeseen delays.

Finally, I proclaim my love and gratitude for Patricia, from whom I was apart more than I had intended or wanted to be while writing the book. After thirty-eight years of marriage, I am no longer surprised at the uncomplaining patience, steadfast encouragement, and loving companionship she manifests when I am deeply immersed in a project, but not for a moment do I fail to recognize the value of such a treasure.

INTRODUCTION

A RIGHTEOUS EMPIRE

It is no simple matter to decide just where a history of the Religious Right should begin. This book focuses primarily on the period from 1960 forward, but the New Christian Right, as the movement is also known, is the lineal descendant of an older Christian Right whose roots run back to the early years of the twentieth century. Understanding that movement requires some sense of what it inherited from its predecessors, and any discussion of foundational religious influences inevitably leads Americans all the way back to the Puritans. While we cannot do justice to these shaping influences, we can at least acknowledge some of the main ones.

Historians of American culture vary in their affection and admiration for the Puritans, but few fail to recognize their profound and apparently permanent effect on American culture. Based on their reading of the Old Testament, the Puritans believed that the only divinely ordained form of civil or religious government was one in which qualified individuals voluntarily entered into an explicit covenant firmly grounded in Scripture. Members of such covenant communities would answer not to monarch or pope or bishop or ecclesiastical council, but only to each other and, always and awefully, to God. If they kept their end of the bargain, they expected God to bless them and earthly governors to treat them fairly. If they fell short, they understood that punishment would be their due. The other member of the covenant (or compact or contract) was similarly bound by its terms. God, of course, would never back down on a promise, but earthly rulers might. If that happened, if the government failed to honor its obligations, it thereby lost its legitimacy and could be resisted. Indeed, if its errors were sufficiently grievous, faithful Christians were obliged to resist it.

Puritan towns were not theocracies. Ministers could not hold civil office and magistrates had no jurisdiction over doctrine or criteria for church membership. Still, the overlap of interests and personnel was considerable, since only church members could vote and all agreed that a pure church was essential to a godly society, the goal toward which they should strive. The Puritans were strongly inclined to think of themselves as a people explicitly chosen of God to create a City upon a Hill, a New Israel, a Redeemer Nation raised up for all humankind to behold and emulate. Still, they harbored no illusions about personal perfection, but regarded themselves and all others as deeply flawed creatures whose only hope of salvation was God's unfathomable grace.

This combination of covenantal thinking, conviction of divine mission, and profound awareness of human fallibility have marked American political institutions and movements from the Mayflower Compact to the Declaration of Independence and the Constitution, through the New Deal and New Frontier and Great Society, to the rise of the Moral Majority and the Christian Coalition and the construction of the Republican Party's 1994 Contract with America. The Declaration of Independence proclaimed that Americans were free to revolt against England and to form a new government because the king had abused the freedoms and rights granted them by "the Laws of Nature and of Nature's God." The Constitution, reflecting a pervasive sense of human imperfection, provided for a division of functions and a system of checks and balances that would keep selfish and ambitious parties from gaining excessive power, placed strict limits on what the government could legitimately do, and delineated a set of rights designed to protect minorities against both government authority and the tyranny of majorities.

Throughout the nation's history, its people have repeatedly asserted that, despite the corruption of the current government and the dissolute and ever-worsening moral and spiritual state of the populace, the Newest Covenant they were prepared to implement could help America regain its rightful position as "the last, best hope of earth." Other nations and disputing factions within this nation have viewed such assertions as näive or arrogant or both, but they do not seem in danger of disappearing.

Though its influence was felt elsewhere, true Puritanism was primarily a New England phenomenon, and even in Massachusetts and Connecticut, the piety and fervor that reminded famed cleric John Cotton of "the New Heaven and the New Earth" soon declined. Religious dissent and diversity increased, church membership shrank, and nonmembers complained at being denied full participation in civil government. Levels of devotion in other colonies were even lower and seemed unlikely to rise. Then, beginning in New Jersey in the 1730s, a profound religious revival historians have called the Great Awakening spread through the colonies, with its most marked manifestations occurring in New England under the preaching of Jonathan Edwards and British evangelist George Whitefield. The revival was, as numerous observers described it, "great and general," leading Edwards, like Cotton before him, to declare that the world could not be far away from "the dawn of that glorious day" when the millennium would begin and New England would take its place as the center of "a kind of heaven upon earth."

Despite its strength and momentum, revival gave way to revolution during the latter half of the eighteenth century and the progressive rationalism and optimism of the Enlightenment played a larger role in the thinking of most Founding Fathers than did biblical theology. Still, the changes Edwards and Whitefield and their colleagues had wrought in that brief, glorious period endured. Though the size of the Christian community did not change dramatically as a result of the revival, life within it did. In revivalist churches, power passed from the clergy to the laity. Instead of formal training and theological acumen, the test of leadership became the ability to appeal to the heart, to rouse men and women to seek salvation and a transformed life. Preachers attained authority and power in direct democratic fashion from the people who heard them preach and freely chose to accept or reject what they heard.

This new democratic, independent sensibility carried over to the revolutionary cause. Men and women who were convinced their direct relationship with God gave them the right and obligation to oppose any infringement on their religious liberties could easily transfer that same spirit of independence to the political realm. Consequently, they deemed illegitimate any authority they did not elect or that operated without their consent. Similarly, the Awakening generated millennial expectations that caused people to regard breaking free of England and founding a new republic not simply as a political experiment, but as part of God's great new work on earth.

During the decades that followed the American Revolution, many thoughtful observers concluded that American religion had seen its brightest day, that those who had predicted a secular Constitution would produce a godless nation had been correct. Revival fires had gone out in New England. On the southern and western frontiers, life was hard and rough and almost wholly lacking in the spiritual and cultural influences present in the East, and the mood within the churches was gloomy to the point of desperation. Supreme Court Chief Justice John Marshall wrote that the church in Virginia was "too far gone ever to be redeemed," and Voltaire and Thomas Paine gloated over the prospect that "Christianity will be forgotten in thirty years."

As the new century dawned, however, America experienced what historians have called the Second Great Awakening or, more simply, the Great Revival. The first phase of this revival, the southern and western camp meetings, turned the American South into perhaps the most distinctively and self-consciously religious region in Christendom. The second phase came remarkably close to achieving the evangelical dream of making America a Christian nation.

Once again, revival stirred millennial expectations, especially in the North, but its more immediately important theological product was a vigorous emphasis on "sanctification," often called "perfectionism." The belief that Christians should live sinless lives was pushed most strongly by the Methodists, but soon became a central preoccupation of all evangelical Christians. In its individualistic concern for personal piety and its opposition to such vices as alcohol, gambling, fornication, profanity, and dishonesty, perfectionism could exempt devout believers from feeling responsible for political decisions, economic policies, or such egregious social ills as slavery. It could also produce a narrow legalism and nearsighted hypocrisy. Still, the pervasive concern for purity helped civilize the frontier and encouraged pioneers to live sober and decent lives.

It is difficult to overstate the impact of the Great Revival on the development of Southern culture. Southern religion, which thoroughly permeated and informed Southern culture, was characterized by its absolute and unquestioning confidence in the Bible, its emphasis on piety and purity, and its unswerving dedication to the primary task of the revivals: the winning of lost souls. It tended to ignore or slight intellectual currents that might conflict with evangelical dogma, and to support slavery with the belief that the Bible sanctioned it. In recent decades, immigration, urbanization, industrialization, and a host of other forces have broken evangelicalism's tight grip on the region, but no attempt to understand the American South can hope to succeed if it does not recognize the truth in historian Kenneth K. Bailey's observation that "nowhere else, almost surely, is there a Protestant population of equal size so renowned for its piety or for its commitment to old-fashioned Scriptural literalism."

In the North, after a series of successful revivals in upstate New York and in major population centers along the Eastern Seaboard, Charles Finney came to New York City to help write a new, vital chapter in evangelical history and usher in a new phase of the Great Revival. During the first half of the nineteenth century, evangelical Christians were so convinced their efforts could ring in the millennium, a literal thousand years of peace and prosperity that would culminate in the glorious second advent of Christ, that they threw themselves into fervent campaigns to eradicate war, drunkenness, slavery, subjugation of women, poverty, prostitution, Sabbath-breaking, dueling, profanity, card-playing, and other impediments to a perfect society.

In the vanguard of these millennialists marched a phalanx of wealthy New York entrepreneurs and bankers calling themselves the Association of Gentlemen, and it was they who persuaded Finney to join their cause. Every subsequent major evangelist has enjoyed the patronage of wealthy business people who supported and encouraged his ministry as an instrument to accomplish religious and social goals they espoused. Since the Civil War, these "angels" have usually been conservatives hoping to return America to simpler, purer times. In marked contrast, the "Gentlemen" were genuine social radicals, and when Finney entered their circle, he became part of a progressive evangelical network whose closely knit members took leading roles in a linked chain of major ventures—a kind of "pious power elite" that would come to characterize evangelical Christianity.

Finney believed and preached that "the great business of the church is to reform the world—to put away every kind of sin," and that true Christians must be "useful in the highest degree possible" and are "bound to exert their influence to secure a legislation that is in accordance with the law of God." He asserted that new converts should set about immediately to improve their society and, in the process, to bring in the millennium. In a famous burst of optimism, he estimated that, if the church would only do her duty, "the millennium may come in this country in three years." It is no surprise that Finney's converts became active participants in most of the progressive social movements of their era. By the mid-nineteenth century, America had become, more fully than ever before or again, a Christian Republic, and the dominant expression of that Christianity was Protestant, evangelical, and revivalistic. Church membership stood at record levels, with virtually all the new growth occurring in evangelical ranks. Individuals and churches exposed to revival preaching were energized with new hopes, new drives, a sense of community with others of like belief, and a conviction they were engaged in a grand effort to save the republic and, with it, the world.

Driven by the desire to present their Heavenly Father with the Righteous Empire he obviously intended America to be, exuberant evangelicals pioneered the development of voluntary associations whose focused attention to single issues made them highly efficient instruments of reform. This kind of organization would still be a prominent feature of evangelicalism 150 years later. Evangelicals learned how to raise money, how to advertise and promote their enterprises, how to use Sunday schools to reach and instruct the children of unchurched parents, how to entertain people who eschewed most popular amusements, and, above all, how to use revival to swell and replenish their ranks. Such was the remarkable legacy of the Second Great Awakening.

As the nineteenth century wore on, however, evangelical Christianity began to stumble. Baptists, Methodists, and Presbyterians split over slavery, and the Civil War and Reconstruction left scars that have never disappeared from the body and soul of the nation. Ultimately more upsetting, however,

were the combined forces of industrialization, urbanization, and immigration, which replaced the relative homogeneity and social cohesion of an
earlier time with multiple subcultures divided by class, ethnicity, language,
and religion. Extensive immigration brought an influx of Jews, Roman
Catholics, and Orthodox Christians who weakened Protestant control of the
nation. Urbanism and an attendant increase in secularism also alarmed evangelical Protestant leaders. A growing interest by churches in social service,
often called the Social Gospel, undercut evangelicalism's traditional emphasis
on personal salvation.

Two challenges stood out above others as posing singular threats to the
then-dominant form of American Christianity. The first was the Darwinian
theory of evolution, which constituted a direct challenge not only to the
biblical account of creation, but also to traditional Christian understandings
of human nature and destiny, and even to theism itself. An even more
serious threat came in the form of historical criticism of the Bible. Imported
from German universities into American seminaries and pulpits, this approach challenged the inspiration and credibility of the entire corpus of
Scripture, the bedrock foundation of evangelical Christianity.

Many Protestants, including some from the revivalist tradition, adjusted to
these challenges. They set forth theories of "theistic evolution" and interpreted the "days" of the Genesis creation story as "ages" that were as long as
God needed to get the job done. They declared bravely that Christians need
not be discouraged by news that the Word of God was shot through with
internal contradictions, factual errors, and supernatural foolishness, since it
still contained an abundance of useful moral instruction that could be applied to the pressing social problems of the day. This accommodation often
included enthusiastic endorsement of the Social Gospel. In marked contrast,
most evangelicals chose to ignore, deny, or simply declare vigorously that
these "modernist" ideas could not be true, no matter what the evidence.
The Bible could be taken at face value, they insisted; it still said what it
meant and meant what it said. The old virtues were not dead and those who
adhered to them could still expect success and enjoy it when it came. The
poor, if they would work, could be rich; the rich, if they were kind and kept
their promises and avoided strong drink, need feel no shame that the Lord
had chosen to prosper them. The vehicle they used to deliver this reassuring
message to the new urban frontier was the same one they had used on other
frontiers: revival. And the men who epitomized anti-modernist revival for
nearly fifty years were Dwight Lyman Moody, whose triumphs came in the
1870s, and the Calliope of Zion, Billy Sunday, whose heyday came during
and immediately after World War I.

.   .   .

A NATIVE NEW Englander who established his early reputation as a YMCA worker and lay church leader—he was never ordained—in Chicago, and who went on to become the leading revivalist of his era, D. L. Moody subscribed to "dispensationalist premillennialism," a relatively new scheme of biblical interpretation that would have an incalculable impact on evangelical theology. The millennialism espoused by Finney included the näively optimistic belief that American society was improving so rapidly that God would soon bring ordinary history to a conclusion and inaugurate a thousand years of peace and prosperity, after which Christ would return to reign forever with his faithful saints. Because the Second Coming would occur after the millennium, this view was known as *post*millennialism. Premillennialists rejected this view, contending that the world was not getting better, and that the only real hope for Christians lay in Christ's coming back to transform a wicked creation and personally inaugurate the millennium—that is, his Second Coming would be *pre*millennial. This doctrine holds that careful attention to biblical prophecies, particularly those contained in the books of Ezekiel, Daniel, and Revelation, can yield clues as to approximately when Christ's second coming will occur, enabling those who possess this knowledge to be ready. In all versions, the relevant "signs of the times" are bad news—political anarchy, religious apostasy, increased wickedness, earthquakes, plagues, and the like. As a consequence, premillennialism has usually fared better in bad times than in good, because it offers believers a shining ray of hope in an otherwise dismal situation. It has also acted as a brake on reform efforts, since it regards such efforts as little better than fruitless attempts to thwart God's plan for human history.

Dispensationalism's distinctive contribution to premillennial thought was its positing of a series of distinct eras ("dispensations") in God's dealing with humanity. The triggering action for the beginning of the millennial age, the last dispensation, will be "the Rapture," at which point faithful Christians will be "caught up together to meet the Lord in the air," leaving the rest of humanity to face an unprecedented congeries of calamities known as "the tribulation." The main protagonist of the seven-year tribulation will be the Antichrist, who will seek total control by requiring every person to wear a mark or number (probably 666, "the mark of the beast" [Revelation 13:16–18]). The tribulation period will end with the Second Coming of Christ and the battle of Armageddon, to be followed by the millennium, the Final Judgment, and an eternity of bliss for the redeemed and agonizing punishment for the wicked.

One of the most important legacies of dispensationalism was its insistence on biblical "inerrancy." If Scripture is to provide a precise blueprint for understanding the present and predicting the future, dispensationalists held,

it must be absolutely reliable in all respects. Closely related to dispensationalism's emphasis on inerrant scripture was its encouragement of separation
from all forms of error. To be fit to ride the Rapturing cloud, one must
identify those whose doctrine is impure and "come out from among them,"
either joining some ostensibly untainted group or establishing a new and
independent body dedicated to impeccable belief and practice. In future
decades, this separatist tendency would become almost as intrinsic to Christian Fundamentalism as its commitment to biblical inerrancy.

Moody disagreed with some of the details of dispensationalism, but he
fully accepted the view that the world was rushing headlong toward moral
and social disaster, from which only the Second Coming and subsequent
millennial reign of Christ offered hope for the redeemed. The task, then,
was to help as many people as possible to prepare for that blessed event. In
perhaps the most frequently quoted of his observations, Moody said, "I have
felt like working three times as hard ever since I came to understand that my
Lord was coming back again. I look on this world as a wrecked vessel. God
has given me a lifeboat, and said to me, 'Moody, save all you can.' " Since he
realized the battle could not be won without more trained warriors, he
created the Chicago Evangelization Society, aimed at rapidly transforming
eager laymen into consecrated minutemen who would "stand in the gap"
for God, both at home and abroad. Later renamed the Moody Bible Institute
and characterized as the West Point of Christian Service, this school served
as a model for dozens of similar institutions and still exercises great influence
in Evangelical circles.

Other evangelists followed in Moody's train, some with notable success,
but the country's enthusiasm for revivals seemed clearly on the wane.
Churches began to question whether revivals actually produced much long-
term growth; evangelicals more attuned to the social gospel grew uncomfortable with the one-sided emphasis on personal morality; and many pious
souls were put off by the flamboyance and secular nature of evangelistic
services. In addition, some evangelists fell under suspicion because of excessive emphasis on collections and alleged inconsistencies between public and
private behavior. Those ready to pronounce itinerant evangelism terminally
ill, however, soon learned that the sound they heard in the distance was not a
dirge sung by mourners of the late revival tradition but the tooting and
blaring of "the Calliope of Zion," the Reverend Billy Sunday.

Billy Sunday grew up in Iowa, played baseball in the National League,
and found Jesus in Chicago by listening to a street preacher outside a saloon.
Still at the peak of a solid major league career, he left baseball in 1891 to
work full-time for the Chicago YMCA, where he came in contact with
some of Moody's friends. That led to a stint as advance man and manager for

a prominent evangelist, and ultimately to his own career as the premier revivalist of the first two decades of the twentieth century.

No theologian, Sunday was content to let others do his deep thinking. Though he peppered his sermons with jokes, mimicry, mockery, dialects, homey illustrations, and slangy outbursts that newspapers reprinted as "Sundayisms," he preached the same simple Gospel that the more dignified and serious Moody had proclaimed: "With Christ you are saved, without him you are lost. . . . You are going to live forever in heaven or you are going to live forever in hell. It's up to you and you must decide now."

His distaste for complexity extended beyond theology to the major intellectual problems that were racking fundamentalism at the time. Of biblical criticism, he concluded, "When the Word of God says one thing and scholarship says another, scholarship can go to hell." And of evolution, he ventured, "If by evolution you mean advance, I go with you, but if you mean by evolution that I came from a monkey, good night!" His attitude toward all forms of higher learning seems well-summarized in his observation that if he had a million dollars, he would give all but one dollar to the church, and the rest to education.

Sunday's meager theology made it possible for him to cooperate with most name-brand Protestant groups and avoid conflict with Catholics. As for Jews, he accepted the stereotype that "Jew blood means the capacity for making money," but spoke against the anti-Semitism some fundamentalists were fomenting. These conciliatory stances may have reflected a recognition of Catholic and Jewish social power more than a heartfelt ecumenism, since Sunday frequently displayed a narrow intolerance toward more marginal groups such as Mormons or Christian Scientists.

Sunday thought the Christian life required little more than adhering to dominant political and economic orthodoxies and upholding the moral standards of the Anglo-Saxon Protestant middle class. In all of these, he tried to set the proper example. In addition, he asserted that "there can be no religion that does not express itself in patriotism." To express his own patriotism during World War I, he appeared with Will Rogers at "Wake Up America" rallies, vehemently damned the Germans (even teaching children to hiss the German flag), encouraged young men to volunteer for the army, recommended jailing people who criticized President Woodrow Wilson and his policies, and, at the president's request, helped sell an estimated $100 million in Liberty Bonds. His economic views consisted of an unreflective espousal of laissez-faire free enterprise. He occasionally acknowledged the distortions unchecked capitalism had produced, but opposed any government interference and insisted that anyone who made a reasonable effort could succeed in America. He characterized the Social Gospel espoused by the new Federal Council of Churches (forerunner of the National Council of Churches) as "godless social service nonsense," un-American in motivation and result. His positive assessment of capital made him a darling of those well-endowed with it, and he counted among his friends and benefactors such names as Rockefeller, Morgan, Carnegie, Wanamaker, McCormick, Armour, Swift, Edison, and Marshall Field. It would be unfair, however, to see him simply as a tool in their hands, since he no doubt truly believed his pronouncements. Still, his wealthy backers must have found it comforting—and useful—to have the best-known religious figure in the nation championing economic principles that sanctioned their favored position in society.

Sunday's economic agenda may have been vaguely conceived, but he knew precisely what he wanted in the more obviously moral realm. He saw a once-strong, once-moral America as flabby and dissolute, consumed with lust, addicted to alcohol, sapped of courage, and unable to resist the evil that assailed from within and without. What the situation called for, he proclaimed, was real men, men who were strong and righteous, men whom women and children and other men could look upon as heroes, men who could lead and inspire; in short, men like Jesus Christ and Billy Sunday.

For the most part, Sunday's prescriptions amounted to little more than a kind of muscular perfectionism, with an emphasis on conquering such personal vices as illicit sex, profanity, smutty stories, a taste for pool halls and the theater, and, above all, the use of alcohol, which Sunday saw as the vilest of villainies, the source of war and crime. (Wherever he went, Sunday cooperated with Prohibitionist forces, and his "booze" sermon was often the high point of his revivals.) Renouncing these "manly" vices would not make a man a Milquetoast, but a fighting saint, a Christian soldier ready and willing to smite the enemy. By being pure and tough, Sunday asserted, the good people of America could regain control of their lives and their country. The crowds, who wanted a hero to show them it was possible to stand firm against the tides of secular modernity, loved it and looked to him as a symbol of the way they felt American life ought to be. Despite the scorn he drew from some religious and political critics, Sunday was unquestionably a national hero. Laudatory books about him became best-sellers, public-opinion polls regularly placed him high on the lists of Greatest Living Americans, national and state legislative bodies invited him to pray or speak at their assemblies, and presidents received him at the White House.

As Sunday rode the crest of his popularity, evangelical Christianity seemed to have regained its stride. Between 1910 and 1915, a widely distributed set of twelve volumes entitled *The Fundamentals: A Testimony to the Truth,* published by a press associated with Moody Bible Institute and financed by California oilmen Lyman and Milton Stewart, not only set forth basic doctrines in the words of some of the most respected men in the movement, but proved crucial in getting the name "Fundamentalist" established as the most common appellation for the conservative Protestant wing of the church. The term gained further currency by the founding, in 1919, of the World's Christian Fundamentals Association (WCFA) at a Philadelphia meeting attended by some 6,000 delegates and led by such notables as Sunday, New York preacher John Roach Straton, Paul Rader of Chicago, and William Bell Riley of Minneapolis. Fundamentalists of this period were fond of drawing up lists of "Fundamentals of the Faith," from which no deviation could be tolerated. The lists varied in length but most included the inerrancy of Scripture, the deity of Christ, the Virgin Birth, the substitutionary atonement (the belief that, by dying on the cross, the sinless Christ took upon himself the punishment rightly deserved by sinful humans), the resurrection, and the imminent return of Christ. The keystone was and is the inerrancy of Scripture, meaning not only that the Bible is the sole and infallible rule of faith and practice, but also that it is scientifically and historically reliable. Thus, evolution could not be true, miracles really did happen just as the Bible describes them, and on Judgment Day all who have ever lived will be assigned for eternity to heaven or hell, both of which really do exist. Any attempt to interpret these or other features of Scripture as myths or allegories strikes at the very root of Christian faith and must be resisted with every fiber of one's being.

World War I and the Bolshevik Revolution of 1917 provided fundamentalism with what was to become one of its major elements: religious nationalism. Sunday, Riley, and other fundamentalist leaders declared that Satan himself was directing the German war effort, and hinted strongly that it was part of the same process that had begun with the development of biblical criticism in German universities. Modernism, they asserted, had turned Germany into a godless nation, and would do the same thing to America. The combination of prewar nativism, war-heightened patriotism, the rise of communism, and the rash of strikes, bombings, and advocacy of radical causes after the war helped produce the Red Scare, an atmosphere of aggressive suspicion that saw communists as responsible for many of the nation's troubles (particularly those associated with labor) and hell-bent on gaining control of all major American institutions.

Anti-Semitism also flourished in this intolerant climate. Jews were portrayed as supporters of labor and other movements considered radical, as greedy and unethical moneylenders and business people, as amoral libertines (in large measure because of their association with the entertainment industry and their limited support for Prohibition), and, in more extreme versions, as the secret string-pullers behind Congress, capitalism and communism, all mere tools to further their plans for world domination.

The two major published sources of anti-Semitism were the infamous *Protocols of the Learned Elders of Zion* and *The International Jew.* The first was a bogus document, written in Russia around the turn of the century and quickly disseminated to anti-Semites everywhere, that purported to reveal the secret plans of a Jewish conspiracy to destroy Christian civilization by undermining its morality, its religion, its economy, and its political culture, ultimately paving the way for Jewish control of the world's major powers. In 1920, this theme was picked up and elaborated with details relevant to Americans by Henry Ford's newspaper, *The Dearborn Independent,* which ran a two-year series of articles titled "The International Jew: The World's Problem," later gathered into a four-volume set titled *The International Jew.* According to Leo Ribuffo, who has carefully traced the influence of these volumes, *"The International Jew's* perverse accomplishment was to combine Anglo-Saxon chauvinism, anti-Semitic motifs common during the Progressive era, and the comprehensive conspiracy theory sketched in *The Protocols."*

These volumes lashed out at the cultural changes increased Jewish immigration was bringing to America, at the "Hollywood lasciviousness" encouraged and engaged in by Jews determined to undermine American morals while fattening their pocketbooks, at Jewish bankers involved in the creation of the Federal Reserve Board, at powerful Jews in President Woodrow Wilson's inner circle, and, most importantly, at the Jewish "hidden hand" whose grip could be felt in virtually every adverse development, especially those difficult to explain in ordinary terms. Scurrilous as they were, the books drew praise from the likes of J. P. Morgan and other prominent Americans, and they fueled anti-Semitic prejudice for decades.

Fundamentalism was not intrinsically anti-Semitic, but it could and often did reinforce nativist tendencies. Because Jews were explicitly not Christians, they could be depicted as enemies of Christianity, and, since being a Christian was virtually synonymous with being 100-percent American, it was difficult to regard them as fully American. Even those who did not regard Jews as a major menace often felt little guilt over excluding them from their clubs, neighborhoods, schools, or professions.

The turmoil of the World War I years benefited fundamentalists by calling into serious question the assumption of the Social Gospelers that the Kingdom of God was just around the corner. In light of national and world events, the fundamentalist contention that things would get steadily worse until Jesus came to usher in the millennium no longer seemed so far-fetched. The dispensationalist scenario gained added plausibility when, after the British recaptured Jerusalem in 1917, the Balfour Declaration gave Jews the right to return to Palestine, which dispensationalists saw as a direct fulfillment of Bible prophecy.

Finally, fundamentalists participated heavily in bringing about Prohibition—when it became a legal fact on January 16, 1920, Billy Sunday celebrated by holding a mock funeral for John Barleycorn. So, in 1920, fundamentalism appeared on the surface to be in reasonably good shape. It had its intellectual act together, it was riding a crest of patriotism, and it had shared in what was apparently a stunning moral victory. Yet within ten years, this formidable movement would be devastated by defeat and dissension.

AFTER A TEN-WEEK New York City revival that marked the apex of his career, Billy Sunday lost his grip on the national consciousness. His less attractive characteristics grew more pronounced, and his star faded. He stepped up his jingoistic attacks on foreigners, Bolsheviks, bootleggers, modernists, evolutionists, dissenters, radicals, and virtually anyone else who did not espouse a rigid Republican party line, which he explicitly regarded as the appropriate political and economic position for true Christians. As part of his increasingly intransigent fundamentalism, he interpreted the grim political and economic news of the 1930s in the light of dispensationalist teaching and predicted the Antichrist would arise in 1935. Sunday remained active on the revival field until his death in 1935, but the great cities of the North and East stopped inviting him, and he played out the rest of his career in smaller cities and towns of the South.

Sunday's disappointing and disillusioning twilight years mirrored deep difficulties within the fundamentalist movement. The most serious of these revolved around two issues still crucially important to fundamentalists in the 1990s—the teaching in public schools of scientific theories thought to be incompatible with Scripture, and the increased influence of biblical criticism in churches and seminaries.

The first and most familiar of these battles focused on Darwinian evolution. According to fundamentalist reasoning, if Darwin's view of the evolution of species was correct, then the Bible's account of creation as having occurred in six 24-hour days could not be true. Since the Bible is true, fundamentalists reasoned, evolutionary thought is therefore false and must not be taught. Some liberal Christians thought it might be possible to reconcile the biblical account with current scientific theory, but most fundamentalists would have none of this. Their most notable champion, former Secretary of State and three-time presidential candidate William Jennings Bryan, declared flatly that "all the ills from which America suffers can be traced back to the teaching of evolution. It would be better to destroy every other book ever written, and save just the first three verses of Genesis." Bryan not only contended that evolution was a pernicious doctrine, but believed Christians had a perfect right to suppress it if they were able. In true populist fashion, he argued that when religion and science come into conflict, the issue should be decided by the will of the common people, not by "those who measure men by diplomas and college degrees." "Why," he asked, "should the Bible, which the centuries have been unable to shake, be discarded for scientific works that have to be corrected and revised every few years?" This question moved social commentator Walter Lippmann to observe that "the religious doctrine that all men will at last stand equal before the throne of God was somehow transmuted in Bryan's mind into the idea that all men were equally good biologists before the ballot box."

In keeping with this attitude, anti-evolutionists throughout the South and Southwest made concerted efforts to prohibit the teaching of evolution in the public schools—just as the teaching of German had been banned during the war. Some of these ran aground rather early. Virginia, West Virginia, South Carolina, Georgia, and Alabama, for example, refused to pass restrictive acts, despite strong affirmations of orthodoxy. In other states, academic freedom and science escaped more narrowly. In Kentucky, a teacher was brought to trial in 1922 for teaching that the earth was round, and was dismissed from his job when the plaintiff, using Scripture, convinced the judge that it was flat. Sensing the presence of kindred spirits, Bryan lent his influence to the cause in Kentucky, and a bill that would have restricted the teaching of evolution was defeated in the legislature by only one vote.

In some states, restrictive measures were enacted. Oklahoma prohibited evolutionary texts from 1923 to 1925. "Ma" Ferguson, governor of Texas, adopted a policy of selecting textbooks that did not mention evolution and of snipping objectionable passages from books that did, and of threatening teachers with dismissal and prosecution if they used unapproved texts. By 1927, however, Texas teachers were free of legal constraints on their scientific instruction. During the same period, Mississippi passed a law against the teaching of evolution, and both Arkansas and Florida placed some restrictions on science teachers. But the most notable success of the anti-evolution forces occurred in Tennessee, where the state legislature overwhelmingly passed a bill making it illegal "for any teacher in any of the universities (or public schools) of the state to teach any theory that denies the story of the divine creation of man as taught in the Bible and to teach instead that man has descended from a lower order of animals."

Probably because the lopsided vote in the Tennessee legislature reflected popular sentiment reasonably well, the passage of this bill did not stir great public reaction, but it became news all over the world when a young biology teacher in the town of Dayton agreed to let a friend test the law's constitutionality by challenging his use of an evolutionist text. Assured of legal support from the fledgling American Civil Liberties Union, John T. Scopes was subsequently indicted by a grand jury and shoved into the middle of one of the more remarkable arenas of intellectual and spiritual conflict in American history.

Scopes's defenders included Maynard Shipley, the most noted fundamentalist fighter of the time, and famed lawyer Clarence Darrow. The fundamentalist prosecution, with William Jennings Bryan in the lists, felt up to the challenge. The lines of conflict were clearly drawn. The prosecution had merely to show that Scopes had broken the law, which was not really under dispute. The defense would argue that the law was unconstitutional because it violated the mandate of the Tennessee constitution to "cherish literature and science" and, further, that it ran counter to U.S. constitutional guarantees of religious and intellectual freedom.

The trial turned into a public carnival and media circus. Darrow made Bryan look shallow and foolish, and journalists led by arch-cynic H. L. Mencken sent derisive reports of Southern and fundamentalist backwardness to newspapers throughout America and Europe. Since both judge and jury were solidly against Scopes, he was convicted and ordered to pay a fine of one hundred dollars, but he soon received a scholarship to pursue graduate studies at the University of Chicago and enjoyed a successful career as a geologist. William Jennings Bryan left town the following day and died unexpectedly within a week while resting at a friend's house after the trial.

Though it had ostensibly won the case, the fundamentalist movement was severely wounded in the Scopes trial, both by the loss of its most dynamic and respected leader and by the ridicule to which it was subjected in the national and international press. Within less than five years, despite strong feelings by millions of Americans that evolutionary teaching was diabolical and false, all legislation forbidding its being taught in the public schools and colleges was repealed, and no further serious efforts to legislate the content of scientific instruction was mounted for half a century.

A less visible, but probably more important fundamentalist struggle centered around increased acceptance of biblical criticism in Protestant churches and seminaries. Some churches escaped great turmoil: Congregationalists and Methodists were barely troubled, mainly because "modernism" (as it was called) was so widely accepted in their circles. Similarly, Lutherans and Southern Baptists escaped serious upheaval because their ranks contained so few who had extended the right hand of fellowship to the new ways of thinking. Holiness and Pentecostal churches, which were experiencing notable growth but were not really part of the fundamentalist movement, were untouched by the whole controversy. The key struggles came within the Presbyterian Church in the U.S.A. and the Northern Baptists, and the battle sites were not backwater burgs in the South, but New York, Princeton, and Philadelphia. Heady with the success they had enjoyed during the second decade of the century and bolstered by the show of strength at the founding of the World's Christian Fundamentals Association in 1919, the fundamentalists set about to root out error wherever they found it and to separate themselves from its perpetrators. Throughout both denominations, fundamentalists demanded public tests of orthodoxy for ministers and seminary professors, called on liberal editors and officers to resign their posts, and succeeded in getting their denominations to withdraw from the ecumenical Interchurch World Movement.

The story is too long to tell here, but the result can be summarized. Efforts to cleanse the Presbyterian Church in the U.S.A. of its liberal elements failed, and in 1929 a group of fundamentalist scholars led by J. Gresham Machen withdrew from Princeton to establish Westminster Theological Seminary in Philadelphia. One of the handful of students who followed them was an aggressive, articulate young man named Carl McIntire, and this would not be his last act of separation from a body he found imperfect. In 1936, after continued intemperate attacks on their denomination, Machen and McIntire were expelled from the denomination and soon formed the Presbyterian Church in America, later named the Orthodox Presbyterian Church. Within a year, McIntire found Machen and Westminster insufficiently pure and split off to form the Bible Presbyterian Church and Faith Theological Seminary. Machen died in 1937, leaving his wing without strong leadership and McIntire without strong opposition. These struggles left scars in the Presbyterian body, but it was clear who had won. The fundamentalists, intent on driving out the liberals and seizing control of the denomination, had themselves been driven out and more moderate forms of Christianity had prevailed.

Similar events occurred within the Northern Baptist Church. As the denomination's leading seminaries—Newton, Colgate, Rochester, Crozer, and the University of Chicago Divinity School—moved more and more to the liberal camp, leading fundamentalists such as Straton, Riley, and Amzi Dixon, who helped edit *The Fundamentals,* struggled furiously to demand adherence to rigid doctrinal statements and to eliminate heretics from the mission fields and seminaries. After a decade of acrimonious strife, it was clear by 1930 that Northern Baptists, like the Presbyterians, had opted for a more flexible form of Christianity than suited the fundamentalists.

At the end of the decade of the twenties, then, fundamentalism appeared to have been defeated and relegated to a minor position. It had not only lost virtually every confrontation it had created but had been exposed to ridicule by its tendency toward intellectual rigidity and obscurantism, by its intemperate actions, by its propensity for attracting and lending support to anti-Semitic, anti-Catholic, and other nativist and right-wing political elements, and by its assertion that only Christians could be 100-percent American. The onset of the Depression had diverted attention from theological wrangling, and it was becoming clear that the great victory of Prohibition would soon be overturned. It appeared that increased acceptance of science and modern biblical criticism would continue inexorably until the last fundamentalist had withered and died. This expectation was so strong that some noted historians as much as declared that it had happened, despite considerable evidence to the contrary.

FUNDAMENTALIST CHRISTIANITY DID indeed pass through a wilderness, but it did not enter the grave. In fact, it not only failed to disappear during the 1930s, but underwent a transformation that left it in a reasonably strong position by the end of the decade. That transformation involved shifting, realigning, and reorganizing its base. Since they had lost the fight for control of denominations and seminaries, fundamentalists set about creating a whole new set of institutions and structures in which the true, pure, and unadulterated Christian message could be preserved and preached.

In keeping with a tendency to lionize its most vocal and sometimes most outrageous leaders, fundamentalists often formed independent congregations centered on a notable hero of the faith. Straton in New York, Rader in Chicago, Riley in Minneapolis, McIntire in the Philadelphia area, J. Frank Norris in Fort Worth, "Fighting Bob" Shuler in Los Angeles, and many other lesser lights gathered the faithful into enclaves of aggressive purity. With the leadership of men such as these, individuals and congregations formed fundamentalist alliances which they hoped would multiply their strength and effectiveness. The World's Christian Fundamentals Association, the National Federation of Fundamentalists, and the Baptist Bible Union were the most notable of these coalitions, but there were dozens of others. Some catered to churches within a particular denomination; others comprised independent congregations, and still others consisted primarily of individuals from various denominations, many of whom felt a call to one particular segment of the battle for truth.

Another crucial development, far more lasting in impact than the various alliances, was the substantial increase in the number of Bible colleges and institutes favoring impeccably orthodox teaching and practical instruction in Christian service over the liberal arts they felt had undermined commitment to truth more narrowly conceived. The model, of course, was the Moody Bible Institute, which by 1930 had trained over 69,000 students to be ministers, church musicians, educational directors, Sunday-school teachers, and missionaries, and which also operated a vigorous press, sponsored numerous conferences, and ran a radio station dedicated to Christian programming. The Bible Institute of Los Angeles (BIOLA) enjoyed a similar status on the

West Coast. The number of these institutions increased from 49 in 1930 to 144 by 1950.

Finally, fundamentalists made extraordinary use of publications and the new medium, radio. Fundamentalism seemed to bring out the editor and pamphleteer in its leaders, who conveyed their message in publications with names like *The Christian Beacon, Essentialist, Crusaders' Champion, King's Business, Conflict, Defender,* and *Dynamite.* Some were inflammatory and irresponsible; more were unimaginative, repetitive, and dull. But they were publications, and fundamentalists were forming a habit of reading. One result of this is that today, books sold by and to evangelical Christians regularly outsell those that appear in the *New York Times* best-seller lists.

Perhaps even more significant, fundamentalists quickly seized the opportunity offered them by radio. With their emphasis on proclamation and the prospect of a vast and ever-growing audience, they immediately saw radio as a tool of great potential. By 1925, one in ten of the 600-plus radio stations in America was owned and operated by a church or other religious organization. Tighter licensing regulations led to half of these being sold off by 1933, but the potential had been seen. Dozens of fundamentalist preachers had successful radio ministries, but without doubt, the most effective of all was Charles E. Fuller, whose *Old Fashioned Revival Hour* was heard over all 152 stations on the Mutual Broadcasting System in 1939, reaching an estimated ten million listeners. By 1943, that program and a second Fuller offering, *The Pilgrim's Hour,* were being heard over 1,000 stations, and Fuller's Gospel Broadcasting Association was buying fifty percent more radio time than the secular company in second place. His success soon led him to found Fuller Theological Seminary, which has become one of the most respected and influential of evangelical schools.

Historians, liberal clergy, and learned professors in major seminaries may have believed, and certainly hoped, that fundamentalism was dead. Millions of Americans knew better. Not only had the writers and editors and radio preachers kept evangelical doctrines before the people, they had, by their astonishing success, made it clear that unnumbered legions still built on the firm foundation, still walked on the ancient pathways, and would teach their children to do the same.

Independent congregations, widespread publications, and religious broadcasting not only helped see fundamentalism through a troubled time, they also gave men like Father Charles Coughlin, Gerald Winrod, and Gerald L. K. Smith license and opportunity to tout racist, anti-Semitic, and pro-fascist views virtually without check.

In Royal Oak, Michigan, Roman Catholic priest Charles Coughlin expanded a children's story program, begun over one station in 1926, into a nationally heard and highly controversial mix of religious, economic, and political comment that moved his listeners to send money to support his broadcasts. As his eloquent preaching drew larger audiences, Coughlin added stations in Chicago and Cincinnati and, in 1930, signed a contract with the CBS network. With the onset of the Depression, Father Coughlin began to criticize "unregulated capitalism" and to castigate people of wealth and power who were "dulled by the opiate of their contentedness." His attacks on President Herbert Hoover led CBS to ease him off the air in 1931, but he quickly developed a network of independent stations that carried his program throughout the eastern half of the United States. His audience was phenomenally large—one estimate, perhaps exaggerated, placed it at 45 million—and one sermon alone drew a response of 1.2 million letters.

Coughlin used his tremendous popularity and brilliant rhetorical skills to achieve great political power. He was credited with being the one man most responsible for the election of Franklin D. Roosevelt to the presidency. He organized a political lobby of five million members, and in 1934 got his listeners to flood Congress with 200,000 letters protesting the establishment of the World Court. By this time, Coughlin was receiving more mail than any other individual in the world, and the mail contained more than five hundred thousand dollars a year. As the 1930s progressed, Coughlin grew increasingly intemperate and began to engage in personal attacks, particularly against President Roosevelt, on whom he had cooled considerably. He began to characterize the president as "Franklin Doublecrossing Roosevelt" and threw his support behind the unsuccessful Union Party in the 1936 election. When Roosevelt appointed former Klansman Hugo Black to the Supreme Court, Coughlin denounced the president as "stupid," a remark that led to a reprimand from the bishop of Detroit and the cancellation of his broadcasts. Late in 1938, however, Father Coughlin returned to the air, but instead of moderating his approach, he became even more radical, speaking out in sympathy for Nazis, blaming Jews for economic problems in the United States and the war in Europe, and, in his newspaper, *Social Justice,* calling for Roosevelt's impeachment. This time, Coughlin's excesses cost him his audience. Contributions from listeners dropped precipitously and, under pressure from the National Association of Broadcasters, most stations refused to sell him any more time. In 1942, the government threatened to charge him with treason, and his bishop offered him the choice of keeping silent on social issues or leaving the priesthood. Coughlin chose to remain a priest and continued to serve his parish until his retirement in 1968, but he was never again involved in politics, even on a local level.

Unlike Coughlin, who was Catholic, Gerald Winrod began his public career as a standard-issue fundamentalist. In 1925, he and a small group of colleagues formed an association known as Defenders of the Christian Faith. The following year, he established *Defender* magazine as the primary outlet for his views. In the early years, Winrod's causes were the typical fundamentalist concerns—biblical criticism, evolution, the Social Gospel, alcohol, modernists in control of churches and other key institutions, etc.—and he enjoyed the support and cooperation of other fundamentalist luminaries. After the Scopes trial, he and a band of Christian pilots known as the "Flying Defenders" toured the Midwest and California in a continuing effort to ban Darwinism from the schools.

A dispensationalist, Winrod saw the fulfillment of prophecy in current events and thought it probable that Mussolini would prove to be the Antichrist. In 1928, he opposed Democratic candidate Al Smith, largely because of his Catholicism and his opposition to Prohibition, but he showed little enthusiasm for Herbert Hoover either. Four years later, he declared Franklin Roosevelt's election to be a disastrous mistake, condemned the president for his failure to confront "the international banking fraternity" (a common code phrase for Jewish financiers) for their alleged role in engineering the Depression, pronounced the New Deal a "Red program," and predicted that "America will never be the same again" after FDR's depredations. By 1934, Winrod had emerged as a full-fledged anti-Semite, now discerning the hidden hand of the Elders of Zion behind revolutionary agitation, the Depression, and the New Deal. He praised Hitler's efforts "to defy Jewish occultism, communism, and finance" and looked with favor on the Nazi regime.

Winrod gained a considerable hearing for these views during the mid-1930s, but when he ran for the U.S. Senate in the 1938 Kansas Republican Primary, he was trounced, his only significant support coming from German-origin Mennonites and counties where the Klan had been prominent. Though he toned down his anti-Semitic and pro-Nazi statements after World War II began, he was still regarded as a threat to national unity and security and was the lead defendant in *United States v. Winrod,* a 1942 sedition case charging twenty-eight German agents, members of the German-American Bund, and other rightist agitators with "conspiracy to cause insubordination in the armed forces" by such actions as urging Roosevelt's impeachment and endorsing Nazi policies. After two years of Justice Department vacillation and bungling, the case ended in a mistrial and charges were eventually dismissed, but few doubted the defendants were less than model patriots.

After the end of World War II, Winrod turned his attention to combating communism and during the 1950s applauded Senator Joseph McCarthy's ruthless search for Reds. Winrod died, ironically, on November 11, 1957, a day on which Americans commemorate victory over Germany.

Winrod's primary competition for the post of America's leading Christian bigot was Gerald L. K. Smith. An eloquent speaker—H. L. Mencken once called him "the damnest orator ever heard on this or any other earth"—from a Disciples of Christ background in Wisconsin, Smith was not a classic fundamentalist. Though opposed to Al Smith in 1928, he also criticized the bigotry of the anti-Catholic Ku Klux Klan. Typical of most Disciples ministers, he had no interest in dispensationalism and never associated with the World's Christian Fundamentals Association. During a term as pastor of a Louisiana church, he displayed an unusual ecumenical streak, even exchanging pulpits with a local rabbi. Leo Ribuffo argues plausibly that the famous men who paid approving attention to Smith may have played a greater role in shaping his unusual career than any deep personal search for a consistent ideological stance.

The first of Smith's key influences was the notorious Louisiana governor and senator, Huey Long. Leaving his pastorate to work with Long, Smith became an avid devotee of his new hero's Share Our Wealth plan, which called for a dramatic redistribution of income. After Long's assassination in 1935, he began simultaneously to move away from the cause of redistribution and to espouse anti-Semitic and pro-fascist themes during his popular speaking tours and radio broadcasts. In 1936, a "March of Time" newsreel feature titled "The Lunatic Fringe" portrayed Smith as a charismatic but sinister enemy of freedom, a man in whom "serious commentators see the making of a fascist dictator." The newsreel probably exaggerated Smith's positions and potential, but it also helped drive him farther to the right, as more moderate supporters cut their ties to him and right-wing extremists embraced him as a new champion.

In 1937, Smith began a series of Sunday-night radio broadcasts over the independent network Father Coughlin had assembled, claiming financial support from hundreds of business leaders opposed to the New Deal. In 1939, he moved to Detroit and began broadcasting regularly over WJR, a powerful station known for its opposition to the Roosevelt administration. From this platform, he assailed communism and championed the virtues of private enterprise, calling for lower taxes, fewer bureaucratic regulations, and a return to rugged individualism and the American work ethic.

While in Detroit, at least partially as a result of a friendship with Henry Ford, Smith began to drink more deeply from this poisoned well of anti-Semitism. In 1942 he founded the *Cross and the Flag* monthly magazine and, after an unsuccessful run for the U.S. Senate, he devoted the rest of his career to anti-Semitism and anti-communism. By the late 1940s, Smith had lost all credibility and most of his audience, but he continued to publish *Cross and the Flag* for the few who cared. Like Winrod, he believed Joseph McCarthy was doing the work of God in trying to root out communists, and he regarded Eisenhower as foolish and inept. During the 1960s, his star shone a bit more brightly, as the chaos he had predicted for years seemed to be occurring. Predictably, he denounced the civil rights movement and its primary leader, Martin Luther King, whom he labeled a "Moscow-trained revolutionist," while praising the obstructionist efforts of southern governors Orval Faubus and George Wallace and assisting the work of the racist White Citizens Councils. Consistent with these positions, he also damned Lyndon Johnson and regarded Barry Goldwater as the first presidential candidate in decades to deserve his support.

Smith played out the last years of his life in Eureka Springs, Arkansas, where he established and gathered support for a Bible museum, a Christ-only art gallery, a passion play, and the Christ of the Ozarks statue, all of which drew hundreds of thousands of visitors to Eureka Springs. At the time of his death in 1976, he was planning a theme park that would feature an extensive replica of the Holy Land as it had been at the time Jesus lived.

FOR COUGHLIN, WINROD, and Smith, political and social issues overshadowed theological concerns. This was not the case for Carl McIntire, despite his fervent anti-communism. McIntire was a true fundamentalist, for whom purity of doctrine was paramount and to whom few besides himself appeared pure. By the beginning of the 1940s, McIntire recognized that fundamentalism was stronger than it had been in over a decade and moved to establish a national fundamentalist organization that would be "militantly pro-gospel and anti-modernist." Despite a desire for numbers, it would also be separatist, barring any churches or denominations that associated with modernists or that belonged to the liberal Federal Council of Churches. In 1941, the American Council of Christian Churches (ACCC) came into being, with McIntire as its first president. It was, from the beginning, a protesting council. It badgered the radio networks to give it a share of airtime equal to that given the Federal Council of Churches. It obtained a quota of chaplaincy slots from the armed services. And, through McIntire's paper, the *Christian Beacon,* it mounted unending attacks on the Federal Council and on any other group or individual less pure than itself. In 1948, McIntire broadened his reach and formed the International Council of Christian Churches (ICCC), whose acknowledged purpose was to oppose the World Council of Churches, formed the same year.

Some fundamentalists, exposed by schools and conferences and radio to gentler spirits, were able to see that the quarrelsomeness of men like McIntire seemed inevitably to result in an endless sequence of splittings into units that grew smaller and smaller, in spirit as well as in number. Less than a month after McIntire's American Council was formed, a group of more moderate conservatives met at the Moody Bible Institute to establish an association that could represent evangelical believers in all denominations, including those affiliated with the Federal Council of Churches. The new group, formalized in the spring of 1942 and called the National Association of Evangelicals (NAE), was, they said, "determined to break with apostasy but . . . wanted no dog-in-the-manger, reactionary, negative, or destructive type of organization," and was "determined to shun all forms of bigotry, intolerance, misrepresentation, hate, jealousy, false judgment, and hypocrisy." It was, in other words, determined not to be like Carl McIntire and the ACCC. Having decided what they did not want to be, these men turned to the greater challenge of shaping a new form of conservative Christianity and, with it, new ways of relating to the larger culture.

BILLY GRAHAM—
GEARED TO THE TIMES

THE SOCIAL, ECONOMIC, and psychic dislocations created by the twenties, the Great Depression, and global war generated enormous concern over the welfare of the young. In addition to the common struggle to keep food on the table and the fear of the loss of loved ones in the war, conservative Christians faced a danger even more troubling: the possibility that their beloved children would abandon faith in God, live and die outside the church, and spend eternity in hell. To ward off this specter, evangelical and fundamentalist leaders all over the country began holding Saturday-night rallies that offered young people a blend of wholesome entertainment, patriotic fervor, and revivalist exhortation.

One of the first of these was a New York City bandleader-turned-minister named Jack Wyrtzen, whose *Word of Life* radio broadcast and rallies began in 1940 and, by 1944, were packing Carnegie Hall and Madison Square Garden. In Chicago, a dynamic visionary named Torrey Johnson, who wanted to do something for the thousands of servicemen who spent their free weekends aimlessly wandering that city's downtown streets, leased the 3,200-seat Orchestra Hall, next door to the U.S.O., and invited a young suburban pastor and radio preacher named Billy Graham to speak at the inaugural rally of the "Chicagoland Youth For Christ."

By the fall of 1944, similar meetings were occurring in at least two hundred other cities and Torrey Johnson spent much of his time on the telephone, helping ministers across the country start still more programs. The movement continued to mushroom and, in July 1945, more than six hundred youth leaders from all over North America met at a fundamentalist conference center at Winona Lake, Indiana, and formed Youth for Christ International. They elected Torrey Johnson president and Billy Graham became the organization's first official field representative, a role he had already been filling unofficially for several months, having been lured from his pastorate by Torrey Johnson's vision of fields white unto harvest.

These were heady days for the energetic young movement. To underline their announcement that Christianity did not have to be drab and dismal, YFC leaders adopted slogans like "Old-fashioned Truth for Up-to-date Youth" and "Geared to the Times, but Anchored to the Rock," implying that they were modern without being "Modernist." YFC leaders also made their point by wearing colorful suits and sportcoats, neon "glo-sox," garish hand-painted ties, and gaudy bow ties, some of which lit up. The rallies themselves were a sort of evangelical vaudeville, with musical performances that might include not only choirs and other traditional groups but also "smooth melodies from a consecrated saxophone," Bible quizzes, patriotic and spiritual testimonies by famous and semifamous preachers, athletes, entertainers, military heroes, business and civic leaders, former hoodlums and miscreants, and such specialty acts as magicians, ventriloquists, and a horse who would "kneel at the cross" and tap his foot twelve times when asked the number of Christ's apostles or three times when asked how many persons constituted the Trinity.

The sermon, of course, was the climax toward which all the preliminaries pointed. As Billy Graham has observed, "We used every modern means to catch the attention of the unconverted—and then we punched them right between the eyes with the gospel." To those who recall these services, listening to the sermons was not a letdown, something to endure in exchange for a good time. Jon Braun, who attended YFC gatherings in Oakland and later became a youth leader himself, remembers being "awestruck at these really phenomenal speakers. I mean, whatever else they did, they could communicate with kids. They were spectacular."

Part of YFC's appeal lay in its unabashed patriotism. At a Soldier Field rally in Chicago on Memorial Day, 1945, as the first troops were returning from Europe after the German surrender, seventy thousand young people sang the "Star-Spangled Banner" while facing an abundant display of flags, after which four hundred white-clad nurses formed a marching cross that entered the field as the band played the "Battle Hymn of the Republic." Then, while every serviceman stood to receive the applause of the grateful and admiring throng, a soloist sang "God Bless Our Boys," and four hundred high-school students saluted the war dead by placing a memorial wreath on a platform crowned by a large blue star. YFC leaders always used emotion to press for a tangible response. After a few moments of silent prayer and the playing of "Taps," Lieutenant Bob Evans, a chaplain who had been wounded several times and had pledged to return to Europe to preach the gospel in the very places where he had fallen, appealed to the crowd to buy war bonds and urged them to sign bond applications while a lone drummer played a dramatic solo from the middle of the field.

William Randolph Hearst liked YFC's emphasis on patriotism and high moral standards, and shortly after the Soldier Field rally, all twenty-two papers in the Hearst chain carried a full-page story on the movement, apparently at the reclusive publisher's instruction. Other papers picked up the story and in February 1946 *Time* devoted four columns to YFC, quoting President Truman as saying, "This is what I hoped would happen in America." *Time* also noted that some Americans viewed "the pious trumpetings of the Hearst press on YFC's behalf" as ominous, apparently fearing the movement might become an instrument of Hearst's generally conservative social and political views. Others, with memories of the Hitler Youth fresh in their minds, feared that the rallies, which by 1947 were attracting perhaps a million young people each week, could easily be manipulated by political opportunists whose hand-painted ties barely covered hearts of darkness.

Insofar as YFC had a political orientation, it was largely conservative, but apart from a decided anti-communist and a strong patriotic strain, politics was neither its manifest nor hidden agenda. It was, as it purported to be, a religious movement, a resurgence of the fundamentalism that had been licking its wounds for two decades, awaiting just such an opportunity to challenge the liberal Protestantism that had held undisputed sway since the mid-1920s. Professors and students in liberal seminaries criticized it for what they regarded as simplistic theology and embarrassing techniques, but the premier journal of liberal Christianity, *Christian Century,* grudgingly acknowledged that "the fact that [YFC] has gone so far as it has is proof that something close to spiritual famine exists among large sections of our population, including the rising generation, who are more hungry for faith than their elders. The churches are not feeding these starving people and they cannot be indifferent to the challenge which this attempt to use the new channels of communication for preaching the Gospel offers them. They should do likewise, and better."

To the young participants themselves, perhaps the greatest impact was in eradicating any feelings of cultural inferiority they may have harbored. As Jon Braun put it, "to be a part of something with two, three, four, five thousand kids every Saturday night was a significant experience. You never felt you were part of a minority, because no one else had anything that big. No one did anything that was that consequential. And you met kids from all over, so it had a great social impact. I felt very much a part of something that was significant, and that was very, very important to me."

Youth for Christ was attracting thousands of teenagers to rallies all over the country and nurturing a cadre of leaders who would join Billy Graham in the ranks of evangelical leadership. But while YFC focused on high-school students, and various Christian missions were working in jails and on skid row, until 1951 no one had staked out college campuses as a primary mission field. That year, a young man named Bill Bright founded an organization that would focus primarily on college students and would eventually eclipse Youth for Christ to become one of the largest and most influential parachurch organizations within the orbit of evangelical Christianity.

While studying at Fuller Seminary, Bright fell under the spell of Henrietta Mears, a dynamic woman who taught a hugely popular Sunday-school class for young adults at the Hollywood First Presbyterian Church and who was also an enthusiastic supporter of Billy Graham's ministry. Mears encouraged Bright to fashion some kind of evangelistic enterprise that could capitalize on his obvious talent and drive. As he later told it, the vision for a ministry to college students and, through them, to the world, came to him late one evening while he was studying for a Greek exam during his last year at Fuller. He regarded the experience as a definite commission directly from God, and he set about to act upon it. Drinking deeply from the currents of the evangelical revival swirling about him, Bright believed that committed Christian young people would provide the strongest bulwark against secularism, moral decay, and communism, and could enhance America's ability to play a critical role in redeeming the world. In the service of this vision, he formed a witnessing team, which he dubbed the Campus Crusade for Christ, and turned it loose on UCLA.

Like Charles Finney long before him, Bill Bright put a high value on organization, technique, and straightforward attempts to move people to make a rational decision. He installed and still maintains a tight chain of command in which lieutenants defer to captains and all ranks acknowledge that Bright holds the ultimate power of decision. He requires his workers to commit themselves to a life of strict moral and spiritual discipline, and to spend many hours each week in the one-on-one task of talking to individuals about their need to be saved. Often adopting the language of warfare—enlist, advance, rally, campaign, blitz, warrior, etc.—Campus Crusade representatives pursue a four-point strategy of evangelism (Penetration, Concentration, Saturation, and Continuation) until satisfied that every student on a given campus has been exposed to their understanding of the gospel, which they present initially in the form of Four Spiritual Laws: 1) God loves you and offers a wonderful plan for your life; 2) Man is sinful and separated from God; 3) Jesus Christ is God's only provision for man's sin; 4) We must individually receive Jesus Christ as Savior and Lord. This simple step-by-step approach is explained in pamphlets, books, speeches, and a continual round of meetings that serve to strengthen faith and maintain commitment.

·   ·   ·

BILLY GRAHAM HAD at least some inkling of what was happening and what his role might be. He believed Modernism was on the ropes and that evangelicals had a real chance to deliver a knockout blow. To a post-Depression, post-war nation that welcomed whatever help it could get in its efforts to reset its anchors and reattach its roots, his bold and confident assertion that a virile, athletic, victorious, freedom-creating Christ was the answer held enormous appeal. By 1947, warnings against communism began to be a regular feature of Graham's preaching. As he noted the rapid spread of the atheistic ideology, he announced that "unless the Christian religion rescues these nations from the clutches of the unbelieving, America will stand alone and isolated in the world."

This message took on new urgency during a 1949 revival in Los Angeles. Just two days before the campaign began, President Truman announced that the Russians had successfully tested an atomic bomb and for two years had been building a nuclear arsenal that would drastically alter the imbalance of power America had enjoyed since the end of World War II. Graham seized upon this stunning revelation and expounded on it throughout the crusade. The line had been drawn, he thundered, between communism and Western culture, and no accommodation was possible. "Western culture and its fruits had its foundation in the Bible, the Word of God, and in the revivals of the Seventeenth and Eighteenth Centuries. Communism, on the other hand, has decided against God, against Christ, against the Bible, and against all religion. Communism is not only an economic interpretation of life—communism is a religion that is inspired, directed, and motivated by the Devil himself who has declared war against Almighty God." The fire of that war, he told his stunned listeners, would fall directly upon them, because communists were "more rampant in Los Angeles than any other city in America. . . . In this moment I can see the judgment hand of God over Los Angeles. I can see judgment about to fall." The only reason America had escaped the ravages and destruction of World War II, he declared, was because "God's people prayed," and its only hope now lay in repentance and revival. Messages such as this doubtless played an important role in spurring William Randolph Hearst to order his editors to "puff Graham," the two-word directive that put the evangelist on the front page of every Hearst newspaper. As the Associated Press and other wire services picked up the story, it brought him to the attention of the entire nation.

Graham hammered the same themes during subsequent crusades in New England and Columbia, South Carolina, early in 1950. While in Columbia, he stayed in the governor's mansion at the request of Governor Strom Thurmond, who invited him to address the state legislature and various high-school assemblies, then provided a police escort for a quickly arranged two-week preaching tour of the state. Thurmond also facilitated a meeting between Graham and Henry Luce, publisher of *Time* and *Life,* which soon began to give prominent attention to Graham's activities.

During the summer of 1950, Graham managed, after repeated requests and intercession by Massachusetts congressman John McCormack, to obtain a brief visit with President Truman. The meeting went well enough, but when Graham and his three associates not only told reporters all that had been said but allowed themselves to be photographed while kneeling in prayer on the White House lawn, Truman was infuriated. It was years before the evangelist was able to repair the breach.

The incident did not, however, deter Graham from attempting to forge links with political power. As his fame spread, aided by his hugely popular radio program, the *Hour of Decision,* his widely publicized pronouncements on the Satanic evils of communism, the God-blessed superiority of the free-enterprise system, and the need to return to the old-fashioned values and virtues of individualist America attracted the favor of some wealthy and influential folk. During Graham's 1951 Fort Worth crusade, Texas oilman Sid Richardson, though not famous for his piety, took a special liking to him and began to introduce him to other rich and powerful men. Given the friendship and support of such people, it was hardly surprising that the first two fictional features produced by Graham's studio were "Mr. Texas," the story of a hard-drinking Texas cowboy who found Christ, and "Oiltown U.S.A.," which tells of a millionaire Houston oilman's conversion and was promoted as "the story of the free-enterprise system of America. . . . of the development and use of God-given natural resources by men who have built a great new empire."

BY THE FALL of 1950, just five years after the end of World War II, many of the nation's young men were bound for Korea, a distant land most Americans knew or cared little about, to try to rescue it from communist invasion. A nation so recently proud and confident had been cast anew into turmoil and perplexity. In this anxious state, it was vulnerable to two ancient and proven defenses: scapegoating and assuring itself that old familiar truths were still valid. Billy Graham instinctively understood this. While he accused communism of trying to undermine the very foundations of Western civilization and damned any effort at appeasement or compromise, he assured his audiences that those who trusted in the great truths of Christianity could be confident that God was on their side and would see them through the worst of trials.

Graham's most important campaign in 1952 was a five-week crusade in Washington, D.C. He preached to a packed armory in virtually every service, and a climactic rally on the steps of the Capitol that, despite rain, drew a crowd estimated at forty thousand. When he first broached the idea of preaching at this location, he was told it would be impossible to arrange, but a call to Sid Richardson, one of House Speaker Sam Rayburn's key support-ers, led to an act of Congress permitting Graham to hold the first-ever formal religious service on the Capitol steps.

That Graham was able to achieve such a coup signaled his growing influ-ence in the political realm. He had been invited to hold the crusade by a bipartisan group of senators and representatives, and he used his sojourn in the capital to forge further links to power. President Truman remembered the prayer on the White House lawn and repeatedly refused to attend a service or to grant the evangelist another audience. Other politicians, how-ever, saw Graham either as a kindred spirit or as someone with whom it would be prudent to identify. Approximately one-third of all senators and one-fourth of House members asked for a special allocation of seats for crusade services, and scores of congressmen attended the Capitol rally.

During these weeks, Graham also met two men who would become close and controversial friends, Richard Nixon and Lyndon Johnson, the latter another favorite of Sid Richardson's. With the help of such allies, Graham got permission to hold prayer sessions at the Pentagon each noon through-out the crusade. Virginia Senator A. Willis Robertson, father of religious broadcaster and 1988 Republican presidential candidate M. G. "Pat" Rob-ertson, boosted Graham by authoring a unanimous Senate resolution, to be read at a crusade prayer-service, urging Americans to pray that "God may guide and protect our nation and preserve the peace of the world."

This attention and encouragement apparently convinced Graham that he and his supporters had considerable political clout. Late in 1951, he had expressed the opinion, foreshadowing later predictions by the Religious Right, that "the Christian people of America will not sit idly by during the 1952 presidential campaign. [They] are going to vote as a bloc for the man with the strongest moral and spiritual platform, regardless of his views on other matters. I believe we can hold the balance of power." This bloc, he suggested, would put forth a coordinated effort in which church members would follow "the instructions of their religious leaders."

During the Washington crusade, Graham announced his desire to inter-view every potential candidate from both parties. Though careful to note that he would not make a public endorsement, he told reporters that he might well share his personal choice with a number of religious leaders "who probably will use my views as a guide." He was also willing to com-mend his views to candidates. "If I could run for president of the United States today," he volunteered, "on a platform of calling the people back to God, back to Christ, back to the Bible, I'd be elected. There is a hunger for God today."

At first, Graham brushed off any suggestion that he had any personal desire for political office, but statements such as this stirred some imaginations and, a few months later, he told reporters that "numerous congressmen" and a former member of Roosevelt's cabinet had approached him to run for the United States Senate from North Carolina, or perhaps even to consider the presidency in 1956. He continued to disavow interest in holding public office, but apparently did not consider such suggestions farfetched. America had not yet reached a crisis that demanded he sacrifice his work and enter politics, he said, but if that should happen, he stood ready to help: "If the country ever comes close to communism, I will offer myself in any capacity to lead the Christian people of this country in the preservation of their God-given democratic institutions." In the meantime, he estimated he could probably swing at least sixteen million votes to the cause or candidate of his choice.

Despite Graham's profession of neutrality during the early stages of the presidential campaign, it appears he already suspected who his choice would be. After speaking positively of Dwight Eisenhower to Sid Richardson, he followed Richardson's suggestion that he write the general and let him know that millions of Americans would like to see him seek the presidency. When Ike responded positively, Graham followed up with a visit to his European headquarters near Paris, where he encouraged Eisenhower even more strongly to enter the campaign. Graham has minimized his role in Eisenhower's decision, but his visit obviously did not dissuade the general from moving forward.

Though he continued to claim he was impartial, Graham repeatedly criticized the Truman administration for thrusting America into the Korean conflict without a clear declaration of war and for its lack of resolve in pursuing victory in the manner recommended by General Douglas MacArthur, whom he praised as a peerless leader and great promoter of Christianity. Throughout the spring and summer, he echoed the sentiments and, sometimes, the exact phrases of the Republican campaign, observing that it was "time for a change," time to elect new leaders who would "clean up the mess in Washington," time to get "a new foreign policy to end this bloodletting in Korea," time to elect "a strong spiritual leader" who has "the fortitude and moral courage to clean out the 'grafters and hangers-on'."

After Eisenhower gained the Republican nomination, Graham visited him at the Brown Palace Hotel in Denver and presented him with a red Bible, which Ike apparently kept with him and read frequently throughout the campaign. The evangelist not only continued to make Republican-flavored comments but, a few days before the November election, revealed to the press that a personal survey of nearly two hundred churchmen and religious editors from thirty states and twenty-two denominations indicated that seventy-seven percent favored Eisenhower for president, while only thirteen percent expressed an intention to vote for Democratic candidate Adlai Stevenson. Predictably, such gestures won Eisenhower's appreciation and affection and, after his thumping victory in the election, led to Graham's being asked to serve as a religious consultant for the inauguration ceremonies. After Eisenhower became the first president ever to lead a prayer as part of his own inauguration and followed this with being baptized in the White House, Graham told his radio audience that, "I have been deeply impressed by [the President's] sincerity, humility, and tremendous grasp of world affairs. I also sense a dependence upon God. He told me on [two] occasions that the hope of building a better America lay in a spiritual revival." He added, "Another thing that encourages me about Mr. Eisenhower is that he is taking advice from some genuine, born-again Christians." The election of Dwight Eisenhower, he asserted, was a signal that "God is giving us a respite, a new chance." After Eisenhower's first talk on foreign policy, Graham compared the address to the Sermon on the Mount. This effusive support of Eisenhower's cause laid the groundwork for what would become the first in a remarkable series of close relationships between Billy Graham and the Presidents of the United States.

IN BOTH AMERICA and Europe, Graham was widely perceived to be a staunch conservative and vigorous opponent of communism and socialism. Although he occasionally conceded that organized labor had helped ameliorate exploitation and insufferable conditions in the workplace, his reference to the Garden of Eden as a Paradise in which there were "no union dues, no labor leaders, no snakes, no disease," reflected a preference for a world free of unions and the conflict they produced. While noting that employers should treat their workers with fairness, generosity, and respect, he clearly felt there was more to fear from labor than from management. After all, hundreds of Christian businessmen supported his work and he knew what kind of men they were. "Some of the finest men I know," he said, "are men of means, but their bank accounts, like their lives, are consecrated wholly to God."

Graham regarded communism as so unqualified an evil that attacking it barely counted as a departure from his ostensible political neutrality. During his 1950 Portland crusade, he told news people that "not once will you hear from this platform an attack, by implication or otherwise, against any religious or political group. The only one I mention from the platform occasionally is communism, which is anti-God, anti-Christ, and anti-American." On the *Hour of Decision* he declared that the struggle between communism and Christianity was "a battle to the death—either communism must die, or

Christianity must die, because it is actually a battle between Christ and Anti-Christ." In keeping with that conviction, the first printed sermon he distributed to his radio listeners was "Christianity versus Communism." He characterized communism as a religion "created and directed by Satan himself," and proclaimed that there is but "one antidote for the poisonous venom of Sovietism, and that is the truth of the gospel of Christ." If America moved to the left, he warned, "it will plunge into the dark abyss of totalitarian despair and gloom, and ultimate annihilation. If it turns to the right and takes the way of the cross, we well might be entering the greatest economic and spiritual renaissance that modern man has known."

In addition to sermons explicitly focused on communism, Graham managed to work references to the Red Menace into a wide range of contexts. In speaking about hell, he opined that Stalin would doubtless be there. In a sermon, "Are You Getting What You Want?" he criticized communism for promising "material prosperity without spiritual satisfaction." When he preached on "The Home," he charged communism with a plan to abolish the family. Weaknesses in American education, he said, would make the nation vulnerable to a better-trained army of young Russians. Thus, revival was needed not only to save individual souls, but also to stop the spread of communism.

Taking the line popular with communist hunters, the most notorious of whom was Wisconsin Senator Joseph McCarthy, Graham stirred fears of communists and communist sympathizers who had wormed their way into America's key institutions and were, at that very moment, eating away at the nation's vitals, ready to betray it into enemy hands at the first opportunity. He warned darkly of "over 1100 social sounding organizations that are communist or communist-operated in this country. They control the minds of a great segment of our people; the infiltration of the left wing . . . both pink and red into the intellectual strata of America [is so extensive that] our educational [and] religious culture is almost beyond repair. . . ." He asserted that communism "has attracted some of our famous entertainers, some of our keenest politicians, and some of our outstanding educators," and charged that "there is a cancer eating at the heart and core of the American way of life, subversive groups seek to destroy us, communists are doing their deadly work in government, education, and even in religion."

Graham thought it imperative that this cancer be forcibly removed and, like many Americans, expressed an early admiration for those who claimed to be finding subversives in government and elsewhere in American society. When McCarthy, frustrated by witnesses who cited the Fifth Amendment's protection against self-incrimination in their refusals to answer his badgering questions, called for changes in the amendment, Graham recommended that, if that was what it took, "Then let's do it." Even after McCarthy's senate committee and its counterpart, the House Un-American Activities Committee (HUAC), came under heavy fire for their abusive and demagogic tactics, Graham persisted in his admiration. In a 1953 sermon, a year before the Senate condemned McCarthy's activities by a three-to-one vote, he said, "While nobody likes a watch dog, and for that reason many investigation committees are unpopular, I thank God for men who, in the face of public denouncement and ridicule, go loyally on in their work of exposing the pinks, the lavenders, and the reds who have sought refuge beneath the wings of the American eagle and from that vantage point, try in every subtle, undercover way to bring comfort, aid, and help to the greatest enemy we have ever known—Communism."

Graham by no means believed that all of America's problems were caused by communists themselves. Equally at fault were American leaders who, however patriotic and well-meaning they might be, had underestimated the threat posed by communism, had listened to bad advice, and had followed a course of appeasement that had encouraged communist aggression of the very sort that had led to the war in Korea. "There can be no bargaining," he warned; "there can be no parlaying or compromising with evil." America must stand firm in its resistance to communism, "no matter what it costs." Firmness did not necessarily entail support of the United Nations. On the contrary, Graham criticized the U.N. during the Korean conflict for its failure "to stand up to Russia" and ventured that a root cause of its sometimes spineless behavior was its lack of a clear theistic foundation: "At the first meeting of the United Nations in San Francisco there was no prayer made to God for guidance and blessing. We were afraid that the Godless, atheistic communists would not like it, so we bowed in deference to Russia." These unrelenting attacks enhanced Graham's recognition as a staunch anti-communist. The *Chicago Daily News,* reporting on his 1955 European tour, called him "Communism's public enemy number one" and ventured that his message was "serving as an antidote to the Communistic Anti-Christian and purely materialistic gospel of the Russians."

ANOTHER NOTABLE ANTI-COMMUNIST in conservative Protestant circles in the post-war period was the redoubtable Carl McIntire, leader of both the American and International Councils of Christian Churches (ACCC-ICCC). During the mid-1940s, McIntire published a trio of books, *Twentieth Century Reformation, The Rise of the Tyrant: Controlled Economy vs. Private Enterprise,* and *Author of Liberty,* which, along with regular articles in his periodical, *Christian Beacon,* laid down positions he would expound for the rest of his long life. McIntire believed the American system of government and free enterprise comprised "the most ideal conditions ever known for advancing God's Word," and must therefore be guarded against any and all threats. (He believed the Roman Catholic church was an even greater threat to freedom, but it was his tireless opposition to communism that attracted most attention.) In 1948, before the Soviets revealed that they possessed nuclear weapons, McIntire and the ACCC called for "a complete and frank showdown with Russia," declaring that "for us to have the atom bomb and in the name of a false morality, born of a perverted sense of self-respect and pacifist propaganda, to await the hour when Russia has her bombs to precipitate an atomic war, is the height of insanity and will, when the fateful hour comes, be a just punishment upon us. We believe that Almighty God holds us responsible." A few months later, the executive board of the ACCC removed any lingering doubt about what such a "show-down" involved. America, it said, had "a moral responsibility to strike first using adequate and necessary ways to thwart the maddened purpose of the enemy."

Such thinking is undergirded by what Erling Jorstad calls "ultrafunda-mentalist" political ideology, which has three theological factors. Confidence in verbal inerrancy—the doctrine that precipitated McIntire's break with Princeton Seminary—assures that the Bible can be trusted to convey God's will for the present age. Separatism, the distinctive trait that repeatedly moves fundamentalists to withdraw from those deemed insufficiently pure in heart and mind, bolsters confidence in one's special capacity to see and follow the proper path. Finally, dispensationalist premillennialism assures that history is firmly in God's hands and that Armageddon, probably nuclear in nature, is scheduled to occur in Palestine, not North America. As we shall see, all three of these doctrines still figure prominently in the ideology of the contemporary Religious Right.

Because America had just won the greatest war in human history and was the strongest nation in the world, McIntire reasoned, one could account for communism's advance only by positing the existence of traitors and dupes within the U.S. government and other key institutions. He felt that Franklin Roosevelt's New Deal, with its substitution of government programs for individualistic reliance on self-discipline, hard work, and free enterprise, had sapped America's will and blinded it to the eroding effects of liberalism, socialism, and communism, leaving it an easy prey for Soviet agents and their American fellow-travelers. By midcentury, the idea that America was falling victim to massive internal conspiracy struck millions of Americans as eminently plausible. Casting doubt on the integrity of all major social institutions became a key feature of right-wing religious efforts during this period.

The formation of the World Council of Churches in 1948 and the transmutation of the ecumenical Federal Council of Churches into the National Council of Churches in 1950 convinced McIntire and his fellow premillennialists that the one-world church identified in the book of Revelation as the Whore of Babylon and the tool of the Antichrist was coming into being. It followed naturally that, as the enemy of God and his people, these ostensibly religious institutions must also be permeated with communist influence. In 1950, McIntire joined forces with two other religio-patriots, Verne Kaub and J. B. Matthews, to produce a tract, *How Red Is the National Council of Churches?*. Not surprisingly, they concluded it was scarlet indeed.

Publication of this tract coincided neatly with the first notorious attacks by Senator McCarthy on government and other leaders he accused of being "Reds." One of McCarthy's most ardent admirers was another preacher, the Reverend Billy James Hargis. After serving briefly in a series of pastorates in Arkansas, Missouri, and Oklahoma, Hargis devoted himself to what he calls the "God and Country" ministry, traveling from town to town and spicing up his straightforward presentation of the fundamentalist version of the gospel with long commentaries on current events and harangues about the urgent need for Christians to be concerned about the deteriorating state of their nation. "I had to put some fear into them," he recalled. "I had to tell them some of the terrible things that were happening. I spoke for hours and hours. There was no one else doing that and they would come to hear this fat kid talking about God and country. And I gained friends. I really believe the Lord was giving me the words to say for God and country. I believe Christian people have to be political as well as religious. I don't think we are full Americans if we're not concerned about our nation and our politics as well as about our faith. I believe the Bible teaches us to respect our government. And I really believe the New Testament teaches free enterprise." In 1947, Hargis established the Christian Echoes Ministry, which later became the Christian Crusade, with headquarters in Sapulpa, Oklahoma, and began espousing his views in a monthly newspaper with the same name.

Hargis soon offered his services to McCarthy, as did McIntire's followers, and the senator publicly credited them with providing him with research and speech writing assistance. McCarthy's ability to destroy reputations with unproved allegations during this period was enormous, and association with such power energized his new associates. McIntire continued to assert that the World and National Councils of Churches were stacked with communist traitors, even declaring that the new NCC-sponsored Revised Standard Version of the Bible was an unholy, un-American, communist-inspired translation designed to undermine authentic faith. J. B. Matthews, coauthor of *How Red Is the National Council of Churches?*, gained considerable notoriety for his claim that "The largest single group supporting the communist apparatus in the United States today" comprised "at least seven thousand Protestant clergymen" recruited by the Communist party to abet its nefarious schemes. McCarthy appointed Matthews to head his investigative team, but public opposition, including criticism by President Eisenhower, was so intense that Matthews was forced to resign after only seventeen days on the job. McCarthy's attack on the churches came to a head in a 1953 speech in which, using materials furnished to him and HUAC by McIntire and Hargis, he accused G. Bromley Oxnam, a prominent Methodist Bishop active in both the World and National Councils, of being a communist. Oxnam, who had been one of McCarthy's most vocal critics, volunteered to appear before the HUAC and to respond under oath to any questions they wished to ask him. After an intense ten-hour grilling, the committee voted unanimously to absolve Oxnam of all charges of communist ties.

The Oxnam hearing effectively ended government-sponsored searches for pink pulpits, and in December 1954, the Senate overwhelmingly condemned McCarthy for using investigative tactics "unbecoming a senator." Hargis and the ACCC-ICCC lost some credibility by being linked with McCarthy, but that did not cause them to turn against their champion, who died shortly after his colleagues repudiated him. More than forty years later, Hargis reminisced warmly about McCarthy. "After I wrote the speech for him, exposing the World Council and the National Council of Churches, he invited me out to his home. He lived in a very humble house in Washington. He did not have anything that looked like riches. He was like my dad. He wasn't a Harvard voice. He didn't speak in the terms of Princeton. But he had convictions. And you know, when they put his body in the Rotunda [of the Capitol], it drew the biggest crowd ever to see a body there, other than MacArthur, I think. So you can't say he was hated by the majority of the people of the United States. He was a wonderful man."

As McCarthy had grown more intemperate, and as his opponents began to demonstrate that he was a liar and a charlatan, Billy Graham had begun to back away from him. When pressed, he had admitted that, while there might be some Marxist thinking in American churches, as McCarthy and others had charged, he did not know of any such cases personally. When asked his opinion of McCarthy by reporters in London during the spring of 1954, he said, "I have never met McCarthy, corresponded with him, exchanged telegrams or telephoned him. I have no comments to make on the senator." Graham's broad, irenic spirit kept him from countenancing McCarthy's excesses; at the same time, his deep and abiding conviction that the free world was locked in a death struggle with Satan's own ideology made it hard for him ever to declare flatly that McCarthy had also been an enemy of freedom.

Though they had failed to convince most Americans that communists were running churches and their government, McIntire and his cohorts did manage to attract increased financial support from those who believed in them. That enabled the ACCC-ICCC to hire Hargis and Fred C. Schwarz, an Australian physician whose articles in *Christian Beacon* and appearances on McIntire's radio program soon won him a following large enough to enable him to move out of the ACCC-ICCC orbit and establish the Christian Anti-Communism Crusade, which he was still leading in 1996. Another McIntire associate and researcher, Major Edgar C. Bundy, became executive director of the Church League of America, a research organization that amassed files on thousands of individuals and organizations it suspected of communist activities or leanings and made its findings and interpretations available to like-minded clergymen. Unlike Schwarz, Bundy has maintained strong ties to McIntire and the ACCC-ICCC. Verne Kaub, a major contributor to the *How Red Is the National Council of Churches?* pamphlet, also continued to work closely with the ACCC-ICCC as leader of the American Council of Christian Laymen, a group that professed to find communism in the public schools as well as in the churches. In this connection, Kaub produced a pamphlet, *How Red Are the Schools?* and advocated a wholesale return to the traditionalist nineteenth-century McGuffey Readers. Older than his colleagues in the ACCC-ICCC orbit—he died in 1964 at age eighty—Kaub had belonged to several anti-Semitic organizations in the 1940s, but this was not a component of McIntire-brand fundamentalism, and his anti-Semitism surfaced only sporadically in his later years. Communism apparently satisfied his quest for conspiracy.

Hargis continued to build the Christian Crusade through his newspaper, personal appearances, and nightly radio broadcasts on super-power Mexican stations, but he also maintained close ties to McIntire. Beginning in 1953 and continuing through most of the rest of the decade, he spent his summers supervising what he still regards as one of his most effective exploits, the ICCC-sponsored Bible Balloon Project. From various points along the German/Czechoslovakian border, he and a crew of assistants used more than a million hydrogen-filled balloons to float portions of scripture to countries behind the Iron Curtain. Though some of it was derisive, the publicity generated by this project enhanced Hargis's reputation among those who believed that the only lasting antidote to communism was the knowledge of God's Word.

THE DECADE OF the fifties had seen Billy Graham emerge as the unquestioned leader and exemplar of evangelical Christianity, particularly that segment of the movement that identified itself as the New Evangelicalism, as distinguished from the Old Fundamentalism represented by Carl McIntire and men of his ilk. In most respects, the basic theology of the two groups was essentially the same, but the New Evangelicals tended to be rather tolerant of minor theological differences among themselves, whereas fundamentalists felt compelled to withdraw fellowship from any suspected of even the slightest deviation from their version of orthodoxy. Both groups deemed modernist theology to be erroneous and threatening to true Christianity, but the opposition of the New Evangelicals lacked the hysterical brittleness characteristic of the fundamentalists. To the New Evangelicals, it was more important to proclaim the gospel than to defend it.

The New Evangelicals were also more positive toward social reform than fundamentalists had been during the previous twenty-five years. By the mid-1950s, with Billy Graham moving easily in the corridors of political power, they had begun to believe they might have an outside chance to regain a kind of cultural hegemony evangelicals had not known, outside the South at least, since the Civil War. As part of a general willingness to take a hard look at positions long held, some key New Evangelical leaders began to reject or at least de-emphasize that hallmark of Fundamentalist doctrine, "dispensationalism." While still believing that Christ would return to bring human history to a divinely ordained consummation, probably including a glorious millennial reign, they cooled on the dispensationalist notion that history is following a blueprint so detailed and immutable that human attempts to affect its course are futile.

Speaking directly to this issue, Harold John Ockenga, a key leader of the movement, asserted that the New (and true) Evangelical "intends that Christianity will be the mainspring in many of the reforms of the societal order. It is wrong to abdicate responsibility for society under the impetus of a theology which overemphasizes the eschatological." By de-emphasizing dispensationalism, which was, after all, a relative newcomer on the theological scene and not part of classic Protestant theology, the New Evangelicals left themselves room to assert some responsibility for shaping the culture, as Luther and Calvin had clearly advocated, and as, just a century earlier, Charles Finney and the Evangelical United Front had accomplished in America. And as their strength grew, they dared hope that, with God's help, they might revitalize evangelical Christianity, and through it, America and the world.

Graham was not alone in his efforts to inject evangelical Christianity into the veins of the body politic. In Washington, a seldom-publicized organization known as International Christian Leadership set up a "Christian Embassy," under the low-key but effective direction of Abraham Vereide, known in evangelical circles as "Mr. Christian of Washington." Vereide's primary strategy was to organize breakfast prayer groups for government leaders and workers, and, more dramatically, to conduct "spiritual installations" for government officials entering new positions or feeling the need for a spiritual booster shot. Vereide also organized, in 1953, the first of what would become annual Presidential Prayer Breakfasts. These breakfasts

brought leading evangelicals together with some of the nation's most powerful figures. At the 1954 edition, which doubled as the opening meeting of
the organization's annual conference, Eisenhower, several cabinet members,
and a flock of influential senators and representatives attended; featured
speakers included hotel magnate Conrad Hilton, Richard Nixon, and Chief
Justice Earl Warren. Billy Graham did not speak at the breakfast, but he was
prominently present and, at the close of the session, his associate George
Beverly Shea led the six hundred guests in singing President Eisenhower's
favorite hymn, "What a Friend We Have in Jesus."

Billy Graham liked to say, and at times perhaps even believed, that he was
completely neutral in politics, but he freely admitted his fascination with the
political realm. Primarily because he was a Southerner, he registered to vote
as a Democrat, but his political and economic views were usually more
closely in tune with those of Republicans. Without much question, however, his overriding political concern was not the brand name of the party in
power, but how that power was and could be used in the service of Christianity. Political leaders who showed little interest in religion, or whose
beliefs or lives openly contravened evangelical preferences, were not likely to
find favor in his eyes, and might even become the targets of some rather
pointed criticism. Fortunately for the New Evangelical strategy of influencing the larger culture, Graham got along marvelously with both Dwight
Eisenhower and Richard Nixon.

Graham and Eisenhower had regular, if not particularly frequent, contact,
which led in turn to a long and fateful friendship with Richard Nixon. Prior
to the 1956 elections, Graham revealed that he was suggesting to friends in
"high ecclesiastical circles" that Nixon be invited to address various religious
assemblies during the following year. Given the likelihood that Nixon would
run for president in 1960, Graham felt the vice president needed to pay close
attention to his public image. "Governor Dewey said to me a few weeks
ago," he confided, "that you were the most able man in the Republican
party. He has great confidence in you, but seems to be a little fearful that
you may be taken over unwittingly by some of the extreme right-wingers.
He feels that in order to be elected President of the United States, a man is
going to have to take a middle-of-the-road position. I think he is right!" He
then cautioned Nixon against drawing too heavily on his anti-communist
credentials. "In my opinion, there is so much good will bubbling out of
Moscow that the issue of communism is no longer as potent as it was
politically in the U.S." The Reds were still a menace, he conceded, but it
might not be wise to harp on it too loudly.

True to his word, Graham arranged to have Nixon, whom he characterized as "a splendid churchman," speak at major Methodist, Baptist, and
Presbyterian conferences in North Carolina during the summer of the 1956

campaign and, to enhance his chances of pushing the right buttons, supplied him with an unsolicited speech he thought the vice president might want to use. He also offered to invite several key religious leaders, including a Methodist and an Episcopal bishop, the president of the Southern Baptist Convention, and the Moderator of the Presbyterian Church in the United States (South), to have lunch with the vice president at the Graham home. Graham felt exposure to these and other religious leaders would help Nixon immensely over the long term. Though he made no official public endorsement during the 1956 campaign, Graham assured Eisenhower that he would do "all in my power . . . to gain friends and supporters for your cause," and such pointed comments as his lament that divorce no longer seemed to disqualify a person from being a presidential candidate—Stevenson was divorced—left little doubt as to where he stood.

In 1956, Graham founded *Christianity Today* magazine, which quickly became the flagship publication of mainstream evangelicalism. As part of its mission to influence national policy, the magazine was first headquartered in Washington, D.C. Graham had once considered moving his organization's offices from Minneapolis to Washington—he thought it would be impressive to tell his radio listeners to write to "Billy Graham, Washington, D.C. That's all the address you need." It was even more important, he believed, for the capital to serve as *CT*'s home base. "I felt a magazine coming from Washington would carry with it an unusual authority," he recalled. "We also wanted our editor to mingle with congressmen, senators, and government leaders so he could speak with first-hand knowledge on the issues of the day." Certainly, the editors must have felt they were at the center; from their tenth-floor offices at the corner of Pennsylvania Avenue and Fifteenth Street, they looked down on the White House lawn and the treasury building.

FOR ALL THE seriousness of the communist threat, attacking it was a relatively risk-free enterprise for conservative Protestant preachers, since not many communists wandered into their services and few fundamentalists held up a hand to argue that their communist friends had been misunderstood. Racism was a different matter. While many Christians felt Graham ought to use all his influence to denounce segregation and prejudice, many of his supporters, particularly in the South, continued to defend racist policies and practices and did not want him to meddle with what they regarded as a God-ordained system. To complicate matters even further, blacks were increasingly relying on various forms of public protest, which troubled Graham, who abhorred conflict and impropriety. The complexities of that problem would dog him for decades.

A native North Carolinian, Graham accepted segregation without question but, like many Southerners, was not exposed to a particularly virulent or hate-dominated form of racism. During the early years of his ministry, he took the easy route by following local custom, even though preaching to a segregated audience increasingly pricked his conscience. In 1952, he startled some of his brethren at the annual meeting of the Southern Baptist Convention by asserting that it was the Christian duty of every Baptist college to welcome academically qualified Negro students. In Jackson, Mississippi, that same year, he named segregation as being one of that city's two greatest social problems, along with illegal liquor. He declared that "the ground at the foot of the cross is level," and said, "it touches my heart when I see whites stand shoulder to shoulder with blacks at the cross." In 1953, after the sponsoring committee of his Chattanooga crusade balked at his demand that seating be open to all, he went to the crusade tabernacle and personally removed the ropes marking the section reserved for blacks. After a bit of backsliding later that year, he never again permitted any of his crusades to be segregated, and he began to call on the church to demonstrate its commitment to racial justice and equality. He would never be comfortable with violent protest or even with nonviolent socially disruptive measures aimed at changing the standing order, but neither would he ever retreat from the higher ground he had seized.

Graham was not the only evangelical concerned about racial justice. In fact, two of his significant institutional anchors, the Southern Baptist Convention and the National Association of Evangelicals, endorsed the Supreme Court's 1954 decision in *Brown v. the Board of Education of Topeka,* which called for an end to school desegregation. Over the next several years, at Eisenhower's specific request, Graham met with a wide range of black and white Southern religious leaders, both in groups and privately, sharing with them his suggestions for improving race relations. He had little doubt that, like President Eisenhower and himself, God approved of a gradual approach to integration. "I believe the Lord is helping us," he ventured, "and if the Supreme Court will go slowly and the extremists on both sides will quiet down, we can have a peaceful social readjustment over the next ten-year period."

In an article for *Life* magazine in the fall of 1956, Graham issued a plea for an end to racial intolerance. He assured a national audience that most Southern ministers believed segregation should be ended on buses, in railroad and bus stations, in hotels, and in restaurants, but that it was "far too early to implement school integration in some sections of the deep south." He also charged that efforts to push too fast had produced a situation much worse than had existed before the Supreme Court handed down its 1954 decision. Still, not all the blame could be laid at the feet of extremists and outsiders.

"We have sown flagrant human injustice," he confessed, "and we have reaped a harvest of racial strife." He stressed that racism could not be justified from Scripture—"Let's not make the mistake of pleading the Bible to defend it"—and called on parents to teach their children to love people of other races, lest they pass on the sin of prejudice. He exhorted all Christians to "Take a stand in your church for neighbor love. . . . Take courage, speak up, and help the church move forward in bettering race relations." It was hardly a pathbreaking statement, but it was a statement, and it called on Christians to take responsibility for building a better world.

During 1956 and 1957, racial tension continued to mount in the South, and Martin Luther King's boycotts, sit-ins, and other forms of nonviolent resistance were turning up the pressure. Graham sincerely believed the proper way to change a society is to change individual hearts, and he could imagine no route to racial harmony that did not run past the foot of the cross. In keeping with that conviction, he felt confrontation was a perilous tactic, but he began to acknowledge that something more than preaching might be required to secure basic civil rights for minorities. In an interview with the *New York Times* a few weeks before his 1957 crusade in Madison Square Garden, he characterized King's controversial tactics not as hostile or disruptive, but as "setting an example of Christian love." When the crusade got underway, he invited King to talk with him and his team about racial issues, and to lead the audience in prayer at a crusade service, a gesture that let both whites and blacks know that he was willing to be identified with King's cause.

Endorsing Martin Luther King and the cause of integration disappointed and angered many of Graham's Southern supporters, but it won him favor with mainstream national media and liberal church leaders who had often criticized his simple theology and conservative political views. Though he would never truly be comfortable with protests and conflict-producing demonstrations, he did not back down on his support of equality and integration. In September 1957, when President Eisenhower called to tell him he was thinking of sending federal troops into Little Rock, Arkansas, to override Governor Orval Faubus's prolonged defiance of a court order to desegregate that city's Central High School, Graham told him, "Mr. President, I think that is the only thing you can do. It is out of hand and the time has come to stop it." The following year, when South Carolina Governor and hard-shell segregationist George Bell Timmerman refused to allow him to hold an integrated rally on State House grounds, Graham agreed to move the rally to Fort Jackson army base, but made it clear that blacks were as welcome as whites. The rally, attended by sixty thousand people, was described as "the first nonsegregated mass meeting in South Carolina's history."

In other actions, Graham joined with newspaper columnist Drew Pearson to raise money to rebuild a Clinton, Tennessee, high school bombed by racists shortly after it was integrated, and held two rallies in Little Rock in which he urged citizens to cleanse their hearts of hatred and bitterness and learn to live in peace with one another. Such activities spurred vitriolic attack from the Ku Klux Klan and White Citizens Councils, anger from politicians who resented his taking the side of the federal government in the most notable challenge to the autonomy of the southern states since the Civil War, and bewildered disappointment from countless Christians who had never imagined that the command to love one's neighbor as oneself had implications for their treatment of blacks. The disaffection of such a large segment of his constituency troubled Graham deeply, and he took care not to offend unnecessarily, but he did not surrender his convictions or apologize for his actions.

BILLY GRAHAM'S INCREASING acceptance as a mainstream figure, albeit one who often stood somewhat right of what the media and other dominant cultural forces defined as the center, was not unique for evangelicals during the 1950s. Bill Bright's Campus Crusade for Christ had met with great success over the decade, enrolling substantial numbers of students in its programs and winning support from wealthy backers who applauded its anti-communist, pro-capitalist, up-with-America ethos. By 1960, it boasted a paid staff of more than one hundred, with ministries on forty campuses in fifteen states. The following year, it purchased a $2 million resort in Arrowhead Springs, California, which served as its headquarters until a recent move to Orlando.

Youth for Christ was also flourishing at the end of the fifties. Staffed mainly by graduates of evangelical and fundamentalist colleges, its main effort at that point was sponsorship and encouragement of weekday Bible clubs in thousands of high schools, but it also sponsored summer camps and youth conferences. During the last week in 1959, approximately ten thousand teenagers descended on Washington to attend YFC's Capital Teen Convention at the National Armory and to usher in the 1960s, which they dubbed "The Decade of Destiny." President Eisenhower was so impressed by their presence that he invited them onto the White House lawn and spoke to them as they stood around the National Christmas Tree.

Graham, the young evangelicals to whom he was a hero, and the millions of conservative Protestants who supported and applauded the evangelical enterprises still felt threatened by the spread of communism, but their concern was less desperate and consuming than it had been earlier in the decade, and their closer association with cultural power and influence reduced their antagonism toward it. By 1960, ardent anti-communism, as well as extreme suspicion of existing major institutions and calls for a return to ostensibly purer forms of Americanism, were largely the preserve of Carl McIntire, Billy James Hargis and others stalwarts of the hard right. It was Graham's less hard-line approach that would dominate evangelicalism in the decade to come.

CHAPTER

2

WARFARE
OF THE
SPIRIT

THE FIFTIES WERE an extraordinarily successful decade for conservative white Protestant Christians in America. Not for more than a century had they felt so closely in tune with and wielded as much influence over the national ethos and culture. Their churches and colleges grew, their books and magazines sold phenomenally well, and their young people were part of the largest youth movement in the country. Their chief spokesman and symbol, Billy Graham, not only was the nation's best-known preacher and one of its most admired men but had the ear of the world's most powerful leader, the president of the United States. Racism still pervaded much of the country, especially in the region most self-consciously pious and moralistic, the South, but the president, the Supreme Court, most national leaders, and most major religious bodies had declared segregation to be indefensible, and the end of American apartheid seemed inevitable, as the civil rights movement emerged and gained momentum. Even the threat of communism, still real and quite fearsome, was diminished somewhat by the confident assurance that God was on America's side. No one imagined America was perfect, but few had any inkling of the radical upheaval that lay just ahead.

For many conservative Protestants, the first sign of major cultural change came in the summer of 1960 when the Democratic Party nominated Massachusetts Senator John F. Kennedy, a Roman Catholic, to be its candidate for president. Al Smith, the only other Catholic to win the nomination of either major party, had been defeated in a landslide by Herbert Hoover in 1928, and his religion had played a significant role in that defeat. It was clear from the beginning that Kennedy's Catholicism also made him suspect in the eyes of many Protestants. This was especially true of evangelical and fundamentalist Christians, many of whom—especially premillennial dispensationalists—viewed the church of Rome not simply as a repository of false doctrine, but as the institution identified in the book of Revelation as the Whore of Babylon, an integral part of the Antichrist's evil plan for world domination. Father Peter Gilquist, now an Orthodox priest, but then a fundamentalist student at Dallas Theological Seminary, a center of dispensationalist thought, recalled that "a guy stood up in the chapel and said that John F. Kennedy was 'the Beast' of Revelation, that he was the Antichrist, and under no circumstances could anybody vote for him. The faculty didn't like it, but they didn't shout him down." (That apprehension was not easily shaken. Gilquist also remembered that, after Kennedy's assassination three years later, he had watched the funeral procession with a fellow graduate of Dallas Seminary "who was fairly sure [Kennedy] would rise out of the coffin and be the Antichrist.")

Billy Graham's clear favorite in the race was his old friend, Richard Nixon. For several years, he had been giving Nixon advice on how to position himself for the 1960 campaign, and he had done his best to allay President Eisenhower's misgivings about Nixon's fitness to succeed him. Aware that religion would be an important factor in the election if Kennedy gained the Democratic nomination, Graham had written Nixon in 1959 to suggest that he make a point of attending church regularly, to keep "the religiously minded people in America" solidly behind him. In May 1960, Graham gave what one newspaper called "an implied but unmistakable endorsement of Vice President Nixon" when he said, "This is a time of world tension. [It] is a time for a man of world stature. I don't think it is a time to experiment with novices." When he followed that with a coy, "But I'm not taking sides," the reporters roared with laughter.

As the Nixon campaign effort gathered steam, Graham continued to offer tactical advice, not always limiting himself to matters of faith. When he did speak of religion, his tone was often more tactical than pastoral. He told Nixon that if Kennedy were nominated, he was certain to capture virtually all the Catholic vote. To counter this, the vice president would have to "concentrate on solidifying the Protestant vote." Choosing a Catholic running mate, as some had apparently suggested, would only "divide the Protestants and make no inroads whatsoever in the Catholic vote." It would be far better to choose a person widely respected in Protestant circles, "someone the Protestant church can rally behind enthusiastically." Graham's choice was Dr. Walter Judd, a former evangelical missionary then serving in the House. "With Dr. Judd," he ventured, "I believe the two of you could present a picture to America that would put much of the South and border states in the Republican column and bring about a dedicated Protestant vote to counteract the Catholic vote." Aware that this kind of specific political advice ran directly counter to his claim of nonpartisanship, Graham added,

"I would appreciate your considering this letter in utter confidence. You would do me a favor by destroying it after reading it."

After the Democrats nominated Kennedy in July, with Lyndon Johnson as his running mate, Graham wrote to Johnson, asking him to assure Senator Kennedy that he did not intend to raise the religious issue "publicly" and that he hoped "to stay out of the political campaign as much as possible." It was a pledge imperfectly kept. Graham never actually gave Nixon an official endorsement, in spite of several assurances that he was about to do so. Still, no one doubted where he stood and, behind the scenes, he continued to offer his friend advice and to work on his behalf. He reported that "throughout Protestantism there is running a question as to your religious convictions," and urged Nixon to weave more references to religion into his speeches. As for tactics, he reported that he felt he had been trying to "neutralize" Martin Luther King's positive feelings toward Kennedy, but recommended that Nixon arrange a meeting with the black leader. "It might swing him," he said, adding that "he would be a powerful influence." He also informed Nixon that he had recently written to the two million families on his mailing list, urging them to organize their Sunday schools to get out the vote, and had advised other religious organizations to do the same. While many of these folk were registered as Democrats or Independents, Graham felt his well-known friendship with the vice president would influence them in Nixon's favor, and that a concerted effort to turn out the vote might well produce a significant surge of votes for the Republican ticket without his having to make an explicit endorsement. In a similar transparent ploy, Graham invited Nixon to visit him in his Montreat, North Carolina, home. Such a visit, he wrote, "would certainly be a dramatic and publicized event that I believe might tip the scales in North Carolina and dramatize the religious issue throughout the nation, without mentioning it publicly. This is just a suggestion, and we would be delighted to cooperate in it if you think it has any merit."

Kennedy had anticipated the anxieties his candidacy was sure to create and had addressed the issue head-on during the West Virginia primaries in May. Noting that the president's oath of office includes his pledge to uphold the Constitution, which mandates the separation of church and state, he pointed out that, since that oath is customarily sworn upon the Bible, "if [the official so swearing] breaks his oath, he is not only committing a crime against the Constitution—for which Congress can impeach him and should impeach him—but he is committing a sin against God." This oft-repeated statement did not quell all doubt, and even such liberal clergymen as World Council of Churches president G. Bromley Oxnam, whom Joseph McCarthy had accused of communist sympathies, and Eugene Carson Blake, president of the National Council of Churches, expressed their concern that Kennedy might find it difficult to square his political duties with his obligations to his church when it came to such matters as parochial schools, birth control, and the separation of church and state.

As the campaign progressed, Graham recognized that Kennedy stood a good chance of winning the election, which troubled him, for religious as well as political reasons. In a letter to Eisenhower in early August, he noted that, if Kennedy and Johnson were elected, Roman Catholic Mike Mansfield would be in line to become senate majority leader. With Massachusetts congressman John McCormack serving as floor leader in the House, Catholics would hold two powerful positions and, Graham warned, "The Roman Catholic Church will take advantage of this." A few days later, the evangelist was quoted as having said, "A man's religion cannot be separated from his person: therefore, where religion involves political decision, it becomes a legitimate issue. For example, the people have the right to know the views of a Quaker on pacifism or a Christian Scientist's view on medical aid, or a Catholic's view on the secular influences of the Vatican." He had then added that "some Protestants are hesitant about voting for a Catholic because the Catholic church is not only a religious, but a secular institution which sends and receives ambassadors from secular states." When he saw his words in print, however, he dispatched statements to both *Time* and *Newsweek,* denying he had been thinking of John Kennedy when he had made these observations.

Many of Graham's fellow religionists saw no reason to pretend they were speaking hypothetically. While acknowledging that a Catholic had every right to seek the presidency, Harold John Ockenga pointed out that the Roman Catholic church had never shown much appreciation for the separation of church and state, particularly when it was able to use temporal power to support its own institutions and doctrines, and observed that several Catholic publications had criticized Kennedy (identified only as "a prominent candidate in this coming election") for his repeated insistence that his private religious beliefs would not take precedence over his oath as president. A strong individual might ignore such criticism, Ockenga admitted, "but the pressures would always be there for him to succumb, especially when there is the possibility of excommunication for disobedience and such excommunication could mean the loss of his soul." Because the Vatican and the American Catholic hierarchy seemed unwilling to acknowledge that America is a pluralistic society in which religious bodies are enjoined from seeking control over the temporal realm, Ockenga urged Protestants not "to aid and abet [the movement toward 'Roman Catholic domination of America'] by electing a President who has more power to advance such a goal than any other person."

Ockenga was hardly a voice crying in a wilderness. James Dunn, a prominent Texas Baptist, recalled the misgivings he and his fellow Baptists, historically strong supporters of church-state separation, had felt. "There was a lot
of anxiety about his being Roman Catholic," he said. "A Roman Catholic
Cardinal had, some years not long before that, said that the separation of
church and state is 'a shibboleth of doctrinaire secularism.' We reacted very
negatively to that. We saw it rather as the American contribution to good
government, which is just the opposite of that view. And the Roman Catholic Church's record in regard to individual freedoms and religious liberty is
not without some very serious blemishes—they finally got around to forgiving Galileo [in 1993], after 350 years. So there was a tremendous amount of
anxiety." Campus Crusade staffer Jon Braun agreed: "I remember all the
rhetoric about how bad it would be. And I remember being told that this
was the last free election that the United States would ever see."

In the fundamentalist camp, the widely circulated journal, *Sword of the
Lord,* published Dallas pastor W. A. Criswell's doom-laden article, "Catholic
President?" and offered new subscribers a free copy of a pamphlet entitled,
Kennedy for President?. Bob Jones, Sr. and Carl McIntire echoed these warnings in even more ominous language; McIntire's ACCC passed a resolution
to the effect that "we do not want to see the spectacle of a President kissing a
Cardinal's ring as an act of obeisance to Roman Catholic temporal authority." Closer to the center, the executive director of the National Association
of Evangelicals wrote a moderate but clearly pessimistic booklet entitled, *A
Roman Catholic President: How Free from Church Control?,* and sent a letter
urging evangelical pastors to warn their parishioners of the dangers of Roman Catholicism. "Public opinion is changing," the letter warned, "in favor
of the Church of Rome. It is time for us to stand up and be counted as
Protestants. We dare not sit idly by—voiceless and voteless—and lose the
heritage for which others have died." The inaugural issue of Billy Graham's
new *Decision* magazine also declared that "we Christians must work and pray
as never before in this election or the future course of America could be
dangerously altered and the free preaching of the gospel could be endangered."

Christianity Today reflected fear of a Catholic's occupying the White
House, but made no formal endorsement, despite an ardent Republican
courtship that included a long meeting between Nixon and the magazine's
editor, Carl F. H. Henry. Henry recalled that Nixon emphasized the personal commitment to Christ he had made as a teenager at a Los Angeles
revival, as well as his staunch opposition to communism. Based on that
conversation, Henry observed wryly, "One would not make the leap to the
Nixon of the Watergate years." At the end of the interview, Henry told
Nixon only that *"Christianity Today* has high standards. Whoever rises to

those standards will inherit its influence." With respect to Kennedy, Henry admitted that "We had our anxieties," not only because of the candidate's Catholicism, but also because "we had information from sources that I could not gainsay, that Kennedy was playing fast and loose with his marriage vows. I wrote one of our board members and asked him what I ought to do with that information, and his answer was: 'Do nothing with it in *Christianity Today*. We were not formed for that purpose.' " The magazine did not raise the issue, and did not run an article submitted by a former Catholic priest who raised the specter of Vatican influence over the White House. Though he had no doubt the magazine's staff favored Nixon, Henry explained that "[we] wanted a good conscience with regard to the magazine and its religious and political ties."

BILLY GRAHAM SPENT most of August and September 1960 holding crusades in Europe, but evangelism was not his only concern. On August 18, a group of approximately twenty-five evangelical leaders answered his invitation to join him in Montreux, Switzerland, to discuss various issues of importance to their movement. Norman Vincent Peale, though not usually a member of their circle, was vacationing in Europe at the time and was invited to sit in. Whatever the original impetus for the meeting, it apparently turned into a session focused on ways to thwart John Kennedy's election. Peale had already been quite outspoken in his opposition to Kennedy, in part because of the famed preacher's Republican sentiments and a longstanding friendship with Richard Nixon, but primarily because of his fear that a Catholic president's primary allegiance would be to "an authoritarian hierarchy" and "a supposedly infallible man," rather than to democratic principles he felt owed their existence—and future health—to Protestantism. Because of this history and his prominence, Peale was assigned responsibility for arranging a meeting between Nixon and a small committee of clergymen, and also to preside at an all-day meeting organized by Citizens for Religious Freedom, an offshoot of the National Association of Evangelicals. The NAE-sponsored "Study Conference on the Relationship of Religion and Freedom," held in Washington on September 7, stressed the political nature of the Roman Catholic church and the threat it posed to democracy. Dr. L. Nelson Bell, Billy Graham's father-in-law and mentor and executive editor of *Christianity Today,* delivered an address entitled "Protestant Distinctives and the American Crisis," in which he charged that American Catholics followed the rules and conventions regarding religious freedom only because they had to. The Roman Catholic church, he said, is "a political system that like an octopus covers the entire world and threatens those basic freedoms and those constitutional rights for which our forefathers died in generations past." The higher the percentage of Catholics in a nation, he warned, the greater the likelihood that tolerance will recede and oppression increase. "Rome," he declared, "never changes." Other speakers played similar themes.

Although Peale had not organized the meeting or set the program, his role as presider and spokesman at a post-session press conference made it appear he was the ringleader. The press regularly referred to the Citizens for Religious Freedom as "the Peale group," and his fellow clergy, particularly such liberal leaders as Union Seminary's Reinhold Niebuhr and John C. Bennett and the editors of the *Christian Century,* subjected him to withering attack. Newspapers dropped his syndicated column, organizations canceled his speeches, and Peale himself became seriously depressed and so convinced he had done irreparable harm to his ministry that he offered to resign his pulpit at New York's Marble Collegiate Church. Remarkably, Billy Graham's role in the whole affair was never mentioned publicly. Graham, still in Europe, did not attend the Washington meeting and, for several months, denied he had known anything about it before the unfavorable publicity broke. He later retracted that assertion in a private letter, professing to have suffered an unaccountable lapse in memory, but the Montreux meeting and his role in encouraging Peale to speak out against Kennedy's Catholicism did not become public knowledge until documented by Peale's biographer, Carol V. R. George, in 1993.

Despite his genuine concerns about Kennedy's religion, Graham was uncomfortable with much of the anti-Catholic rhetoric and, on September 1, informed Richard Nixon that he was "detaching myself from some of the cheap religious bigotry and diabolical whisperings that are going on." He also urged Nixon "to stay a million miles from the religious issue at this time." As he had feared, Kennedy's forthright treatment of what was clearly on the minds of many Protestants was playing well. Then, in a bold gamble that paid off handsomely, the senator arranged to meet with a large group of ministers in Houston, where anti-Catholic sentiments ran high. Repeatedly and without hesitation or ambiguity, Kennedy assured his interrogators that if in the role of president he faced a conflict between his obligation to America and his obligation to the Vatican, he would either give precedence to his obligation to America or he would vacate his office. "I believe in an America," he declared,

> that is neither Protestant, Catholic, or Jewish, where no public official either requests or accepts instructions on public policy from the Pope, the National Council of Churches, or any ecclesiastical source, where no religious body seeks to impose its will, directly or indirectly, upon the general populace or the public acts of its officials, and where reli-

gious liberty is so indivisible that an act against one church is treated as an act against all.

Kennedy was so effective in this mid-September meeting that any subsequent attempt to portray his religion as a threat to America was depicted as naked prejudice and served only to enhance his appeal. Billy Graham regarded this defense as cynical manipulation of public opinion, but conceded there was little he could do about it. Sobered by the vehement criticism Norman Vincent Peale had drawn for expressing his doubts that Kennedy could govern free of Vatican control, Graham informed Nixon that he would have little further to say regarding the election and would definitely avoid mentioning religion. "Not only would they crucify me," he explained, "but they would eventually turn it against you, so I must be extremely careful."

As election day approached, Graham wrote an article for *Life* magazine, offering a warm appraisal of Nixon and, without naming Kennedy, observing that it would be inappropriate for a candidate to win because he was "more handsome or charming" or because he happened to be richer, better organized, and more ruthless. Before the article could appear, however, Graham got cold feet and persuaded publisher Henry Luce to pull it and to run instead a nonpartisan article on why Christians should vote. When word of what he had done leaked out, Graham told reporters that "I have come to the conclusion that my main responsibility is in the spiritual realm and that I shouldn't become involved in partisan politics." Given that the election was one of the closest in American history, many observers, including Richard Nixon, believed such an article could have brought victory to the Republican ticket.

John Kennedy could hardly regard Billy Graham as an ally, but he was sufficiently astute to recognize that it would be unwise to alienate the evangelist and his huge following. In January 1961, a few days before the inauguration, Florida Democratic senator George Smathers arranged for the two men to have lunch together in Key Biscayne and to play a round of golf at Palm Beach. That evening at a press conference, Kennedy announced to reporters that Dr. Billy Graham was present and would make a few comments on the religious issue that had drawn so much interest during the campaign. Graham had been given no warning and was flabbergasted, but he rose to the occasion, saying what Kennedy undoubtedly wanted him to say. A *New York Times* article titled "Dr. Graham hails Kennedy victory" reported that:

The Reverend Dr. Billy Graham declared tonight that the election of John F. Kennedy, a Roman Catholic, had promoted a better understanding between the Protestant and Catholic churches in the United States. Dr. Graham, the evangelist, said Mr. Kennedy's victory had proved there was not as much religious prejudice as many had feared, and probably had reduced forever the importance of the religious issue in American elections.

Despite the service Graham had performed by making this statement, the president-elect and his team were not particularly anxious to forge stronger ties. In granting approval to send photographs of the two men taken at the press conference, Press Secretary Pierre Salinger told the photographer that it should be made clear "in writing" that "it is our understanding that these pictures are for Mr. Graham's personal use," and not for reproduction in his magazines or other publications.

THE KENNEDY YEARS hardly qualified as Camelot for evangelical Christians. In the South, they continued to grapple with the civil rights movement and its unrelenting charge that segregation, which generations of their forebears had defended by appeals to Scripture, was un-Christian, unjust, and immoral. Many white Christians, of course, also abhorred segregation and welcomed change, despite the disruption it was sure to bring. And many black Christians saw the movement as fulfilling the Scripture, "Proclaim liberty throughout the land, to all its inhabitants." These differing, but related, strands of religious faith played themselves out during the 1960s in Lynchburg, Virginia, a city that twenty years later would become a major staging ground for the Religious Right.

Lynchburg, Virginia, is perhaps best known to most Americans as the home of Jerry Falwell's Thomas Road Baptist Church, Liberty University, and the now-defunct Moral Majority lobby, but it was also the site of many clashes over civil rights in the 1960s. As such, it was a microcosm of what was going on throughout much of the South: resistance from white segregationists, including prominent clergymen and leading laypeople; nonviolent, often spontaneous, defiance of established norms by African Americans, again including prominent clergy and devout laypeople; and, ultimately, grassroots mobilization of political and legal resources that helped bring down or dramatically change an unjust and oppressive system. Also, despite the common complaint that the movement was conceived and controlled by "outside agitators," nearly all the protagonists in the Lynchburg struggle were home-grown products.

Jerry Falwell was born in Lynchburg in 1933 and, except for a brief period when he attended Baptist Bible College in Springfield, Missouri, has lived there all his life. Falwell is a common name in Lynchburg and a good many Falwells have money. Nobody seriously doubts Jerry could have become rich if he had set his mind to it, and little in his childhood seemed to be aiming him toward the ministry. To the best of his knowledge, his daddy, a heavy drinker, was never in a church building for a regular service in his whole life, though he did experience deathbed repentance and salvation three weeks before his death. His mother claims to have received "assurance of her salvation" in 1956, but she must have had some hints of it before then, since Jerry recalls her listening to pioneer religious broadcaster Charles E. Fuller's *Old Fashioned Revival Hour* when he was a teenager. Though Jerry joined the local Baptist church at age twelve, he did so "because it was the thing to do" rather than out of any deeply felt conviction about the condition of his soul. A more profound conversion experience followed when he was nineteen, but this, too, entailed no great emotional upheaval and was accompanied by a parallel intention to seek not only Christ but also the church pianist, Macel Pate, whom he later married.

In high school, Jerry was an excellent student and an outstanding athlete who played baseball well enough to receive an invitation from the St. Louis Cardinals to attend spring training. He also showed good promise as an engineering student at Lynchburg College for two years, but transferred to Baptist Bible College when he decided to become a minister. After graduating in 1956, he was about to accept a pastorate in Macon, Georgia, when a small band of people who had split off from the Park Avenue Baptist Church in Lynchburg persuaded him to help them establish a new church. According to the official story, the energetic and ambitious young pastor personally called on every family in Lynchburg, inviting them to the new Thomas Road Baptist Church. (Since the church had no black members for fifteen years, one assumes the visits were restricted to white families.) Despite the effectiveness of this technique, Falwell quickly moved to magnify his voice and multiply his image through broadcast media. In September 1956, he began preaching over a local radio station. Three months later, he expanded to television, at first with just a studio sermon, then eventually to a broadcast of Thomas Road's Sunday morning service. At the height of the program's success in 1980, he was heard daily on 280 radio stations and seen weekly on more than 300 television stations, and his church became one of the largest Protestant congregations in America.

The little band of charter members who first sought Jerry Falwell out and who witnessed his phenomenal success were, as their famous pastor describes them, "sort of grassroots, typical Southern people, blue-collar—few exceptions—sincere, honest, God-fearing people who were willing, though they didn't have a great deal of this world's goods, to invest what they had in building a new church. "No family, perhaps, exemplified Thomas Road better than the Godseys. The late Emmitt Godsey, a factory worker with little education, led the singing, visited the hospitals, preached at the nursing home, and helped Falwell baptize new members until a stroke disabled him. His wife, Nancy, was one of a cotton-mill worker's seven children and dropped out of high school to work for the telephone company in 1945. Emmitt and Nancy's children, Melody and Bill, are both teachers.

The picture the Godseys paint of their family and church life was typical for many conservative Christians in the 1950s. Emmitt Godsey taught his boys the value of work and the importance of minimizing debts and paying those they could not avoid. The only debt that remained constant was the Lord's "tithe," the tenth of total income that was pledged to the church, no matter what. "My husband went for thirty years, Sunday morning, Sunday night, and Wednesday night, without missing one meeting," Mrs. Godsey recalled, "and, as far as I know, all five of the children had perfect attendance for nineteen years." All the children memorized Scripture verses on a regular basis, and friends knew not to call the house at nine o'clock, because that was the time the family gathered to read three chapters of the Bible and pray. "That was a special joy to me," Melody recalls. "There were no excuses."

Melody, who married a divorced former Catholic with four children—"but he had already become a Christian"—admits it is difficult to replicate those conditions in her own home. "It's totally different as far as the influences of the world," she observed. "Sometimes it really gets to you, the things that are being shown on television." Bill Godsey sounded a similar note, but emphasized values and self-control more than external influences. "When I was growing up," he said, "you not only had values, but you had limits. You might want to hit somebody, but because you were a Christian you didn't hit them, or you might want to say something that was really ugly about a person, but because you were a Christian, you held your tongue. Today, a lot of folks do not have those limits. And I think you need them; otherwise, you're going to be doing things that you shouldn't do. That doesn't mean [we were] perfect or anything. It just means that there are some values taught within churches such as Thomas Road that I think are very important, and they taught them. That was something that was always discussed and talked about—you treat other people as you would want them to treat you. We could do away with jails tomorrow if everybody would just follow that simple little rule."

Yet however much it was stressed in Jerry Falwell's church, the Golden Rule was applied selectively, and Falwell did little to alter that fact. In 1958, he preached a sermon, titled "Segregation and Integration: Which?," in which he asserted that integration was not only wrong but would lead to the destruction of the white race. To his credit, Falwell makes no attempt to hide what he did. "As I recall," he said, "everyone who had taught me was a segregationist. As far as I knew at the time, every minister in this town was a segregationist—I mean among the white pastors. So that was no big deal. That kind of sermon was preached everywhere." He added, however, that he soon changed his mind on this vital question. "Not much later, within a year's time from preaching that sermon, I was coming to different conclusions, until finally I told the congregation, 'I've been wrong on that.' That wasn't a popular thing to say. But the real test came—it was probably 1960 or '61—when a black family came forward to join our church and wanted to be baptized. I said, 'All right, I'll baptize you,' and I did. But I told them that night, as we were about to go down in the water, I said, 'Neither one of us may come up out of that water, so I hope you're right with the Lord. I am.' And I baptized them. We lost a couple of families over that, but just that quickly it was all over. And as far as I know, we became the first church in this town to aggressively begin ministering to everyone. That doesn't sound like a big deal in 1996; in 1960 in the South, it was a big deal. And it caused criticism—in the city, in the community, not just in the church. There were people wondering, 'What is this young preacher trying to do, ruin our town?' "

This inspiring story has one significant flaw: It is almost certainly inaccurate. It is difficult to know just when Jerry Falwell changed his mind or his public position on integration, but Thomas Road Baptist Church remained segregated until 1968, and the first baptism of an African-American person appears not to have occurred until 1971.

IF A YOUNG white preacher could draw widespread approval for a sermon defending segregation in 1958, one might assume that a young black preacher would have little interest in leaving a comfortable pastorate in Providence, Rhode Island, to occupy a pulpit in Lynchburg. But Virgil Wood had grown up in Virginia, and he wanted to come home to be part of what was happening in the South. Martin Luther King's bus boycotts had gained a major victory for blacks in Montgomery and the year-old Southern Christian Leadership Conference (SCLC) was gearing up to press for similar gains throughout the South. Fully aware of the dangers that could befall black people who chose to exercise their citizenship rights, but suffused with "a kind of euphoria about what we could do with the whole of the South," Wood felt that "I needed to be back in my native Virginia, to be a part of the engagement that was taking place." In the spring of 1958, he came to the thriving Diamond Hill Baptist Church, with its long tradition of community service. After a year in the city, he also joined the faculty of Virginia Seminary, a school for African Americans.

In Lynchburg, as elsewhere, churches played the key role in "birthing" the civil rights movement, and the name old-timers speak with the greatest reverence is Vernon Johns, a compelling figure James Earl Jones portrayed in the 1994 television movie, "The Vernon Johns Story." As pastor of Court Street Baptist Church, Johns began to preach about civil rights as early as 1939. M. W. Thornhill, a Lynchburg funeral director who grew up under John's preaching, recalls that "we would get a sermon at least once a month on civil rights, civil disobedience, and respect as a man. We heard that constantly, and it was instilled in us. We felt we got more civil rights than any other church in America." Johns eventually left Lynchburg to pastor the Dexter Avenue Baptist Church in Montgomery. His uncompromising sermons there so discomfited that congregation that they accepted his resignation in 1952, replacing him with a young man they thought would be less likely to cause trouble: Martin Luther King, Jr.

To Virgil Wood, "Martin Luther King exemplified a person who faced the Southern terror. The Southern apartheid was a terrorist kind of thing. You had people doing anything necessary, including killing folks and burning down churches and killing children, clergy, grandmothers, to stop this incipient movement. So I had certain fears, just growing up as a black man in the South. Black men in the South were particularly vulnerable. If you wanted just to keep your life, you had to be totally compliant, acquiescent."

Wood readily agreed that black churches and their understanding of the Christian gospel provided the major impetus to the civil rights movement. "Black Christians," he explained, "saw in the gospel the polar opposite of what their oppressors saw. That comes through in many of the spirituals, which grew out of that long midnight in American history. The spirituals embody a certain spiritual genius, a certain wisdom, about how you survive this whole thing. They had to keep the faith when it didn't appear that any effort would make any difference at all. They had a kind of cultural ethos based on the gospel." Operating from this base, "the black church was the incubator of this new way of carrying the gospel into the streets, doing it in such a way that when we got into the streets we were no longer just the black church. We were Catholic nuns, we were Catholic priests, we were Jewish rabbis, and so forth. People from the broadest spectrum of the interfaith community were there. The only survival for America is to have a way of life that looks at the plight of all poor folks, all folks who are left out, black or white. I think that's been the genius of the black church's involvement with America."

Wood recalled that "Lynchburg had a wide-awake core group of people from probably a dozen local black churches" who were already working to improve the situation of blacks. The largest group belonged to the NAACP, which concentrated on changing things through the courts—the "legal beavers." Students and other young leaders such as Wood found the SCLC's confrontational tactics more appealing. Wood joined SCLC's national executive board in Virginia, and worked closely with his fellow Lynchburg pastor, Dr. Wyatt Tee Walker, who belonged to Dr. King's inner circle. With connections such as these, it was inevitable that Lynchburg would eventually have to deal with SCLC's nonviolent, but hardly passive, techniques for effecting change.

In other parts of the South, students inspired by the SCLC began staging "sit-ins." In February 1960, the civil rights movement entered a new and dramatic phase when four black students from North Carolina A & T College attempted to obtain service at a Woolworth's lunch counter in Greensboro, North Carolina. From that beginning, sit-ins became a favored means of challenging segregation in public facilities. Sit-ins occurred in perhaps a hundred southern cities during the next ten months. In December, the movement came to Lynchburg, and brought together two women, one black, one white, in a pivotal protest at a local drugstore lunch counter.

As one of nine children in a Holiness minister's family, Barbara Thomas Shannon grew up poor, wearing hand-me-down shoes and dresses made of feed sacks. She resented not only her family's poverty but the subservience and humiliation the color of their skin forced on them. She bridled at having to help her mother clean white people's houses and burned with embarrassment when she was not allowed to enter those same houses except as a servant. "I also resented it," she recalled, "when I would go downtown and there would be the four bathrooms: the 'white men,' 'white ladies,' 'colored men,' and 'colored women'—not 'colored ladies,' but 'colored women.' I never had an inkling that I would be able to change anything—it was there, had always been there—but I never felt it was right." When she graduated from high school in 1956 at age sixteen, Barbara attended all-black Virginia State for a brief period, dropped out, spent time with an older sister in Baltimore, then returned to Lynchburg in 1960 to enroll at Virginia Theological Seminary and College, the city's only institution of higher learning open to blacks.

Rebecca Owen grew up in Saluda, a tiny village in southeastern Virginia where her father worked in the bank and her mother taught Sunday school at the Methodist church. Like Barbara Thomas, she also quickly learned the rules about who was welcome where. "On my third birthday," she recalled while sitting in her Manhattan apartment, "an Afro-American woman who had been my primary caretaker made me a birthday cake, and I wanted this woman whom I loved very dearly to stay and have dinner with the family and have cake with us, and I asked my mother if Estelle could stay to dinner. I don't know exactly what was said to me, but I do know that I was made to feel very ashamed that I'd asked this question. I was told that Estelle wouldn't like to stay to dinner, that this would somehow embarrass her or be uncomfortable for her, and that I was extremely bad to have wanted this. It's one of my earliest childhood memories, and it was the beginning [of my awareness] of a very, very deep breach between feelings and conventions, feelings and thoughts, feelings and rules, that's a part of what I consider to be a really psychotic culture."

As a little girl, Rebecca Owen saw a marked disjunction between the gospel of compassion she absorbed in Sunday School and the inequality she saw in Saluda. "I was just puzzled as hell," she said, "that there seemed to be such a gap between what I was hearing about the gospel and what I saw people doing. I remember as a very young child asking questions like, 'This family's so poor; why're they so poor? Why don't rich people give them enough so that they're not poor?'" Despite her perplexity, Owen did not give up on the gospel. She remained active in her church, attended Methodist church camps and conferences, and worked at a Methodist mission school for disadvantaged children in eastern Kentucky the summer after finishing high school. At the end of that summer of 1957, Owen enrolled at Randolph-Macon, a Methodist-supported women's college in Lynchburg. "Going from this struggling mission school to this upper-middle-class, good academic college that was very concerned with the conventions, with making us 'ladies,' was a big culture shock for me. I think I had somehow imagined the church was more of a unified institution than in fact it was."

Rebecca Owen's years at Randolph-Macon did not dim her religious ardor nor her passion for equality. As president of both the Virginia Student Ecumenical Movement and the Virginia segment of the Methodist Student Movement, one of the more liberal religiously based student organizations of that era, she had occasion to interact with some of the black students who had participated in the Greensboro sit-ins. Fired by their example, she resolved to take some kind of decisive action in Lynchburg, feeling that "I would have to do this or leave the church. I did it primarily because I was a very fundamentalist Christian. I really felt very strongly that to think of myself as a Christian meant to be involved in the struggle there. It just seemed like this was the time and this was the place that God's will was being manifest."

After school started in the fall of 1960, Owen contacted several ministers, black and white, about setting up interracial discussion groups. By November, she and other members of the Randolph-Macon Human Relations Council started meeting with their counterparts from all-white Sweet Briar, Lynchburg College, and Virginia Seminary. Most of the meetings took place at the Diamond Hill or Court Street Baptist churches, or at a black-owned restaurant known as The Mecca. Barbara Thomas attended several of these gatherings. She remembered that "most of the white students actually had no contact with blacks except for domestic 'help,' and they genuinely wanted to know just what we were going through and what we felt. I never felt at any time that they were just being nosy or just wanted information in order to put us down. I felt a genuine concern, and it really made me feel good."

During the Thanksgiving break, Rebecca Owen went to New York to meet with the Methodist Board of Missions and the National Student Christian Federation to discuss how various groups could provide strategic and financial support, including legal counsel and bail, to civil rights demonstrators in the South. When she returned from that errand, she was ready to move. A couple of weeks later, at one of the student meetings, someone—no one seems quite sure who—brought up the possibility of trying to integrate some of the businesses in Lynchburg. In casting about for likely targets, they soon hit upon Patterson's drugstore. Patterson's was probably the largest drugstore in Lynchburg and Mr. Patterson gave credit to black customers, which helped him attract a large black clientele. Still, when the students tried to set up a meeting to discuss desegregation of the store's lunch counter, he told them he was not interested in talking to them "then or at any other time." When additional efforts failed, they decided to go to the store in a group and, if he still refused to talk, to sit in.

They fully understood that such an action would violate a new Virginia trespass law, passed in the wake of the Greensboro demonstrations, that made it a felony offense for a black person, or whites acting in concert with that person, to attempt to be served in a segregated establishment. Understandably, Barbara Thomas admitted, "I was kind of hesitant because I had seen the police dogs, the fire hoses, all that went with sit-in demonstrations, and I probably would not have gone, except that there were four white students who were willing to go. I felt that if they were willing to go, I had to go. This was something totally new, to stand up to a law that I felt was unjust. We were taught, 'You accept it. That's just the way it is.' I was petrified."

Mr. Patterson may have been hard to catch on the telephone, but the six students had no trouble finding him in person. When they first sat down at the counter, the clerks ignored them, then finally said, "Coloreds aren't served here." To subvert that rule, the white students ordered coffee and Cokes, then passed them to Barbara Thomas and a black male student. At that point, Patterson emerged, asked them several times to leave, growing angrier with each request. Playing out what had become ritual across the South, Patterson finally called the police, who arrested the students for trespassing on private property—even though the property was a business establishment that ostensibly welcomed the public—and carted them off to jail, where they remained for a few hours before being released.

The protesters came to trial in early January. Rebecca Owen remembers it as an exciting, shocking, thrilling event. "I'd never heard this level of discourse openly taking place in the South. The judge was rampantly prejudiced in expressing his views, and both of our lawyers were speaking very strongly about civil rights. People just didn't talk about these things in the South. All of this had been so covered, so unspoken. It felt really extraordinary. The judge was totally perplexed and puzzled and unprepared for it, and both of our lawyers were prepared to make very strong statements about civil rights in general. They had sermons to give as much as they had defendants to defend. And that was very exciting, to hear what they had to say in that particular context, kind of *in vivo,* with all of these people there from Lynchburg."

Whatever the level of their lawyers' skill and eloquence, the students were easily convicted; they had, after all, deliberately violated the law. Still, though they could have been fined one thousand dollars and sent to jail for twelve months, they were sentenced to only thirty days in jail, the maximum penalty under the previous trespass law. In a public statement printed in the Lynchburg *News* on January 4, 1961, they defended their action by saying, "We have taken seriously the most basic principles of our Judeo-Christian heritage. . . . These, we believe, represent a Higher law than the law of governments." For a few days, the group remained free on bail—posted by members of the black community—while their lawyers appealed the constitutionality of the trespass law in federal courts. Then, fearful the appeals process had insufficient dramatic impact, they decided they could make a stronger statement by going to jail. "We were quite familiar with the slogan, 'jail, not bail,' " Rebecca Owen explained. "It was very much in the air that this was the strongest statement one could make." Virgil Wood approved of their decision. "Oh, that was great. The movement protocol was that, if you went to jail, you stayed there. That's where the point was made. Every day you're in jail, it puts a certain kind of pressure on the local establishment. They want you out of jail. In fact, we even had cases where the judge himself or someone close to the court paid people's fines just to get them out of jail."

By all accounts, their nineteen days in jail (they only served two-thirds of their sentence) were far from dreadful for the students. Jailers were careful not to do anything that could possibly be construed as brutality. In addition, neighbors came by to chat, and black churches sent their choirs over to sing for their young heroes. But not all the visitors were so welcome or benign. A delegation from the Virginia State Assembly came to see Rebecca Owen, strongly suggesting she was a communist and telling her that if she did not leave the state at the end of the school year, she would be tried for sedition. "And I believed them," she said, "so I told them I thought I would leave. That was pretty menacing. They were scary men."

Apart from that singular encounter, Owen admitted that her time behind bars "was in many ways a very sweet time. Dr. Wood and other African-American ministers in the community mobilized their congregations to write these enormously touching letters to us. There was a telegram from Martin Luther King. I felt blessed to be a part of that, to share it and live it." Owen realized, of course, that her situation was both voluntary and temporary, which reduced most of the sting, but she and her friends also felt they were engaged in a righteous cause. On the day they went to jail, they issued a statement declaring that "we are confident that no person of good conscience will idly stand by . . . while we students who sought to speak against the destruction of human potential which results from racial discrimination are punished for completely implementing our faith in Christian-democratic principles." A few days later, in a statement published in the *Washington Post* and the black newspaper, the *Lynchburg Advance,* they expressed similar sentiments, adding that "as we accept the penalty of this law, we feel it is not so much we who are on trial as it is insensitive Lynchburg society that is on trial."

After the jail lifted an initial ban on reading matter, Barbara Thomas concentrated on her Bible. Rebecca Owen's reading matter included the Bible, Dostoyevsky, and Dietrich Bonhoeffer, the German pastor who had been imprisoned and eventually executed for his resistance to the Nazi regime. She was already in the midst of writing a senior thesis on Bonhoeffer's life and thought, and reading his moving *Letters and Papers from Prison* seemed particularly fitting. "Bonhoeffer had helped me very much in my own thinking when he said, 'God calls us to be fully in the world and active for the world,' not to be separated somehow from the world in some kind of piety. His words there were a real liberation to me personally, having grown up in a pietistic, moralistic church."

Rebecca and Barbara and their comisdemeanants may have been at peace, but the world outside was not. Reactions to what they had done were as varied as attitudes toward integration itself. Owen remembers that "my father blamed it on the Methodist Church—he'd been born a Southern Baptist. He said I'd been brainwashed, but there wasn't any real rift between him and me. My mother was more ambivalent. She kind of believed it was the right thing to do, but I think she was absolutely, totally disgusted that I had done it. She really felt socially stigmatized by it. My sister, who was three years older than I, was very much against it. The summer after the sit-in, she systematically destroyed a lot of things of mine that were in the house—just burned them—including a telegram from Martin Luther King, one from Robert Kennedy, and many, many letters from Dr. Wood's church. Her husband said I was becoming more and more like Eleanor Roosevelt every day. I thought, 'What a wonderful compliment!' My grandmother, though, had unqualified congratulations for me and thought I was doing God's will. So the family was a mixed bag."

Barbara Thomas did not know what to expect from her family, because they had never discussed civil rights, "but to my surprise, they were supportive. I was afraid of the repercussions that might come onto the family, maybe some type of violence, and I felt that might have been their main concern. But they were very supportive. My father said he wished he had done something before that himself." Thomas herself, however, never again took part in any civil rights activities. Dissension within the ranks of the NAACP and SCLC and fear of involvement with other groups about which she knew little frightened her. "I was so confused," she explained. "While we were in jail, we got correspondence from every organization you can think of—there was ACLU, there was CORE [Congress on Racial Equality], there were so many groups approaching me—and I had heard about some of these groups having communist involvement, and I was totally afraid of communists. So, not knowing which group was which, I never really got into any of them. Also, I've never been a very public person. I was embarrassed by all the publicity, and with the dissension among the different groups of leaders, I just felt that I no longer wanted to be involved."

Most Lynchburg whites, at least as Virgil Wood remembers it, were less ambivalent than the Owen and Thomas families. Wood described the students' challenge to the dominant mores as "like pouring ice water on a hot stove. Looking back, it seems so innocent and benign, but at the time, it was like declaring war on a way of life, and there were people who said, 'By golly, we're not going to let this happen.' And you had the mobilization against what we were doing by the top echelons of power in the region. So it was somewhat frightening at first."

The more moderate elements in the city, white and black, including many who believed in integration, disagreed less with the students' aims than with their choice of tactics—"We honor what you have done, but this is not the way to do it." Rebecca Owen found that message of moderation particularly galling. "The thing I was sickest of by the time I finally left Lynchburg," she said, "was the number of people of 'good will' who told us they 'revered and respected our convictions,' that we were these 'holy children with right convictions,' but that they despised our behavior, that we shouldn't be doing these indiscreet things, because it 'set back race relations' ten years, or decades, or a hundred years. That just seemed so totally lukewarm and wimpy. I felt so strongly that my behavior and my convictions could not be pulled apart that way, that they were integrally matched with one another. As I look back on that now, I still totally support my behavior, but my firm knowledge of God's will and my certainty about exactly how things should go seem [in retrospect] a little more naïve, a little more 'iffy.' I feel a little embarrassed about that."

NAACP leaders avoided the confrontational approach that Rebecca Owen took, preferring legal challenges and behind-the-scenes negotiations. Virgil Wood, his colleagues in the SCLC, and many Lynchburg blacks, young and old, did not concur. When it became increasingly clear that neither the Council nor the NAACP would ever be comfortable with confrontational tactics, Wood took the lead in establishing the Improvement Association, which comprised leading lay people and pastors from many of the black churches and which began immediately to twist the thorn in Lynchburg's festering side.

Wood and his colleagues had realized that the community had gotten over the initial shock of the first sit-in quickly, "So it was clear that we needed to escalate the pressure. We needed to hit another lick at the same target." Within a few days of the first sit-in, another group of black students and a group of theological students and pastors attempted to integrate Patterson's drugstore; in both cases, they were arrested and jailed. Other groups visited other stores, with varying results. The stepped-up campaign had an effect. On February 25, the same day Rebecca Owen, Barbara Thomas, and their four friends were released from jail, five Lynchburg businesses quietly opened their lunch counters to blacks. Still, the struggle was just beginning. In the weeks that followed, the Improvement Association announced its intention to file an omnibus suit against the city of Lynchburg, calling for the desegregation of all public facilities. In response, city officials announced they would permanently drain both of the two white swimming pools and the one Negro pool rather than permit them to be integrated. The Association shot back with an outline of steps for renewing "all-out warfare" against discriminatory practices in Lynchburg, including boycotts and picketing of offending businesses.

The jailing of respected pastors and seminarians, even for a few days, was, Wood recalled, "a new moment of consciousness-raising and education for the community as a whole—spiritual leaders in jail because they had decided to break the law and to accept the consequences of their decisions! Needless to say, the broader black community was thrilled." However broad-based, that thrill was not universal. Wood lost his post at the seminary and the students who had joined the protests were not allowed to re-enter in the fall. "It was a sad chapter in the life of the president of the school," Wood noted. "He had always been what we call a 'good race man,' somebody who stood for his people no matter what, but the pressures from downtown were just too much for him and for others who had to depend on the good will of downtown interests."

Wood himself came under heavy criticism within his own congregation, but was spared from getting fired by strong expressions of support from what he called "the ordinary people" in the church, as distinguished from "the elites" who were more beholden to "downtown" interests. Not that he won everybody over. "I wish I had a dollar," he mused, "for every time I was told, 'The church is for saving souls, not for politics. Stay out of politics and stick to the gospel. Stay out of economics and stick to the gospel.' One of the answers I've always had for that is that our Lord said far more about taking care of people, feeding the hungry, economic justice, even about business, than He did about love. I don't think you can have an authentic gospel if it ignores politics and economics."

OVER THE NEXT two years, sit-ins, swim-ins, pray-ins, boycotts, pickets, and suits continued. Virgil Wood occupied the center of the storm and, not surprisingly, sometimes felt its full fury. Haywood Robinson, a Lynchburg native then pastoring a church near Pittsburgh, recalled with amusement that on several occasions when he returned home to preach at Diamond Hill, "at least one night or one day during that week, Virgil would be in jail. He'd been arrested for leading a demonstration or he'd have to go to court to stand trial for a previous arrest for leading a demonstration. And the very next day, if it could be arranged, he'd be back in the streets carrying the banner again. And there was always very warm and fervent and special prayer for him at that time." Inevitably, such activities got Wood labeled as a "Communist agitator" or "sympathizer," and laid him open to attacks by outraged bigots. "I had a young family," he recalled, "two children, then of first grade and kindergarten age. And the calls would come, the nasty calls: 'Nigger, we gonna kill you.' You can't imagine what that does to you, having someone say, 'I'm gonna kill you,' even when you know they are the hate-mongers. We had to find a way to deal with it that did not deteriorate our spirit, so my wife and I developed a strategy of reading the Bible to them. The Bible stayed open by the phone. They'd call and start spewing out their venom; we'd start reading from the Psalms, just starting where we'd left off the last time. Eventually, out of exasperation, they would just call us a name and hang up. Those kinds of things can be very demoralizing, especially when it's directed at your family, like the time they threw bricks through the windows of the parsonage—bricks in my little daughter's bedroom. And the time they shot through my car, and I'd just been out of it a few moments. But we found out in the movement that if you lingered at the level of your fear—and there was a lot to be afraid of—you became a prisoner, you became paralyzed, so you managed to keep on going and trusting in the Lord."

When Virgil Wood left Diamond Hill for an experimental inner-city parish in Boston in November 1963, Lynchburg had a different look. School integration, though still in its infancy, was well underway and most public facilities were open to all. The "White Only" and "Colored Women" signs that had offended young Barbara Thomas had disappeared. The Promised Land was still far in the distance, but, as Wood modestly put it, "Change was in the air, and people were reasonably certain that much of it, at least, was permanent." Wood's successor, Haywood Robinson, was pleasantly surprised to see that "the Joshua development," the bringing down of the walls of segregation, had been mostly accomplished. He realized, however, that having the walls down "did not necessarily mean that people knew how to live with one another or that person-to-person contacts were being made or established. So I began to see myself as a person whose job was going to be to try to build bridges across those chasms left when the walls fell. The people who had been divided by legal and self-erected and institutionally imposed barriers for so many years needed some bridges to bring them together. And I wanted to be one of those bridges and help build others."

JERRY FALWELL'S THOMAS Road church expanded rapidly during the 1960s, adding staff, starting a youth camp on an island in the middle of the James River, and launching a building program that included a one thousand-seat sanctuary and several adjoining structures. Falwell's later accounts to the contrary, however, none of this impressive growth included black folk, and none seemed to be in the plans. When the 1963 March on Washington drew more than two hundred thousand people to hear Martin Luther King deliver his famed "I have a dream" oration and to urge Congress to pass President Lyndon Johnson's sweeping civil rights legislation, Falwell spoke against the measure in the pulpit and, after it passed, declared that "it should be considered civil wrongs rather than civil rights" and labeled it "a terrible violation of human and private-property rights."

Most Americans, including many Southerners, hailed the Civil Rights Act of 1964 as the beginning of a new era. M. W. Thornhill remembers feeling a great sense of hopefulness: "We're going places; we'll get jobs; we're going be treated as decent human beings. Our way of life has changed. I'm glad to be a citizen." But not everyone shared those sentiments. Barry Goldwater, the Republican nominee for the presidency that year, voted against the act, contending that the federal government had no authority to regulate such matters as employment and public accommodations. Goldwater later felt he took "a bum rap" from opponents who tried to paint him as a racist. Critics charged him and the Republican Party with exploiting white backlash generated by racial conflict. For Haywood Robinson, there is no question that Goldwater's backers represented "an organized political effort to turn back the sociological clock," to reverse the march of black progress. Virgil Wood agrees, noting that talk of states' rights and objections to federal regulations were often little more than code words used to make old-style racism seem respectable. They did not exempt Jerry Falwell from that accusation.

In July 1964, less than three weeks after Johnson signed the historic act and asked all citizens to "close the springs of racial poison" and help "eliminate the last vestiges of injustice in America," one black and three white high school students, all apparently associated with the CORE and brandishing a sign that asked "Does God Discriminate?," staged a "kneel-in" on the steps of Thomas Road Baptist Church. Police evicted them and, according to one account, threatened to shoot them if they returned the following Sunday. Falwell took the incident lightly, criticizing the boys for interfering in the life of his church but observing that there was nothing wrong with them that a haircut couldn't cure. Looking back years later, he acknowledged the courage the boys had shown and recalled that when, a few days later, an elderly black man who shined his shoes every Saturday asked him, "When will I be able to join your church?," the question hit him "like a boxer feels a bad blow to the stomach."

Whatever his gut feelings, Falwell did not immediately soften his stance toward the civil rights movement. He resented feeling "bullied and attacked by white Northern demonstrators" who "demand we follow their dictates," and was angry at Congress and the Supreme Court for assuming rights that belonged to the individual states. He especially resented Martin Luther King and distributed anti-King literature furnished him by King's longtime nemesis, FBI Director J. Edgar Hoover. But his most famous attack on the movement came in a March 1965 sermon, "Ministers and Marches," in which he leveled a broadside at King, his black ministerial colleagues, and the Northern clergy whose liberal theology made them fully as suspect as their politics. Although he acknowledged that "many sincere persons are participating" in the movement, he questioned "the sincerity and nonviolent intentions of some civil rights leaders such as Dr. Martin Luther King, Jr., Mr. James Farmer, and others, who are known to have left-wing associations. It is very obvious that the Communists, as they do in all parts of the world, are taking advantage of a tense situation in our land, and are exploiting every incident to bring about violence and bloodshed." Speaking of the role ministers should properly play, he declared that "our only purpose on this earth is to know Christ and to make him known. Believing the Bible as I do, I would find it impossible to stop preaching the pure saving Gospel of Jesus Christ and begin doing anything else—including the fighting of communism or participating in the civil rights reform. . . . Preachers are not called to be politicians, but to be soul winners."

Falwell has long since repudiated that famous sermon, even calling it "false prophecy," but his 1995 account of how he regarded it then is nonetheless surprising. "I was saying to pastors that we should not be involved politically; we should not be out leading marches, we should not be out demonstrating, doing lie-ins and pray-ins and sleep-ins and so forth. We should be preaching the gospel and changing people's hearts. And I used my own testimony in that sermon about how, in the early days, we had refused to accept black members in our church and how, when I came to the conviction of the wrongness of that position and baptized the first black family here, we had lost people over it. But I still had the confidence then that government, the courts, the Congress, would correct these social ills; I had the confidence that we could trust government to make the difference. I was wrong, and later, of course, became very involved."

A plausible account of a man dealing with a complex set of issues, but again, an account that does not match the data. Falwell's distribution of material attacking Martin Luther King and preaching against integration and the Civil Rights Act were fully as political as supporting the movement would have been. His "testimony" about accepting blacks from the early days at Thomas Road neither appears in the printed version of the sermon nor squares with the facts. And his admitted anger at Congress and the Supreme Court hardly sounds like that of a man who felt he could "trust government to make the difference."

Within the black community, Jerry Falwell and the Thomas Road church were viewed less as vehement opponents to civil rights than as folk who, like many other whites they knew, were likely to stand on the wrong side of the issues that concerned them most. Falwell's next major project did nothing to alter that impression. In 1965, impatient over the slow pace of school integration, Commissioner of Education Francis Keppel ordered all public schools to establish and implement plans for substantial integration by fall of 1967. In November 1966, Falwell announced plans for the formation of Lynchburg Christian Academy, which would open as a kindergarten-through-fifth-grade institution in the fall of 1967 and would subsequently add grades until it reached K-12 status. Falwell named a Board of Directors and declared he would serve as president himself. At the time of the announcement, Falwell refused to say whether the school would be integrated or segregated, claiming that administrative policy had not been fully formulated, but a subsequent story in the Lynchburg *News* described the academy as "a private school for white students."

Falwell attributed his interest in building a school to the 1962 and 1963

Supreme Court decisions that banned school-sponsored prayer and Bible reading, as well as to other developments he felt indicated that "the Christian world view was not only going to be pushed back but eliminated, and that another might replace it." Not surprisingly, he had anticipated the question of motivation. "There were those who thought we were probably starting Lynchburg Christian Academy to have a white-flight school—that kind of thing—but from day one I made it clear that Lynchburg Christian Academy (and we had a college in mind at the time, and a seminary) would be for any and all who loved Christ and who wanted to study under born-again teachers in a Christian environment with academic excellence." As for the "whites only" designation, Falwell has insisted since at least 1982 that the newspaper made a mistake.

If the Lynchburg *News* erred, it apparently published no retraction. When the school began to accept applications in April 1967, the board of the black Lynchburg Ministerial Association issued a statement to the effect that, because of its concern for "our Lord's inclusiveness," it "deplored the use of the word 'Christian' in the title of a school which excludes Negroes and other non-white people." The *News* noted that the statement "does not mention by name the Lynchburg Christian School Corporation which has announced plans to construct a segregated school on Evergreen Farms."

Whatever Falwell's deepest motives in founding a school, it is surely the case that, for many who had been part of the burgeoning Christian school movement, other factors were more important than avoiding association with blacks. Pierre Guillermin, who came to Lynchburg in 1967 to help Falwell found the academy, played a crucial role in launching Lynchburg Baptist College (subsequently renamed Liberty Bible College, then Liberty University), articulated a philosophy of Christian education widely held in conservative religious circles, Protestant and Catholic. "I came to Lynchburg primarily to train young people to serve God in all walks of life, whether [as] a doctor or lawyer or educator or businessman. I wanted them to carry with them belief in God and Christ and in the basic principles of Christian living that are in the Scriptures. When we started the academy, we made certain definitive decisions. We said that we were going to employ only those who were Christian . . . to integrate into our curriculum as much as possible the Christian principles of life and the Scripture so that a student would understand that 'these are the very foundations of your faith. These are the principles by which you are supposed to live.' . . . I think there was a concern on the part of Christians, regardless of where they lived, that we were losing a sense of our values and standards and principles in the United States. To maintain the strength of what all of us feel America was established upon, the Christian principles of life, it was necessary to focus our attention on education, because that was the heart of the nation."

The academy's white-only policy apparently lasted no more than a year or two. According to Falwell, who said the school had no black students the first year "because none applied," three were admitted the second year—and blacks and other minorities have been accepted since that time. The Reverend Haywood Robinson seemed willing to view this change in policy in a positive light. Readily acknowledging that many of the private schools that sprang up throughout the South in the 1960s and '70s were "segregation academies," he pointed out that "a number of them have changed focus through the years, some of it market-driven, but some because of a change in conscience and heart. I'd like to think that they have become more 'embracive,' and if that is the case, I truly applaud it."

LIKE MOST OF the South, Lynchburg did indeed begin to change, slowly but surely. In the early seventies, a secret gathering of black and white community leaders led to a public statement by Mayor Leighton Dodd that discrimination in Lynchburg must come to an end. In 1976, M. W. Thornhill would be elected to the City Council, and in 1990, he would become Lynchburg's first black mayor.

Thomas Road Baptist Church participated in Lynchburg's changes in the 1970s. It began a "bus ministry outreach" to minority neighborhoods and, in 1968, that effort bore fruit when the first black family to apply for membership at the church was unanimously accepted by the board of deacons.

The Godsey family, who seem representative of the early, all-white Thomas Road congregation, has adapted to these changes with minimal trauma. Bill, now a teacher in the public schools, finds it difficult to believe he went to segregated schools until the eleventh grade. "It's just mind-boggling. I have a classroom of students that's almost fifty-fifty black and white, and I mention something like that, and they look at me like, 'Really? Golleee!' " As for the church that nurtured him, Godsey observed, "I remember when people from different cultures came to Thomas Road and caused quite a stir, because maybe they dressed a little differently. Fact is, I remember a time when if you grew a mustache, you weren't in total favor. It's not perfect yet, but I think the church has gone through the same evolution as society has." As for Jerry Falwell's evolution, Godsey suspects that, today, his pastor might "rephrase" some of the things he said in the 1960s, "or he might be on a different side. He probably was like most people in the South, and did not realize the importance of the civil rights movement till later on. We're talking about millions and millions of people."

Bill's mother has less trouble remembering the old order and the difficulties change posed for black and white alike. "It really was hard to accept," she acknowledged, "because the older, wonderful black people didn't approve of their children pushing and wanting to sit at the front of the bus or go into the cafeterias and restaurants with everybody else, because they were raised to be with their own people and to stay with themselves and not mingle with the white people." She mentioned a woman, college-educated herself, who was disappointed at her daughter's involvement in the civil rights movement, "because she wasn't raised that way. She was raised to stay in her place. But I presume somebody had to take the stand, so she did it. It took off from there, and then it just became a normal thing. I think they've come a long ways. They're able to do 'most anything and go anywhere that we can go. So we have to treat them that way."

Looking back on this tumultuous time, Haywood Robinson, who grew up in Lynchburg and has been pastor at Diamond Hill Baptist Church for more than thirty years, reflected on the civil rights movement and its inextricable connection to the Christian church. "There was a feeling of great hope," he said, "a feeling of specialness, of history in the making. You could feel the energy of change in the air. But it was also a time of real frustration, a time of one step forward and two steps backwards, a time of wondering 'when?', and a time of a great deal of suffering. You could feel the real anguish of spirit over 'How long, how long, Lord?' Because the walls were real, the battles were real, the discouragement was real, the bruises were real, and the pain was very real. This wasn't a great stage production. This was real, this was battleground, this was a kind of warfare of the spirit, and there was a feeling of 'Now or never. We've come too far to turn back.' And without the involvement of the black church, the movement not only would not have been successful; I'm convinced it never would have been born. My first hope about the possibility of change in this area took place under the dome of a church and within a religious atmosphere, and practically every time I heard it, I heard it foremost and most memorably from the pulpit from a black preacher, or from some committed soldier of the Cross talking about it and testifying in a black church. To think of the civil-rights movement—that whole panorama of events and emotions and energies that took place particularly in the Sixties and in the early Seventies—without thinking of the church is, for me, inconceivable. I don't think the movement could possibly have been born in any other way. And that was the defining moment, a pivotal time. The victories achieved at that time—while blacks and other minorities might have been the immediate beneficiaries—actually represent the shining moment of glory for this nation as a nation."

CHAPTER

3

A MAN
ON HORSEBACK

THE EXHILARATION FELT by Lynchburg's Haywood Robinson, though shared by millions of Americans, black and white alike, was not universal. And the "whole panorama of events and emotions and energies" that marked the 1960s was, for many, anything but "a shining moment of glory." On the contrary, the changes occurring in America in that period seemed to them to point toward chaos and destruction of all they cherished. They had no intention, however, of giving up without a fight. They preferred an America they had known, and not that long ago. They determined to recover and conserve it, however long that might take.

In 1960 virtually everyone had known that Richard Nixon would be the GOP candidate. Still, a small group of delegates to the Republican National Convention had regarded the Eisenhower/Nixon administration as insufficiently conservative and had nominated Senator Barry Goldwater of Arizona. Goldwater understood he had no chance and quickly withdrew from the race in a stirring speech in which he not only offered the expected encouragement to Nixon, but also declared, "The Republican Party platform deserves the support of every American over the blueprint for socialism presented by the Democrats. We have been losing elections because conservatives too often fail to vote. Let's grow up, conservatives. If we want to take this party back, and I think we can some day, let's get to work."

Despite the closeness of the election, President Kennedy proved so appealing, particularly in his public addresses and encounters with the press, that many Americans who had opposed him or supported him only with reluctance, actually began to ask themselves what they could do for their country—in the Peace Corps, in government, in the race to the moon, in the struggle for civil rights. Some even came to believe that the road through the New Frontier might ultimately lead to Camelot, a kind of secular equivalent to the Kingdom of God. In truth, despite the fact that communism was still a powerful force and the Soviet Union still posed a major threat to national security, a movement whose central theme was that the nation was going to hell in a handbasket seemed a little out of step. And indeed, those who sounded such pessimistic notes most shrilly appeared to be losing ground. After Robert Welch, head of the strongly anti-communist John Birch Society, labeled Dwight Eisenhower "a dedicated, conscious agent of the Communist conspiracy," such conservative notables as *National Review* publisher William Rusher and Barry Goldwater distanced themselves from that organization. For his part, Ike bluntly observed, "To try to make politics completely black or completely white is simply stupid." Billy Graham, still viewing the advance of communism as "almost surely a sign of the Second Coming," nevertheless repudiated the still-common right-wing charge that America's pulpits were filled with legions of covert communists, noting that he had never met a single minister in the United States whom he suspected of being a communist. He also commended President Kennedy's Peace Corps and recommended that the United States send massive quantities of surplus food to communist China during a famine that blighted that nation in 1961. "We are not at war with the people of China," he said. "I feel we have a moral and spiritual responsibility to share our surpluses with them. We cannot compromise with their ideology, but we should feed them when they are hungry."

The thunder on the right, however, did not grow quiet. As historian Erling Jorstad observed, Kennedy and his clan made a perfect target: "Roman Catholic, Harvard, intellectual, Boston-accented, sophisticated, very wealthy, liberal, and consistently good copy for the mass media." Right-wing leaders understood how poorly this image played with their own constituencies and learned to exploit it to raise money and enlist followers "by presenting themselves as America's only real antidote to the venomous New Frontier."

In response to the barrage of attacks that Billy James Hargis, Carl McIntire, and their brethren launched at him, Kennedy proclaimed:

[T]here have always been those on the fringe of society who have sought to escape their own responsibility by finding a simple solution, an appealing slogan or a convenient scapegoat. . . . Men who are unwilling to face up to the dangers from without are convinced that the real danger comes from within. They look suspiciously at their neighbors and their leader. They call for a "man on horseback" because they do not trust the people. They find treason in our churches, in our highest court, in our treatment of water [a reference to the common conservative opposition to fluoridation]. . . . Let our patriotism be reflected in the creation of confidence in one another, rather than in crusades of suspicion.

Kennedy doubtless hoped his listeners would apply the "crusades of suspicion" label to Hargis's Christian Crusade and Fred Schwarz's Christian Anti-Communist Crusade without his having to specify them. Hargis, in a pointed response, left less to chance:

This nation today is in the hands of a group of Harvard radicals who have long ago been "hooked" by the insidious dope of socialism and view human life from the international standpoint. . . . They are a dangerous scourge—and they are so deeply entrenched in power that they can be removed only by a nationwide upsurge of conservatism—which, please God, will come in the elections of next November. It makes no difference that these Harvard eggheads call themselves Democrats or Republicans. This has now become a distinction without a difference. They are liberals; liberals are socialists; and Khrushchev himself said that socialism is "the first phase of communism."

This was red-meat rhetoric, and Hargis and his ilk could roar without respite. While it marginalized them in the eyes of the major media and much of the general populace, it caused their circulation lists to grow and their incomes to swell as they attracted people who had not shown much interest in dispensationalist premillennialism or arguments for the inerrancy of Scripture. Between 1960 and 1964, subscriptions to Hargis's *Christian Crusade* grew from 58,000 to 98,600, and McIntire's *Christian Beacon* rose from a circulation of 20,000 to 66,500. The Christian Crusade's income averaged about $800,000 over that same period, but contributions to McIntire's Twentieth Century Reformation jumped from $635,000 in 1961 to more than $3 million in 1964. The John Birch Society experienced a similar increase, from just under $600,000 in 1960 to $3,200,000 in 1964. In addition, Hargis proclaimed "the Bad News" on his *Christian Crusade* broadcast, which aired seven nights a week on super-power Mexican radio stations, and McIntire expanded his radio ministry from one station in 1958 to 540 in early 1964. By the end of 1962, *Life Line,* a 15-minute radio program begun and heavily supported by Texas billionaire H. L. Hunt, carried a similar (though less explicitly religious) message to 42 states over a syndicate of approximately 300 stations. These and dozens of smaller organizations helped keep conservatives across the country in contact with one another and stirred up about issues that troubled them.

Conservatives were deeply concerned about the Red Menace and the national government's failure to resist it. The fact that Fidel Castro had

managed to install a communist government in Cuba, just ninety miles off
the coast of Florida, had helped support the John Birch Society's charge that
Dwight Eisenhower was in league with Moscow. The fiasco at the Bay of
Pigs, when lack of American support made it easy for Castro's troops to rout
invading anti-Castro rebels, coupled with the discovery that Russia had nuclear missiles based on the island, seemed clear proof that Kennedy was also
taking orders from the Kremlin. In the same spirit, when Khrushchev subsequently caved in to the president's demand that the missiles be removed, it
was seen as just another orchestrated ploy to lull Americans into a false sense
of security.

If the government was serious about fighting communism, the argument
ran, why not send in the Marines to kick Castro into the Caribbean? Why
not tear down the Berlin Wall? Why had we allowed Mao Tse-tung to oust
Chiang Kai-shek and cast the communist mantle over the most populous
nation in the world? Why were we selling wheat to Russia? Why were we
helping train soldiers of our putative "allies," when they were certain to use
these same skills against us? And why, most of all, why were we muzzling
those who tried to warn and protect us, such as Major Edwin Walker, whom
the Air Force fired for subjecting his troops to a "citizenship education
program" that included materials prepared by the John Birch Society and
lectures by the Church League of America's Edgar C. Bundy? (After Walker
was forced to resign, Hargis signed him up for a cross-country speaking tour
he dubbed "Operation Midnight Ride," in which the two of them called
for an invasion of Cuba and inveighed against the National Council of
Churches and the Harvard radicals in the White House.)

The right wing, political and religious, also inveighed against the "Warren
Court," whose decisions ordered the end of segregation, banned illegally
obtained evidence (making it harder to convict criminals), placed restrictions
on McCarthy-type congressional investigations of subversion, and lifted restrictions on issuing passports to suspected communists. Conservatives put
up billboards demanding that Congress "Impeach Earl Warren!" But nothing, perhaps, generated more lasting resentment against the Supreme Court
and stirred more concern among conservative Christians than the 1962 and
1963 decisions banning officially sponsored prayer and Bible reading in public schools. The Court claimed such practices violated the historic First
Amendment prohibition against government establishment of religion. Its
critics viewed the decision as a declaration of war against Christianity, a
conviction that has not diminished over time.

Billy James Hargis's son, Bill, an opera singer and entertainer in Houston,
recalled the day in 1962 when his father got the news of the Court's decision
outlawing school-sponsored prayer. "We were in Colorado Springs"—Hargis owned a hotel and youth camp in nearby Manitou Springs—"and had

gone to an ice-cream parlor. As we were leaving, we saw the newspaper machine and the headline that said the Supreme Court had ruled against prayer. All the way home, my dad talked about how this was really the beginning of the end for America, that the country had turned its back on God, and that any country that did that couldn't stand. As I sat there in the back seat listening to him—he probably wasn't even aware I was paying attention—I remember being dramatically upset. It made a profound impression on me and really put the fear of the Lord in me. I felt like this was a tragic event and, looking back on it, I still do. Back in the hotel, I dissolved into tears and my mother came and found me and she took me to my father's office there in the hotel, and he opened up the Bible with me, and that's the day I accepted Christ as my personal savior and became a Christian." The senior Hargis's subsequent fulminations against the Court and his overt support for the "Becker Amendment," which sought to exempt school-sponsored prayer and Bible reading from the Court's prohibitions, led the IRS to revoke his organization's tax-exempt status in 1964.

Conservatives saw further proof of government's persecuting them when John Kennedy was assassinated in 1963. Because the killing occurred in Dallas, a hotbed of right-wing activity at the time, some early reports blamed far-right extremists for the deed—much as Middle Easterners were initially suspected of the 1995 Oklahoma City bombing. When the assassin, Lee Harvey Oswald, turned out to be a minor-league malcontent with well-documented communist ties, the Right was quick to capitalize on the opportunity to blast anti-right-wing sentiment. Carl McIntire offered radio listeners a packet of materials entitled, *A Communist Kills Our President but the Right Wing Is Blamed*. Robert Welch and University of Illinois classics professor Revilo P. Oliver contended that the Kremlin had ordered Kennedy's death because he had not been sufficiently effective in carrying out his assignment to convert America to communism. Hargis took a similar tack in a 1964 book called *The Far Left*. When President Lyndon Johnson appointed Earl Warren to head the commission to investigate the assassination, the picture of a massive, Soviet-engineered conspiracy was complete. Placing the blame on a nondescript loner, even one branded as a would-be communist, was construed as a transparent attempt to protect gullible Americans from the true nature of their sinister opponent, the federal government.

The remaining major ingredient fueling right-wing resentment was the civil rights movement. Part of the opposition was explicitly racist. Though Hargis rejected this label and insisted he knew it was "wrong to deprive the Negroes of their constitutional rights," he also declared that segregation "is one of Nature's universal laws. No intermingling or crossbreeding with animals of widely different characteristics takes place except under abnormal or artificial conditions. It is my conviction that God ordained segregation."

Carl McIntire and the ACCC had also stipulated that "Segregation within the church on racial, linguistic, and national lines is not unchristian nor contrary to the specific commands of the Bible. . . . Segregation or apartheid is not sin per se. . . . The love which Christians have for one another does not in itself demand an integrated church." As for love between Christians and non-Christians, both Hargis and McIntire repudiated the popular notion of "the Fatherhood of God and the Brotherhood of Man" as unbiblical, and McIntire explicitly declared the golden rule to be irrelevant to civil rights legislation.

In addition to indulging in unabashed racism, many opponents to the civil rights movement, especially after Kennedy introduced sweeping civil rights legislation in the spring of 1963, marched under the banner of state and individual rights. When the federal government commanded individual states to desegregate their schools and told individual business people that they could no longer "reserve the right to refuse service to anyone," as signs posted prominently in virtually every restaurant in the South put it, many Southerners declared it a grave offense against the Constitution. When Alabama Governor George Wallace ostensibly defended this position against federal troops with his infamous "stand in the schoolhouse door" speech in 1963, the *Christian Beacon* pronounced its approval and the Christian Crusade named him "Christian Patriot of the Year."

Whatever their feelings toward blacks' and states' rights, nearly all conservatives of the day disapproved of civil disobedience of the sort engineered by Martin Luther King Jr., whom Hargis once labeled "a stinking racial agitator." Even Billy Graham, who told a 1962 press conference that "Jim Crow must go" and who counted King as a friend, cautioned that Freedom Rides and other confrontational measures might create resistance that could never be broken down. "I am convinced," he said, "that some Negro leaders are going too far and too fast." Even while Dr. King languished in the Birmingham jail in the spring of 1963, Graham advised him to "put on the brakes a little bit," calling his timing "questionable" and suggesting that blacks and whites alike would benefit from "a period of quietness in which moderation prevails." In his eloquent "Letter from Birmingham Jail," King responded by saying he had never participated in "a direct-action campaign that was 'well-timed' in the views of those who [had] not suffered unduly from the disease of segregation." That summer, Graham not only declined to take part in the most memorable civil rights demonstration in American history, the March on Washington, but elected to challenge what was perhaps Dr. King's most arresting image. King had said, "I have a dream that my four little children one day will live in a nation where they will not be judged by the color of their skin, but by the content of their character." Graham had no quibble with the dream, but his theology and philosophy of change had no room for such a vision of harmony. "Only when Christ comes again," he said, "will the little white children of Alabama walk hand in hand with little black children."

THE GROWTH OF conservative organizations during the early 1960s clearly reflected serious dissatisfaction with the direction the country was moving. Conservatives groped for ways not only to express this dissatisfaction, but also to do something about it. When John Kennedy used the image of a "man on horseback" in 1961, he alluded to perhaps the most enduring icon of American popular culture, the plainspoken Western gunfighter who rides into a troubled, lawless town and brings order out of chaos, using methods that, if not always genteel, are straightforward and effective. Kennedy seemed to be saying that no such rescuing, conquering hero could be expected. Conservatives didn't buy it. They not only longed for such a man; they knew who he was—Arizona senator Barry Goldwater—and they admired that picture of him on the cover of *Life,* the one that showed him with his horse, Sunny.

The closer conservatives looked at their Western hero, the better they liked what they saw. In his blunt speeches, his three popular books, and the positions he took in Congress, Goldwater held aloft what Ronald Reagan called a "bright banner" of conservatism, as distinguished from "pale pastels." Believing as he did in an active communist conspiracy eating at the entrails of American society, he had supported Joseph McCarthy's efforts to root out subversives and peppered his own speeches with allegations of red influence in churches, the media, the military, and, of course, the government. He proposed that the U.S. withdraw from the United Nations if communist China were allowed to join, and he warned China that "if they ever should push the button" on the nuclear weapons they were developing, "we would destroy them." On domestic issues, he regarded integrated schools as "wise and just" but opposed federally mandated desegregation as a violation of state sovereignty and voted against the 1964 Civil Rights Act. He was, predictably, an ardent champion of free trade and laissez-faire capitalism. His religious credentials were the weakest part of his appeal to conservative Christians—an Episcopalian, he averred that religion had more to do with ethics than with "how often [a man] gets inside a church," and he had too much integrity to feign piety—but he pleased religious conservatives by his strong support of the Becker Amendment, which favored school prayer and Bible reading.

Goldwater's views, of course, rankled many high-level Republicans. At a July 1963 press conference, New York Governor Nelson Rockefeller blasted what had come to be called the "radical right," warning that the Republican

Party was "in real danger of subversion by a radical, well-financed, and
highly disciplined minority." But the Arizona senator had never counted on
party elites to back him. In his 1960 convention speech, he had asserted that
"conservatives too often fail to vote." He believed that if he could reach that
nonvoting, frustrated, dispirited minority, he could recapture the Republican party for true conservatives.

Unlike Nelson Rockefeller, who commanded great personal wealth, had
ready access to that of others, and enjoyed the confidence of Eastern establishment Republicans, Goldwater depended heavily on grassroots backing
from ordinary folk. The 1964 California primary campaign illustrated this in
notable fashion. Shortly after the 1960 convention, James Townsend, an
arch-conservative activist in Anaheim, joined with another Orange County
Republican to form what they called the Citizens Committee of California,
whose purpose was to back Barry Goldwater for president in 1964. Their
success in gathering approximately a million signatures on petitions to qualify Goldwater to run provided the little push he needed to defeat Nelson
Rockefeller.

Goldwater received another powerful boost from an admirer who was
destined to become the best-known woman in the Republican party. Phyllis
Schlafly says she does not remember a time when she was not a conservative.
As a young woman, she researched and wrote about politics, economics, and
foreign policy for a newsletter published by the St. Louis Union Trust Company. After obtaining a master's degree at Harvard in 1945, Schlafly worked
for a time at the fledgling American Enterprise Institute in Washington,
analyzing bills and ghostwriting speeches for conservative congressmen, then
moved back to Alton, Illinois, across the river from St. Louis. In 1952, she
attended the Republican National Convention, where she "watched the
New York kingmakers steal the nomination away from [Ohio Senator] Bob
Taft, who was the choice of a clear majority of the delegates at that convention." In 1956, after reading an article by Fred Schwarz, Schlafly invited him
to come to St. Louis to deliver a series of lectures on communism. "I put on
the first workshop on communism that Fred Schwarz gave," she said.

In 1960, Mrs. Schlafly was president of the Illinois Federation of Republican Women. In that capacity, she arranged a luncheon for Republican
women during the national convention in Chicago and invited Barry Goldwater to be the speaker. "I gave him his first national Republican audience,"
she said. "He was a big hit. I chose him, and I was very happy with everything he said. Goldwater was an authentic conservative. He didn't pussyfoot
around or muddle up the issues. He was just a very straightforward guy who
called it the way it is."

In 1964, Schlafly wrote and published *A Choice, Not an Echo,* a little book
that eventually sold three million copies. In it, she provided a detailed expla-

nation of how liberal Eastern elites, whom she characterized as "secret king-makers," had controlled Republican conventions since 1936, frustrating efforts of rank-and-file party members to nominate an authentic conservative, selecting instead liberal or middle-of-the-road candidates who differed little from the Democratic standard-bearer and who could be counted on not to oppose the internationalist policies that helped them maintain their wealth and power. She described how, in 1960, Richard Nixon had sacrificed his independence and his Republican principles when he went to Nelson Rockefeller's Fifth Avenue apartment to hammer out a compromise platform so liberal that Barry Goldwater labeled it "a surrender to Rockefeller" and the "Munich of the Republican party." When Nixon selected as his running mate Henry Cabot Lodge, Jr., *National Review* publisher William Rusher characterized Lodge as "a Boston Brahmin" even more liberal "if possible" than Rockefeller. It seemed clear, once again, that the Eastern elite controlled the Republican party.

Schlafly wrote her book, she explained, because: "I realized that most of the delegates had not been to conventions before and they needed to know the tactics by which they could be cheated out of the nominee they really wanted. It was clear that Barry Goldwater was the grassroots choice. All I wanted to do was tell them what went before. . . . [My book] took people who were Nelson Rockefeller supporters or Lyndon Johnson supporters and turned them into Barry Goldwater supporters. People in California credit it with winning the California primary for Goldwater over Rockefeller, which was the crucial turning point of that campaign. Grassroots Goldwater workers would buy two or three hundred of these books and they would distribute them in their precincts. And when they would go re-poll their precincts, they would find that they had Goldwater votes. *A Choice, Not an Echo* had another, more far-reaching and long-lasting effect: It brought people into the conservative movement. Every week of my life I meet some public official, some older person, who says to me, 'Mrs. Schlafly, I came into the conservative movement [because of] *A Choice, Not an Echo* in 1964.' It made people believe they could accomplish something, that they weren't just nobodies, that they could do something which would elect the public officials they wanted and, bring about the policy changes they wanted."

The book's popularity was reflected in the fact that "A Choice, Not an Echo" became, along with "In Your Heart, You Know He's Right," one of the two most popular slogans of the 1964 Goldwater campaign. "It meant," Schlafly said, "that we wanted a Republican nominee who was somebody different from the Democratic nominee; we did not want the Republican nominee to be a 'me too' person or an echo." Theodore H. White, in *The Making of the President 1964,* seconded Schlafly's contention. Goldwater, he said,

proposed to give the nation a choice, not an echo . . . a whole system of ideas which clashed with the governing ideas that had ruled
America for a generation: a choice on nuclear weapons, a choice on
defense posture, a choice on the treatment of Negroes, a choice on
dealing with Communism, a choice on the nature of central government. There were many choices, but the rub was that no voter could
pick at will among those choices. A voter must buy the entire Goldwater package of ideas—or reject them entirely. . . .

GOLDWATER ENTERED THE 1964 Republican National Convention,
held at the Cow Palace in San Francisco, with a commanding lead, but his
supporters, duly warned by Phyllis Schlafly, still worried that the "Eastern
kingmakers" would somehow manage to cheat them out of their prize.
They had reason for concern. The liberal wing of the party could not defeat
them, but it made no attempt to hide its displeasure with the course events
had taken. The first assault came in Oregon Governor Mark Hatfield's keynote address.

"A keynoter traditionally is supposed to be the cheerleader," Hatfield
observed, "to start the convention off with the theme of the coming campaign, to mobilize and organize the party, and to set forth the indictment
against the other party. Now you have to understand that it was a predeter-
mined situation. Barry Goldwater had the votes before I ever hit the platform, and everybody knew that. So it seemed to me I had to add another
dimension, and that was to try to [correct] the concept that the Republican
Party was all thinking the same as Senator Goldwater. Oregon was the only
primary Governor Rockefeller won, so I was a Rockefeller delegate keynot-
ing a Goldwater Convention. . . . I remember the line that gave me a
distinction that no other keynoter in history has ever had: I was booed by
my own Convention. . . . because I warned the Convention that we
should beware of extremists from the left or from the right 'who spew forth
their venom of hate, such as the Communist Party, the Ku Klux Klan, and
the John Birch Society.' Well, a third of the delegates were members of the
John Birch Society, so that 'boo' really responded a very strong response.
But I still felt it was a message we had to communicate, not to the people in
that auditorium but to the public out there that would be going to the polls.
I still feel we had put ourselves into such a very narrow image of thought
and were noted more for what we were against than what we were for, and I
felt constrained to bring that into my keynote speech."

A day later, Nelson Rockefeller was also drowned out with boos and
hisses after he complained that the convention and the party were being
taken over by "a minority wholly alien to sound and honest conservatism."

To complete the rebuff, just as Rockefeller was moving to the climax of his speech, a horde of Goldwater enthusiasts—bearing tickets furnished them, according to James Townsend, by an ardent Goldwater backer named Ronald Reagan—entered the Cow Palace and began parading around noisily. Townsend gleefully recounted Rockefeller's plight. "He couldn't stop them. He just threw up his hands and quit. It ruined his whole deal. It was a lot of fun."

The highlight of that memorable convention, of course, was Barry Goldwater's acceptance speech. As expected, he sounded all the notes in the familiar conservative litany—"We are plodding along at a pace set by centralized planning, red tape, rules without responsibility and regimentation without recourse. . . . There is violence in our streets, corruption in our highest offices, aimlessness among our youth, anxiety among our elderly, and . . . a virtual despair among the many who look beyond material success toward the inner meaning of their lives. . . . We have an administration which seems eager to deal with Communism in every coin known, from gold to wheat." He also pledged that a Republican administration under his leadership would reverse this tide of decline, win the day, inspire the world, and show the way "to a tomorrow worthy of all our yesteryears."

These lines were popular, but they were also standard fare. Then Goldwater intoned the two sentences that would be associated with him for the rest of his career. "I would remind you," he said, "that extremism in the defense of liberty is no vice! And let me remind you also that moderation in the pursuit of justice is no virtue!" This paean to unrestrained patriotism unleashed a sustained storm of applause and cheers, to which the candidate responded with uplifted arms. As the television cameras caught Richard Nixon in the audience, smiling awkwardly but not applauding, a reporter remarked to campaign chronicler Theodore White, "My God, he's going to run as Barry Goldwater!"

Unfortunately for Goldwater, a generation of voters who had grown up in fear of a nuclear holocaust found him more frightening than inspiring, and not without some justification. He had, after all, clearly indicated in a 1963 press conference that he favored giving NATO commanders the power to use tactical nuclear weapons on their own initiative in an emergency. This widely publicized statement underscored the Western gunfighter image and fed what Theodore White called the "primordial issue [that] overshadowed all others."

Lyndon Johnson's campaign, at the urging of press secretary and adviser Bill Moyers, took full advantage of Goldwater's vulnerability on this score. In one of the most notorious political commercials ever seen—it aired on television only once in 1964, but has been shown many times since in retrospective accounts of campaign advertising—a young girl plucks petals from a daisy until her image is obliterated by a mushroom cloud. In a second commercial, a girl licks an ice-cream cone while an announcer talks about Strontium-90 and notes that Barry Goldwater had voted against the Nuclear Test-Ban Treaty. In his autobiography, Goldwater asserts, "Those bomb commercials were the start of dirty political ads on television. It was the beginning of what I call 'electronic dirt.' Bill Moyers and the New York [advertising] firm will long be remembered for helping to launch this ugly development in our political history." In addition to these commercials, anti-Goldwater slogans and placards reminded voters that "In Your Heart, You Know He Might"; ironically urged Americans to "Stamp Out Peace—Vote Goldwater"; and bluntly advised the senator to "Keep Your Atom Bomb in Arizona." One of Goldwater's campaign managers expressed his frustration to Theodore White: "My candidate had been branded a bomb-dropper—and I couldn't figure out how to lick it."

Goldwater also complained that he was misrepresented on the issue of civil rights. Though he voted against the historic Civil Rights Act of 1964, arguing that the act contained "no constitutional basis for the exercise of Federal regulatory authority" in the areas of employment and public accom-modations, he claimed to favor integrated schools. In an October campaign speech written by William Rehnquist, he condemned both compulsory segregation and compulsory integration, insisting he believed in a society in which people were free to associate or not associate with whomever they wished. He and his supporters knew, of course, that Southern racists had long used these same arguments to resist integration and they doubtless hoped to capitalize on resentment of the new legislation and anger over the disruptive movement that had helped produce it. The senator was correct when he noted, "Civil rights was a big problem for me in the campaign"; his claim that he took "a bum rap on the issue" is less persuasive.

By all accounts, Goldwater's campaign was not well organized, and the candidate was not a skillful campaigner. Thirty years later, James Townsend continued to marvel at the ineptitude of the whole enterprise: "They took him into Tennessee to the [Tennessee Valley Authority, the huge govern-ment-owned utility] and he said, 'Get rid of it.' Then they'd take him into some state where there's a lot of retired people and he wants to get rid of Social Security." In fact, Goldwater did not advocate ending Social Security, but he did mention possible changes, including making it voluntary, and that was close enough to generate fear in the hearts of pensioners, especially after the Johnson camp ran a commercial that showed a Social Security card being torn up. On other economic issues, Goldwater took a consistently conserva-tive line, criticizing farm subsidies, attacking the National Labor Relations Board, and arguing for unfettered free trade.

As the campaign moved into its final stages, Goldwater sought to attract traditionalist voters, including conservative Christians, by further criticizing centralized government, attacking the integrity and ethics of President Johnson and key associates such as Bobby Baker (for improper exploitation of his ties to the president) and Walter Jenkins (for a homosexual encounter in a YMCA men's room), and blaming the Supreme Court's banning of school prayer and Bible reading for much of the general down-turn in morality. In a stump speech delivered in the Mormon Tabernacle, typical of the tone Goldwater took late in his campaign, he asked:

> Why do we see wave after wave of crime in our streets and in our homes? Why do we see riot and disorder in our cities; a breakdown of the morals of our young people; an alarming rise in juvenile delinquency; an increasing flood of obscene literature; corruption around our highest offices, erosion of the honor and dignity of our nation and of the individuals who compose it? Something basic, something dangerous is eating away at the morality, the dignity, and respect of our citizens—old as well as young, high as well as low. My fellow Americans, is this the time in our nation's history for our federal government to ban almighty God from our schoolrooms? I'll remind you that for almost nine score years in the life of our country, children regularly said prayers in the public schools of states permitting it.

To lend weight to this approach, Richard Nixon joined Goldwater in a televised dialogue and speech on the critical importance of character for the job of the presidency. As a further effort to reach the same audience, the campaign produced a thirty-minute documentary called "Choice." Ostensibly backed by Mothers for a Moral America, a front group created specifically to serve as its sponsor, the film featured pictures of rioting blacks, topless models, nightclub patrons dancing the Twist, and other scenes calculated to offend a conservative audience. According to producer Rus Walton, an evangelical Christian, the intent was to "take this latent anger and concern which now exists, build it up, and subtly turn and focus it." To his credit, Senator Goldwater judged the film to be inappropriate and refused to let it be shown.

As ELECTION DAY drew closer, it appeared certain Lyndon Johnson would win in a landslide, but the Arizona gunslinger had one more card up his sleeve, and it was an ace. Goldwater's "moderation-is-no-virtue" convention speech, popular as it was inside the Cow Palace, effectively ended his chances of becoming president. But on October 27, 1964, another speech, equally stirring and ultimately more important, thrust a well-known but seriously underrated conservative communicator into an orbit whose path would mark a fundamental change in the shape of American politics. To raise money for the campaign's final push, Ronald Reagan, former movie actor, former host of TV's *General Electric Theater* and *Death Valley Days,* and former liberal Democrat, delivered a nationally televised fundraising speech entitled "A Time for Choosing." The speech was a classic jeremiad, perhaps the oldest and most American of speech forms, in which the speaker—originally a preacher, but eventually including politicians able to sound like preachers—delineates the signs of a corrupt society, excoriates his audience for their contribution to or acquiescence in this damnable state of affairs, warns of the only end possible if they do not turn from their wicked and ignorant ways, then points to the one avenue of escape, the sole path to salvation, and demands that they choose, now, in this moment, while there is yet time. The content was familiar; Barry Goldwater had been saying the same things for months. But Reagan's style was stunning. Syndicated columnist David Broder, generally considered a moderate, judged the speech to be "the most successful national political debut since William Jennings Bryan electrified the 1896 Democratic convention with the 'Cross of Gold' speech."

Phyllis Schlafly remembered that Reagan's speech "just went through the country like electricity. As soon as it was shown on television, all of these unorganized grassrooters went around raising their last dollar to keep putting it on again." The response, in fact, was so overwhelming, that the campaign was unable to spend all the money and wound up with a substantial surplus. Had Reagan's performance caused Schlafly to think of him as a potential Republican politician? "No," she admitted with a laugh. "It made me think, 'Why didn't Goldwater put him on earlier in the campaign?' "

Originally, Goldwater had pinned his hopes on winning all eleven states of the Old South and enough other states to gain an electoral majority without a single contribution from the Eastern Seaboard. In the end, he took only six states—Arizona, Alabama, Georgia, Louisiana, Mississippi, and South Carolina. Some observers viewed this loss and the rise of right-wing Republicanism as twin misfortunes from which the party might never recover. Theodore White declared that "Goldwater's campaign was hopeless to such an extent that it not only destroyed him as a political figure but profoundly undermined the worthy cause he had set out to champion, the cause of American conservatism . . . ." Morton Blackwell, the youngest Goldwater delegate at the convention but now a seasoned Republican organizer and leader, challenged White's assertion. "A lot of people don't understand," he observed, "that in politics, sometimes you win by losing. You lose the battle, but you set up the potential for future winning, and that's how I look at the Goldwater campaign. It brought a lot of people into politics, and we developed expertise." Among those attracted to Goldwater's views, Blackwell asserted, were many conservative Christians. "The religious leaders who were deeply committed to the values of traditional morality began to say, 'Hey, if we're not careful, this country's going to be changed in ways that we don't like at all.' It was clear that the Republican party was the party that was most hospitable to them, and there were people like me out there working to recruit them."

Phyllis Schlafly agreed with Blackwell's assessment. "Nineteen sixty-four," she said, "was the year when grassroots conservative Republicans took control of the Republican Party, and they've had it, more or less, ever since. You have to realize that 27 million people who voted for Barry Goldwater in 1964 don't regret it. He was a strong, clear voice for the conservative philosophy, and we were very proud to have supported him. I have never talked to anyone who said, 'I wasted my vote.' And they remain constant. They built their strength and they continued to work and to build the conservative movement until twenty years later, by 1984, the numbers had doubled, to 54 million. He can be very proud of the part he played in that. I doubt if there's ever been anybody else who lost an election who had as big an impact as Barry Goldwater did."

Ironically, one of the most dramatic transformations of the Republican Party came in reaction to the Goldwater campaign's preference for nostalgic symbolism and damn-the-torpedoes rhetoric over rational organization and technological expertise. However appealing the image of "a man on horseback," Richard Viguerie, executive secretary of the ardently pro-Goldwater Young Americans for Freedom, soon persuaded conservatives that what they really needed was a man with a computer. Shortly after the election, Viguerie went to the General Accounting Office in Washington and, with the help of a team of Kelly Girls, hand-copied the names and addresses of approximately 7,500 people who had contributed fifty dollars or more to the Goldwater campaign. To these he added names collected from such conservative organizations as the American Economic Foundation, the Committee of One Million, and the newly formed policy think tank called the Philadelphia Society. With those names as his basic resource, Viguerie launched the era of computer-managed political fundraising, eventually building a direct-mail empire that would raise untold millions of dollars in support of organizations, candidates, and causes that made up what Viguerie dubbed the New Right, by which he meant a conservative movement more focused in its aims and more committed to winning than the "echo" Republicans whose day, he felt, was over.

Viguerie's determination to mobilize committed conservatives signaled a

new approach for Republican politics. As Morton Blackwell, the youngest
Goldwater delegate at the convention, said, "After 1964, conservatives got
tired of losing and decided that perhaps being 'right' in the sense of being
correct was not sufficient to win. Conservatives came to the understanding
that we owe it to our philosophy to study how to win; that we had to
become proficient in campaigns, and in recruiting candidates and we had to
be active in party structures." Republican leaders encouraged this line of
thinking. Dean Burch, chairman of the Republican National Committee,
assured Southern party-members that their success on Goldwater's behalf
had not been "one-shot victories," but had helped make the GOP "a feature of the whole Southern landscape." In 1965, Goldwater campaign workers took the lead in forming the American Conservative Union, a broad-
based organization that took care to distance itself from the Birch Society
and other elements on the extreme right.

The Goldwater campaign also generated another development of im-
mense long-term importance to the Republican Party, and ultimately to the
Religious Right, by the exposure it provided to Ronald Reagan. Conservatives were thrilled by the content and effectiveness of Reagan's eleventh-
hour speech during the campaign, but they could not help wondering how
deep his convictions ran, how much of the performance was simply an actor
delivering his lines. When word spread that Reagan was considering a run
for the governorship of California, James Townsend, whose Citizens Committee had helped Goldwater win the California primary, was among the
skeptics.

He was particularly troubled that Reagan was getting advice from the
same public relations firm that had managed Nelson Rockefeller's 1964
campaign, a possible sign that he had not completely renounced the liberal
Democrat views he had held as a younger man. On learning of Townsend's
reservations, Reagan called and asked for the opportunity to meet with him
and discuss his ideas and plans. Townsend invited him to dinner and originally intended to have no guests other than Sam Campbell, the hard-right
editor of the *Anaheim Bulletin,* and his wife, but as word of the meeting got
out and people Townsend knew to be effective grassroots political activists
asked to be included, the meeting site was shifted to a prominent dentist's
backyard, and Reagan found himself facing a crowd of seventy-five or so
curious conservatives.

"We didn't know if we wanted to back Reagan or not," Townsend explained, "because he'd been a Democrat, so we set it up that, after he spoke
we went into question-and-answer, people would stand up and ask a question and then they would just sit down and give him the 'fish-eye,' no
matter what he said, whether it was what they wanted to hear or not. Now
[those were] the ground rules, but Reagan didn't know that. Well, this went

on and, every once in a while, a question would be asked of the public-relations man. And if Reagan felt [the P.R. man] hadn't given a complete answer, he would step in and finish answering it. That's when we realized that Reagan wasn't just a tin-horn movie star that was playing around with being governor, that he really did know his politics. Finally, we couldn't contain these grassroots leaders any more. As the evening wore on, they started to jumping around and smiling and making various moves. Now, Reagan had told me before the meeting that he had to be back in Los Angeles by 10:30, so I said, 'We've got time for two more questions, because Mr. Reagan has to get back to Los Angeles,' and he said, 'No, no, nope, nope.' This is where the actor came in. He had a tough audience and he had started to crack them and he didn't want to stop until he finished. And he did. He stayed there and posed for pictures with various candidates. He couldn't have been more congenial.

"That meeting in Anaheim was the first time Reagan ever spoke as a candidate. Later on, the P.R. guy called me up and said, 'I never did thank you for the meeting you set up in Anaheim. It was the most important one we had in the whole campaign. We went up North and set up exactly the same kind of meeting, brought in the same type of people, and we won the state with just two meetings. After that, we just spent the whole primary campaigning against [Democratic Governor Edmund G. "Pat"] Brown.' And that's true. They didn't even bother with the other Republican candidates, because we were working with very dedicated people who knew how to organize and how to use their opportunities. And it was written up in the newspapers after he was elected President how his trek to the White House started in Anaheim, and it told about the meeting I just described."

Townsend remembered that most of the issues Reagan discussed in the 1966 election were same ones Republicans were stressing thirty years later: big government, the right to bear arms, lower taxes, and welfare reform. In addition, however, he had the advantage of being able to campaign against the dramatic changes occurring among young people, and nowhere more visibly than at the University of California at Berkeley. Townsend readily agreed that the turmoil helped Reagan. "Absolutely! No question. The Berkeley campus had exploded with the free-speech movement, marijuana, LSD, the whole drop-out deal, the long hair, the hippie movement. This was very frightening to the older generation. We didn't have eighteen-year-olds voting then, so most of the people who were old enough to vote had not been a part of this movement and had been raised in the old school of apple pie and motherhood and the Constitution, and things like that. This was something new that had suddenly been thrust into the public eye and represented a great threat. It was a hell of a campaign issue, and it was ready-made for somebody like Ronald Reagan, with the ability to speak and the brains to use this issue."

Reagan did, of course, possess formidable skills as a communicator. In stump speeches the *New York Times* described as having a "moralistic, highly simplified and emotional appeal," he declared, "I am not a politician. I am an ordinary citizen with a deep-seated belief that much of what troubles us has been brought about by politicians," and warned that "if we ordinary citizens don't run government, government is going to run us." He talked of the spread of "sexual orgies and behaviors so vile I cannot describe them to you" and called for a "moral crusade" against such evils, to close the "morality and decency gap" between good people like his listeners and the wicked minority of students who were wrecking the University of California. And, in a line that brought wild applause, he challenged Governor Brown to deal forcibly with those students—"And if that means kicking them out, kick them out!"

RONALD REAGAN WAS not the only conservative to see opportunity in the student turmoil of the late sixties. Youth for Christ maintained its essentially conservative ethos, but had so restricted its mission to high school students that it had less occasion to confront the major political currents of the sixties youth culture. Other youth organizations, such as the Navigators and InterVarsity Fellowship, had more contact with collegians, but concentrated on personal evangelism and individual spiritual development. By far the most energetic and visible challenge to the radical student movement came from Bill Bright's Campus Crusade for Christ (CCC).

Though its primary emphasis had always been on winning individual souls, Campus Crusade had been from its beginning a politically conservative organization. In part, this was simply a manifestation of the generally Republican sentiments common to many evangelical Christians, especially outside the traditionally Democratic (but still conservative) South. It also reflected the strong convictions of its authoritarian leader, Bill Bright, who flatly told staffers that "this is not a democratic organization" and explicitly regarded criticism of himself, his lieutenants, or the ministry as "evidence of disloyalty to Christ" and warned that such disloyalty "shall be accepted as an act of resignation." Given that Bill Bright has, in the words of a former Crusade staffer, "always been Republican, always been politically conservative, and feels that's consistent with his understanding of the Gospel," loyalty to Bright effectively ruled out a liberal political stance.

For the first decade of its life, self-conscious political activity played little role in Campus Crusade's mission. Governor Mark Hatfield and Congressman Walter Judd were on its board, but a pietistic emphasis on holy living and separation from "the world" in anticipation of the imminent Second Coming far outweighed any desire to transform social structures. By the mid-1960s, however, that began to change. A number of Crusade staffers campaigned vigorously for Goldwater in 1964. At about the same time, a dynamic young speaker and writer named Hal Lindsey joined the organization and began to interpret current events by means of a dispensationalist premillennial framework congenial to right-wing sentiments, serving to spur greater awareness of political realities. (In 1970, Lindsey would incorporate these views into *The Late Great Planet Earth,* which would become the best-selling book of that entire decade.)

Also of critical importance was the fact that Campus Crusade depended for its livelihood on donations from Christian business people whose political views were decidedly conservative. Jon Braun, who by this time had become the organization's National Field Coordinator, candidly noted, "You find out who butters your bread. It's nice to say that it's God who butters your bread, and in a sense that's true, but we didn't get a lot of financial support from left-wing people. We were 'protecting the world from Communism,' and we were forever quoting Abraham Lincoln—'The philosophy of the classroom in one generation is the philosophy of government in the next.' We would quote President Eisenhower—'Without a moral and spiritual awakening, we will awaken one day to find ourselves disappearing in the dust of an atomic explosion.' Or we would quote MacArthur. We had all of these little sayings that we used to approach those who were going to support us. What we represented was not just something spiritual, but a way of life [our followers] wanted to maintain. We weren't as willing to admit the political overtones as much as we should have, but yes, we were very aware of those things. We were a right-wing movement and we were supported by right-wing money, and the movement against prayer in the classroom and all the sexual liberation that was taking place on campus actually helped us gain a great deal of the financial support we needed to stay out there."

The turmoil of the mid-sixties did not cause Bill Bright to reject his conservative politics, but it did move him to retool his rhetoric and to adopt new approaches. In 1966, a traveling musical group known as New Folk began holding largely secular concerts during which the musicians gave a low-key pitch for establishing a personal relationship with Christ. The following year, a CCC ministry called Athletes in Action formed a basketball team that traveled about the country, playing local college teams and presenting a Christian message at half-time. Other sports were soon added until, by the mid-seventies, Athletes in Action was one of CCC's most visible efforts, and was far more active in evangelistic efforts than its older counterpart, the Fellowship of Christian Athletes.

Predictably, such approaches struck many students as old-fashioned, corny, and embarrassingly out of synch with the spirit of the times, but, perhaps just as predictably, they proved enormously appealing to thousands of youngsters who felt quite at home in traditional American society and had little impulse to "Tune in, turn on, and drop out." Campus rallies featuring such popular evangelical speakers such as Jon Braun and Josh McDowell often drew several thousand students, many of whom made or renewed a profession of faith in Christ. Hundreds of those eventually joined the staff of CCC or other parachurch organizations and hundreds more went to seminary.

The most ambitious attempt to reach college youth was a 1967 effort remembered in CCC circles as the Berkeley Blitz. Just as he insisted that staffers concentrate first on reaching campus leaders—the student body president, the editor of the school newspaper, the captain of the football team, the head cheerleader, the fraternity or sorority president—in the reasonable expectation that others would follow their lead, Bright decided to take on the most important campus in the University of California system, and one of the most prestigious in the world. Berkeley, of course, gained enormous notoriety during this period for the raucous demonstrations in the plaza in front of Sproul Hall, where Bettina Aptheker extolled the virtues of communism and Mario Savio, in the name of free speech, railed profanely against anything that smacked of conventional virtue. Bright decided that, if his Crusaders could conquer Berkeley for Christ with a prototype campaign, other campuses would fall like dry sheaves cut down by the double-edged Sword of Truth.

To show that he was in tune with the times, Bright had already begun to use such terms as "Revolution Now!" and to assert that "we need dissent in our society," even though he would not permit it in the organization he ran. Instead of encouraging Crusade-affiliated Berkeley students to live in apartments owned or rented by the organization, as had been their separatist practice, he urged them to move back into regular dormitories and let their lights shine "in the world." Then, after months of careful preparation, approximately six hundred students and staff members converged on the campus for a full week in an intense effort "to confront the hotbed of sixties radical campus activism with the radical message of the gospel."

Under the aegis of the campaign's slogan, "Solution: Spiritual Revolution," Crusaders carried their message to athletic teams, clubs, fraternities and sororities, dormitories, student centers, coffee shops, and open-air meetings. Jon Braun recalled, with some amusement, addressing several thousand young people from the steps of Sproul Hall. "The day before, the [regents] had dismissed the chancellor of the entire system, and these kids were out there because they thought it was a demonstration against the university. They hadn't really come to hear someone preach the gospel. But we had relatively little choice. I remember being surrounded by a group of very large football players from various universities around the country, and that comforted me a little bit. But that was probably the worst experience I've ever had in my life in evangelism."

The climax of the blitz came at the end of the week, when Billy Graham addressed a large audience at Berkeley's Greek Theater. On the surface, the effort seemed a modest success. More than seven hundred students and faculty members "received Christ" and approximately two thousand others indicated a desire to hear more. The surface, however, was thin. According to Peter Gillquist, another CCC staffer assigned to Berkeley, "we know of only two [students] who really followed through." A second attempt at the "blitz" strategy had similar results at UCLA. "Dollar for dollar," Jon Braun admitted, "I think it was one of the weakest things we ever did."

Weak though it may have been, the Berkeley Blitz did leave its mark. One CCC staffer, Jack Sparks, a former Penn State professor, became so convinced that standard Crusade tactics could not penetrate the radical student movement that he essentially "went native." He let his hair and beard grow out, exchanged his Brooks Brothers suits for bib overalls and a chambray work shirt, and founded what he called the Christian World Liberation Front, which published a newspaper called *Right On!* and consistently spoke of Jesus as a revolutionary. By all accounts, Sparks was not engaged in a charade, but came to share many of the counterculture's socially radical values. In addition to baptizing new converts in the fountain on the Berkeley mall, the group provided medical care to the sick and strung-out, dispensed food and clothing to the needy, and helped support an agricultural commune in nearby Humboldt county. Before it disbanded in the early seventies, the CWLF came to be regarded as a prominent component of the Jesus Movement, whose cultural outlook and lifestyle often seemed closer to the counterculture than to the Campus Crusade for Christ.

A surprising secondary footnote to the Berkeley Blitz came as a result of efforts by a small group of CCC staff members to assess why they had not been able to crack the student culture. Instead of trying to revise their approach and sales pitch, they began to study the Book of Acts, where they rediscovered the importance not just of evangelism, but of the church. "We called ourselves an arm of the church," Gillquist observed, "but we were amputated. We had no real connection to it. We said, 'We've got to be church. We can't just go out and be hit men for Christ, with no sense of follow-through or permanence or historicity.'" The effort to learn more soon led to a study of early church history. Six men, including Braun, Gillquist, Sparks, the directors of CCC's African and Canadian programs, and the coordinator for the southeast region of the U.S., pledged to meet for one week every three months, to study Scripture and church history to see where it might lead them. After several intermediate steps, all six were eventually ordained and currently serve as priests in the Eastern Orthodox Church.

REAGAN'S 1966 VICTORY over Pat Brown in the California governor's race, accompanied by conservative victories in several other key states, provided solid evidence that Goldwater Republicanism was still alive in America. As they recognized their considerable and growing strength, many of the people who had supported Goldwater hoped they might be able to gain the nomination for Ronald Reagan, who had the support of *National Review* publisher William Rusher, veteran Republican operative Clifton White, and several other strong conservative voices. They soon recognized, however, that it was not yet the right time for Reagan. Southerners approved of Reagan's narrow view of the federal government's proper role and of his "antipathy for demonstrators of all varieties," but many who had voted for Goldwater in 1964 were sure to back Alabama's segregationist Governor George Wallace in 1968. (Billy James Hargis claims that Wallace asked him to be his running-mate on the Independent Party ticket, before finally settling on General Curtis LeMay.) More importantly, however, Richard Nixon had decided he was willing, after all, to let his critics kick him around some more, and announced he would once again seek the nomination. Nixon had been a faithful party member in the eight years since he had left office, traveling about the country to raise money and speak on behalf of Republican candidates, and he was ready to call in his chips.

Though he owed the former vice president nothing in particular, Billy Graham proved to be a significant asset to Nixon's cause. Graham had enjoyed a close relationship with Lyndon Johnson during Johnson's term in office. He had offered his services to the new president in the days immediately following Kennedy's assassination and had seen his offer hungrily accepted. In their first visit, scheduled for fifteen minutes but stretched to five hours, the two farm boys who had ridden their talent, ambition, and energy to the pinnacle of their respective professions found they had more to offer each other than either had ever imagined. For Billy, just to be welcome once again at the White House meant that he and his people—good, decent, God-fearing, Bible-believing, patriotic, middle-class, middle-American folk—were back in charge, or at least back in favor, as many felt they had not been during the Kennedy years. More specifically, the legitimation evangelicals had worked for and won in the fifteen years after World War II had not been lost. Now, their plans to rekindle a spirit the nation had not known since the days of Charles Finney could proceed apace.

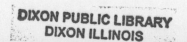

For his part, Lyndon Johnson understood the advantages of being Billy's buddy. If Billy Graham was the president's friend, then millions of Americans would conclude that the president must be a good man, a decent man, a noble man, perhaps even a Christian man. And if he possessed those qualities, then his causes—his War on Poverty, his Civil Rights act, his effort to preserve freedom and democracy in Southeast Asia—must also be good, decent, noble, perhaps even Christian, and therefore precisely the causes Christian folk ought to support.

Over the next five years, Graham visited the White House and Johnson's Texas Hill country ranch on numerous occasions and the two men regularly exchanged letters, cards, and small gifts. In a singular demonstration of loyalty, Graham withstood an astonishing attempt to pressure him into endorsing Goldwater—in the few days just before the election, he received over a million telegrams, some bearing hundreds of names, and tens of thousands of additional messages delivered by airplane and surface carriers. Perhaps not completely sure of his friend's allegiance, Johnson not only called Graham to say, "Now Billy, you stay out of politics," but also invited him to spend the weekend at the White House, where he would not be tempted to read his mail.

Even though he no longer attacked communism with the fervor he had shown in earlier years, Graham still regarded it as a global menace and for that reason defended American involvement in Vietnam, especially during the early years of the war. As the deadly conflict dragged on, he developed misgivings and tried to avoid dealing with it in press conferences, but was regarded by both the president and the public as generally supportive of U.S. policy in Southeast Asia. He was more comfortable with Johnson's Great Society programs, since they were easier to square with Jesus's own concern for the poor, the sick, and the mistreated. He continued to call for racial understanding and harmony, and for obedience to the new civil rights laws, but stopped short of approving protests and demonstrations that created unseemly disruptions and openly questioned whether pastors and leaders of denominations and such bodies as the National and World Councils of Churches had the right to make statements as if they were speaking for their entire constituencies. He also doubted that most ministers had the requisite expertise to offer an opinion on many nontheological issues. "I fear," he observed, "that if the church, as the church, begins to try to dictate in politics, we're way off the main track."

Lyndon Johnson's announcement that he would not seek re-election in 1968 freed Graham from having to make a painful choice between the president and old friend Richard Nixon. He had already obliquely encouraged Nixon to seek the Republican nomination and, though he refused to say whom he would vote for, he did concede publicly that he would like to see Nixon at the top of the Republican ticket. Then, throughout the primary and election campaigns, he made so many favorable comments about Nixon, his high principles, and his deep religious convictions that a formal endorsement would have been superfluous.

At a September crusade in Pittsburgh, Graham invited Nixon to take a prominent seat in the VIP section, where the cameras could easily find him, and lauded him from the platform as one of his most cherished friends. Graham also noted that he sensed a significant rightward trend among "a big segment of the population," a segment that would not be seen participating in riots or protest marches, but were nonetheless ready to take action, "a great unheard-from group" who were likely "to be heard from loudly at the polls." No one sensitive to campaign rhetoric would likely have missed the similarity between this group—presumably people Billy Graham had seen in his own audiences—and the "Silent Majority" the Republicans were courting so assiduously.

In a final boost to his friend's cause, Graham sat in the studio audience of one of the carefully managed televised question-and-answer sessions Nixon used during the campaign. When asked by reporters if Graham was supporting him, Nixon replied that he felt safe in saying that was true. A few days later, Graham himself revealed that he had already cast his absentee vote for Nixon, an acknowledgment the Nixon forces used in the campaign right down to the wire on election day.

Richard Nixon's term in office initiated a new era for "civil religion," that blend of religious and political culture that has potential both to call a nation to acknowledge and honor its transcendent ideals and to delude it into thinking it has already done so. Every president in American history had invoked the name and blessings of God during his inauguration address, and many, including Billy Graham's friends Dwight Eisenhower and Lyndon Johnson, made some notable public display of their putative piety, but none ever made such a conscious, calculating use of religion as a political instrument as did Richard Nixon.

Like other presidents before him, Nixon appeared at prayer breakfasts and made the standard salutes in heaven's direction, but the keystone of his effort to present himself as a man deeply concerned with religion and religious values was the White House church service, which he initiated on the first Sunday after his inauguration, with Billy Graham as the preacher. Other presidents had held religious services in the White House, but none before Nixon had ever sponsored a regular schedule of Sunday services. Throughout his presidency, an uncommon amount of his staff's time and attention went into the White House Sunday services. Not surprisingly, Nixon's critics saw this as a blatant play to the pews and an unhealthy blurring of the line between church and state, but Graham did not concur. "Some people thought it was practicing civil religion," he acknowledged. "Mark Hatfield had that view. But I never thought of it in those terms. I just thought it was a great idea that the President of the United States would have services in the White House. I don't think there was any political connotation. There might have been, but I think Nixon was being very sincere. He wanted to set an example for the whole country."

Documents from the Nixon archives make it clear that piety was not the only item on the president's agenda. An early "action memo" to Charles Colson instructed him to get moving on the "president's request that you develop a list of rich people with strong religious interest to be invited to the White House church services." Colson and his colleagues apparently performed quite admirably; the guest list for a subsequent service included the president or board chairman of a dozen of the nation's largest corporations. In another memo, Nixon's Chief of Staff H. R. Haldeman observed that "we are now covering the members of the regulatory agencies" and pointed out, "It isn't going to do us one bit of good to have a member of a regulatory agency at the Church Service or any other function. If they are to be invited, please limit the invitations to the Chairman or to an appointee we [are] working on for a specific purpose."

Colson, who had been the most cynical of Nixon's aides but experienced what appears to be a thoroughly genuine religious conversion and has subsequently spent years leading the Prison Fellowship ministry, believes that Nixon's interest in religion had an authentic aspect. "Sure," he admitted, "we used the prayer breakfasts and church services and all that for political ends. I was part of doing that. But Nixon was an interesting guy. There was an ambivalence about him. There were times when I thought he was genuinely, spiritually seeking. The things he'd believed as a young man, he said he no longer believed. He didn't believe in the Resurrection, or in Jonah's being swallowed by the whale. He believed those were symbols. But then, he'd talk about Catholics and how they had a set of firm beliefs. He'd say he wished he could be a Catholic because they had a set of beliefs and were comfortable with them. You could tell he was struggling inside. That was probably his mother's influence working on him.

"At the same time, Nixon was a very shrewd politician. He knew how to use religious people to maximum advantage. He recognized that there were voting blocs that were enormously influenced by their religious leaders. He recognized that the blue-collar, white ethnic group in the North that had been a pivotal vote for Democratic majorities in the past was open to wooing by Republicans, that they were identifying with us on more social issues—the great 'Silent Majority.' And he recognized that many of them were Roman Catholics. Early in 1969, he said, 'I want an executive order [saying that] we are going to begin to recognize aid to parochial schools. We want to do something for the Catholics.' We got Cardinal Krol in from Philadelphia and took him out on the Sequoia [the presidential yacht], and the Cardinal was just absolutely mesmerized by Nixon. Needless to say, we got a lot of help in some of the Catholic precincts around Philadelphia, because the Cardinal put the word out. At the same time, Nixon recognized that the evangelical vote was the key to the Southern strategy, so he began to invite evangelical leaders in. And one of my jobs in the White House was to romance religious leaders. We would bring [religious leaders] into the White House and they would be dazzled by the aura of the Oval Office, and I found them to be about the most pliable of any of the special interest groups that we worked with." As for the church services in the East Room, Colson said, "We turned those events into wonderful quasi-social, quasi-spiritual, quasi-political events, and brought in a whole host of religious leaders to [hold] worship services for the president and his family—and three hundred guests carefully selected by me for political purposes."

How does Charles Colson feel today about the role he played in attracting conservative Christians to the Republican side? His response was direct and sobering: "One of the reasons I have written books and given speeches warning Christian leaders not to be seduced by the wiles and the attractiveness of power in the White House, and to keep our distance and never mix the gospel with politics, is that I saw how well I exploited religious leaders when I was in that job. But that's what politicians do."

THE BATTLE
OF ANAHEIM

WHILE CAMPUS CRUSADERS were blitzing Berkeley and presidential aides were romancing the reverend clergy, many other Americans were working in more mundane settings to stop what historian Allen Matusow aptly characterized as "the unraveling of America." In a decade marked by assassinations, protests, riots, war, drugs, and sweeping changes in major social and economic arrangements, few changes troubled conservative Christians more than the seismic shift in sexual attitudes and behavior. They could not approve of what they saw happening. Some dared to hope they could stop it.

So seriously is sexual sin regarded in evangelical circles that, when the term "immorality" is used without elaboration, it almost always refers to intimate sexual relations outside the bonds of one's own marriage. And to many conservative Christians, even "immorality" seems too gentle a term when speaking of homosexual behavior. Though Scripture contains far more condemnations of adultery and fornication than of homosexuality, they are more easily understood and forgiven. Heterosexuals can imagine themselves overwhelmed by the temptation to commit fornication or adultery; that, after all, has been the source of prohibitions against dancing and "mixed bathing" and "immodest apparel," of efforts to ban or restrict motion pictures and books calculated to stir the blood, of constant warnings against the dangers of necking and petting, and of dating rules designed to keep young people within the sight of their elders and the glow of bright lights. But homosexuality, to many Christian people who are not homosexual, is of a different order. In their eyes, to engage in sex with a member of one's own gender is not just immoral, or a lamentable but understandable weakness, but a perversion of nature, an abomination in the sight of God, an act deserving of imprisonment and perhaps even death. Given these realities, it is no surprise that the religious right has repeatedly rallied around issues involving human sexuality.

When the sexual revolution of the 1960s had run its course, both private and public sexual mores had changed dramatically, but signs of that change had been posted prominently throughout the preceding decade. In 1948, Alfred Kinsey's bombshell best-seller, *Sexual Behavior in the Human Male*, focused unprecedented attention on sexual behavior. Most Americans were surprised by the large numbers of people who admitted to engaging in sex outside the home, but the revelations about homosexuality were truly startling. According to Kinsey's data, half of all males acknowledged erotic responses to other males; over a third reported at least one post-adolescent homosexual episode leading to orgasm; and, most astonishing, four percent of adult males reported they were exclusively homosexual. Those four percent, of course, could be found throughout American life, in families, professions, and institutions—including churches—that had never allowed themselves to face such a reality. Social scientists challenged the validity of Kinsey's data, noting particularly that, since it was not based on a carefully selected random sample, those who volunteered to be interviewed about their sexuality might be somewhat more sexually active and uninhibited than the population in general. Still, it seemed clear that many people, far more than anyone had imagined, were having sex in circumstances not blessed by clergy.

In the late 1950s and on into the sixties, the Warren Court progressively lifted prohibitions against books and movies and other materials previously banned or severely restricted as obscene. Then, in 1960, the Food and Drug Administration gave its approval to "The Pill," the female oral contraceptive, which would not only facilitate more reliable family planning but would greatly reduce a significant barrier to nonmarital sex. Times indeed were a-changing.

As Americans tried to come to grips with greater public attention to sexual behavior, growing recognition of sexual variety within the general population, and increased freedom to engage in sex without fear of pregnancy, many thought it crucially important that young people receive more extensive and systematic education about sex. Numerous prominent organizations, including the National Education Association and the American Medical Association, publicly endorsed the idea of sex education in the public schools. No one took the need for increased sex education more seriously than Mary Calderone, medical director of Planned Parenthood. Because executive director Alan Guttmacher and the board of Planned Parenthood felt a major sex-education initiative would dilute its primary work of encouraging contraception, Calderone left the organization in 1964 to form the Sex Information and Education Council of the U.S., better known simply as SIECUS (pronounced "seek us"). Dr. Harold Leif, one of the founders and eventually president of SIECUS, observed, "The level of ignorance in the sixties was greater than it is now. In 1963 or '64, I wrote an article for *Harper's* called 'What Your Doctor Probably Doesn't Know about Sex,' the point being that, if your doctor doesn't know about it, what can you expect of ordinary laymen?"

According to Leif, the founders of SIECUS saw themselves not as providing "disaster insurance" against pregnancy or disease, but as promoting "sexual health" by "raising the consciousness of people about the value of human sexuality as an integral part of personality development and an important source of either marital health or disharmony." Various opinion polls indicated that most parents were in favor of school-based programs to help prepare their children for responsible sexual behavior in the changing social climate, and SIECUS set about to develop such programs.

Though widely regarded as responsible in its approach, SIECUS quickly became a lightning rod for opposition from conservative political and religious groups, who regarded it as libertine, communistic, perhaps even satanic. But SIECUS was not the only player in the field or the only target in the fight. In fact, one of the earliest and most important struggles over sex education involved a home-grown program in Anaheim, California.

AS A YOUNG school nurse in California, Sally Williams was fascinated by the bizarre theories kindergarten children had for where babies come from. Those experiences eventually led her to write a master's thesis on ways to integrate sex education into family life, and also to a position on the Sex Education Committee of the American School Health Association. When she went to work in the Anaheim Union High School District in 1961, Superintendent Paul Cook asked her to chair a committee to develop a sex education curriculum for grades 7–12, a curriculum local parents were eager to see developed and implemented.

Despite the support of the parents, however, neither Cook nor Williams assumed such a venture was risk-free. Throughout the country, school-based sex education was coming under fire from conservative groups who feared that explicit instruction in sexual behavior would erotically stimulate students and encourage them to put their newly acquired information to an empirical test. California's conservative and controversial Superintendent of Public Instruction, Max Rafferty, openly criticized such programs as inappropriate for public schools. Even closer to home, Sam Campbell, the ultra-conservative editor of *The Anaheim Bulletin* and no friend of public schools to begin with, viewed them as one more facet of a governmental conspiracy to gain control over all aspects of private life. His best reporter and writer,

John Steinbacher, also wrote occasional pieces critical of sex education. And in 1962, a small program in two of the district's junior highs had been discontinued after protests led by a priest from St. Boniface's Roman Catholic parish. Subsequently, however, a committee of community representatives had conducted a survey of parents who participated in school functions and found that ninety percent of them favored including sex education in the curriculum.

Williams's committee worked for over a year, examining available materials and developing the protocols under which the program would operate. Although most parents who responded to the aforementioned survey had expressed a preference for sex-segregated classes, the committee recommended the classes not be segregated, feeling that the clear communication necessary for healthy sexual behavior would be best fostered by exposing boys and girls to the same material simultaneously and opening up dialogues between genders. They also insisted that the classes not be turned over automatically to coaches and other physical education personnel. Rather, they wanted them led by instructors who had been specially trained to present the materials and conduct classes in a manner that would minimize embarrassment or unfortunate revelations about the personal lives of students. Instructors were to guide rather than lecture authoritatively, and to stimulate discussion, set up role-playing exercises, serve as a resource, even offer personal opinions, but refrain from imposing their own moral judgments on their students. By filling in boxes on a questionnaire, students could ask potentially embarrassing questions anonymously and instructors could provide proper terminology for activities and anatomy for which students knew only slang terms. Students would receive no grades for the course.

The stated goal of the program, which came to be known as Family Life and Sex Education (FLSE), was to prepare students for the task of forming "a family with strong bonds of affection, loyalty, and cooperation," and its four-and-a-half-week curriculum focused far more on developing healthy family relationships than on the mechanics of sex.

The committee enthusiastically endorsed the new curriculum and it caused little concern during the first three years after its introduction in 1965. Inevitably, some parents were apprehensive about the course, but teachers and principals had anticipated most objections and found that by explaining their rationale, they were able to address parents' concerns. In fact, because numerous assignments required students to ask their parents questions prior to class discussions, parents often reported that the classes had improved their communication with their children.

Few programs, of course, accomplish all their goals or are implemented flawlessly. Eleanor Howe, a conservative Catholic and concerned parent, discovered this one evening at dinner in 1968. Almost off-handedly, her twin sons, Rick and Rob, asked for notes excusing them from the Family Life and Sex Education class that semester (participation had always been contingent on parental approval). Puzzled, she began to interrogate them. When she asked what was taught in the course, they told her, "Nothing. Kids just get into class and talk about how many girls they have had, how easy it was, and what they did." Howe hammered away at her sons for four hours, then noticed that her daughter, a year older, had quietly slipped away to her bedroom. Suspicious, Howe went to the girl's room and confronted her: "Anne, did you have this class last year?" When the girl admitted she had, Mrs. Howe demanded to know why she had not told her mother about the class. Anne replied that their teacher had warned them not to tell their parents about what went on in the classroom, because they were sure to be upset.

Incensed, Mrs. Howe went to the school the next day and asked the principal for permission to monitor one of the classes, which he arranged. She also obtained a copy of the curriculum and spent the next several afternoons at the school district office, reviewing films, books, and other materials used in the course. In addition to sexual descriptions more explicit than she thought appropriate, she found books that took a positive view of masturbation and that, in her opinion, encouraged boys not to feel guilty if they had engaged in sex with animals. "After I went through all of that," she said, "I just refused to believe what they were doing. And I was angry. I was angry because no love attachment was mentioned anywhere. No closeness, no love, no marriage, nothing that depicted my values. I resented it that they took from my boys and my daughter that beautiful wedding night that their mother experienced, and I resented it because . . . because they didn't have to know all that they were told. It wasn't so much the information. It was the shift in values."

Howe also confronted her sons' teacher, who told her he did not try to inject his own values into the discussion—"They're your children, not mine"—but let the youngsters clarify their own values through discussion. He told his students they should not accept a value system simply because their parents or grandparents held it, but should "decide for yourself what is right and what is wrong for you." Howe informed him, "That was not the way my family was raised, period, that we had a value system in our home that I expected them to follow, and that I resented what they were doing in that course."

Determined to counter what she regarded as a frontal assault on her family's values, Howe photocopied excerpts from materials in the FLSE curriculum and pasted them together to create a single publication that she labeled *Adult Bulletin* and passed out to a small group of mothers to distribute to their friends. Reaction was immediate and strong. "I had parents calling me till two and three o'clock in the morning," she recalled. "They had questioned their children and found out that, yes, the children were familiar with what was in my scrapbook of curriculum excerpts. So then we had a big meeting [at my house]."

At the meeting, held in the middle of the summer of 1968, Mrs. Howe informed her friends that she intended to get on the agenda at the August school-board meeting and would raise questions about the FLSE curriculum at that time. She urged them to attend and to invite like-minded parents. "I had no idea," she recalled, "if there would be ten people there, or twenty or a hundred. And of course I was quite nervous because I was never a public speaker. This was my first time to get involved, really, so I was plenty nervous. Well, so many people turned out that they had to put speakers outside. We couldn't get all the people inside the board room."

Mrs. Howe had help in drawing the crowd. Most of the people who had come to the meeting in her home were religious women—Catholic, Baptist, Presbyterian, Methodist, Church of Christ, Mormon. "Just the people," Howe explained, "not the churches per se. All of us were in our own churches, but we didn't discuss religion that much." But also attending was James Townsend, the erstwhile Goldwater enthusiast, who had come at his wife's behest. Townsend had been aware of the circumstances surrounding the development of the FLSE program and had been generally favorable toward it. At that meeting, however, when he saw the materials Howe had gathered, he changed his mind. "I couldn't believe what was being taught in this program," he said. "They were shoving things in front of me so fast, you couldn't believe it. When I left there six hours later, I actually staggered out of the house. There wasn't anything that was *verboten*."

Like others at the meeting, Townsend was particularly upset at the course's treatment of homosexuality. Sally Williams was fully aware that homosexuality was a potentially explosive topic, but felt it was critical for students to have some understanding of it. Her outlook had been heavily influenced by personal knowledge of a friend of her children's who had been so incensed by a homosexual's approach to him at a local ball park that he and two of his friends killed the man. "They were unaware," she observed, "that they didn't have to do that, that they could just say no and walk away. His life was practically destroyed by being sent to prison." She explained that, as Kinsey and others have shown, a substantial percentage of adolescent males have had some sort of homosexual contact, often ambiguous in nature and quite inconsequential. "If my students didn't understand what that was all about, they might think they were choosing that route." Understanding that such episodes are reasonably common, she reasoned, might relieve a great deal of anxiety. Opponents of the program, however, insisted that treating homosexuality as variant rather than deviant behavior, without rendering moral judgment, was to condone behavior they regarded as particularly sinful. Jim Townsend spoke for others when he charged that "there were more homosexuals made in that sex-education classroom than would have ever been here today if they hadn't told them, 'If you haven't tried it, don't knock it; it's just an alternative lifestyle.' Well, they tried it, and they didn't knock it, and a lot of them became homosexuals as a direct result of being taught that in the classroom. That's a fact."

Both the cause and the prospect of a good fight appealed to Townsend. In a 1995 interview, Townsend characterized the FLSE curriculum as a pilot attempt by SIECUS to sell its ideas on sex education, using Sally Williams to lead the offensive. "They had this huge staff of writers," he explained, "and they're all getting rich making speeches and selling their books. It was a very profitable deal for many of these people in SIECUS." SIECUS, however, did not exist when the Anaheim program was commissioned and developed in 1962. Sally Williams's association with SIECUS came well after FLSE had achieved recognition as a model program. But by 1968, SIECUS experts did have some role in training FLSE instructors, and that was enough to sustain the connection in the minds of those disposed to regard the New York–based organization as a sinister force.

Consequently, says Townsend, "I agreed to head the program [against FLSE] and we put it under my umbrella, which was the California Citizens Committee [organized to support Goldwater and active in the Reagan campaign]. Our membership had dropped from some 50,000 to about 3,500 more or less inactive people who still had their name on our mailing list, so we really didn't even care about those people. It was the name of the Citizens Committee [that was important]. I could issue a press release—just phone it in to *AP* or *UPI*—and hear [it] on the news forty-five minutes later. That's the kind of power we had after our involvement with the Goldwater and Reagan groups."

At the August school-board meeting, Mrs. Howe asked the board to allow her and her friends to make a special presentation regarding their views of the FLSE program. The board's decision not to grant the request probably helped her and her group gain far more attention than they would otherwise have received. At subsequent board meetings, the group continued to attack the FLSE program, always referring to it not as "sex education" but as "sex instruction," or simply "the sex program." A favorite tactic involved simply reading aloud from curriculum materials. "There were things they wouldn't let us read," Howe recalled. "They said, 'We can't use that kind of language in here.' I said, 'Well, why don't you monitor the classrooms? It's being used there.' We got our point across." When the board tried to curb this practice by allowing protesters only two minutes at the microphone, they simply lined up and, when their time was up, passed the book to the next person, who continued the reading at that point. "We had all of our members briefed," one objector recalled, with obvious pleasure. "They all had their little part to play in this drama, so the board couldn't get on with their school business until after twelve or one o'clock. They were so dang tired by the time they got to the real school business, they couldn't see straight. We turned their meetings into fiascoes." Resentment of such tactics became so strong that, before one meeting, Mrs. Howe received a telephone call warning her that if she showed up at the meeting, a gun would be pointed at the back of her head. "That didn't bother me," she said. "I never told my husband, because he probably would have said, 'You can't go.' "

At a kinder, gentler level, Howe was eased out of three bridge clubs to which she had belonged. "I was really a social outcast," she said. "It tore friends apart. It was not nice. But I felt, as did so many others who helped me, that this was a necessary evil. We had to follow our value systems. . . . If thirteen, fourteen, fifteen-year-olds get that [sex] drive, which they do, they're not supposed to inhibit that? They're supposed to satisfy it? That's what I couldn't understand."

However unpopular Howe's tactics were, they proved successful. The board caved in and agreed to sponsor a "workshop" at which she would be able to make a presentation. At that meeting, held in the Grand Hotel in Anaheim, State Senator John Schmitz spoke against sex education and Howe presented a film called *Pavlov's Children*. The film's premise was that Russian communists, through the agency of UNESCO (the United Nations Educational, Scientific, and Cultural Organization), were using Pavlovian conditioning techniques, in sex education and elsewhere, to render American youth susceptible to totalitarianism. While the connection between a repressive totalitarian political ideology and sexual libertinism might appear tenuous, anti-communist groups regularly asserted that sex education advocates were communists, communist sympathizers, or dupes of clever communist manipulators. More theologically oriented sex-ed opponents believed Satan was behind sex education, and was using communists to work his evil will. Jim Townsend, Sam Campbell, John Steinbacher, and the John Birch Society all thought it likely communists were involved, but no one played both the communist and satanic themes as adroitly as Billy James Hargis.

As the controversy over sex education had begun to heat up around the country, Hargis had hired a Michigan educator named Gordon Drake to come to work with him in Tulsa. "He was a brilliant man," Hargis said, "and his whole creed was that what was wrong [with society] was that the emphasis was on sex instead of on spiritual things or patriotism. I had never thought about it. He gave me the whole idea. He was an expert. He was a Ph.D. So he wrote a little book, which I published, called *Is the School House the Proper Place to Teach Raw Sex?* I sold one million of them, and then I hit the road with him. I would do my thing and he would deliver his message, two a night. We'd start with him, on the chance that they'd stay to hear me, since they'd heard of me before, and then I'd bring my message on God and Country, always God and Country."

The narration for *Pavlov's Children* included passages from *The Little Red Schoolhouse* and, as luck (or Providence) would have it, the Hargis & Drake Sex-God-and-Country road show came to California during the first two weeks of October 1968, organizing a statewide anti-sex education movement known as California Families United. Although Townsend belittled Hargis's real contribution to the fight against sex-ed in California schools—"His book wasn't worth a damn and we didn't have any help. It was our group."—the presence of a figure so well known in conservative circles undoubtedly provided a boost to the opposition cause.

The cause of the "Antis," as Sally Williams and FLSE supporters referred to their opponents, gained a further major boost from *The Anaheim Bulletin*. First, editor Sam Campbell inflamed opposition passions by printing sample questions from a "sex knowledge" test that had been used in the course—one time, before administrators withdrew it, not because it was inherently objectionable, but because they rightly feared that questions such as, "Will having sexual relations several times before marriage enable a couple to judge whether they are likely to be sexually well-mated?" might raise suspicion that the program was condoning premarital sex. Teachers were explicitly instructed not to use the test again, a fact Campbell did not mention. Then, in December, John Steinbacher wrote a three-part series that was reprinted and distributed around the country. In the first article, entitled "School Sexology Plans Charted at Hush-hush Session," Steinbacher quoted a critic who alleged that sex-ed advocates could initiate such a program by "sneaking it in." The Anaheim program, which had been mandated by the school board and approved by a representative committee of citizens, did not fit this description, but the assertion fit popular theories that perverse educators were scheming to ruin the morals of American youth. According to Steinbacher, nearly ten million copies of the series were distributed in the year after it appeared.

As the Antis turned up the heat, backers of the program rallied to its defense. Townsend recalled that, at first, "It looked like everybody was in favor of it, and immediately they started issuing statements against us. We were a group of wild-eyed, extremist, rabble-rousing, Bible-thumping, right-wing kooks and nuts. So I said, 'If these people are going to play this game and support this raunchy program, let's give them a little publicity.' So the first thing we did was take excerpts from all these books and other things that were being taught in the class. We got the stuff from non-sex-education teachers who resented the program because it took money away from their class, and they were having to pay for school supplies out of their own pockets. They were finding all the raunchy things and supplying us with them."

Townsend and his collaborators used these materials to produce more fliers, which they put on windshields and handed out at churches on Sunday mornings, whether or not they were welcomed. At St. Boniface, the priest who had led the protest against the early sex-ed program had been replaced by a man Townsend described as "unbelievably liberal." The new priest favored the FLSE program and posted a guard at the literature table in the foyer of the church, to keep the "Antis" from placing their fliers there. "You could see [the table] from the parking lot," Townsend recalled with amusement, "so one of our people just sat out in the car and watched, and when the guard left, he went in and put our literature on the table." This and other tactics gained Townsend and his allies much publicity.

All the media coverage necessitated changes in the scope of the operation. Demand for the still-photocopied *Adult Bulletin* grew so great that Eleanor Howe and her coworkers simply could not keep up. To rescue them, Townsend agreed to put the material into a newspaper format that could be mass-produced and more easily mailed. He saw it initially as a one-time publication, but soon began to receive requests for subscriptions. "The dumbest thing I ever did," he said with a laugh, "was not sending the first three hundred of them back, because that's about all I got in the next two years, and once you get subscribers, you're obligated to them, so you keep on going." He named the new publication *The Educator*—"just to gig the educators who were pushing sex education"—and hired John Steinbacher to be its managing editor. With the exposure provided by the paper, Steinbacher began building a reputation as one of the most articulate and effective opponents of school-based sex education nationally.

ELEANOR HOWE BECAME a celebrity of sorts, and for a while she spoke frequently to groups on both sides of the issue. "When I gave talks," Mrs. Howe said, "they were not very long. I enjoyed questions." She knew where she stood and felt fully capable of holding her ground. At a teachers' seminar at the University of California at San Diego, a young teacher observed, "I gather from what you're saying that everything is black or white, and you see no gray." Not fazed for a moment by the charge of moral rigidity, Howe replied, "Oh, I'm so glad I made that point. Would you like to give me an example of where you think gray should have a place in my value system?"

The young woman raised a standard ethical poser: Would it be wrong for a man to break into a home to steal food to feed his starving children? Howe's response was immediate and unambiguous: "I'd prosecute him to the hilt. But if he waited till I came home, I would drive my car full of groceries to his house, or if he went to either one of my neighbors on my street, he could have had all the food he wanted. But he did not have a right to break into my house and steal even one can of beans." She recalled that the teachers had difficulty seeing her point. "I knew then that the values were changing, and that teachers were influenced to accept humanistic ideas and situation ethics—'If it's right for you, do it.' "

On another occasion, at Long Beach State, Howe was greeted with such mocking rudeness that she walked off the stage. She routinely declined remuneration beyond travel expenses, but she informed her hosts on this occasion that the next time they invited her, the honorarium would be ten thousand dollars.

Eleanor Howe's umbrage would not impress Sally Williams. "They were so unfair," Williams said. "It was unbelievable. It started with John Steinbacher, who began writing nasty things about our program, accusing us of doing terrible things that nobody in his right mind would even imagine an adult would do to children. [The accusations] were totally unfounded, but I had to investigate each [one]. Of course, newspapers have you over a barrel. They ask you something that is totally outrageous, something that never did happen, never would happen, never could happen, and then they say, 'She denied it.' As the group grew bigger, they began attacking individual teachers. It just snowballed until we couldn't believe what was happening. When I was invited to speak to churches and community groups, I always went and answered their questions and told them our philosophy of the program. But after a while, adversaries of the program would be in the audience, so that I couldn't really work with them. They have no integrity. They do not care what they accuse you of, and they are adamant. They will not discuss it. There is no way to deal with them except to refuse to meet, and that is what I had to do."

Harold Leif also noted the difficulty of dealing with the zealous "Antis," observing that interviews conducted by SIECUS in an effort to understand the opposition to sex education programs repeatedly turned up the same set of charges. In addition to the ever-popular report that FLSE materials advocated bestiality, respondents frequently claimed that a teacher in New York—"They always cite New York"—had taken off all her clothes in front of her junior high class, and that in some other school a couple had sexual intercourse right in the classroom. "Whenever there was a newspaper article in which the reporter interviewed people [about the Anaheim situation], that was an inevitable part of the piece—some allegation that was absolutely untrue. And yet, people who had a mindset to think of sex education as inherently evil were ready to believe these stories. The teacher or the super-intendent could say that nothing like that had taken place, but by that time the damage was done, and the corrections were unheard."

James Townsend acknowledged that the stories might have been untrue, but seemed untroubled by that possibility: "There was a class back in New York or somewhere where a teacher engaged in intercourse for the benefit of her students. And some of them stripped. Unless these were all lies. I'm sure the opposition will say, 'That's a damn lie. It never happened.' But if it didn't happen, it certainly was out as happening, and was being run around the country and talked about on radio and TV. So—happened or didn't happen—in the minds of the people, it happened."

Whether or not they fully believed every story they spread, the Antis clearly believed the FLSE program was evil and wanted it out of their schools. To that end, they were determined to gain control of the Anaheim school board. At the next election, in April 1969, only 14,250 of 100,000 eligible voters went to the polls, and the well-organized movement managed to win two of the three contested positions. The president of the five-person board opposed the program, but wanted to pursue a different strategy. Rather than simply call for a vote to cancel sex education classes, he persuaded them to join him in a subtler approach that would strangle the program without drawing public resistance.

As a first step, the board imposed a gag rule forbidding instructors in the program to talk about it publicly, or even to defend it or themselves against charges brought by individuals. Then, Sally Williams was dismissed from her position as director, a move that caught her quite by surprise. "I knew it was controversial, and I was concerned about the gag rule—it was very difficult to have all of these accusations being made, and no one in the district allowed to defend our program—but I didn't see it coming. . . . We had put our heart and soul into this program. We had spent about twenty hours a day working on it. And our students were so receptive. [On their evaluations,] they told how the course had helped straighten out some of their thinking, had made them realize how much thought and care they need to put into their decision of whom to marry and when to marry, and how they had reacted to the parenthood portion of the units. I couldn't believe the community would destroy all that. It felt awful. I cried."

Because she had tenure in her position as a school nurse, Williams was able to keep that job, but she was forbidden to accept any of the many invitations she received to help other schools set up sex-education programs, and whenever she spoke to groups of school nurses as part of an effort to bring them under the aegis of the National Education Association—without reference to the sex education—her visits were regularly preceded by a barrage of letters to local newspapers, coughing up the familiar charges that had been raised against her in Anaheim. "It's like every community that I went to had a drawer full of letters that they pulled out in anticipation of my coming, while I was there, and after I left. They had such rapid communication. There was such an efficient organization behind this. We were just flabbergasted." Before the beginning of the next school year, she asked for and received a transfer to another high school in the district.

The Antis' juggernaut continued to gain momentum. State Superintendent Max Rafferty, railing against the moral relativism he believed to be the source of the upheavals on college campuses, told the California state board of education, "The SIECUS program is not appropriate for California schools." In response, the board, which was also being pressured by the Drake and Hargis group, California Families United, banned the use of SIECUS materials in the state's public schools—an easy ban to enforce, since SIECUS did not produce materials for classroom use. That summer, an anti-sex-education gathering called The National Convention on the Crisis in Education met in Chicago, attracting approximately three hundred and fifty representatives from parent groups in twenty-two states. In addition to their opposition to sex education, the group also announced its intention to halt sensitivity training for teachers and to get prayer back into the classroom, and at least one leader also spoke of her opposition to busing for the purposes of integration.

Such attention eventually led to ten days of hearings before the House Education Committee in Washington. "Antis" around the country swamped committee members with telegrams urging them to see *Pavlov's Children* and other materials that had been provided to them. Back in Anaheim, Jim Townsend's California Citizens Committee organized a successful campaign to force Superintendent Paul Cook's resignation, charging that he had "introduced material of questionable merit," subjected Anaheim to national ridicule by promoting sex education, downgraded parents in the eyes of their children by implying they were not honest with their children about sex, and had misrepresented the district's connection with SIECUS. Cook, age sixty at the time and understandably resentful at what had happened to him and the program he had championed, observed that

a man in Germany fifty or forty years ago . . . proved beyond a shadow of a doubt that if you tell big enough lies and tell them frequent enough, there're a lot of fools who will believe 'em. And we're seeing this every day. There are people right in this town who could go right down and look at our books and look at our films who won't do it. Even though we could demonstrate that the savage lies and falsehoods that are being told are utterly and completely false. And yet people won't bother to come and find out about it.

He added that, since eighty percent of Anaheim students had parental permission to take the FLSE course, it seemed clear the opposition was in the minority. He thought it particularly unfortunate that a small group of people—he estimated the core group numbered no more than twenty-five—aided by *The Anaheim Bulletin,* had been able to thwart the obvious will of the majority through efficient organization and what he deemed to be unscrupulous tactics.

With both Cook and Sally Williams out of the way, the school board was able to move forward with dismantling the FLSE program. For an entire semester, it directed instructors in the program to submit, then repeatedly resubmit, drafts of the curriculum to fit a revised set of guidelines. When it finally restarted, it was a mere shadow of what it had been. Instead of the thirty-four books, forty-four films, nineteen film strips, and twenty pamphlets that were part of the original program, it now included only five books and two films. All books written by SIECUS directors or endorsed by that organization were explicitly banned from use. Discouraged by this maneuver, most of the teachers in the program asked to withdraw from participation in it. Thus, as Sally Williams pointed out, the board did not actually kill it, which might have given parents who supported it something to protest; "They just quietly let it go away."

In the months that followed, State Senator Schmitz successfully backed a law that did away with mandatory sex education in California schools, and John Steinbacher gained national renown in conservative circles as a speaker on sex education and author of a book called *The Child Seducers,* which charged that John Dewey, communist agents, and sex educators were part of a conscious movement to subvert the morals of America's youth and alienate them from their parents, leading ultimately to the collapse of the nation. The jacket cover for a record by the same title, and for which Steinbacher had written the narration, pictured an obviously terrified blond schoolgirl wearing only a slip and tied to a chair beneath an unshaded light bulb, with pictures of Marx, Lenin, Hitler, Trotsky, and Castro on the wall behind her. It purported to be "A factual EXPOSE of America's Sexploitation conspiracy." The reverse side of the jacket proclaimed, in large yellow letters against a black background, "THE CHILD YOU SAVE MAY BE YOUR OWN."

DESPITE THE FACT that a solid majority of parents throughout America continued to approve of sex-education programs, the conservative victory in

"The Battle of Anaheim" was replayed again and again. Jim Townsend admitted, "It went very much the way we wanted it to go and much, much faster than we had anticipated. And our group was in other communities, whether it was Camarillo or Bakersfield or Huntington Beach or wherever. We had little Citizens Committee groups that went to board meetings and put the pressure on. It scared the living daylights out of superintendents in other schools around the nation. It killed other programs."

Townsend was not simply bragging. Harold Leif recalled that when he testified at New Jersey state legislature hearings on whether to initiate sex education in public schools, he was greeted by a large gallery of women who booed loudly when he began to speak. They eventually quieted down, but they apparently had their effect. "They were middle-aged white women," Leif recalled. "Homemakers for the most part, I would think. I didn't see many, or any, that I would have said, 'Here is a businesswoman.' It would be my guess that they were mobilized through some local churches, or maybe the John Birch Society. I don't know the answer to that. But they were voters, and I think the legislators were influenced by them. At any rate, the bill did not pass."

As in California and New Jersey, so it went throughout the nation, as conservative religious people, mostly women at this point, learned that by marshaling their arguments, organizing their forces, and stomping on the hottest buttons, they could exert influence out of all proportion to their numbers or the true popularity of their positions.

As a founding member of SIECUS and its president from 1969 to 1971, Leif grew accustomed to hostile reaction from right-wing groups. "Their argument," he explained, "was that if you teach kids about sex, they'll want to engage in it and that will lead to abuse—more teenage pregnancies, unwanted babies, more abortions, etc. They felt sex ought to be buried, repressed, not expressed. Theirs was a prohibitive culture; ours was expressive. Our view was that knowledge of sex and its natural development will lead to responsible sex and appropriate use. They saw sex education as a threat to what we now call 'family values.' That's why they attacked us as ferociously as they did. Their view is no sexual activity until the wedding night. We [at SIECUS] feel that, in our day and age, 'Just say no to sex' doesn't work. The abstinence model is not a workable model. My own slogan is 'Wait a few years until it's appropriate for you emotionally and in terms of your capacity for responsibility.' I think that would have a wider audience than abstinence. Just postponing sexual activity for a few years would work wonders in terms of reducing teenage pregnancy."

Leif theorized that the attacks on sex education during the sixties were "part and parcel of the whole social fabric of the time." Riots, assassinations, student protests on college campuses, the war in Vietnam, growing distrust of government—all these were put in the same bag with sex education, "and the John Birch Society and others linked with them managed to reinforce this notion. Liberals were painted as 'Red sympathizers' or 'pinkos.' [Former Planned Parenthood director] Mary Calderone and I were called communists. There was a kind of delusional mindset at work. Back in Salem, they believed in witches, and more recently there's a belief in alien abductions, or memories from a past life, or satanic ritual abuse. Thousands of people believe these myths. There's always a certain segment of the population that is willing to believe the most outlandish ideas."

Leif noted that SIECUS has always maintained good relationships with what he called "mainstream religious groups," and had recently formed a Center for Sex and Religion, to help churches and denominations deal with problems related to sexuality. "It has mainly been the fundamentalist churches that have tried to demonize sex education and claim we were in league with Satan. You can get analytic and say they are dealing with their own impulses, which are scary to them, and that they project that outward and make part of the population into demons rather than deal with their own inner conflicts, but that's not easy to grasp, and even more difficult to prove. But the fact that whole segments of society could subscribe to irrational ideas and that reason could be swept aside left me with some concern about what else of a similar nature could happen in our society."

JAMES TOWNSEND, SAM Campbell, and John Steinbacher all seemed to share, or at least to exploit, the notion that sex education was part of a plot hatched by communists. Interestingly, despite having used *Pavlov's Children* in her presentations, Eleanor Howe does not hold this view. "Why should it be communist-inspired?" she asked. "I never could latch onto that. The Birch Society wanted me to be a speaker for them, but I refused, because I never believed in the conspiracy theory." To Howe, sex-education proponents are simply "people of the liberal bent who allowed themselves to be brainwashed into accepting the theory of situation ethics and the humanist philosophy. The humanists don't mind telling you that there are no absolutes, that they have to destroy religion per se—not any one in particular, but religion, period. You have that in their own words, in writing, in their own material."

Howe does not feel any strong impulse to become a long-term crusader, either. When the school board gutted the FLSE program, she withdrew into private life. "That was it," she said. "I had spent enough time away from my family, although I managed. My children never needed clean clothes or a hot meal [but] I wasn't there. . . . I figured that, once we got this over with, I was through. Phyllis Schlafly was writing, and other people were doing a good job, and that was enough for me. But I've been vindicated. I made the statement at a school-board meeting that if they continued with this type of sex instruction—I never called it education—that they were going to find it necessary to distribute condoms and other birth-control devices in our junior-high schools, and everybody laughed. They just thought that was the funniest thing. And yet that's precisely what they're doing now." Not long ago, she recalled, she had overheard her six- and seven-year-old grandchildren become excited by a television program. "One of them said, 'Come on, quick! They're getting into bed and he's going to pound her!' Something like that. I didn't say anything. I didn't want to make an issue of it, but I thought, 'God, what they've done. Even these little innocent kids will leave their toys because someone on TV is about to have sex.' That's how far this whole thing has gone toward changing the values of an entire society. That's what I foresaw, and now all I can say is, 'I told you so twenty-some years ago.' "

Beginning in New Jersey in the 1730s, a profound religious revival called the Great Awakening spread through the colonies, with its most marked manifestations occurring in New England under the preaching of British evangelist George Whitefield, shown here preaching to a group of soldiers.

As the nineteenth century dawned, America experienced the Second Great Awakening (or Great Revival), which produced a vigorous emphasis on "sanctification," the belief that Christians should live sinless lives. Although pushed most strongly by the Methodists, sanctification soon became a central preoccupation of all evangelical Christians.

In the late 1800s, Dwight Lyman Moody, a native New Englander who began as a YMCA worker and lay church leader in Chicago, became the leading revivalist of his era. Moody created the Chicago Evangelization Society—later renamed the Moody Bible Institute—and by 1930, this institution had prepared over 69,000 students to enter religious callings.

Billy Sunday was one of the most popular and charismatic preachers of the early twentieth century. A former National League baseball player, Sunday's theology was a kind of muscular perfectionism, with an emphasis on conquering such vices as illicit sex, profanity, and drinking alcohol, and on accepting the simple gospel that "With Christ, you are saved, without him you are lost."

To prevent Christian youth from abandoning faith in God in the rocky years that followed the Great Depression, evangelical and fundamentalist leaders began holding Saturday-night rallies that offered them a blend of wholesome entertainment, patriotic fervor, and revivalist exhortation. These meetings became immensely popular, and by July 1945, six hundred youth leaders from all over North America gathered together and christened their movement Youth for Christ International.

Youth for Christ leaders sought to show that Christianity did not have to be drab and dismal, and appealed to their youthful audience with catchy slogans such as "Old-fashioned Truth for Up-to-Date Youth" and "Geared to the Times, but Anchored to the Rock." As Billy Graham has observed, "We used every modern means to catch the attention of the unconverted—and then we punched them right between the eyes with the Gospel."

Apart from its strongly patriotic and anti-communist stance, Youth for Christ had no manifest political agenda. The growing size and splendor of its rallies, however, proved that its religious and moral message held sway over a considerable proportion of American youth.

Billy Graham was one of YFC's most inspiring, visionary, and devoutly anti-communist preachers, and his thundering sermons rapidly brought him to national attention. At a 1949 Los Angeles rally, Graham warned that communists were "more rampant in Los Angeles than in any other city in America," that "judgment [was] about to fall," and that the city's—and the country's—only hope now lay in prayer, repentance, and revival.

Billy Graham's crusades took him all over America and the world. Pictured here with a young American soldier during a tour of Korea, Graham (right) continually warned against the spread of communism's atheistic ideology, noting that, "unless the Christian religion rescues these nations from the clutches of the unbelieving, America will stand alone and isolated in the world."

In 1950, Graham obtained a brief meeting with President Truman to discuss the communist threat, the Korean conflict, and the country's spiritual health. The meeting went well enough, but when Graham (third from left) and three associates allowed themselves to be photographed while kneeling in prayer on the White House lawn, Truman was infuriated. It was years before Graham was able to repair this political breach.

Joseph McCarthy (left) inveighed against the satanic evils of communism with even more vigor and determination than Billy Graham. The Reverend Billy James Hargis (right) was one of McCarthy's most ardent supporters, and his association with the Wisconsin senator at the height of his influence raised the profile and membership of Hargis's own hard-right "Christian Crusade" ministry.

Fear of communism remained high among conservative Christians well into the 1960s, but what inspired even more concern—and resentment—in their ranks were the 1962 and 1963 Supreme Court decisions that banned officially sponsored prayer and Bible-reading in public schools. The Court claimed such practices violated the historic First Amendment prohibition against government establishment of religion, but its critics viewed the decision as a declaration of war against Christianity.

The 1950s were an extraordinarily successful decade for conservative white Christians in America, but the first sign of major change came in 1960, when the Democratic Party nominated Massachusetts Senator John F. Kennedy, a Roman Catholic, to be its candidate for president. Shown here giving a historic speech to the Houston Ministers' Association, Kennedy declared, "I am not the Catholic candidate for president; I am the Democratic party's candidate for president. . . . I do not speak for my church on public matters, and the church does not speak for me."

When John F. Kennedy used the image of a "man on horseback" in 1961, he alluded to the most enduring icon of American popular culture: the plain-spoken Western gunfighter who rides into a troubled, lawless town and makes order out of chaos. In Barry Goldwater, conservative Christians found their no-nonsense hero, and his "In your heart, you know he's right" campaign made him the most influential Republican never to be elected president.

Lyndon Johnson's announcement that he would not seek reelection in 1968 freed Billy Graham from having to make a painful choice between the president, with whom he was on excellent terms, and his old friend Richard Nixon. Graham had already obliquely encouraged Nixon to seek the Republican nomination, and though he refused to say whom he would vote for, he did concede publicly that he would like to see Nixon at the top of the Republican ticket.

CHAPTER

5

CULTURE WAR

ALICE MOORE READ about the Battle of Anaheim in the *Saturday Evening Post* in 1969, while sitting in a beauty shop in St. Albans, West Virginia. "I was shocked at some of the things I read," she recalled, "but I wasn't that concerned about it, because I knew this was West Virginia, not a radical state like California. I thought, 'It's not going to happen here.'" Not long afterward, however, she saw a newspaper story announcing that sex education was going to be introduced in Kanawha County schools. "That concerned me a little bit," she said, "but not all that much. And then I noticed that there was going to be a parents' meeting in a little restaurant in South Charleston, so I decided I'd go." That simple decision set Alice Moore on a course of action that erupted into a full blown "culture war," a violent and prolonged upheaval that laid bare deep fissures in the county's social structure.

In 1969, Kanawha County, West Virginia, was predominantly white, Anglo-Saxon, and Protestant—folks who, one would think, should find it easy to get along. But cutting across those broad categories were divisions of religion, class, and world-view that made real community for whites, much less for whites and blacks together, all but impossible. By its residents' own account, the county had at least two distinct populations of whites: the reasonably well-educated middle-class citizens of Charleston and the rural Appalachians who worked in the chemical plants and refineries of Nitro, St. Albans, and Dunbar, or carved a living out of the sometimes wild, coal-filled mountains gorged by hollows and creeks that drain into the Kanawha River. The social and cultural chasm between the capital city and the surrounding Upper and Lower Valleys is sufficiently wide that, at times, some have thought the county should be divided into two. Just about the only governmental jurisdiction that treated the area as a single unit was the Kanawha

County school district, and in the 1970s that could serve more to divide than to unite. The closing of dozens of small schools during the 1950s and '60s had thrown more rural children into contact with urban culture, thereby undermining their own folkways. The changes wrought by the upheavals of the sixties also threatened the fragile peace that masked quite different ways of perceiving reality.

Alice Moore was a relatively new resident of the area, having moved there when her husband became minister of the fundamentalist Church of Christ in St. Albans, an industrial suburb south of Charleston. Though she had no deep roots in the county, she did have a great concern for children and strong convictions about how they should be reared. Nevertheless, while the leaders of the meeting in South Charleston were uneasy about the proposed sex-education program, Mrs. Moore tried to keep an open mind. "When I listened to some of the things they were saying," she remembered, "I still wasn't convinced that everything was necessarily true, because people get excited about things sometimes. So I decided I would go to the Board of Education and just ask to see the materials myself. Many of the pictures I had seen at the meeting simply weren't there. Many of the things they had said were in the materials, I didn't see." Later, she alleged, she learned that some of the more controversial materials had been withdrawn after the first flurry of objections. Even with those items removed, however, she still found the proposed curriculum disturbing. "What concerned me was that this wasn't just a sex education course. It dealt with every aspect of a child's life. It dealt with their attitudes. In fact, the stated purpose of the course was to teach children how to think, to feel, and to act. And it covered everything, from their relationship with their parents, to their attitudes toward the use of drugs and social drinking, to their attitudes toward sexual conduct. So that concerned me."

The curriculum, a comprehensive health education program, had been prepared with the aid of a U.S. Office of Education grant and approved by the Kanawha County Board of Education and a Curriculum Advisory Committee of interested citizens—none of whom represented the county's more conservative rural population. To express her concern, Moore called Superintendent of Schools Walter Snyder and explained her feeling that the proposed curriculum would intrude into "our relationship with our children, what we wanted to teach them, what we wanted them to believe, how we wanted them to behave." His reply, by her account, amounted to little more than, "I'm sorry, Mrs. Moore, but there's absolutely nothing you can do about it."

Alice Moore did not accept Snyder's reading of the situation. Instead, she began speaking to various groups around the county and lobbying members of the state legislature to look into the matter. When her efforts seemed ineffectual, Moore and a few of her friends decided she should run for the single contested spot on the Board of Education. "We went down there with just minutes to spare and signed up to run," she recounted with a laugh. "It was really a spur-of-the-moment decision." A newspaper poll conducted a week before the election gave the incumbent nearly a third of the vote and Moore about eighteen percent, with the remainder split among seven or eight other candidates. Moore credits the newspaper poll, which indicated she had at least some chance, with rallying much of the anti-incumbent sentiment behind her. She also bought space on seventeen billboards, something no one had ever done for a school-board election, though it cost only $1,750. Opponents charged, with some evidence, that parent organizations backed or encouraged by the John Birch Society helped mobilize support for Moore's candidacy. Whatever the role of newspapers and billboards and Birchers, she took thirty-four percent to the incumbent's thirty-three, defeating him by approximately four hundred votes.

Within months of taking office in early 1970, Moore managed to overcome opposition to her view that the sex-ed curriculum was anti-Christian, anti-American, and indoctrinated students with an "atheistic and relativistic view of morality" that ran counter to her own firm conviction that "God's law is absolute." She acknowledged, "We pretty well won our case. Everything wasn't exactly to my liking, but we no longer had a program that was as disturbing to people as that one had been." In the course of this conflict, Superintendent Walter Snyder resigned and was replaced by Kenneth Underwood. These accomplishments made Alice Moore a champion in some circles. When she ran for re-election in 1976, she received 25,000 votes, two-and-a-half times her total in 1970 and 7,500 more than the nearest competitor. Moreover, she pointed out, most of the eight or nine people running against her shared her basic stand on most issues. Clearly, the rural "creekers" and factory workers, as well as a substantial number of white-collar city folk, felt they now had a voice on the Board of Education.

"Sweet Alice," as both friends and critics came to call her, though with different inflections, next made big news in 1974, when the school board sought to adopt 325 titles for its K–12 language-arts curriculum. In standard fashion, the books had been chosen by a school-system textbook committee. Under Superintendent Underwood, the Curriculum Advisory Committee had become dormant, so the textbook committee's recommendation reached the board in March and received rubber-stamp preliminary approval at a meeting Alice Moore missed. In keeping with the times, the books included substantial selections from black, Hispanic, and other minority writers, as well as a much greater than usual variety of other materials, all designed to help teachers create individualized programs of instruction that recognized differences in student interests, outlooks, and aptitude. The board followed established policy and put the books on display at the Kanawha County Library, to allow any citizen who wished to look them over to do so. They apparently drew almost no attention. When the time came to finalize adoption, however, Moore complained that not enough time had been allowed for inspection and persuaded her colleagues to extend the period of inspection until the June board meeting.

Mrs. Moore was particularly concerned about a growing toleration of "non-standard English" and had read articles, she explained, "to the effect that it was as important for a child who spoke standard English to learn to speak ghetto English as it was for a child of the ghetto to learn to speak standard English. That was an outrageous idea. If that's the case, why do we hire English teachers? Why do we even bother?" She listened to English teachers tell the board about a broadening approach to teaching, and, she recalled, "The more they talked, the more I realized they were talking about teaching non-standard English. So I suggested we postpone the adoption."

Objection to "non-standard English" can be a coded way of registering dislike of blacks and other minorities. It can also be precisely what it purports to be: objection to non-standard English. Those to whom the substitution of "lay" for "lie" and the use of nominative pronouns after prepositions sound worse than fingernails on a blackboard need not be racist to hope their children will not "axe" such questions as "Do he have your grammar book?" Whatever Alice Moore's true motivation on that score, she soon found even more substantial problems with the new books. Indeed, moments after the April board meeting adjourned, her husband, who had been leafing through some of the books, said, "I want you to look at what you just adopted." The selection he handed her, she remembered, "was written by a man who said, 'Thank God' he had gotten out of the South, because if he hadn't, he'd 'still be a blankety-blank Christian.' "

MOORE EXAMINED AS many of the books on the adoption list as she could. She also contacted Mel and Norma Gabler of Longview, Texas, to ask for their help. The Gablers, staunch fundamentalists themselves, have been called the two most powerful people in American education. That may not be an exaggeration, because the Gablers have enormous influence over Texas textbook adoptions, which has far-reaching repercussions for other states. Texas, like many states, including West Virginia, uses an adoption system in which local school boards must select books from an approved list if they are to receive state money for their purchase. Since Texas is the nation's largest single purchaser of textbooks, making its list is practically a guarantee of profit for a publisher; failure to make it can doom a book. Most publishers are understandably sensitive to pressures to make their books acceptable for use in the Lone Star state's nearly eleven hundred public school districts. Each year, as books are being considered by a committee appointed by the state board of education, citizens are invited to examine the books and to submit written "bills of particulars" containing specific complaints they may have. Since 1962, the Gablers have been subjecting every book under consideration to a painstaking line-by-line examination, ferreting out what they regard as unsound or harmful material and preparing "bills of particulars" (lists of objections) and reviews that sometimes run to hundreds of pages. In some years, their objections have been instrumental in getting more than half of the books under consideration stricken from the Texas list.

The Gablers believe the purpose of education is "the imparting of factual knowledge, basic skills, and cultural heritage" and that education is best accomplished in schools that emphasize a traditional curriculum of reading, math, and grammar, as well as patriotism, high moral standards, dress codes, and strict discipline. They also believe the kind of education they value has all but disappeared and that textbooks have played a crucial role in that disappearance. They quote textbook publisher D.C. Heath's dictum, "Let me publish the textbooks of a nation and I care not who writes its songs or makes its laws," and evince no doubt that inferior, improper, and blatantly destructive textbooks are responsible for leaving young people unprepared to face the challenges of adulthood, for destroying confidence and pride in America, for undermining Judeo-Christian values, and for creating a society in which crime, violence, drugs, pornography, venereal disease, abortion, homosexuality, and broken families have become facts of everyday existence. "TEXTBOOKS," one of their information sheets declares, "mold NATIONS because they largely determine HOW a nation votes, WHAT it becomes, and WHERE it goes!"

The Gablers were already heroes of the New Right in 1974, and they share most of that movement's conservative positions. They criticize material that seems to encourage or condone change, dissatisfaction, rebellion, or protest, even though the major part of their lives is spent protesting and encouraging others to protest against the standing order in education. On matters of economics, they stand foursquare on the side of free enterprise and regard as inept any text that notes its shortcomings or fails to take a hard line against socialism and communism. They regard sex education as a parental right that should not be usurped by the school, even if the home is failing to provide it. They insist that any science book dealing with evolution contain a statement that it is a theory, not a fact. They disapprove of books containing language they find offensive and of stories whose tone strikes them as "morbid" or "negative"—for example, they dismiss Edgar Allan Poe's classic tale, "The Cask of Amontillado," as "gruesome, murderous, bizarre content. Not suitable for a literature class. The murderer shows no sign of regret!'' They object to material that draws parallels between Christianity and other religions, since that seems to downplay the unique validity of Christianity, and to material that contains any hint of moral relativity. ''To the vast majority of Americans,'' one of their pamphlets proclaims, ''the terms 'values' and 'morals' mean one thing, and one thing only; and that is the Christian-Judeo morals, values, and standards as given to us by God through His Word written in the Ten Commandments and the Bible. . . . After all, according to history these ethics have prescribed the only code by which civilizations can effectively remain in existence!''

Because Texas was considering many of the books on the West Virginia list, the Gablers were able to provide Alice Moore with numerous bills of particulars. With these and her own notes in hand, she met privately with other members of the board, most of whom apparently shared her amazement at what she was finding, and with Superintendent Underwood, who suggested that the board meet with the teachers' committee that had selected the books, to allow them a chance to defend their choices. Moore insists that she hoped the matter could be handled quietly—''I knew that as soon as I started raising objections, I was going to be hit with accusations of book burning, of Nazism, so I didn't want anybody to know what I was doing.'' But word of the meeting leaked out and local newspapers gave it front-page treatment, pointedly alluding to Nazi Germany.

At that well-attended meeting, Moore showed a fine flair for playing to the crowd. With unconcealed delight, she recalled having held up a selection from one of the books and explaining, ''We have a lot of people from the community sitting here who have no idea of what we are talking about.'' She said she would be uncomfortable reading the item herself, but asked if someone from the selection committee would volunteer to read it for the audience. ''If we're going to put this in the classroom, for students to read,'' she said, ''surely someone here will read it.'' After a long silence, a board member agreed to read the item—a poem by e. e. cummings. ''It was dealing with sexual intercourse,'' Moore explained, ''and pretty explicitly. He read the poem, and there was kind of a stunned reaction. No one was saying anything. And then he said, 'Well, I think it's talking about sex.' And the whole room broke up in uproarious laughter. It was a great moment. I had made my point.''

NOW THAT A public struggle was inevitable, Mrs. Moore began to marshal the troops. She put a selection of books on display at the St. Albans library. She made her case to the newspapers. She spoke at churches and parent organizations around the county. She produced fliers listing quotations from offending books and detailing objections to them. She stirred up self-ordained fundamentalist preachers whose zeal and passion, untempered by education or habits of analysis, allowed them to stoke fires of angry resentment in their flocks of "creeker" parishioners.

She also recruited allies who could reach people that she could not. The most important of these was Elmer Fike, owner of a small chemical company and a hard-line conservative well known for newspaper columns he wrote, then periodically collected into a pamphlet-type publication called *Elmer's Tune,* which he printed and distributed at his own expense. Fike helped Moore identify material he regarded as "extremely liberal" and agreed to head a new organization called the Business and Professional People's Alliance for Better Textbooks. "We put ads in the paper," he recounted, "and it's just unbelievable the response we got, because people were looking for intelligent people who were not radical or rabid."

Moore used her tie to Elmer Fike to good advantage. When a local television station's evening news program ran a five-night segment in support of the books, she asked for and received a seven-minute slot in which to respond. Moore simply read one of Elmer Fike's columns, followed by a short piece from one of the books up for adoption. In it, a man fantasized that his daily bus ride would be livened up if all his fellow passengers took off their clothes and started making love with everyone else on the bus. When she finished, she said, "You know what Elmer Fike thinks about this, and you know what I think about it. Now, it's your decision. You decide what you think about it and let the school board know how you feel about putting this in your child's classroom." When she got home, she said, "My phone started ringing and it didn't stop for two days, and it took off from there."

As Moore and Fike and their cohorts constructed their case, their complaints about the textbooks fell into categories familiar to anyone who knew the Gablers' work or was aware of similar struggles in other states. The objecting parents sought to shield their children from anything that smacked of a lack of patriotism or, in their oft-used phrase, "disregard for government authority." Mike Edds, an inner-city youth pastor who rallied to Moore's side early in the protest, explained that, "Those books challenged the sacredness of everything that we believed about America. I'm sure America's wrong at times, but we believe it's the best thing we've come across in this world. They never brought out what America did do that was good. They said the flag was just a piece of cloth. Well, that's not what we believe. We have a lot of relatives who died under that banner. To us, it's like a sacred symbol. You don't burn the flag; you don't challenge what our Founding Fathers have done, or the Constitution. If there're things that're wrong, you work to change [them] and make it better." Closely related to charges of a lack of patriotism were complaints that the books contained criticism of the free-enterprise system. Elmer Fike regarded some of the readings as "obviously liberal, socialist, even communist-inspired." Alice Moore was less in-clined to think actual communists were involved, but she did believe the books bore the marks of "people in our country who are maybe leftist leaning, who think socialism is a better system than we have. They were radical books."

In addition to these fears, Mrs. Moore voiced concern that the books might create "more race consciousness than they would otherwise have had." Numerous parents were disturbed by material written by such black writers as Nikki Giovanni, Alice Walker, James Baldwin, and Gwendolyn Brooks. Ruth Davis, an English teacher who was also active in the local NAACP chapter, recalled her pleasure at seeing the work of black and Hispanic authors in the series: "I felt we had moved forward. We had faced integration and here we were now, teaching all students, and we were going to be able to have the black students see some of their culture within the textbooks for once in our career." Repeatedly, however, these writers were criticized for profane or negative language, for depressing content, and for exposing children to realities from which they should be shielded. Ms. Davis felt this was a transparent effort to hide the fact that many white parents did not want their children exposed to black influences, even in books.

Although selections by black authors contained some strong language and gritty scenes, racism could not account for all the discomfort over "realism" in the books. Board-member Matthew Kinsolving acknowledged that the books contained some "cuss words" and such terms as "tits" and "piss," which some parents found objectionable, but Alice Moore thought it more serious than that. "The books were filled with all kinds of profanity," she insisted. "It wasn't just an occasional thing." She felt the stories not only contained inappropriate vocabulary, but their content was often quite un-suitable for youngsters. "There was a play in a junior high book," she recalled, "to be acted out in a classroom, and it was a story of a fifteen-year-old boy's first visit to a prostitute. Now this was a book for junior high children! It was almost as if they were stretching the limits, to see how far they could go, to see what they could do."

Echoing a common Gabler objection, Moore and her backers charged the books with being pervaded by a "morbid," "negative," "depressing" tone. "There's more to life than negative things," said Mike Edds. "The sun shines sometimes; it's not always rain and clouds and darkness and sadness. They said, 'We want to introduce you to real life.' Well, I thought I was living real life. Most of us were happy people. Maybe we were happy in our ignorance, but we were happy people. We were happy in our homes; we were happy with what we were teaching our children. I wasn't really con-cerned with what was taking place on the streets of New York City."

James Moffett, the editor-in-chief of a collection of books called *Interac-*

tion, which comprised 172 of the 325 books on the adoption list, thought the matter more complicated. He noted that much literature and drama, including the ballads of Appalachian folk culture, has long dealt with dark subjects. He said, "We had a book called *Monologue and Dialogue* that had a lot of old chestnuts of English literature in there—Robert Browning, William Blake, Matthew Arnold, T. S. Eliot. But they said 'Trash, trash from beginning to end' about this book. They said it was 'morbid.' That criticism—that things were 'negative,' 'morbid,' 'depressed'—made me do a lot of thinking about what was in their mind. The psychological research on the authoritarian personality indicates that it's based on a very negative view of the world—'The world is a fearsome place and I'm not going to make it'—and on low self-esteem, low self-confidence, a view that mankind is evil, a feeling of being unable to cope. I think that comes out in their criticisms."

Since one aspect of a fearsome world is the absence of reliable road signs, the textbook critics assailed readings that smacked of moral relativity, that is, the belief that there are no definite right and wrong answers. Closely related was a distaste for symbolism, irony, satire, ambiguity, or role-playing, since all these invite interpretations that diverge from a literal reading of the text. In their view, schoolbooks—like the Bible—should have one meaning and one only, and it should be obvious to all. Cultivating a taste and talent for multiple interpretations can only increase the likelihood of thought and behavior that call into question the settled and dependable nature of one's community and religion.

Alice Moore believed the assault on the truth of Christianity begins in the primary years. As an example, she pointed to the way the familiar story of Androcles and the Lion was presented in one of the language-arts books. In the recommended discussion, she noted, "the teacher explains to the children that some stories are true, and some stories are just fables and make-believe. One way we can tell the difference is if an animal in a story doesn't act like an animal would really act, then we know it's a fable or make-believe story. For example, would a lion really remember Androcles, and remember that he had pulled the thorn from his paw, and then not kill him in the arena? And the conclusion is obvious: of course not. Therefore, we know this is a fable. Now, then, let's discuss the story of Daniel in the lions' den, which every one of these children had heard from the time they'd just been little things. In the Bible, the lions didn't kill Daniel, because he was under the protection of the Lord. And they're saying, because the lions don't act as they do in real life, we know it's a fable.

"Now, that kind of thing doesn't happen by accident. Their intent was obvious. Deliberate. . . . We had a situation where the school system was, in effect, attacking their religious convictions by compelling their children, by law, to be in that classroom, and then undermining everything they believed in. Books from several different companies, from all over the country had a definite anti-Christian slant. I'm not talking about ignoring Christianity; I'm talking about attacking Christianity. In one book, every selection, without exception, would present Christianity in a bad light. Christians were always hypocrites. Only old people believed in God. Young people sneered at religion. Even Christ was mocked. It couldn't be by accident. It was by design."

At higher levels in the curriculum, the objectors criticized the teaching of classical mythology, because, as Ruth Davis explained, "myths indicate that there were gods and goddesses back then who may have caused something to happen, and they didn't want us teaching that to students. If you weren't teaching about the one true God, then you couldn't teach about those myths and legends." Myths also drew fire because they invited comparison with the stories of the Bible. Mike Edds acknowledged that "the word 'myth' means different things to different people, but to West Virginians, a myth is a made-up, make-believe story. We believe the Bible is the inerrant Word of God, that it is true, that it's not a fable. We didn't want our children taught that the Bible's a myth."

BY THE TIME of the June 27 school board meeting, Alice Moore had convinced most parent-teacher groups and numerous conservative white churches to line up against the textbooks. On the other side, the West Virginia Human Rights Commission and the chapters of the NAACP and YWCA endorsed the adoptions, as did the *Charleston Gazette,* the *Charleston Daily Mail,* WCHS television, and most black churches. A coalition of clergy representing the West Virginia Council of Churches, Roman Catholic churches, Jewish synagogues, most Episcopal, Presbyterian, and Methodist churches, and some Baptist congregations, issued a statement acknowledging that any wide-ranging set of books is likely to stir controversy but asserting that their own investigation had found the books "not nearly as bad as portrayed." The issues objected to, they said, must be discussed openly if students are to be prepared to face the challenges of living in a multifaceted world. "We know of no way to stimulate the growth of our youth if we insulate them from the real issues. We feel this program will help our students think intelligently about their lives and our society." In response, a conservative coalition organized by a Baptist pastor and members of the Dunbar Ministerial Association issued statements critical of the books. And in the most impressive show of opposition, the Magic Valley Mother's Club gathered twelve thousand signatures of Kanawha County citizens urging the board to rescind the adoption.

The June school-board meeting drew more than one thousand people. In the end, the five-member board voted three-to-two to approve the original list, with the exception of eight books from the *Interaction* series. Joining Alice Moore in casting a negative vote was Matthew Kinsolving, who admits he was less concerned about the content of the books than about peace in the county. "On the basis of what she had upstirred," he said, "I voted against adopting those books at that time." Kinsolving's apprehensions were to prove more than justified.

Some citizens expected the objectors to accept their defeat with resignation, if not with grace. The response, however, involved neither. During July and August, an organization called Christian-American Parents initiated a letter-writing campaign, bought newspaper ads, held a large public rally, picketed a board member's company, and held a demonstration in front of the governor's mansion. (Eventually, a different group of parents came together and called themselves Non-Christian American Parents, to make the point that people other than fundamentalists opposed the books.) Another new group, Concerned Citizens, picketed the Board of Education. And various parties, not all identified but definitely including the American Opinion Bookstores, continued to circulate copies of material calculated to stir anger even further.

Some of the most inflammatory material, blatantly sexual in nature, was not even in the books that had been adopted, but few bothered to check; some of those who did check, and did not find the controversial passages, concluded that a deceitful administration was hiding the material until the furor died down. Because nearly all attacks on the books emphasized the profanity and sexual content, the entire collection soon came to be known as "the dirty books."

As summer wore on, Alice Moore began to urge parents to hold their children out of school in September if the board tried to force them to use the new books. On Labor Day, September 2, the day before schools were scheduled to open, Concerned Citizens sponsored a rally at which fundamentalist preacher Marvin Horan fervently urged the crowd of eight thousand to boycott the entire school system the next day. Tuesday morning, with national news media on hand to watch, approximately twenty percent of the district's forty-five thousand students stayed home. In the Upper Valley, where Horan and other fundamentalist preachers had been most vociferous in their objections to the books, some schools had absentee rates above eighty percent. Some parents doubtless kept their children home out of fear of what the protesters might do to those who violated the call for a boycott—this was, after all, strong union territory—but most observed the boycott because they believed it was a righteous cause.

The following day, the boycott received a tremendous boost when an estimated thirty-five hundred coal miners struck in a show of solidarity with the protesters, despite orders from United Mine Workers officials not to do so. Within a week, the number of striking miners in Kanawha County and seven surrounding counties ran as high as ten thousand. Meanwhile, protesters picketed schools, school-bus garages, businesses, and various other sites, sometimes erecting barricades to keep people and vehicles from passing through. Thousands of people mounted daily demonstrations at the school district's main administration building. On September 10, Charleston bus drivers honored the picket lines, leaving more than ten thousand regular riders without service.

On September 11, the school board caved in, announcing it would withdraw the disputed books from use and submit them to examination by a new Textbook Review Committee, to which each board member would be allowed to name three individuals of his or her choosing. Alice Moore credited the miners with having forced this semicapitulation. She had asked them to strike and felt they made a tremendous difference. "They added a power," she said. "That coal mine strike was costing millions of dollars a day. And shutting down the mines, of course, grabbed national attention. That was probably the first and only time they ever went on strike for anything other than their salaries or working conditions." James Moffett pointed out that the miners were in a contract dispute at the time, and that reducing coal reserves placed additional pressure on negotiators, providing an extra incentive to strike. But he did not doubt their genuine sympathy for the protest. "I think they really felt they should cast their lot with these book objectors," he said. "I think they thought the same way, and many of these children were their own children. There was a strong identification there, and miners don't have a lot of power. Part of the way they can assert power is to strike." Marvin Horan offered a similar explanation when he told Superintendent Underwood, "The common man don't know what to do except what he's done, and that's to go home and sit down."

Perhaps to Moore's surprise, the troops she had mobilized were not content with a partial victory. At a large rally on the evening of the board's concession, the crowd jeered when she called the agreement "the best we can expect." Marvin Horan, who had signed the agreement on behalf of Concerned Citizens, reversed himself and joined the crowd's call to continue the boycotts and pickets until the offending texts were permanently removed from the schools and the superintendent and school board members who approved them swept out of office.

The protests not only continued after the rally, but quickly turned to ugly violence over the next few weeks. While the Textbook Review Committee formed and began its work, one school was dynamited, two others were firebombed, and several were damaged by gunfire and vandalism. Two men were wounded by gunfire, one as he tried to cross a picket line and the other, a protester, shot through the heart by a pro-book demonstrator who said he thought he was being attacked. CBS News reporter Jed DuVall and his television crew were badly roughed up. School buses were fired upon while returning from their rounds, and at one point most of the buses in the upper part of the county were disabled by vandals. Protesters stoned the houses and broke car windows of parents who defied the boycott and sent their children to school. Teachers and administrators were repeatedly threatened. Shots were fired into a car belonging to the president of the Classroom Teachers Association. And someone set off fifteen sticks of dynamite under the gas meter at the school board building just minutes after Underwood and the board had left.

Supporters of the books were also guilty of violence. The car of one protester was destroyed by fire. Alice Moore was repeatedly threatened, guns were fired in front of her house, sugar was put in her gas tank, and police bodyguards stayed with her during times of greatest threat. At one point, concern for student safety moved Superintendent Underwood to cancel all classes and extracurricular activities for several days, during which he and several board members, including Mrs. Moore, left town for reasons of personal safety. All attacks on schools and school buses occurred when no children were present, but one man eventually convicted in the bombings testified that he and others had considered bombing carloads of children as a way to stop "people that was sending their kids to school, letting them learn out of books when they knew they was wrong."

Alice Moore admitted, "I never dreamed it would come to this," and professed to be appalled by the violence. She noted, however, that both sides had been involved, that a tiny minority can create great havoc, and that most protesters had posed no physical danger to anyone. "It got to be a very emotional time," she said, "with very angry, explosive feelings, and those were just some sad things that happened." Citing the dynamiting of the school-board building, she pointed out that "it was played up as if textbook protesters were trying to kill the superintendent, but nobody knows who set that off. I was at that meeting. Were they trying to kill me? The papers didn't report that I was there. There was some troublemaking going on, some of it to give the protesters a bad name, but the violence got played up out of proportion to what was taking place here."

Emmett "Lefty" Shafer, who was principal of the Midway Elementary School, where Marvin Horan's children attended, remembered that he had not been afraid of violence—until his school was hit by a Molotov cocktail and a dynamite bomb. "It was frightening," he admitted. "I think they were trying to let the board know that they were going to be doing whatever was necessary to see to it that those books were not used." Ruth Davis agreed that "it was scary, it was frustrating, it was nerve-wracking. You would think that if they were Christian people, they would not have used those types of tactics. You really didn't know what to expect when you went to school the next day. You didn't know whether you were going to be able to find the building there or not, especially in the upper end of the county. We always tried to travel together. Nobody would travel alone. We had a sort of cama-raderie among ourselves, in that we would talk on a daily basis, to make sure everything was all right, and we would get together in the evening, after school or at church, just to keep the lines of communication open among ourselves."

THE RENEWAL OF hostilities triggered by the boycott drew new adver-saries into the arena. Joining Marvin Horan were three other fundamentalist preachers—the Reverends Avis Hill, Ezra Graley, and Charles Quigley—who quickly assumed leading roles in court-defying mass protests at school headquarters, which resulted in their being arrested, jailed, fined, or released on bail, and accorded martyr status among their followers. Quigley gained early notoriety when he declared, "I am asking Christian people to pray that God will kill the giants [the three board members who voted for the books] who have mocked and made fun of dumb fundamental-ists."

On the other side of the aisle, the Reverend James Lewis, rector of St. John's Episcopal Church in Charleston, emerged as a key leader of pro-textbook forces. Lewis was a newcomer to Charleston who had paid little attention to the textbook controversy before the boycott began. At the request of several student council leaders who objected when the new texts were withdrawn, Lewis, along with a rabbi and a Baptist minister, met with a group of students to see what might be done to get the books back into the classrooms. That meeting led to others and, soon, to the formation of the Kanawha County Coalition for Quality Education, which sought both to defend the new books and also to avoid further damage to the social fabric. One of the coalition's first steps was to hold meetings throughout the county to give citizens the opportunity to examine the books for themselves, to show that much of what they had been told about the books was simply not true. "Everyone was so frightened," Lewis said, "as though somehow the children would die if they read these books."

Lewis's meetings were reasonably effective in easing the minds of some parents, particularly those primarily concerned with the presence of graphic sexual material, but they did little to mollify those who disagreed with the overall multicultural thrust and innovative approach of the books. Lewis felt that stories depicting other cultures might cause Kanawha County children to become more aware and appreciative of the distinctive Appalachian sub-culture and stimulate them to reflect on their own history and lives and tell their own stories. Instead, he quickly learned that stories he considered "absolutely marvelous" and "wonderful" were viewed by many parents as "depressing, offensive, and ungodly," and that he was engaged in something that could not be resolved by pointing out errors in propaganda fliers.

"What we saw in that struggle," he said, "was a real religious crusade. If you stepped in front of it and challenged it in any way, you were immediately demonized and seen as the enemy, as the Antichrist. When you move into that kind of demonization, you are just a hair away from killing the person or people associated with that view, because to kill something evil becomes something good. That was the aura and the mood of that whole struggle. A woman stepped up to me at a meeting one time and put her face up against mine, quoting Scripture in my face as though somehow I didn't read Scripture, and she said to me, 'We shouldn't cast our pearls before swine' as though I were swine. There's a sense in which this passion turned into a terrible crusade that got violent very quickly in a self-righteous way. That's the thing you could feel in that valley all the time: you could be killed 'for Christ's sake.' "

Following a telephoned death threat, Lewis's family and friends urged him to step away from the controversy, but he felt that was not an option. Comparing the struggle to an explosion outside the church door, he said, "You have to go to it. People were warring with one another. This was Bosnia. This was a deeply tribal struggle, and there was no way to stay out of it." Lewis consistently described the conflict as a clash between cultures. "It was a struggle," he said, "of people from lots of different persuasions. My concern was always, 'How can all of us in this valley study and work and live together and not kill one another, particularly over these textbooks?' It was crystal-clear to me from the very beginning that we were in a major struggle with folks who saw life from a different perspective. The seeds had been there for a long time, but something new was happening." In an article carried by newspapers across the country at the time, Lewis wrote, "The anti-textbook people of Kanawha County are confused and angry about everything from marijuana to Watergate. Feeling helpless and left out, they are looking for a scapegoat. They are eager to exorcise all that is evil and foul, cleanse or burn all that is strange and foreign. In this religious war, spiced with overtones of race and class, the books are an accessible target."

Like James Lewis, evangelical youth pastor Mike Edds also felt he had no choice but to take a stand. "We'd been taught in the Bible Belt," he explained, "that there is a higher law, that if the civil law is contrary to biblical law, then we have to obey the higher law. I felt something great was at stake. That's where the majority of parents and many of the educators who grew up in West Virginia were. Our whole belief system was at stake, and we had to take a stand. That was the first time in my life I had ever known Christian people to march in a protest or resist something. Before that, Christians did nothing; whatever came down the pike—fine, good, bad, or in-between—it was 'Just don't bother me.' But this was striking at their very soul.''

Edds agreed with Jim Lewis's assertion that the struggle over the books stemmed from cultural differences, but viewed it from a different angle. Recalling a report that Superintendent Underwood had remarked in exasperation, ''These fundamentalists: How can we live with them?,'' Edds said, ''That's where the split came. There was an elitism in the central office that saw the majority of the county's population as ignorant, uneducated folks. I'm sure some of the folks didn't use proper English; I speak with a little bit of hillbilly lingo and slang. Some of these folks maybe didn't finish high school, maybe some of them didn't go on to college, but that's not a mark of a person's intelligence. People in Kanawha County are very pro-American, very patriotic—it's apple pie, Mom, the flag, and the church. These textbooks struck at every area of that belief system, and parents felt like, 'We cannot just avoid this conflict; we have to face it; we have to do something about it.' It was a terrible time. It was almost like a civil war. The community was just split down the middle.''

Mike Edds clearly felt that a reconciling spirit could have accomplished more than elite snobbery or wild-eyed anger. He told of an assistant superintendent named Marian Ashley—''good Christian lady, tremendous influence on my life''—who had driven out one night to a rural church where she knew a protest meeting was being held. ''A minister with his army fatigues on,'' Edds recalled, ''was spouting, 'It's time for war,' which was totally absurd, and she walked into that place and said, 'I'm an assistant superintendent from Kanawha County schools. I'm here to listen.' In a situation that could have become violent, she totally defused it, and she handled herself with grace. They yelled, they screamed, they complained, but she listened. When she left there, every one of those people came up and shook her hand and said, 'Thank you for listening. Thank you for coming.' Most of the trouble would have never happened if the superintendent would have climbed down out of that ivory tower and said, 'I'm here to listen to you, not as your superior, but as an equal, as a fellow citizen. Express your concerns. How can we address it?' ''

James Moffett agreed that social class and culture played a major role in the conflict, noting that support and opposition typically broke along lines that divided rich and poor, urban and rural, black and white, educated and uneducated, but he also noted that a good bit of demographic line-crossing occurred. Columnist Elmer Fike played an important role in reaching higher-status people who were uncomfortable lining up with fundamentalist "creekers." Fike observed, "There were some hillbilly preachers who took this thing and really made a career out of it," volunteering that, though a churchgoer, he was "anything but a fundamentalist" and believed in evolution—his daughter was getting a doctorate in entomology at Berkeley at the time. To him, opposition to the textbooks was a way to further a larger conservative agenda more than as a life-or-death struggle in itself. Still, he professed to have great sympathy for "the religious people" and wondered, "Why the hell do we have to indoctrinate our children out here in semi-rural communities with the problems of the inner city?"

Fike preferred to think of himself and those who shared his views as "traditionalists." To them, he wrote in one of his columns, "The job of the schools is considered to be the transmission of the tradition of the parents to the children in order to preserve society. Books and supplementary materials should be chosen to promote that end. While other cultures and governmental systems should be considered, the American system should always be the yardstick by which others are measured." By contrast, those he characterized as "progressives" regard this approach as "indoctrination" and "prefer that the child be allowed to examine all philosophies with a minimum of guidance." They see the task of education as teaching the child "how to think, not what to think." Fike found this approach wanting because, among its other faults, it "subtly attacks traditional ideas."

In spite of his opposition to the textbooks, Fike met regularly with Jim Lewis and Superintendent Underwood and other school administrators, working to stem the violence and also to help them understand the arguments of the protesters. Lewis, he remembered, was deeply concerned about divisions in the community and wanted to explore ways to resolve the conflict by helping the textbook critics understand that the books would be good for their children and that the school system and the pro-book people were not their enemies. Fike thought Lewis failed to recognize the importance of the traditional/progressive chasm he had delineated. "I told him, 'I think the problem is a difference of opinion as to what the purpose of education is. How can you have unity if you don't work out an agreement on what you're trying to do?' But we didn't get anywhere on that."

Fike's organization, the Business and Professional People's Alliance for Better Textbooks, established an office in Charleston and stayed in touch with people dealing with similar issues throughout the country. A *60 Minutes* story about the conflict depicted him as a major player but, according to him, "I never got the kind of publicity that the people who wore the coonskin hats got. The local paper wouldn't even carry my name. Media love a radical, wild person, but somebody like me, who was reasonable, they don't give us much space, because we're not good copy."

James Moffett noted that many of the more affluent and better-educated citizens who sided with Fike were business people whose conservative views included a desire to reduce and limit government taxation and regulation of their enterprises. At lower levels in the status hierarchy, he contended, mountaineer folk "don't like central government because it disrupts their folk ways and has never, throughout their history, seriously come to their aid. They felt their children were being mentally kidnapped by people of a larger, dominant culture. They've always been pushed around. Outsiders have always come in and grabbed the land and siphoned the money from the mines, so they've never felt included or protected by the federal government or larger social entities. They had their own culture, and they wanted to keep it that way."

Moffett's comments about the mountaineer attitude toward government point to an interesting paradox that can be seen in many situations of religious and cultural conflict in this country. While vehemently resisting efforts of governmental agents to regulate their lives, culture warriors may feel quite justified in using government to impose their own views and standards. In Kanawha County, the protesters raised the quite legitimate question of what role legally responsible parents should have in determining what their minor children are taught in tax-supported schools. (In fact, the authors and publishers of most of the disputed books had explicitly expected teachers to tailor the wide range of materials in the texts to their students' particular needs.) Those same protesters, however, were quite willing to use their power to decide what all children, not just their own, should be allowed to encounter in school. A journalist who attended one of numerous anti-textbook rallies told a friend, "I looked around at the people there, and I could feel for them and with them. I felt like there was room for them in my America, but I didn't feel there was room for me in their America."

Protesters who actually had a measure of power occasionally used it in creative ways. On one occasion, a meeting arranged by a Methodist bishop in an attempt to find common ground between factions in the controversy was broken up when constables, dispatched by a disgruntled mayor, arrived to arrest Superintendent Underwood and several board members on charges of contributing to the delinquency of minors by exposing them to pornographic books. No action was ever taken on the charges, but such harassment and intractable hostility eventually led to resignations, first by the president of the school board and later by Kenneth Underwood. In an extreme instance of political hubris, the mayors of several upper valley towns seriously threatened to withdraw their towns from Kanawha oversight and form an entirely new county.

.   .   .

AS NEWS OF Kanawha County's culture war spread, a variety of allies joined the side of the protesters. One of the first groups to offer support, at Elmer Fike's invitation, was the Heritage Foundation. A fledgling Washington think tank, it had been established, with generous support from Colorado brewer Joseph Coors, during the Nixon administration, by a group of young conservative thinkers and activists that included Paul Weyrich, Ed Fuelner, Lawrence Pratt, and James McKenna. McKenna, a lawyer, had been recruited to the organization in part because of his success in a string of cases in which he had defended the right of parents to educate their children at home, and he came to Kanawha County to provide legal assistance to the fundamentalist preachers and other protesters who had been arrested for violating one or another city ordinance in the course of their anti-textbook activities. He explained why the Heritage Foundation decided to aid the protesters: "It was consonant with their ideological concerns. The conservative element in the society, then and since then, has had a continuing suspicion about the education establishment." The foundation was "espousing causes which were very much in line with what these 'creekers' were doing, and they had hired someone with a substantial amount of experience in that field, so they had a 'win/win' situation. A number of organizations felt very strongly about what was being done to these 'creekers.' Heritage just happened to have the right equipment at the right time." In addition to McKenna's efforts, Larry Pratt—the same Larry Pratt who in 1996 would be forced to withdraw from his position as Pat Buchanan's campaign manager after being accused of having ties to white supremacist groups and the militia movement were revealed—came to Charleston to help Elmer Fike and his colleagues map out long-range strategy.

Additional help came from a group known as Parents of New York United, whose spokesperson, Janet Mellon, helped draw further national attention to the controversy. "She was a really expert controversialist," McKenna remembered. "She was well-connected—her husband was related to the money family—and a knife-fighter of some considerable proportion. She brought in a number of educators, writers, and controversialists and got them writing about the subject." Other supportive groups of similar nature included the John Birch Society, a Louisiana-based anti-sex-education organization known as the Hard Core Parental Group, and an organization that called itself the Guardians of Traditional Education. On October 6, 1974, an estimated eight thousand protesters attended a mass rally at which the featured speakers included McKenna, textbook evaluators Mel and Norma Gabler, and Robert Dornan, who represented a California organization known as Citizens for Decency Through Law. The Gablers stayed on for a week, speaking to groups up and down the valley and tutoring anti-text members of the newly appointed advisory committee in the fine points of finding and documenting objectionable materials in textbooks. Dornan later returned to offer further aid to the protesters, before going back to California to mount a successful campaign for election to the U.S. House of Representatives from the congressional district that includes Anaheim and Orange County.

James Moffett suggested that conservative interests such as the John Birch Society, the Heritage Foundation, and Bob Dornan used the Kanawha County situation to appeal to a working-class population for whom their conservative economic views held little attraction, and that the Gablers and Mrs. Mellon saw it as a prime opportunity to strengthen their network of textbook critics and advocates of traditional education. "There was an exuberant build-up of rightist forces during this period," he explained, "and the Kanawha County controversy was one episode in an accumulation of things. The numbers were not that large, but it got huge publicity all through the fall of 1974, and I think it did swell the constituency of rightists during that period."

The boycotts, strikes, pickets, demonstrations, rallies, newspaper ads, violence, and harassment had a decided effect. A September poll conducted by the *Charleston Gazette* had found forty-one percent of county residents opposed to the books, with thirty-one percent undecided or unconcerned. Follow-up surveys in December and January revealed that most of the undecideds had become opponents, with seventy percent opposing their use in elementary schools, though less than thirty percent thought them inappropriate for secondary students.

Given the emotional climate, tensions ran high in anticipation of a public meeting the school board scheduled for November 8, at which time it planned to reach a final decision on the Textbook Advisory Committee's recommendations. Expecting a huge turnout, the board rented the Charleston Civic Center and had thousands of seats set up. To discourage violence, guards armed with metal detectors and guns were stationed at entrances; additional guards kept watch on the auditorium floor from positions in the rafters. These elaborate preparations proved to be superfluous. Alice Moore and a minister from the pro-book forces had both used radio and personal contact with various groups to urge citizens not to attend the meeting, lest trouble break out. As a result, the board conducted its deliberations in the huge hall before an audience of no more than fifty people. By a four-to-one margin, with Moore as the lone dissenter, it ruled that the books would be returned to the schools, but that no school or child would be forced to use them. Parents would have to provide written permission for their children to be assigned the books, and children whose parents objected would continue to use the old books or some acceptable alternative. Some books, including James Moffett's *Interaction* series, would be restricted to library use. Two weeks later, the board agreed that future texts would have to meet criteria set forth in a set of restrictive guidelines Alice Moore had prepared with the aid of the Gablers.

One might imagine that both sides would conclude they had done about as well as could be expected. Traditional parents could protect their children from the new books, and future books would be more to their liking. The children of more progressive parents could use the controversial books until they wore out and, if not too many of them turned into communists or criminals, a future board might relax some of the restrictions it had placed on itself. Ideological struggles, however, seldom end quite so peacefully, especially when they involve fundamentalists, for whom half-measures and partial victory are regarded as little better than defeat. Near the end of November, at what was billed as a national rally, the Reverend Carl McIntire came to Charleston to blister local politicians for their failure to back the folk who were standing up for God and the American Way by trying to ban the controversial texts. Marvin Horan, who had told Lefty Shafer he could be content with a decision that allowed individual parents and schools to make their own decisions—"if that'd take place," he had said, "that'd fix everything up real fine. We wouldn't have anything to protest over"—changed his mind and started circulating fliers that asked protesters, "Why have you stopped fighting?"

On December 1, the Reverend Avis Hill led a demonstration in which two thousand people marched through the Charleston shopping district waving flags and carrying placards that read, "Trash Is for Burning," "No Peaceful Co-existence with Satanic Communism," and "Wish We Had More People Like Sweet Alice." A few days later, Hill and fellow fundamentalist preacher Ezra Graley went to Washington to discuss their concerns with conservative Indiana Congressman Roger Zion, who registered their complaints in the *Congressional Record*. On December 12, during a televised school-board meeting, protesters physically assaulted Superintendent Underwood and all the board members except Alice Moore. And on Christmas Eve, worshipers leaving a family service at St. John's Episcopal Church, which had backed the pro-book forces, found the church door decorated with stickers that announced, "You Have Been Paid a Visit by the Klan." On the other side, the National Education Association held hearings and issued a report that criticized the board both for not being more sensitive to the concerns of a significant part of its constituency and also for caving in to most of the objectors' demands.

Early in January, Concerned Citizens and the Business and Professional

People's Alliance, with considerable assistance from the Heritage Foundation and Janet Mellon, held a three-day seminar that brought in such noted speakers as California's conservative Superintendent of Public Instruction, Max Rafferty, and representatives of the National Parents League, an Oregon-based group that showed churches and parents how to set up private schools free of government control, as well as prominent education experts and activists from several states and Washington, D.C. That experience helped establish Heritage as a significant force in the field of traditionalist education. Seminars, however, were only one weapon of choice. On January 17, a grand jury indicted preacher Marvin Horan and five others for "conspiracy to blow up two elementary schools and other School Board property." The next day, nearly two hundred protesters, including Horan, welcomed several delegations of the Ku Klux Klan who gathered on the steps of the state capitol for a full-hood rally, followed by a larger gathering at the Civic Center, where Imperial Wizard James Venable darkly predicted that the "Communist, socialist, nigger race is going to dominate this nation," and other Klansmen declared their support of the protesters and invited them to join the Klan.

With the exception of some of the fundamentalist preachers, most leaders of the anti-textbook forces professed to be disturbed by such support. Elmer Fike acknowledged he was sympathetic to much the John Birch Society stood for, but volunteered that "sometimes they get a little bit out of line, and it did not give us the kind of image we wanted." As for the Klan, "We didn't want anything to do with them. We wouldn't touch them with a ten-foot pole." Mike Edds was even more pointed: "We're not ignorant people. We felt like we were fully capable of representing ourselves. I was appalled when the Klan got involved. They just found a good thing going, that was getting some national attention, and they jumped on board. A lot of us dropped out toward the end. We were tired of other groups wanting to speak for us, trying to promote their organization's agenda, which wasn't the agenda that had us out on the streets. There is a religious right and a political right, and they're not one and the same."

The intrusion of uninvited outside forces and the arrest of Marvin Horan and his coconspirators, together with the increased presence of West Virginia State Police, soon brought an end to the boycotts and demonstrations and violence. After Horan was found guilty of conspiring to bomb the schools, the Reverend James Lewis appealed to the federal judge to give Horan a probated sentence, so he could remain in the community and use his influence to help try to heal fractures and restore peace to the valley. The judge sentenced Horan to three years in the federal penitentiary; his five accomplices received various lesser sentences.

. . .

BY SOME ACCOUNTS, the pro-textbook forces won the Kanawha County textbook wars; most of the offending books were restored to the classrooms and the most vociferous of their enemies went to jail or prison. The apparent victory, however, proved hollow. In schools where opposition ran high, the books were typically not used at all. When opinion was mixed, as was often the case, teachers found it difficult to devise comparable assignments and often abandoned attempts to use the new materials at all.

Because the Kanawha County conflict created such upheaval and was so widely publicized, its effects were felt throughout the country. To avoid similar problems in their own districts, many school boards and administrators refused even to consider adopting the controversial *Interaction* series, and competing publishers' salespeople quite happily spread the word that the books had been condemned as immoral in West Virginia. As a result, books languished and died before their time. Since then, publishers have been unwilling to produce books containing the range of subjects and ideas found in the books vilified and crippled in the Kanawha County struggle.

Though no battle has come close to the Kanawha County episode in intensity or scope, hundreds of school districts throughout the nation have experienced protests, usually initiated by small groups of conservative Christian parents, against textbooks and other books assigned in classes or available to students in school libraries. The protests are part of a general campaign. "They're the same old books all the time," James Moffett noted, referring to such titles as John Steinbeck's *Of Mice and Men,* J. D. Salinger's *The Catcher in the Rye,* Mark Twain's *Huckleberry Finn,* Shel Silverstein's *A Light in the Attic,* Judy Blume's *Forever,* Judith Guest's *Ordinary People,* Madeleine L'Engle's *A Wrinkle in Time,* and Maya Angelou's *I Know Why the Caged Bird Sings.* "I can think of much worse books to censor, but they're on a standard list that circulates throughout the censorship network. These parents just pick these books off the lists, look for them in their schools, and then complain."

As evidence of the growing power of the Religious Right, book banning efforts intensified after Ronald Reagan's election in 1980. A 1981 survey by the Association of American Publishers, the American Library Association, and the Association for Supervision and Curriculum Development estimated that more than twenty percent of the nation's school districts and thirty percent of school libraries experienced challenges to literary works and textbooks. Four years later, in 1985, *USA Today* reported a thirty-seven percent increase in censorship efforts over the previous academic year, with incidents occurring in forty-six states.

The textbook controversy spurred another development that has had many counterparts throughout the country: the growth of private Christian day schools and an increase in home schooling. Kanawha County teacher

Ruth Davis regarded this as an unfortunate turn for American education. "Students are segregated," she said; "We need to expose students to all types of literature and to people working together. They need to be able to see how people in different cultures can come together and work together and live together and go to school together." James Moffett agreed. While appreciating the desire to protect one's culture against a perceived invasion, he felt that establishing private schools tailored to subcultural preferences "sets a time bomb for the future" and "will seriously deepen community and national divisions. Children who grow up apart will probably fight as adults. Not having grown up learning to share resources despite personal differences, they will be unable to live, let live, and unite to solve common problems. Not speaking the same language, they will not talk together."

School principal Lefty Shafer made his peace with the protesters, not only by agreeing not to use the books in his school, but also by donating some old books to a new church school—"they called it the Christian school; I always called it 'the church school.' " Still, he never came to approve their tactics, and he offered a rousing defense of intellectual freedom. "I never thought much about the textbooks," he said. "I knew they weren't objectionable because I'd looked through them carefully. It really didn't matter to me whether the books were put in the classroom or not, but any time you start banning books, you're headed for trouble. If you start banning a book, any book, pretty soon you've got to ban another. And the first thing you know, where are you?"

EVEN MORE THAN the Battle of Anaheim, the Kanawha County culture war was a true grassroots movement, with thousands of people energetically involved before any outside forces showed up to capitalize on the situation. The Gablers provided importance early assistance, but only after being asked to help with a problem Alice Moore and her supporters had found on their own. Some, such as Lefty Shafer, suspected that Mrs. Moore had been sent into Kanawha County to foment discord, probably by the John Birch Society, but there is no more evidence for this than for the Reverend Ezra Graley's charge that the original adoption of the textbooks was a communist conspiracy. Still, there is little doubt that Kanawha County was an important episode in the rise of the New Christian Right, that it had a lasting impact in the long-term battle to retain or restore a traditionalist approach to education, and that individuals and organizations with designs that reached far beyond West Virginia used it to broaden their base and further their larger agenda.

The Heritage Foundation's Jim McKenna acknowledged, "We learned that picking your fight is important, that if you pick the right fight at the right time, it can be profitable . . . you can make your political points, you can help the people involved, and you can become a force in the political community." James Moffett was inclined to view the involvement of Heritage and similar groups in a somewhat dimmer light, but felt liberals must share the blame. "Political conservatives don't have a lot of appeal on practical terms to the working class. They don't have much to offer them, and they know that, and they want to deflect them from thinking about the practical disadvantages of conservatism. They want to win them over, and the only way they can is through social or moral issues. Nobody's against family values, and I think these people know that, but they're trying to pretend that some are for the family and some are against it, that if people don't go to church they're against family values. . . . But I do feel liberals are making a big mistake in ignoring the spiritual dimension. They have too much faith in courts and legislatures. They leave themselves open by having nothing to offer people who want some kind of spiritual dimension and to whom liberals seem materialistic. Liberals have a big hole there, and some adept conservatives are taking advantage of it."

Looking back at Kanawha County twenty years later, Alice Moore noted, "There'd been attempts for a long time to get this movement going, but it reached a head about the time I was on the school board of Kanawha County. And today, the fight goes on. People out there aren't ready for the schools to institute social change contrary to what they are establishing in their own homes and their own families and their own communities. For years the schools had been undermining what parents want to teach their children, but they crossed over the line with this. They went beyond what people could accept. And at that point, people had to take a stand. I think that was sort of a beginning, and if other things have grown out of it, I'm glad."

Mike Edds has not identified with the Christian Right or the Religious Right, but he acknowledged that the textbook struggle was the first time he had ever seen "Christian people getting involved in resisting and taking a stand. And since then it seems like it has mushroomed throughout the country. There are some things I agree with, some things I don't, but on the whole, I think it is positive. Christian people are a part of this country. I get so disturbed that, when Christians speak up and resist something, we're labeled as 'the Christian Right' that wants to impose our agenda. Well, who doesn't? Humanists are doing the same thing; socialists have their agenda; the people on the far left have their agenda. That's what this country's about: people trying to make their agenda known. . . . That's what America's about."

Reflecting on his experiences in Kanawha County, Jim Lewis said, "I learned that it doesn't take but a second for a community to be blown wide open, whether it's with a bomb or a book. And suddenly, people who are neighbors and who shop together and work together and live together are enemies, and everybody's got to make a decision about whether you're 'on God's side' or not. It's a terrible moment. But you learn at that moment that if you're going to exist in a community and celebrate all your differences, you've got to face down the kinds of intolerance that all of us are capable of and deal with them." Lewis did not feel he and those who stood with him had been remarkably successful at this task, nor that Kanawha County was better off from having gone through its culture war. "It's probably weaker," he conceded. "Divisions are still as deep as ever, people living up the creeks are still getting a bad deal, and people living on the hill are still getting a better deal. It was so tragic."

Lewis acknowledged, however, that something new seemed to be taking place in Kanawha County in 1974. "It was being perceived by so many people in the country as some kind of crazy hillbilly battle, but it was much deeper than that. Right-wing politics and right-wing religion were coming together. Over and over, we saw people coming in from various organizations, with church ties connected to the right. Bob Dornan came in [from California], as some sort of knight on a white horse to help solve the problems of Kanawha County. And the Heritage Foundation came in. Those groups came in with their banners and slogans and terms. It didn't take long before I realized that we were seeing a new wedding here, an important wedding of right-wing religion and right-wing politics. And it was speaking to the fear people had, and increasing that fear. They took so much language away from us. We were 'for pornography,' we were 'anti-God' and 'anti-Christian.' We were all sorts of bad things. They claimed the titles. Something new was happening in that folks were beginning to get organized from the right and utilizing all the tools, all the symbols, all the words, from religion, bringing them together so that a political program was being fashioned with the blessing of the religious symbols—a very dangerous combination. We could move toward a kind of religious fascism that could be deadly to us all, and it would behoove us all to face up to that. Fascism doesn't just have to do with Nazi Germany. We could see a different kind of fascism here, and it could have its roots and its blessing right at the heart of religion."

But Mike Edds is no fascist. "What's made this country great," he said, "is its inclusiveness, its diversity, its allowing me to be a Christian, a Protestant, a Catholic or whatever. The America I grew up with was a melting pot, but today it has turned into a bunch of little pots. Maybe the America I grew up in no longer exists, but it still exists in my heart. I wish we had leaders today who would stop being politicians and care about the people of this country. I've watched all of them, Republicans and Democrats, and I haven't found any that really do. I guess my idealism has died. I was a child of the Sixties—'Let's change the establishment. Let's set up a new order.' Naïve, very naïve. At forty-seven, I've become a realist. I don't think you can reform the system. I've become polarized too, and it just breaks my heart."

Clearly, the textbook struggles of 1974–75 took a toll on the idealism of people like Mike Edds and Jim Lewis. Just as clearly, if a truce is to be reached in the cultural conflict that continues to threaten the domestic tranquility of this nation, men and women like them must not lose heart.

CHAPTER

6

BORN AGAIN

THE POLARIZATION AND disillusionment that occurred as Kanawha County tore itself apart were, unfortunately, not unique. The 1960s had brought dramatic improvement to the lives of millions of blacks, other minorities, and poor whites, but that turbulent decade had also fostered epidemic use of illegal drugs and had encouraged patterns of sexual behavior that did not seem conducive to strengthening the family. Widespread resistance to American policy in the war in Vietnam had critically weakened the legitimacy of the government and corporations believed to be profiting from the war. At the same time, backlash to the civil rights and anti-war movements had created disenchantment with other institutions, liberal universities and churches foremost among them. The early years of the seventies offered scant indication of respite or renewal.

Any hopes that things would improve in the new decade were quickly dashed by events of the early 1970s. U.S. Army Lieutenant William Calley was court-martialed for his role in the massacre of 347 Vietnamese civilians in My Lai. At Kent State University in Ohio, National Guardsmen killed four students and wounded eight others while quelling a protest against the sending of American troops into Cambodia. Nine of the FBI's sixteen "most wanted" suspects were political radicals, and Angela Davis, an academic and a leader in the American Communist Party, was booked for murder, kidnapping, and conspiracy for allegedly playing a role in the attempt to free a fellow radical from a California prison (a jury found her not guilty). In New York, Detective Frank Serpico testified to widespread corruption in that city's police department. In Maryland, former Alabama Governor George Wallace, a candidate for president, was crippled for life by a would-be assassin's bullets. And in Washington, D.C., on June 17, 1972, five burglars were arrested and charged with breaking into the executive offices of the Democratic National Committee, in the apartment complex known as The Watergate. Seen at first as perhaps little more than a pimple of runaway zeal in the service of a political campaign, it eventually festered into a plague of boils that, for the first time in American history, drove a sitting president from office.

The trauma of Watergate shook the entire nation, but few people who were not directly involved felt its effects more powerfully than did Billy Graham. A trusting man and loyal friend, Graham remained close to Nixon throughout the president's first term in office, with benefit to both parties. As the war in Vietnam dragged on and draft boards began to tighten up, Graham used his influence to help gain draft exemptions for Campus Crusade staff members, contending that, though unordained, they were doing the work of ministers. Foes of Nixon and Graham criticized the evangelist for not pressing the president harder to end the war and for being too comfortable with a government they felt paid too little attention to continuing problems of racial injustice and poverty. They also registered disappointment at Graham's efforts to use his reputation and prestige to legitimate Nixon's regime and enhance his chances at reelection, as when he invited the president to address a huge stadium audience at his Knoxville crusade in 1970, then included the appearance in a nationally televised broadcast of the event, making certain that vigorous protests from a segment of the audience were deleted. In return for such favors, Nixon traveled to the evangelist's hometown of Charlotte in 1971 to help celebrate Billy Graham Day. Even though Southern Baptists ranked among Graham's most devoted supporters, even some of them worried that he was "too close to the powerful and too fond of the things of the world, [and] likened him to the prophets of old who told the kings of Israel what they wanted to hear."

Nixon got more than symbolic benefit from his relationship to Graham. Because of his peerless reputation and international contacts, Graham was often able to serve in an informal ambassadorial role in situations in which a member of the diplomatic corps might have been less effective. But the assistance that Nixon and his aides valued most was Graham's ability to influence his admirers to vote for the president's reelection in 1972. Early in 1971, White House chief of staff H. R. Haldeman wrote himself a memo: "Graham wants to be helpful next year. . . . Point him in areas where do most good. He thinks there are real stirrings in religious directions, especially re young people. I call him and set up date. No other level—can't have leak." Two days later, Haldeman scribbled a follow-up reminder: "Must mobilize [Graham] and his crowd."

In February 1972, Graham met with Nixon to discuss ways he could be helpful during the campaign. Subsequently the president directed his aides, particularly Haldeman, to keep Graham posted on various developments within the administration and the campaign, and to sound him out for his reading of public opinion. In turn, Graham urged Nixon to attend church and to use more biblical quotations in his speeches, to enhance his appeal to conservative religious people he believed were increasingly anxious to become involved in the political arena. Graham also indicated to Nixon that he and Bill Bright could provide entree to fifty major conservative religious organizations with massive mailing lists.

Like most Americans, Graham initially regarded the Watergate break-in as an act of no great consequence and felt certain Nixon would emerge unscathed when all the facts were in. As it became clear that the burglary and subsequent cover-up constituted a scandal of major proportion, he called for the punishment of the perpetrators but remained confident that the president's "moral and ethical principles wouldn't allow him to do anything illegal like that." By the end of 1973, Graham sounded less confident that his friend's hands were entirely clean but pledged his support and his prayers and urged all Americans to do the same, noting that, "in all probability, Mr. Nixon will be the only President we have for the next three years." In a January 1974 interview published in *Christianity Today,* Graham edged further away from Nixon, calling Watergate "not only unethical but criminal," and declaring that "I can make no excuses for Watergate. I condemn it and I deplore it. It has hurt America." He still doubted Nixon was directly involved, but ventured that if he was, admitting his mistakes would help restore public confidence in him and the government. Some of Nixon's supporters, including Graham's old friend Norman Vincent Peale, thought the evangelist was deserting the president like a rat leaving a sinking ship. But Charles Colson, regarded as one of the toughest and most cynical of Nixon's inner circle before experiencing a life-changing religious conversion, agreed that what the White House and the nation needed most was an admission of wrongdoing, a sincere manifestation of repentance, and a rebirth of faith and commitment to God.

In the months that followed, the president was named a Watergate co-conspirator, his top aides were sentenced to federal prison, and, after resisting a House Judiciary Committee subpoena on grounds of executive privilege, Nixon finally released extensive edited transcripts of tape recordings secretly made of virtually all conversations that occurred in the White House during the period of the break-in and cover-up. When the first excerpts began to appear in the news media, Graham admitted his surprise and disappointment, although he gave more attention to the president's profanity than to his association with burglary, bribery, extortion, and perjury. When he was able to read the transcripts more fully, what he found there devastated him. "Those tapes revealed a man I never knew," he admitted. "I never saw that side of him." Still, he reiterated his claim to be a faithful friend and said he had no intention of forsaking the president at this trying moment. And indeed they remained friends until Nixon's death in 1994.

Watergate sobered Graham mightily and made him more wary of patrolling the corridors of power in Washington. Looking back on his association with prominent politicians, Graham conceded that some members of the White House staff may have tried to use him at times. "Sometimes I knew it, and sometimes, in hindsight, I can see that I didn't know it. I wasn't used most times, I think. I'm sure there were a few times when I was." On being made aware of memos that showed the attempts to use him had been more numerous and calculating than he had imagined, he confessed that "I knew what I had said to the President, and I knew what he had said to me. But I was unaware of all those memos circulating in the background. When I [learned] about that, I felt like a sheep led to the slaughter." Graham maintained a friendly relationship with subsequent presidents, but never again did he permit himself to be quite so tempted by what the New Testament calls "the kingdoms of the world and their glory."

IN 1976, AS America prepared to mark the bicentennial anniversary of its founding as a nation consciously and formally based on lofty ideals and noble principles, the national mood was hardly one of celebration. The war in Vietnam had finally ended, but in what amounted to bitter defeat. Moreover, the policies that had driven it had been exposed as deeply flawed, increasing the sense of guilt and bitterness over losses of life on both sides. The economic crisis created by the 1973 OPEC oil embargo had battered illusions of self-sufficient independence. Gerald Ford had restored a measure of honor and respect to the presidency after Nixon resigned in 1974, but his pardoning of Nixon and the fact that he had ascended to both the vice presidency and presidency as a result of the misdeeds of his predecessors made it impossible for him to dispel the clouds hanging over the White House, and he enraged hard-core Republicans when he appointed Nelson Rockefeller to be his vice president. At age two hundred, the nation sought more than improvement; it longed to be born again.

Today, it may be difficult to remember how devastating it was to learn that the president of the United States and his closest associates were guilty not just of poor judgment, but of a conscious attempt to deceive the nation, even at the cost of subverting the Constitution. No circle escaped impact, but evangelicals, always concerned with morality, were particularly stunned. James Dunn, executive director of the Christian Life Commission, the social action agency for Texas Southern Baptists, recalled his own dismay over Watergate: "After Watergate broke, the commission spoke out, calling for a time of repentance and revival in our land, a commitment to honesty and integrity and fair dealing in the political realm. There was a kind of looking inward, at how we got in a mess like this as a country, at whether we maybe ought to rethink our basic values. As we looked at it seriously, we could see it was a devastating blow to the appeals we were making to young people all over the state, as we'd speak on college campuses. That was the main impact we felt from Watergate. It didn't have particularly partisan overtones. We just thought, this is going to make it harder than ever to convince people that politics isn't dirty. [It was] a Polaroid snapshot of politics at its dirtiest."

Few people better understood how much the nation longed for a time of healing than did Jimmy Carter. Though he had served as governor of Georgia, Carter was not well known outside the South; when he announced that he wanted to be president of the United States, seasoned political observers found it difficult to take him seriously. It soon became clear, however, that Jimmy Carter knew America. He knew how to present himself as the embodiment of the bedrock values, deep concerns, and honest aspirations of millions of his fellow citizens, and he knew, as his detractors did not, that his own quite genuine religious faith was an asset. Stuart Eizenstat, who served as Carter's chief adviser on domestic affairs, during the campaign, observed, "Somehow the notion of a man grounded in solid family and religious values gave a certain amount of confidence that this was the kind of person who could do the healing the American people expected in the wake of Watergate. Jimmy Carter perceived this mood in the country before some of us who were more public-policy-oriented did. We didn't sense the pulse of the public as well as he did. But it became obvious as we got into the primary campaign that in fact this had a real resonance." Jody Powell, Carter's press secretary, put even more emphasis on religion. "For a lot of people," he said, "the idea that this was a man of religious faith gave them some measure of hope that he meant what he said, that he would do what he said, that he would abide by the law, that he would behave in a way that was moral and decent and just. That is one of the things religion is supposed to do for us."

Carter did not overstress his religious faith. In most of his campaign speeches, he talked of his childhood on a peanut farm in Plains, Georgia, of the comfort and stability he had derived from always knowing where his mama and daddy were and being able to turn to them if he had a problem, of his empathy for blacks and poor people, as well as of his experience in the Navy, his training as a nuclear engineer, and his connections with international leaders. Again and again, he promised his audiences he would never lie to them, and he affirmed their virtue and integrity by calling for "a government as good as its people." Still, he was known to be an active layman in the Baptist church—he taught Sunday school, went on retreats and participated in short-term missionary programs, and had chaired an ecumenical evangelistic effort that used films produced by Billy Graham's organization—and he made no effort to hide his convictions. Kenneth Briggs, then chief religion reporter for the *New York Times,* recalled that, early in the primary campaign he casually mentioned that he was an evangelical and a "born-again" Christian. According to Briggs, "The mainstream press in this country didn't really know what an evangelical was. And what they did know harkened back to the days of the Scopes trial and fundamentalism and a kind of backwoods yahoo-ism that they found very distasteful. No one was sure that a presidential candidate should be talking about such things as private 'born-again' experiences and conversions."

Within days, news media that seldom paid serious attention to religion were abuzz with questions: What, precisely, did it mean to claim that one had been "born again"? Interest was further heightened by the appearance of Watergate felon Charles Colson's best-selling book by the same title. Jody Powell, a Southern Baptist himself, remembered with amusement that "I ended up spending a good portion of that campaign, certainly far more than I would have expected as a candidate's press secretary, attempting to provide some rudimentary understanding to journalists about Southern Baptist theology." Jim Dunn had a similar experience: "I was asked by the American Jewish Committee to come and speak to their state meeting and explain what being 'born again' meant. I was interviewed by the press and local television all over the place about 'What's an evangelist?' 'What's an evangelical?' 'What's a Baptist?' 'What does "born again" mean?' 'Where does this come from?' "

The terminology, while perhaps alien to many journalists and others outside religious circles, could hardly have been more familiar or less controversial to evangelical Christians, who could easily have echoed Jody Powell when he said, "That phrase is as familiar and as uncontroversial to me as almost anything—as 'Our Father Who art in Heaven.' " And, though perhaps surprised that a major touchstone of their faith was being examined as if it were some kind of occult cipher, they relished the opportunity to explain. In a nationally televised crusade service in May 1976, Billy Graham observed that "everybody is asking, 'What does it mean to be "born again"?' " and proceeded to cite the biblical origin of the phrase. In the third chapter of the Gospel according to John, Jesus informs Nicodemus, an inquirer who has heard him speak and wants to learn more, that "except a man be born again, he cannot see the Kingdom of God." To Nicodemus's understandably puzzled response—"How can a man be born when he is old? Can he enter the second time into his mother's womb and be born?"—Jesus answered, "Verily, verily, I say unto thee, except a man be born of water and of the spirit, he cannot enter into the Kingdom of God. That which is born of flesh is flesh. That which is born of spirit is spirit. Marvel not that I say unto you, 'Ye must be born again.' "

Many, but not all, evangelicals associate being "born of water" with baptism. In some circles, "born of spirit" carries expectations of some dramatic kind of personal spiritual experience; in others, it may mean simply—but not trivially—a conscious decision to acknowledge one's sinfulness and the need for God's grace, to effect forgiveness of sin and to equip one for righteous living. Graham himself acknowledges that he experienced no great turmoil at the time of his own conversion, and the title of his magazine, *Decision,* reflects the fact that responding to the invitation he offers at the end of his sermons involves conscious volition far more than seizure by some irresistible force. But whatever the version or nuance, to those who use it, the term "born again" refers to the point in their lives at which they began seriously to consider themselves Christians. Thus, as Jesus advised Nicodemus, they "marvel not" when someone professes to be a "born-again Christian," because to be one is to be the other. And, though they may have disliked what some heard as a condescending tone, Christians could hardly quibble when NBC anchor John Chancellor informed his audience, "We have checked on the religious meaning of Carter's profound experience. It is described by other Baptists as a common experience, not something out of the ordinary."

While Carter never pretended his experience was out of the ordinary, he did profess that it was real and lasting. He explained that in 1967, while dealing with his disappointment over having been defeated in his first try for the Georgia governorship, "I realized that my own relationship with God and Christ was a very superficial one." A series of experiences that included mission work among some extremely poor people and a walk in the woods with his evangelist sister, Ruth Carter Stapleton, enabled him to form "a very close, intimate, personal relationship with God, through Christ, that has given me a great deal of peace, equanimity, the ability to accept difficulties without unnecessarily being disturbed, and also an inclination on a continuing basis to ask God's guidance in my life." And he told more than one audience, "The most important thing in my life is Jesus Christ."

Jody Powell often remarked that Jimmy Carter "probably quoted less Scripture and read more than any public official we've had in a long, long time." Since the days of their colonial ancestor Roger Williams, Baptists in America had insisted on the separation of church and state, contending that both realms flourish best when not entangled with the other. Jimmy Carter subscribed to this position, made it clear he did not believe God had ordained him to be president, and said he would never mix religion and politics to get votes. When *700 Club* host Pat Robertson asked him if he would bring godly men into his inner councils or Cabinet to advise him, he replied, "I think it would be a mistake for me to define the qualifications of a public servant according to what kind of a church they attend or what their denomination is. Obviously, a commitment to the principles expressed to us by God would be an important prerequisite." Such careful answers justified Powell's observation that Carter "was always exquisitely sensitive to the fact that there are many in America who don't necessarily share the specifics of his faith, maybe almost none of it." Still, Carter understood that, to most Americans, his profession of deep religious faith would strike a reassuring chord. As *New York Times* religion reporter Kenneth Briggs noted, "The idea of some kind of personal conversion certainly wasn't new, and it was very much associated with the heartland of this country, and it had a very rich American heritage. I think for that reason it had currency right away with people who understood it."

Billy Graham, who had devoted his life to conversion, understood it. He told his Seattle and television congregations that America was experiencing "a deeper national yearning, a turning toward spirituality, a yearning for morality. Americans want more than anything else in their president, this year, the spiritual qualities." Robert Maddox, a Baptist pastor who would later join the Carter administration as a special liaison to the religious-community, agreed: "It was a brand-new phenomenon to have a man running for president who would so clearly state his faith, and clearly coming out of the religious community. Many of us, as Baptists, were very excited about that possibility and had great hopes that as president he could leverage the country spiritually and morally in ways that we had not seen in a long time."

A young Nebraskan named Guy Rodgers also understood it. After his parents divorced while he was in high school, Rodgers became a Christian through his association with Young Life. In college, he prepared to be a teacher, convinced he could be a greater influence for good in that role than in any other. During the summer of 1974, while traveling in Europe with his brother, he watched Nixon's resignation on television. "I was somewhat separated from it, being overseas, and yet there was a sense of 'What is happening at the top of our nation? The President!'" When Carter emerged in 1976, Rodgers was elated. "He was the first political figure of any kind of national stature I had ever seen who was open about his faith. He said, 'I am an evangelical; I'm a born-again Christian.' That was impressive to me in my young Christianity—I'd only been a Christian for three years—so I helped out in his campaign."

Another heartlander who responded positively was Evelyn Davis, a black Baptist woman from Iowa. "I loved Jimmy Carter," she said with unmistakable feeling. "In the United States of America where we say we allow people the privilege of their religion, but very few of us say anything about the Lord or Jesus, here was a man running for President, and he said 'born-again Christian.' I can remember the night I heard it, and I was shocked, but I knew what I had to do: I had to work for him." Ms. Davis also liked the fact that Carter was a Southerner. "One of the things about Southerners," she said, "is they believe what they say and do, really, and I thought, coming out of the South, he knows minorities, he knows the poor, and he talked like he was going to do something."

Evelyn Davis was hardly unique. Eizenstat, who admitted he had been unaware of the millions of Americans who considered themselves to be born-again Christians, quickly recognized the appeal Carter's religion had in the black community. "The Baptist background was a very important thing in establishing the chemistry between black voters and Jimmy Carter. You could feel it when you came into a black church, a sort of instant sense of communication. It had a deeply felt resonance among black voters."

Guy Rodgers was voting for the first time and Evelyn Davis was a Democrat, but Carter was also garnering support in fields formerly left for Republicans to harvest or largely ignored by both parties. Jerry Regier was working with Campus Crusade for Christ and well remembers "a number of fellow staff members who were very excited about Jimmy Carter. And it was all built around the fact that he had talked about being 'born again.' It's the first time any of us had remembered any national leader using the term, understanding the term."

It was people like Regier—conservative Christians who were inclined either to vote Republican or to stand clear of the political process entirely—on whom Carter's public acknowledgment of his faith had perhaps the greatest impact. Evangelical journalist and filmmaker Rus Walton characterized the evangelical community as the "sleeping giant of American politics" and had begun to produce literature and audio-visual materials designed to rouse the giant from its slumber. More systematically, the Christian Freedom Foundation (CFF), established after World War II to promote what chief supporter J. Howard Pew regarded as "Christian Economics," but now supported primarily by Amway president Richard DeVos, had begun to disseminate materials designed to demonstrate a unity between evangelical Christianity and a conservative political agenda. In addition to laying out broad themes, the CFF materials also contained nuts-and-bolts information about how people could get involved in local and state politics—qualifications for various positions, how to file for office, how many signatures are needed on a petition, where to file petitions, and the like. Arizona Congressman John Conlan, who oversaw this project, explained that "you don't get this in high-school civics classes. You don't even get it in Poli Sci 101 or 501 at the university, [because] the professor has never worked a precinct. He doesn't know how an election operates. He doesn't know how anyone gets in or how they get out; he only knows the theory of it. It's like a bowling ball going down the alley. If it goes in the right place, it knocks down all ten pins, so if you have the voters voting your way in the precincts, that will determine who your county government is, who your school district leaders are, who your legislators are at the state level, and it'll determine on up the line who becomes your national Congress, your national president, who appoints your judges and other elements of your society." To make sure these lessons were thoroughly absorbed, Conlan and old friend Bill Bright recruited and trained regional directors whose assignment was to mobilize people in every congressional district and teach them how to use the materials to start home study groups modeled on Bible study sessions with which most evangelicals were quite familiar.

In a similar 1975 move, an organization called Intercessors for America, with which Bill Bright was also associated, had sent a letter to 120,000 clergymen, urging them to order materials that would teach them how to take over local precincts and elect only "godly" Christians to public office. That action, according to *Newsweek,* moved Billy Graham to announce that he was "opposed to organizing Christians into a political bloc" and would endorse no candidate in the 1976 election. "I learned my lesson the hard way," Graham said, in a transparent reference to his disappointment in Richard Nixon.

Some evangelicals apparently concluded that Billy Graham's problem had been the horse he rode, not the fact that he had saddled up. In a full-page ad in *Christianity Today,* an organization calling itself Citizens for Carter asked the question, "Does a Dedicated Evangelical Belong in the White House?" and answered with a resounding yes. The ad, which Carter aides insisted they had not placed, noted that "in this post-Watergate era, people throughout the country are disillusioned with the moral corruption and incompetent leadership they see in the political arena. Citizens for Carter believes that a return to decency and integrity in government can begin this election year. As an evangelical you can play an important part in this restoration of confidence. . . . America's problems are the result of a spiritual crisis at its heart. . . . Citizens for Carter supports Jimmy Carter because he stands for a return to open government, competence, honesty and an abiding sense of the importance of morality in our national life."

Catholic theologian and social critic Michael Novak recognized the long-term implications of these developments when he observed, "There is a hidden religious power base in American culture which our secular biases prevent many of us from noticing. Jimmy Carter has found it." Even Sam Donaldson, arching his eyebrows mischievously as he spoke of Carter's well-publicized practice of reading a chapter of the Bible in Spanish each night before retiring, conceded that "there does seem to be a yearning for some kind of spiritual revival in this country, and planned or not, it could turn out that Jimmy Carter's religion will be a net plus in this campaign for the presidency."

More than one reporter likened the 1976 Democratic National Convention to a revival meeting. Texas Congresswoman Barbara Jordan, daughter of a Baptist preacher and heroine of the Watergate hearings for her stirring defense of the Constitution, delivered the keynote address with both the voice and authority of God. When Carter came to the hall to accept the nomination, he entered from the rear so he could walk through the crowd, touching hundreds and smiling at all, embodying his well-developed persona as an outsider, a humble man of the people who would emerge from their ranks to lead them on to higher ground. In his acceptance speech he spoke of his own humble origins, criticized abuses of privilege by "the establishment," promised to work for a fairer tax system, and asked for help in making his presidency a time of healing. Republicans might continue to charge Democrats with holding radical political and social views and abandoning traditional values, but millions of Americans could not help hoping, perhaps even believing, that Martin Luther King, Sr., was right when he stepped to the microphone at the end of the evening and said, slowly and majestically, "Surely the Lord is in this place. Surely the Lord sent Jimmy Carter to come on out and bring America back where she belongs. I'm with him. You are too. But as I close in prayer, let me tell you, we must close ranks now. If there's any misunderstanding anywhere, if you haven't got a forgiving heart, get on your knees. It's time for prayer." As Daddy King spoke, television cameras caught the next president of the United States quietly mouthing an amen.

ON THE CAMPAIGN trail, Carter continued to speak forthrightly about his religious faith, but he appealed to an even wider audience of voters by promising to do what he could to help strengthen the American family. During the New Hampshire primary, he told an audience, in his low-key, earnest way, "I've got a good family. I hope you'll be part of my family." Back in Manchester in August, he was less a Good Father inviting all who would to come in than a concerned Elder Brother warning his siblings to shape up. "The American family," he said simply, "is in trouble. I have campaigned all over America, and everywhere I go, I find people deeply concerned about the loss of stability and the loss of values in our lives. The root of this problem is the steady erosion and weakening of our families." He supported this contention by ticking through a dismal list of statistics—a rising divorce rate, an increase in unwed motherhood, decline of the extended family, millions of children living with only one parent or in foster homes, and alarming rises in juvenile crime, venereal disease, alcohol and drug abuse, and suicide. "There can be no more urgent priority for the next administration," he concluded, "than to see that any decision our government makes is designed to honor and support and strengthen the American family."

Charging that government policies often did just the opposite, he affirmed his desire to reform the welfare system so that it "encourages work and encourages family life and reflects both the competence and the compassion of the American people"; reshape the tax system in ways that would help families stay together; encourage a national health-care program; develop a comprehensive program of family planning that would prevent the need for abortion; and institute a national day-care program. He gave his approval to running mate Walter Mondale's recommendation that each federal program should present a "family impact statement" that showed what effect it had on American families, and he announced the appointment of Joseph Califano, Jr., as a special adviser to oversee such matters. (Califano would later become the first secretary of the Department of Health, Education, and Welfare.) "The family unit," Carter concluded, "is the best way for men and women to live their lives, the best way to raise children, and the only solid foundation upon which to build a strong nation."

In a similar speech to the National Conference of Catholic Charities in October, Carter added two new items to his list of promises. He would, he said, try to find "ways to provide aid to parents whose children attend non-segregated private schools, so that those children can benefit fully from federal education programs." That pledge, of course, had great appeal to Catholics, who had long sought government support for their parochial schools. It was also one in a list of aspirations Carter would be unable to fulfill. In a second new pledge, Carter told that group that, shortly after becoming president, he would convene a "White House Conference on the American Family" that would bring together government leaders, representatives of family-related professions, and ordinary citizens and parents to discuss ways of supporting and strengthening families and "restoring the public-private partnership in social services that has been so hampered by Republican neglect." This was a promise that, if he could have foreseen the outcome, Jimmy Carter might not have made.

Carter's stress on the family played well among Catholic voters; his stand on abortion was less successful. Catholics played the major role in generating the anti-abortion movement spawned by the Supreme Court's 1973 *Roe v. Wade* decision. By contrast, conservative Protestants seemed hardly to recognize it as a major issue. In 1971, the Southern Baptist Convention (SBC) had voted almost unanimously in support of a resolution affirming a woman's right to have an abortion if giving birth would pose physical or emotional danger. In 1975, Billy Graham, evangelical theologians Harold O. J. Brown and Francis Schaeffer, and pediatrician C. Everett Koop helped form the Christian Action Council, which produced a newsletter and lobbied Congress for measures to curb or prohibit abortion. Given that lack of in-depth attention to abortion in his own circles, combined with the strong support of abortion rights by most liberal Democrats, Carter found it awkward to deal with the issue during the campaign, and wound up with a straddle position that both camps found troubling. At one point, he implied he might favor an anti-abortion amendment, then backed off. Eventually, he took a disapproving pro-choice stance, opposing both legal prohibition and federal funding of abortion, declaring that the fornication and adultery that lead to most abortions are "not acceptable on any sort of measurement of moral standard," and pledging to do whatever he could "to minimize the need for abortions, which I think are wrong." This effort would take the form of "better education on sex, better family-planning procedures, and access to contraceptives for those who believe in their use." It was, Stuart Eizenstat conceded, "an issue that gave Jimmy Carter a great deal of difficulty."

AS THE CAMPAIGN picked up steam and it became clear that a Baptist Sunday-school teacher might actually be elected president, evangelical Christianity received increased and more respectful attention. News media turned their attention to gospel music concerts, the booming religious book market, the phenomenal growth and success of religious radio and television, and even the existence of Christian supper clubs, where pious folk could enjoy a good meal, listen to music that did not assault their eardrums, and laugh at comedians who told jokes about preachers' kids, all in a smoke-and-alcohol-free atmosphere. The high point of this attention came when George Gallup reported that as many as fifty million Americans could fairly be described as evangelicals and *Newsweek* ran a cover story in which it dubbed 1976 as "The Year of the Evangelical."

Given this kind of attention, evangelicals began to feel they had come into their own once again, and to dream about further power and glory. Evangelical social critic Os Guinness perceptively observed, "One of the features of the seventies was nostalgia. The fifties were the last decade in which traditional Americanism was largely innocent and largely intact. . . . And, of course, if you go back to the nineteenth century, you start harking back to 'Christian America.' Now, who were the natural heirs of Christian America? The evangelicals thought they were." As if to illustrate Guinness's observation, Christian Broadcasting Network founder Pat Robertson volunteered, on the network's flagship program, the *700 Club,* that he believed "in the next five years we have an unprecedented opportunity for America to fulfill the dream of the early settlers who came right here to Virginia in 1607, that this land would be used to glorify God." And a secular TV journalist doing a story on CBN concluded his piece by saying, "The driving ambition is to bring Jesus to America and America to Jesus."

Exuberant Christians showed their appreciation for Jimmy Carter's contribution to their new celebrity. In a keynote address to fifteen thousand pastors and lay persons of the Southern Baptist Convention, the organization's popular future president, Bailey Smith, proclaimed that this country needs "a born-again man in the White House . . . and his initials are the same as our Lord's." Jimmy Allen, who became SBC president in 1977, also weighed in on Carter's side. As journalists pressed harder and Carter spoke more, however, it became clear that the candidate did not subscribe to an inerrantist view of Scripture, that he admired the writings of Reinhold Niebuhr, the liberal theologian who had been one of Billy Graham's harshest critics during the 1950s, that he occasionally took a drink, that he was basically pro-choice on abortion, that he (like many Southern Baptists) did not favor returning prayer to the public schools, and that his views on several other social issues did not jibe with their own. Inevitably, his evangelical support began to erode. The fact that Democratic party leaders, like Republican regulars in 1964, made little attempt to incorporate evangelicals into the party structure did not help. Then, in its November issue, which appeared in October, *Playboy* magazine ran a long interview Carter had given one of its reporters.

The interview got wide media play, largely because of Carter's voluntary admission that, despite remaining faithful to his wife throughout their marriage, he had "looked on a lot of women with lust. I've committed adultery in my heart many times." That particular locution puzzled some, who wondered if he was referring to some kind of sexual irregularity, and amused others, who took it as another sign of the candidate's lack of sophistication. Evangelicals instantly recognized the reference to the Sermon on the Mount, in which Jesus declared that a person's attitude is as important as his or her behavior, and that a man who looks at a woman "with lust in his heart" is as guilty of adultery as the man who actually gets into bed with her. In practice, evangelicals apply sterner sanctions to physical adultery than to unconsummated lust, but they perfectly understood what Jimmy Carter was saying: He adhered to a strict moral code but was not trying to pass himself off as a plaster saint who had never felt temptation. Some even commended him for his candor. What scandalized them was both the frank language he used in this context—"Christ says, Don't consider yourself better than someone else because one guy screws a whole bunch of women while the other guy is loyal to this wife. . . ."—and, more importantly, the very fact that he had even spoken to *Playboy,* the cultural embodiment and advocate of a lifestyle about as unevangelical as one could adopt.

The reaction to the interview was immediate. Carter's own pastor said, "I do wish he would have used different words." W. A. Criswell, pastor of Dallas's First Baptist Church, the SBC's largest congregation at the time, announced that he was "highly offended." Criswell subsequently allowed the Ford campaign to run an ad in which, with President and Mrs. Ford seated in the congregation, the venerable shepherd told his flock of a conversation in which the president had revealed that he had also been asked to give *Playboy* an interview, but had responded "with an emphatic 'No!'" Jerry Falwell summed up the feelings of many when he said, "Like many others, I am quite disillusioned. Four months ago the majority of the people I knew were pro-Carter. Today that has totally reversed."

The reversal, of course, was not total. Carter received a tide of support from regular Democrats, Southern and other Republicans who found his appeal to traditional values convincing, blacks who believed he understood them and their needs, and millions of evangelical and charismatic Protestants, who may have disagreed with his political philosophy but still saw him as one of their own. Consequently, Jimmy Carter won the presidency, if only by a scant three-percent margin over Gerald Ford. At his inauguration, after taking the oath of office on a Bible his mother had given him, Carter—like every president since George Washington—made reference to the importance of God's blessings on America and quoted the timeless admonition from the prophet Micah: "He has showed thee, O man, what is good; and what does the Lord require of thee but to do justly and to love mercy and to walk humbly with thy God." In that spirit of justice, mercy, and humility, Carter thanked "my predecessor for all he has done to heal our land" and extended his hand to Gerald Ford, whose eyes welled with tears as waves of warm applause billowed forth from the multitude. ABC news reporter Jim Wooten, who was not a Carter admirer and was inclined to regard the gesture as insincere, nevertheless recognized that the new president was impressively and successfully presenting himself as a man of Christian grace and compassion who, by this gesture, was pronouncing "the final benediction on Watergate and Vietnam," and promising America that a new day lay ahead.

In the early months of Carter's presidency, he continued to display the populist characteristics that had helped reshape the anti-establishment, anti-traditional, even radical image the Democratic Party had acquired, the characteristics that had brought many middle- and working-class people back into the Democratic camp. He held town meetings and call-in talk sessions, sometimes asking callers, in good Southern fashion, if they happened to be kin to some folk of the same name that he knew down in Georgia. He wore a cardigan sweater in the White House and mended his clothes while talking to reporters on the presidential plane. He carried his own luggage and stayed in the homes of ordinary people when he traveled about the country. He had the Allman Brothers Band and James Cleveland's gospel group, The Mighty Clouds of Joy, perform for families sitting on blankets spread out on the White House lawn. In short, he helped convince millions of people who had felt shut out of the political process that the richest, most powerful nation in the world was being led by a humble, everyday man—a man much like themselves. By helping to put him in office, they had done what Jesus had told them to do: They had taken their light from under a bushel and put it on a stand, for all the world to see.

JIMMY CARTER, of course, was not the lone voice calling conservative Christians to a larger role in public life. Another extraordinarily important figure was a little-known American evangelical, Francis Schaeffer, who for many years had operated an unusual religious community in Switzerland, dedicated to thinking about and embracing Christianity across the spectrum of human experience. At L'Abri, Schaeffer's community, devout believers, doubters, hippies, miscellaneous seekers, and curious intellectuals of several stripes came to hear Schaeffer lecture and to engage him in searching discussions. Schaeffer attempted to show his audience and followers that the Christian faith was relevant to every aspect of human culture and could engage it without being swallowed up by it. Os Guinness, who spent considerable time with Schaeffer, observed, "The challenge is always to be 'in' but not 'of' the world, to be committed to thinking about all that's going on in the culture, yet keeping a critical discernment, knowing what's good and what's bad. Schaeffer was very much for a critical discernment. Francis, for me as for thousands of young English and American students who were Christians, was a door opener. It was not only okay but right and proper and responsible, as a Christian, to understand the whole of life—'All truth is God's truth,' as the early Christians said. So whether it's art or philosophy or culture or the films of Ingmar Bergman or the music of John Cage, the whole of life is fair game to think about freely as a Christian." Mel White, a former Youth for Christ leader who had gone on to a career as a well-known teacher, filmmaker, and ghostwriter, agreed: "Francis was pointing at art, at music, at film, at theater, at government; he was talking about polity and all of these issues that had been on the off-list for evangelicals. We didn't go to movies when I grew up. And now he was talking about the great films and the way they've changed our lives. We didn't go to Florence to look at the statues with leaves—we stayed home and looked at the head on Christ on a flannelgraph. And suddenly Francis was opening the whole world to us and saying, 'We're Christians; this all belongs to us; this is all God's. Every realm is His.' I think Francis was that first voice that said, 'Reclaim everything in God's Creation: It's yours.' We had just talked about souls until then."

In the early 1970s, Schaeffer decided he needed to return to America to spread his message of cultural relevance, a decision that would have profound effects on conservative Christianity in this country. In the longish hair, goatee, and knickers that were his eccentric trademark, he addressed these issues in a book, *How Should We Then Live?*, and in lectures. In one such lecture, he asserted, "The Bible is not a great book simply because it's printed on Indian paper and has a leather cover and gold edges. There's only one reason the Bible is worth listening to—only one—and that's because the Bible is the truth which God has given us, not only as it speaks of religious things, but [of] the totality of life. It stands there as that which we must use to judge every aspect of life across the whole spectrum of life, in our individual lives, what we are taught in the classroom, and when we go out into the poor broken culture that surrounds us. Do not think Christianity is a small thing. Do not sell it short. Christianity is intellectually viable. Christianity is intellectually salable to our generation. Christianity covers the whole spectrum of life. You need never be ashamed of it. No matter how far you go, you will never sail off the end of the world. The Bible is there and it covers the whole spectrum of life. God has given us a beautiful thing. Please do not truncate it. Do not sell it short."

Schaeffer was, despite his catholic interests and cosmopolitan outlook, quite conservative in his theology, and those who heard his lectures and read his books often understood him to be saying that relating to the world meant conquest, not compromise. Pat Robertson's Christian Broadcasting Network, with its high production values and increased emphasis on news and commentary, was a serious attempt to convince conservative Christians that they could master a sophisticated medium and compete with their secular counterparts on equal terms. Jimmy Carter's election also seemed consistent with that aim for a while, but many who supported him because of his espousal of Christianity and family values soon became disillusioned as they learned that he was, after all, still a *bona fide* Democrat. He did not abolish or seriously reform welfare. He did not overhaul the tax structure. To make things worse, instead of flourishing in a new populist economy, farmers, wage-earners, and small-business people found themselves struggling to keep up with double-digit inflation. As promised, Carter did establish a department of Health, Education, and Welfare and named Joe Califano to head it, but creating a new government bureaucracy was not the way to win conservative hearts. Further, in addition to his pro-choice leanings, he appeared to believe, as most evangelicals emphatically did not, that homosexual men and women should not be discriminated against because of their sexual orientation. And, almost as objectionable to them, he favored the Equal Rights Amendment, which many Christian conservative viewed as an affront to the divine order of relationships between men and women.

Some contemporary biblical scholars profess to find New Testament support for social equality between the sexes, but a straightforward reading of Scripture—and evangelicals definitely prefer straightforward readings—gives considerable support to a patriarchal order, particularly in the writings of the Apostle Paul. Consider, for example, the following:

> "As the church is subject to Christ, so let wives also be subject in everything to their husbands." (Ephesians 5:24)
> "As in all the churches of the saints, the women should keep silence in the churches. For they are not permitted to speak, but should be subordinate, as even the law says. If there is anything they desire to know, let them ask their husbands at home. For it is shameful for a woman to speak in church." (I Corinthians 14:33–35)
> "Let a woman learn in silence, with all submissiveness. I permit no woman to teach or to have authority over men: she is to keep silent. . . . [w]oman will be saved through bearing children, if she continues in faith and love and holiness, with modesty." (I Timothy 2:11–12, 2:15)

Christians who regard Scripture as a response by believers to what they understood to be the work of God in their individual and communal lives can excuse Paul's evident patriarchalism by noting that he was reflecting the culture of his time and that, if he were alive today, he would doubtless say something quite different. Conservative Christians who regard Scripture as a direct revelation from God, every word inspired and applicable for all time, have no such option. And a person who believes that God Himself—God's gender is not in question in evangelical circles—has ordained that the proper role for a woman is to be quiet, have babies, and do what her husband tells her is not a prime candidate for feminism.

The Equal Rights Amendment, endorsed by the National Organization for Women (NOW), passed both houses of Congress by 1972 and was allotted seven years to achieve ratification by three-fourths of the states. The wording seemed innocuous and unobjectionable: "Equality of rights under the law shall not be denied or abridged by the United States or by any State on account of sex." Polls consistently showed that two-thirds of the public favored the amendment and twenty-two states ratified it the first year. The pace slowed noticeably in the second year, however, then dropped to a trickle, picking up only two states in 1975–1977. Meanwhile, five states rescinded their previous approval. At the end of 1977, the amendment was stalled at three states short of ratification, and it was not at all clear where three more positive votes would come from. Feminists tended to blame men for the sluggish pace and stalemate, noting that women were under-represented in state legislatures and that businesses, still mostly male-led, benefited from sex discrimination. Careful observers, however, noted that some of the strongest and most effective opposition came from women—women of the political and Religious Right.

Early in 1972, Phyllis Schlafly began to oppose the amendment in her *Phyllis Schlafly Report*. In 1975, she founded the Eagle Forum, a women's organization whose primary purpose was to fight the amendment's ratification. Whereas ERA backers depended heavily on public rallies, impassioned rhetoric, and organizational endorsements to carry their cause, Schlafly and other anti-ERA forces displayed a keener understanding of the political process. The feminists failed initially to recruit nonworking and minority women and often tried to bully legislators into voting for ratification—in an egregious example of arrogant ineptitude, pro-ERA workers in Florida "banged on doors of legislators' homes at seven A.M. to hand them literature, a state senator's driveway was painted with pro-ERA slogans, and the white facade of the state capitol was defaced with pro-amendment mottoes."

In contrast to these ineffectual tactics, Schlafly and her "Stop ERA" brigades took legislators loaves of homemade bread—"from the breadmakers to the breadwinners"—and politely pointed out to them that the amendment was, at best, unnecessary and probably harmful. They contended that the Fourteenth Amendment already offers equal protection to "all persons," making a new amendment superfluous. They argued that enforcing the amendment would entail an expensive and indefensible increase in the federal bureaucracy. They also managed to depict the amendment as leading inevitably to unisex toilets, legal homosexual marriages, women on the front lines of battle, and husbands freed of the responsibility to support their families. Its passage, Schlafly contended, would be a step backward for women. Jerry Falwell declared, "Of course, Christians believe in equal rights. As a matter of fact, Christians believe in superior rights for their women. We believe in opening the door for our women, helping them with their coats, providing them with their living, and protecting them from their enemies. We are against the Equal Rights Amendment because we believe it degrades womanhood, and may one day cause our women to use unisex toilets and fight in the trenches on the battlefield, where men belong. Yes, we believe in superior rights for our women."

Pro- and anti-ERA forces squared off, though at a distance, when the National Women's Conference, part of the International Women's Year, met in Houston in November 1977. Congress had provided five million dollars to fund the conference, and asked it to "identify barriers that prevent women from participating fully and equally in all aspects of national life" and to recommend ways to eliminate them. State and territorial conventions that attracted 130,000 women had elected 1,442 delegates and a national commission had appointed an additional 400. At least 12,000 other women showed up just to be there. The organizers took care to assure diversity, and what was described as a "rainbow of women" did indeed include most of the main hues and views.

Some women found the diversity required an expansion of consciousness. Sharon Overcast, a registered nurse, a member of Jerry Falwell's Thomas Road Baptist Church, and a woman of gentle manner and generous spirit, recalled her own reactions. "I didn't have a real wide view of society. I grew up in Montana with just ordinary people. The women that were showing people where to go and that sort of thing, their uniform was hard hats, white T-shirts, and jeans. To me, it didn't look very feminine. Not that they should be running around in skirts, but it was interesting to observe. Then to see groups that were actually parading down the street with big placards—the Socialist Party and lesbians, and there was a group of prostitutes, as well as others. These sort of things kind of made pictures in my mind. I hadn't ever seen that before. But we do have the freedoms pretty well to express ourselves, and that's the beauty of America. So it was a broadening experience."

Mrs. Overcast quickly discovered that not everyone took such an ecumenical view. When she visited the exhibit hall and noticed that each state had a booth, she headed for the Virginia exhibit. "At the outset," she recalled, "the women there were very friendly and handed me this beautiful red, shiny Delicious apple from Virginia. They asked me, 'Where do you stand on the Equal Rights Amendment?' and I said, 'Well, I'm opposed to the ratification of it.' And they didn't pursue the why or anything else. They said, 'What about abortions being paid for by Medicare?' I said, 'Oh, I do oppose the destruction of our unborn children,' and I said, 'I'm a registered nurse, if that gives me any credibility.' I was eager to continue to talk to them about these issues, but they reached over and took my shiny red apple back, and that was the end of our conversation."

When the conference convened, New York congresswoman Bella Abzug served as chairman; Rosalynn Carter, Betty Ford, and Lady Bird Johnson were featured guests; and Barbara Jordan gave the keynote address. After three days of ebullient celebration and efficient politicking, the conference passed a twenty-five-point National Plan of Action, most of which had been formulated by the national commission prior to the conference. Its recommendations typically received near-unanimous support, as both liberal and conservative women approved of extending Social Security benefits to housewives, expanding bilingual education for minority women, government-funded programs for victims of child and spousal abuse, increased education in rape prevention, and the like. Three hot-button issues—the ERA, abortion, and lesbian rights—faced more opposition and created support for a counter-rally led by conservative Christian forces.

Time estimated that perhaps twenty percent of the delegates, mostly from Southern and Western states, opposed these measures, but were steamrolled by a majority that not only knew it had the votes, but used its superior numbers and parliamentary procedure to squelch opposition voices. Some women on the winning side voiced unease at the lack of respect for minority viewpoints. It was no surprise that a conference chaired by Bella Abzug and featuring such noted feminists as NOW pioneers Betty Friedan and Eleanor Smeal and ERAmerica's leader, Liz Carpenter, would offer strong endorsement of the ERA and, given its increased identification with feminism, the right to abortion. How the group would vote on homosexual rights was less certain. The issue had not been on the original agenda suggested by the national commission, but when thirty-six state conventions asked for its consideration, it was added, and passage of a resolution calling for an end to any sort of discrimination against lesbians, including judicial prejudice in child-custody suits, created a lasting identification between the Houston conference and the gay rights movement. According to *Time,* when the resolution eventually passed, by a margin nearly as large as that for other measures, "Lesbians in the galleries roared their approval: 'Thank you sisters!' Pink and yellow balloons were released with the message WE ARE EVERYWHERE." Beverly LaHaye, who later founded and now heads Concerned Women for America, with a membership and budget far larger than NOW's, observed, "The lesbians flooded into that conference and attached themselves to the feminist movement, and never again were the feminists able to shake the lesbians from their agenda."

Phyllis Schlafly agreed: "I remember the impassioned pleas by Betty

Friedan and Eleanor Smeal from the floor of that conference saying, 'Yes, we have to work with the lesbians and they have to be part of our movement.' They did that on national television, and the American people saw it and they didn't like it. A few months later a reporter asked the Governor of Missouri, 'Governor, are you for the ERA?' And he was a savvy Democratic politician, and he said, 'Do you mean the old ERA or the new ERA?' He said, 'I was for equal pay for equal work, but after they went down to Houston and got all tangled up with all those lesbians, I can tell you Missouri will never ratify ERA.' " And Missouri did not. Rosalynn Carter obviously held a similar view. Though declining to be more specific, it seemed clear she had abortion and gay rights in mind when she said, "The ERA is important to me. My only reservation is that some of the more controversial issues have been mistakenly identified with the amendment. And these issues have absolutely no relevance to the ERA."

As this conference progressed, an estimated fifteen thousand women, men, and children packed the Astro Arena across town in a gathering its leaders dubbed the National Pro-Family Rally. (According to Phyllis Schlafly, "that's when 'pro-family' came into common usage as a term to describe our movement.") The key figure in organizing this meeting was Lottie Beth Hobbs, a woman well known within the quite conservative Churches of Christ as a writer of devotional and inspirational books. Hobbs had opposed the ERA from the time of its passage by Congress. In 1974, she began publishing a widely distributed leaflet called "The Pink Sheet" (because "the color is feminine") that asked, "Ladies, have you heard?" and explained why women should oppose ratification. She also founded a traditionalist organization called Women Who Want to Be Women, and helped mobilize a corps of "Pink Ladies" who lobbied Texas legislators to vote against ratification. When she learned of plans for the National Women's Conference, she attended state-level meetings and quickly discerned that women holding traditional views would have no effective voice in its deliberations. Declaring that "I'm a woman and they don't speak for me," she set about to organize a counter-rally in which more traditional views could gain a hearing. In the weeks prior to the conference, she traveled extensively, mobilizing groups of women from all fifty states. In contrast to the heavily funded conference downtown, the Pro-Family Rally was financed entirely by contributions taken at the end to cover expenses associated with rental of the hall and Kentucky Fried Chicken for fifteen thousand.

The three-hour rally featured a succession of speakers who were allowed to hold forth for five minutes apiece. *Time* observed that the gathering "easily matched the ardor of its counterpart in the Sam Houston Coliseum, and its rhetoric was substantially greater." Phyllis Schlafly charged that "the

Equal Rights proponents want to reconstruct us into a gender-free society, so there's no difference between men and women. I don't think babies need two sex-neutral parents. I think they need a father and a mother." Clay Smothers, a black Texas state representative, said, "I have enough civil rights to choke a hungry goat. I ask for public rights, Mr. Carter. I ask for victory over perverts of this country. I want a right to segregate my family from these misfits and perverts." Anita Bryant, who had gained notoriety for her fight to repeal a gay rights ordinance in Dade County, Florida, bestowed her blessings on the gathering via videotape, and a delegate who said he had been a homosexual for twenty-six years before his conversion testified that "the Lord Jesus Christ is the only one who can deliver you from homosexuality." Other speakers included Lottie Beth Hobbs, California Congressman Robert Dornan, and a representative from Senator Jesse Helms's office.

Observers called the National Women's Conference "a crash course in practical politics" and noted that delegates committed to translating its resolutions into legislation would return home to work in grassroots political efforts that would announce to their elected officials, "Unless you listen to our demands, we are going to get you out of office." For perhaps the first time, however, the national media paid attention to the anti-feminist forces, noting that "they too are on the march as never before," and quoting conservative women who also claimed, in the words of one, to have "strengthened my communication with other pro-family delegates. I'll be corresponding with all of them this month." While generally viewing the empowerment of both liberal and conservative women in a positive light, *Time* conceded, "Women on both sides are repelled by what they consider to be the abstract, unfeeling rhetoric of the extremist opposition."

Jimmy Carter appeared to share his wife's ambivalence about the conference. Doubtless aware that implementing its long list of resolutions would create staggering demands on the federal budget, and perhaps not eager to align himself with its more controversial social positions, he allotted only fifteen minutes to members of its National Advisory Committee, who wished to discuss the conference and its recommendations with him. That dismissive gesture so infuriated the women that they canceled the meeting altogether. Further to the right, the Houston conference provided conservative religious leaders with delicious fodder for their cannons. Pat Robertson, who said he had "done everything this side of breaking FCC regulations" to elect Carter, felt personally betrayed. "I wouldn't let Bella Abzug scrub the floors of any organization I was head of, but Carter put her in charge of all the women of America, and used our tax funds to support that convention in Houston." Jerry Falwell attacked the conference as being "anti-family, anti-God, and anti-America," called the ERA "a delusion," and characterized the feminist movement as "full of women who live in disobedience to

God's laws." And Texas evangelist James Robison described the resolutions adopted by the conference's resolutions as reading "like a summary of the feminist/humanist movement's grand design for destroying the American family."

For years, and with good reason, committed feminists and zealous pro-family Christian women alike would look back on three days in Houston as a time when both their movements entered a new era. By most reckonings, the feminists outpointed their rivals in the Houston match-up. When they squared off in a rematch three years later, their conservative sisters were ready.

CHAPTER

7

WE—SOME OF US— ARE FAMILY

Beginning in the mid-1960s, many evangelical and fundamentalist churches, particularly in the South, established private schools as part of their overall programs. Without question, many of these schools were "segregation academies," designed to thwart the racial desegregation mandated by the federal government. But most scholarly investigations have concluded that other trends also figured importantly in their rise, and that by the mid-1970s integration was no longer a significant factor in their continued proliferation. More important were concerns of an increasing secular bias in the public schools, symbolized most dramatically by the banning of school-sponsored prayer and devotional Bible reading, but also by the teaching of evolution, the spread of sex education courses, the adoption of textbooks thought to demean or distort American history and traditional values, and exposure to a hedonistic youth culture. Many parents also felt, with documentable good reason, that public schools simply were not providing their children with a fundamentally sound education.

In response to the situation in the public schools, concerned parents and church leaders formed thousands of new private schools expressly designed to correct these defects. With teachers and other staff who typically received far lower salaries than they could have earned in public schools, and with substantial volunteer assistance from parents, these private academies provided a well-ordered atmosphere in which religious beliefs, patriotic sentiments, and conservative behavioral patterns were reinforced rather than challenged. Curriculum materials were developed to inject specifically Christian content and values into normally neutral subject matter. Arithmetic, for example, might be taught by adding the number of people saved on successive nights of a revival meeting; a geography lesson might include spotting locations where missionaries were needed. Critics could charge that the new schools were inferior and that much of their curriculum was irrelevant to the modern world, but it was hard to make those charges stick. In standardized tests, students from private Christian schools performed as well as or better than students in the schools from which the families had seceded. Furthermore, parents were unlikely to be upset by warnings that their children might not be admitted to secular universities. For these reasons, Christian schools were multiplying at a reported rate of more than one per day during the 1970s—Jerry Falwell often proclaimed the rate to be one new school every seven hours.

Christian school officials bridled at any outside interference and engaged in running skirmishes with state boards of education over the government's right to oversee hiring policies and set curriculum standards. Because of these battles, they were generally not friendly toward Jimmy Carter's campaign promise to establish a separate Department of Education, seeing this as yet another encroachment by the federal government into matters they felt should be managed at a local level. The major conflict, however, occurred in 1978 when the Internal Revenue Service announced plans to revoke the tax exemption of private schools that did not meet certain standards of racial integration. This move was based on a 1972 case, *Green v. Connally,* in which a district court had decided that a school that practiced segregation no longer fit the definition of a charitable institution and was therefore not eligible for tax exemption. Efforts to broaden its application had been in the works for several years before Carter came into power and were part of a general attempt by the Equal Employment Opportunity Commission (EEOC) to broaden the reach of the 1964 Civil Rights Act. In a widely publicized 1975 case, the IRS had revoked the tax-exempt status of Bob Jones University, which had denied admission to blacks until 1971 and which still forbade interracial dating and marriage. The university had sued to regain its status, but the case would not reach the Supreme Court until 1983. Regardless of the history behind the IRS threat, Carter was blamed for it. After all, he apparently agreed with its intent, and those whom it could affect saw it as further evidence that the president had betrayed the very people who had helped elect him. They also saw it as a transparent attempt by their government to impose a secular philosophy on their children by using the excuse of racial discrimination to obstruct Christian education.

One of the pioneers of the Christian Day School movement was Robert Billings, whose book, *A Guide to the Christian School,* was a basic reference work in the field. When the IRS declared its intention, Paul Weyrich invited Billings to come to Washington to help orchestrate a response. This, Weyrich sensed, might be the opportunity he had been seeking for years. He had been reared in Wisconsin in a working-class family led by a Catholic German immigrant father who scoffed at the notion that polite people do not discuss religion and politics—"Politics determines your temporal life and religion determines your eternal life," he would point out, "so what else is there to talk about?" Weyrich cut his intellectual teeth on rousing dinner-table conversation about both realms and their relation to each other.

In 1960, at age seventeen, on a visit to Philadelphia during the presidential campaign, Weyrich amazed a gathering of relatives and their neighbors with his political observations. Mostly Catholics, they told him, "You're the first Republican we've ever visited with. We've never met anyone who told us these things." As he pondered that bit of intelligence, Weyrich realized that his mother's relatives, mostly evangelical Protestants whom he described as "perfectly good people who had sound moral values," had also never been sought out by politicians with a conservative outlook. He "began to think about what you could do if you could reach both groups and get them to work side by side." Two years later, Weyrich tried to get Republican leaders to protest the Supreme Court's decision banning officially sponsored prayer in schools. "I was completely unsuccessful," he noted; the chairman of the Wisconsin Republican organization asked him, "Why would we want to involve ourselves in that? That's crazy. Are you out of your mind?" Weyrich did not press the matter further at the time, but he did not abandon the idea of reaching a united working- and middle-class Catholic and evangelical audience.

In 1969, after moving to Washington to indulge his passion for politics, Weyrich received a revelation of how he might accomplish his dream when he attended a political strategy session run by liberal operatives. "I wasn't supposed to be there," he admitted. "I won't go into all the details of how I got there, but there before my eyes was revealed the modus operandi of the left. They had all these different groups, including religious groups, networking with people on the hill, formulating strategy for offering amendments, and then executing that strategy with media, with demonstrations, with lawsuits, with studies, with political action, by targeting people—all the different elements of the political process. It was a magnificent display of how they operated and it changed my life. From that moment on, people didn't want to see me coming, because all I talked about was, 'This is what they're doing. This is what we have to do. How are we going to replicate what they're doing so that we are competitive? Because we're not even playing on the same ball field.' " By his own account, Weyrich spent the early part of the 1970s working "to get these people who really have the same morals, who have the same ideals, but who came at it from different traditions to work together. I thought to myself, 'Why are these people going in different directions politically? This doesn't make any sense. The country is falling apart, and they're going in opposite directions. They ought to be working together because they agree on essential things.' "

In 1971, with generous support from Colorado brewer Joseph Coors, Weyrich had taken the lead in establishing a low-profile policy analysis organization that, in 1973, became the Heritage Foundation. According to Weyrich, the aim of this enterprise was to "provide some intellectual underpinnings for some members of Congress who wanted to articulate a different approach from the Nixon administration. We did not regard the Nixon administration as conservative on many issues and we wanted to provide an alternative course. There were any number of members of Congress who were interested in taking that alternative course; they just didn't have the staff and the intellectual back-up to make that happen." To provide that back-up, foundation staffers began churning out position papers opposing, among other things, Nixon's views on welfare, Secretary of State Henry Kissinger's policy of *rapprochement* with Eastern European Communists, and what they regarded as misguided attempts to manage the economy through wage and price controls.

In 1974, Weyrich established a political action committee, called the Committee for the Survival of a Free Congress, the first of several organizations to bear the "Free Congress" label, which he calls "the worst political name in history. I probably should have bitten the bullet and changed the name years ago, but I never got around to it. My wife reminds me of it periodically." That same year, Weyrich's close friend Howard Phillips, who had worked in the Nixon administration, founded a political action organization known as the Conservative Caucus. In addition to turning out policy papers and setting up political action groups, Weyrich and his friends met from time to time to discuss various topics and hammer out a long-range agenda.

The Heritage Foundation's participation in the Kanawha County conflict had helped give it visibility and legitimacy in evangelical circles. The IRS threat to the Christian schools did much to enhance the foundation's image even further and to establish Weyrich's reputation as a skilled political operative. One of the first things Billings did was to arrange for a group of pastors associated with Christian schools to meet with Weyrich. The meeting took place in a large Senate caucus room and Weyrich recalled, "I didn't know what to expect, but I went over there and explained to them what was going on and I attacked it in rather fierce terms, and these people jumped to their feet and started cheering. I was absolutely astounded. I'd never encountered an audience like that, because conservatives are rather reserved."

Despite their enthusiasm, the pastors resisted Weyrich's urging to get involved in the political process, arguing that their members would not tolerate such activity. "I told them, 'You're dead wrong.' Of course, I didn't know that, but one thing I had learned over the years is that if you sound as if you are morally certain, people will tend to believe you. So whether or not I know what I'm talking about, I always try to sound morally certain. In any case, I told them, 'You are dead wrong, and we will prove it, and moreover you are going to pay to prove it.' So I went around like it was an Israeli bond meeting and collected $1,000 from each one of these people, to pay for a national study of the evangelical population and what they wanted their church leadership to do about the moral issues of our time. Lance Tarrance and Associates did an excellent study, and a man came to a big meeting in Washington and made a presentation. He revealed that not only was the evangelical community anxious for their leadership to come forth on these issues, but they were sort of angry at them for not having come forth. Moreover, they were willing to pay to support these activities, in addition to what they were giving to their churches. You could see the wheels turning at this meeting, and from that moment on you had a commitment on the part of lots of different people to be involved in the political process, because they knew they wouldn't lose their ministries. They knew there would be a financial base to do this, and they knew their people were clamoring for them to do it."

With Weyrich's help, Billings began Christian School Action, which later became the National Christian Action Coalition, and recruited Jerry Falwell to the cause. The proposed action by the IRS to revoke tax-exempt status from segregated Christian schools also drew fire from James Dobson, a California-based Christian psychologist whose tradition-oriented books, films, workshops, and radio programs on child-rearing and other aspects of family life were fast becoming instructional staples in evangelical circles. While Billings traveled extensively and used his newsletter, *Christian School Alert,* to warn Christian-school leaders and supporters about the IRS threat, Falwell and Dobson reinforced his message through their broadcasts and publications. (Falwell called the IRS plan "sneaky" and complained, "In some states it's easier to open a massage parlor than to open a Christian school.") Religious broadcasters Pat Robertson and Jim Bakker booked school activists and Christian attorneys on their respective television shows, the *700 Club* and the *PTL Club,* to inform their audiences about the federal government's intentions. The grassroots organization Christian Voice, whose largest constituency was composed of members of the Assemblies of God and other Pentecostal churches, also joined the fray.

Within weeks, the White House, the Director of the IRS, and members of Congress received at least half a million pieces of mail protesting the new regulations. This outpouring of opposition led to several days of hearings—at which Catholic and Jewish leaders joined the protest—before both the IRS and a congressional subcommittee, and ultimately to an agreement by the IRS that it would not attempt to carry out its plans. To make sure, North Carolina Senator Jesse Helms got an amendment passed that prohibited use of federal funds for investigating or enforcing alleged violations of IRS regulations by Christian schools.

Several key figures on the Religious Right credit the 1978 IRS/Christian School battle with playing a pivotal role in bringing together conservative Christians and creating a genuine politically effective movement. Paul Weyrich emphatically asserted that "what galvanized the Christian community was not abortion, school prayer, or the ERA. I am living witness to that because I was trying to get those people interested in those issues and I utterly failed. What changed their mind was Jimmy Carter's intervention against the Christian schools, trying to deny them tax-exempt status on the basis of so-called de facto segregation." Weyrich explained that while Christians were troubled about abortion, school prayer, and the ERA, they felt able to deal with those on a private basis. They could avoid having abortions, put their children in Christian schools, and run their families the way they wanted to, all without having to be concerned about public policy. But the IRS threat "enraged the Christian community and they looked upon it as interference from government, and suddenly it dawned on them that they were not going to be able to be left alone to teach their children as they pleased. It was at that moment that conservatives made the linkage between their opposition to government interference and the interests of the evangelical movement, which now saw itself on the defensive and under attack by the government. That was what brought those people into the political process. It was not the other things."

Robert Billings's son Bill, who was involved with his late father's efforts in this period, agreed with Weyrich on the importance of the 1978 protest, but suggested the concern was not entirely ideological. Parents who were already spending thousands of dollars on their children's education had no trouble understanding the financial implications. "If the Christian schools were to lose their tax-exempt status," Billings explained, "their tuition could conceivably double. When it becomes not just a moral or a conservative/liberal issue, but a pocketbook issue, you definitely take an interest. And they did. I don't know if I was really surprised. I knew that somewhere there was going to be something that would jolt some people into action. We'd been trying to encourage that."

DURING THE FIRST two years of his presidency, Jimmy Carter saw much of his evangelical and other conservative support slip away because people felt he had not lived up to the promise of his campaign. In 1979 and 1980, he lost even more support, this time because he did keep a campaign promise. In October 1976, he had told the National Conference on Catholic Charities of his intention to convene a White House Conference on the

American Family soon after his inauguration. That promise went unfulfilled during 1977, in large measure because more pressing policy matters—tax issues, energy problems, job creation, inflation, and the Middle East—crowded it off the agenda. But in January 1978, Carter announced that a conference "to help stimulate a national discussion of the state of American families" would take place in December 1979, then nearly two years away. The conference did not actually occur until the summer of 1980, but it was preceded by extensive preparation, a fact apparently overlooked by critics who claim Carter whipped up the conference in 1980 to improve his re-election chances by appealing to Catholic and evangelical voters.

Carter appointed former Arkansas Congressman Jim Guy Tucker to chair the conference and, after an initial appointment went sour, named John Carr as executive director. Carr had worked with the Catholic Diocese of Washington and was keenly aware of conservative sensibilities on such issues as family planning, abortion, and gay rights. The controversy that accompanied the National Conference on Women had demonstrated that what looked like safe terrain could be sown with land mines, and at one point it appeared the White House conference would be postponed until 1981, to avoid having it damage the president's bid for re-election. Bill Billings acknowledged that announcement of the conference gave conservatives new life. "We had resolved a lot of the problems with the Christian schools," he explained, "and in a way we were almost like the March of Dimes. They raised enough money and found a cure for polio, then decided they didn't want to go out of business, so they found another cause. Now it's all birth defects. Well, by this time we had motivated and spurred a lot of Christians to involvement, so we had a small army and needed another battle to fight."

A key figure in alerting conservative Christians to the opportunity for involvement in the conference was a young woman named Connaught "Connie" Marshner. Marshner had been involved with Young Americans for Freedom while attending the University of South Carolina and, after graduating in 1971, had gone to Washington to work for YAF's magazine, *New Guard*. That soon led to a close association with Weyrich, Phillips, and other figures in the New Right. In one of her earliest independent initiatives, she prepared a three-page analysis and critique of a liberal "child-development bill" proposed by then-Senator Walter Mondale and sent it out on the letterhead of The Emergency Committee for Children, an organization of which she was the only member. "We sent this out," she related, "to every conservative newspaper columnist, and random mailings to newspapers, not knowing what would happen with it. To our total amazement, Richard Nixon got an unprecedented amount of mail and he vetoed the bill on December the 9th, 1971, which some books regard as the birth date of the 'pro-family' movement."

Where had the letters come from? "We were as baffled as anybody else," Marshner admitted. "And we didn't know the answer for several years, but what had happened was that those mailings had gotten into the hands of somebody who passed it on to her cousin, who read it and said, 'This is pretty horrible,' and then she took our three-page summary and made it into maybe a one-page or half-page summary and mailed it to her cousins and sisters and uncles and aunts, and then they did the same with it. All over the country there were little clusters of evangelical and fundamentalist Moms' groups—it was mainly mothers. They were unstructured, they didn't have an organization; they were just in touch with each other, and they were beginning to be aware that there really was a problem here.

"This totally informal network of parents out there in real America—we called it 'the floating crap game' for years—those real, true grassroots Americans are the ones who provided the blood and the bones for what became an organized movement. When we realized that there were people like this all over the country, it was sort of a political light bulb turning on. Paul Weyrich was the one who said, 'Wait a second—these folks are numerous and they're out there and they're not organized. Let's get them in, let's get them organized, and let's get them voting, and see what happens.' So it really was a discovery. These were the forgotten Americans, and when somebody began paying attention to their worries and their concerns, they responded in droves. Up until then, nobody had paid attention to them. They weren't on the radar screen of the policy wonks in Washington. I don't think they had any glimpse of a significant number of people out there who didn't think government was an extension of themselves, who didn't think government was always to be trusted and looked to. I don't think they realized there were intelligent, articulate, credible people out there in large numbers who had a totally different point of view."

To keep in touch with this constituency, Marshner began editing a newsletter called the *Family Protection Report,* whose purpose was to monitor the impact of government policies on family life and to stay in touch with members of the pro-family floating crap game. She also spent time on other New Right projects, including a brief stint in Kanawha County in January 1975, to help organize a seminar for textbook protesters.

When President Carter announced plans for the White House Conference, Marshner and her associates urged the people in their network to get involved in state conventions that would elect delegates to the national conference and help decide what items would be on the conference agenda. She observed that the National Advisory Committee for the conference was heavily weighted with "leaders of the social-welfare establishment, because to their way of thinking, the good of the family is co-terminous with the good of the social-welfare profession." In fact, Carter had insisted that the advisory committee not be one-sided, and less than a third of the forty-member group could be described as part of "the social welfare establishment," even by quite broad criteria. The remainder consisted of people representing an impressive diversity of backgrounds and viewpoints. Moreover, there was a conscious effort to include as much listening as possible, to get an accurate feel of what ordinary families saw as their greatest needs.

From the beginning of his involvement, John Carr wanted to "decentralize" the conference, to "spend less of their energy on a big Washington meeting and more on real dialogue about how families are helped or hurt by government and how society can do a better job of supporting parents and churches in their important roles in society." In keeping with that philosophy, conference leaders decided to hold three regional conferences—in Baltimore, Minneapolis, and Los Angeles—rather than a single conference in Washington. Carter's domestic policy adviser Stuart Eizenstat candidly offered an additional justification for this decision: In light of growing agitation over family issues, there was a concern that a single conference would concentrate "all of the energy" and could lead to a nationally televised fiasco, "blowing up in the administration's face rather than bringing some degree of honor to it for having brought these issues to the public fore."

To minimize the possibility that the conference would be too narrow in its composition or would appear to be manipulated from the top down, states were told that at least thirty percent of their delegates had to be chosen through some sort of open process, such as public balloting, voting at the state convention, or even a random drawing. Governors were to choose an additional thirty percent, with an eye toward achieving diversity. Each state then had the option of deciding how it wanted the remaining forty percent of delegates to be selected.

As soon as procedures for delegate selection were announced, Marshner and her growing network attempted to capture as many spots as they could. Their first effort, in Virginia, was phenomenally successful; mobilized through churches, Bible study groups, parents' organizations, and other pro-family bodies, they packed the convention and walked away with twenty-two of twenty-four elective positions (governors were able to appoint additional delegates). One participant, who preferred not to be identified, still keenly remembers the frustration she felt. "Evangelicals came by the busloads," she recalled. "They all wore blue dots. People from Lynchburg were very much involved. The buses had 'Lynchburg' on them. They came in with their agenda and tried to 'X' out most of the things we had formulated. They didn't want anything about family planning, no family-life education in the schools. Their picture of the family was Mom, Dad, and kids, with Mom at home—the 'traditional family.' I heard that term till I thought I was going to die. And blue dots on everybody. It was one of the most frustrating experiences I have ever had. We lost all rationality."

Marshner's contacts in Michigan rallied members of Phyllis Schlafly's Eagle Forum, Beverly LaHaye's Concerned Women for America, the League of Catholic Women, Right to Life, Stop ERA, several groups with names such as Mothers on the March (MOMS) and Happiness of Womanhood, as well as the Michigan office of Ronald Reagan's campaign organization, and managed to dominate that state's convention in similar fashion. They won all the spots in Oklahoma and a majority in Oregon. In New York, feminist groups used similar tactics to elect a predominantly liberal slate, and liberal leaders in other states also tried to be sure that a solid majority of participants shared their views. In light of these experiences, some governors and state leaders tried to avoid domination by one point of view by limiting the number of elected delegates to the required thirty percent and exercising greater control over the discretionary spots. Predictably, this led conservatives to complain that the deck was being stacked against them. In the end, approximately two hundred fifty of some fifteen hundred delegates came from conservative Christian ranks. Some of those, including Connie Marshner, were at-large delegates appointed by Jim Guy Tucker and John Carr, to insure that their views were adequately represented.

In addition to seeking to control delegations, pro-family representatives also raised objections over the same set of issues—the ERA, abortion, gay rights, pornography, limiting government involvement with the family, etc.—again and again, often in virtually identical language. One participant remembered a meeting in Seattle at which she asked a woman in the restroom what she thought of the conference. "It doesn't matter what I think," she replied. "I came to read the script." It turned out the woman was part of a Mormon contingent that had been bused in with detailed instructions as to what to do. Such tactics alerted liberals and moderates to the existence, energy, preparation, and determination of the conservative movement. "When there's an ice storm," one participant noted, "the liberals stay at home, but these guys rent a bus."

It surprised no one that the ERA, abortion, and gay rights would stir debate in a conference on the family. Planners and many participants were caught off guard, however, by the bitter wrangling that ensued at the state-level meetings over the definition of "family." The first stirrings of trouble came in reaction to an early decision to change the operative word in the conference's title from "Family" to "Families." In a 1979 proclamation kicking off National Family Week, President Carter had said, "We are a nation of families. All families are important, but the extended family, the foster family, and the adoptive family play a special role by relieving the isolation of those who lack the comfort of a loving nuclear family." Jody Powell claimed that the decision to speak of "families" was in this same expansive spirit. "When I think of the term 'family,' " he said, "I don't just think of my wife and my mother and my daughter and my grandchildren. I think of hundreds of people—cousins and aunts and uncles and now two sets of in-laws and all of that. And my guess is that when Jimmy Carter spoke of family and healing wounds and divisions and so forth, he was thinking of family in that broad sense."

Whatever Jimmy Carter had in mind, the conservative forces sought to limit application of the term to people related by blood, adoption, or marriage, and to establish the basic unit of husband, wife, and children as the norm to be adhered to whenever possible. A key reason for their concern, of course, was to make sure that unmarried partners, unwed mothers and their offspring, and, most particularly, homosexual relationships were not recognized as legitimate.

Beverly LaHaye summarized well the concerns of many conservative Christians: "We came to realize that this White House Conference was really geared up toward changing the definition of the family. It wanted to include any two people who chose to live together, regardless of their sexual orientation. Early in 1980, we saw that homosexuals were driving in, because they wanted to be part of the whole definition of the family. And we objected to that." Pro-family delegates liked to ask if the Manson Family would qualify for inclusion under the broadened definition—"Is he going to a parent conference for the children of the girls in his so-called family? Is that a family?" Sharon Overcast, whose brusque treatment by her fellow Virginians in the National Women's Conference had moved her to get involved in the Virginia convention, avoided such rhetoric, but acknowledged her preference for a limited definition. "I think from the beginning of time," she said, "a family has been looked at as a Mom and Dad and children with marriage bonds. Now, I'm aware that there are a lot of differences in various cultures and societies around the world. Of course, I feel that God has ordained this family unit as His pattern." Beverly LaHaye agreed. She and her Concerned Women for America, she said, were determined "to hold onto the real true meaning of the genuine family, as God intended it to be."

People whose "normal" families had been broken by death, divorce, or other unfortunate circumstances, were understandably hurt. Mary Robinson, a black single mother who was studying to become a lawyer, objected strongly to the notion that she was not part of a family—"What are these people talking about?" Feminists who saw little need for a husband to help rear a child, and homosexual couples, with or without children, were affronted by the open censure of their lifestyles. In the middle, many people who were working with severely dysfunctional families found the struggle over definitions quite bizarre. Sam Clark, then-executive director of the Connecticut Child Welfare Association, and also a gay man who had long served as a foster parent to two homeless youngsters he had taken in after they were released from a residential treatment center, admitted his bewilderment. "I guess I was a little sheltered," he said. "Broken families, single-parent families, foster families, adoptive families, same-sex couples—those are things I had dealt with on an on-going basis in my work. For me, that was the reality. To argue that somehow the only real family is Mom and Dad and two or three kids was completely unrealistic in terms of my experience. I'd not had that fight with anybody. For me, it was a given that there's a whole range of families out there, and that's America. That's the reality, and I'm not sure we're going to 'turn it around.' I think the question is how we make it healthy and functional and positive for those people who find themselves in those many situations. The question for me was 'How do you make that work?' not 'How do you make that bad?' But for a lot of people at that conference, the traditional, stereotypical American family was their reality, or the reality [they believed] America ought to be returning to, and they felt very strong and very emotional about that issue."

Eventually, the conference settled on a nondefinition. Mary Robinson summarized the result: "Because it was so diverse that it was not going to be possible to affirm everybody's lifestyle, what we ended up doing was listing the various definitions that had come out and saying, 'This is what this group wants and this is what that group wants.' That was about the best we could do." That dropping of boundary lines rankled pro-family participants, but they resented even more the sense, not entirely imaginary, that their own view of the family had been marked as narrow and stultifying, a source of inequality and oppression, rather than being seen as a basic and vital foundation for a moral and democratic society.

Not persuaded that their representation in the delegate corps was adequate and fearing their voices would be muffled at the regional conferences, conservative forces sought greater input at a higher level. Jerry Regier had moved from Campus Crusade's college ministry to work in its Christian Embassy, which Bill Bright had established in Washington in 1975 as an evangelical outreach to government officials. More moderate and optimistic than Connie Marshner, Regier approached John Carr to express his concern over the lack of evangelical representation among conference leaders. "In the evangelical world," he explained, "family seminars, marriage seminars, children's seminars, parenting courses, those kinds of things, were natural and normal, and speakers traveled all over and tapes were disseminated. It was just a natural part of our world. To see that a White House conference on the family was going to take place and that these people weren't even a part of it created a feeling that 'Something's wrong here. Either it's being rigged or they genuinely don't know what they're doing.' " Regier thought the consternation was worsened by the fact that "we had a President who initiated this conference, who said he was 'born again,' and yet that whole world was being left out. Had it been a President that wasn't at all familiar with people in that world, it might have been a little different response."

Carr, who had been taken aback by evangelical criticism of the conference, candidly admitted he was unaware of the world Regier was describing. Connie Marshner has reported that Carr told Regier, "When we want to hear the lesbian point of view, we know where to get that, and when we want to hear the point of view of a commune or something, we know where to get that. But to get a Christian point of view, we don't know where to go." That perception is clearly distorted. Carr himself was and is a devout Catholic, and the forty-member National Advisory Committee included many religious leaders, including a Catholic bishop, a Catholic charities director, Lutheran Pastor Richard John Neuhaus (now also a Catholic), a high-ranking Mormon official, a representative of the Church of the Brethren, the Reverend Jesse Jackson, Coretta Scott King, and the head of the Christian Life Commission of the Southern Baptist Convention.

Carr urged Regier to assemble a group of people to meet with Jim Guy Tucker and other members of the National Advisory Committee. Regier invited such well-known evangelicals as James Dobson, NAE executive Robert Dugan, Bill Gothard, whose family life seminars regularly attracted huge crowds all over the country, and Jay Allen Peterson, who had led an evangelical "Continental Conference on the Family" in 1976. After the meeting, which went well, Jim Guy Tucker told Dobson, "I've been in and around Washington for years. Where have you guys been?"

Consequently, both Dobson and Regier were named at-large delegates to the conference. Although Regier felt that people in Tucker's position should have known about Dobson and his colleagues, he admitted his own ignorance of their world. At a subsequent meeting at the offices of the Department of Health and Human Services, Dobson appeared on a panel with famed child psychologist Urie Bronfenbrenner. "He is very well known in secular circles," Regier said, "but I don't think I'd ever heard of him, just like other people had never heard of Dr. Dobson. I began to see immediately that these spheres of influence were intersecting a little bit, but generally they were totally separate worlds."

The welcome Regier and Dobson received fit Tucker's announced philosophy of "Ask and you shall receive." At a White House reception for the National Advisory Committee, Tucker said, "I don't want any crybabies coming to me after the conference saying they were excluded. If you want to participate, you've got to build your own coalitions and jump into the process." Connie Marshner was also appointed to be a delegate, had several meetings with John Carr, and was named to a conference panel that included Children's Defense Fund director Marian Wright Edelman. "We did not suffer from the absence of advice from Connie Marshner," Carr said wryly, "but it was usually delivered through a press release rather than through dialogue or meetings."

Just asking to be involved, however, did not guarantee an invitation. When Phyllis Schlafly sought to have the Eagle Forum included in a coalition of nongovernmental agencies involved in the conference, she was turned down, not only because she and her organization had been seeking either to dominate or criticize the conference almost since the beginning of the process, according to coalition chairman Joseph Berg, but also because she refused to provide information required of all such groups. In response to this rebuff, Schlafly, Marshner, Robert and Bill Billings, the Heritage Foundation's Onalee McGraw, and others formed what they called the Pro-Family Coalition. Bill Billings explained that the group hoped "to do with family issues what some other groups had done with defense issues or with tax issues or whatever: to provide an opportunity to share information, share resources that we knew about, share people we knew to be experts in a particular field, and work toward making sure that whatever came out of that White House Conference on Families was something that we could be comfortable with."

Most of the same people formed the Library Court Group, an aggregate of people and organizations focusing on family issues under Connie Marshner's leadership. Finally, perhaps remembering the success of the counter-rally at the 1977 women's conference in Houston, this circle decided to organize, under the aegis of Paul Weyrich's Free Congress Foundation, an American Family Forum, billed as the first "Pro-Family Movement" national convention, to be held in Washington in the summer of 1980, a month after the first regional White House Conference was scheduled to occur in Baltimore.

THE BALTIMORE CONFERENCE, which attracted approximately seven hundred delegates, opened grandly, with a stirring speech by President Carter, but the same issues that had created tension and animosity in the state conventions soon erupted here as well. Connie Marshner labeled the make-up of delegates "a liberal stacked deck" and repeated her charge that the conference had been devised primarily to help re-elect Jimmy Carter by making it appear he was concerned about the family. In the same vein, participants fell to arguing over the same old issues: definition of a family, gay rights, abortion, and the ERA. David Cunningham, a gay man who worked on issues of child abuse, juvenile delinquency, and child welfare in Connecticut, remembered the resentment he felt at "this temper, with people being irate, outraged if the issue of gays and lesbians came up. It stepped outside of any kind of professional conversation and turned into a personal conversation. There I was, an American human being—I apologize for the corniness of that—and I was being told I had no right in my own country to be recognized as a family. When someone would stand up and say something clearly insulting to gay and lesbian people, and they would say it with what I would characterize as a venomous kind of spitting and shouting and red-faced yelling, I'm embarrassed to say it, but I reacted. I did take that personally, and I got mad at it. And I didn't make sure that I kept my respect in place for their right to speak as well as mine. Frankly, I wished they would shut up."

Professional facilitators in most of the various work groups managed to keep the definition issue from bogging their sessions down by reaffirming the preconference decision not to produce a restrictive definition of family, but that only angered conservatives further. At the end of the first day's meetings, Connie Marshner complained bitterly that discussion of the definition of the family had been stifled and reasserted her belief that "Families consist of people related by heterosexual marriage, blood, and adoption. Families are not religious cults, families are not Manson families, families are not heterosexual or homosexual liaisons outside of marriage." She charged that, instead of grappling with this fundamental issue, the conference had become a "working out of the hidden agenda that has been there all along: guaranteed annual income, guaranteed jobs, national health insurance, federal involvement in child care, federal involvement in housing, and so on down the line. Just increase, increase, increase, in federal programs, supposedly for families. Expanding the federal bureaucracy, expanding the inflation rate, expanding the tax rate, and not helping families solve their own problems." In her view, "Families are strong when they have a function to perform. And the more government, combined with the helping professions establishment, take away the functions families need to perform—to provide their health care, their child care, their housing—the less purpose there is for the family, per se, to exist."

Marshner also complained that efforts to discuss the pivotal issue of abortion were repeatedly ruled out of order. John Carr did not deny that possibility, but explained that group facilitators had been instructed to restrict discussion to the specific topic they had been assigned. Two segments of the conference made that difficult. Committed feminist delegates tried to inject the ERA into every session, and pro-family forces tried to turn every group into a forum for discussing abortion. The heat with which both sides argued their cases made calm consideration of other issues difficult. Sam Clark remembered his disappointment with the process and, ultimately, with himself: "I'm a person who believes in discussion and negotiation and compromise, that anything can be worked out, that somewhere we can come to a middle ground and agree and come up with a solution. I had been working on public policy for children, youth, families, those kind of things, and whenever we worked in the legislature, we worked both sides of the aisle. You never worked one side and not the other. We built bi-partisan support and moved things forward through the General Assembly. So I had done a lot of that, but it became clear to me that this was not the way this thing was going to end up. There were hard, staunch positions and people were not budging or moving on those issues, and I began very quickly to see coalitions taking shape, and rump meetings and side meetings, and finding myself actually caught up in that process. It became kind of like we'd just go ahead and do it and 'Screw 'em.' There was not discussion that would somehow bring things together. That concerned me, but you get caught up in a group process of 'win and lose,' and lots of people, including myself, wanted to win. But it seemed like maybe there could have been some middle ground, and that was not achieved at all. From the point of view of the 'pro-choice' delegates, who clearly were going to win the vote, it was almost like chastising the 'pro-family' group. When you're dealing with policy issues I'm not sure that there's a lot of value in making the losers feel bad. And I think that's part of what was happening—'Ehh, you're losing, so get the hell outta here.' "

On the second day of the conference, Connie Marshner instructed her circle of pro-family delegates to let her know what went on in their morning sessions. During the noon hour, she stationed herself near some potted palms and waited for the reports. She recalled that every delegate had the same report: " 'We weren't allowed to talk.' 'We were gaveled down.' 'We were told another workshop would deal with that, but the people in that workshop weren't allowed to bring it up either.' So people started gathering there by the potted palms, and everybody was having the same disgust with the whole thing and it was clear—'This isn't gonna work.' A couple of people said, 'Wait a minute, you don't want to discredit the whole process,' and I said, 'Why not?' You know, 'Why not?' So we just said, 'This is ridiculous. This is just a travesty. Let's not give this any more legitimacy than it deserves.' And we walked out en masse." Before leaving, Marshner and Larry Pratt registered a protest at a conference luncheon. Pratt wrested the microphone from Jim Guy Tucker and said, "We decided this delegation is stacked and we should walk out." Marshner declared that "by walking out now the point will be made that the conference doesn't have credibility. We have become a pitiful minority and we're walking out on principle. . . . Only the point of view of the conference staff could be heard."

Approximately thirty delegates left with Marshner and Pratt. Some probably would not have left on their own, but suspected it was the right thing to do. "It was just such an unwinnable situation," Sharon Overcast reflected. The group's leaders, she felt, "probably knew more than I did" and "felt nothing was going to be accomplished anyway, so it was futile. In an uncomfortable situation, we did what we could, and it was just time to leave." Others thought it better to remain at the table and continue to present their point of view. Both Jerry Regier and James Dobson chose that route. Regier acknowledged that it had been "a very uncomfortable feeling to stay when people I agreed with wholeheartedly on what we believed about families [had walked out], but they felt like they needed to make a statement for other purposes."

Regier's reference to "other purposes" is telling. By several accounts, the walkout was not as spontaneous as it seemed. Regier remembers having been "invited to a meeting previous to that where they were strategizing, and I said that I wasn't going to walk out," and that Connie Marshner had replied, "We have to walk out. We're not going to change anything here. We're too small a group. This place is stacked." John Carr noted that pro-family delegates staged similar protests at both the Minneapolis and Los Angeles conferences and charged them with "trying to make a point for the press rather than anything else." Sam Clark insisted that "we all knew it was going to happen before it happened. It had been in discussion probably for twenty-four hours before that, and there was an attempt on some people's part, including myself, to have that not happen. It was symbolic of the breach of the process. But as I got into discussions back and forth, it became clear that it was going to happen, and nothing could prevent it. The feelings were so strong that people were going to walk out."

Ironically, Marshner's charges that the conference staff had total control of the outcome and that she was part of "a pitiful minority" were quite mistaken. John Carr was and is staunchly opposed to abortion, but did not believe that should be a major issue for the conference. He pointed out that when pollsters ask people what they consider to be the greatest threat to their families, they talk about economic pressures, work pressures, lack of adequate housing, and the like. Social conservatives "may be disappointed that abortion and homosexuality do not surface very highly" in such polls, he said, "but the idea that George Gallup would try to help us predetermine our agenda lacks some credibility." More notably, a resolution that lent the conference's endorsement to the ERA, abortion on demand, and gay rights passed by a single vote. Had Marshner's band of angry warriors not decamped, they could easily have defeated it.

Looking back, Regier does not necessarily feel his friend Connie Marshner made a mistake. "Sometimes you have to do things that will mobilize people," he observed. "And 'Conservatives Stage Walk-Out' was front-page news. It woke people up all across the country to what was going on. So, sure, we may have lost something by one or two votes in the short run, but from their perspective, which was much more politically seasoned than mine, they may have won the war down the road." Marshner conceded. "It wasn't that walking out changed the outcome; it probably didn't, but it delegitimized the process; it showed the world that this process was flawed and didn't deserve their respect."

Pro-family tactics may have had another, supremely unintended effect in that they provided a significant boost to the gay rights movement. The National Gay Task Force's request for a spot on the National Advisory Committee had been denied, but they were given representation at the conference. The gay publication, *The Blade,* reported that only seven of 671 delegates were openly gay at the beginning of the conference, but one delegate had reported that approximately thirty other men and women had "come out" to him during that week. Delegate David Cunningham was one of those who decided to go public with his homosexuality, a gesture that involved considerably more personal risk in 1980 than it does today. "For me," Cunningham said, "the White House Conference was my Stonewall," a reference to the New York City gay bar that was the site of a police raid commonly regarded as having triggered the gay-rights movement. "I wasn't at Stonewall in 1969, and I hadn't gotten involved in gay political organizations. I was just living a pretty comfortable life in Connecticut, very accepted by my family and friends. But just like the people at the Stonewall, something about the attacks at the White House Conference had me say to myself, 'I am not going to put up with this!' "

Cunningham did not imagine that Jimmy Carter was placing his seal of approval on gay relationships, but he did think it significant that homosexual men and women were able to have their views represented at a conference convened by the president of the United States. "We had never in history been able to have our debate at that level," he noted, "and here we were actually able to debate issues central to gay and lesbian life at the national level, at something called a White House Conference on Families. That brought immediate stature to gay politics. I was fascinated by the amount of coverage. Gay politics on the front page of my newspaper? I was thrilled." Not surprisingly, perhaps, Cunningham did not regret the departure of the pro-family dissenters. "It was not an enlightened attitude," he said with a laugh, "but my feeling was 'Yeah. Fine. Go. Good riddance. Now we can stop the yelling and get some serious work done.' "

Cunningham's pleasure was magnified at the closing ceremonies, which featured a slide presentation of scenes from the conference and wound up with delegates holding hands in a line that snaked throughout the ballroom, while Sister Sledge's "We Are Family" washed over the crowd like a warm, healing stream. Some delegates may have associated the song with the Pittsburgh Pirates, who had used it as their theme during their 1979 championship season. David Cunningham recognized it as a favorite song in the gay discos of that era. "It was like being at home," he said. "All of a sudden, our music, so to speak, was being used to close the conference. It was clear that people were really ready to celebrate the entire conference. I wasn't sure how the delegates from my state would feel about my having become active on the gay issues, but everything became okay in that closing ceremony. I was going to go home and work with them on children's issues and they would celebrate who I was and everything I brought to the party. That was an important moment."

The Minneapolis and Los Angeles conferences drew less media attention than the Baltimore meeting, but followed much the same pattern, with pro-family delegates arguing furiously for their positions, decrying the gathering as a transparent attempt to boost Jimmy Carter's flagging stock and promote alternative lifestyles, and staging a midpoint walkout to express their frustration at the short shrift their views had received. Befitting its Midwestern setting, the Minneapolis meeting produced a slightly more conservative set of resolutions than the other two, but the overall agreement was impressive. The final report placed greatest emphasis on such recommendations as the flexible hours for working parents, the need for increased efforts to stem alcohol and drug abuse, changes in the tax code to eliminate the "marriage penalty," tax policies to encourage home care of the elderly, and increased financial assistance to families with handicapped members. Support for the ERA, abortion, and sex education were included, but listed among secondary recommendations. The only reference to gay rights was the inclusion of gays in the definition of the family. James Dobson wrote a minority report that became a part of the final document. On receiving the report, President Carter thanked the 125,000 Americans who had helped produce it, observing that "the consensus on the major recommendations is a remarkable achievement and shows how Americans of different backgrounds and beliefs can unite around specific programs."

In early July, nearly one thousand representatives of more than three hundred pro-family groups gathered in Washington for the American Family Forum. Speakers and other luminaries included Weyrich, Phillips, Marshner, Schlafly, Dobson, Falwell, Bright, Beverly LaHaye and minister husband Tim, evangelical theologian Harold O. J. Brown, and Senators Jesse Helms and Paul Laxalt. The meeting produced no surprises—conservative columnist James Kilpatrick called it "as one-sidedly conservative as the Baltimore affair was one-sidedly liberal"—but the fervor of its sessions made it clear that the pro-family forces were geared up for the long haul.

· · ·

LOOKING BACK ON the White House Conference fifteen years after it occurred, Connie Marshner dismissed it as an event of little lasting consequence. "You can probably find a copy of the White House Conference Report if you need to see one," she said, "but it's not going to be cited as a seminal document in the development of family policy in this country." The main benefit she felt it provided was to serve as a training ground for pro-family activists. "It got our people involved in a process that they hadn't been involved in before, but they also had a clear look at the results of that process, and they realized, 'Wait a minute—we can't play by the old rules any more. We've got to get onto a playing field where we help write the rules,' because the people who were writing the rules were keeping our issues off the agenda. That's the way politics is played, and if you can't get in there and inflict consequences for bad behavior, for wrong votes, etc., you are not taken seriously. And the consequences that a politician pays attention to is something that compromises his re-election."

Marshner was inclined to regard John Carr as "a nice guy" with a wrong-headed philosophy. "John grew up in a world which believed that the government could carry out the exhortations of Scripture. When Jesus Christ said, 'Feed the poor'—John believes government can do that. I can pay my taxes and give it to the government and the government will feed the poor, and this cleanses my conscience, and therefore a welfare state is a good idea. From my point of view, when Jesus Christ says, 'Feed the hungry,' he means me. He means, 'Go in your kitchen and cook a meal and take it down to the homeless shelter.' He doesn't mean, 'Pay some taxes and let somebody else do it.' And I think that's a really important difference in the mind of liberals and conservatives." Families, Marshner believes, can solve their own problems if the government will just leave them alone.

Carr acknowledged the need for personal responsibility and readily admitted that "the Left really blew it, and has continued to blow it with its uncomfortableness in dealing with family issues." At the same time, he viewed Marshner's outlook as simplistic and symptomatic of an unfortunate polarization of thought. "It's not either/or," he said. "What we've got in family policy and so many other areas is one group that says what we really need are better values—more personal responsibility, more time with our kids; children need to stop having children; we need more sexual restraint; we need good old-fashioned morality. Then another group says that what we really need are better policies—better jobs that pay a living wage, better child care, better health care, less homelessness and hunger. The fact is we need both better values and better policies. We need policies that reflect our best values. Churches can't feed every hungry person in America. I go down to the soup kitchen and I bring my kids. I think that's part of what I'm called to do as a believer, but as a society we have got to do something about millions of hungry kids, and that's not only by making lasagna and bringing it down to the soup kitchen. It's also by deciding what kind of policies, what kind of budget priorities we're going to have, what kind of supports we're going to give to families. So we have to get over the unnecessary, the unreal, the unhelpful polarization that says we've got to have better values or better policies, when in fact we need both. And we have to understand that those who would seek to polarize us, those who would use whatever forums available to advance their own ideological cause, are standing in the way of the pursuit of the common ground and the search for the common good that could help us move forward on better values and better policies. If we began with the needs of families instead of the needs of the interests groups and the needs of the politicians, we'd be a lot better off."

Carr believed some of the dissent within the three meetings stemmed from a cynical agenda. He told of troubled pro-family delegates to the Minneapolis conference who knew of his anti-abortion convictions and approached him to report that they had been instructed by other pro-family delegates to vote in favor of the pro-abortion resolution. They explained that since the resolution had passed by only a single vote in Baltimore, if the Minneapolis conference took a pro-life position, it would undermine the dissenters' claim that the conference was biased against conservative views. Carr was quick to note, however, that the press had concentrated far more on dissension within the conference than on a much more pervasive cooperative spirit, and that "the vast majority of people who participated in this process," including James Dobson and other pro-family delegates who declined to join the walkouts, "were trying to find the common ground and trying to build bridges, and were really pleased and satisfied that despite the enormous diversity and differences of opinion, that on a whole range of important concerns for families they did find common ground on issues that crossed the liberal/conservative, Democrat/Republican lines."

Evelyn Davis had greater regard for the idea of the conference than for what it actually accomplished. As one of relatively few black delegates at the Minneapolis assembly, she perceived that "really, it was a battle of the haves against the have-nots," and the have-nots were hopelessly outnumbered. "Where it should have been a conference of understanding one another, of trying to work out some women's issues and some minority issues, it was really a thing of middle-class women getting together and putting their agenda on the table. And some of us were kind of in the way."

Robert Maddox reserved most of his regret for the unfair treatment he felt Jimmy Carter had received. "What he intended for good was turned against him," he said, "and the very people that we invited to come and help with the conference pulled out their long knives and began to slash at him and the conference, and had no compunction whatsoever about using every media outlet they could find, not only to trash the conference but to trash him, in a way that not only questioned his policy, but questioned his faith. My political naïveté was pretty well shocked right there. I thought people of faith sat down and worked out differences for the common good. That pretty well blew that out of the water."

CARTER'S INABILITY TO hold on to the evangelical constituency that had helped elect him in 1976 was pointedly illustrated in a breakfast he held for a small group of prominent conservative ministers that included Jerry Falwell, Oral Roberts, Rex Humbard, Jim Bakker, D. James Kennedy, Charles Stanley, and Tim LaHaye. The day before, he had made a highly successful address to four thousand members of the National Religious Broadcasters and had hoped to use this occasion to mend some key fences, but he misfired from the start. When someone pointed out that thousands of people were gathering across the street for the annual March for Life, held on the anniversary of the *Roe v. Wade* decision, Carter made a statement on abortion that they considered vague. When asked about the lack of evangelicals in his administration, he hedged again. Finally, Tim LaHaye asked "why he as a Christian and a pro-family man, as he protested to be, was in favor of the Equal Rights Amendment in view of the fact that it would be so harmful to the family, and he gave some off-the-wall answer that the Equal Rights Amendment was good for the family. Well, I knew when he said that that he was out to lunch. We had a man in the White House who professed to be a Christian, but didn't understand how un-Christian his administration was." Afterward, LaHaye recalled, while waiting outside for a limo to take him back to his hotel, "I stood there and I prayed this prayer: 'God, we have got to get this man out of the White House and get someone in here who will be aggressive about bringing back traditional moral values.' And little did I know that several others prayed essentially the same prayer. We got into this limousine, and here were some of the leading ministers of America, and they were stone silent. It was just like depression had settled on all of us. We all had made a commitment to God that day that, for the first time in our lives, we were going to get involved in the political process and do everything we could to wake up the Christians to be participating citizens instead of sitting back and letting other people decide who will be our government leaders. And ever since then we've been trying to get people involved by just waking Christians up to the realization that we can no longer vote Republican or Democrat or Independent. Christians have to vote for the candidate most deeply committed to moral values, because if he's going to represent us, he's going to have to represent our moral values, and our moral values are the same traditional values our country was founded on."

Not everyone, of course, gave up on Jimmy Carter. Evelyn Davis observed, "It seemed as if he had a plan put together that helped both of us, conservatives and liberals. And I think he did more for the nation in his little country way of being president than the rest of them did with all of their army backgrounds and things, because he looked at the total plate." Mary Robinson, whose experience as a delegate to the White House Conference led her to abandon her law studies and enter the ministry, agreed with this assessment. She had voted for Carter in 1976, she acknowledged, "and I voted for him for re-election. I really think he was a fair, gentle man. I'm sure he could be hard and ruthless when it was necessary, but I think he attempted to be fair and to show that he cared, and it was unfortunate that in this country, for a president to have that kind of image was somehow deemed a weakness. I never understood that. In my opinion, Jimmy Carter did and still does have a heart for people, and you can't beat that. In a real sense, the White House Conference on Families was one piece of that. If nothing else, it let me know about the way people are hurting and how we need to be sensitive and inclusive. It helped prepare me to be a pastor and listen to people's hurts and fears and dreams, and to help bring the message that Jesus is real and God is love. We're so diverse here in this country, and our laws and our policies and our practices need to reflect that diversity. It helped me to recognize that America is not just for a few on the political right or left, or even in the middle, but it's for all of us."

CHAPTER

8

MORAL MAJORITY

WHEN TIM LAHAYE and his colleagues vowed to work for Jimmy Carter's defeat after their unhappy breakfast at the White House, it was the culmination of a long process, and they had received expert assistance in arriving at that point. After watching his ideologicals suffer massive defeat in 1964, Barry Goldwater's young admirer, Morton Blackwell, recognized that hard-line conservatives had little chance of seeing their candidate elected unless they recruited legions of new Republican voters and developed more effective strategies for deploying them. As he explained thirty years later, "If you can identify some segment of the population which is not active and can be activated, or some segment that is miscast in their current party affiliation and can be switched over to your side, you're going to change things dramatically." The group he regarded as most promising were fundamentalist and evangelical Christians, whom he characterized as "the greatest tract of virgin timber on the political landscape." And, he said, "We set about quite systematically to identify leaders, to teach them how to become effective, how to organize, how to communicate, how to raise funds, how to use direct-mail technology—skills that would make them more effective."

Others who saw potential for some heavy logging in the evangelical forest included former Arizona Congressman John Conlan and Ed McAteer, a Memphis layman with extensive contacts in evangelical circles. Conlan became a popular speaker in Christian circles throughout the country through association with other evangelicals who belonged to two organizations. The first, known only as The Fellowship, was low-profile, based in Washington, and focused on prayer groups and personal support for people in government; the second was Bill Bright's more activist Christian Embassy. At Conlan's urging, McAteer came to Washington in 1974 to open an office of the Christian Freedom Foundation. From this organization, he set up speaking engagements for Conlan and arranged showings of Rus Walton's politically flavored films at evangelical churches. Moving in these circles brought Mc-Ateer into contact with Howard Phillips, who soon persuaded him to leave the foundation and become field director for Phillips's Conservative Caucus, which led in turn to closer association with Paul Weyrich, perhaps the most important figure in the small constellation of leaders who were consciously referring to themselves as the New Right. The textbook wars in Kanawha County had provided the Heritage Foundation with a good example of what grassroots organization could accomplish at a local level. With Weyrich's counsel and assistance, Robert Billings had led the successful effort to make the IRS back down from its attempt to regulate Christian day schools. The Lance Tarrance survey had uncovered a willingness by evangelical church members to become more involved. And Connie Marshner, another Heritage veteran, was gearing up to disrupt President Carter's Conference on Families. But Weyrich and his cohorts had their eyes on the largest of political prizes: the conservative capture of the White House and Congress.

Hard-line conservatives in this period were almost uniformly critical of the Supreme Court, disagreeing not only with the substance of some of its more famous decisions, but also with what they took to be a disregard of the original intent of the Constitution and a dangerous usurpation of power from Congress and the individual states. The 1962 and 1963 decisions that ended officially sponsored prayer and devotional Bible reading in the public schools had been met by howls of outrage and predictions of every sort of evil consequence, such as rampant drug use, sexual promiscuity, high crime rates, disrespect for authority, and widespread loss of a sense of right and wrong. Though the causal connection may have been tenuous, the undeniable appearance of all the predicted phenomena not only convinced critics of the Court that they had been right, but made the restoration of school prayer an evergreen item on the conservative agenda. It may be, however, that no decision—not even *Brown v. the Board of Education,* which sounded the death knell for legally segregated schools in 1954—would create as big a rift in the nation, and as great an opportunity for political exploitation on both sides of the divide, as the Court's landmark 1973 ruling in the case of *Roe v. Wade.*

When the Court published its decision, which essentially removed all existing legal barriers to abortion in the United States, an ardent supporter of abortion rights observed, "We neither asked for nor expected this much." Small wonder, since, as a result of that single decision, the United States suddenly found itself with abortion laws more lenient than those of any noncommunist country in the Western world. Though individual states and physicians could impose restrictions on late-term abortions, the Court itself did not, and nearly a quarter-century later, it is quite clear that it was not just abortion advocates who got more than they asked for or expected. Few issues in American life stir more passion, generate more high-profile political activism, and appear less amenable to satisfactory resolution than abortion. Stuart Eizenstat observed that the abortion question gave Jimmy Carter "a great deal of difficulty" in 1976. In 1980, it was one of the major factors that led to his defeat.

The strongest opposition to abortion prior to and immediately following the Court's decision came from Roman Catholics. Many liberal Protestants were uncomfortable with the massive numbers of abortions that were soon being performed each year and were willing to recommend some restrictions, but most affirmed a pro-choice position. Evangelical and fundamentalist Protestants, many of whom now consider abortion a litmus test of extraordinary importance, had little to say about it one way or the other. It appears, for example, that Jerry Falwell did not preach a sermon on abortion until 1978. Harold O. J. Brown, a Harvard-trained evangelical theologian and ethicist who was one of the first prominent evangelicals to address the issue, has suggested that lingering anti-Catholic bias may have played a role in their late espousal of the pro-life position. "At that point," he said, "a lot of Protestants reacted almost automatically—'If the Catholics are for it, we should be against it.' That proved to be a very unwise position, but it took a while to realize that. The fact that Catholics were out in front caused many Protestants to keep a low profile."

Brown, then an associate editor of *Christianity Today,* immediately wrote a thoughtful editorial for the magazine, contending that abortion constitutes a repudiation of the Hippocratic Oath and Judeo-Christian ethics. In the months that followed, he was surprised that the astonishing increase in the number of abortions—740,000 in 1973, 900,000 in 1974—failed to produce in others the disquiet it caused him. In February 1975, at a New Orleans conference for Christian men, he met the prominent pediatric surgeon, C. Everett Koop. Aware that Koop had issued a strong condemnation of abortion in a 1973 commencement address at Wheaton, the prestigious evangelical college, Brown suggested to Koop that they devise a strategy for enlisting evangelicals and other Protestants into the anti-abortion movement. Koop agreed, and became even more positive after learning that Billy Graham was willing to place his imprimatur on the effort. The task was not as easy as Brown and Koop had imagined.

Most of the leaders who attended a meeting Graham convened were, as Brown put it, "still of the older non-interventionist persuasion." They viewed abortion as morally unacceptable, but saw no prospect for doing much about it and thought it inappropriate to take political action to oppose it. Brown and Koop moved ahead, however, and formed the Christian Action Council, which at first did little more than publish a newsletter and lobby Congress for measures to curb or prohibit abortions. "We really thought it wouldn't take much to get the general Christian community in the United States really upset about this issue," Brown recalled, "because it seemed so horrible to us. We thought, 'Once people realize what's going on, there will be a spontaneous upheaval.' That didn't happen."

Brown soon realized that many people, including many Christians, found it difficult to single out abortion as uniquely evil. "Many people," he acknowledged, "would like to see abortion as a trivial sort of issue—one among many. But others of us see it as a crucial issue, because it affects what you think human beings are, and what you think they're worth, and what you think should become of them." The tide finally began to build in 1977, when, by coincidence, Koop was invited to address the Canadian Theological Society about abortion and euthanasia. To his surprise, he discovered that Francis Schaeffer, the evangelical theologian and philosopher, was speaking to another group on the same subject on the same campus at the University of Toronto. After a young man in the audience who was aware of Schaeffer's lecture pointed out "he's speaking in the abstract and you have all the examples," he asked, "Why don't you guys get together?" Koop had been a friend of the Schaeffer family for years and, as he remembers it, "I walked over and repeated that conversation to Francis."

That led to a meeting at L'Abri Schaeffer's compound in Switzerland three weeks later and a long conversation with Schaeffer and his son, Franky, a filmmaker. Excited by the challenge of depicting the horrors of abortion and providing Christians with a biblical framework for opposing it, the three men outlined and subsequently produced a five-segment film and companion book, both titled, *Whatever Happened to the Human Race?* The central theme of both film and book was that abortion is both a cause and a result of the loss of appreciation for the sanctity of human life, and that widespread acceptance of abortion would eventually lead to acceptance of infanticide and euthanasia. Schaeffer, who had begun to spend more time in the U.S., visited churches throughout the country, showing the film and urging Christians to work for the prohibition of abortion. On numerous occasions, Koop appeared with him. As word spread, the films circulated widely in evangelical circles, with tremendous impact. Conservative Christians not only developed a revulsion for abortion but, as Koop put it, they also "began to associate the need for tying their faith to social action." Brown agreed: "I wouldn't say it's the only thing that influenced the 'pro-life' movement, but nothing has had an impact across the board that compares to the Schaeffer-Koop series. Today, you won't find many who call themselves evangelicals who don't hold a very strong 'pro-life' position."

.   .   .

WHATEVER HAPPENED TO the Human Race? was not Francis Schaeffer's first foray into film. In 1976, he and Franky, with extensive assistance from ghostwriter Mel White, had collaborated on another film/book combination, titled *How Should We Then Live?* That effort not only laid important groundwork for acceptance of Schaeffer's views on abortion, but helped introduce evangelicals to secular humanism, an elastic concept that would eventually supersede communism as their prime ideological enemy.

Humanism, of course, was an old philosophy, associated particularly with the Renaissance and the classical ideals whose rebirth gave that era its name. As the term suggests, humanist thought focuses on human values and capabilities. Some outstanding Renaissance thinkers, such as Erasmus, were Christians who saw no conflict between a high view of God and a high view of humanity, since humans were the capstone of God's glorious creation, made in his image and designed for dominion over the earth. Other humanists, however, saw little need for God. In modern usage, many who speak of themselves as humanists (with a small "h") place a high value on enduring human values, scientific knowledge, and cultivation of literature, arts, and philosophy, without feeling the need to reject all religious authority or deny the existence of God. Those who pointedly identify themselves as Humanists, however, are quite likely to have no room in their scheme for the divine, though they may regard themselves as religious; those who answer to "secular humanist" explicitly reject the existence of God or gods, and profess to feel no need for religion. The secular humanist view is epitomized in the *Humanist Manifesto*, first issued in 1933, then revised and reissued in 1973, and signed by a number of prominent educators, including John Dewey, and other leaders. This document, to which evangelicals have paid far more attention than most other Americans, asserts that "the traditional dogmatic or authoritarian religions that place revelation, God, ritual or creed above human needs and experience do a disservice to the human species. . . ."

Though Francis Schaeffer held a high view of humanity and insisted that Christians should feel at home in God's world and should embrace and transform every realm of culture, he felt secular humanists commit a calamitous error by failing to acknowledge God as their Creator and Sovereign and, as a consequence, by surrendering belief in absolute standards of right and wrong. He was convinced that this surrender to secularity, this abandonment of belief in transcendent reality, would lead humankind to a dreadful future devoid of ethical and moral restraint. *How Should We Then Live?* laid out Schaeffer's thesis, warned Christians of the dangers threatening their children, their churches, and their world, and urged them to take appropriate action to turn society from its headlong plunge into self-destruction. Mel White, who was called in to rescue the project when it seemed about to fall apart, does not regard the films as especially compelling. "Francis was all

over the place," he observed, "philosophically, ideologically, theologically. I never could follow him. I still can't. But it was the first time that evangelicals started looking at the world issues of hunger and pain and war and nationalism and race and so forth. It wasn't what he said but what he was talking about that made the difference."

As fundamentalists and evangelicals saw Schaeffer's films and read his numerous books, secular humanism came to be regarded not simply as an increasingly widespread way of looking at the world, but as a coherent movement diabolically bent on luring their children into every sort of immorality and unbelief in the course of undermining America's moral and spiritual foundations. This view was abetted by a 1961 Supreme Court decision in which Justice Hugo Black included secular humanism among "religions in this country which do not teach what would generally be considered a belief in the existence of God." That a search for churches or other meeting halls belonging to this destructive sect is likely to prove fruitless can be seen as another sign of its cleverness. According to their despisers, secular humanists, like communists before them, perform their work in ways so subtle that only those with eyes to see and ears to hear can recognize and resist their blandishments. The results, according to this view, are patently obvious. In the words of a "Special Report on Secular Humanism vs. Christianity," published in a Christian magazine, "To understand humanism is to understand women's liberation, the ERA, gay rights, children's rights, abortion, sex education, the 'new' morality, evolution, values clarification, situational ethics, the separation of church and state, the loss of patriotism, and many of the other problems that are tearing America apart today."

Schaeffer popularized the idea of secular humanism as a destructive, anti-Christian religion in his twenty-plus books, which sold an estimated three million copies before his death in 1984. His ideas gained their greatest exposure, however, through his influence on other men who had access to even larger audiences. In the late seventies, Tim LaHaye regularly gave extensive attention to secular humanism in his and his wife Beverly's two-day Family Life Seminars for Christian couples. In 1980, he turned these into a book, *Battle for the Mind,* which went on to become a best-seller. LaHaye's book was important in that it described secular humanism and its dangers in terms easily grasped by people to whom Schaeffer's more difficult prose, abstract conceptions, and wide-ranging illustrations posed more of a challenge. By the time *Battle for the Mind* appeared, however, the term was already in widespread use, and no one had done more to popularize it than Jerry Falwell.

Though lacking a broad liberal education, Falwell is an intelligent man, and found Schaeffer's efforts to broaden the intellectual horizons of conservative Christians appealing. He invited Schaeffer to visit Liberty University on several occasions and instituted a practice, still in force, of requiring every freshman student to see and discuss the film, *How Should We Then Live?* Schaeffer urged Falwell to make Liberty a kind of fundamentalist Harvard, equipping its students to defend the faith against the strongest assaults the larger academic community and intellectual world could offer. Falwell took this challenge quite seriously for a while. In recent years, however, he has replaced his ambition to have Liberty equal Harvard in academic achievement with the more modest goal of fielding a Division I football team capable of beating Notre Dame and Brigham Young. As a Liberty official explained, "We want to be to that fundamentalist or evangelical young man or woman what Notre Dame is to young Catholics and Brigham Young is to young Mormons: the place to go, the school that stands for excellence in every area. Since Dr. Schaeffer's death, I see Dr. Falwell's goals as being much broader than just academic elitism."

OF MORE LASTING impact than his effort to shape Liberty University was Schaeffer's increasing emphasis on the need for evangelicals to plunge into the public arena and try to redirect the course the nation was taking. In the late 1970s, Schaeffer urged Falwell to use the recognition he had gained through his popular television program, *Old Time Gospel Hour,* to draw more evangelicals into political activity. When Falwell expressed doubts that there were enough evangelical Christians to change the nation, Schaeffer snapped, "Listen, God used pagans to do his work in the Old Testament, so why don't you use pagans to do your work now?" The two men then discussed the concept of cobelligerency, by which they meant aligning themselves with people who might differ with them theologically or on certain key issues, but who were willing to fight on the same side in pursuit of specific goals. To veteran politicians, this was an old idea; to fundamentalists accustomed to severing ties over the smallest of disagreements, it was revolutionary.

The notion of using his influence for political purposes was not entirely new for Falwell. Ed Dobson, one of Falwell's closest aides during most of the 1970s, remembered how surprised the preacher was when Jody Powell called to register a complaint about Falwell's criticism of Jimmy Carter's *Playboy* interview. "In my opinion," Dobson volunteered, "that was a catalytic triggering event. He was very surprised that what he said on a religious television program would be watched by the Democratic political campaign and that they would in fact respond to it." The next year, Falwell branched out a bit further when he answered Anita Bryant's request for help in her crusade to repeal a gay-rights ordinance in Dade County, Florida. He not only invited Bryant to appear on the *Old Time Gospel Hour,* but staged an anti-gay rally in the Miami convention center. Falwell had little difficulty entering this battle since, like many fundamentalists, he regarded homosexuality as unspeakably evil, in the same category with rape, adultery, and incest. In keeping with that view, after the assassination of San Francisco Mayor George Moscone and Supervisor Harvey Milk, the city's first openly homosexual elected official, Falwell told his television audience that the murders, committed by a man who acknowledged that opposition to homosexuality had prompted his action, were a judgment from God.

Since *Playboy* and homosexuality both came under the heading of morality, Falwell may hardly have imagined that by criticizing them he was engaging in political action. Nevertheless, when he and his fellow religious broadcasters stirred up enough response to cause the IRS to back down on its proposed regulation of private schools in 1978, and to stall ratification of the ERA, Falwell realized he was moving into new territory, and he liked the lay of the land. He also recognized he was not alone. He and his friends and fellow broadcasters Charles Stanley, D. James Kennedy, and James Robison had discussed ways they might respond to what they regarded as a growing crisis in American life, a crisis they viewed as a serious threat to Judeo-Christian values, and they were beginning to take action. By spring of 1979, Stanley, pastor of the First Baptist Church in Atlanta, had already sent hundreds of thousands of viewers a videotape of his sermon, "Stand Up, America," in which he had urged Christians to become more active in politics. Kennedy, pastor of Coral Presbyterian Church in Florida, was also introducing more political content into his widely televised sermons. And down in Texas, Baptist evangelist Robison was engaged in a fight for his preaching life.

Robison, at thirty-one, was a big, raw-boned, ruggedly handsome, compelling speaker regarded by many as among the very best "crusade evangelists" in America. He had launched a weekly television program at the specific urging of Billy Graham, who regarded him as a major preaching talent. Robison had been conceived in a sex act forced upon his mother and spent most of his childhood in abysmal circumstances. The struggle to overcome that background left its mark. Though he could be gentle and genuinely funny, he was an obvious fighter who often displayed such ferocity in his attacks on sin that he was sometimes referred to as "God's Angry Man."

Robison traces his politicization to February 1979, when Dallas's ABC affiliate, WFAA, decided to pull his nationally syndicated television program from its lineup after he charged that gays sometimes recruit children to participate in homosexual behavior. "It hurt me deeply when they did that," he recalled. "I went to them and said, 'This won't be accepted. I wish you hadn't done it.' It became a rallying point. Catholics, Church of Christ, Jews, every religious segment said, 'This is wrong. This man has spoken on a moral issue he feels strongly about, and you've taken him off the air.' I designed a bumper sticker that said 'Freedom of Speech, the Right to Preach,' and it just went everywhere. We held a rally that overflowed the Dallas Convention Center. Dr. Falwell was there. Dr. Criswell introduced me, and he looked right at the WFAA cameras—they had a microwave feed right to the station—and he said, 'Channel 8, go look at the people whose cause you champion.' The people at the station told me later that they just about got under the table. They said, 'My goodness, they're going to come carry this station off, brick by brick.' And to be honest with you, the potential for that kind of thing was there. They had pushed good, caring people too far, and there was a ground swell of people saying, 'Everybody else is coming out of the closet; let's come out from under the pew, stand up, and take this country back.' Big advertisers told me they would stop advertising on Channel 8 or in the *Dallas Morning News*. I'm talking about millions of dollars in advertising. And then Mary Crowley [a prominent Dallas businesswoman] and a lot of fine women from First Baptist Church in Dallas surrounded Channel 8 and said, 'Put the man back on.' Well, they put me back on. As I look back, probably more than anything else, that incident caused me to realize that we could in fact lose our freedom to preach and speak publicly."

The Dallas rally did more than get Robison back on the air. It put him in touch with Paul Weyrich and Howard Phillips, who showed up at the urging of Ed McAteer, who felt they needed to meet the evangelist. "They looked at me that night," Robison recalled, "and said, 'This is the beginning.' And they were crying. Here's Howard Phillips, a Jew, and he's crying. He says, 'This is the hope to turn our nation back to the values upon which it was built—these people, this kind of attitude.' Again, I didn't know these men, but something really happened." Indeed it did. A few months later, when McAteer founded the Religious Roundtable, with a view toward mobilizing Southern Baptists and other mainstream evangelicals, Robison would become its primary public spokesman. On the West Coast, Robert Grant and Richard Zone, with cooperation from Robert Billings, ran Christian Voice, a group that described itself as working toward a "Christian majority in a Christian Democracy" and was most effective among the Assemblies of God and other Pentecostal denominations. From time to time, it gained notoriety for issuing "Biblical Scorecards" that rated legislators according to their stand on a list of issues of interest to Christian conservatives. The remaining aggregate of Christian conservatives to be targeted were various independent Baptist bodies and an ever-growing number of one-shot fundamentalist "Bible churches." Mobilizing that sector required a visit to Lynchburg.

Several versions of the story exist, but the essentials seem reasonably clear. Falwell had told McAteer of his budding political interest, but, according to

Weyrich, "he didn't know what he wanted to do and he certainly didn't know how to do it." In May 1979, Weyrich, Phillips, McAteer, and Robert Billings met Falwell at the Holiday Inn in Lynchburg and told him what role they thought he could play. At McAteer's suggestion, Weyrich began the conversation: "I said, 'Out there is what one might call a moral majority—people who would agree on principles based on the Decalogue [the Ten Commandments], for example—but they have been separated by geographical and denominational differences and that has caused them to vote differently. The key to any kind of political impact is to get these people united in some way, so they can see that they are battling the same thing and need to be unified.' Falwell stopped me and said, 'Go back to what you said earlier.' I misinterpreted him and started to say something, and he said, 'No, no. You started out by saying that there is something out there . . . what did you call that?' I had to think of what I had said, and finally I said, 'Oh, I said there is a moral majority.' And he said, 'That's it!' And he turned to his guy and said, 'That's the name of the organization.' And that's how Moral Majority got its name."

The remainder of the conversation dealt with issues on which such an organization could focus, with abortion at the head of the list, and on plans to influence the Republican platform in 1980. According to Falwell biographer Dinesh D'Souza, Weyrich believed that a strong anti-abortion plank in the platform would attract many Catholic voters who normally voted Democratic. A few weeks later, in June 1979, Moral Majority officially came into being, with headquarters in Washington. Charles Stanley, James Kennedy, Tim LaHaye, and Greg Dixon, pastor of the Baptist Temple in Indianapolis, joined Falwell on its board. Robert Billings was named executive director.

When Falwell broke the news of his plans to key members of his staff at Thomas Road, not everyone was pleased. Ed Dobson remembered that one associate "begged him not to do it, that he would be departing from the Gospel, he'd be wandering off the path, it'd be the worst thing he could do. When this person got through with his impassioned appeal, Jerry said, 'Well, I appreciate what you say, but this is what I'm going to do.' You have to understand how Dr. Falwell historically has operated. My observation is that the deterioration of American culture compelled him to do something, and he did it before he thought through precisely what he was going to do. I don't know if it was a Monday or a Thursday or a Saturday, but one morning he woke up and said, 'If not me, then who? And if not now, when?' and decided he had to do something. And then we all woke up one morning and realized we had founded the Moral Majority. It was kind of a 'ready, fire, aim' approach. No one sat around for a lengthy period of time to discuss it, to analyze it, to come up with an ideology. I think Jerry was politically naïve. I don't think he had any anticipation of where it would go, but there was a clear sense of a window of opportunity to deal with the issues [that concerned us]."

Not long afterward, in *Listen, America!* a book designed to articulate the new organization's rationale and purpose, Falwell characterized Moral Majority as "pro-life, pro-family, pro-moral, and pro-American." (Similar lists often added "pro-Israel," a reflection of the dispensationalist premillennial view that a complete restoration of the nation of Israel, including the rebuilding of the temple, is a prerequisite to the Second Coming.) He explained that the organization's work would fall into three categories: Registration, Information, and Mobilization. Citing a report that eight million evangelicals were not registered to vote, he declared such dereliction of civic duty to be "one of the major sins of the church today" and urged pastors to help eradicate it. (In personal appearances, he would inevitably draw laughs by describing a minister's duty as "getting people saved, baptized, and registered to vote.") Under the rubric of Information, Falwell wrote that Moral Majority's goal would be

> to exert a significant influence on the spiritual and moral direction of our nation by: (a) mobilizing the grassroots of moral Americans in one clear and effective voice; (b) informing the moral majority what is going on behind their backs in Washington and in state legislatures across the country; (c) lobbying intensively in Congress to defeat left-wing, social-welfare bills that will further erode our precious freedom; (d) pushing for positive legislation such as that to establish the Family Protection Agency, which will ensure a strong, enduring America; and (e) helping the moral majority in local communities to fight pornography, homosexuality, the advocacy of immorality in school textbooks, and other issues facing each and every one of us.

In a related listing of major evils threatening America, Falwell also named abortion, divorce, and secular humanism. As for Mobilization, he urged Christians who shared Moral Majority's views to become familiar with the way government works, from the precinct to the presidency; to make their views known to relevant public officials; to attend precinct, county, and state meetings of political parties; and to consider becoming a delegate to party conventions.

Falwell recognized that riding into the political arena in such a visible vehicle constituted a direct challenge to fundamentalist pietism, which traditionally manifested itself not only in disciplined devotional practice and strict standards of personal morality, but also in a general stance of separation from "the world." As Dobson explained, pietists felt that "the political world—the public square—should not be part of a Christian's priority. Our priority is to love God and to love our neighbor. Forget about politics. That pietistic idea was predominant in the mind of the average person in the average pew in a fundamentalist church in America. The miracle of the Moral Majority was that, in just a matter of months, that whole concept was shattered, and [fundamentalists] began registering to vote and getting involved." In accounting for this remarkable shift in attitude, Dobson made a telling observation: "Fundamentalists are absolutist on issues and moral principles, but the fundamentalist movement has always been innovative in its methodology—willing to try new things, do new things, break old stereotypes, because we're not bound by centuries of tradition. That carried over into politics. There was an underlying pragmatism that asked, 'How can we ultimately accomplish our goals?' "

Falwell agreed that pragmatism was crucial to the stunning triumph over pietistic separatism and helped him cancel the effect of his earlier criticisms of ministers who participated in the civil rights movement. "I had preached many, many sermons at pastors' conventions," he admitted, "saying, 'Fellows, don't lead marches; don't get involved politically; focus on your pulpit; don't get caught up in the [temporary causes] of the day.' Later, when I got into politics personally, it was morally necessary for me to say out loud that 'I have misled you on that issue. I never thought the government would go so far afield, I never thought the politicians would become so untrustworthy, I never thought the courts would go so nuts to the left, and I misjudged the quality of government that we have. Our lack of involvement is probably one of the reasons why the country's in the mess it is in. We have defaulted by failing to show up for the fight.' It didn't take long. When you're honest about something and say, 'I was heading in the wrong direction, and you followed me; let's go in the right direction,' most will say, 'Let's do it.' "

FALWELL'S OWN CONGREGATION took his turnabout in stride. Some of the old-timers missed the comfort of having their pastor at home and on call, but most trusted his judgment. "I had the advantage," he said, "of being the founder of the church and their only pastor, and I'd led most of them to Christ, so it was a lot easier for me than for the average minister out there who had become pastor of an established congregation filled with people with diverse political leanings." He also had the advantage of being part of an ecclesiastical tradition—independent fundamentalist churches—that magnifies the power of the preacher. "God's plan," he liked to say, "is that his flock is to be led by shepherds, not by a board or committee." Nancy Godsey, one of the church's charter members, doubtless spoke for many when she said, "Somebody had to take a stand. I think Dr. Falwell was the one to do it because he gets his wisdom and knowledge from God.

That's why we're for him a hundred percent. It's not just his point of view. He goes back to God's word. None of us is perfect, and we don't worship Dr. Falwell, but we love him because he preaches the Bible. And right off the top of my head, I can't think of anything that he's ever tried to teach us that was wrong, because he is inspired of God, and we just trust him."

Ed Dobson believed Falwell's pastoral authority extended well beyond Thomas Road Baptist Church. A man like Paul Weyrich, he explained, could not have done what Falwell was about to do, "because he's not a pastor. Jerry Falwell understood that the only person who could beat the drum to get Christians out of their lethargy was a pastor. Christians tended not to listen to or were suspicious of people who didn't bring the authority that a pastor would bring. He understood that to garner a force of Christians for good probably required an ordained person."

Throughout the remainder of 1979 and 1980, and indeed for the next several years, Jerry Falwell spent most of his time on the road, traveling upwards of three hundred thousand miles per year, often speaking several times a day at churches, public gatherings, luncheons, dinners, and press conferences, and meeting privately with the network of people who were helping set up Moral Majority chapters throughout the country. Almost always, however, he swooped back into Lynchburg to preach at the Sunday service, which was the heart of his weekly television program. Keeping the television program going was vital not only as an evangelistic effort, but because Falwell constantly used it to raise money for Liberty University. In addition, of course, it played a major role in keeping him in touch with the very people he was trying to recruit into politics.

Since the bicentennial year of 1976, Falwell had been holding "I Love America" rallies on the steps of state capitols throughout the country. The rallies, which often drew thousands of people and dutiful coverage by local news media, featured a band and chorus of squeaky-clean Liberty students who performed rousing renditions of religio-patriotic songs, followed by a stirring Falwell jeremiad and call for national repentance and, typically, warm endorsements of the event by high-ranking state officials and other well-known local figures. Falwell characteristically concluded the rallies by quoting II Chronicles 7:14: "If my people which are called by my name, shall humble themselves and pray, and seek my face and turn from their wicked ways; then will I hear from heaven and will forgive their sin, and will heal their land." The rallies increased and legitimized Falwell's public stature. These gatherings were strategically more important after the founding of Moral Majority. Falwell usually invited all the pastors present—often several hundred—to a complimentary luncheon where he explained the rationale and strategy of the Moral Majority. He urged them to establish local chapters and to use their churches as a base for registering people to vote and providing them with basic information on such issues as abortion, pornography, homosexuality, and the ERA. Only the modest expense of the meal had to be paid for by nonexempt Moral Majority funds. Other costs were paid for by tax-exempt contributions from supporters of the *Old Time Gospel Hour* and Liberty University.

In his meetings with fundamentalist pastors, Falwell worked hard at breaking down their separatist impulses. He recalled, "When we announced that Moral Majority was a political organization, not a religious one, and that we welcomed Jews and Catholics and Protestants and Mormons and even non-religious people who shared our views on the family and abortion, strong national defense, and Israel, a great deal of opposition erupted inside our own ranks. [Arch-fundamentalist educator] Dr. Bob Jones thought it was the most heretical thing he'd ever heard of. And many, many pastors across the country in the evangelical/fundamentalist camp shuddered to think of sitting at the same table with a Roman Catholic or a Jew or, God forbid, a Mormon." Explicitly following and often citing Francis Schaeffer's notion of "cobelligerency," Falwell repeatedly stressed that "it is not a violation of your convictions, nor does it displease the Lord, for you to work with people who don't agree with you theologically, if in so doing you improve your country, improve your society, help families, and accomplish things collectively that you could not have accomplished apart from each other." It was a big barrier to bring down, he said, but "it didn't take very long. After one year of Moral Majority's explosion, our people realized that this is what the opposition had been doing all along. To move them away from single-issue politics into collective negotiating and bargaining was about a one-year process, but it's been done, and it doesn't have to be done again."

Perhaps even more effective and efficient than his personal appearances was Falwell's use of direct mail. At the Holiday Inn meeting, Falwell had spoken of the seven million families on his mailing list—perhaps an exaggeration, since his regular audience comprised less than a million families—and of similar lists controlled by other television preachers. This was no revelation to Richard Viguerie and his colleagues. They were fully aware that such lists existed, but access to them had been difficult. Both to protect their supporters from appeals for causes inconsistent with their own, and to protect their list from poaching by competitors, most of the larger ministries would not share their list with others. John Conlan observed that Viguerie and other conservative direct-mail experts had never been able to tap the Christian market. "They couldn't get into Billy Graham's list, and they couldn't get into others," he said, "so Jerry became a very convenient vehicle for them."

Direct mail is expensive and often turns little actual profit for anyone other than the mailing company, but it can be effective as a self-supporting means to advertise, raise consciousness, and create constituencies. It also enables its users to say things they could not easily say in more public media. Viguerie has likened it to having a water moccasin for a watchdog: It is quiet, deadly, and leaves no tracks. By using his huge list, Falwell was able to warn his followers that "our Grand Old Flag is going down the drain" and "we are losing the war against homosexuals," citing as proof of both the news that "gays were recently given permission to lay a wreath on the Tomb of the Unknown Soldier at Arlington Cemetery to honor any sexual deviants who served in the military. That's right—the gays were allowed to turn our Tomb of the Unknown soldier into: THE TOMB OF THE UN-KNOWN SODOMITE!" Another favorite tactic was to send questionnaires that were to be returned, along with a donation, then passed along to members of Congress. The following questions were typical:

> "Are you in favor of your tax dollar being used to support abortion on demand?"
> "Do you agree that voluntary prayer should be banned from the public schools?"
> "Do you believe that smut peddlers should be protected by the courts and the Congress, so they can openly sell pornographic materials to your children?"
> "Should school systems that receive federal funds be forced to hire known practicing and soliciting homosexual teachers?"
> "Do you approve of American flags being burned in liberal and radical anti-American demonstrations?"
> "Do you approve of the ratification of the Equal Rights Amendment, which could lead to homosexual marriages, unisexual bathrooms, and the drafting of women into combat?"

Decorated with flags and made vivid with capital letters and extensive red underlining, the letters were not geared to stimulating thoughtful reflection.

Such tactics proved remarkably effective. By September 1979, Falwell claimed to have contacted seventy-two thousand preachers and acquainted them with Moral Majority and its purposes, and provided them with materials that would help them explain to their flocks why fundamentalists had to change their old attitude toward politics and register to vote.

WHILE JERRY FALWELL took the lead, several well-known colleagues gathered in Dallas for two days of prayer and discussion. James Robison described the meeting as "one of the most significant things that ever happened in the life of our country." As Robison told it, "Bill Bright called and said that he and Billy Graham had talked, and that they had a great concern for the future of our country. He said there were ten or twelve of us they wanted to meet with at a hotel by the Dallas–Fort Worth airport. [Prominent Southern Baptist pastors] Charles Stanley and Adrian Rogers were coming, Pat Robertson, Rex Humbard, some others. I asked if I could bring my pastor, Dr. Jimmy Draper, who later became president of the Southern Baptist Convention, and he came too. Clayton Bell [Billy Graham's brother-in-law] from the Highland Park Presbyterian Church came in and visited with us for a few hours." (Robison could not remember why Jerry Falwell was not present.)

The men discussed what they saw going wrong with America: moral decay, negative trends in entertainment, the continuing threat of rapacious communism, loss of spiritual values, complacency on the part of Christians. "There was a broken, contrite heart on the part of those who attended," Robison remembered. In what seems to have been the critical point of the gathering, "Billy Graham said, 'I believe God has shown me that unless we have a change in America, we have a thousand days as a free nation . . . three years.' Bill Bright said, 'I know. . . . I do not believe we'll survive more than three years as a free nation. It's that serious.' And Pat Robertson said, 'I believe the same thing.' Charles Stanley was standing there and I can just remember so well, he put his hand down on the table with resolve and said, 'I'll give my life to stop this. I'll give everything I've got to turn this country.' And I said, 'Me too. I'll die to turn this country. Whatever it takes. We can't lose the country.' And each man around the room said, 'We're going to get involved.' Except Rex Humbard. He said, 'I'm uncomfortable politically. I really am very uncomfortable.' And Dr. Graham said, 'I cannot publicly be involved. I can only pray. I've been burned so badly with the public relationships I've had. I can't afford it, but I care so much.' We had an awesome time of prayer; it was one of the most moving things I've ever seen. All of those men would definitely remember how vitally important those two days of prayer were, because I'm telling you, we came out of that meeting determined. Determined. It's possible that few people have ever had more positive effect on a country than those men in that room."

Charles Stanley began to fulfill the pledge he had made at the Dallas gathering by inviting scores of Georgia preachers to meet at his church for a "Campaign Training Conference" at which Paul Weyrich, among others, would show them how they could register their flocks to vote and insert them into the political process without jeopardizing their churches' tax exemption. Weyrich remembered it as a singular occasion. "It was an odd gathering because the speakers were a professor from Notre Dame, an Anglican priest, and me. So you had a high-church Anglican, a Roman Catholic, and a Greek Catholic addressing a group of Baptist ministers who were effusive in their 'amen-ing.' I had [newspaper columnist] Bob Novak with me and he was absolutely in a state of shock. It was at that moment, he told me, that he decided Carter was going to lose, because minister after minister stood up and said, 'I was part of Carter's team in 1976. I delivered my congregation for Carter. I urged them all to vote for Carter because I thought he was a moral individual. I found out otherwise, and I'm angry.' This was months before the election, and Novak said, 'I decided at that point that Jimmy Carter's goose was cooked because I saw the intensity of those people.' That was really an extraordinary moment. At one point, something was said about baptism, and Paige Patterson, who is now very big in the Southern Baptist Church, and some of his buddies lifted me up, physically, and started to carry me backwards to dunk me in the baptismal well there in the church. It was a humorous moment, and all the guys in the audience were cheering. But it was all done in good fun. It was a remarkable day, really."

By November 1979, the conservative Christian infatuation with Jimmy Carter was indeed quite over. Some, such as Falwell, had kept up a drumbeat of criticism and mockery, much of which appealed to the pietist sense of personal holiness, as when he volunteered the following observation on White House hospitality: "I don't know why every one of our presidents thinks he has to wine and dine every drunk who comes over here from some other country and dance with his wife. It seems to me that if a president is a Christian, he can offer that foreign head of state some orange juice or tomato juice, have a good minister come in and read a few verses of Scripture, and if he doesn't like that, put him on the next plane home." Laughing at such memories, Thomas Road Baptist Church member Bill Godsey acknowledged that his pastor "had a good time with Jimmy Carter during that period. Some of it was honest and, well, Jerry has a sense of humor and is full of practical jokes, and I think sometimes things come out of his mouth that, if he could go get them again, he would do it and rephrase them. I don't think he really disliked Jimmy Carter personally, but Carter practiced a version of Christianity that, if you used the term 'liberal,' you would probably be close to what he was, and that was not popular with evangelicals and fundamentalists. That got him into trouble with Jerry and the people who were with him at that particular time." But disenchantment with Carter was not the only force leading inexorably to political divorce. Fully as important was a budding romance with Ronald Reagan.

Though defeated in his efforts to replace Gerald Ford as the Republican nominee in 1976, Reagan had never stopped running, and he had a plan he believed could overcome the strong resistance to him within his own party. Reagan understood that Richard Nixon had won the presidency by using a "Southern Strategy" that involved both explicit and coded appeals—to segregationist sentiments, to resentment of federal interference in state and local institutions, to anxieties over changes in traditional social and moral norms—that caused many Democrats to cross long-honored lines to cast Republican votes. He also understood that a major reason Gerald Ford had lost the presidency in 1976 was Jimmy Carter's ability to use another set of appeals to drag many of those same voters back into Democratic ranks. The implication was obvious: To win the presidency, Reagan would have to put together a coalition of people who normally voted Republican and another group of people who were conservative but who normally voted Democratic. Given that premise, avid courtship of Christian conservatives would be essential.

Reagan's record would seem to have marked him as an unlikely suitor. He had divorced and remarried, his performance as a parent was clearly subpar, his children were hardly models of fundamentalist piety, and he had won his first fame in the movie and television industries, both regularly excoriated for their contribution to moral decay. As governor of California, he had signed relatively liberal abortion measures and had opposed legislation that would have barred homosexuals from teaching jobs. His 1979 tax return revealed that he contributed less than one percent of his adjusted gross income to charitable and religious causes. And, though reared in the Disciples of Christ by an ardently devout mother, he was not a regular churchgoer and would surely have been soundly defeated by Jimmy Carter in the "Sword Drills," contests Southern Baptist youngsters used to sharpen and show off their knowledge of Scripture. Reagan had met Billy Graham in the 1950s and they had discussed Bible prophecy during his tenure as governor, but evangelical shibboleths did not trip lightly off his tongue. Charles Colson remembered an incident when, during the 1976 primary campaign, a reporter held a copy of Colson's new book up to Reagan's face and asked, "Are you born again?" According to Colson, "Reagan shrugged, like the fellow had landed from Mars. He didn't know what he meant."

By 1979, Reagan had learned how to answer such questions. His longtime aide Michael Deaver remembered an incident in a Fort Worth mall, when a young woman approached the candidate and asked him point-blank, "Do you believe?" Reagan, Deaver said, "must have seen this fervor in her face, and he said, 'Yes, I do.' She said, 'No, I mean do you really believe?' And Reagan very seriously looked her right in the eye and said, 'Yes, I do.' There was something about Reagan that made you know it was in his bones." Some cynics suspected it was only in his script, but no one doubted he knew how to play the role this time around. *New York Times* religion reporter Kenneth Briggs observed that "Reagan very definitely played to the evangelical constituency, and did it rather skillfully. He had a feel for who evangelical people were and what they valued, and I think he spoke very directly and effectively to those people. I don't recall his identification with a 'born-again' experience as such, but he played the themes—the personal-morality themes, his opposition to abortion, his emphasis on the family. There were lots of ways in which, through direct address and perhaps through some code words, he conveyed to them that he was one of them, and that they could count on him to deliver what they were looking for in their national life and in their community life. So it was very clear that he knew where he was going with that group. And he got there. He was very successful."

Knowing the code could be crucial. John Conlan told of a gathering of evangelical leaders John Connally assembled on his South Texas ranch in the summer of 1979 for the purpose of persuading them to support Connally in 1980. At this point, many evangelicals regarded Connally as an extremely attractive alternative to Reagan, even though he upset Falwell and others by asserting that the main reason the U.S. should support Israel was to protect access to Mid-East oil, as if fulfillment of biblical prophecy was not even a consideration. During the discussion, James Kennedy asked, "If you were to die tomorrow, Governor, and you wanted to go to heaven, what reason would you give God for letting you in?" According to Conlan, "Connally said, 'Well, my mother was a Methodist, my pappy was a Methodist, my grandmother was a Methodist, and I'd just tell him I ain't any worse than any of the other people that want to get into heaven.' Well, that fell like a stone on all these Christian leaders." Shortly afterward, Conlan invited many of the same people to visit with Reagan at the Capitol Hilton hotel in Washington. When Kennedy asked the same question, "Reagan dropped his eyes, looked at his feet, and said, 'I wouldn't give God any reason for letting me in. I'd just ask for mercy, because of what Jesus Christ did for me at Calvary.' And, hey, BOOM! To a man and woman in that room, they said 'Let's go!' and they went all out for him."

Television preachers were by no means the only conservative Christians to convert to the Reagan cause. Conlan told of a time during the primary campaign, when Michael Deaver told him the Reagan organization was running out of money and asked him to help. "So I brought in about fifty top Christian businessmen from around the country who committed to raise ten grand, or half a million, for Reagan, to tide him over and help get him through the Iowa primaries. Most of these men were participating for the first time, and about eighty percent of them fulfilled their commitment. That was just the beginning. They helped out and then asked what else they could do. So I took a leaf out of the liberals' page—bless their hearts, they're innovative too—and we used non-profit foundation money to register voters we thought would go our way. Now if you wanted to do the same thing today, and you had an outstanding candidate with solid Christian moral values, there are five thousand Christian businessmen and women around the country who could easily raise ten grand apiece and put a $50 million kitty together."

Reagan also did well with nonevangelicals who were not normally attracted to Republican candidates, but found his message resonant. Faith Whittlesey, an avid Reagan backer who would eventually hold a key White House post, remembered having trouble recruiting her neighbors on the Philadelphia Main Line to work for Reagan, "but in blue-collar areas, we had people lining up to make phone calls for him. They sensed that he had a belief in the wisdom and good sense of ordinary people. He wasn't patronizing. He honestly wanted to explain to the lowest person in the country why he thought his solution was the right one. That's the dichotomy in the Republican Party that exists to this day: Wall Street vs. Main Street. That struggle goes on, but Ronald Reagan was able to bring the two together, because he could relate to ordinary people in a way that the Republican establishment could not and never would."

JERRY FALWELL AND his cobelligerents may have been drawn into politics by issues clearly related to "family values," but they quickly fleshed out their platforms to include positions not ordinarily dealt with in Sunday School. Both Moral Majority and Christian Voice went on record as opposing the strategic arms limitation treaty (SALT II), economic sanctions against Rhodesia, abrogation of the U.S. military treaty with Taiwan, and relinquishing control of the Panama Canal. On the positive side, they regularly lined up in favor of increased spending for national defense. In *Listen, America!,* Falwell lamented that, whereas the United States could have destroyed much of the population of the USSR just ten years earlier, "the sad fact is that [in an exchange of missiles] today the Soviet Union would kill 135 million to 160 million Americans, and the United States would kill only three to five percent of the Soviets because of their antiballistic missiles and their civil defense."

Falwell associate Elmer Towns offered a rationale for such forays into extra-ecclesiastical territory. "In the late seventies," he said, "the threat of communism was great, whether it was seen as a 'hot' war or an undermining action to take over this country by giving away our freedoms and our rights, including the freedom to preach and the freedom to have a church and be separate and be different. Now whether that was real or not, it was perceived as real by fundamentalist people. We felt a threat. We really had a fortress mentality: 'Let's hang on. We are losing ground every day to society, to the world, to bureaucracy, to the federal government.' It was a very real threat, and Falwell had an easy time rallying people for a strong America."

Jody Powell regarded such talk as either hypocritical cant or ignorant rationalization. "Our principal problem with the Reverend Falwell and the leaders of that very politicized religious movement on the right," he said, "was that we were not dealing with honorable people. Whatever their motivation may have been, I think it's obvious in retrospect that religion either fell into or was delivered into the hands of people who had a rather clear political agenda. Inevitably, when religion allows itself to become the handmaiden of politicians, more damage is done to the church than to the government. Nothing gives more comfort to the hardened skeptic or unbeliever than to have religious leaders chasing around the country invoking God's name on behalf of what are clearly secular causes. I remember Mr. Falwell and his crowd, in the name of Christianity, attacking people who had voted against the B-1 bomber, for heaven's sake! That is not [an issue] on which I could imagine the good Lord took a position."

Powell was not alone in questioning Jerry Falwell's honor. At a January 1980 White House breakfast described by Tim LaHaye, Falwell had asked permission to tape the discussion. Robert Maddox, Carter's liaison to the religious community, had arranged the meeting and readily granted his request, but had an aide record it as well, as a precautionary measure. Not long afterward, at a Moral Majority rally in Alaska, Falwell told a large audience, "I was at the White House not long ago and I asked the president, 'Sir, why do you have homosexuals on your senior staff in the White House?' " As Falwell told it, Carter had said that since he wanted to represent everyone, he had to hire some homosexuals. The story apparently drew the reaction Falwell wanted in Alaska, and he subsequently printed it in the *Moral Majority Report*. The problem was that the conversation had never occurred. A Carter supporter who had been present at the Anchorage rally obtained a tape of Falwell's speech and sent it to Bob Maddox, who complained to Falwell's associates about the false allegation. Maddox remembered that, "at first his people said, 'No, he didn't say that.' Then I played them the tape and they said, 'Oh my God, that is Jerry saying that.' " Maddox saw to it that several newspapers, including the *New York Times* and the *Dallas Morning News* got transcripts of both the breakfast discussion and Falwell's sermon. When confronted with the evidence by veteran reporters, Falwell tried to excuse his action by characterizing what he had said as a "parable" or "allegory," which Southern Baptist James Dunn called "a new name for a lie." Maddox recalled his hope that the incident would cast Falwell into "utter and everlasting ill repute, which it did not, but it did cause some doubts about him, because it made the national news. For a few days it was everywhere that Falwell had plainly lied about the meeting with the president."

Though less controversial than Falwell, James Robison also continued to make news, addressing twenty-eight thousand anti-abortion marchers at a

March for Life in Washington and appearing on *60 Minutes, Bill Moyers' Journal, Donahue,* Tom Snyder's *Tomorrow,* and the *700 Club.* More significantly, he took a prominent role in "Washington for Jesus," a mass rally he described as "one of the first times that mainline denominations joined hands with charismatics and Pentecostals and said, 'Let's stand up together.' That was significant. That was sort of a coming together of a lot of different groups." Bill Bright and eight religious broadcasters, including charismatics John Gimenez (who first suggested such a gathering be held), Pat Robertson, Jim Bakker, and Demos Shakarian (the leading figure in the Full Gospel Businessmen's Fellowship International), and evangelicals D. James Kennedy, Adrian Rogers, Charles Stanley, and Robison used their television programs, mailing lists, and personal contacts to persuade people from all over the nation to gather for a day-long prayer meeting on the Mall on April 29, the anniversary of the date in 1607 when the first settlers landed at Jamestown and erected a cross on the Virginia coast to symbolize their determination to dedicate their new homeland to God.

Conspicuously missing from the leadership ranks was Jerry Falwell, who reportedly had doubted the event could succeed and feared a small turnout would make his movement seem ineffectual. Falwell miscalculated. The event drew at least two hundred thousand people and, by some estimates, the crowd exceeded five hundred thousand, which was not only larger than the March on Washington that featured Martin Luther King's famous "I have a dream" speech, but, if true, made it the largest public gathering ever held in Washington to that point. The success of the march convinced Pat Robertson, apparently for the first time, of "the potential of a unified evangelical response to political problems," according to biographer David E. Harrell. However, despite the large turnout, "Washington for Jesus" drew little more than cursory attention from national news media, and a few months later, Pat Robertson decided to withdraw from the political arena, declaring that "active partisan politics is the wrong path for true evangelicals. . . . There's a better way, fasting and praying."

Before he stepped back from politics for a season, Robertson had observed that "sometimes the perception of power is equal to the reality of it, and if people perceive it's there, maybe we can have some influence." After years of having regarded television preachers as some kind of aberrant novelty act, the mainstream media not only began to give them unprecedented attention, but began to accord them even more influence than they apparently had. In 1979, National Religious Broadcasters executive director Ben Armstrong asserted that approximately 130 million people listened to religious radio and television programs every week. Subsequent studies showed the regular audience for religious programs to be about one-tenth that size, but in their haste to be exciting, all manner of major media publicized versions of Armstrong's exaggeration.

As the most visible of the television preachers, Jerry Falwell drew special attention; estimates of his audience ranged between six and thirty million. Falwell abetted such extravagant claims by estimating his audience at fifteen million, though he sometimes admitted he had no idea as to how many people actually watched. Similarly, publicists for James Robison claimed that his television show had a potential audience of fifty to sixty million people, failing to add that fewer than a million actually tuned in. Eventually, a closer look at Arbitron and Nielsen ratings—which had been available all along to any reporter who bothered to check them—revealed that no television preacher had an audience larger than 2.5 million, that the top four televangelists (Oral Roberts, Robert Schuller, Rex Humbard, and Jimmy Swaggart) included little or no politics in their programs, that the audience for Falwell's *Old Time Gospel Hour* stood at approximately 1.4 million, while James Robison drew less than six hundred thousand. Obviously, such numbers were not inconsequential, but the potential impact of the television preachers would depend more on organization, dedication, and diligence than on overwhelming numbers of viewers. Their resources in those areas were harder to overstate.

Whether accepting the numbers at face value or simply hedging their bets, the Republican Party did pay formal attention to the new members in its ranks, as well as to Goldwater-era hard-liners. At the July 1980 Republican convention, they overrode objections to having Henry Kissinger speak, but decided against a tribute to the late Nelson Rockefeller. In contrast to the Democratic platform, whose only reference to family issues was a single sentence pledging support to "efforts to make federal programs more sensitive to the needs of the family, in all its diverse forms," the GOP platform dropped earlier support of the ERA (to the decided displeasure of many party regulars), favored a constitutional amendment to outlaw abortion, and recommended that opposition to abortion be a prerequisite for an appointment to a federal judgeship, a stance Illinois Senator Charles Percy called "the worst plank that has ever been in a platform." In addition, party co-chair Mary Crisp was asked to step down because she supported the ERA.

Overall, however, the convention was an exercise in decorum and courtesy, in keeping with Pennsylvania Governor Richard Thornburgh's observation that, in contrast to 1964, Republicans had no desire to "leave the battlefield littered with the wounded from an ideological tong war." In his acceptance speech, Reagan played the role of healer, demonstrating that pragmatism in the service of politics is no vice. By his words and relaxed, reassuring demeanor, he assured his party and the nation that they could trust him to restore the nation to its God-ordained greatness. He ended the speech by asking, in an emotion-choked voice, for a moment of silent prayer. When he brought that pious pause to an end with the official benediction of the nation's civil religion, "God bless America," the throng rewarded him with a twenty-minute ovation. Party chairman Bill Brock accurately observed, "This party is a new party—we are on our way up."

"Pro-Family" forces did not imagine that Ronald Reagan's emergence as the Republican standard-bearer meant their job was over, particularly since it was clear that many establishment Republicans were scarcely more comfortable with him than they had been with Barry Goldwater in 1964. In midsummer, the *New York Times* reported that the leaders of approximately thirty family-issue organizations had joined to form the Library Court Group. Closely aligned with the Heritage Foundation, this group would conduct research, provide materials to legislators and activists, and exert a constant pressure on political leaders in a position to implement its programs.

The Reagan campaign did not take this religious regiment lightly. When Reagan appointed Mary Louise Smith, a former International Women's Year commissioner and a strong supporter of the ERA, to head his Women's Policy Board, the Library Court Group deluged his campaign headquarters with protests, moving him to compensate by establishing a Family Policy Advisory Board that would include staunch abortion foes Harold O. J. Brown and Illinois Congressman Henry Hyde, anti-feminists Lottie Beth Hobbs and Beverly LaHaye, and all-purpose Carter critic Connie Marshner.

ANY LINGERING HESITATION the New Evangelical Right had about backing Ronald Reagan was swept away on August 21 at the National Affairs Briefing, a Dallas event sponsored by the Religious Roundtable and led by James Robison, who described it as "something God put on my heart." Robison's plan, devised with the help of Ed McAteer, was to invite leading political figures, including Reagan, Carter, independent candidate John Anderson, and Henry Kissinger, to articulate their views in some detail before a large gathering of conservative Christian pastors and leading laypersons. When he broached the idea to Paul Weyrich and Howard Phillips, "They were blown out; even appalled." They talked him out of inviting Kissinger, and both Carter and Anderson declined, perhaps because they recognized their views would receive few endorsements from a list of speakers that included Weyrich, Phillips, McAteer, Robison, Phyllis Schlafly, Connie Marshner, Tim LaHaye, Jerry Falwell, Pat Robertson, Senator Jesse Helms, and Congressman Phillip Crane, not to mention Ronald Reagan. (Conspicuously absent were Billy Graham, Jim Bakker, Oral Roberts, Rex Humbard, and Robert Schuller, an enormously popular television preacher who sometimes wove patriotic themes into his basic "possibility thinking" message, but had not joined his theologically more conservative colleagues in their political adventure.)

In Robison's mind, Reagan's appearance was the key to the event's success, and no final date was set until he agreed to speak. The two-day conference attracted approximately twenty-five hundred pastors from forty-one states; for the major speeches, local church members joined them to fill Dallas's new seventeen-thousand-seat Reunion Arena. Robison and McAteer, however, never imagined that the event's impact would be limited to those physically present. Robison estimated that, when the assembled ministers' radio and television audiences were added to the numbers in their congregations, as many as fifty to sixty million potential voters were represented. While that number may have been a bit optimistic, the actual figure was unquestionably quite high. In addition, more than four hundred journalists, the major television networks, and a double handful of foreign correspondents were on hand to cover the event.

In addition to receiving more information about how to register and mobilize voters, conferees heard strongly worded depictions of America's sins and listened to last-chance exhortations on how to halt the country's disastrous decline by seizing the reins from the hands of treacherous secular humanists. They also attended sessions at which experts talked about such matters as the SALT II negotiations and America's military preparedness. But the conference received immediate and lasting fame from two brief statements, one negative and one positive, that rocketed around the nation. All who heard them, which was nearly everyone who was paying attention, pondered seriously the nature of this new political force.

The statement reported most widely outside evangelical circles was made by Dr. Bailey Smith, president of the Southern Baptist Convention. An engaging and popular pastor and evangelist, Smith offended millions of people when he observed, "It is interesting at great political rallies how you have a Protestant to pray, a Catholic to pray, and then you have a Jew to pray. With all due respect to those dear people, my friends, God Almighty does not hear the prayer of a Jew." Not surprisingly, Smith's comment was interpreted as an egregious example of anti-Semitism, but this was not quite accurate. Instead, it was more a manifestation of fundamentalist exclusiveness than of any particular animosity toward Jews. If Muslims, Buddhists, and Hindus were routinely invited to pray at American political rallies, Smith would doubtless have included them in the list of those to whom God is deaf. Note his own explanation of what he had said: "For how in the world can God hear the prayer of a man who says that Jesus Christ is not the true Messiah? That is blasphemy. It may be politically expedient, but no one can pray unless he prays through the name of Jesus Christ."

The last point is the operative one: One cannot reach God without going through Jesus. Had he been pressed, Smith—and if not he, then surely many in his audience—might seriously have doubted that Catholic prayers were any more efficacious than those of Jews. But whatever Bailey Smith's true feelings about Jews, underneath the scandalized public reaction was a legitimate concern: How can members of a pluralistic society be comfortable with a political movement whose leaders declare that they alone are on God's side?

The second pronouncement associated with the Dallas meeting was uttered by Ronald Reagan and was received far more positively. Though it garnered less immediate attention than Smith's notorious line, it was, in the judgment of many observers, the single most important statement of the entire campaign. As James Robison remembered, "Governor Connally and I picked Mr. Reagan up at the airport, and we had a private meeting with him. I told him that, since we could not and would not endorse him as a body, it would probably be wise if his opening comment would be, 'I know this is non-partisan, so you can't endorse me, but I want you to know that I endorse you.' Oh, he loved that. He wrote that down and said, 'That's great. I'm going to use it.' "

Realizing that Reagan's speech would be the high point of the briefing and would draw the largest crowd, Robison scheduled himself to give the speech just before Reagan's. He was remarkably candid about that decision: "It was my brainchild, and I really wanted to speak. I felt I could say what we were thinking about as effectively as anyone could, and I definitely desired that opportunity. A lot of other people wanted that opportunity and were unhappy they didn't get it, but you have to make decisions, and we made that one."

Robison was indeed in fine form that evening. In an earlier address, Pat Robertson, perhaps reconsidering his warnings against political involvement, had declared that God was telling Christians, "Be fruitful and multiply. Take dominion. Subdue the land in [His] name. We are to fight a war. Our weapon is faith. We are salt and we are light. We can move the hand of God in a mighty crusade of holiness." Robison was not to be topped. In one memorable passage, he announced, "The stage is set. We'll either have a Hitler-type takeover, or Soviet domination, or God is going to take over this country. It is time to crawl out from under the pews and stop looking through the stained-glass windows. . . . We've had enough talk. If we ever get our act together, the politicians won't have a stage to play on. We can turn to God or bring down the curtain. We can sound the charge or play taps." Such militaristic assertions of power led James Dunn to characterize Robertson, Robison, and colleagues as "egomaniacs who don't have a compassionate connection with people" and to charge that "we've got a bunch of TV preachers who want to establish a theocracy in America, and each one of them wants to be Theo."

Arizona Senator John Conlan was present that evening and remembered not only Robison's performance, but the reaction to it by Reagan aides Michael Deaver and Ed Meese. "James was making some real fiery statements," he recalled, "triggering the crowd, who would respond to him, and Mike Deaver and Meese were cringing and saying, 'Where the heck did that guy come from?'" *New York Times* reporter Kenneth Briggs saw it a bit differently. "James Robison is one of the most powerful preachers I've ever seen," he said. "He could preach the wax off chairs. He had people in the palm of his hands."

The crowd, accustomed to such preaching, loved it, and they noticed that Reagan apparently loved it too. The original plan had been for Reagan to wait backstage until it became time for him to speak, but Connally and others urged him to go out and sit on the platform. Robison explained that "Governor Connally told Mr. Reagan, 'I'd like you to hear James. You're going to really like this. And it will say a lot to people to watch how you respond to the values he's going to emphasize. Your countenance is going to do a lot.' Well, Deaver was very upset about that. He said, 'You can't go out there on the platform.' But out he came, and he sat there and he clapped, and that said a lot to people. I was talking but they were watching him, and he responded in a way that made people think, 'He agrees with some of these things that are important to us.' Then he gave a wonderful speech, and he opened with 'You can't endorse me, but I endorse you.' Well, you can imagine what that did for caring, traditional-values people. He endorsed us. It was a big impetus." Ed Dobson agreed with Robison's assessment. "I don't think people understand," he said, "that the average fundamentalist felt alienated from the mainstream of American culture. That was a significant moment, because the candidate came to us; we didn't go to the candidate."

The candidate had already come to this constituency in a prespeech press conference in which he had urged that the biblical story of creation be taught in the public schools as an alternative to the theory of evolution, which he said was being increasingly discredited by scientists. They also knew and loved his endorsement of tuition tax credits, his complaint that the Supreme Court had "expelled God from the classroom," and his oft-made observation that everybody in favor of abortion had already been born. As a kind of capstone to these comments, Reagan sealed his identification with this crowd by calling attention to the challenge facing "traditional Judeo-Christian values" and by asserting that if he were shipwrecked and could choose only one book to read for the rest of his life, he would choose the Bible, adding that "all the complex questions facing us at home and abroad have their answer in that single book." To no one's surprise, that remark brought a thundering standing ovation. Republican activist Morton Blackwell thought Reagan's performance and the crowd's reaction to him so significant that he deemed the speech "a turning point in America," because "vast numbers of religious leaders were deciding whether to get involved . . . ; as a result of that meeting, they decided to."

Their decision, however, was not without qualification. In the same conversation in which James Robison had fed Reagan the "I endorse you" line, he had said, "We really like you. We like the principles you espouse. But you need to understand something about the nature of this group. We're not partisan. We're not pro-party. We're not pro-personality. We're pro-principle. If you stand by the principles you say you believe in, we'll be the greatest friends you'll ever have. But if you turn against those principles, we'll be your worst nightmare."

ROBISON'S IMPORTANCE TO the campaign had reached its apex at the Dallas meeting. Most of the public attention thereafter went to Jerry Falwell and Moral Majority. Like Robison, Falwell had a talent for stirring the crowds and began enlivening his rallies with a ninety-minute audio-visual presentation that included images of Charles Manson, Times Square "adult" theaters, aborted fetuses in bloody hospital pans, nuclear explosions, statements by American Communist Party leader Gus Hall, and other offenses ostensibly chargeable to the accounts of communists, secular humanists, and, by implication, Democrats. Predictably, such tactics drew fire from critics and increased attention from the media. A coalition of church leaders, including some from evangelical denominations, criticized Moral Majority and Christian Voice for their tactics. While freely granting the right of Christians to engage in political activism on behalf of justice and peace, they declared, "There is no place in a Christian manner of political life for arrogance, manipulation, [and] subterfuge. . . . There is no justification in a pluralistic society for demands for conformity along religious or ideological lines."

In Paul Weyrich's estimation, Moral Majority "was by no means the most important of the groups that had been formed," but the media focused on it because its name was so boldly self-righteous and because "Falwell was a good target. He was very visible and he was willing to talk to the media. So they seized upon [Moral Majority] to explain to America that 'this is what is happening. If you want to know who these people are and what they are about, there you have it.' Also, the opposition seized on [the name]. Liberals came out with their bumper stickers, 'The Moral Majority Is Neither,' and so on. It became symbolic of the Religious Right, of the involvement of those people in the political process."

As journalists probed into Falwell's past, they quickly uncovered his less-than-admirable record on civil rights and his "Ministers and Marchers" sermon. To his credit, Falwell faced his past squarely and apologized for it. He went to individual black ministers, told them he had been wrong in some of his past attitudes, and asked for their forgiveness. Ed Dobson, who was present on one of those occasions, described it as "a very gripping and moving moment." More publicly, Falwell attended a meeting at Court Street Baptist Church, where Jesse Jackson had been invited to preach a sermon criticizing Moral Majority, and the two men struck a remarkable bargain. Falwell told Jackson that in the past he had been "reflecting the culture, and I was wrong," adding, "You've said things you know were wrong. We both have an apology to make to our people." That night, Falwell stood before a fair representation of Lynchburg's black community and said, "I have said things that're wrong; I have done things that're wrong; and I apologize and ask you to forgive me." The next morning, Jesse Jackson spoke at Thomas Road Baptist Church on the subject of brotherhood.

Falwell made amends for his "Ministers and Marchers" sermon in similarly open fashion. He called a press conference at which he explicitly repudiated the assertions that ministers ought to stay out of politics as "false prophecy," and declared not only that ministers have a responsibility to be involved in struggles involving moral and social issues, but announced his own intention to engage in civil disobedience if Congress voted to draft women into the armed forces. Skeptics in Lynchburg and elsewhere saw Falwell's actions as impelled by political expediency rather than any significant change of heart. It is worth noting, however, that a genuine change of heart is possible, and that it might well have moved Jerry Falwell to do exactly what he did.

AS THE CAMPAIGN moved closer to November 4, indeed as late as election eve, the major media and most pollsters deemed the election too close to call. Voters who had made up their minds were about evenly split; pollsters and pundits assumed the undecideds would also split somewhere along the middle. Instead, they broke heavily for Reagan, giving him forty-four states and ninety-one percent of the electoral votes. With the exception of blacks and Hispanics, virtually every significant bloc of normally Democratic voters saw substantial numbers defect to the Republican ticket. This rightward surge spilled over into other races as well, giving Republicans a majority in the Senate for the first time in twenty-six years.

Remembering the many times he had been told that people of different theological opinions could never be brought together, Paul Weyrich found great satisfaction in the news from around the country. "My proudest moment," he remembered, "was when an article appeared that said right there—jumped out of the page—that Catholics in areas like Dubuque, Iowa, had helped elect the evangelical [Charles] Grassley, and evangelicals in places like Mobile helped elect the Catholic [Jeremiah] Denton. And I looked at that article, and I stared at it, and I said, 'By golly, it really has happened.' "

Given the fact that, despite his sweeping victory, Reagan was elected with the highest negative ratings of any successful presidential candidate in the nation's history, it was clear the election represented rejection of Jimmy Carter as much as approval of Ronald Reagan. Subsequent analysis also indicated that Reagan's margin of victory was sufficiently great that he might have been elected even if he had not had the votes of the Religious Right. But without question, their enthusiastic support was part of the wave that bore him upward and moved other voters to take him seriously. Awareness of what they had helped accomplish came early as, long before voting had ended, exit polls made it clear Reagan had won. Ed Dobson remembered driving to Thomas Road Baptist Church to pick up his children, and seeing Jerry Falwell sitting in his truck, listening to the radio. "I walked over and sat in the front seat of the truck [with him], just the two of us. It was one of those moments of 'Can you believe what we did?' I'll never forget that moment. The most cynical of the press were admitting that the Religious Right, or whatever they called it back then, had at least influenced the election. Others were saying we had swayed it. We chose to believe we swayed it." Falwell was also willing to take considerable credit, calling the election "my finest hour."

James Robison, who watched the election returns in his home, his reactions filmed by WFAA cameras—"the very people who took me off the air"—admits he was elated. "I think it was the Harris Poll that said the next day, 'The preachers gave it to Reagan.' There was no question in my mind that we had really contributed. Just like religious leaders delivered in the civil-rights movement, the Religious Right—whatever you want to call them, New Right, Christian people, caring people, family people, people with traditional values, and, yes, outspoken preachers—impacted the direction of this country, and they impacted the election. There is no doubt about it."

With God on its side once again, it seemed America might last longer than a thousand days.

© Larry Pierce/Charleston Gazette

In the late 1960s and early 1970s, the teaching of sex education and the adherence to "traditional" curricula in public schools became two of the most controversial issues for conservative Christians. In Kanawha County, West Virginia, Alice Moore, a school board member and the wife of a fundamentalist minister, was instrumental in bringing about a full-fledged culture war on what she considered to be inappropriate, unpatriotic, and blasphemous books adopted by the public school system.

During the summer of 1974, Alice Moore encouraged parents to keep their children out of school in September if the Kanawha School Board tried to force them to use the new books. On Labor Day, Concerned Citizens sponsored a rally at which fundamentalist preacher Marvin Horan urged a crowd of eight thousand to boycott the entire school system the next day.

On the Tuesday morning after the Concerned Citizens rally, approximately twenty percent of Kanawha County's forty-five thousand students stayed home. Some parents kept their children home out of fear of what the protesters might do to those who crossed the picket line, but most observed the boycott because they believed it was a righteous cause.

On September 4, the boycott received a tremendous boost when approximately ten thousand coal miners from Kanawha and seven surrounding counties struck in a show of solidarity with the protesters. On September 10, city bus drivers honored the picket line, leaving more than ten thousand regular riders without service. On September 11, the school board caved in, announcing that it would withdraw the books.

No president ever made such a conscious, calculating use of religion as a political instrument as did Richard Nixon, pictured here at a prayer breakfast with his wife, Pat, and Billy Graham. Nixon instructed his aides to sound out Graham for his readings of public opinion, and Graham in turn counseled the president on ways to enhance his appeal to conservative religious people.

After Watergate, America hungered for a return to honesty, integrity, and fair dealing in politics, and few people better understood this need than Jimmy Carter. Seen here with wife, Rosalynn, and daughter, Amy, on the steps of Plains Methodist Church, Carter knew how to present himself as the embodiment of bedrock values, deep concerns, and honest aspirations. And he knew—as his detractors did not—that his own quite genuine religious faith was an asset.

Jimmy Carter was not the only voice calling conservative Christians to play a fuller role in public life. For many years, the American evangelist Francis Schaeffer had operated an unusual religious community in Switzerland. L'Abri, as it was called, was dedicated to showing that Christianity was relevant to every aspect of human culture and that believers could embrace their faith without being swallowed by it.

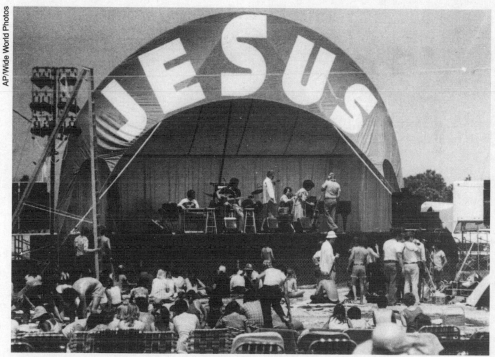

After Jimmy Carter was elected president, evangelical Christianity received increased and more respectful attention. News media began to report on the booming religious book market, the phenomenal growth and success of religious radio and television, and religious concerts and gatherings such as the "Jesus Festival '78," shown here.

In the first half of his presidency, Jimmy Carter's evangelical and conservative support eroded because people felt he had not lived up to his campaign promises. In 1979 and 1980, he lost further support by keeping a campaign promise: convening a conference to stimulate a national discussion of the state of American families. Carter is shown here with his hand-picked Advisory Committee, which included Coretta Scott King (far left) and Jesse Jackson (second from left).

Jimmy Carter intended the White House conference to be a forum in which all types of people could discuss their different ideas about the meaning of the word *family*. By no means did the president place his seal of approval on gay relationships, but his refusal to exclude homosexual men and women from the conference was enormously significant and brought immediate stature to gay politics.

Despite President Carter's attempts to discuss families in their most inclusive sense, conservative forces sought to limit application of the term to people related by blood, adoption, or marriage, and to establish the basic unit of husband, wife, and children as the norm. Unmarried partners, unwed mothers and their offspring, and homosexual relationships were not recognized as legitimate.

Connaught "Connie" Marshner (left) was a key figure in alerting conservative Christians to the opportunity for involvement in the White House conference. She and her associates—who included Phyllis Schlafly and the groups Right to Life and Stop ERA—fought hard to become delegates, and Marshner was ultimately elected to a panel that included Children's Defense Fund Director Marian Wright Edelman (right).

During the 1970s and on into the 1980s, Phyllis Schlafly became one of the most vocal and influential members of the Christian hard right. She vigorously opposed the Equal Rights Amendment and President Carter's Conference on Families on the grounds that they would bring forth a "gender-free society, [with] no difference between men and women. I don't think babies need two sex-neutral parents," she declared. "I think they need a father and a mother."

CHAPTER

9

PROPHETS AND ADVISERS

THE ELATION FALWELL and his colleagues felt at the Republican victories in the 1980 election soon gave way to the realistic recognition that, significant as their contribution had been, they had achieved something less than revolution. At the 1979 meeting when Reagan told the ministers his only hope of heaven was the blood of Christ, he had promised that the number of evangelical Christians in his administration would be proportionate to their strength in the population. John Conlan, who had helped arrange that meeting, saw immediately that this pledge could not be kept. "George Gallup had just finished doing a study that said forty percent of the country considered themselves 'born-again' Christians," Conlan observed. Because evangelicals had not participated extensively in government, they had nowhere near the number of qualified and experienced people to fill that kind of quota. But even if they had, Conlan charged, there was little hope such people would have been appointed in substantial numbers. "The core group around Reagan—the Mike Deavers of the world and the others—were not at all interested either in appointing evangelical Christians into the administration or in concentrating on their values, because they didn't understand. Their hearts were not with the middle-class, upper-working-class, or even the poor classes that were oriented to church and moral values. There was no money to be extracted from those people, there were no titles, no fancy dinners, no private concerts at the Corcoran Art Gallery or anything else, so they were not interested."

The problem of inexperience went beyond evangelical Christians. Morton Blackwell, who had worked for Richard Viguerie's direct-mail operation, contributed frequently to the Viguerie-published *Conservative Digest,* and edited another publication called the *New Right Report,* was part of Reagan's transition team. He agreed that "there were very few people who were available for appointment whose résumés indicated they could run a major department or agency. How do you fill an entire administration with people who have never managed large staffs or handled huge budgets?" Blackwell also confirmed Conlan's view that Deaver and other members of Reagan's inner circle had little interest in catering to either the conservative Christian constituency or the hard-line "movement conservatives" of the New Right. In the end, evangelicals received few appointments. James Watt, a member of the Assemblies of God, was named Secretary of the Interior; Robert Billings became a special assistant to Secretary of Education Terrel Bell, an ironic choice in light of the fact that one reason Billings had come to Washington was to work for that department's abolition; and Jerry Regier was appointed director of the Office of Families. New Right conservatives fared no better, prompting Richard Viguerie to complain that "the appointments are largely a disaster from the true conservative standpoint." Howard Phillips weighed in with a similar lament: "They promised true conservative government, but they didn't deliver."

Shortly after the election, both Reagan and Senate Majority Leader Howard Baker announced that serious consideration of the "social agenda" would have to be deferred for at least a year, to give the new administration time to focus on economic recovery. "In response to that blow," Paul Weyrich recalled,

> evangelical and fundamentalist leaders refused to say anything. Imagine a President Cuomo getting elected with the help of the civil-rights movement and then announcing that civil-rights issues were nonsense and he wasn't even going to address them. We all know what the ensuing activity would be like.
>
> Well, I had a conference call with the leadership of the Religious New Right . . . and I said, "This cannot be tolerated. If the idea that economic issues are more important than moral issues takes hold, then it says something about what we stand for." The leaders told me that I was much too harsh and that they rather agreed with the notion that economic issues were important. They thought Reagan had a good point, that he had to deal with the economy first.

Weyrich said he told them, "No, you settle matters that pertain to God first—that's the proper order." Weyrich compared the preachers' docility to a ghetto mentality.

> What overshadowed all their concerns was simply their pleasure in being able to get in even the back door of the White House. They didn't want to do anything to jeopardize that. They were willing to put

aside what minimalistic ideas they had on their so-called "agendas"—and with the exception of their pro-life position, they were trivial—to safeguard meaningless access.

Weyrich's reference to "the back door" had an antecedent. With members of their own ranks essentially shut out of the administration, evangelicals felt their only hope for moving their social-issues agenda forward was to take their concerns to Reagan himself. That proved to be no easy task. The Reagan White House was controlled by the triumvirate of Chief of Staff James Baker, Deputy Chief of Staff Michael Deaver, and "counselor to the president" Edwin Meese. Jerry Falwell believed that Meese shared the views of Christian conservatives on such issues as abortion but was outweighed by Baker's focus on other issues, particularly the economy, and by Deaver's obsession with enhancing Reagan's image and chances for re-election. "Mike Deaver," he volunteered, "probably couldn't spell 'abortion.'"

Falwell claimed not to have been terribly surprised by the Reagan administration's focus—"I had no illusions that when we elected Ronald Reagan, we had changed America. We had only changed the direction America was taking; we had not saved the country"—but he was clearly rankled at the thought of having his access to Reagan cut off after the election. Shortly after the inauguration, he recalled, "Someone called me one morning and read a squib out of the *Washington Post,* where Michael Deaver had said—talking about the Religious Right—'They'd be welcome in the White House, but they'd need to come in the back door.'" Falwell called Morton Blackwell, who was serving as the administration's special liaison to conservative groups, and said he wanted to talk to the president. "A week or two later," Falwell said, "I was in the Oval Office. I got there five minutes early and I was standing there outside with [Blackwell] and suddenly here comes Deaver running up. He said, 'Jerry, that so-and-so newspaper misquoted me. You know I wouldn't say a thing like that. Please don't mention that in there.' I said, 'Michael, I don't know whether you said it or not, but I want to get some things cleared up today.' He was a very nervous man, and he left. When I was in the Oval Office, I said, 'Mr. President, I read this comment that Michael Deaver made,' and obviously he'd never seen it or heard it. And he said, 'Did you come in the back door today?' I said, 'No, I came in the front door.' And he said, 'Feel free. That door is open.' And he meant it, through eight years. I wasn't really mad, but I wanted to make sure we weren't getting off on the wrong foot. We never had any more problems with Deaver from that time on."

Deaver has denied ever having made the "back door" statement, defending himself by noting that it would make no sense, since the White House has no back door. He acknowledged, however, that, given the myriad requests the White House Public Liaison office receives for meetings with the president, some lower-level functionary may have made such a comment. Faith Whittlesey, who directed the Public Liaison office for a little over two years, saw the Reagan White House as the scene of a struggle between two distinct camps, one led by Baker, with Deaver as a close ally, and the other by Ed Meese, with neither being conservative enough to suit Reagan's true believers. Baker, Whittlesey said, genuinely believed it was in Reagan's interests to downplay the "values" issues. "There was a continual effort to minimize not only the issues themselves but the people who were promoting these issues, so there was a kind of White House underground of people who were known to be supporters of the 'pro-life' position, of school prayer, of tuition tax credits. We all knew one another." Those opposed to highlighting these positions thought Reagan's chances of re-election would be damaged "if he appeared to be too much influenced by people of deep religious faith, that he would be described as a zealot, an extremist—the same terms they use today. They didn't want to make any effort intellectually to explain the basis for his positions, and they didn't want him to do that.

"People who were part of this coalition would find themselves seated way in the back at presidential appearances, and instead of being in car number four, where you might be because of your official position, you'd be in car number fourteen. Or when I arranged a small luncheon for Paul Weyrich, on the tenth anniversary of the Free Congress Foundation, to recognize all the foundation had done in those ten years, the Chief of Staff did not show up. I don't think any other member of the senior staff appeared, and the president was persuaded not to attend." Similarly, Whittlesey said, requests to have Reagan appear at gatherings designed to rally support for parts of the social-values agenda were systematically turned down, a program to furnish speakers to various groups almost never included "values proponents," and when a request came for an administration representative to address such topics in a television interview, "they would pick one of their people who would present the position at its weakest or wouldn't even mention it."

Michael Deaver, whom Reagan biographer Lou Cannon called "the grand producer of the Reagan presidency," freely admitted to much of what Whittlesey had asserted. "Faith felt very strongly about getting the president's ear on issues of 'family values,' " he said, "so from the early days of the first term there was pressure on the scheduling office to make time available for those people." Deaver viewed such visits as a misuse of the president's time. "The only way I knew to communicate to the American public what we wanted to do," he said, "was through television. And in my mind, that meant coming up every night, or as many times as possible, with a visual that was attractive, entertaining, stimulating, interesting, so that the producers of the networks couldn't refuse to put that picture on television. There was only one priority in the first term, as far as I was concerned, and that was the economy. So I would say, 'Unless you can show me how this thing plays to the economic-recovery issue, I don't want to see it on my desk.' I would even go to the point of saying, 'If you can't describe a visual for me, if you can't give me a venue that provides a sixty-second television sound bite that has to do with the economic recovery issue, don't even bother to bring a request to me.' I was pretty brutal, because I was absolutely convinced that we had to make the economic turnaround or he was going to be a one-term president. Unless we got a handle on that, it didn't make any difference about abortion or prayer in schools or gun control or all the rest of it. It wasn't going to happen. So there was only one priority, as I saw it."

Despite this kind of resistance, Whittlesey and Blackwell did manage to gain some hearing for Christian conservatives. During Whittlesey's two years as Director of the Office of Public Liaison, substantial numbers of major and minor evangelical leaders and pastors were invited to the White House and had their picture taken with the president. For many, that was enough reward for their efforts on Reagan's behalf. Syndicated columnist Cal Thomas, who had signed on as vice president of Moral Majority early in 1980, observed that "politics is a great seducer. As I'd travel around the country, I'd go into churches and I'd see featured prominently in the office or the hallway a picture of the pastor with Ronald Reagan. Nothing wrong with that, but that happened so many times that I think Christian people were sucked into the political process so that it became primary in their lives, and the moral and spiritual power that should have been theirs, to [enable them to] speak truth to power, seemed to be put on the back burner, because Ronald Reagan became the surrogate messiah."

Ed Dobson acknowledged his own bedazzlement at feeling he was near the center of world power. "One of the things that drove fundamentalists to get involved," he ventured, "was the feeling that they were a disenfranchised people. They didn't belong in the mainstream. No one invited them to the banquets in the public square. They were just kind of idiots, basically. The 1980 election affirmed us as more than an inconsequential splinter group in America culture. In spite of the media, in spite of what everybody said, we had made a difference. Then Ronald Reagan and others recognized that we had made a difference, so we were affirmed as legitimate partners in the democratic experiment. We were invited to the table for the first time. And that was a great feeling. I remember the first time I went to the White House with Jerry Falwell and ate at the mess hall with two key people in the president's inner circle, and I'm thinking, 'Wow, I am sitting here at the White House.' And I remember the time a group of about fifteen of us spent two hours with Menachem Begin at Blair House. I remember the night at

Vice President George Bush's house when we spent the whole evening. This was heady stuff for people who, one or two years earlier, had been unnoticed and unheard of, and nobody had cared about us. Now all of a sudden the gatekeepers of culture had invited us in. It meant we were somebody, that we mattered, that we cared, that we were making a difference, that all of the years in the back woods of the culture were over. We had come home, and the home was the White House."

Dobson admitted that his wide-eyed response was in part a sign of his naïveté about politics and the way things get done in Washington. "I assumed," he said, that "if you elected the right person, all your problems were solved, not realizing that one election is probably not going to make a long-term difference in anything." This naïveté involved "getting caught in the euphoria and failing to ask, 'What's the next step?' We were carried along and seduced by success and never asked the tough questions: 'In the nitty-gritty of politics, what do we need to do to accomplish certain objectives?' "

THE FIRST SIGNIFICANT loss of innocence came about when the Reagan administration failed to stem the tide of abortions. While it is doubtful that leaders of the Religious Right would have appreciated Weyrich's characterization of their agenda as largely trivial, they certainly agreed that abortion was its most important issue and the obvious choice as the first item on which they sought results. The early signs were excellent. Two days after his inauguration, Reagan met with a group of right-to-life advocates in the Oval Office, a gesture Dr. Jack Willke, president of the National Right to Life Committee, regarded as extremely encouraging. "It was a signal," he said, "because we were the first citizens' group in the White House. The one historical parallel is when the civil rights leaders were brought into the White House under Kennedy." In addition, Richard Schweiker, the new Secretary of Health and Human Services, addressed the crowd of more than sixty thousand people who participated in the annual March for Life, the first cabinet member ever to do so.

Given such encouragement, determined anti-abortion forces began to put forth various legislative proposals during the spring session of Congress. The most substantial was a bill known as the Human Life Statute, cosponsored by two Republican stalwarts, North Carolina Senator Jesse Helms and Illinois Congressman Henry Hyde, whose successful amendments to various appropriations bills had reduced the number of federally funded abortions from 295,000 in 1976 to only 2,400 in 1979. Few pro-lifers thought it possible to secure a "human life" amendment to the Constitution at this juncture, but they hoped the Helms-Hyde bill, which could become law by a simple majority vote in both houses, would accomplish much the same purpose. Writing for the Court in the *Roe v. Wade* decision, Justice Blackmun had acknowledged the Court's inability "to resolve the difficult question of when life begins." If it could be determined that a fetus is indeed a "person," he conceded, its right to life would have to be guaranteed. Using that opening, the Helms-Hyde bill declared straightforwardly that "human life shall be deemed to exist from conception."

If passed, such a bill would clear the way for states to define abortion as murder. Even such anti-abortion constitutional experts as Robert Bork felt confident the Supreme Court, seeing its role as guardian of the Bill of Rights threatened, would deem such a statute unconstitutional. Jesse Helms, a canny parliamentarian, acknowledged that possibility, but observed that the statute would doubtless encourage some states to pass bills outlawing abortions and that, while the challenges to those bills worked their way up to the high court, abortions would be stopped. Further, if the court did rule against the statute, pro-life forces would see that their only hope lay in a constitutional amendment and would redouble efforts to obtain one. In Helms's view, the statute was "a necessary step to have some movement on this question prior to the adoption of a constitutional amendment."

Reagan had indicated he believed human life begins at conception, but the White House offered no assistance in support of the Helms-Hyde bill, which baffled and frustrated most anti-abortion activists, and the bill failed. Cal Thomas did not find this particularly surprising. "Political people," he observed, "have a marvelous way of stroking you and making you think they are really on your side, and they can get you to believe this for a month, two months, six months, a year, sometimes longer, depending on how good they [are] at the stroking and how naïve you are at being stroked."

The Religious Right's sense of having been beguiled and betrayed grew during the summer of 1981 when Reagan had his first chance to fill a slot on the Supreme Court, which had been vacated by retiring Justice Potter Stewart. He had indicated during his campaign that he planned to appoint a woman to the High Court, so when the opportunity arose, Reagan insisted that his staff find a suitable female candidate. John Conlan remembered being asked by a Reagan aide for his opinion of Reagan's choice, Judge Sandra Day O'Connor of Arizona. "I said, 'Well, I was chairman of the Judiciary Committee in Arizona, and Sandra is a wonderful girl, handsome and beautiful-looking, articulate, smart as a tack, Stanford Law graduate. But she comes from upper-class landed aristocracy, [from a] ranching family, and there is a tendency for people to feel that she's somewhat of an economic oligarchist. She has no religious orientation, she fought hard for the Equal Rights Amendment, and very hard for the legalization of abortion when she was in the State Senate. Are you sure you want to put someone with that position on the Supreme Court?' I never actively campaigned against her; I just alerted them."

According to Michael Deaver, the pitfalls inherent in judicial appointments had been driven home to Reagan when a man he had appointed as Chief Justice of the California Supreme Court reversed himself on capital punishment six months after joining the court, "so he was very leery about court appointments and wanted to be sure he got the right person." The president was familiar with O'Connor's record, discussed it with Attorney General William French Smith and Ed Meese, and with O'Connor herself, finally satisfying himself that "he was still making the right appointment, that her instincts and values were consistent with his, that some of [what had been reported] could be a matter of interpretation, that it wasn't enough to be a red flag for him, that she was going to pass the test of time as far as his philosophy was concerned."

When word of O'Connor's nomination and legislative record spread through the conservative Christian network, it met with less equanimity. In keeping with his threat to be the president's worst enemy if he abandoned his principles, evangelist James Robison recalled that he had "hollered and screamed" at Ed Meese about the nomination, and quickly collaborated with Religious Roundtable leader Ed McAteer to mount an anti-abortion/anti-O'Connor rally in Dallas on Labor Day. Jerry Falwell, both calmer and more influential than Robison, responded more cautiously. "I was in Myrtle Beach, South Carolina, with my family on vacation," he recalled, "when the phone rang in the condo. It was Ronald Reagan, and he said, 'Jerry, I'm going to nominate Sandra Day O'Connor to the Supreme Court. We've done a pretty good background study; we feel very strongly that she represents the views and values that I campaigned on, and I would simply ask you to give us a little time to develop that through the hearings before taking a position.' I agreed to that and did in fact keep quiet, and once she was examined, I became one of her supporters . . . and still am. I read several places where I allegedly had commented, but I had not. I promised the president not to comment, and I did not comment." In fact, his only reported comment seems to have been the noncommittal observation, "I do not believe [Reagan] would intentionally appoint someone who supports abortion."

A week after Reagan's announcement, Moral Majority issued a statement expressing "substantive concerns" over the nomination and declaring that the organization "believes without equivocation that the questions Moral Majority and other traditional pro-family groups have raised about O'Connor's position on abortion need to be answered." Cal Thomas, who issued the statement, also observed that, to those who had "been waiting patiently for [Reagan] and supporting him on the economy, this [was] not a very good signal." Moral Majority, however, did not work against the nomination.

For Ed Dobson, the difference between Robison's and Falwell's responses can be understood as the difference between the roles of prophet and adviser. "If you choose to be a prophet," he explained, "you don't have a lot of influence on the political reality, but you're always free to speak what you perceive to be the truth for the current historical moment. Or, you can be an adviser with a sense of truth, a sense of value, but your objective is simply to influence the process. I think the Moral Majority moved from a prophetic role into more of an adviser role and lost some of its ability to speak against the administration. So when a Sandra Day O'Connor comes along who has both positive and negative issues, if you're the adviser the tendency is, 'Because we understand who the president is and what his commitments are, we may not entirely agree with his nomination, but he deserves our support and we will stay true to him in order to ultimately advise and influence him.' Whereas the prophetic role would have been to say, 'No way.' I think the Moral Majority chose the adviser role, which is the danger of politics: Once they invite you up to the Big House, then you have to go by the rules of the Big House."

Conservatives of the New Right, pragmatic though they were, reacted more like Robison. "That was a very eye-opening experience," Connie Marshner observed. "With this nomination, the Administration effectively said, 'Good-bye, we don't need you.'" Reagan, she charged, "had not consulted with his allies, had not checked with his conservative friends. They got a phone call saying, 'This is who it's going to be,' but there had not been any opportunity for input, and no care had been paid to the fact that she had a pro-abortion voting record in Arizona. It was just, 'That's it. Take it or leave it.' That was one of the first breaks that a number of us had with Reagan."

Cal Thomas, though not enthusiastic about O'Connor's record on the Court since her appointment, criticized Reagan primarily for what he did not accomplish at such a propitious moment. "At a time when you had a Republican Senate and pretty much a free ride for anybody Ronald Reagan would nominate," he noted, "there was really no excuse for not nominating someone with the convictions of Judge [Robert] Bork early on. Many of us were advocating precisely that, because we knew that it would be much easier to get someone with deep moral and intellectual and legal convictions and credentials through [the confirmation process] early on, when Ronald Reagan was going down the track like a freight train, getting virtually everything he wanted, from tax cuts to reducing government to firing the air controllers and making it stick, one thing after another, and the Democrats in the House were in full retreat, signing off on just about everything.

Instead, he picked somebody who might have been better picked later when the Senate was controlled by Democrats—a woman, a seeming moderate on some of the issues." Thomas hardly overestimated the Reagan momentum; the Senate confirmed Judge O'Connor by a vote of ninety-nine to zero.

AS PAUL WEYRICH witnessed the dismay and sense of betrayal Christian conservatives felt over the failure of the Helms-Hyde bill and the O'Connor appointment, he stepped up his efforts to teach them "how government really works." He organized discussions under the aegis of the Library Court Group, which focused on family issues. He also showed them how the legislative process works, and put together intensive workshops that focused on mastery of the political machinery. "I think the greatest thing these meetings accomplished," Weyrich said, "was teaching many of these people *realpolitik,* because many of them learned how things actually happen. The amount of naïveté, politically, in the evangelical community was extraordinary. You have sixth-graders who have just learned civics that have a better clue than many evangelical leaders as to how things actually went on in the country. They were really babes in the woods. And by sitting through meetings, they saw the progression of legislative battles, they saw who did what, they saw the level of betrayal, they saw the level of participation by various groups, and they saw what it took to win. All of this taught them what you have to do if you are going to be a serious player." Connie Marshner agreed. "They did not realize," she said, "the degree of depravity of most politicians, [who make] decisions on how they are going to vote based on 'Who can put the most pressure on me? Who can cause me the most difficulty in my re-election campaign?' rather than 'What do I think is right?' Leading somebody to salvation is very different from leading them to vote your way. You don't lead them; you force them."

One of the first lessons Weyrich sought to instill in his new pupils was the need to play offense rather than defense. "Two years earlier," he explained, "we had decided that we needed a vehicle to be proactive, because in most cases we were reacting to the initiatives of the left, who would get a policy adopted or get a Supreme Court decision in their favor, and then we would be stuck with the consequences of that in trying to fight a rear-guard action. And of course no defensive movement ever survives." He had brought together a working group of conservatives, including Mormons, Catholics, evangelicals, fundamentalists, and "movement conservatives" that, with help from Robert Billings, Connie Marshner, and Nevada Senator Paul Laxalt, had produced a piece of legislation known as the Family Protection Act. It went down to swift defeat in 1979, but was resurrected in 1981, this time with Iowa Senator Roger Jepsen as its chief sponsor—perhaps as penance for having belonged to a "spa" that was later shut down as a house of prostitution. Variously described as "a mish-mash of New Right wishes" or a "grocery list of extremist panaceas that only the Moral Majority could love," the bill provoked the observation that "the New Right is more skilled at denouncing laws than at writing them." Its thirty-one provisions included measures that would prohibit abortion; bar the provision of contraceptive information to teenagers without parental consent; restore school prayer; offer tuition tax credits and other benefits to parents with children in private schools; give parent or other community groups the right to review and block adoption of books used in public schools; permit the segregation of sexes in school sports activities; forbid the use of federal money to promote homosexual or feminist values or to pay for educational materials that do not "contribute to the American way of life as it has been historically understood"; and support "traditional families" and the role of women "as historically understood" by offering tax breaks to non-working female spouses, as well as to multigenerational families and families who adopt.

In keeping with his announced policy of concentrating on economic issues, President Reagan did not endorse the Family Protection Act and, despite efforts to drum up support through their publications, direct mail, television appearances, and telephone campaigns, it appears none of the New Right insiders believed an omnibus bill with so many controversial provisions had any chance of passing. Instead, they used it as a device to identify and label allies and opponents of their movement during the 1980 elections and thereafter. According to the Washington publication, *City Paper,* Marshner readily acknowledged that the bill's more controversial provisions were designed to provoke liberal outrage, which could be used to paint the liberals as anti-family. This, in turn, might convince moderates that conservatives were trying to help them preserve their traditional families, while liberals were interested only in aiding gays, abortionists, sex educators, and critics of the American way of life.

Conservatives frustrated by the O'Connor appointment and the failure of their legislative efforts were somewhat assuaged when Reagan named Dr. C. Everett Koop, the evangelical anti-abortion advocate, to the post of Surgeon General (Koop will be discussed in greater detail in the ensuing chapter), but they continued to register disappointment at the president's lack of interest in their agenda. Though Falwell repeatedly expressed confidence in Reagan's good intentions, the *Moral Majority Report* regularly complained about lack of influence in the White House, and a *Conservative Digest* poll revealed that New Righters now rated Reagan as their second favorite conservative, behind the Lynchburg preacher. (Nancy Reagan also slipped to second, behind Phyllis Schlafly. Schlafly scored a final decisive victory over the ERA in 1982, when the time allotted for its ratification, though extended three years beyond the normal seven, finally elapsed with the proposed amendment still three states shy of the thirty-eight needed for it to become law.) Morton Blackwell tried to reassure his friends in the New and Religious Right that the president had not forgotten them, but their confidence was wearing thin.

As the 1982 elections approached, Richard Viguerie wrote an open letter in the *Conservative Digest,* urging the president to "take a highly visible national leadership role promoting issues that will defeat liberals and elect conservatives such as. . . . school prayer, tuition tax credits, [etc.]. . . . Millions of people supported you in the '60s, '70s, and '80s elections solely because of your position on these issues." Nellie Gray, organizer and president of the March for Life, held annually on the anniversary of the *Roe v. Wade* decision, scored the White House staff for its "untenable excuses for keeping the president from speaking to the huge pro-life gatherings." Joining the chorus, even the patient Jerry Falwell declared, "It is absolutely imperative that the president aggressively address the social issues which were a part of his campaign in 1980." Abortion, school prayer, and tuition tax credits, he said, simply must "be put on the front burner." In July, Moral Majority and Weyrich's Free Congress Foundation cosponsored "Family Forum II," where five hundred participants from thirty-seven states discussed strategies for overcoming Reagan's apparent lack of interest in the social issues. The grumbling eventually grew so loud and so public that some liberal activists began to assert that perhaps they had overestimated the clout of religious conservatives.

Ranking just after opposition to abortion and homosexuality on the conservative social-issues agenda was, and continues to be, the restoration of devotional prayer exercises in public schools, on the grounds not only that the Supreme Court's 1962 decision banning such practices violated First Amendment guarantees of freedom of religion, but also that their absence has played a major role in rising rates of crime, drug use, promiscuous sex, and other social pathologies. Since the Court has ruled that such practices are unconstitutional, the obvious—though quite difficult—remedy is to change the Constitution. Public polls regularly indicate that a strong majority of Americans favor a return to voluntary prayer in the public schools, though not all of those see it as of paramount importance. In both his 1976 and 1980 campaigns, Ronald Reagan promised to support a prayer amendment. It was natural, then, for religious conservatives to focus on school prayer as an issue on which to force his hand.

During the summer of 1981, Jesse Helms introduced a bill that would ban the Supreme Court from reviewing cases dealing with school prayer. That dubious proposal, which the White House opposed and the Supreme Court would almost certainly have tossed out, got bottled up in committee, but it increased the pressure for some kind of action, and Reagan eventually offered his standard response: symbolic gestures with little follow-up action. At the National Prayer Breakfast in 1982, he complained that "God, the source of all knowledge, has been expelled from the classroom." A few days later, however, in an address to the National Religious Broadcasters, he made no mention of school prayer.

Social-issue conservatives wanted more. An organization called the Leadership Foundation distributed more than forty-two million pieces of material backing school prayer and produced a one-hour television special, *Let Our Children Pray,* which was shown on more than a hundred religious, commercial, and public stations. Jerry Falwell also produced an *Old Time Gospel Hour* special on the subject, and busloads of students from Liberty Baptist College came to Washington to form a human chain between the Supreme Court and the Capitol as a way of pleading for a school-prayer amendment.

In May, Reagan finally took concrete action; with Falwell and other leaders of the Christian Right standing alongside him in the Rose Garden, he announced he was recommending that Congress take action to pass a prayer amendment. After a laborious process that involved extensive consultation with Christian conservative leaders and Constitutional lawyers, the White House legislative office sent a proposed prayer amendment to Congress. It contained two straightforward clauses: "Nothing in this Constitution shall be construed to prohibit individual or group prayer in public schools" and "No person shall be required by the United States to pray."

Hearings on the proposal were held during summer of 1982, but Congress adjourned before any action was taken. When the 1983 session opened, the White House resubmitted its proposal. After months of wrangling, and a plea for its passage by the president in his State of the Union speech, the Senate finally voted on the proposed amendment in the spring of 1984. The count was fifty-six to forty-four in favor, eleven votes short of the two-thirds majority needed. Morton Blackwell pointed to the prayer amendment campaign as an example of the strategy of using defeat to enhance the possibility of long-term success. "We didn't really expect that it had a good chance of passing," he admitted, "but there was something highly desirable about coming up with a good initiative and forcing a vote on it, then allowing members of Congress who voted the wrong way to be held accountable by the voters next time around." Whatever the realistic expectation of the amendment's chance of passing, the White House did not put real weight behind it, at least in part because a number of prominent Republicans considered it a bad idea and did not wish to be put on the spot.

Some Christian conservatives may have accepted Blackwell's reasoning. Others were growing decidedly impatient with the administration's tactic of fending them off with pointless attempts to amend the Constitution. In August 1982, Ron Godwin, then-executive director of Moral Majority, asked, "Why does Reagan think symbolic gesturing will keep him in office?" and suggested that "the next two years may well be the last two years of the Reagan administration." During a visit to the White House a few months later, Falwell gave Reagan a list of twelve issues Moral Majority thought he must address if he hoped to keep his 1980 coalition intact. Reagan responded by mentioning several of the items in a speech a week later. In addition, Vice President Bush and Interior Secretary James Watt both spoke at Liberty Baptist College later that spring. Sidney Blumenthal, a perceptive observer of the New and Religious Right, wrote that the Republican Right strategy that led to the founding of the Moral Majority was to use social issues to separate the evangelicals, mostly southern Baptists, from their historic allegiance to the Democratic Party. After winning the White House in 1980, the strategy was then to keep the Religious Right "in a state of perpetual mobilization" and give support to versions of their bills which would ultimately fail, or to support constitutional amendments that were sure to fail but would rally the troops.

To make sure that Southern Baptists didn't slide back into the Democratic Party, Morton Blackwell and Ed McAteer cooperated with fundamentalist forces that were engineering a stunning takeover of the nation's largest Protestant denomination. In a well-orchestrated strategy first unfurled at the denomination's 1979 convention in Houston, hard-line theological conservatives had captured the SBC presidency—and with it, the power to make crucial appointments that would affect key agencies throughout the denomination—from the moderate forces that had long held sway. The president they chose that year was Adrian Rogers, Pastor at the Bellevue Baptist Church in Memphis, where Ed McAteer was a member. The next was Bailey Smith, who served two one-year terms (1980, '81) and was succeeded by James Robison's pastor, Jimmy Draper (1982, '83); Charles Stanley (1984, '85) followed Draper, and, in an unusual move, Adrian Rogers was re-elected for two terms (1986, '87). In short, the first four presidents of the SBC's new fundamentalist era were all closely aligned with the Religious Right. It showed. In the past, the SBC had affirmed a woman's right to abortion under certain circumstances and, in keeping with historic Baptist thought on the separation of church and state, had repeatedly given its approval to the Supreme Court's ruling that school prayer is unconstitutional. Under the new leadership, these positions were reversed. Similarly, Southern Baptist seminaries and colleges came under attack for theological liberalism, the ordination of women was discouraged, and churches that "affirm, approve, or endorse homosexual behavior" could no longer be part of the convention.

· · ·

As the 1984 campaign season rolled around, both the New Right and Religious Right felt they had been let down by Ronald Reagan and, especially, the men around him. Their most aggressive ally in the White House, Faith Whittlesey, had been appointed ambassador to Switzerland, at least in part, it was said, because James Baker had grown weary of dealing with her importunate demands. (Interestingly, she had become an evangelical Christian in the process—in considerable measure, she said, because of watching Jerry Falwell respond graciously to what she regarded as rude and ungrateful treatment from her colleagues.) Morton Blackwell continued to take the evangelicals' side, but always in the service of a larger strategy. Their demands for a move from symbolism to substance on social issues grew louder and Reagan's "Morning in America" theme did not exactly fit their dark view of the nation's moral and spiritual health, but in the end, they had no place to go, especially after the Democrats chose Walter Mondale and Geraldine Ferraro as their candidates. Reagan might not be perfect, but they needed him more than he needed them, and both he and the Religious Right knew it.

Jerry Falwell was still inclined to be generous to the president. At a press conference, he declared that "Ronald Reagan is the finest president in my lifetime. . . . If we are to give grades to a president, I could give him nothing less than 'A+'." At a later, more private event, Paul Weyrich chided Falwell for grading too easily, adding that he would give the president "about a 'B–'." Falwell covered himself by saying, "I graded on the curve, comparing [him] with previous administrations." Reagan no doubt received extra credit just for keeping the White House door open. Even on the off-chance that Ed Dobson was correct in asserting that Falwell was unfazed by his association with power, Falwell himself surely knew that countless members of his flock shared Thomas Road Baptist Church member Nancy Godsey's awe-filled assessment of her pastor's peregrinations. "It was just unbelievable," she said, "that our pastor, this little guy here in Lynchburg, was off in Washington, right up there with the president in the White House, having meetings and giving advice, and even going overseas and speaking to leaders over there. I think it's just great that he was able to do that. We just thought it was an honor for our pastor to be associated with the president and to encourage him on the right, from our Bible point of view."

At the Republican National Convention in August, Reagan told a prayer-breakfast audience, "The truth is, politics and morality are inseparable. And as morality's foundation is religion, religion and politics are necessarily related. We need religion as a guide. We need it because we are imperfect. And our government needs the church because only those humble enough to admit they're sinners can bring to democracy the tolerance it requires in

order to survive. Without God, democracy cannot and will not long endure." Both W. A. Criswell and James Robison offered prayers at plenary
sessions of the convention, another sign to the Religious Right that Ronald
Reagan still endorsed them. Robison prayed, "We thank you, Father, for the
leadership of President Ronald Reagan."

By 1984, Ed Dobson had lost some of the giddy thrill of standing close to
power and began to have second thoughts about the efficacy of what he and
Moral Majority were doing. Looking back on what the Christian Right
accomplished in these heady years, Dobson said, "Did we have access? Yes.
Did we have influence? Yes. Did the president and vice president attend our
events? Yes. Were we invited to theirs? Yes." But how much of the Religious Right's social agenda has actually been accomplished since 1980?
"Very little, other than that they have become points of discussion in every
election, which was a positive. As far as significant political change, there
really hasn't been a lot of that."

Part of the problem, he thought, lay in the way politics is played. "The
White House, whether Republican or Democrat, operates [by] throwing
bones and dog biscuits to the wild dogs out there. They invite you to an
event, they bring you in, they affirm you, and hand you a dog biscuit,
assuming that when the next election comes around, you'll vote for them. I
think the Republicans did that and I think the Democrats do that. That's
politics." But he also thought that fundamentalism itself contributed to the
problem. "Because the nature of the American political system makes it
difficult to do anything, politics is essentially the art of compromise and
negotiation, and fundamentalists don't place a high value on compromise
and negotiation." Moral Majority, he said, was "good at being *against* something. We never were good at being *for* something. We were much better at
being an antagonist, a confronter, than at having a larger, coherent political
philosophy that articulated what we were for." Fundamentalists honestly felt
they were fighting for lost or endangered rights, he said, but "a fighting
mindset will often get you in trouble. In the history of fundamentalism, it
was a fighting spirit that caused them not only to fight theological liberalism,
but to end up fighting each other. I think the same is true in the political
arena; what propelled us was the chance to have a fight over issues. But the
truth is we just want to keep on fighting." Dobson is now a pastor in Grand
Rapids, Michigan, serves on the editorial board of *Christianity Today,* and is
no longer involved in electoral politics.

James Robison has also stepped back from the political arena and, in the
process, has mellowed noticeably. Noting that he was only thirty-four in
1980, he said, "I was riding the crest of incredible success for a very young
man, and I don't think I handled it the best way, and I regret that." Participation in politics "thrust me into being a champion of causes, perhaps more

than being an example of Christian life. I really do believe that my desire to
see America turn was one hundred percent right. I thought we were deteriorating. I thought the communist menace was very real. We were in trouble.
So here I was, a young man with all this 'influence,' and perhaps I contributed positively in some way. I don't question that. My motive started out
pure, but power corrupts. Some people are terribly affected by it. I could
have been. I found myself saying hard things about Jimmy Carter—hard,
mean, cruel things. I found myself caught up in that, but the closer I got to
it, I was frightened of it. I watched what it did to people. I watched how it
fed, how it would drive them, to the point that I felt like principle could be
sacrificed for power, even on the part of good, quality people. I thought,
'What is wrong with us?' And when I wanted to repent of all that, the
Christian crowd that was supposed to be my friends got mad at me."

   In the mid-1980s, Robison found his way through some personal and
spiritual difficulties with the aid of people from the charismatic movement.
It was clearly a kind of conversion experience and the demeanor he displays
on his low-key interview program bears little resemblance to the angry
tirades that marked his preaching fifteen years earlier. "I experienced a glorious deliverance," he testified. "I was a changed person. God put so much
love in my heart for people that it was just absolutely incredible. I want to do
so much more to help the suffering in this world, and to encourage other
people to do it. We're a house divided. We're racially divided, we're politically divided, we're divided along party and ethnic lines. I wish we could
[just] be Americans and really love each other. I wish the Houses of Congress could just sit down and really talk about the positive things that could
be done, and that Christians would do the same thing. I want to see people
involved, but not because they want to be king-makers. I want them to
influence policy because they really care. I want to see this country better."

   The lust for power and the lure of battle may have diminished for Ed
Dobson and James Robison, but as the Reagan administration entered its
second term, millions of politically active religious conservatives still had
plenty of fight left in them. Frustrated by their inability to make headway
against what they called the holocaust of abortions, they found themselves
faced with the devilish task of coming to terms with a new enemy, the
plague of AIDS.

THE UNTOUCHABLES

Dr. C. Everett Koop was something of a hero to evangelical Christians. A graduate of Dartmouth and Cornell University Medical School, with further training at the University of Pennsylvania, he emerged not only with gilt-edged credentials but with his evangelical Presbyterian faith intact, a feat accorded special respect in conservative Christian circles. He quickly displayed formidable skill in the then-underdeveloped field of pediatric surgery and was named surgeon-in-chief at Children's Hospital in Philadelphia in 1948. He also held a faculty position at the University of Pennsylvania Medical School. During his long tenure at Children's, Koop established the nation's first neonatal unit, perfected delicate techniques for correcting undescended testicles and undeveloped esophaguses, and performed one of the first successful separations of Siamese twins. These impressive accomplishments, combined with his large frame and patriarchal beard, lent weight and authority to his words, and evangelicals, sensitive to assertions that they were an intellectually backward tribe, were pleased to call the good doctor one of their own. When Ronald Reagan announced in 1981 that Koop was his choice to become the thirteenth Surgeon General of the United States, it seemed certain that this was more than a minor gesture. Surely, this was an attempt by the new president to make clear his genuine commitment to addressing the concerns of his evangelical constituency, and particularly their consuming determination to combat abortion.

The expectation that Koop would launch a crusade against abortion was shared by both his supporters and his critics, with good reason. In 1975, he had joined with Billy Graham, evangelical theological Harold O. J. Brown, and his long-time friend and the evangelical icon Francis Schaeffer to form the Christian Action Council, whose sole reason for being was to bring pressure on Congress to stem the tide of abortions that followed the 1973

Roe v. Wade decision. Then, believing it would be more effective to stir a much more broadly based response, he teamed with Schaeffer in 1977 to coauthor an anti-abortion, anti-euthanasia book, *Whatever Happened to the Human Race?*, and take a prominent role in a companion film with the same title. As noted earlier, the combination of the film and book, together with the extensive promotional tour in which both men participated, is often credited with having been the single most important factor in bringing evangelicals into the fight against abortion.

Whatever Happened to the Human Race? was not a subtle production. In one arresting scene from the film, Koop stands in shallow water near the shoreline of the Dead Sea, which he identifies as the site of the former city of Sodom. As Koop intones, "Sodom comes easily to mind when one contemplates the evils of abortion and the death of moral law," one notices that all about him in every direction are hundreds of dolls, representing the one million babies aborted each year in the wake of the *Roe v. Wade* decision. No one had to wonder where Everett Koop stood on the question of abortion. Precisely because his position was well known, several Republican friends had sounded out Koop during the fall of 1980 to see if he might be interested in the post. One of the first of these was Carl Anderson, a deeply conservative Roman Catholic who had come to Washington to work against abortion as an aide to Senator Jesse Helms. Koop's involvement in politics had been limited to a bit of poll-watching during elections in Philadelphia, but because he was near retirement age at the University of Pennsylvania Medical School and the Children's Hospital of Philadelphia, he was open to a new challenge. After Reagan was elected, Koop contacted the people who had called him and announced, "Instead of being a reluctant suitor, I am now enthusiastically seeking that job."

Though designated as Reagan's choice in February, Koop served as Deputy Assistant Secretary of Health for nine months while waiting to be confirmed by Congress. He recognized that his views on abortion would create serious opposition to his candidacy, and on the day he arrived in Washington in March, he told the Secretary of Health and Human Services, Richard Schweiker, that he did not intend to use the Surgeon General's post as a bully pulpit to oppose abortion and would not continue to be a speaker on the pro-life circuit. Though his convictions on the subject had not changed, he felt "the law of the land said abortion on demand was legal. The Supreme Court had decided that, and I didn't think it was up to me to lead an insurrection within government against the Supreme Court. I think those things have to play out. When you have a social issue of such tremendous importance, that has separated the people of this country more than any other issue since slavery, you're not going to settle it by having one man, the Surgeon General, saying something about it. It's one thing to come to

Washington and have firmly held positions, but it's another thing to take an oath of office to uphold the Constitution, and there may be times when, without abandoning your beliefs, you have to make a political compromise to get the best possible solution to a problem that you can."

Such moderate, pragmatic statements, if they were heard at all, were not taken seriously. Nellie Gray, the organizer of the annual pro-life march held in Washington on the anniversary of the *Roe v. Wade* decision, brought her troops out in support of Koop's nomination. Illinois Congressman and ardent abortion foe Henry Hyde earnestly lobbied the White House on Koop's behalf. Less helpfully, a well-meaning group of Pentecostal Christians purchased time on a Washington television station to show long excerpts of *Whatever Happened to the Human Race?* These gestures, intended to bolster Koop's stock, had the opposite effect of rallying the forces against him. The American Medical Association, the American Public Health Association, the National Organization for Women, Planned Parenthood, Women and Health Roundtable, the National Abortion Rights Action League, the United Mine Workers, the National Gay Health Coalition, and thirteen major daily newspapers, including the *New York Times* and *Los Angeles Times,* all made public statements opposing Koop's nomination. In the House, California Congressman Henry Waxman led the opposition, derisively referring to the physician as "Dr. Kook" and observing that "he's a frightening individual. I don't find the man [to be] the kind of person I'd like to see in a position of high authority in this country." Going even further, the Director of the American Public Health Association said he would rather see the position of Surgeon General abolished than to see Koop confirmed. The process lasted a grueling nine months, but in the end the Senate confirmed Koop by a solid sixty-eight to twenty-four majority.

To the disappointment of such associates as Harold O. J. Brown, Koop kept his pledge not to use his post to campaign against abortion. In part, he stepped back because of the distinction he drew between his personal convictions and his public obligation to uphold the Constitution, but he had also grown weary of the fruitless quality of the debate over abortion. He recalled that he had "told both the pro-life and the pro-choice forces that I was dropping out of this controversy until they talked to each other. As you read the papers about the plans of either side, it sounds like World War II. It's always 'battle' and 'war' and 'confrontation,' and I just don't think that that ever leads to amicable conclusions. And there are many things that I think they could get together on. If the pro-life people in the late 1960's and the early 1970's had been willing to compromise with the pro-choice people, we could have had an abortion law that provided for abortion only for life of the mother, incest, rape, and defective child; that would have cut the abortions down to three percent of what they are today. But they had an all-

or-nothing mentality. They wanted it all, and they got nothing." Foremost among those who felt they got nothing were Everett Koop's friends. For the rest of his eight years at his post, the man who had spoken eloquently, even apocalyptically, about abortion, seldom mentioned it in public again.

The same people who were upset with Koop because they felt he did too little regarding abortion became even more upset when he did far more than they wanted regarding AIDS. Given the attention this devastating disease has received in the last fifteen years, it is stunning to realize that, when Dr. Koop was first approached about being Surgeon General in February 1981, neither he nor anyone else had ever heard of AIDS. In June of that year, the Centers for Disease Control (CDC) reported that five homosexuals had contracted a rare form of pneumonia. A month later, the Public Health Service reported that forty-one homosexual men had an uncommon cancerous condition known as Kaposi's sarcoma. Common to both sets of men, it appeared, was a virus that destroyed the immune system, leaving them vulnerable to diseases that a healthy immune system would easily resist. By August, the condition had been given a name—Acquired Immunodeficiency Syndrome—and the CDC knew of 108 cases, of which 43 had already proven fatal. Though he was preoccupied at the time with the brutal confirmation process, Koop remembered feeling that "if there ever was a disease made for a Surgeon General, it was AIDS. The Surgeon General is mandated by Congress to inform the American people about the prevention of disease and the promotion of health. If ever there was a public in need of education and straight talk about AIDS, it was the American people."

The mysterious disease continued to spread. By the end of Reagan's first term, the CDC had recorded 5,527 deaths from AIDS. By the end of his second term, nearly 103,000 cases and more than 60,000 deaths had been confirmed, and doctors estimated that the number of people infected with the virus was at least ten times greater than the number of confirmed cases. Given such startling numbers, and the enormous stir they generated, one can understand Koop's consternation that "for an astonishing five and a half years I was completely cut off from AIDS." He was directed not to make speeches about the disease, and when he appeared at press conferences or on television interview programs, the media were explicitly told that questions about AIDS were off limits. When Assistant Secretary of Health Ed Brandt created an Executive Task Force on AIDS in 1983, Koop was not asked to be part of it. Not surprisingly, Koop found this situation embarrassing and irritating, since he was made to appear either ignorant or unconcerned about a disease he regarded as the most important health problem facing America.

Koop professed not to be certain as to why he had been shut off from AIDS, but he felt surer about the overall character of the controversy sur-

rounding the disease. "Within the politics of AIDS," he wrote in his memoir, "lay one enduring, central conflict: AIDS pitted the politics of the gay
revolution of the seventies against the politics of the Reagan revolution of
the eighties." Elaborating on that statement, he explained that demands by
gays for an end to legal and social barriers to their full and free participation
in society created confusion and hostility that reduced sympathy for their
calls for greater attention to AIDS. At the same time, the Reagan administration and a major segment of its constituency contained many people
whose attitude toward homosexuals and homosexual behavior was decidedly
hostile. Quite plausibly, the White House saw less risk in ignoring a relatively small constituency than in offending a demonstrably large one.

That some offense was likely to be involved became increasingly clear. In
1983, researchers in France and the U.S. identified the specific human immunodeficiency virus (HIV) that caused AIDS. By mid-1985, they had concluded that the virus could be transmitted only by introducing semen or
blood from an infected person into the bloodstream of another person. With
the possible rare exception of transmission between two open wounds,
which could result in mingling of blood, there were only four known ways
of getting the disease: 1) sexual intercourse with an infected partner (usually
but not exclusively anal intercourse, which is practiced mainly by homosexual and bisexual males); 2) intravenous use of needles and syringes previously
used by an infected person; 3) transmission from an infected mother to her
baby during pregnancy or delivery; and 4) transmission of infected blood
through transfusion. Prior to the development in 1985 of a screening test to
detect the presence of the virus in blood supply, an estimated twelve thousand people, including ninety percent of severe hemophiliacs, were infected
as a result of blood transfusions. After measures were taken to protect the
blood supply, an overwhelming proportion of the remaining cases could be
traced to homosexual activity and intravenous drug use. As Koop observed,
the strong negative reaction to AIDS reflected not only fear of a deadly
disease, but also abhorrence of the behavior patterns that cause its transmission. "Most people get AIDS," he pointed out, "by doing things that most
people do not do, and do not approve of other people doing."

Fear and revulsion regarding AIDS took several forms. Predictably, many
saw the disease as a just punishment for wicked behavior. Pat Buchanan
wrote, "The poor homosexuals. They have declared war on nature and now
nature is exacting an awful retribution." Though he denied it, numerous
reporters claimed to have heard Jerry Falwell call AIDS "the wrath of God
upon homosexuals," and that was certainly a common sentiment in fundamentalist circles. Others saw AIDS as an opportunity for political gain. Appearing at a conference on "How to Win an Election," sponsored by Tim
LaHaye's American Coalition for Traditional Values, Newt Gingrich said of

AIDS, "It's something you ought to be looking at. . . . AIDS will do more to direct America back to the cost of violating traditional values, and to make America aware of the danger of certain behavior than anything we've seen. . . . For us it is a great rallying cry."

Some members of the Religious Right called for a quarantine of those afflicted with the disease. Jerry Falwell asserted that quarantining people with AIDS was no more unreasonable than quarantining cows with brucellosis, but acknowledged that such a measure was not likely to be taken, since "homosexuals constitute a potent voting bloc and cows do not." The American Family Association, headed by the Reverend Donald Wildmon and known mainly for its boycotts of companies that sponsor television programs regarded as morally offensive, circulated a petition calling for a quarantine of "all homosexual establishments," which it regarded as "crucial to your family's health and security." William Buckley suggested that AIDS sufferers be given a readily identifiable tattoo, to protect others from being infected. Dr. James O. Mason, director of the CDC, acknowledged that the Reagan administration was considering a quarantine of people with AIDS as late as 1985, after the facts about how AIDS is transmitted were known and the AIDS blood screening test had been developed. And as late as 1988, a *Los Angeles Times* poll revealed that forty-five percent of the general population and fifty-seven percent of fundamentalists favored a quarantine of people with AIDS. Koop commented that "in the very early days and then even after people should have known better, they refused to believe that it was passed only by sexual transmission, by blood products, by birth, and by intravenous drug abuse, and they would much rather have preferred that it came from typewriter keyboards and handles on briefcases and doorknobs and toilet seats—the usual stuff about sexually transmitted disease. The problems people faced were terribly severe. If you were a waiter and you turned up HIV-positive, you would lose your job. You might find yourself locked out of your apartment house. If you had a child, he might not be able to go to school. In Florida, a family with three little hemophiliac boys had their house burned down. It was just a very unreal situation."

NO QUARANTINE LAW was ever passed, but AIDS sufferers were nonetheless shunned and isolated. Certainly, few families have suffered more because of the calls to quarantine than the Reverend Jimmy Allen's. President of the Southern Baptist Convention from 1977 to 1979, the dynamic Texas preacher was a leading light among the moderate evangelical forces that resisted the SBC's takeover by fundamentalists. For a while, the bitter dissension and politicking that wracked the denomination he loved must have seemed the worst thing that could happen to him. Then, in 1985, his daughter-in-law Lydia learned that a blood transfusion she had received in 1982, just prior to the birth of her and Scott Allen's first child, had been infected with the AIDS virus. Blood tests revealed that Lydia, her son Matthew, and a new baby, Bryan, were all HIV-positive. Scott, an associate minister at the First Christian Church in Colorado Springs, tested negative. In a terrible coincidence, his brother Skip, a gay man, was also found to be HIV-positive.

In search of solace and support, and also feeling an ethical responsibility to inform people with whom they had been in contact about their condition, Scott Allen shared his news with the senior pastor of the church he was serving. "During that initial conversation," he said, "he asked for my resignation." Allen told the pastor that he did not want to resign and that his family was in great emotional and spiritual need. The next day, he found a letter on his desk, saying, "Thank you for your resignation. We'll be praying for you as you seek God's will." When he did not tender the desired resignation, the church board informed him that he was being given a "leave of absence," effective immediately. Stunned, the Allens left Colorado in the middle of the night and drove to Dallas, to be near their families.

Scott was able to find work with the AIDS project of the Mission Service Corps of the Southern Baptist Convention of Texas, but he and his family had less success in finding a church that would take them in. They were particularly interested in finding a church that would accept Matthew, who was three at the time, into the Sunday school. Repeatedly, Disciples, Baptists, Methodists, and Presbyterians told them there was no room at the altar. Jimmy Allen, who had moved to Fort Worth in 1980 to help launch a national religious cable television network, imagined he could help in this effort.

"I didn't want to lay an unbearable burden on a fellow pastor," he said, "because I knew the pragmatic responsibilities of pastoral ministry. So what I tried to do was to pick people who were progressive, involved, compassionate, concerned pastors, and I sat with them to talk to them about this family and this child and his need to be in a Sunday School. I made a canvass of several whom I knew and who I really felt would be as eager to do this as they possibly could be. Each of them said, 'You're right; we need to do this. We'll try to get it done.' Each of them had his own way to go at it, and I don't know what all the processes were, but all of them took it seriously enough to try. None of them managed it. One after another would come to say it hadn't worked. 'We had a doctor who was scared and couldn't give a thousand-percent assurance,' or 'we had this' or 'we had that,' so it didn't work. It ultimately meant that there was no place for Matthew to go to Sunday School. There was a silence after that. I didn't feel that I ought to hound them about it, but I think of all the wounds that we had, that was the deepest one. I know it was the deepest one for Lydia and for Scott, and it was as deep a wound for me as I ever encountered. What we saw was a reversal of the New Testament concept of 'Perfect love casts out fear.' In our case, fear cast out perfect love. I think that's a universal experience of humanity. When you're afraid, love dries up and you begin protecting rather than giving yourself away. And love means giving yourself away. A year or two later we did find a Church of Christ that would allow Matt to come to their summer day school, and he did that. The pastor just declared it an [HIV-positive] zone and just wrote and told everybody he'd done that, and he had a good response to it. By that time, though, the emotional and spiritual damage was so great that this couple had given up hope; therefore, Matt has never had the kind of Sunday School kind of nurture that he needed."

MATTHEW ALLEN, REJECTED by one church after another, finally found an accepting community in the institution regularly reviled by the right: a public school. The Lakewood elementary school in Dallas "not only allowed him to stay," noted ABC News reporter Peggy Wehmeyer; for six years "they surrounded him with love and support." Jimmy Allen gratefully agreed. "The most Christian institution we found for our little boy was the Lakewood public school . . . a place where people know how to love."

Scott Allen, though not infected with the disease, was nevertheless ravaged by it. "The two things I had dedicated my life to," he said, "were God and my family. This whole thing destroyed my view of God, and it takes away my family little by little, inch by inch, day by day." Bryan died first, when he was a little over nine months old. Scott noted that "he weighed only ten pounds. Very, very small. He never grew. He could never crawl, he could never hold his head up on his own. And he lived with an enormous amount of pain all of his life." Lydia died in February 1992. Matthew hung on bravely until late 1995.

In 1987, the *Baptist Standard* published anonymously an essay of Lydia's, which she called "Wearing the Scarlet Letter 'A'." In it, she told of teaching phonics to Matt and asking him if he could think of a word that begins with A. His poignant answer was, "A is for AIDS." From that beginning, she gave a brief account of how she had gotten the disease, of Bryan's death, and of the disease's devastating toll on their family's daily life. "We are the new UNTOUCHABLES," she wrote,

> The few relationships I have had are superficial and almost totally
> based on fabrication. How could I truthfully answer simple questions:
> "Why did you move here?" "What was wrong with your baby?" I

couldn't talk about the fact that my heart was breaking every time I looked at my little boy. I couldn't share the fact that my marriage was fragmenting from the incredible stress in our lives. I couldn't "act sick" lest someone get suspicious. So I hid my symptoms and my pain.

I didn't dare reveal anything about the severity of my son's illness lest my child be totally ostracized from all socialization. I couldn't even contact former coworkers to explain why I had suddenly disappeared.

Telling of the painful and fruitless attempt to find a church that would accept them, she revealed,

We do not attend church now. The rejection runs too deep. To Christians, I would say that AIDS cripples not only the body but the heart. At a time when the AIDS victim is dealing with death and dying, heavy financial burden, and physical debilitation, they need support, care, and concern—not rejection. If there ever was a time to reach out and touch the "lepers" of our day, it is now.

She concluded by saying,

I have done nothing immoral or illegal to contract this disease, but those who HAVE hurt just as deeply as I. Their needs are as great or greater than mine for a compassionate and loving response to AIDS.

Jimmy Allen found Lydia's comparison between AIDS and leprosy deeply moving. "Jesus," he noted, "was the first man in recorded history to reach out and voluntarily touch a leper, and when Jesus touched lepers, it didn't give him leprosy; it gave lepers healing. He reached past the barriers of fear, past the cries of 'unclean,' and he moved because he was love and is love. We don't touch lepers, and somehow that separation, that refusal to touch, contaminates us with a deeper virus than leprosy: the virus of indifference, of hard-heartedness. You see, any time you need to reach out and touch and do not, something hardens the arteries of compassion in your spirit. And that shrivels the soul."

As of mid-1996, Jimmy Allen was still dealing with the impending death of his son Skip. He acknowledged that dealing with Skip's homosexuality had been difficult for him, but felt they had worked through that. "He is my son, and I love him," he said, "but he is going to die one of these days, and he is absolutely unafraid about it, because he has such an absolute belief that God is working in his life." Any of his early judgmentalism has been softened by experience, and he observed that "when you die of a heart attack, nobody blames you for the fact that you overate all of your life. If you die of lung cancer, folks may lament the fact that you smoked all your life, but they don't blame you for it. But if you die of AIDS, they ask, 'How did you get it? Maybe you really deserved it.' I think the attitude of rejecting people, of deciding that God is bringing judgment specifically to individual AIDS victims or to AIDS families is an inadequate and incorrect interpretation of God. The biblical view I have is that evil came into the world in man's rebellion against God, and that God is working at being on our side, seeking and saving all that he had lost. He is walking with me, and he loves me enough that he actually enters into my pain. He feels as I feel it. You can't decide that because we have a disease that can be traced to misbehavior that God is socking us. God doesn't say 'gotcha.' Alcohol does befuddle the brain, fat cells do create heart attacks, sexual misbehavior often creates an atmosphere in which AIDS is transmitted, but it is not because God is bringing a vindictive judgment on an individual. When you have a twisted idea about God's being a 'gotcha' kind of God, you have lost the spirit of the Gospel. There is in this world, in every religion, a fundamentalist judgmental mindset: You find it in Shi'ite Islam, in some forms of Buddhism, in some forms of the Jewish faith, and you find it in some forms of Christianity. That is a mindset that I reject."

Former Falwell associate Ed Dobson shared Allen's rejection of the view that God created AIDS to punish homosexuals. "I find it impossible to draw that conclusion from the Bible," he said, adding that "this would mean that it's also God's judgment on people in Thailand, on hundreds of thousands of people in Africa, on people who are hemophiliacs. I don't agree with that at all. Are there potential consequences to risky behavior? Yes. You can't deny that. But when you begin declaring things as the judgment of God, you have presumed yourself to be God's spokesperson, and that's pretty dangerous territory. I believe sexuality is a gift from God to be expressed exclusively within the commitment of heterosexual marriage, but I do not believe that gives us a license to hate people, including homosexuals. Christians have not been very good about loving gay people. Oh, they'll tell you they hate the sin but love the sinner, but I don't see much love for the sinner. I cringe at some of the language and rhetoric [I hear] regarding the gay community."

Though most evangelicals, whatever private feelings, felt no compulsion to take overt action against gays, there were occasional sorry episodes of intolerance by professed Christians, reflecting a general increase in anti-gay violence.

Anti-gay violence also increased noticeably in the mid-eighties, and the potential for even more was obvious. A Nevada newspaper ran a full-page "AIDS Alert" ad in which one of the sponsoring ministers was quoted as saying, "I think we should do what the Bible says and cut their throats." Such extreme statements were not restricted to the fundamentalist fringe.

Koop told of discussing a proposal for widespread AIDS screening with California Congressman William Dannemeyer. When he asked the congressman what he would do if it were possible to identify every HIV-infected person in the country, Dannemeyer replied, "Wipe them off the face of the earth."

If Jerry Falwell ever spoke of AIDS as God's judgment on homosexuals, as reporters assert, he denies it, although perhaps he has merely recanted a bit. In any case, he now says, "I believe that AIDS and syphilis and all the sexually transmitted diseases are God's judgment upon the total society for embracing what God has condemned: sex outside of marriage." He explicitly believes that homosexuality is both sinful and curable. "We lead gays to Christ," he said. "We rehabilitate them, we help them, we marry them to persons of the opposite sex, we minister to their families. It's something from which a person can be delivered and recovered. We do it on a regular basis, as do most Christian ministries. But to say 'Gay is okay. It's fine. You don't need to be changed. Just go do it.' No. While we need to love the homosexual, and I work with them on almost a weekly basis, we must tell them that what they're doing is wrong. AIDS has been communicated everywhere, but it had its origins, clearly, within the homosexual community. While we should spend whatever it takes to find a cure, we should also be telling folks, 'Don't do what causes AIDS.' To me, that's just common sense. We should tell people who are doing things that can make them sick, 'Stop doing it.'" Falwell did not think AIDS sufferers should be ostracized. "We've had AIDS patients at Liberty University," he revealed, "we do right now. We look at the health issue, and if there's any danger to another student, we take all of the prudent measures, but we don't deny them admission. At Thomas Road Baptist Church, we've had three members with AIDS that I know of, all of them in good standing until the day I preached their funerals."

E. V. Hill, pastor of the Mt. Zion Baptist Church in the Watts area of Los Angeles and one of few African-American ministers to align himself with the Religious Right, takes a similar approach to AIDS and those it affects: offering help while warning against risky behavior and reserving the right to behave in a guarded fashion. "I believe," he said, "that God's judgment is becoming clearer and clearer by becoming more severe. And I don't know of anything that should speak [more] loudly to us than the problems of AIDS, that God is dissatisfied and is very definitely warning us that He can get rougher." He added that he felt Christians have an obligation with regard to AIDS—"Raising funds? Trying to help? Trying to counsel? Count on me."—but that the obligation *is* limited by a rational prudence that people with AIDS should respect. "I have said to people who have been members of this church and have AIDS, 'Don't try to act like people are bad by not coming up and hugging and kissing you.' I have said from the pulpit, 'If I come down with AIDS, whichever way I catch it, you don't have to come kiss me or hug me or come to the hospice to see me. You just don't have to do that.' I've also said [to people with AIDS], 'There is a responsibility on your side not to indulge in things that can bring AIDS. And if you are an AIDS victim, then be careful.''

A S A W A R E N E S S O F the scope and seriousness of the AIDS crisis spread, public demand for some kind of response from the White House grew intense, generating charges that the government was either cooperating with homosexuals to downplay the seriousness of the epidemic, presumably to dampen anti-gay sentiments, or was deliberately ignoring the disease in the hope that it would wipe out the homosexual community. In July 1985, after Koop told his superiors at Health and Human Services that he simply could not remain silent about AIDS any longer, he was finally made a member of the AIDS task force and given permission to say whatever he felt was appropriate regarding the disease. The real breakthrough, however, came in February 1986, when the president asked him to prepare a special report on AIDS.

Since the overwhelming portion of AIDS cases were the result of what Koop called "a conscious decision to carry out a specific form of personal behavior," he believed that, in the absence of effective treatment, the only way to combat the disease was through education. That meant his report would need to be frank, forthright, and written in simple language. Koop realized that "telling the truth about AIDS, the truth, the whole truth, and nothing but the truth would not be well received in some places. One of those places would be the White House, at least in those offices where ideology would be the main concern."

After consulting with numerous organizations and experts—and preparing twenty-seven drafts—Koop released his report on October 22, 1986. The report made explicit the ways in which the disease could be contracted and clearly recommended against sex outside monogamous relationships and use of illegal drugs. Descriptions of such behavior as anal intercourse may have made his conservative constituency uncomfortable; his recommendation that people determined to have sex outside of marriage use condoms and that children receive sex education made them livid. "I used the real terrible word 'condom,' " he recalled, "and that was probably the most serious word that I used in my entire tenure as Surgeon General. It absolutely inflamed part of the president's constituency and certain parts of the White House. It was not easy for [me, as] someone then in his seventies, married for fifty years, with children and grandchildren, to be talking about those things in public. But somebody had to talk about them, and nobody was. I made it a point never to talk about condoms without going through the whole litany of my firm belief in abstinence for young people and mutually faithful monogamy for older people, and I never said anything about condoms until I talked about those things, and then I said, 'But if you persist in a promiscuous lifestyle and you haven't heard these good-health messages, you are in danger, and the only thing we have to offer you is a condom. It's not one hundred percent safe, but it's better than nothing."

Catholics, of course, objected to condoms as part of their official but widely ignored prohibition against contraception. However, both Catholics and conservative Protestants felt that, instead of telling people how to protect themselves while engaging in immoral behavior, the report should simply have condemned the behavior; urging the use of condoms or sterile needles, they argued, was tantamount to approval. Even more troublesome was the report's recommendation of early sex education. In answer to a question posed at a press conference to announce release of the report, Koop had said he favored beginning sex education by as early as the third grade. Richard Viguerie's *Conservative Digest* immediately charged that Koop was "proposing instruction in buggery for schoolchildren as young as the third grade on the spurious grounds that the problem is one of ignorance and not morality," and Viguerie himself said, "I don't think he is the Surgeon General of all the people. I think he is the Surgeon General of the far left. He is the Surgeon General primarily of the homosexual lobby. He is not a person who is being responsive to his boss, Ronald Reagan." The *National Review* pronounced Koop guilty of "criminal negligence" in recommending the use of condoms. Paul Weyrich and Phyllis Schlafly wrote that "Koop's proposals for stopping AIDS represent the homosexuals' views, not those of the pro-family movement." In another article, Schlafly said the AIDS report, perhaps because it included the telephone numbers of several homosexual resource centers, "looks and reads like it was edited by the Gay Task Force."

Koop knew, of course, that both the political and religious right had long opposed sex education, but asked, sensibly enough, "How can you talk to children about the dangers of a sexually transmitted disease that is fatal if you don't let them understand something about their own sexuality? It's an absolute insanity to try to do that. And I didn't feel I was out of place at all as Surgeon General to say that sex education should take place as early as possible." He also believed it was unrealistic to expect parents to perform this necessary task. "I was in pediatrics all of my professional life," he said, "and I never met a mother or father who didn't say, 'The sex education of my children is my privilege and my obligation,' but practically none of them ever did it. It seems to me that if parents will not advise their children about what might threaten their lives, then somebody else has to do it, and the schools seem a logical place." He acknowledged that a child might learn something that would clash with the parents' moral beliefs, but felt this could provide an excellent opportunity for parents to make their position clear. Instead, he said, most parents teach their children little or nothing about sex and "as a result, the children of America are educated by television and in the streets."

Koop suggested that part of the negative reaction to his recommendations stemmed from the mistaken belief that "if condoms are available and young people know about it, they are going to go out and use them right away, and a promiscuous generation will develop. No studies have ever indicated that." Schlafly, he said, "went on television and essentially said that she would rather see her children become infected with sexually transmitted diseases than for [them] to know there was such a thing as condoms. My comment is that they're probably in the garage filling them with water to see how big they can get before they rupture, but she doesn't know it." Schlafly also charged that the report amounted to "multimillion-dollar free publicity" for condom manufacturers and claimed that some schools were using Koop's message as an excuse for teaching children how to perform both heterosexual and homosexual acts while using condoms. In a rare display of pique, Koop described Schlafly as "beneath contempt" and a woman "whose idea of sex education was something like 'Don't let anyone touch you where you wear your swimsuit.' " He offered a similar assessment of conservative columnists Rowland Evans and Robert Novak, charging that one relatively short article they had written about him contained "seventeen factual errors and twenty omissions that distorted the truth." Perhaps, he suggested, "their vitriolic behavior was . . . only compensation for their lack of real influence."

Inside the White House, the strongest opposition to the report came from Koop's old ally, Carl Anderson, who had lobbied to get Koop appointed Surgeon General, and from Gary Bauer, a key adviser to the president regarding family policy. Pat Buchanan, White House director of communications, shared their views. Anderson objected to a statement in the AIDS report that "Most Americans are opposed to homosexuality, promiscuity of any kind, and prostitution." According to Koop, "He wanted me to say 'All Americans . . .' and did not seem to understand that I could not say it because it was not true." In less than three weeks after the report was released, Bauer suggested to Koop that it might be time for a second edition. Since the report was new and two million copies were ready for distribution, Koop asked what he had in mind. The only "update" Bauer sought, according to Koop, was removal of references to condoms, which Koop dismissed as ridiculous. At a later meeting, Bauer argued against teaching children about AIDS by trotting out a white notebook containing what Koop described as "bad semi-pornographic sex education material," claiming that he did not want his daughters to be exposed to such materials. Koop's response to Bauer was that there are many things parents might prefer their children not know, such as the possibility that a stranger might try to abduct them and sexually molest them, but that such knowledge might save their lives. Bauer also told of a Christmas dinner at which members of his family had said, "Koop wants to give condoms to kids in the third grade." When Koop said that anyone who had made such a statement had not read the report, Bauer acknowledged that was true. Such encounters led Koop to observe that "the Reagan White House, including the president himself at times, reasoned anecdotally instead of examining the evidence and drawing conclusions."

AS TIME PASSED and Koop continued to speak about AIDS and his report, his critics on the right grew more strident. After a speech at the National Press Club in which he acknowledged that an AIDS-infected pregnant woman could legally choose to have her baby aborted, March for Life organizer Nellie Gray called for Koop's resignation and "symbolically withdrew" an award her organization had given him to honor his long-time opposition to abortion. Obviously more nettlesome to him was Phyllis Schlafly's campaign to sabotage a 1987 "Salute to the Surgeon General" dinner that some of his "faithful conservative supporters" arranged to honor his contributions. Schlafly and Paul Weyrich wrote a letter to the event's sponsors, which included every man who expected to be a serious candidate for the 1988 Republican nomination, strongly suggesting that they dissociate themselves from the event. In addition, according to Koop, Schlafly circulated a petition at a Republican fund-raising meeting, asking people to sign their names if they wished to receive information about sex education. ("Was she going to send them a picture of a swimsuit?" he wondered.) "Then," he said, "without the knowledge of those who signed the request form, she instead appended their names to a petition denouncing me and urging a boycott of the dinner in my honor." Bob Dole, Jack Kemp, Pete DuPont, and Pat Robertson all withdrew their support. George Bush did not attend, but sent a warm letter of encouragement. Jesse Helms did not attend, but remained a sponsor. Of the major Republican stalwarts who had been expected to show up, only Orrin Hatch appeared. Asked about this episode, Phyllis Schlafly replied, "Oh, yeah, that was pretty funny. I did have a hand in getting all the presidential candidates to find another engagement that evening. So the dinner turned out to be just a disaster. I think there were about five presidential candidates who reneged on going." Koop's

comment was crisp: "I didn't think people who would follow Phyllis Schlafly in that kind of a campaign were of presidential caliber."

In the hope that he might be more successful at communicating with the
Religious Right than he had been with veteran ideologues, Koop set aside
seven weeks in 1987, during which he spoke only to religious groups. "I
chose," he explained, "to speak to the very people who didn't seem to
understand what the stakes were." His first speech was to the National
Religious Broadcasters, to whom he said, " 'If you believe homosexuality is
a sin, I know that, wherever you learned that, you learned an equivalent
Christian doctrine, and that is your obligation to separate the sin from the
sinner, and therefore you have no right to point a finger at somebody and
say this person should not be cared for because of the manner in which he
got into trouble.' I think that had a telling effect on them, because I used
their teaching to teach them. I said, 'If you believe this, you've got to believe
that, because you learned them in the same place. You can't have it both
ways.' "

Koop used that occasion to make an additional point. In a speech directly
preceding his, Vice President George Bush had referred to an incident in
which a group of Christians had burned some books in the public square of
a Southern town because they objected to their being in the town library.
"There are those," Bush said disapprovingly, "who would seek to impose
their will and dictate their interpretation of morality on the rest of society."
Building on Bush's comments, Koop told the broadcasters, "Initially, you
sought freedom. In the process, you gained power. And with power, a small
minority now want control." Religious Roundtable leader Ed McAteer
pronounced this statement "absolutely dead wrong" and declared that such a
comment "makes me reticent about giving him my support." Others, however, responded positively, and invited Koop to appear on their broadcasts
and in their churches.

Again and again, whether on Jerry Falwell's *Old Time Gospel Hour* or in a
chapel service at Liberty University or over the Moody Bible Institute's
radio station or as part of a Billy Graham television special or on PBS or
HBO, Koop delivered his message of morality, values, and the need for
compassion. He repeatedly pointed out that leprosy provided much of the
impetus for Christian missionary work in the nineteenth century. "That was
the great issue," he asserted. The attitude of Christians then had been, " 'We
will leave the shores of England and Belgium and Holland, and we will go to
Africa and India, and we will treat leprosy patients because, first of all, they
have a disease they don't understand, they are outcasts, they are pushed out
of their families, they are desolate, and they're dying.' And my plea to the
Christian church was, 'AIDS is modern-day leprosy as far as the challenge

for social service is concerned. Respond in the 1980's as you did in the 1860's. That's your obligation.' "

What Koop was doing, Ed Dobson observed, was a practical application of Martin Luther's concept of Two Kingdoms. "It was easy for people to say, 'We are against condom distribution, period, as a matter of principle. But we have an obligation both to God's Kingdom and to human kingdoms. In our obligation to God's Kingdom, we are obviously going to promote sexuality as we understand it and as Scripture teaches it as the best prevention to the spread of HIV. But C. Everett Koop introduced the other concept: What about our commitment to public health, and what about those who choose not to believe our values? Are we willing to let them die for the sake of our values?" Mel White, who had been apprehensive about Koop's appointment, applauded his approach: "This open, loving evangelical doctor did what so many other evangelicals like Jimmy Carter had done. He showed that evangelical Christians can be warm and loving and accepting, too. I was afraid he'd be a fundamentalist in that position, but he wasn't at all."

Based on an unscientific survey of what he heard on Christian radio stations, Koop was convinced his report was having some positive effect, but it was clear the reaction on the Religious Right was mixed, and several TV preachers weighed in against Koop's position, if not against the Surgeon General himself. D. James Kennedy aired a program featuring Gary Bauer and Secretary of Education William Bennett. Here and elsewhere, Bauer contended that one reason sex-education courses in the 1960s and '70s had not stopped teenage pregnancies was because they made no effort to inculcate a sense of right and wrong. Bauer also believed that having an adult tell children, "If you can't take the advice [not to engage in sex] and you're just unable to control yourself, here's the way to avoid some of the consequences," would undermine the efforts of parents who wanted their children to abstain from sex until marriage. Bennett also stressed that the key issue regarding AIDS was morality, not prophylaxis. From the beginning of the controversy, he had contended not only that sex education should be in his domain rather than the Surgeon General's, but also that such education was inappropriate for grade-school children. Bennett was also a proponent of widespread mandatory testing for AIDS, which Koop opposed.

Jerry Falwell, despite his openness to Koop's appearance in Lynchburg, sent out fund-raising letters alleging that homosexuals "have expressed the attitude that they know they are going to die and they are going to take as many people with them as they can," and arguing that legislation granting increased civil rights to gays would "force morally upstanding citizens to work alongside homosexual AIDS carriers." In a similar vein, Pat Robertson allowed that quarantining homosexuals "might not be a bad idea." Interestingly, the religious broadcaster who showed the greatest empathy for people with AIDS seems to have been the much maligned and ridiculed Tammy Faye Bakker, who insisted on having AIDS patients on her television program *Tammy's House Party* and wept—no surprise—as she spoke of a young man who had told her the saddest thing about his plight was that his parents and sister were afraid to touch him. "How sad," she said, "that we as Christians, who ought to be the salt of the earth, and we, who are supposed to be able to love everyone, are afraid so badly of an AIDS patient that we will not go up and put our arm around them and tell them that we care." Mel White observed appreciatively, "Tammy insisted on talking about how Jesus would treat people with AIDS on her program. Tammy Bakker would not be shamed into silence."

Koop admitted that it would have been helpful if President Reagan had assumed some leadership on the issue, but pointed out that talking about diseases was not customarily considered to be part of a president's job, and that AIDS presented a devilishly difficult problem. "No think tank," he asserted, "could have concocted a more difficult disease to deal with—politically, medically, socially, and economically—than AIDS." When Reagan finally agreed, at the First Lady's request, to address the American Foundation for AIDS Research, the original draft of his speech was watered down to remove references to condoms and to Ryan White, the young hemophiliac who had been infected with HIV during a blood transfusion and who had become a national and widely admired spokesman for AIDS sufferers. Many in his audience booed when the president revealed he had added AIDS to the list of diseases for which immigrants and aliens could be denied admission or residence in the U.S., as well as for his approving remarks regarding mandatory testing of federal prisoners. There was relief, however, that he did not call for widespread testing, which the Public Health Service opposed on the grounds that the suffering experienced by people falsely identified as HIV-positive would far outweigh the gains of any such effort. They also applauded the president's assertion that, because AIDS could not be transmitted through casual contact, "there's no reason for those who carry the AIDS virus to wear the scarlet A." According to biographer Lou Cannon, Reagan had barely participated in preparing the speech, which he delivered on May 21, 1987—just seven weeks after addressing AIDS for the first time in public.

This lack of concern or will to engage the issue more seriously was seen even more clearly, Cannon noted, when, two months later, Reagan "appointed an AIDS commission that included opponents of AIDS education and was devoid of physicians who had treated AIDS patients or scientists who had engaged in AIDS research. The commission appointments reflected the influence of conservatives who feared not only AIDS but homosexuals. In naming this body, Reagan sent an unfortunate message to the public that he did not care enough about the AIDS problem to muster the best scientific information available."

Distribution of the Reagan commission's thirty-six-page report on AIDS was uneven and perhaps deliberately impeded at times. The Public Health Service wanted to mail a copy to everyone on the IRS mailing list, but that would have been prohibitively expensive. But, perhaps embarrassed that western countries with a far smaller AIDS problem had done a better job of public education, Congress appropriated money early in 1988 to send a six-page flier, "Understanding AIDS: A Message from the Surgeon General," to 107 million addresses, making it the largest mailing in American history. Naturally, much of the response continued to be negative. One critic doubtless spoke for others when he marveled that "a guy who looks like an Old Testament prophet [would] end up selling the gospel of sodomy to the entire country with a mailing of 107 million advertisements for condoms!" On the other hand, Koop's stature in Washington and throughout the nation unquestionably was rising significantly. One of his strongest allies in gaining congressional approval for the mailing had been his old critic, Henry Waxman, who had also come to admire him for his strong anti-smoking stance. AIDS sufferers and gays likewise applauded Koop's performance. Randy Shilts, author of *And the Band Played On,* the definitive account of the early stages of the scientific assault on AIDS, declared with wonder that "it took an ultra-conservative fundamentalist . . . to credibly call for all of America to take the epidemic seriously at last. Unwittingly, the Reagan administration had produced a certifiable AIDS hero."

Whether in response to Dr. Koop's call for compassion toward AIDS sufferers or simply as part of a more general public understanding of the disease, the Reverend Jimmy Allen acknowledged that Christian churches have gotten better at dealing with people with AIDS. Even the evangelical and fundamentalist community did gradually face the disease with more sensitivity and courage than it had shown in the early years. Of the churches that had turned his son's family away, Allen said, "Nobody went on record as saying they were not going to take care of ministering to an AIDS child. They just didn't minister to him." Eventually, however, "each of those churches faced up to their responsibility, and each one of them is now ministering to AIDS people." Allen also spoke graciously of individual Christians who had offered love and support. "God has a lot of people scattered all through the Christian community," he said, "who belong to Jesus Christ and have his spirit about them. We had churches and Christians who would get together and come do things like cleaning the house. Some of them were doing it by their own initiative because they were in churches that were not going to respond in corporate ways, and they were just determined to respond. That happened with a lot of folks. That was a very encouraging thing. I really don't want to give the impression that conservative Christians don't care. There is lots of caring going on, but corporate structures have a hard time making those decisions. That's what's been the barrier. But we are now at a point at which a lot of corporate structures are making positive decisions. I'm in churches all the time where there are caring ministries that are doing things with AIDS [patients]. They are putting together support groups. Their nursery policies have been worked out so that they are able to handle any kind of person with an infectious disease in a reasonable manner."

As part of their response to AIDS, churches have also begun to minister to the families of homosexuals. "You must remember," Koop said, "that the families of AIDS patients [often] learn two things on the same day: 'My child is dying of AIDS, and he is also homosexual.' For many people, the diagnosis of homosexuality is worse than facing the death of their child. These people are devastated, and one of the things the Christian church has done is to provide group therapy to help them come to terms with the fact that their children are still their children." Jimmy Allen was grateful for such developments, but regretted they did not come sooner. "It is changing," he said. "It's just so far behind the timeline for our need that it [was too late to help] our woundedness."

Scott Allen has turned away from Christianity to seek solace in Eastern religious traditions. Jimmy Allen tries to count his blessings. "The secret," he said, was "a burden. The sharing of the secret is an opportunity. The Father with whom I've walked all this time has revealed a lot more of his presence and love. Suffering has been there, but I do not ask for pity. I do not even ask for all the answers. I ask for strength to deal with the Mystery. And the marvel of it is that it's a joyous journey. The Bible says that Jesus endured the cross; he did that for the joy that was set before him. There is a joy about living life to its fullest, and that means suffering is a part of it, laughter is a part of it, harmony and happiness are part of it. All of those things are in the mix. All of us hurt, everybody has about as much capacity for pain as he can handle. What we do with our pain is the answer, and what God has given me is a sense of absolute energy and victory in dealing with our pain. I've asked him not to waste this pain, to let me learn from it, and let me share the good news of hope with people who are feeling their own kind of pain."

THE INVISIBLE ARMY

WHEN JERRY FALWELL and his New Right associates formed Moral Majority, they invited Charles Stanley from Atlanta, D. James Kennedy from Florida, and Tim LaHaye from California to be part of it, but they consciously left Pat Robertson off the list, even though he lived right there in Virginia. Simple rivalry may have played some part. Falwell had called most of the shots at Thomas Road for nearly twenty-five years and may not have wanted to contend with Robertson, who was known to want and usually get his own way. Despite what appears to be astonishing self-confidence, Falwell may also have felt insecure in standing beside a man like Robertson. Falwell's father was a drunkard who killed his own brother in a gunfight; Robertson's father, A. Willis Robertson, served in the United States Congress for thirty-four years. Falwell had gone to Baptist Bible College in Springfield, Missouri; Robertson was a Phi Beta Kappa graduate of Washington and Lee, Yale Law School, and New York Theological Seminary. Falwell had a popular syndicated weekly television program; Robertson had a flourishing cable network and his *700 Club* aired for an hour every day. Without much question, however, the major reason for Robertson's exclusion was his theology.

Though ordained as a Baptist, Robertson had long been a prominent figure in the charismatic wing of evangelicalism, exercising such spiritual gifts as speaking in tongues, healing, prophesying, and the increasingly common "word of knowledge," which enabled him to announce with authority that "someone out there in Iowa has just been healed" of cancer, liver problems, female trouble, or, most famously, hemorrhoids. Like most Baptists, Jerry Falwell thought the possession of such gifts had ended with the death of the apostles and regarded charismatics and Pentecostals as guilty of grievous error or, at the least, errant nonsense—Falwell once facetiously attributed tongue-speaking to eating bad pizza. Baptist churches and associations often expelled charismatics as heretics; to have asked one of the best-known tongue-speakers in the country to help him recruit fundamentalists into politics would have doomed Falwell's effort from the outset.

It is quite possible that, even if asked, Robertson would have declined an invitation to join Moral Majority, since he had long held an ambivalent attitude toward political involvement. In 1966, he refused to use his growing influence to support his father's campaign for re-election; the elder Robertson lost by only six hundred votes. In his 1972 autobiography, *Shout It from the Housetops,* he explained that he had "yearned to get into the fray and start swinging, but the Lord refused to give me the liberty," telling him, "I called you to My ministry. . . . You cannot tie My eternal purposes to the success of any political candidate . . . not even your own father." Robertson backslid in 1976 when he offered strong support for Jimmy Carter, but his disappointment with Carter rekindled his wariness of politics. In 1980, he participated in "Washington for Jesus" and attended the National Affairs Briefing in Dallas, then stepped back once again, declaring that "active partisan politics is the wrong path for true evangelicals." The following year, he formally resigned from the Religious Roundtable, informing Ed Mc-Ateer that "your objective is to change America through political means. Mine is through spiritual means."

Robertson either had unconventional definitions of "political" and "spiritual" or gave in to withdrawal pains even more quickly than usual. Within months of making this statement, he established an organization called the Freedom Council, whose purpose, he said, would be "to fight for the rights of believers and to teach evangelical Christians, primarily, but also Orthodox Jews and Roman Catholics, how they could be effective in the political process. There are 175,000 political precincts in America. My goal was to have ten trained activists in each precinct. I was playing for the long haul, and I knew the answer was to move into the precincts, get to know the people and understand their needs and desires, and to build an organization that would be effective for local school-board races, city council races, legislative races, Congressional races, and ultimately the presidency." The council did its work through political units consisting mainly of Pentecostal Christians contacted through *700 Club* mailing lists or local churches, and organized by precinct and congressional district. Though it was accurately described as a grassroots operation, the Freedom Council's precinct leaders received instruction from headquarters in Virginia Beach, most of its financial support came from the Christian Broadcasting Network, and no one doubted that Pat Robertson was in charge.

Despite an attempt to have a nationwide presence, the group did not try to draw attention to itself. "We're not running ads in papers to recruit people to our cause," a California coordinator said. "We get less pressure from the news media that way, so people don't know where you're at, what you're doing." The main thing the Freedom Council was doing from 1981 until 1985 was getting organized. Its first and, apparently, only significant project, which had its focus in Michigan, played a crucial role in laying the groundwork for Pat Robertson's presidential campaign.

Lori Packer learned about the Freedom Council while she was still a student at the University of Michigan. An evangelical who had participated in several political campaigns, Packer was attracted to the Freedom Council's emphasis on responsible participation and prayerful concern for government leaders. Because she had a modicum of experience, she was hired to recruit people to attend training seminars in two congressional districts. Using lists supplied by other activists, she would "just call people up and let them know that 'there is this new organization that we're starting' and ask them to come out to an informational meeting. From there it grew to encouraging people to become involved as precinct delegates in either the Republican or Demo-cratic Party. That was kind of the entry-level position for partisan involve-ment. Most of them got involved in the Republican Party—probably ninety percent—but we recruited for both parties."

Just as not all members of the Freedom Council were Republicans, not all of its leaders were evangelicals. The state director for Michigan was Marlene Elwell, a Roman Catholic whose initiation into politics had come in 1972 when she took part in a successful effort to defeat a state referendum to legalize abortion. That effort, of course, was overturned by the *Roe v. Wade* decision the following year, but Elwell was hooked on politics. The daughter of a truck driver, she was reared as a Democrat: "In the neighborhood where I grew up," she said, "if you voted Republican and let anyone know it, that was cause for Confession." That changed in 1980 when the GOP decided to hold its national convention in Detroit. With Ronald Reagan as the likely nominee, Elwell saw an opportunity "to get pro-life language into the platform of the Republican Party." When the party, influenced at least to some degree by the efforts of the Pro-Life Impact Committee Elwell organized, adopted an anti-abortion plank, she was converted: "I've been a Republican ever since."

As she got to know more Republicans, Elwell discovered that many of them were pro-abortion. Disillusioned by this, she saw a need to recruit more pro-life Christians into politics. Catholics were typically anti-abortion, but also more likely to be Democrats. Conservative Protestants were likely to be pro-life, but less likely to be involved in politics. The solution, she con-cluded, was to mobilize evangelical Christians. When a black evangelical pastor from Detroit learned of her intentions, he said, "Marlene, there's a guy named Pat Robertson who wants to do exactly what you're doing," and recommended that she meet him. Elwell had never heard of Robertson or the *700 Club,* but a trip to Virginia Beach convinced her that Robertson's vision for getting Christians involved in politics was the same as her own. Quite sensibly, she decided that, since "he had more money and more clout, rather than start my own organization, I would just join his." Because she already had considerable experience at grassroots organizing, she was appointed coordinator for a congressional district early in 1985 and, not long afterward, became the Freedom Council's director for the entire state. Elwell insists that when she first began working for the Freedom Council, she had no idea that Pat Robertson might be considering a run for the presidency. That changed in 1986, and Michigan was the place where the change first occurred.

The 1980s were an odd decade for both the Democratic and Republican parties in Michigan, with each trying to gain an edge on the other and both seeking to upstage their counterparts in other states. Michigan Republicans had resurrected an unusual procedure that called for presidential delegates to be selected at a state convention; the peculiar aspect was that delegates to that convention were to be selected approximately two years prior to the Republican National Convention. This meant that a well-organized candidate might sew up most of Michigan's seventy-seven delegates a full two years before the GOP convention, thus gaining a significant head start. Some canny Republican leaders saw this as a golden opportunity for George Bush, who was sure to run in 1988, to launch a first strike that would discourage would-be challengers. Others saw it as a chance for the more conservative Jack Kemp to prove himself a viable candidate, even against a sitting vice president. Almost none of the party regulars, it appears, gave Pat Robertson a second thought—which is precisely what Robertson wanted.

Robertson's mailing list and extensive television exposure were of great value in organizing the the Freedom Council, but he did not rely on them exclusively. Instead, he spent an enormous amount of time traveling from place to place, visiting personally with individuals and groups at every level. This labor-intensive process not only helped recruit thousands of people—a high proportion of them contributors to the *700 Club*—into the Freedom Council, but generated a great deal of personal appreciation for Robertson. In March 1985, the *Saturday Evening Post* ran a long, highly flattering piece in which a variety of prominent people spoke glowingly of how Robertson was fit for the presidency. Paul Weyrich volunteered, "Among potential candidates today, political or nonpolitical, there is no one with a higher rating in education, experience, family background, name recognition, popularity and vigor. . . . If I thought Pat wouldn't repudiate it, I'd lead a draft movement."

As Robertson spoke of his vision for the country and as people responded to his leadership, he was repeatedly asked if he would consider running for the presidency. Whether or not that was the true reason he had founded the Freedom Council, the organization soon became the lead float in his parade, and he became an increasingly willing Grand Marshall. He did not find it easy to walk up to strangers and repeat the would-be candidate's mantra, "I'm Pat Robertson and I'm thinking of running for president," but as he forced himself to do it, he found that people warmed to him and that he was quite good at it. Within a few weeks, one associate observed, "Pat was behaving like a very old-fashioned politician."

At about this same time, Robertson looked into the possibility of making the Freedom Council more than a voter-education effort. To protect its tax-exempt status and to avoid other legal difficulties, he sought the advice of Marc Nuttle, an Oklahoma Republican who moved in Paul Weyrich's circles and was thoroughly conversant with federal election laws, with particular expertise in the ways tax-deductible corporate contributions could be used to fund political-education organizations and grassroots lobbying efforts. An astute and experienced political operative, Nuttle was also an evangelical Christian and became, at first informally, then later officially, Robertson's national campaign manager.

THOUGH GEORGE BUSH had not officially declared himself a candidate for 1988, it was clear he planned to run, and he had strong backing from mainstream Republicans in Michigan, where he had defeated Ronald Reagan in the 1980 primary. The election of precinct delegates who would attend the state convention in 1988 was scheduled for August 5, 1986; to be eligible to run in that election, one had to file a petition by May 27. Often, no more than one person filed in a given precinct, and in 1984, no one at all filed in nearly a third of the state's 12,700 precincts.

Most veterans in the Bush camp, led by Lee Atwater, expected supporters of the vice president to dominate the filings and the precinct elections, despite vigorous efforts by Jack Kemp. Bob Dole was so convinced Bush had Michigan sewn up that he decided not to waste time and money on a fruitless campaign. The lone Bush insider to see a cloud on the horizon was Doug Wead.

Wead, the son of an Assemblies of God minister, was cofounder of a famine-relief organization called Mercy Corps International. Because his work often involved coordination with political and religious leaders in various countries, which could have implications for American foreign policy, he had worked with both Democratic and Republican administrations. A chance conversation with the vice president early in 1985 led to his giving help on a speech Bush was delivering to the National Religious Broadcasters and, soon afterward, to a post in the Bush campaign. "There was a tremendous vacuum in Washington and New York in general," he said, "about who evangelicals are, and a tremendous ignorance. National periodicals, the greatest newspapers in America, routinely misspelled the theological terms. They didn't know the difference between a fundamentalist and an evangelical. And suddenly, with evangelicals increasing in huge numbers and involved in politics, there was almost a panic. I wasn't so smart or hot or sharp, but I was an evangelical who understood those numbers, and I was a friend they trusted. So I began to pour into this vacuum information they needed and didn't have."

Over the next several months, Wead prepared a number of detailed memos—one ran to 161 pages—instructing Bush and his staff on the opportunities and pitfalls involved in dealing with the large and varied evangelical community. He recommended that Bush, a theologically moderate Episcopalian, establish an early and close relationship with evangelicals, then back off a bit as the election approached, to avoid appearing to have been captured by them. He thought it prudent for Bush to read at least the first chapter of C. S. Lewis's popular defense of Christian beliefs, *Mere Christianity,* and scan "a highlighted copy of one or two books by Francis Schaeffer," and that he refer to these frequently in meetings with evangelicals, a gesture he said "would be a superb compliment to evangelicals and sincerely appreciated by [Billy] Graham, [Charles] Stanley and others. It would also afford the Vice President a feel [for] the evangelical rationale of faith." He urged Bush to get a thorough briefing, perhaps from Billy Graham, on such matters as the born-again phenomenon and evangelical eschatology, which could help him understand why evangelicals think it so important for America to have a strong pro-Israel policy.

Wead particularly stressed the importance of Bush's being able to handle what he called the "born-again question." The vice president would undoubtedly be asked, by conservatives and liberals and secularists alike, if he had been born again. To say "no" or to finesse the question would cost him dearly among evangelicals, who would conclude that he had either "considered the claims of Christ and rejected them" or was "superficial, carnal, and indifferent to one of the major religious revivals of his generation." On the other hand, to offer a simple "yes" would alienate nonevangelicals who viewed the born-again movement with suspicion and offend evangelicals who would wonder why this information had not come to light earlier. The best approach, Wead thought, was for Bush to offer a two-part response. When speaking to evangelicals, he should say, "I have a definite trust in the Lord as my Savior," then add that he had some difficulty with the term "born-again," because it seemed to call for a dramatic crisis experience, and that it had troubled him when his devout Christian mother had been questioned about her faith because it had grown incrementally, without such an experience. The first phrase, Wead observed, was close enough to the evangelical formulation, "I have accepted Jesus as my personal savior" to be acceptable. The second part of the answer would not only serve as evidence to nonevangelicals that Bush "had turned down the born-again notion," but would also ring true to millions of evangelicals who, if pressed, would have to admit that their own spiritual biographies lacked a critical turning point. Wead recommended that "if the Vice President feels comfortable with this response, he should continue to try it out in small meetings with evangelical leaders across the country until he learns how to harden it and protect it from probing questions that could make it come unstuck."

Anticipating objections from those who thought he was taking such matters too seriously, Wead offered a cautionary reminder: "Remember, Governor Reagan's early encounters with evangelical leaders developed into little stories and legends that passed by word of mouth through the whole movement. Some of these stories took on a life of their own, making Baptists, or Charismatics, or some other category of the Evangelical Movement feel especially close. The Vice President must be careful that his own early encounters with leaders of the Evangelical Movement do not reveal a lack of understanding of their values and develop into similar legends that pass through the movement as examples of the Vice President's indifference or ignorance of their way of life."

One of Wead's early projects was to see to it that such favorable items got planted where they would do the most good. "Early in 1986," he recalled, "we made a videotape. I interviewed the vice president and we were going to show the tape in selected television markets in the South. It was about his life, but tucked away in the middle were a few little evangelical buzz words and a few key questions that we wanted evangelicals in the South to hear. They were the real reason for the tape, even though they took up only a small part of it." Everyone on the Bush team knew that his answers on abortion would be crucial, since his position on the thorny issue had been somewhat consistent, and it was feared that a stumble could prove disastrous. The suspense did not last long. At the taping session, when Wead asked the abortion question, Bush replied without hesitation: "I'm against abortion, and I favor a Constitutional amendment against abortion except in the cases of rape, incest, or to save the life of the mother." Wead recalled that other staffers in the room sucked in their breath. "I thought, 'You'd better be comfortable with that, because that's where you're going to have to stay the rest of your life.' The vice president had been reading and studying about it, thinking about it, talking to people, and finally came to that decision. That videotape settled a lot of issues. The debate had ceased. From then on it was 'this is what we have to work with. This is where he is going to stand. So let's go.' "

Wead quickly became known as "the evangelical in the Bush campaign," a role that brought mixed blessings. "There were people in the campaign who thought I was having too much influence with George Bush," he recalled, "and yet they were afraid to keep my memos away from him because he was demanding them. Normally, if you have a good idea in politics, someone above you will co-opt the idea and put it on his letterhead and send it on in, and get credit for it. My ideas and suggestions were so bizarre that they'd go through untouched. I guess they were thinking, 'Give this guy enough rope and he'll hang himself.' "

One of Wead's earliest bizarre ideas was that an evangelical was almost certain to seek the presidency in 1988, and that the most likely possibility was Pat Robertson. As it became increasingly clear that Wead was right, his stock within the Bush camp rose and he was assigned the task of keeping track of what evangelicals were up to. Wead paid no attention to polling data, which consistently showed Bush with a lock on Michigan. Instead, he and a handful of helpers made thousands of telephone calls to ministers of evangelical and charismatic churches throughout Michigan, to find out what was going on. What they found during the spring of 1986 astonished them. For months, Marlene Elwell and her counterparts all over the state had been quietly marshaling their troops in preparation for an ambush on the Republican election apparatus.

Republican leaders in Michigan knew of the Freedom Council's grass-roots organizing and were generally pleased to see Republican ranks grow. And in some locales, as Peter Secchia, then Republican National Committeeman from Michigan, explained, some experienced Republican leaders affiliated with them, just to have some troops to lead. Secchia admitted that the Freedom Council also attracted "the fringe people, the people who always wanted to fight over some single issue. They had been without respect, without leadership, and without troops for so long. All of a sudden, ten or fifteen people from local churches showed up and wanted to work."

Sometimes, the identification with local churches was not obvious. According to Republican officials, the Freedom Council distributed an instruction sheet in Iowa that included such advice as, "Give the impression that you are there to work for the party, not to push an ideology," "Try not to let on that a close group of friends are becoming active in the party together," and "Hide your strength." A similar set of instructions warned Minnesota evangelicals that "experience has shown it is best not to say you are entering politics because of your Christian beliefs." In Michigan, it is clear that the Freedom Council members caught many by surprise. On May

1, 1986, the Detroit *News* reported that the organization had requested twenty-five thousand petitions to be used to nominate precinct delegates for the August election. An astonished county clerk called the number "unprecedented," noting that "never in our history has anybody or [any] group asked for that many petitions." A few days later, Pat Robertson spoke to approximately three thousand people in Detroit's Cobo Hall and to at least another four thousand watching by satellite hookups in thirteen sites across the state. He told them, "You have an extraordinary opportunity in Michigan . . . to influence the whole nation." Marlene Elwell followed up by explaining to the crowd, most of whom were contributors to the *700 Club,* how they could become precinct delegates by following instructions found in packets that had been placed on each of their chairs.

Such developments and gatherings troubled Bush. Wead remembered a social event at the Bush home when the vice president asked him to stick around after others left. "We were picking food off the table and chatting and he said, 'What's going on up in Michigan?' I said, 'Everybody I talk to in the evangelical community is supporting Robertson. They're just falling into line.' He said, 'I can't get over this. I haven't met a single person who supports Pat Robertson. I've talked to every county chairman up there and they don't know of a single person who's supporting Robertson. I can't figure it out.' I said, 'I can't figure it out either, Mr. Vice President. Apparently they live in two separate worlds and they're not talking to each other. But they're out there.' "

As Wead continued to sift through the information he was receiving, he concluded that as many as five thousand Freedom Council people might file petitions on May 27 and wrote a memo to that effect. Despite the fact that Wead had names and addresses, no one believed him, and a friend on the campaign warned him such claims would destroy his credibility. "Atwater's got great information," he said. "If you know of some that we haven't found, you'll look good if you tell the vice president there're going to be six hundred, or seven hundred. But don't tell him there're going to be five thousand Robertson delegates." Soon afterward, on a trip to Boston aboard *Air Force 2,* Bush summoned Wead to the front of the plane to ask how many precinct delegates he expected Robertson to file the following week. "I said, 'Five thousand,' " Wead recalled. "He said, 'Five thousand? Atwater's telling me five hundred. There's a big difference between five thousand and five hundred.' I'm thinking, 'I know.' And he said, 'Five thousand? That's just not possible.' I said, 'Well, we broke them down. We even took sample counties where we identified them. I can give you their names and addresses. There's going to be five thousand.' He was upset, and there were those on the plane who were upset with me. But all of that strengthened my relationship with him."

On the evening of May 27, Doug Wead got a frantic call from Lee Atwater, who had just learned that Robertson people had come into the Michigan Secretary of State's office and had delivered thousands of precinct-delegate filings at the last minute before the deadline. "Atwater was really nervous," Wead recalled. "He called me back two or three times that night. He was running scared. He was saying, 'You gotta get back here. We gotta talk.' "

When the results were in, more than nine thousand people, far more than in previous years, had filed petitions indicating they wanted to run for precinct delegate. Those who filed were not required to say whom they would favor in a presidential election, but a close look at the numbers indicated that Freedom Council candidates probably did constitute close to half of the nine thousand, and that many of them would be running unopposed, since the organization had made a special effort to target precincts that had gone unrepresented in 1984. Bush had apparently gotten the lion's share of the rest, with Kemp a poor third. The *Washington Post* aptly observed that "the anecdotal evidence suggests that Robertson stunned both of the more conventional politicians with an avalanche of last-day filings." The same county clerk who had been astonished by the the Freedom Council's request for twenty-five thousand petition forms said, "When a person of Robertson's newcomer status is able to best the vice president of the United States and one of the most prominent Republicans in the House of Representatives, he's hit a home run." Quite clearly, George Bush faced the prospect of an embarrassing upset in the August election, and even if he emerged with a majority of delegates, it was obvious he would not get the thumping victory he had counted on. Nearly two years before the official campaign would get underway, he had already been marked as vulnerable.

AT SEVERAL PUBLIC appearances during the spring, Robertson had teased his audiences and fed his ego by asking if he should run for high office, a question that invariably drew enthusiastic applause. On at least one such occasion, he responded by saying, "The Lord has spoken here tonight." Two weeks after the May precinct filings, while he spoke to a cheering crowd of more than six thousand ardent supporters who had gathered at Nelson Bunker Hunt's ranch in Texas, an airplane flew overhead, dragging a banner that said, "Pat, Go For It!"

Kathy Potera, a young Pennsylvania woman, explained her own enthusiasm for Robertson in terms that must have fit many others. "I'm Pentecostal," she said. "I'm what you call a tongue-talking Bible-believing Christian. It was very exciting that Pat chose to run, because he not only was a Christian, but he was a Pentecostal Christian, and he wasn't ashamed of his roots and his background, and he gave Pentecostals, for the first time, a voice, an opportunity to say, 'this is someone that we adhere to.' What you find with conservative Christians is that they're very much segmented, and everybody sort of has their own champion. And although many Pentecostals had no problem supporting the Moral Majority, many of the Moral Majority people had a problem really giving voice to Pentecostal Christians. We weren't really accepted in their ranks. So I was thrilled that Pat was involved, even though I felt it would be extremely difficult for him to be elected."

Once it appeared Robertson might be a serious candidate, the media began paying more attention to him and digging out morsels to feed a curious public. Many of those keyed off his Pentecostal faith. A favorite was a segment of a 1985 *700 Club* program during which Robertson had ordered Hurricane Gloria to turn away from the Virginia coastline. "In the name of Jesus," he had said, "we command you to stop where you are and move northeast, away from land, and away from harm. In the name of Jesus of Nazareth, we command it." It did move—eventually hitting Long Island—and Robertson pronounced the incident "extremely important" to his political plans, "because I felt, interestingly enough, that if I couldn't move a hurricane, I could hardly move a nation. I know that's a strange thing for anybody to say, and there's hardly anyone else who would feel the same way, but it was very important to the faith of many people." Though his prayer was widely publicized, usually in a spirit of derision, Robertson never tried to minimize it. In 1995, when another hurricane was approaching the East Coast, he referred to his success in warding off the advance of Hurricane Gloria and indicated he stood ready to repeat the performance.

If Robertson saw no problems in mixing faith and meteorology, it is hardly surprising that he regarded the wall between church and state as permeable. Perhaps to prepare his viewers for the surprise showing in Michigan, he announced on May 1 that "God's plan, ladies and gentlemen, is for his people to take dominion." Two weeks later, he said, "The evangelicals [are] a force that nobody else really has been reckoning with, but they're going to be one to be reckoned with because God is establishing this." Following the precinct filings, the Freedom Council sent out a letter proclaiming that "the Christians have won." Then, at a June rally, Robertson declared, "It was no coincidence that Ronald Reagan was elected president. It was the direct act of God. . . . The Republican takeover and reversal of direction in this country is no coincidence."

As such statements came to light, Republican regulars found it increasingly difficult to take Robertson seriously. Almost anyone could file for election, but surely sensible Michigan Republicans would not actually vote for such people. The Freedom Council forces, however, were more inclined to agree with a delegate who asked a crowd gathered at a rally a few days before the August 5 election, "If God is for us, who can be against us?" When the votes came in, it appeared that the answer to that question was "the Republican establishment." The mechanism for gathering reports from hundreds of precincts around the state was woefully inadequate, and the true numbers would not be verified for several days, but the Bush forces took advantage of the situation to deprive Robertson of his due.

As a way to exert influence over information, the Bush campaign set up an unofficial "election central," complete with facilities for the media, in the Clarion Hotel in Lansing. As results were phoned in from various precincts, they were fed into computers and analyzed—by Bush staffers. According to them, Bush was winning handily. The Freedom Council forces were getting a different picture. Their sources indicated that Robertson delegates were not only controlling the uncontested precincts, but were beating both Bush and Kemp delegates in some hotly contested races. But their notebooks, maps, and voting lists seemed primitive in contrast to the computers, and when the Bush people finally declared their man the victor, the reporters accepted it as true and the media announced it.

Marc Nuttle was later quoted as having credited the Bush forces with "a masterful job of 'spin control.' " Doug Wead put it more bluntly: "It was a lie. And the media bought it. They accepted it. They reported it." In part, Wead surmised, the reporters were seduced by the appearance of sophistication: "We had all kinds of technology. How can you doubt technology?" But they were also influenced by personal predilections and a desire to be seen in a favorable light. Some members of the media, he speculated, may have known the Bush camp was lying, but "they didn't like evangelicals, they didn't like Robertson, they didn't want to believe he could win in Michigan, and they didn't want to give him a bump. They liked us. They loved Lee Atwater, who was a lovable, funny, witty, talented guy. He was a charmer. And they needed him. He was going to be a friend of the future president. So they wrote what we wanted." Asked how he felt about such a tactic, Wead replied, "I wasn't personally a part of that. I wouldn't have advocated it, and I had mixed emotions, as an evangelical, seeing it happen. But it was not especially eye-opening. I'd already seen a lot before then. It was typical. It was politics." Eventually, the Freedom Council was able to prove that it had managed at least a tie with Bush, with Kemp running a distant third. The *New York Times* reported the more accurate data; most papers did not.

DURING THE SPRING, a religion reporter had revealed that the Christian Broadcasting Network's tax returns showed it had contributed or loaned more than eight million dollars to the Freedom Council between 1984 and

1986, and the IRS had warned that the Freedom Council's tax-exempt status barred it from supporting federal candidates. At Marc Nuttle's suggestion, Robertson formed an "exploratory committee" called Americans for Freedom; a political action committee called the Michigan Committee for Freedom, which could endorse state and local candidates but could not accept corporate contributions; and the Civic League, which could accept such contributions. Technically, they were separate operations; in fact, they all served to boost Robertson's candidacy. In October 1986, after it had been acknowledged that the Freedom Council had spent four hundred thousand dollars on the Michigan elections, Robertson closed the organization down. According to one account, former employees "were offered $100 to sign a confidentiality agreement that banned them from discussing the Council's activities."

Flush with his remarkable showing in Michigan, Robertson decided to continue his "exploration" in a major way. In September, in a three-hour closed-circuit telecast that originated in Constitution Hall in Washington but was fed by satellite to 220 cities around the nation, he announced that he would run for the presidency if he received three million endorsing signatures by September 1987, a year away. *New York Times* religion writer Dudley Clendinen wrote that, with this meeting, Robertson had "[made] history by applying the tools and skills of modern television evangelism to presidential politics." But as Robertson's star was rising, other parts of the Religious Right looked less robust.

The Religious Roundtable had been dormant since shortly after the 1980 election. Christian Voice also appeared to be little more than a shell. In December 1985, Tim LaHaye's American Coalition for Traditional Values had held an impressive conference on the theme, "How to Win an Election," but the revelation by *Mother Jones* magazine that one of the organization's biggest supporters was the Reverend Sun Myung Moon's Unification Church damaged its credibility, and LaHaye closed ACTV's doors shortly after the 1986 elections. The 1986 elections themselves were a disappointment to conservatives, with Democrats regaining control of the Senate, thus making it quite unlikely that the Religious Right's social agenda would make any progress for at least two more years.

Jerry Falwell clipped his own wings in 1986. In January, he announced that Moral Majority would be folded into a new entity known as the Liberty Federation. In effect, this was a face-saving way for both Falwell and Moral Majority to withdraw from an arena in which they were no longer effective. The Liberty Foundation proved to be a cipher—after two articles at the time of its inauguration, the *New York Times* never mentioned it again during the entire year, a marked contrast to the enormous amount of attention Moral Majority had received during its early years. But Moral Majority's day was clearly over. Public opinion polls repeatedly indicated that a substantial majority of the population held negative views of Falwell and his organization, no doubt partly because they had been subjected to such an intense barrage of scrutiny and criticism. In addition, many of Falwell's long-time supporters had never approved of his political activities, with the result that contributions to the *Old Time Gospel Hour* and Liberty University had suffered precipitous declines. Jerry Falwell had played a critical role in mobilizing conservative Christians, but it was time to pass the torch. Falwell understood that and seemed quite willing to step back from the fray, but he appeared to be less enthusiastic about ceding his leadership position to Pat Robertson. He had already said he intended to support George Bush in 1988; when Robertson made his aim apparent, Falwell remarked dryly, "He's probably the best-trained television personality running for president."

BACK IN MICHIGAN, both the Robertson and Kemp forces quickly recognized that if they joined forces, they had a good chance of keeping George Bush from winning the state in 1988 and, in the process, of gaining control of the Republican Party in Michigan. Less openly, each side believed the other would eventually fall by the wayside, enabling it to emerge with a winning margin. Operating with these assumptions they formed a "marriage of convenience" whose working motto was "Anybody But Bush." The Bush forces, also confident they would eventually win, did not want to alienate the impressive regiment of newly minted Republicans. In counties where none of the three camps had a majority, Bush supporters agreed to send representatives to the county and district conventions, to be held in February 1987, on a proportional basis, even if Bush controlled the largest number of delegates. The Robertson camp happily accepted this arrangement, but refused to reciprocate. In counties in which they had a majority of precinct delegates, they "changed the rules and adopted a winner-take-all approach, shutting out the Bush side."

Peter Secchia described one tactic the Robertson forces used to outmaneuver competitors. "Early in the campaign," he said, "we came across a Robertson document that said, 'When you go to a county convention, stall. Ask for a vote on everything. Try to delay the ending of the convention, because these people are used to having a convention that starts at seven-thirty and ends at ten at the latest. They have baby-sitters, they have commitments, they have habits, they have traditions, they will all start to go home around 9:30 or 10:00, and if you delay the important votes till the end—if you were thirty out of a hundred [at 7:30], you will be thirty out of fifty by 10:30.' It worked. We would hear, 'Gee, so-and-so got deposed as the county chairman,' or that 'three out of five members of the State Central

Committee from this county or this district are Robertson people.' So para-
noia developed. It was like 'The Invasion of the Ants.' These people were
coming after us, and they were everywhere. And they had money. They
were well-organized and well-paid."

Such unexpected tactics enabled the Robertson-Kemp coalition to dominate a majority of county and district conventions and to seize control of the
Republican Party's state central committee, but they set off a year-long series
of conflicts that created deep rifts within party ranks. Not surprisingly, such
goings-on shattered illusions that the newly enlarged Republican Party in
Michigan would be a unified, decorous organization. Kemp Republicans,
while happy to shunt Bush down a sidetrack, did not want to blow up the
train, and were troubled that the Robertson forces did not share that concern. Bush campaign adviser Mary Matalin recalled that Robertson backers
would show up at political meetings and say, "We don't really care if
Republicans or Democrats are in there. What we care about is advancement
of Christian philosophy." Expression of that philosophy sometimes took
unusual forms. At one meeting, an elected official complained to Marlene
Elwell that he had been hit over the head with a Bible. When she gathered
some of her brood into an impromptu meeting and asked if anyone knew
anything about such an incident, "This guy raised his hand and said, 'Yes.
He was in front of me and used some profanity, so I just took the Bible and
hit him in the head and told him we don't talk like that.' He was pretty
proud of himself. I told him, 'Well, we don't do that here.' Other people,
from faiths where they don't drink, saw people having a drink and that was
foreign to them. So there was a good bit of back-and-forth 'learning the
system,' you might say."

David Walters, who ran the Michigan Committee for Freedom PAC,
which became the major instrument of Robertson's campaign, remembered
being badgered by Secchia, Governor John Engler, former Governor
George Romney, and other party stalwarts for behaving badly. "They said,
'David, why are you doing this? It is George Bush's turn to be president.' I
said I didn't understand this 'It's his turn' business. They said, 'He's paid his
dues, he's gone up the ranks, he's been a good VP.' I said, 'Well, the last
time I checked, it's the guy with the most votes who wins; it's not whose
turn it is.' To me it was ridiculous that it was all wrapped up and that
anybody else was an interloper, whether you were for Dole or Kemp or
Robertson. The Republican Party was a very close-knit group and their
philosophy was 'Keep it small and keep it all.' There was a sense of entitle-
ment these people had that was quite amusing to me—'We've been Republicans all our lives, and these are new Republicans. What right do they have
to a position?' "

As Michigan's national committeeman, Secchia was often the brunt of criticisms and complaints about the new Republicans. "They had found us asleep and had moved in and taken our turf," he said, and party regulars asked him, "Where were you, Secchia? Why didn't you see this coming?" Looking back, he said he recognized that "these were just decent, God-fearing people who had a lot of the same dreams and desires that most Republicans had, but they went about it a very different way. That's not to say their way was wrong, but it was different from our way. I [was working] for Bush. These people felt they were working for God, and if I was on the other side, who was I really working for? It was a little scary for some of us. It was pretty hard to tell them they were wrong, because they were 'working for the Lord' and we were working for somebody who wasn't on that level. But we had to stop them, because if we didn't, Bush would not win. It wasn't because they were religious; it was because their candidate was not our candidate. They were a threat to us, and we had to win. The national party was watching. How could I be an effective committeeman if I lost control of my party to some new people—outsiders? We just had to circle the wagons and shoot out, and protect what it was we had." On the other side, Robertson deeply resented Secchia's efforts on Bush's behalf and vowed to unseat him from his position as national committeeman, once even swooping in to a state convention by helicopter to berate him in front of stunned colleagues.

THE STRUGGLE IN Michigan absorbed far more energy, time, and money than anyone had anticipated, but it was not the only front in the campaign. For Robertson, it was crucial that he succeed in his effort to obtain at least three million signatures of people who would pledge to support him if he entered the race officially. He realized he needed far more than his *700 Club* fans to accomplish this task and, in November 1986, sought professional advice. The advertising firm of Young and Rubicam was already helping him with the metamorphosis of his old CBN cable network into the new Family Channel, and the person handling his account, Constance Snapp, was both a Virginian and a newly reborn Christian. After one conversation, he persuaded her to join his campaign as National Director of Communications. In that role, which she assumed in January 1987, her two major tasks were to help garner the three million names and to help the public understand just who and what kind of man Pat Robertson was. Snapp explained, "He didn't care that I didn't know politics. He was looking for someone who knew how to market with a database. He knew he was going to have to go directly to the people—he certainly couldn't count on the press to communicate his message, at least not intact. He also knew we were going to have to count, because politics is a numbers game. You have to know who they are, where they are, and how you can reach them, so you can get out the vote and win caucuses. Pat knew that if he could get three million names and they were in the right precincts, that could carry him to the convention. And, of course, it wasn't just to get them to sign a petition saying he should run; we had to find people who would be willing to support him financially, pray for him, or volunteer for him. It meant they would take it very seriously."

Getting three million people to sign petitions would be a significant accomplishment, but it would not win the big prize. For Robertson to have any chance at the nomination, millions more would have to rally to his cause. And as Peter Secchia pointed out, to those who did not know him or knew him only through what they had heard about him through the mainstream media, Robertson took some getting used to. "We had had candidates who took positions on Vietnam and abortion and public schools and charter schools," Secchia said, "but we had never had one who said he could move a hurricane, and that the Lord was going to solve our problems." For Connie Snapp, the twofold challenge was to overcome Robertson's consistently high unfavorability ratings and to let the public know what kind of man he was and what he stood for.

To find out why the negatives were so high, she assembled "focus groups" of the sort advertisers use to test reactions to sales pitches or new products. The groups proved enlightening. Snapp remembered that "one guy looked at a tape of Pat from the *700 Club* and said, 'Well, gosh, every time I've seen him, he's sweating and marching across the stage and he's got that handkerchief.' He thought he was Jimmy Swaggart! That's the way it was across every group. People didn't really know who he was. They thought they knew who he was, but they had him confused with everybody but himself. I thought, 'This is great. It's not that they don't like him; they don't know him. If we can find a way to let them see who he really is and not confuse him with other people, we have a much better chance of getting them to listen.'" That led to a campaign in which the emphasis was on getting people simply to listen to Robertson before making a decision about him. Several television spots, in fact, showed Robertson saying, "I'm not asking for your vote right now; I'm just asking you to listen." Snapp rejected the suggestion that she was "repackaging" Robertson. Instead, she insisted, she was simply trying to get people to see the truth about him—his education, his business and media experience, his having grown up in the home of a powerful U.S. Senator. "If I had to make up a guy," she said, "I couldn't make up one any better. He was perfect. He was an advertiser's dream. But we had to communicate that. We had to tell the real story."

Snapp's task was complicated by the fact that Robertson was perceived to be a preacher, and quite a conservative one at that. "The press corps and ultimately many people in the public thought it was a case of church and state getting too cozy," she said. "They characterized him as someone who would tell us how to run our personal lives, which wasn't the case at all." She pointed out that the *700 Club* was not an evangelism show but an information show, a news and current events show. He always had the Lord as the focus and forefront, and he was good at interpreting life in the light of what the Scriptures tell us, or in the context of our faith, but millions of Christians in this country appreciate and want that perspective. I thought, 'If the public could know what I know, I think they would have a different opinion of whether he was qualified to be president. They still may decide they don't want to vote for him, but it won't be because they have falsely perceived him to be this preacher who's going to tell them how to live. So the goal for the early part of the campaign was to debunk the myths. That's why our advertising, our Sunday newspaper inserts, our twenty-eight-minute video all had the theme, 'Who is this man, Pat Robertson?'"

As it happened, the spring of 1987 was not an optimum time to be brushing up the public image of a religious broadcaster. First, Oral Roberts brought ridicule upon himself by announcing that God had put a price on his head and would "call him home" if his followers did not pony up eight million dollars. (He did eventually raise the money, with a considerable boost from a dog-track owner who recommended that he see a psychiatrist.) Then came the soap opera known as PTL. Almost everyone connected with Christian media had known for some time that Jim and Tammy Faye Bakker, their PTL Network, and their Heritage USA amusement park and resort complex were heading toward some kind of embarrassing disaster. The enterprise had been the subject of investigations by the IRS, the Justice Department, and the Federal Communications Commission, its financial operations were known to be chaotic at best and perhaps blatantly dishonest, and former employees told stories of irresponsible spending, deceptive fund-raising tactics, "and *worse.*" The Charlotte *Observer* had long stayed on the case and finally, in March, reporter Charles Shepard, who would win a Pulitzer Prize for his work, broke the first phase of the story: Jim Bakker had not only engaged in a brief tryst with Jessica Hahn, a former church secretary and future *Playboy* and jeans model, but his copastor had paid Ms. Hahn $250,000 not to mention the occasion to anyone.

This was followed by stories of deception, gross exploitation of trusting supporters, outrageous mismanagement and misuse of funds, exorbitant salaries, unconscionable luxuries, additional sexual shenanigans, even some drug dependency—prior to the revelations about Jim and Jessica, Tammy Faye had checked into the Betty Ford Clinic, in an effort to deal with a drug problem; Jim later admitted to regular use of Valium. The national media pounced on the story and rode it for months, none more avidly than Ted Koppel, whose extra-length interview with Jim and Tammy racked up the largest audience *Nightline* had ever drawn to that point.

Before the story finally died from overexposure, Jim Bakker inexplicably turned PTL over to Jerry Falwell, who oversaw it long enough to recognize it was a hopeless situation and surrendered it to the court that was overseeing the debacle. (The sight of the stout Baptist preacher, fully clothed in a dark business suit, arms folded across his chest as he plunged down a Heritage water slide, deserves a spot in TV history, alongside Lucy in the pie factory and the death of Chuckles the clown.) Eventually, the IRS revoked PTL's nonprofit status and sued the bankrupt ministry for $56 million for taxes from 1980 to 1987, and Jim Bakker was sentenced to forty-five years in federal prison for having defrauded his supporters of $158 million. The sentence was almost universally regarded as unusually harsh for white-collar crime, and Bakker was released in 1994.

The protracted attention given to these matters dealt a crippling blow to many religious broadcasters. A March 1987 *New York Times* poll found that sixty-five percent of Americans had an unfavorable opinion of most television evangelists. Nearly every major broadcast ministry reported a significant drop-off in contributions. Falwell claimed a dip of $2 million per month and Pat Robertson reported that CBN revenues dropped $12 million during the first two months after the PTL scandal broke and were expected to fall an additional $16 million by year's end. Announcing that CBN would have to lay off 470 employees, Robertson said, "In the history of American Christianity, we have never seen anything like this. The scandal has hit the evangelical world like a bombshell."

Though neither Robertson nor CBN was involved in any aspect of the scandals, his campaign must have seemed like ground zero. A July *Los Angeles Times* poll reported a sharp rise in the proportion of people who said they would not be likely to vote for Robertson if he decided to run for president, and fifty-two percent of respondents in a *USA Today* poll indicated they thought the scandals had diminished his electability. "We had to fight it for months," Connie Snapp admitted. "Pat would never have been in such a mess, but it was guilt by association, stereotyping. Every question became: 'What about the scandal?' 'What about Jim Bakker?' 'When he worked for you, was he a crook?' Our strategy was to say, 'We'll answer one or two questions, but we're not going to let it dominate an entire press conference. We've got to get our message out to the people.' We only had so many days, so many hours. It was hard. It was a thorn in my side. But it did get better, at least with the national press, and sometime around late August, I remember saying to Pat, 'Did someone write down the minute when we actually had a whole press conference and nobody asked about PTL?' It just sort of happened one day, and we were like, 'Oh, wow!' "

The timing of the media's loss of interest in the telescandals was fortunate. After the Freedom Council had closed down in 1986, Marlene Elwell stepped away from the Robertson organization, but when she decided to rejoin the team after a few months, she was elevated to Midwest political director for Americans for Robertson. Aware that Iowa's early caucuses typically drew considerable attention and that grassroots organization paid its greatest dividends in caucus states, she set about to see what it would take to win in Iowa. Early on, she learned that, unlike most states, Iowa holds an informal straw poll in September, several months before the actual caucuses. "I didn't know a whole lot about the straw poll," she admitted, 'but I remember calling Pat—he was in a car and I called him on his mobile phone—and saying, 'I found the key. It's going to be the straw poll. We're going to concentrate on that [to get name recognition].' And that really was the key."

Using names gathered during the petition process, Elwell contacted people in all ninety-nine of Iowa's counties and urged them to round up friends and fellow church members and get them to drive to Ames to participate in the straw poll. On the day of reckoning, while Bush, Kemp, and Dole supporters mingled under tents where caterers provided fancy hors d'oeuvres, the Robertson followers, some of whom had ridden for four or five hours in church buses, lined up at a hot dog stand to receive their portion of populist manna. They also contrasted with the other voters in another respect: there were more of them. When the straw vote was held, Robertson beat all three of his better known rivals. Elwell remembered the delicious moment: "Pat was really a joke at that time. I remember reporters coming up and kind of laughing. They had to put up with us, because there we were. But when he actually won, it [sent] such a shock wave through the whole nation that pretty soon he had a whole flock of cameramen following him. So it put him on the map. For the first time, he was beginning to be taken a little more seriously and got a lot of headlines out of it. It was quite an exciting time for the whole movement, particularly the Christian community. And Christians really became mobilized. They had a cause now, they had a champion who was speaking to their pain, speaking to their hearts and was willing to speak out loud, publicly expressing that. They had now found someone to do that for them. I think that created this intensity that was second to none." Those who took part in the straw poll went back home to organize their precincts and counties and eventually became the heart of the Religious Right in Iowa. Elwell noted that "it's very exciting today to go to Iowa and see those very people that we trained at the caucus level that year are now in leadership roles in the party. They run for office and are active all over."

Both to take advantage of the momentum gained in Iowa and to distance her client further from the Bakker debacle, Connie Snapp stepped up the campaign to have Robertson seen as something more than a TV preacher, setting up appearances on nonreligious television programs and urging reporters to refer to him as "Mr." rather than "Reverend" and to identify him as a Christian broadcaster, not a television evangelist. Robertson registered particular offense at being labeled an evangelist, and Snapp was correct in noting that, strictly speaking, the *700 Club* was not an evangelistic program. And, though the distinction was often lost on journalists and much of the public, Robertson was also correct in pointing out that he had never filled the role of an evangelist, whose task it is to win people to Christ, after which they will be ministered to by people filling other roles. "In the church," he explained, "there are various offices—apostles and prophets and pastors and teachers and evangelists, administrators, educators, people who do humanitarian work. It's like a football team. One person plays end, one plays tackle, one plays guard, one plays center, some play blocking backs, halfbacks, quarterbacks, etc. If a sports reporter for the *Washington Post* called every person on the Washington Redskins team a center, the man would be fired instantly, but the press thinks it can call everybody in Christian work an evangelist, which is totally untrue. I have not been ordained by God as an evangelist. I have been a pastor, I have been a teacher, I have been other things God has ordained me for, but not an evangelist. It's a special office. But the press was saying, 'We are superior to you yahoos. We will call you whatever we want to, and if you don't like it, tough luck.' That's why I resented it. It was scorn, it was bigotry, it was demeaning and insulting."

Clarifying the nature of his ministerial office did not solve all of Robertson's image problems, since many people, religious and otherwise, thought it improper or unwise for a clergyman of any description to hold the highest office in the land. Both Jerry Falwell and Ed Dobson felt that Robertson—particularly since they judged he had little chance of winning—was diminishing his influence by running. In Falwell's view, a man called to the ministry should restrict himself to the prophetic or advisory roles. "Preach, influence, speak out," he recommended, but "don't ever take an office, don't ever ask for a favor. Be an outsider hammering on the door, but don't ever get inside playing the game with them." Dobson agreed: "When Pat announced he was running for the presidency, I thought, 'That's a terrible mistake. Your calling is significantly different than that. And you can have greater influence by not doing that.' If I am a preacher, then I ought to stick with what God has called me to do. To contaminate that with political engagement seems to me to dilute the Gospel and the ultimate mission."

Jesse Helms's aide, Carl Anderson, held a higher view of politics but felt that Robertson's image as a religious leader was "an insupportable burden." Critics would accuse Robertson of imposing his religious beliefs on issues of public policy. If he tried to address such issues without reference to his faith, his Christian constituency would fault him for not making the connection. "He was sort of caught in the middle," Anderson observed, "so maybe the conclusion is that, in this type of a pluralistic society, a religious leader's stepping into candidacy for political office is not the best idea."

INTERESTINGLY, THE OTHER minister with an eye on the Oval Office, Jesse Jackson, stirred less apprehension. This may have been due in part to the fact that most people did not believe Jackson had any real chance to capture the Democratic nomination, whereas they were not sure just how much punch Robertson and his constituency might pack. In addition, black and white churches operate according to a double standard with respect to politics. Black preachers and churches have long publicly endorsed candidates and contributed money to their campaigns without raising criticism. Such practices have generally been regarded as inappropriate in white churches; indeed, some have been threatened with loss of their tax-exempt status for such behavior. Finally, while Jesse talked about letting "justice roll down like waters" and reflecting God's concern for the poor, Pat spoke in tongues and professed to get special delivery messages from the Holy Spirit. Robertson still chafes at the treatment he received from reporters uneasy with high-intensity religion. "In general," he observed, "the media comprise people who I would consider biblical illiterates. They have no knowledge of historic Christianity, no knowledge of the Old Testament, no knowledge of the New Testament. I was ridiculed, I was castigated, I was held up to all kinds of scorn. I was in one editorial meeting at the Seattle *Post-Intelligencer,* and instead of asking serious questions, they said, 'If the Russians launch a nuclear bomb, and one is falling on America, what would you do, start praying?' They were just baiting me. Now, certain papers—the *New York Times,* the Detroit *Free Press,* the reporter who covered me for Knight Ridder, the *L.A. Times*—were very courteous and gave me a respectful hearing. But there were many who were absolutely rabid about the fact that somebody believed as strongly as I did about religion. I would ask why they didn't parody Jesse Jackson's religion. Well, the difference was that I was supposed to be religious and I really meant it; they didn't think he did.

In addition, he also was enunciating liberal positions, and I was a conservative. And so the two together just made me the object of scorn in a number of circles."

In an effort to dampen some of the criticism he was receiving and to assure voters that he was running for president, not pastor, Robertson took an unusual step late in September 1987: He sent a letter to the Freemason Street Baptist Church in Norfolk, Virginia, where he had been ordained in 1961, announcing that he was resigning his ordination, thereby indicating he no longer wished to be regarded a minister of any description. The Reverend Donald Dunlap, pastor of the church, recalled that "there was some shock that he would want to treat his ordination in this fashion," and felt Robertson's action sent an unfortunate signal, since the Constitution does not disqualify a minister from becoming an active political candidate. At the same time, Dunlap admitted to a concern that "some blurring" of the line between church and state might occur if Robertson were ever elected president, even though one of the reasons the broadcaster had given for resigning his ordination was a desire to send a clear signal of his belief in the importance of maintaining that line. Dunlap observed, however, that Robertson's action probably had little effect. "He had promoted himself as a televangelist prior to his running for president, so when he became a candidate, it was unrealistic of him to expect that perception to change overnight. I don't think it made any difference with the voters."

Dunlap was probably right. But some of Robertson's more ardent supporters felt he had erred in trying to deflect attention from the centrality of religion in his life. "Why should anyone have to resign his ordination to hold any position in public life?" asked James Muffett, a key Michigan backer. "I think that's ridiculous. This culture says so much about diversity and openness and inclusiveness, but that doesn't apply to someone who has Christian credentials. Somehow it's 'We're open to everything except you.' I find that the height of hypocrisy, and I really don't appreciate that aspect of the cultural response to Christians in politics. I feel that's a misinterpretation of what the First Amendment was all about. So I thought, 'Pat, why did you have to do that?' " Robertson's Michigan PAC director Dave Walters agreed with Muffett, noting that "I felt the reason he even had a platform to run for the presidency was because of the fame he had received from being a minister, from being on television, from having a Christian television network. Millions of people supported the ministry and perceived him as a minister, a servant of God. I felt that, by resigning [his ordination] to pacify a group of people who were never going to support him anyway, he would alienate some of his strong base who believed in him, because they would feel he was moving away from his 'calling.' "

Kathy Potera, who had been so pleased to have a Pentecostal champion and who had worked hard on the Pennsylvania campaign, felt Robertson's action entailed a partial surrender of religious freedom. "I felt it would be better for him to be 'the Reverend Pat Robertson,'" she said. "He had a degree and a credential. It was the same as if he had been a doctor. It was the same as Jimmy Carter's being a nuclear physicist; he didn't resign being a nuclear physicist because he wanted to be President of the United States." Potera told of a Jewish friend who informed her that he voted for her as a delegate to the Republican National Convention, but was nonetheless concerned at the prospect of "a tongue-talker in the White House." Potera replied, "I understand that, but if we sat down and talked about the fact that in the Jewish faith you separate your milk and your meat on the plate, it would make Arlen Specter look like a very unattractive candidate, because he's a Jewish person, and people who don't understand Jewish traditions might think that's really weird—'You mean you can't have macaroni and cheese and steak on the same plate just because you're Jewish? How could we have somebody in the White House who can't even eat a normal meal, or what Catholics and Protestants or most of America thinks is a normal meal?' And I said, 'That's your tradition, and I don't criticize you for that. The fact that Pat Robertson is a charismatic should not play into it. If he chooses to pray in tongues in the White House, that should not matter. That should not be a factor in whether people vote for him. He should have the right to pray to God in a prayer language that maybe you don't understand, if that's his religious belief.'"

Regardless of the ultimate effect of Robertson's action, it did draw attention to his formal announcement of what most people had assumed all along—that he was indeed an official candidate. By using the grassroots network the Freedom Council and its successor organizations had built, by direct-mail campaigns, and by such general methods as publishing inserts in Sunday newspapers, Robertson apparently obtained the three million endorsements he had sought—at an estimated cost of ten million dollars. That hurdle safely cleared and his ministerial credentials set aside, he decided to launch his campaign in a way that might add still another dimension to his public image. Instead of holding a press conference at his CBN headquarters or in Washington, Robertson elected instead to return to the Bedford-Stuyvesant neighborhood in Brooklyn, where he had lived and worked for a brief period during the earliest years of his ministry. "Republicans," he explained, "have been portrayed as country-clubbers, silk-stocking elites, Wall Streeters, et cetera, and I'm not that way. I'm a successful businessman, but I am not somebody who is removed from the common man. I had worked in that very neighborhood ministering to the poor and the needy, and I wanted to say that I had a message for the miners in West Virginia, the steelworkers in Pittsburgh, and the auto workers in Detroit, and the inner city black people. I cared about them and I wanted to see a government that would make life better for them."

Perhaps it seemed like a good idea at the time, but a gathering conceived to portray Robertson as a friend of poor and working class Americans turned into a raucous attempt to paint him as a benighted and dangerous bigot. The press conference was held directly in front of the brownstone where Robertson and his family had lived. A platform had been built and media tent erected, and busloads of nicely dressed white Christians had been imported to provide the candidate with a politely enthusiastic audience, but no one had remembered to tell the residents of the area what was happening, which made Robertson's effort to identify with them seem a bit hollow. Mostly African Americans, the neighbors took offense at Robertson's references to the rather well-kept block as a slum or ghetto, but that might have gone unnoticed. The serious protesters, however, were not about to be lost in a crowd, especially not with an estimated three hundred media representatives present. As soon as Robertson approached the microphone to make his speech, he was greeted by a cacophony of shouted questions, angry accusations, loud jeers, and miscellaneous heckling comments from placard-waving demonstrators parading along the sidewalk and surrounding the chairs where the Robertson troops sat looking in baffled astonishment.

The protesters included representatives from various groups, including the National Organization for Women and People For the American Way, which had been formed by Norman Lear in 1980 in direct opposition to Moral Majority and other components of the Religious Right, but the core group came from ACT UP, a largely gay and lesbian organization deeply concerned about AIDS. Ira Manhoff, an ACT UP leader, explained that, disheartened over the Reagan administration's silence about AIDS, the group "had decided we needed to have a presence in the presidential elections coming up, and that we needed to be out there confronting both the Republicans and the Democrats on the issue, because we felt neither group was really dealing with it sufficiently." They were particularly concerned about Robertson's implication that AIDS represented God's judgment on homosexuals and indications that he might favor a quarantine on people with the disease. Manhoff admitted that the group was ecstatic to learn that Robertson was tossing his hat into the presidential ring from the front steps of a Bed-Stuy brownstone, since that meant "we didn't have to go on some long bus ride down to Washington or into his territory, but that he was coming up into our territory, and it was just a matter of a subway ride, and we were going to be able to be there and voice our opinions about what we thought of his running. So people were very psyched up for it."

According to Manhoff, the original plan had been to be present, to make at least some effort to "engage him and dialogue with him about his opin-

ions, and let him know why we were there and what we were offended by."
But the desire to dialogue, if it ever existed, quickly gave way to a determination to drown out. Robertson slogged bravely through a statement, but
protesters carrying such placards as "Pat for President, Tammy Faye for
Vice" and "Hitler in '39, Robertson in '88" kept up a constant din, and
even managed to enlist the help of a few local residents. Manhoff insisted,
"Drowning him out was spontaneous. We were there with our signs, but we
knew that, unless we had a very strong presence, it would be easy for the
news media to not even include us, or maybe have a little side shot of us.
That's why what came off was more or less a drowning out of what he had
to say. He seemed like he was totally shocked. I don't know what else he
could have expected, coming up into New York to announce this."

Robertson, chuckling at the memory years later, acknowledged that the
protesters had "made it a very difficult situation. And of course people said,
'How foolish can you be? Why didn't you go into an area that was very
congenial to your message and surround yourself with your friends?' Well, I
wanted to show people that I didn't mind stepping out in the streets and
taking on the toughest environment there was. That certainly was a baptism
with fire." Manhoff regarded the protest as "an utter success. With only a
few days' notice, we were able to get down there and really become a focus
of the news broadcasts, nationally and local. It made it very clear that a Pat
Robertson candidacy wasn't going to bring people together, but in fact
ignited a lot of strong emotions in people, because of what he was saying and
how he was saying it." He also felt it had forced Robertson to tone down
some of his remarks about gays and AIDS as the campaign progressed.

Though they may have been engaging in spin control or exercising selec-
tive memory, Robertson's campaign staff also found some positives in the
harrowing experience. Connie Snapp, while acknowledging that the event
itself had been spoiled, thought it had served Robertson well in the long run
by garnering sympathy from a sometimes hostile or skeptical press. "They
said, 'We know you guys worked hard on this, and we at least want to hear
what the man has to say. I can't criticize it if I can't hear it.' Toward the end
of the campaign, there was a begrudging admiration—in some cases, just
flat-out admiration—for this man and the message we were trying to communicate. And I could look back and see that at moments like that, they
were starting to connect. So we were upset, of course, but I think it turned
out okay." Marc Nuttle went further than that. He admitted he had not
anticipated such an intense response, but ventured that "to our base it was
wonderful. The announcement, the militant homosexual demonstration,
and the resulting coverage really boosted our organization and intensified
our support in the South."

While the press may have grown more sympathetic toward Robertson, it did not abandon its legitimate role as fact-finder and revealer. Early in the campaign process, Paul Weyrich gave Robertson a useful warning. "Look," he said, "I don't know what it is, but there is some skeleton in your closet. You'd better have discussed it ahead of time and decide how to react to it, because when the time comes, it's going to devastate you if you haven't thought it through." Weyrich's prediction soon came true. Simple checking of a few vital statistics revealed that the Robertsons' oldest son had been conceived well before they were married, a fact Robertson handled reasonably well by acknowledging its truth and noting that this was part of a pre-conversion lifestyle whose shortcomings he had never denied. More damaging was his claim to have been a "combat veteran" of the Korean conflict. Near the time of the 1986 Michigan precinct elections, Congressman Paul "Pete" McCloskey charged that he and Robertson had been on the same troop ship bound for Korea in 1951, and that Robertson's father had used his influence to get his son pulled from the ship, to keep him out of combat. Robertson hotly denied the charge and sued McCloskey for libel. The suit dragged on until the spring of 1988, when a U.S. District Court judge dismissed it, but the prospect of pending litigation gave Robertson a welcome excuse for not talking about the matter until most reporters had lost interest in it.

Somewhat surprisingly, especially considering that conservatives repeatedly assail the media for its leftist leanings, reporters did not make much of Robertson's strong and well-attested propagandist and financial support of rightist, sometimes brutal military regimes in Guatemala, El Salvador, Honduras, and Nicaragua throughout the Reagan years—according to a story in *The Nation,* CBN was the largest single private donor to Contra forces in Honduras, providing between three and seven million dollars in aid. Because Robertson's activities in Central America were in synch with the president's policies, and because all the groups he supported there were ostensibly anti-communist, this aspect of his history, even when it was mentioned, did him little damage with his natural constituency. Somewhat more problematic was his claim that CBN's news department had known the location of American hostages abducted in Lebanon in 1985, in connection with the hijacking of a TWA plane, and his implied accusation that the administration should also have known this and should have rescued them immediately. When the Reagan administration hotly challenged his statements, Robertson at first stuck by his story, then had to back down, admitting that his people had known the names of the hostages, not their location.

In an insightful comment, Paul Weyrich suggested that such apparently reckless statements, which damaged Robertson's credibility with an already skeptical press, may have been attributable to the particular nature of Robertson's experience in broadcasting. Though the *700 Club* regularly dealt with current events in a manner emulating secular news broadcasts, they seldom involved the same kind of critical internal scrutiny that is more common in the secular media. "I [had] thought he would make an excellent candidate," Weyrich said. "I did not take into account one factor, and that is that he had been doing a television show where nobody challenged what he said for many years, and he simply was not prepared for the challenges one gets in the political arena. When you make a statement, you have to back it up. You have to be able to prove it, or they'll slice you into bits. And he really hadn't been challenged for a long time. He used to get on his program and make statements about things he had heard; maybe they were true, maybe they weren't, but nobody challenged him. And so all of a sudden here he was in the political arena, and he would make dogmatic statements about something, and somebody would say, 'All right, prove it,' and when he wasn't able to do that, it really affected the whole campaign psychologically. That was a factor that I hadn't thought about."

TO OFFSET THE errors and onus of inexperience, it was crucial for Robertson to prove he was not simply a novelty act. That meant nailing down an early victory in Michigan, which would be no easy task. A "creative redistricting" scheme (read "extreme gerrymandering") devised by Mary Matalin provided Bush with thirty-seven Michigan delegates, to Kemp's thirty-two and Robertson's eight. Robertson forces, who had unsuccessfully challenged the redistricting scheme in court, held separate rump conventions at both the district and state levels, and Robertson announced that he expected those results—forty-three delegates for him, twenty-one for Kemp, and twelve for Bush—to be honored at the national convention in New Orleans.

Eight years later, Robertson still maintained he had been deprived of what should have been a clear victory. "We won Michigan," he said, "but the 'old guard' was there and they stole it away from us. There is no question that the word 'stole' is an apt description of what happened. We had the state won, but through parliamentary decisions and [with the help of] a couple of judges, they disqualified some of our people. It was a bloody mess. It was 'legal,' but it was unethical. When you're running for the presidency, they hit as hard as they can. They block, they tackle, and sometimes they rabbit-punch. I was rabbit-punched in Michigan. But in fairness, I had won Michigan, and that was a shock to the vice president."

E. J. Dionne, who was covering the midwestern campaign for the *New York Times,* observed that, despite the enormous shock Robertson had given Michigan's Republican regulars, "one of the important things to remember about this insurgency is that it ultimately failed. It was one of the great lessons of the way people with political power and expertise can assume control over a situation. In the end, the party leaders went to those Jack Kemp supporters who were deeply rooted in Michigan politics and said something like, 'You can't let these guys take over the party, no matter what you want to do for Kemp.' They ended up breaking with the alliance and, ultimately, the traditional party prevailed. What happened was very traditional politics: People in the legislature, who did business together all the time, who respected each other and had long-standing relationships, sat down and said, 'This has gone too far.' "

WITH MICHIGAN FINALLY behind, the campaign shifted focus to the rest of the country. The immediate target, and the most important for the Robertson campaign, was Iowa, another caucus state. As Dave Walters explained, "We had a proficiency at being able to get people to turn out for caucus meetings. We could go to any area of the country and find a group of fervent believers in Pat Robertson's candidacy, and get them to work very hard to get their neighbors and aunts and uncles and brothers and sisters to come to these caucuses. We could get the numbers there. So we focused on states that chose their delegates that way. A primary, which is wide open and public, is a totally different ball game. The numbers are much greater and it's not a meeting where you can pack people in and have a majority. It's whoever shows up at the poll and votes. And even though Pat had a group of fervent believers, he also had very high negatives nationally, and that made it much more difficult for him to secure a primary win."

In addition to working through churches, the Robertson campaign in Iowa relied heavily on small group meetings at which Marlene Elwell or one of her associates would talk about their candidate and answer whatever questions people might have about him and his program. While not operating in secret, the campaign generally kept a sufficiently low profile that the state's Republican regulars once again failed to comprehend what was going on, even after the straw poll revealed that Robertson should be taken seriously. Doug Wead, the "evangelical in the Bush camp," recalled that when Iowa party members "just couldn't find evangelicals on the radar screen" they concluded, "Well, they're not in Iowa." Wead knew better: "The data showed there were a lot more evangelicals in Iowa than in Michigan." The Bush campaign was also worried about Bob Dole, whose decision to stay out of the Michigan affray had saved his campaign millions of dollars and immeasurable effort, and had left him free to concentrate on Iowa, where he was already quite popular. They feared not only that Dole would beat them in Iowa, but that he would "stand up and defend the party against this incursion of evangelicals who were stealing our party," a stance that might well win favor among both local and national party leaders whose support Bush had taken for granted.

Perhaps reflecting her years of working with evangelicals, Marlene Elwell claimed that many who attended the small group meetings were "converted . . . to being Pat Robertson supporters," but the questions raised in such groups, as well as the results of public opinion polls, made it clear that many people were still apprehensive about Robertson's charismatic/evangelical beliefs. "We knew that was the problem," Connie Snapp said. "We had people who liked Pat and liked what he stood for, but were just a little afraid of this preacher background, this religious background. It frightened them. We felt we needed to make them pay attention to the fact that he was not going to try to legislate morality or tell them how to run their lives personally from his religious perspective. His faith gives him his integrity, but it wouldn't necessarily direct his decisions about their personal lives.

"As we looked back and asked, 'Who else has faced this?' the comparison to Kennedy kept staring us in the face. We studied what Kennedy had done. I could probably recite that speech he made to that meeting in Houston. He didn't run away from it. He took it head on, so we felt we had to do basically the same thing. So far, our basic advertising strategy had been, 'Don't vote yet; just listen.' Now, we needed something more dramatic."

Since there was no general convention at which Robertson could address the issue, Snapp and a small team of ad specialists designed a double-page newspaper ad, with a picture of Kennedy on one page and Robertson on the other, and the bold headline, "In 1960, the opposition said this man wasn't qualified to be president because of his religion; in 1988, the opposition is saying the same thing about this man." The ad ran on the Sunday before the Monday caucuses. "Just another good old Madison Avenue axiom," Snapp said. "People are home, they have the time, they read it. It was the last thing we would leave them with before caucus night. We were actually trying to influence the press as well. We were hoping we would get coverage of the ad itself, which we did. So more people saw it—because it was news—than we could have afforded [to pay for]."

Like Snapp, Marc Nuttle regarded the ad as tremendously effective. Whatever the crucial factors, Robertson did score a notable upset. Dole came in first, as expected, but Robertson beat both Bush and Kemp, which was not expected. "It was a pretty awesome night," Snapp admitted. "You would have thought Robertson won. We got all the publicity because we beat a sitting vice president. Senator Dole didn't get any publicity. I felt really bad for him—for about two seconds." Doug Wead attested to the jubilation in the Robertson camp. "Robertson was giddy and high," he recalled. "I passed his suite of rooms and he was in there talking to somebody about walkie-talkies for the Republican National Convention. He was getting his electronics in place. It was a nervous time."

E. J. Dionne professes to have been less surprised than some by Robertson's showing, recalling, "Some of the party people, the non-Robertson people, had an uneasy feeling that there was a lot of organizing going on, and when you talked to some of the Robertson people, you had a sense of confidence that they were going to pull it off. You went into the churches, you saw the people in the church parking lots, the kind of leafleting that was going on. People were just around, and the key to caucuses is activism. It's hard to win caucuses with lukewarm support, but you knew these guys were going to go out in the cold, in the snow, in any kind of weather, under any sort of circumstances, to make their point. And that's exactly what they did."

Though neither were victories, the Michigan and Iowa campaigns demonstrated the power of Robertson's appeal and organization. He also came in first or second in Hawaii, Nevada, Alaska, Minnesota, and South Dakota. These achievements, all in small or caucus states, lulled his campaign into forgetting that the game would change dramatically when they moved into larger states or states with primaries. The first of these, of course, was New Hampshire. Marlene Elwell recalled that, when she arrived from the Midwest to survey the situation in New Hampshire, "It didn't take me long to know they were in trouble. They didn't have the organization that we were able to put together in Michigan and in Iowa, and by the time I got there, it was too late. There had been an exaggeration of the support and a misunderstanding of what was actually needed to win that state. My reaction was a feeling of helplessness. There really was not anything I could do."

She was right. When the votes were in, Bush had surprised everyone by beating Dole, thirty-seven to twenty-eight percent. Jack Kemp had finished third, with thirteen percent, and Robertson had come in a weak fifth, with only nine percent of the vote. James Muffett acknowledged that the results were a blow. "In caucus states," he said, "we were able to do the Green Beret thing, and in a small environment, we were able to play on a par with the Bush people. I think that inflated expectations, not only among the staff and others at the national level, but also among the media. They sort of bought into these great expectations. And of course, the difference between the expectations and the results were cataclysmic, and very hard for people to deal with. At that point, I said, 'Well, the jig's up. We've got a long way to go before we have a consensus in America for a person like Pat Robertson.' "

Robertson's last glimmer of hope lay in gaining some victories on Super Tuesday, with its collection of primaries that included key states in the

South, as well as Oklahoma, Missouri, and Texas. He seemed genuinely to feel he had a chance to turn the tide in his direction, in large measure because of the high proportion of evangelical Christians in most of these states. Just as he was gearing up for an all-or-nothing push, however, his colleagues in the electronic church served up another blockbuster scandal: Jimmy Swaggart, perhaps the most watched of all the television preachers and a purported pillar of self-righteous rectitude, had been photographed taking a roadside prostitute into a motel room on the outskirts of New Orleans. Though less complex than the PTL scandal, the Swaggart story was almost equally juicy, and all the old images of Elmer Gantry god-hucksters were dragged out, wadded up, and hurled at Pat Robertson once again.

Aghast at having to defend himself for sins that were not his, Robertson angrily accused the Bush campaign with having released the Swaggart story at this particular moment. According to Doug Wead, it had been leaked by Bakker associate Richard Dortch, who resented the scathing attacks Swaggart had made on the Bakkers and PTL. Wead, however, was nearly fired from the Bush campaign until leaders of the Assemblies of God, who had passed the story from Dortch to Ted Koppel, acknowledged that he had not been their source.

The Swaggart story hurt, to be sure, but it was not Pat Robertson's greatest problem. When Marlene Elwell arrived in South Carolina, she discovered a situation similar to that in New Hampshire: "The organization just wasn't there." To complicate matters further, the Bush campaign had devised an ingenious way to short-circuit intensive recruiting for Robertson through conservative churches. Doug Wead explained: "We identified 160 super-churches in the South—by 'super-church' we meant a large congregation that had a television ministry, schools, staff, a huge budget into the millions of dollars. This was the base of operations for the Robertson campaign and it was easy to neutralize. All you needed was one tithe-paying member of the board who supported George Bush to walk in, sit down with the pastor, and say, 'I notice you had tables out in the vestibule last Sunday for Robertson. I'd like to put a table out there for Bush.' Most pastors would shut it down right there, saying, 'Nope, this is a church, not a political organization. We're not going to do that. We can't do it for everybody, so we're not going to do it for anybody.' And that would shut it down. It sounds simple, but the execution involved a lot of finances, building relationships, a lot of work. But that turned out to be one of our most effective projects."

The Bush team also made inventive use of a ready-made grassroots organization: AmWay distributors. "We had almost a thousand AmWay distributors in thirteen southern states," Wead said. "We used them for crowds. It was really comical. Lee Atwater would call me up and give me twenty-four hours to produce two thousand people to line the route from the airport to the place where Bush was speaking. I'd say, 'Okay, give me ten photos with the vice president as he steps off the plane and I'll get them.' Then I'd call one of the AmWay leaders and say, 'You want your picture taken with the next president of the United States? Well, prove to me that you can get five hundred people on the route from the airport to the hotel, and you can have your photograph tomorrow morning.' They'd call their little network; ten people would call twenty and so on, and they'd be out there early the next morning. And we'd drive by and the media would say, 'Look at the ground-swell for Bush!' We used that all the way through the general election campaign."

Despite such precautions, the Bush camp was not taking anything for granted. Robertson had fooled them before and they feared it might happen again. The media added to their sense of apprehension by dubbing the Robertson troops "The Invisible Army," often portraying them as religious fanatics on the fringe of society. Opponents often went further than that. A South Carolina party official likened Robertson's supporters to Nazis, and vice presidential son Neil Bush, in an unguarded moment, referred to them as "cockroaches issuing out from underneath the baseboard of the South." Predictably, the Robertson campaign collected such comments and made them part of a final leaflet distributed at church parking lots on the Sunday before Super Tuesday. "That hurt us," Doug Wead conceded. "Most evangelicals weren't going to vote for Pat Robertson, for the same reason that non-evangelicals weren't going to vote for him, but when the Robertson people unloaded all this information into the churches, which we knew they would do, many evangelicals saw it and said, 'Well, I'm voting for Dole. I'm not going to vote for Bush.' And we lost support we could have had." Others, he believed, voted for Robertson not because they wanted him to be president, but simply as a protest against having their religion denigrated by Bush representatives. No one had to tell Neil Bush to avoid such comments in the future, Wead said. "He knew. We learned from it. But remember, we won the South."

INDEED, BUSH DID win the South, taking every primary on Super Tuesday. Kemp formally withdrew from the campaign. Robertson, who finished third in his native Virginia and managed to attract only nineteen percent of the vote in South Carolina, a state he had said he must win to justify staying in the race, maintained a symbolic presence but acknowledged he no longer had any chance. George Bush, almost written off after Michigan and Iowa, had bounced back, regained the momentum, and could no longer be stopped. Still, that did not completely discourage Robertson's determined supporters. In Kentucky and North Carolina, and perhaps elsewhere to a lesser extent, they swamped post-primary precinct meetings and district conventions in efforts to elect their own people as delegates to state conventions, where they would have a chance to influence the party platform. It soon became clear to the Republican regulars that these zealous insurgents were going to be around for a while and that they intended to be taken seriously.

To avoid an ugly incident at the national convention in New Orleans, Lee Atwater and other Bush campaign leaders worked out a compromise with Robertson's Michigan forces, who still claimed their rump convention was the valid one, even though they recognized they would not prevail. The agreement was that their slate of delegates would be seated on the convention floor, even though they would not get to vote. Michigan's national committeeman Peter Secchia, who had to persuade the National Committee to go along with the arrangement, had not been part of that negotiation and did not like it. He liked it even less when Republican veterans chastised him for what he had done. A party member from Florida accosted him and said, "You're done. You'll never again get any support in the National Committee if you do this, because it's never been done before. These people do not deserve to be on the floor. They're not credentialed." Secchia explained the man's ire: "In the history of the Republican Party and our democracy, there had never been outsiders on the floor other than Sergeants-at-Arms. People work in politics for fifty years to get to be a delegate to the National Convention. And now, 'You're going to take these thirty or forty or fifty people and plop them right on our floor?' Well, since Bush was the nominee, we prevailed, but that was a very nasty fight. We got seats for them. If I'm not mistaken they were right behind the Illinois delegation, and they were in front of other official delegations. They had pretty good seats. And I remember walking down on the floor with their leadership and saying, 'This is where you'll be,' and it wasn't good enough for them. They wanted to be right up front. I really expended a lot of political capital to make that work."

Despite such efforts, Pat Robertson was not in a conciliatory mood. He had not been able to fulfill his vow to have Secchia removed as national committeeman, and he did not want to cause a rift in the party, but he did manage to extract a bit of revenge for what he regarded as Secchia's favoritism toward Bush. "The day Robertson gave his delegates to President Bush should have been a very exciting day for me," Secchia said, "because this had not been a very pleasant three years. I was tired, I had traveled a lot, we had won through nothing but hard work in the trenches. I had a message in my room to call [Bush's national political director] Rich Bond or Lee Atwater. They said, 'Got to see you right away,' so I went over. And George Bush, Jr., the current Governor of Texas, told me, 'Pat Robertson is going to relinquish the claim on the delegates pledged to him and give them to Dad. He's going to do it on national television. But he has one stipulation—that you not be there.' I think I teared up. Why couldn't I be there? Then it dawned on me that I was the symbol of something that bothered Pat Robertson, and the way George Bush, Jr., explained it was, 'He wants you out of town.' So I drove across the border and sat in a Holiday Inn drinking a cup of coffee, watching on television as Pat Robertson gave his delegates to [Michigan party chairman] Spencer Abraham, who had not committed to anybody, and to [leaders of Bush's Michigan campaign]. That was a sad moment, but I recovered. It was over, and we had won. I'm not proud of how we won, because we won with every trick in the books we could think of. . . . At the time, that was my job."

Not all of Robertson's supporters carried a grudge. Marlene Elwell became cochair of the Bush campaign in Michigan, with special responsibility for bringing Robertson supporters into line behind the Republican standard-bearer. James Muffett and Lori Packer, both ardent Americans for Robertson in the Michigan struggle, easily transferred their allegiance to Bush and worked diligently to get him elected. "A number of us decided," Muffett said, "that there was a clear distinction between [Bush and Dukakis], so we came back and put ourselves into that campaign. That surprised a lot of people from the Bush campaign in Michigan. I felt like it sent a signal to them." Packer concurred: "Bush wasn't my candidate in the primary, but in the general election, I felt very comfortable with him. Certainly against Dukakis."

Some of Robertson's troops were not able to scale down their idealism so easily. Kathy Potera, the Pennsylvania woman who had won the right to cast a vote for Pat Robertson, felt cheated that she was not able to do so. "I took great offense at this," she said. But "never once was I asked my opinion about anything. It's polite to ask somebody if he wants something; that's just general good manners. It was as if we didn't win five slots in Pennsylvania. I said, 'You do not have the right to take my vote. People voted for me and I'm here to represent them.' I wanted to go down for all time and eternity as a vote for Pat Robertson, as a vote for Christian conservative politics, as a vote that really mattered. This was something I had given months of my life to support, a tremendous amount of effort, a great deal of money, to be there representing Christian conservatives, and now all of a sudden I was being asked just to forget everything I had worked for and join the group. I asked why and I was told that Pat had made arrangements with the Republican Party. They told him that if he would give them his support, they would allow him his half-hour or hour of time. They would cheer for him when he stood up, he could make a speech and give everybody a copy of his latest book, everybody would wave their flags and their signs, and it would look

great on TV. He could have his moment in the sun, and then it would be
over. I didn't work for just one moment in the sun. I felt it was wonderful
that we were going to be a united party. It was great that Pat wouldn't be a
political outsider. But if this was all we gained for all of the work that
millions of Christians had done in registering voters and running individual
campaigns, that was a small trade-off. So I was disappointed.

"The only reason I changed my vote was out of respect for Pat Robertson. That was the only reason. I just didn't feel that we were treated fairly. I
believe we brought so much more to the Republican Party. I was very
disillusioned. I thought we were going to have discussions about some of the
issues, but in National Committee meetings, all the decisions were made.
We did not have a vote. I really didn't have to run as a delegate and win. All
it did was get me a seat on the floor and a seat at the inauguration. That was
it. It meant absolutely nothing to win. Christians want a voice. We're not
trying to take over the country, but we don't feel that our views, our
opinions, our beliefs, should be ridiculed. We don't feel they should just toss
us a bone and think we'll be thrilled."

Bone-tossing did seem to be in fashion at the convention, and the bigger
the dog, the more meat on the bone. Once again, Doug Wead was in charge
of scraps for evangelicals. "We were looking for ways to talk to the evangelical community, to say, 'We include you, we respect you, we respect the
support you've given us; we know we need your votes; we won't forget
you,' and to do that without offending the non-evangelical voters that we
had to have. We had to include Robertson. They didn't have to include him
in 1992, but we had to in 1988, because he was a candidate." They also
invited and paid attention to such figures as Robert Schuller and Pat Boone,
whose appeal went well beyond conservative church folk. Potentially more
troublesome were Jerry Falwell and men of his ilk, whose image made many
voters apprehensive and who might say something that would reflect poorly
on Bush or the party. Wead's strategy for dealing with them was disingenu-
ously simple. "Look," he told his colleagues, "if you exclude these guys,
they're going to be interviewed on CNN and the whole country's going to
see them sitting there on a couch, talking about the Republican Convention. They'll get ten minutes of network television time. It would be much
better to bring them in and keep them busy and have them speak to the
Iowa delegation and the Michigan delegation and have them go to a reception in this hotel and that hotel, and have them be with the vice president
and the president. Work them to death as part of the team—and nobody sees
them." When Bush operatives said, "If we don't let Jerry Falwell on the
platform, then America isn't going to see him," Wead countered with,
"America's going to see him unless you bring him into this convention and
work him to death, running him all over the place. If he's got free time, he's

going to end up on network television, talking about 'my good friend, George Bush.' "

Good seats and lackey duty were not all the Robertson forces received at the convention, and Paul Weyrich felt pleased with what he regarded as real gains. Robertson, he observed, "is an attractive fellow. He's very intelligent, he presents himself well, and he has sound ideas. But I never had any illusions that he was going to win in that particular election, because the odds of electing somebody of his views were very small. He told me at one meeting that God had told him he was going to be elected president and I said, 'Did he say when? Because it isn't going to be this year.' Well, of course, he didn't want to hear that. But what I [expected] the Robertson candidacy to accomplish, which in fact it did accomplish, was to move the party in a rightward direction, and you can't have any kind of political effort succeed unless you have a candidate out there who represents your values. He may not win, but if he doesn't embarrass himself and get no votes and have to withdraw, you will end up influencing the outcome. There is no question that Dan Quayle was picked as vice president precisely because Robertson had been in the race. Had he not been in the race, you would have gotten some liberal vice presidential nominee—Alan Simpson, maybe, or someone like that. So I thought that Robertson did quite well under the circumstances."

Quite clearly, the Bush camp did not alienate its evangelical constituency. On the contrary, the largest single group of voters giving the vice president his sweeping victory in November comprised the various groups of white evangelicals, who gave him eighty percent of their votes. To be sure, the Bush camp had courted them assiduously and had been rewarded with what Doug Wead estimated to be the equivalent of one hundred million dollars worth of free publicity in their magazines and newsletters and on their radio and television broadcasts. Still, Wead admitted, "We were shocked to have pulled eighty-one percent of the evangelical vote in the general election. It had never been done before. We always lose the other constituencies, but we had never lost them this bad. We lost the Jewish vote, of course, and the black vote, which we always lose, and the Hispanic vote. And Bush was the first person in modern times to be elected president and lose the Catholic vote." Ironically, the unmistakable importance of the evangelical vote proved unsettling. "Our first concern," Wead said, "was, 'We have to diversify fast. We are too dependent on that vote. It is too controversial and the media hate it.' It was scary, and a bit stunning. All these years, because of doctrinal or cultural differences, they wouldn't unite. Some of them preached that the others were going to hell. But they had come together for self-defense, out of a feeling that they were threatened, that their way of life was under siege. They couldn't come together for

Jesus, but they had come together for Reagan and Bush—in their minds, for survival."

ANALYSIS OF POLLING data from the year's campaigns gave a clearer picture of what Pat Robertson had and had not accomplished. Robertson had apparently believed the "tidal-wave shift of political interest in the evangelical world" might actually carry him into the White House. The data revealed, however, that his strength was confined mostly to the charismatic segment of that larger evangelical world. Political scientist John Green, a careful tracker of voting data on the Religious Right, reported that among the evangelical ministers Robertson had counted on to lead the charge for him, forty-three percent of charismatic and Pentecostal clergy named him as their first choice, compared to only twenty-eight percent of Baptists, eighteen percent of fundamentalists, and ten percent of Holiness and Adventist leaders. In each category, the more education a minister had, the less likely he was to support Robertson. Dave Walters, whose position as head of Robertson's Michigan PAC gave him the opportunity to see where the serious support was coming from, agreed that "Robertson had a base of support that remained pretty steady and constant, a fervent, active, strong base, but it just did not grow. Regardless of the effort, they never were really able to increase that original base of support."

Robertson's lack of support among noncharismatic evangelicals, and thus his poor showing in the South, where many had expected him to manifest his greatest strength, was attributable to several factors. One was theological. As noted earlier, most Southern Baptists—the largest of all Protestant denominations—believe that God's power is unlimited, that "prayer changes things," and that "the fervent prayer of a righteous man availeth much," but they don't really believe they have the power to deflect hurricanes, they are likely to regard tongue-speaking as a self-induced delusionary activity, and they are quite unlikely to expect to see the lame, the blind, and the deaf healed right before their eyes. They were just as uncomfortable as many secular people with the idea of a president who clearly believed all these things.

Some of them were also wary of Robertson's penchant for interpreting international developments in the light of biblical prophecy, and for what sometimes seemed to be a peculiar reading of current events. E. J. Dionne recalled a videotape the Robertson campaign had distributed in Iowa. "He was talking about how liberal ideas were seeping into education and that this would lead us all the way to the Communist International. He took several quick logical leaps, and suddenly communists were running the schools. You thought, 'Gee, after eight years of Ronald Reagan, the communists are running the schools.' It was just very peculiar. I sensed that a lot of his supporters weren't ideological in quite that same way. They didn't have the full-blown right-wing view about communists and how all these things are linked together. They just felt excluded, that their ideas were somehow not represented, that the country was going downhill, and that the place to fix that was politics." In addition, he noted, many of them shared the deep American conviction that both religion and government flourish best at a safe distance from each other. "As long as the Religious Right is a movement of people saying, 'Hey, religious America deserves attention. We shouldn't be ignored. We shouldn't be made fun of,' then it can be very strong. But as soon as it moves to making the stronger claim that 'God's policies should be national policies,' an awful lot of people, including religious people, say, 'No, that's not how I look at the political process.' So the closer Robertson got to victory, the more these kinds of people were going to back off and say, 'Might be willing to vote for him to make a point, but we don't want him to be president.' "

Some observers, including many relieved Republicans, were inclined to write off the Religious Right after Robertson's defeat. Others, more perceptive, knew better. Vicki Kemper, writing in *Sojourners* magazine, a publication of socially liberal evangelicals, presciently observed that "it would be a grievous error to write Pat off as simply another also-ran. Robertson's unsuccessful 1988 campaign will continue to impact the Religious Right and its future role in electoral politics long after the inauguration of our next president. Those observers who would interpret the failure of Robertson's candidacy, and his inability to garner a majority of even the evangelical vote, as proof of the weakening of the Religious Right and the waning of its political influence are sorely mistaken. . . ." Kemper went on to point out that the organizing strategies developed during the campaign would influence the way evangelicals do politics far more than the get-out-the-vote efforts of Moral Majority and Christian Voice had done. "Now," she wrote, "inspired and led by Robertson's candidacy, those same people—and many more—who used to do little more than vote in November have realized that if they really want to change things in this country, they need to be part of a mainstream political party. So thousands of Robertson supporters—most, but not all, of them right-wing evangelicals or charismatics—have flocked to precinct, county and state organizations of the Republican Party. . . . The goal . . . is to reshape and reorient American politics completely by systematically infiltrating and taking over its basic political structures. . . . [T]he Religious Right has discovered grassroots politics, and already it is building a formidable power base . . . their political concerns and their hunger for morality and traditional values have been building for more than twenty years."

Carolyn Sundseth, an evangelical who left the Reagan White House to work on the Robertson campaign, not only agreed with Kemper's assessment, but ventured that getting conservative Christians involved in the details of the political process "may be the purpose for his having run. He may have accomplished what God had in mind for him to do." Connie Snapp concurred: "Pat gave average people a way to participate in politics. First, he was a leader. He was a point behind which they could rally. Secondly, he was very keen on voter education and on setting up political organizations in the communities, helping people define issues, teaching them how to run for office. I think he was saying, 'Get out and solve your own problems. They can't be solved if you're sitting at home and just watching. You have to get out and do it.' And that's what's happening today. They're doing it."

James Muffett pointed out that Robertson had followed his own exhortation. "He didn't have the political credentials or the seasoning to be president, but he was carrying the message and carrying the torch. It gave people something to be for rather than just something to be against, and that is critical for any movement. A lot of people were very disappointed at the time, and some of them would never get involved in politics again because they saw it as a big failure. But I came in with a different set of expectations, so for me, the question after the November elections was, 'What do we do now? I'm here and I'm a player and I want to continue to be involved.' And I have been." Lori Packer (now Lori Packer Wortz) not only continued to be involved but later became chief of staff to the senate majority leader of the Michigan legislature. Marc Nuttle parlayed his experience in the campaign into a position with the National Republican Congressional Campaign Committee, and from there on to other committee posts in the Republican Party. Thousands of similar stories could be told. As Peter Secchia observed, "A lot of these Robertson people have stayed in politics. They are now the regulars. That's the great thing about American politics: It's constantly changing. I've learned there's room for more people within the tent."

Such developments did not surprise Dave Walters, who professed never to have believed that the failure of Robertson's candidacy would have a bad effect on the Christian conservative movement. "I knew," he said, "that the army we had built over those years, with all those resources and all that energy and time, wasn't going to leave the political arena just because Pat Robertson hadn't been elected President. They were going to stay, and they were going to grow, and their influence would increase. I remember a reporter who said, 'Well, Dave, this is the last big year of the evangelical vote.' I said, 'No, you'll see. Just look at your exit polls in '90, '92, '94, '96, and watch the percentage of people who will identify themselves as evangelical Christians. It's going to increase, not decrease.' " To Walters, watching that prediction come true meant the Robertson campaign was a significant success. "My agenda," he said, "was to grow the base of the Republican Party with new blood, with people whose values I shared—conservatives, evangelical Christians, conservative Catholics, whatever—to build that base and get people involved in the party who had heretofore not been involved, and to see that build for the future. I felt Pat Robertson was the greatest cheerleader we could have had at that time, so the credit can largely go to him. Personally, I felt it would have been better had he not chosen to run. He could have been a kingmaker and had an even greater influence than he has had, but the work, effort, and resources he poured in around the country are largely responsible for the results that we see today."

Pat Robertson himself obviously rejects any suggestion that his 1988 campaign was a failure, even though some associates believe he truly thought he stood a good chance of winning. "The theme of my campaign," he noted, "was restoring the greatness of America through moral strength. I sensed in 1986, '87, '88, what has come to full flower today: a moral decline in our nation, the break-up of the American family, the rise of crime and drug addiction and abortion. Those pathologies were full-blown then, but they have gotten much worse; they've become center stage. But I was considered a bit strange to bring those things up. I was also talking about a return to faith in God and individual self-reliance. I thought we had depended too much on big government, on government programs, for the solution, and needed to go back to that sense of pioneering spirit that America had been known for. I was advocating a flat tax and school vouchers and a partial privatization of Social Security. Many of the programs in the Contract with America were things I was enunciating in those days. So out of the seeming defeat of my campaign and the demise of what had been called the Moral Majority came an extremely effective force which I believe is the wave of the future, and which is toppling historic liberalism and will bring about a conservative era in the United States."

Has he ever considered another run at the White House? "I have flirted with the thought for the year 2000," Robertson admitted, "but the flirting goes away very rapidly. I've got more important things to do."

CHRISTIAN COALITION

EARLY IN 1989, Pat Robertson received a telephone call from Billy McCormack, an original core member of Freedom Council and chairman of Robertson's campaign in Louisiana. "Pat," McCormack told his friend, "all that you have done is going to naught unless you provide leadership right now for these people. Hundreds of thousands of people, whom you have brought into politics for the first time in their lives, are looking for leadership. You've got to do something." Robertson already knew that and obviously had some inkling as to what he wanted to do, because he had asked Marlene Elwell to lead and expand the grassroots network developed by Freedom Council and Americans for Robertson. Exhausted and feeling a need for a respite from full-time political activity, she had declined. By so doing, she made room for one of the more remarkable new figures in American politics.

On the last evening of the festivities associated with George Bush's inauguration, Robertson received the "Man of the Year" award from a conservative college political organization known as Students for America. As the honored guest, he sat by the group's founder and president, a fresh-faced young man named Ralph Reed. Apart from a brief encounter in a reception line, this was the first time the two men had met or spoken. "We just began to do what two politicos do," Reed recalled; "we started to talk shop. And as someone outside his campaign—I had supported Kemp, but I thought very highly of Pat—I was offering my view of some things I thought had gone right, and also wrong, in his campaign. I think he was a little taken aback that somebody he had never met before was saying, 'I think your people did the following things wrong.' Then we talked about the future, and we agreed that George Bush was unlikely to bring to the Oval Office the same symbiotic relationship with conservatives and people of faith, the same sort of moral tone and moral tenor that Reagan did, the way Reagan could speak so deeply and so passionately about his own faith and about [moral] issues without really alienating or offending those who did not share those convictions. We both felt Bush would have a difficult time pulling that off, and therefore it was going to be necessary to shift the focus of the 'pro-family' or religious conservative movement out of Washington and away from the Oval Office and get down to the grassroots—school boards, city councils, county commissions, and so forth.

"I also remember his commenting extensively about the movement of his people into the [Republican] party. He felt that as many as a million people who had been Democrats had switched party registration just so they could vote for him. And I remember one other thing he said that I've never forgotten: 'If the Roman Catholics and the evangelicals could get together and agree on a shared agenda, they would be the most effective political force that the country had ever seen.' "

At the end of the dinner, as they were walking toward the elevator, Robertson said, "I've met with a group of potential donors who have indicated they would be willing to provide the seed capital to start a new organization. I think there's a window of opportunity with Reagan leaving, with the Moral Majority closing down, and with the momentum I have coming out of my campaign, to start something new, something different." He invited Reed to take the lead in starting it. Because he was in the midst of writing a Ph.D. dissertation in American History at Emory, Reed "very politely declined" to "come on board and help run an as-yet-unnamed organization that was really, at that point, just an idea," but offered to send him a memo on how to build such a group. "I sent him that memo," Reed said, "and then I didn't hear anything back for nine months. He didn't call, he didn't write. I assumed the project had just been pushed aside and forgotten about." Robertson, however, had forgotten neither the project nor Ralph Reed. He remembered being struck with Reed's presence and potential: "He spoke with unbelievable intelligence and knowledge. I thought, 'This is an extraordinary guy.' "

Indeed, despite a countenance that seems inevitably to remind journalists of choirboys, Reed was, at age twenty-eight, already a seasoned politician. While a student at the University of Georgia and Emory, he had been active in the College Republicans and had attended the Leadership Institute, a political-activist training program Morton Blackwell established in 1979. After successfully spearheading a project supporting Lech Walesa and the Solidarity movement in its efforts to free Poland from Soviet control, Reed had become executive director of College Republicans. His predecessor and mentor, Grover Norquist, another Leadership Institute alum, observed, "It was obvious that Ralph would be the natural successor. He knew all the state and local activists. He traveled, slept on floors—the whole nine yards that student activists do. He put together a 'How to Design, Build, and Burn a Soviet Flag' kit which was mailed out to the College Republicans, because everybody always forgot which way the hammer and sickle go. Ralph was a natural organizer—very aggressive, very hard-working." Reed was also very confident of success. He explained, "Just as my counterparts on the left during the sixties felt that, although they might be in the minority then, the future belonged to them, I felt like the future of the country and the future of my generation rested in the hands of conservatives, and that it was conservatives, not liberals, who had the ideas, the intellectual energy, the vitality, the moral force that would make them the governing movement of the future."

Reared in a devout Methodist home, but admittedly something of a hell-raiser during his college years, Reed returned to religion in 1983. Shortly afterward, he left College Republicans to found Students for America, which shared many of the same aims but concentrated on getting religious students, in Christian and secular institutions alike, involved in politics. During this period, he and Norquist often talked about the political power that could be achieved if Catholics and evangelical Protestants could combine forces, which is why Pat Robertson's insights struck him so forcefully.

When Robertson was finally ready to move, in late September, he contacted Reed and told him, "I'm flying to Atlanta, and I'm going to have a meeting of some of my top political advisors. I want you to be there." The cast of characters was familiar: Charles Stanley, D. James Kennedy, Beverly LaHaye, Marlene Elwell, James Muffett, Lori Packer, and a few other people who had taken a lead role in Robertson's campaign. These insiders met privately for a while, then reconvened with a somewhat larger group, including Reed. At the second meeting, which lasted only two or three hours, some seemed resigned to encouraging the people they had mobilized just to fit into the Republican party and hope for the best, but others found that approach unpromising. Disenchantment with the Bush administration had already set in. Their suggestions for appointments had been largely ignored and it seemed clear the president and his key associates had little real enthusiasm for their agenda. Reed sensed that "the days of kowtowing to Republican presidents had come to an end, and it was now time to build a permanent, separate grassroots structure that would speak for them and be a force unto its own." By the end of the discussion, that was clearly the consensus, and most of those present had pledged to help.

Reed knew few of these people, and they knew little about him. When, as the meeting drew to a close, Robertson introduced him as the first staff member of the still-unnamed organization, Reed recalled that almost everyone in the room looked somewhat surprised, none more so than he, "because when I walked into that meeting I had no idea this would happen and no intention of taking any job, with that or any other organization. The meeting broke up and everybody was heading back to the airport to fly home, and Pat walked over to me and said, 'Congratulations. You have no money, no staff, no budget, and no office. Welcome aboard.' And that was literally how the Christian Coalition began."

Shortly after the Atlanta meeting, Reed and his wife, Jo Anne, moved to the Tidewater area and became the entire staff of the new organization. (In part at Paul Weyrich's urging, a decision had been made to keep the national headquarters out of Washington, to avoid, Reed explained, "getting sucked into the inside-the-Beltway game of doing nothing but going to meetings and news conferences.") Despite their lack of previous contact, Reed and Robertson apparently meshed smoothly from the beginning. Reed valued the lessons Robertson had learned in the campaign. "I remember one night early on," he said, "probably the first week or two I was there. We were going through the old warehouse that had been his campaign headquarters, getting ready to move out of there and set up our own offices, and just rummaging through what remained of the presidential campaign: a few beat-up old file cabinets, a bunch of inflatable elephants left over from some rally, a bunch of old 'Americans for Robertson' bumper stickers—just the afterbirth of a presidential campaign, and a losing one at that. It was not a very optimistic scene.

"It occurred to me at that moment that Pat was only the third explicitly evangelical political figure of the twentieth century to seek the White House, the first being William Jennings Bryan and the second, Jimmy Carter. And he was certainly the only conservative evangelical in the twentieth century to run for President of the United States. By going twelve rounds with Lee Atwater and Charlie Black and Jim Baker and Ed Rollins, he got a Ph.D. in the political school of hard knocks. He learned a lot about how this system works, things most religious conservatives and 'pro-family' leaders have never learned. So I respected his views and would usually call him before I did anything big. We developed a strong relationship early on, and that's never changed. I'm usually on the phone with him two or three times a week, if not more, discussing what we do and how we do it." Still, Reed professes never to have felt he was being stifled or watched too closely. "Pat is an entrepreneur, a founder, a delegater," he said. "He doesn't micromanage. Once he starts something and presents the vision, he lets the person he brought on run the day-to-day operations. So from day one, he was the president and founder and I ran the day-to-day operations. The relationship between us developed very rapidly into a strong collaboration in which I leaned heavily on his wisdom and insight and knowledge, and he leaned heavily on my strategic and tactical mind and my ability to organize politically." (It may be worth noting that several knowledgeable observers, none of whom was willing to be identified in print, regard Reed's description of Robertson's disinclination to micromanage as rosier than the actual situation.)

By all accounts, the Christian Coalition, though inspired and backed by Pat Robertson, received nothing like the eight million dollars or so that CBN had contributed or loaned to the Freedom Council. "Based on the fact that the Christian Broadcasting Network is a $100-million-a-year ministry," Reed observed, "most people probably have a misapprehension that we immediately walked into big offices and that large donors wrote big checks to get it off the ground. That was not the case. It was a very humble beginning. Pat wrote a thousand-dollar personal check. I flew to Atlanta and met some donors I knew personally and several of them wrote checks for five hundred dollars or a thousand dollars. The first month, I think we had a grand total of three to five thousand dollars. That just paid my salary and turned the phones on. They put the deposit for the phones on my personal credit card. That was how it got going."

The new organization's first priority was finding some members, and the obvious place to look was the mailing list of people who had contributed to Americans for Robertson. To generate a response, Reed relied on one of the Christian Right's most dependable ploys: outraging its constituency with sensational accounts of offenses against religion and morality committed by homosexuals, liberals, or the government. The initial mailing, sent to the entire list, which had not been used since the campaign, managed to hit all these buttons at once, attacking the National Endowment for the Arts for subsidizing exhibits of the work of Andres Serrano and Robert Mapplethorpe. The letter attacked Serrano's art for, as Reed put it, "uses of religious imagery in a way that many felt was less than respectful." The most egregious example was the notorious "Piss Christ," a photograph of a plastic crucifix submerged in Serrano's urine. Mapplethorpe's photography, which often featured stark sadomasochistic and homoerotic images, was almost equally sure to offend evangelical and other conservative sensibilities. Christian Coalition asked its audience to join its efforts to combat the use of federal money to fund such exhibits. More importantly, it asked them to volunteer to start local and state chapters of the new organization.

The response was immediate and substantial. Dick Weinhold, a Robertson supporter who attended the Atlanta meeting and subsequently headed Christian Coalition efforts in Texas, recalled that he had loaned the organization money to help pay the postage on that first mailing. "I wish that had been a stock-option deal," he said with a laugh, "because that would have been the best investment I had ever made." According to Weinhold, "Ralph and [his wife] Jo Anne keyed in the names of supporters as they came in.

They sent thank-you letters, signed them, stuffed them, and mailed them. I remember Ralph's telling me that he took letters to his Bible-study group on Wednesday night, and after the Bible study, they would sit around and he would give them pizza, and they'd stuff the letters to donors. It was a very humble beginning, and in those days I think no one really had much faith it would be a successful operation."

Using the money garnered in this first-fruits harvest, the new organization gained national publicity by purchasing full-page ads in the *New York Times, Washington Post, USA Today,* and other newspapers, calling on Congress to prohibit use of National Endowment funds to underwrite pornography, obscenity, or attacks on religion, and warning legislators that, as Reed put it, "If you continue to vote for these things, you're going to face the voters in November of 1992." The ads sparked considerable controversy over the NEA's activities and brought Christian Coalition its first national publicity and additional income.

After that flurry, the organization faded from public view, enabling Reed to begin the more substantial work of building a movement. Traveling a well-marked road, he went first to Orange County, California, "on the theory that if I couldn't start a chapter in Orange County, I probably couldn't start one anywhere in the country." He was not disappointed. "We had a good meeting," he said. "We probably had a hundred twenty people at a breakfast, and we started a chapter."

It did not take the Orange County chapter long to show its muscle. When the City Council of Tustin announced it was discontinuing its long practice of opening its meetings with a prayer, the group organized a letter-writing campaign and began to pack council meetings, importunately demanding that the prayer be reinstated. It was, with petitionary duties passed around among the local clergy. Reed observed that the quick success of this effort vindicated his conviction in the importance of learning how to exert pressure close to home. "It is much easier to move a city council or a school board," he said, "than to move the U.S. Congress. If you're an athlete, you don't begin by trying to bench-press five hundred pounds; you begin with fifty pounds. And the strength you gain by doing that allows you to go up to a hundred and two hundred and so forth. I felt, just as a matter of political strategy, that the religious conservative movement had always gotten it backwards. It always tried to leap-frog over the preliminary steps to political influence with one long bomb: trying to win the White House. But if you win the White House and you don't control anything underneath it, it can be a Pyrrhic victory, as we discovered with Reagan, and as the left is discovering with Clinton. So that Tustin City Council issue demonstrated to us that we were on the right track."

From that beginning in Orange County, Reed began conducting "Lead-

ership Schools" in various states where the response to the first mailing had
been greatest. He would show a seventeen-minute video presentation,
"America at the Crossroads," in which Pat Robertson spoke alarmingly of
the need for Christians to stop the nation's slide into hell. Reed would then
offer detailed instruction on how to participate in local politics and how to
form local, state, and regional organizations throughout the country. During
most of this time, Reed observed, "The media were just completely missing
the story. Very few people called; very few understood what we were building, until many years later."

A S C H R I S T I A N C O A L I T I O N grew, Reed had to delegate some of his
responsibilities. To serve as the organization's first national field director, he
hired Guy Rodgers, who had backed Jimmy Carter in 1976, taken part in
the White House Conference on Families in 1980, and worked with Marlene Elwell on the Robertson campaign in 1988. The two men met at a
Heritage Foundation gathering in November 1990. Rodgers went to work
for Christian Coalition on January 16, 1991, the day George Bush launched
Operation Desert Storm.

"In my first meeting with Ralph," Rodgers recalled, "we spent four
hours and I filled up six or eight pages on a legal pad with various things
they had been wanting to do but simply had not been able to get to. My job
was to take this and start moving it ahead. I looked at the early materials they
had. They had a training manual for organizing the grassroots. They had a
strategy. They had a plan. I was very impressed by the direction they wanted
to go. Columnists were writing the epitaph of the Religious Right but those
of us who had been involved in it at a grassroots level didn't see it that way.
We saw a movement in transition." Rodgers saw that Reed and Robertson
and some of their key advisers shared that perception and wanted to create
"a genuine grassroots organization—not a paper organization, not a mail-
ing-list organization, but a genuine grassroots organization. And that's what
I was hired to do. After I came on board, I dealt with the training programs
and Ralph was able to focus more on dealing with the media and other
things he does now. He was trying to do all those things before, and it was
simply too much for one man to do."

After consolidating the base of previous Robertson supporters, Rodgers
and Reed began to recruit people who had not been part of that effort.
Many of these, predictably, came from other segments of the "pro-family"
movement and might still be involved in James Dobson's Focus on the
Family or Beverly LaHaye's Concerned Women for America. "The message
I carried," Rodgers explained, "was that, if we are going to be successful as a
movement, we have to have a vehicle that can focus what we're doing and

that understands the political realities. I think, as much as anything else, that what sets us apart as an organization is that the people who were at the top of it, from Ralph to me and my staff, were all political people. We had campaign experience, not think-tank experience. That's not to put down the think tanks, but we said, 'Listen, you have these great ideas, these great positions, but how do we turn this into policy? You have to understand political realities. You have to understand how to lobby and how to orga-nize.' That's the type of experience we brought to bear, and that's how I would sell it at the grassroots.

"And that approach was beginning to take hold, because by '91, '92, people in this movement were tired of losing. We came along with our training programs and said, 'Listen, we all agree on these issues. This is how we can turn them into something that is going to be implemented. This is how you can lobby at the local level and do it effectively. This is how you work together with one voice.' That was bringing the right message at the right time, because people were hungry for something that was process-driven even more than it was message-driven. They were ready for some-thing that would take them to that next step."

Dick Weinhold agreed with this assessment. "There was a legacy," he said. "There were people all over America who had been involved politically for the first time, and they had been bitten by the bug. They wanted to keep going." Ralph Reed's old friend, Grover Norquist, concurred. "The Rob-ertson campaign was a building campaign," he said. "It was for the Reli-gious Right what the Goldwater campaign was for the modern New Right. It identified lots of activists; it brought people together; it taught people campaign skills. People who hadn't been political in '64 became politicized [in '88], worked on a campaign, liked it, decided it was important, and thought they could win the next time."

Guy Rodgers also thought they could win, but knew they would have to learn and absorb a great many things that did not come naturally to most evangelical Christians. "Our type of governing system," he explained, "can be responsive to an organized effort from the grassroots if they know what they're doing, and that was one of the main things I communicated over and over and over again: If you're going to play in this game, you have to know the rules. There are certain formal and informal rules of being an activist in politics. My objective was to take people who have things they believe in very strongly, who want to have an impact, but didn't understand the pro-cess. Most people who get involved in this process don't understand that the things they learned in civics class don't go very far when it comes to being successful in advancing things you believe."

Rodgers admitted that the compromises and deals and manipulations that characterize much of politics have been difficult for many of his people to accept. "Most of the Christians we talked to," he said, "had frustrations with things they had done themselves or things they'd seen other Christians do. What we said to them was, 'Listen, government is about public policy. It is not about redemption. It is not about making people moral or better. If you look at the history of governments, you can see that it doesn't do a very good job at that. Don't try to make government do that. Just try to make government reflect policies and values you believe in. If you do that, you will find a lot of people who may not call themselves evangelicals or born-again Christians, but who will share many of the values you have." Rodgers also urged his charges to avoid speaking in what he called "Christianese." Instead, he told them, "Speak the language of the people you're trying to communicate with. If you're in the public-policy arena, which is not church, don't talk like you're in church."

This pragmatic approach permeated Christian Coalition's strategy and style. Volunteers were urged to hold preliminary meetings in churches other than their own, to avoid the appearance of proselytizing; to reserve rooms half the size of the expected crowd, to create an appearance of an unanticipated groundswell of interest and enthusiasm; and to make sure that name tags were written in bold block letters, to enable leaders to call people in the first few rows by their first names, creating a greater sense of community. One moderate Republican who experienced her share of conflict with the Coalition acknowledged her admiration for the organization's cookbook-style approach. "If you take a look at the Christian Coalition organizing manual," she said, "it tells you precisely what to do. I wish the moderates would follow it."

NO ONE, PERHAPS, was more pleased at Christian Coalition's rapid progress than Paul Weyrich. Though he did not make the comparison himself, he seems to have felt that, like Queen Esther in the Bible, Robertson and Reed had "come to the kingdom for such a time as this." "Opposition to the Soviet Empire," he observed, "was a glue that had held all sorts of disparate elements of the conservative movement together, because whether you were a religious-right person or an extreme libertarian or whatever in between, the one thing everybody could agree on was that the Soviet Union was 'the evil empire' and that it had to be opposed. With that disintegrating, you had an entirely different dynamic, and you shifted from the Cold War framework that had dominated American politics from the end of World War II to 1990 or so, to a domestic-oriented political framework. That had a profound impact on the [Religious Right] movement, because it now had to define itself much more carefully than it had in the past, when it could be part of a larger framework."

Weyrich believed Pat Robertson not only perceived this shift, but also recognized what it would take to influence domestic policy. "He learned what all those other [Religious Right] leaders never understood, and that is, if you want to have an influence on politics in this country, then elect people at the local level. Grow the movement from the bottom up. Don't worry about the presidency; the presidency will take care of itself in due course. And train people. Robertson bought that. He chose Ralph Reed and he set up funding to provide training of people at a big-time level. I tried to get the earlier group of religious-right people to do the same thing, and they didn't have a clue as to what I was talking about. They simply did not understand it. To them, having political impact was having a rally with lots of people waving flags. So the great thing, the most important thing to come out of the Robertson campaign was an organization that actually is training people and training them correctly, and is operating not just at the federal level with presidential candidates, but right down to races for local positions. They took seriously my injunction that they should be active in local politics first.

"As a result, we have lots of friends now on city councils and county boards and school boards and in state legislatures—something we never had before. This is why we can seriously talk now about fundamental changes in Washington, because you've got governors and legislators and mayors who are speaking up and advocating [conservative] positions. Heck, when Reagan was president and wanted to do some of the very things we're talking about now, he didn't have a mayor in the country outside of some small town in the middle of Tennessee who was willing to speak out in his behalf. Now you have big-city mayors who are willing to say, 'Yes, we will handle this if you give us greater flexibility,' and governors, including some Democrats, who will say, 'Yes, reform welfare this way and we'll handle it for you and do it more cheaply and serve more people in the process.' In the early eighties, the whole infrastructure was in the hands of the status quo, and they screamed bloody murder when Reagan tried to change anything."

Working under Rodgers, state directors had responsibility for organizing chapters in each of their state's counties. Some directors, such as Marlene Elwell in Michigan, were seasoned veterans. Others, such as John Dowless in Florida, were not. Dowless had little real experience at political organizing, but Christian Coalition hired him anyway. Because of the newness and nature of the organization, he explained, "they obviously couldn't bring in top operatives, so they had to bring in people with a lot of energy and not a whole lot of experience, and make the best of it." Drawing on his enthusiasm and training materials furnished by the national headquarters, Dowless set out to locate people in every county who were willing to lead chapters or to serve as neighborhood coordinators and church liaisons. "I don't know if there is a typical volunteer," he said. "but many are parents and grandparents who are concerned about the next generation."

Once established, Dowless explained, the county and state organizations operate with a fair amount of autonomy, raising their own money and exercising considerable independence as to projects to undertake and alliances to form with other groups. The national organization provides them with legal and strategic advice, enlists and expects their support on national-level projects, keeps them informed on pertinent legislative issues, provides continuing exposure to the work of conservative thinkers and leaders, and helps them stay in touch with what chapters in other parts of the country are doing. It's not a rigid structure, Dowless said. "It's very fluid and flexible. 'Interdependent' is probably the best way to put it." In keeping with the organization's name, local chapters frequently form coalitions with other conservative organizations in their area. In Florida, Dowless said, "We've worked with right-to-life organizations. We worked with Concerned Women for America, with the American Family Association, with Dr. Dobson's groups. We're fairly close. We call each other and ask for advice or say, 'Hey, can you help out with this?' "

One advantage this kind of networking provides is to help organizations decide how best to deploy their resources. If a candidate, however pure in heart and ideology, stood no chance of winning, he or she stood little better chance of getting much help from Christian Coalition. "We have a lot of people calling us to say they'd like to run for office," Dowless explained. "We can determine if we are strong in an area or not. Let's say they're running in certain parts of Miami or West Palm Beach. I can tell them right off the bat, 'That's a liberal area. The issues you represent may not fare well there. We don't have a real strong membership in that area.' Ultimately, a campaign is up to them, but we can determine if they would get much support."

IN THEIR FIRST conversation, Pat Robertson and Ralph Reed had agreed that the newly inaugurated George Bush would have difficulty matching Ronald Reagan's success at capturing evangelical hearts and minds. That this proved to be true was due in some measure to the Great Communicator's ability to convince his admirers that his expressions of conviction and good will were backed up by substance, despite the lack of tangible evidence. As columnist E. J. Dionne pointed out, "It is striking how much loyalty Ronald Reagan won from this constituency without delivering much to them at all—except on judicial appointments, which proved important. There was no school-prayer amendment, no anti-abortion amendment, no school-choice program. Most of their core issues were just not dealt with. I think Reagan sensed, correctly as it turned out, that he could maintain the loyalty of this constituency—because they still thought that, in his heart of hearts, he was with them—without doing much for them." And by not doing much for them, he was able to avoid alienating the more socially moderate-to-liberal wing of his Republican coalition.

According to Dionne, Jack Kemp's press secretary once said that "whenever Ronald Reagan spoke about abortion or spoke to the Religious Right, his younger yuppie supporters always thought they saw him wink. I think it demonstrated Ronald Reagan's skill as a politician that he could keep the trust of both wings of this very complicated coalition he had put together, that he could reassure the more socially liberal/moderate folk and still give these passionate, moving speeches to evangelicals. Bush somehow did not have either this natural gift or the natural sympathy from this constituency, so he paid the price for the troubles that faced an America that Ronald Reagan had led for eight years. It's odd, because, although he didn't seem much like an evangelical Christian, George Bush was a much more observant religious person than Ronald Reagan. Bush went to church every Sunday. He seemed to refer quite naturally to God when he spoke. It didn't seem like an affectation. Maybe it's a lesson in how much of a cultural split there is in the American Christian community, that a reasonably conservative, mainstream Protestant can still be viewed with some suspicion by certain kinds of evangelicals and fundamentalists."

Bobbie Greene Kilberg, a moderate Republican who worked in the White House public liaison office during the Bush administration, sounded a similar note. "It remains quite amazing to me," she said, "that George Bush had problems with the Religious Right, because I don't know what more he could have done. His position on abortion, on prayer in the schools, on guns—another issue they seem to care deeply about—was [exactly the same as theirs]. Yet there was a distrust that was real. I think it comes down to cultural factors. He doesn't wear his religion on his sleeve. His faith was a very deep and real thing, but it was a private thing and he didn't like talking about it much. He is a very modulated person. He is not an ideologue. He is a conciliator, a pragmatist who believes in getting accomplished what he can get accomplished. He is not a 'true believer' in that sense. When other people talked about religion all the time and made it their raison d'être for everything, it made him uncomfortable. It's just not something he did. There really was a disconnect, and it happened time and again. If you pushed people from the Religious Right and asked, 'What is it about George Bush that so bothers you? He's with you on [all the issues]. What more do you want?' And they'd just say, 'He's not one of us.' "

Guy Rodgers tried to explain the same phenomenon. "We are all a product of our experiences," he said, "and George Bush comes from a world that is far removed from that of most evangelicals. Take his involvement in a mainstream church. What's he—Episcopal? That's a different stream from someone who comes from a Foursquare church or a Baptist church or an Assembly of God church. Also, [Bush's] growing up in a political family, a family that was well off financially, that's a different world from the average evangelical out there. And there was a chasm that existed when George Bush tried to communicate, but didn't quite know how to connect. I remember seeing him at a Christian Coalition conference. He was well received, but you could sense that there was a strain; it wasn't his normal comfort zone. That was an area with which he wasn't real familiar or real comfortable, by virtue of his own experiences."

The inability to connect with evangelicals extended beyond Bush to much of his administration. Doug Wead, who worked under Kilberg in the public liaison office, with special responsibility for conservative groups, saw the problem developing but had trouble getting anyone to listen to him. He recalled, "I would come in saying, 'We've got major problems with evangelical voters,' and they would laugh me out of the room, because the polls showed that George Bush was the most popular president in history. They'd say, 'What problems can we be having with evangelicals?' It was so deceptive. It was hard to argue that 'you're doing something wrong' when the polls were saying, 'You're doing everything right,' but I could feel the undercurrent. I felt, 'We're going to pay for this. We're going to pay.' Lee Atwater's vision of the neo-Republican was a young preppie kid in his twenties or thirties, a computer nerd driving a foreign convertible through the desert playing 'Phantom of the Opera.' That's an attractive vision of the modern Republican. Who wouldn't like that? Who wants an old blue-haired lady that's a born-again Christian as the prototype of the Republican Party? But the reality was, the numbers said this was our base. And we let them go."

In part, Wead conceded, the White House could afford to slight evangelicals because they had still not learned how to use their influence to greatest effectiveness. "We were more fearful of someone like Paul Weyrich," he noted, "than someone like Beverly LaHaye, who had the biggest women's organization in the world, Concerned Women for America, because Weyrich was savvy. He knew how to work the national media. If Weyrich attacked a conservative White House on some issue, he would get millions of dollars worth of publicity. The evangelical leaders didn't know how to do that. They were perhaps a bit spoiled because they had such enormous, powerful means of distribution themselves, through radio and television and publications. They had not yet learned how to hold the White House [hostage] by blackmail, or how to threaten the White House with that type of power. The most powerful conservatives in Washington were the ones who knew how to do that."

Wead also put Gary Bauer in the "savvy" category. "When Bauer and the [Dobson-related] Family Research Council came on board in 1989," he said, "they knew what they were talking about. They'd come to the table with facts and they had a well-informed, talented group of young people. They were immediately effective. Gary had an advantage. He had worked in the Reagan administration and he knew how the White House worked. He knew what we wanted and needed, and he had a big impact."

Perhaps because he was a seasoned pro, Gary Bauer acknowledged that he had felt a bit of uneasiness when he first heard about Christian Coalition. "I saw great promise," he recalled, "but also great risk. The promise that I saw then, and continue to see, is that it's a great vehicle for men and women of faith to organize and get involved in public policy. My misgiving is that when you name an organization 'Christian Coalition,' you are indirectly making a religious point. While I can make a faith-based argument on things like the sanctity of human life or some of the other morally based issues, it's harder to make a morally based or Christian argument on what the proper budget level should be for the Department of Education. I've always worried about that, and I think the leadership of Christian Coalition worries about it, too—that they never do or say anything that would in some way set back the cause of Christ as they advance the political cause they're interested in. It's a delicate thing that any of us who are both Christian and involved in public policy have to wrestle with."

Doug Wead did not attribute all of Bush's problems with evangelicals to a cultural gap. Substance also played a role. As had been true of both Reagan administrations, few evangelicals were being appointed to important positions, a fact that contributed heavily to their growing frustration. "The issue that will gain you the support of evangelical leaders," he explained, "is appointments, because they have come to the conclusion that 'people are policy, and if our people aren't in [key] positions, we're going to be abused—in the courts, in the IRS, in immigration, in [other parts of the] bureaucracy.' The solution is to get people in place who understand the way they believe, who are evangelicals themselves. That's a powerful issue with evangelical leaders. If a candidate will make credible promises to appoint evangelicals, that will forgive a lot of sins."

Wead's aims and style caused tension within the Bush administration. Officially, he worked under Bobbie Greene Kilberg, who directed the office of public liaison. Kilberg answered to David Demarest, presidential assistant for communications, and Demarest answered to White House Chief of Staff John Sununu. In recalling his days at the White House, Wead omitted Kilberg from the chain of command, which would not likely have surprised her. "Doug really didn't think he worked for anyone," she observed. "In theory, he worked for me, and his specific role was to deal with conservative groups, particularly within the religious community. But there was a conflict between Doug's perception of his role and virtually everybody else's perception of his role. Governor Sununu, Dave Demarest, and I all had a very clear perception: We needed to represent the president to [a given] constituency in a strong and assertive way, and we also needed to take the concerns of that constituency and bring them back to the White House. We would hear what organizations were saying about issues, to make sure that was factored into the policy process. But once a decision was made, on a piece of legislation or whatever, then it was our responsibility to be the most forceful advocate for the president that we possibly could be, and to go back into those communities and sell those programs and help get them on board to support the president."

Kilberg obviously felt Wead had misplaced his job description. "Doug viewed himself as the conservative spokesman in the White House," she said. "It was very important to him that he be viewed by the religious conservative community as a powerful person in the White House, a real deal maker and power broker. The concept of team playing, which all the rest of us had, was not really there, I'm afraid. Doug had his agenda and he was determined to move it forward, whether it was the president's agenda or not. That caused some problems."

Wead confirmed much of Kilberg's analysis, but felt he had had little choice. "There were titles to these jobs," he said, "but you soon evolve into a job that may not be what the title says. In my case, I became the in-house advocate for all sorts of conservative issues, to make sure they were thoroughly argued. I didn't care what the president's conclusion was; wherever he went, I'd support him, but I wanted to make sure the political consequences were thought out before a decision was made. And it was very lonely. I can't say there was a moment when I came to my boss and there was a *disconnect*. There was almost never a time when I took one of these evangelical issues to somebody on the staff when there was a *connect*. There was never a connect. They didn't understand it. They weren't trained that way." Many times, Wead said, Bush's conservative constituency would have been unnecessarily offended had he not stepped in at the last moment and warned of a proposed policy's troublesome features. Predictably, that led to power struggles: "There were people who said, 'Keep him away, because we've got this settled. We don't want him to get near and have this thing unravel.' "

Wead was convinced this attitude on the White House staff hurt both Bush and, even more importantly, the Republican Party. "It seemed to me," he said, "that here was a chance for Republicans to put down their golf clubs, come out of the country club, and welcome millions of new voters to the party. And if they'd bring them in, there'd be a transition; the rough edges would come off. At the Republican National Convention in 1984, a huge percentage of them were born-again Christians and nobody even noticed, because they had political sophistication. They'd been involved in the political process. The same thing would happen in another four years to these Robertson supporters. They'd learn, they'd become sensitive to other groups and realize what they're sounding like. [They'd see the difference between] what they're saying and what people are hearing. That would happen, and they could be allies. But we didn't [do that]. We played games at the staff level and faked it. We kept them at bay. They were not totally included. They could have been—should have been—but they weren't."

Wead claimed that he did what he could to offset what he regarded as a short-sighted, elitist attitude, slipping evangelical leaders into meetings when their presence was not obviously called for. But, he said, "toward the end [of my tenure in the White House], a real power struggle began and there were people who wanted me out of there, so there was a concerted effort to block the people that I brought into those meetings with the president. That was of a personal nature. The idea was, 'It will make him look bad with his own constituency if we can [prevent] those meetings.' But I worked around it. I would do mass mailings, using that great White House apparatus to mail out 'personal' letters from the president, and that was probably more effective than running people into the Oval Office. But many began to resent my work and wanted me quieted."

Wead's critics did manage to get rid of him, but in so doing they discovered the peril of ignoring the sensibilities of the constituency he represented. On April 23, 1990, President Bush signed a piece of legislation called the Hate Crimes Bill, which mandated stiff penalties for crimes committed against people primarily because they are members of a specific group. The American Jewish community had been the strongest backers of the legislation, hoping it would stem the growing incidence of anti-Semitic acts in various parts of the country. Other supporters of the bill included Roman Catholics, several Protestant bodies, African-American and Hispanic organizations, and, fatefully, gay and lesbian groups. In what was regarded as a routine measure, representatives of the various supporting organizations were invited to the signing ceremony at the White House. Apparently unbeknownst to anyone involved in planning the event, this was the first time gays and lesbians had ever been officially invited to the White House. No special point was made of the invitation but, Kilberg explained, "The president's position was that it would be hateful and wrong not to invite someone because of their homosexuality. That's what the bill was all about and what it was supposed to counteract. So the decision was made very clearly that, yes, they would be included. That did not mean that George Bush shared their views, but it did mean he was going to show respect for the piece of legislation. This group was a covered class within the legislation."

The ceremony itself went off without a hitch. "This was just an event," Kilberg said, "probably one of three or four we did that day. Everybody behaved well and we didn't think anybody had tried to use it as a platform to advance any other agenda. As a matter of fact, I had the leaders of the two gay and lesbian groups in my office on the day of the ceremony, to let them know that this was not in any way an endorsement by President Bush of any of their agenda items, and that they were being invited to the bill signing because they were part of the coalition [that had supported it], and that they should read nothing into it other than that. They were delightful, very polite, and it was a nice ceremony, and we went off to other things.

"And then all of a sudden this firestorm came. We started getting letters and phone calls from people who accused the president of being a 'gay-lover' and saying that, by bringing people with a homosexual or lesbian sexual orientation into the White House, we were 'destroying the moral fabric of American society' and undermining the moral fabric of the Republican party—which I think they thought was worse—and that this was a terrible thing and we should apologize for it. The response from the president's office was clear: The president felt he had carried out the intent of the legislation in the way he held the signing ceremony and had nothing to apologize for."

Before that fire could die down, the White House committed two more sins against its conservative constituency. On July 17, Bush met with a group of magazine executives that included Christie Hefner, daughter of Hugh Hefner and publisher of *Playboy*. "It was not politically sound," Wead said. "[*Playboy*] offends conservatives, it offends women, it offends liberal women. There was no reason for it." Then, on July 26, at the signing of the Americans with Disabilities Act, members of ACT UP were spotted in the large audience gathered on the White House lawn, once again moving conservatives to brand Bush as pro-homosexual. According to Kilberg, no one was invited to represent gays, who were not regarded as disabled, but "somehow, surprise upon surprise, among 3,300 people who walked in the gate, some of them happened to be gay or lesbian, and some of them evidently had their own little Instamatic cameras and took pictures of themselves and showed them to friends afterwards."

As word spread that gays had once again been invited to the White House, the reaction was immediate and unsparing. Richard Land, executive director of the Southern Baptist Convention's Christian Life Commission, told the president that the "active courting of the homosexual lobby by your administration goes far beyond any argument of being president of all the people . . . [and] grievously damaged your administration's standing among many of my constituents." Robert Dugan, director of the fifteen-million-member National Association of Evangelicals, warned Bush that "many evangelicals believe you are sacrificing your claim to be a traditional values president."

After both the April and the July incidents, Doug Wead—on his own initiative and, according to Kilberg, without authorization from his superiors—wrote letters to evangelical leaders, describing the president as "a man who lives as well as speaks about family values" and charging that "quite frankly, the president's staff did not serve him well" by inviting the gay and lesbian people to the signing. In a similar statement to the Baptist Press, a news service of the Southern Baptist Convention, Wead said the decisions "poorly served the president." That, Kilberg recalled, "got Governor Sununu slightly ticked off, since clearly he was the one who made that decision, and I don't think he appreciated having someone who worked for him saying that he was poorly serving the president. He said, 'That's enough,' and he replaced Doug."

Wead denied that his letters were the reason for his dismissal, claiming that both Sununu and David Demarest were fully aware of them and repeatedly instructed him to send such a letter to new complainants. Furthermore, he insisted, placing the blame on the staff was a standard "good cop/bad cop" ploy used to deflect criticism from the president. "We did that sort of thing all the time. A liberal on the staff would say to other liberals, 'That's Doug Wead's horrible influence on the president,' and I would blame liberals when I was talking to conservatives. That was part of the process. The letter wasn't the issue. It was a political struggle, as it always is."

Wead's firing became an immediate cause célèbre in evangelical circles. Gary Bauer not only defended Wead as "one of the people at the White House who understands the coalition that elected President Bush," but asserted that "if anybody should be leaving the White House staff, it should be the individuals who have embarrassed the president by inviting homosexual rights activists who have opposed Bush in 1988 and will oppose him again in 1992." Robert Grant, who headed the American Coalition for Traditional Values, was even more blunt, asserting that "someone in the White House has decided to alienate the conservative traditional values base [estimated at fifty million] in the hope of cultivating the homosexual base that represents less than one million. It's crazy."

That Sununu was irritated more by Wead's behavior and style than by his conservative views and evangelical predilection is indicated by his choice of a replacement. Though initially disparaged by conservatives as too young, Leigh Ann Metzger soon proved to be an able champion of evangelicals. Before coming to the White House, Metzger had been a member of Charles

Stanley's church in Atlanta, had headed Phyllis Schlafly's Eagle Forum, and had served with the National Republican Congressional Committee as a contact with evangelical groups. Kilberg praised Metzger as an effective team player and noted that she and Sununu immediately set about mending fences with their evangelical constituency. "If I remember correctly," she said with some amusement, "they went into a meeting frenzy and brought in virtually all the different Religious Right groups."

Despite her ability to mollify conservative religious groups, Metzger admitted to a certain tone-deafness on the part of the president and her colleagues. Again and again, she noted, the president and his aides would give speeches in which they cited his support of the Americans with Disabilities Act and the Clean Air Act as key accomplishments of the administration, apparently unaware that these raised red flags for many of the people she represented. Doug Wead concurred. "The week after I left the White House," he recalled, "he spoke for a big humanistic organization out in Colorado. That's where he introduced the 'New World Order.' In the minds of evangelicals, that conjured up the anti-Christ systems prophesied thousands of years ago. A collection of Hitler's speeches was titled *My New Order*. It was not a good choice of words, and it frightened evangelicals."

BY THE FALL of 1991, Christian Coalition had more than 82,000 members and was financially secure. A year earlier, it had proved its effectiveness in a major election when it distributed 750,000 voter guides in North Carolina just before election day, helping rescue Jesse Helms from what appeared to be probable defeat. Now, it applied its young muscles on the national level during Senate hearings regarding the nomination of Clarence Thomas to the Supreme Court. "We knew the vote was going to be very close," said Guy Rodgers, "so we did what any good grassroots organization would do. We identified [the Senators] we thought were the swing votes and we mobilized our people in those states to make phone calls. We made tens of thousands of phone calls, and we made the right kinds of phone calls." When Thomas was confirmed, Rodgers continued, "That really impressed people at the grassroots. It hit home that when we told them, 'This is how you do it,' we were saying, 'You have feelings about this. Now you can do something about it. Your voice won't be one voice crying in the wilderness; it will be a collective voice that will ring very loud on Capitol Hill. [Judge Thomas] was the target of a tremendous smear campaign by the liberal establishment. They didn't realize there was a sleeping giant out there that would take this man on as a champion."

On the heels of the Thomas confirmation and just after the 1991 midterm elections, in which Christian Coalition had supported several successful candidates for the Virginia state legislature, Ralph Reed volunteered a now-famous characterization of his low-silhouette politicking: "I do guerilla war-fare. I paint my face and travel at night. You don't know it's over until you're in a body bag. You don't know till election night." Because Pat Robertson and other Christian Coalition leaders also used military metaphors, it was natural for journalists and critics of the movement to repeat them as evi-dence of a belligerent spirit. After a year of having his and other such statements thrown up to him repeatedly, Reed wrote a long memo to the organization's leaders, recommending that they substitute sports metaphors for the language of warfare, as more appropriate to the image they wished to convey. "It was a valuable learning experience for me relatively early on," he acknowledged. "It was an important transition for me to recognize that I was not longer just a bare-knuckled, brass-tacks pol—a Lee Atwater—but that I was now viewed as someone who wore the name of Christ, and that by bearing that name, my speech and my actions had to reflect his charac-ter."

Despite the admitted need for a change of tone, Reed felt his critics had misinterpreted what he had meant by what came to be called his "stealth" approach. Many, he said, "tried to claim that my comments suggested we were trying to hide who we are, which was ridiculous. The only point I had been trying to make was that the things we did, like the things the labor unions and feminists and black churches have done for decades—voter iden-tification, voter education, getting out the vote—are not things you really see until election day. The old modus operandi of religious conservatives had been to hold a news conference and endorse a candidate. We didn't endorse candidates; we simply informed voters on where the candidates stood on the issues and then phoned them and mailed them and urged them to go to the polls. That's just tried-and-true grassroots politics, and it often isn't really visible until an election day."

Interestingly, it appears that the persistent association between Christian Coalition and so-called "stealth" techniques is based largely on the appar-ently mistaken belief that the organization played a major role in a 1990 conservative uprising in San Diego County, when candidates associated with the Religious Right won sixty of eighty-eight races to capture a wide range of positions in local government, including school boards, hospital boards, and city councils. Many of the candidates did indeed take what might be described as a stealth approach, avoiding public appearances and declining to say where they stood on a variety of issues. Instead, they counted on the arithmetic of elections and the power of carefully targeted voter mobiliza-tion. It is common for students of American elections to note that, in a presidential year, approximately sixty percent of those eligible actually regis-

ter to vote. Of that group, only half (thirty percent of the eligible population) actually vote, meaning that as few as sixteen percent of eligible voters
can decide the outcome of an election. In lower-level elections, such as
those for school board and city council, which typically attract smaller turn-
outs, a candidate might well win with the support of only three or four
percent of eligible voters. By extensive telephone canvassing of conservative
churchmembers and widespread distribution of flyers on the Sunday before
the election, the organizers of the 1990 campaign pulled off a remarkable
number of surprise victories, many by complete political novices. So stunning was this accomplishment that supporters, critics, and professional observers of the Religious Right began speaking of "the San Diego Model," as
something likely to be replicated all over America.

While it is true that these election victories were largely engineered by
the Religious Right, it was a California-based organization called Citizens
for Excellence in Education, headed by Robert Simonds, and leaders in the
California Pro-Life Council who took the leading roles. Christian Coalition
was less than a year old and apparently had no part in the campaign, though
one of the key organizers did later become the coalition's director for California. Further, the San Diego Model failed to reproduce itself as predicted.
Indeed, just two years later, two-thirds of the candidates backed by the
Religious Right were defeated, which seems to confirm Ralph Reed's contention that such a strategy cannot succeed over the long term. "It might
work on election day," he said, "but you can't campaign as one thing and
govern as another. Campaigning builds the reservoir of political capital that
you then need to spend when governing. So what I advise candidates to
do—left, right, and center—is to say what you are going to do, run as who
you are, and don't apologize for it. Then, if you get elected, you'll be able to
govern. [A stealth approach] may have happened in one city. It does not
represent where the pro-family movement is going."

This disavowal of stealth techniques and the San Diego Model, however
sincere in retrospect, did not happen immediately. In fact, in at least two *Los
Angeles Times* stories published in the spring of 1992 and apparently based on
recent interviews, Reed was quoted as admitting, "Stealth was a big factor in
San Diego's success," and as once again using covert-operations metaphors:

> [T]hat's just good strategy. It's like guerilla warfare. If you reveal your
> location, all it does is allow your opponent to improve his artillery
> bearings.
>   It's better to move quietly, with stealth, under cover of night.
> You've got two choices: you can wear cammies [camouflage uniforms]
> and shimmy along on your belly, or you can put on a red coat and

stand up for everyone to see. It comes down to whether you want to be the British army in the Revolutionary War or the Viet Cong. History tells us which tactic was more effective.

It is not difficult, of course, to believe that Reed thought stealth and talk of guerilla maneuvers was a grand idea in 1990, but has changed his mind. He has, in fact, denied ever having made the statement quoted by the *Los Angeles Times*. Guy Rodgers, noting the universality of doing and saying things one later regrets, readily acknowledged that he was "sure there are some things Ralph has done that he looks back on and says 'youthful exuberance.' " Still, Rodgers was less inclined to view Reed's famous remarks as a symptom of belligerence than as a manifestation of euphoria. "We became victims of our success," he observed. "When I joined Christian Coalition, we had a ten-year plan. Within a year, we were already doing things that went beyond [that plan]. That [caused] an excitement that sometimes may have led to a little less discretion than would probably have been wise. One of the best ways to understand people in the grassroots of the pro-family movement is to understand their perception of being outsiders, either because they chose to be out of the process or because they wanted to be involved but always met resistance. If you were around this process during the 1980's, you saw defeat after defeat after defeat. To start winning a few and see some candidates you agree with get elected, is naturally something to be happy about. It was sobering for me to see that things I knew could work actually were working.

"And there's a responsibility that goes with that. You're no longer simply a voice crying in the wilderness; you are now moving into the process. I saw that [because I was] the national field director of Christian Coalition, people at the grassroots were looking to what I said, how I acted, what I did. And that is something not many people get in their lifetimes—being able to influence a process in that way."

NOT ALL EVANGELICALS accepted Christian Coalition's assertion that "this is how you do it." Some, particularly those committed to opposing abortion, regard the buttoned-down, political-mechanic approach to social change as likely to prove impotent. Easily the most notable of these is Randall Terry, founder of the confrontation-oriented anti-abortion organization known as Operation Rescue. Terry, a native of the upstate region of New York known as the "burned-over district" because it spawned repeated revivals and novel religious movements during the nineteenth century, was reared in a nominally Christian home, but did not take religion seriously until his midteens, when exposure to students from a fundamentalist Bible

Institute led to a born-again conversion experience. "I was radically converted," he said. "Up until that time, I was part of the rock 'n' roll culture, involved in drugs and immorality, but God just snapped me out of that, and I became a very outspoken witness for the gospel."

Like most fundamentalists at that point, Terry believed his primary duty was to evangelize others, not get involved in controversial social issues. Then, while attending Bible college, he began to see the films and read the works of Francis Schaeffer and became convinced that "there are biblical positions on the issues of the day." Terry recalled that, "When I was a junior, we watched the [film] *Whatever Happened to the Human Race?* When we got to [a particularly gripping scene of an aborted baby] in the last film, I literally sat there and sobbed. I remember praying, 'God, please use me to fight this hideous crime.' The Bible says, 'Rescue the fatherless from the hand of the wicked.' It's my Christian duty to fight abortion. I learned my duty from the Bible." Schaeffer's book, *A Christian Manifesto,* gave Terry instructions in how to discharge that duty. "One of the things it did for me," he explained, "was legitimize the idea that there is a higher law, that God's law is above man's law, to be revered and obeyed before man's law. That had a profound impact on me."

In *A Christian Manifesto,* Schaeffer spells out in some detail that obedience to God's law will sometimes entail disobedience to man's law. Armed with that bit of legitimation, familiar to adherents of classical Christianity but still a novel idea in fundamentalist circles, Randall Terry began to explore ways to fulfill the mission he had chosen for himself. He read anti-abortion literature distributed by the National Right to Life Committee. He read Coretta Scott King's *My Life with Martin Luther King, Jr.* and King's own *Letter from a Birmingham Jail.* He watched *Eyes on the Prize,* the PBS documentary series on the civil rights movement, and he said, "There's something there, in those tactics." More pertinent to his mission, he read *Closed: 99 Ways to Stop Abortion,* by Joseph Scheidler, a Roman Catholic with a long history of vigorous anti-abortion activism in the Pro-Life Action League. By the mid-1980s, Terry and his wife began to participate in Nellie Gray's marches and to picket local abortion clinics.

In 1987, feeling ready to strike out on his own, Terry founded Operation Rescue (OR), which quickly became the most controversial organization in the anti-abortion movement. Headquartered in Binghamton, New York, OR's premise was simple: "Babies are being murdered. We have a duty to save them." In a typical "rescue," usually carried out at a well-known abortion clinic, demonstrators divided themselves into three squadrons. One group, the actual "rescuers," sought to limit access to the clinic by blocking driveways and doors. A second group of "sidewalk counselors" attempted to persuade women not to have abortions and to tell them of alternative services, such as church-run homes and adoption agencies, that would enable them to avoid having an abortion. A third contingent prayed, sang, and quoted Scripture to support their colleagues and bear witness to women seeking abortions.

In addition to rescues, OR drew attention to its cause by sponsoring rallies and high-profile demonstrations, often featuring the fiery rhetoric of its founder. In a typical jeremiad, Terry proclaimed, "Twenty-five million children that are dead are enough to damn any nation to hell and to ultimate judgment. Period. But suffice it to say that the blood that has been shed and now stains the garbage dumps of America, now stains the once land of the free and home of the brave—that blood is crying from the ground to the god of heaven and earth, saying, 'How long, O Lord?' "

Such bold language understandably offended pro-abortion forces, and OR's activities, particularly the blocking of access to abortion clinics, not only drew sharp criticism but led to the jailing of many protesters whose behavior was judged in violation of various local ordinances. Terry himself has been arrested numerous times and spent four months in jail in 1990. Not surprisingly, protesters often compared their actions to the civil rights demonstrations of the 1960s, and Jerry Falwell underscored his repudiation of his "Ministers and Marches" sermon by comparing Terry to Dr. Martin Luther King, Jr.—and meaning it as a compliment. Both Falwell and James Dobson had Terry as a guest on their programs, and the young firebrand also received endorsements from Pat Robertson, D. James Kennedy, and New York Roman Catholic prelate John Cardinal O'Connor.

Legal and financial problems forced the organization to fold in 1990, but it soon reappeared in Florida with a slightly different name, Operation Rescue National, and a different leader. In 1994, it relocated once again, this time to Dallas, and is headed by the Reverend Philip "Flip" Benham. Randall Terry has not been officially connected with the organization since 1990, but the separation was largely a legal fiction. He has continued to be involved in its activities and remained its most prominent spokesman.

The most notable of Operation Rescue's activities occurred in 1991, during what Terry dubbed the "Summer of Mercy." Most news media called it the "War in Wichita." OR targeted Wichita, Kansas, for a weeklong siege against three abortion clinics, in an effort to dramatize the seriousness of abortion for the entire nation. "Wichita was picked for a couple of reasons," Terry explained. "It's the heartland of America and it had an abortionist who kill[ed] babies in the third trimester. So we thought, 'Let's capitalize on the fact that there's a monster there.' And it just went wild. It just exploded. People were, like, 'Yes!' and they began coming in from all over the country. It was awesome. So we thought, 'Hey, why stay a week? Let's stay a month. Let's stay the summer. Let's see how long we can stay.' "

They stayed forty-six days, blocking cars trying to enter clinic grounds, chaining themselves to clinic doors, pleading with pregnant women, haranguing abortion doctors, and mocking the ethics of pro-choice liberals by singing:

> Be a hero, save a whale;
> Save a baby, go to jail.
> Keep your eyes on the prize, hold on.

Operators of the abortion clinics complained to police, asserting that the protesters were violating their and their patients' rights to abortion, a procedure ruled legal by the *Roe v. Wade* decision. Then, federal District Judge Patrick F. Kelly decided enough was enough, warning protesters that he was authorizing federal marshalls to crack down on those who violated the law by attempting to bar people from seeking or performing an abortion. To support his decision with legal precedent, he cited an 1871 law designed to protect freed slaves from intimidation and sometimes known as the Ku Klux Klan Act. Those who persisted in their protests, he warned, "should say farewell to their family and bring their toothbrush, and I mean it, because they are going to jail. . . . Nobody is above the law."

OR volunteers were required to sign a pledge of nonviolence before being permitted to participate in one of its events. "Non-violence of word and deed," Terry noted. "That idea came directly out of the civil-rights activities of Dr. King." They were not, however, bound to obey every human law, precisely because, as Francis Schaeffer and Randall Terry had stressed, "God's law is above man's law." So, day after day, in full view of national news media, hundreds of protesters were handcuffed, dragged to vans or buses, and thrown into jail, many of them softly singing, "Every knee shall bow, every tongue confess, that Jesus Christ is Lord."

At one clinic, pro-choice demonstrators mockingly waved toothbrushes at the protesters as police and marshalls carted them off to jail. Others chanted, "Born-again bigots, go away! Racist, sexist, anti-gay!" A Wichita woman screamed, "I'm tired of the name you're giving to our city. We are law-abiding people. You come from out of state and break the laws." Another complained, "They're dividing my family. They've divided me [from] many of my friends. Neighbors are against neighbors. And it's sad. It's really sad." Speakers at an anti-protester rally that drew five thousand united behind a widely held sentiment: "This is our town. GO HOME!" Asked later if such sentiments had surprised him, Randall Terry said, "Absolutely not. Look at the arrests in the civil rights movement. The majority of Americans were against the tactics of the civil rights workers, the lunch-counter sit-ins, etc. And yet those street-level protests produced political change. Frankly, the fact that twenty percent of the people polled liked our tactics was a shock to us."

The protesters saw a glimmer of hope when, at the request of Operation Rescue lawyers, the U.S. Attorney for Kansas filed a brief opposing Judge Kelly's order, on the grounds that it was based on a faulty interpretation of the Ku Klux Klan Act and, further, that the clinics should have appealed first to the state, not to the federal government. Aware that the Justice Department had filed a similar brief on OR's behalf in a Virginia case, Terry reasoned that the Bush administration might be getting serious about its avowed opposition to abortion and decided to try to meet with the president himself. The president was on vacation in Maine, but that did not deter Terry, who flew to Kennebunkport and accosted Bush on the golf course. When he could not get rid of his supplicants by an appeal to courtesy—"Golf days," he said. "Mean an awful lot to a fellow."—Bush finally told television reporters who had accompanied Terry that he supported the right to protest abortions but believed demonstrators should stay within the law. Later, coming out of church, he said, "Breaking the law is excessive. That's what I think." Randall Terry was already on record as having said, "It is not excessive to save a baby that is about to be murdered," but he indicated he would pester the president no further. Looking back on this episode four years later, Terry offered a realistic assessment: "I think the president and Sununu and his advisers viewed us as a political liability. This is that lukewarm, mealy-mouthed, 'pro-life' Republican position that has no teeth and that is really of very little use to ending this slaughter."

When the War in Wichita finally ended at the close of summer, it marked the occasion with a large rally at which Pat Robertson gave a stirring speech about the moral imperative to rescue the innocent who were being led to slaughter. Randall Terry did not attend, having been warned that he would be arrested if he appeared anywhere in Wichita, but he professed not to have felt cheated. "Big rallies do not impress me," he said. "The issue isn't how many people are at the rally. The issue is how many people are in the street." He conceded, however, that even the Summer of Mercy, which put more pro-life protesters on the street than any other event, had been of limited efficacy. Thirty-four women were talked out of having abortions, but "then it stalled, and now babies are still being killed in Wichita. Babies are being killed all over. We did not obtain our objective."

Terry and his organization may have been disappointed at the limited success they achieved, but they did not abandon the field. In the summer of 1992, Terry tried to embarrass pro-choice Bill Clinton by attempting to hand him a fetus during the Democratic National Convention in New York. Terry and OR cooperated with a Houston-based organization called Rescue America in staging a widely publicized demonstration staged during the

Republican National Convention. And during the fall campaign, he distributed materials to twenty-seven thousand pastors, asserting that "to vote for Bill Clinton is to sin against God." Even more publicly, the Church at Pierce Creek, Terry's home congregation in Binghamton, took out a full-page ad in *USA Today* in which it noted that "the Bible warns us to not follow another man in his sin, nor help him promote sin—lest God chasten us," followed by the pointed question, "How then can we vote for Bill Clinton?" For this action, the church had its tax-exempt status revoked, an exceedingly rare action by the IRS. To pastors who feared their own churches might suffer a similar fate if they opposed Clinton too boldly, Terry said, "Our tax-exempt status be damned if it prevents us from proclaiming God's truth."

E. J. DIONNE's observation that George Bush had to pay for Ronald Reagan's failure to deliver on his implied promises to the Religious Right was even more true in 1992 than in 1988. "You can argue," Dionne contended, "that the Houston Convention was overly orchestrated in the direction of the Religious Right because, after everything Bush did to win the support of this constituency, it still didn't fully trust him, so they pushed the convention further to that side than they probably should have. It was a price Bush kept paying." Ralph Reed testified at Platform Committee hearings prior to the convention, to make sure the party understood that, if it hoped to hold on to evangelical voters, it would need to write key pro-family planks into the party platform. His arguments, which included pointed reference to the importance of evangelical voters to Bush's election in 1988, proved persuasive. Despite strong efforts by abortion-rights Republicans, the platform retained the anti-abortion plank as well as planks in support of the Religious Right's positions favoring public prayer and vouchers parents could use to send their children to parochial schools, and opposing same-sex marriages, programs in public schools that provide birth control information, and the use of public funds to subsidize "obscenity and blasphemy masquerading as art." Reed called it "the most conservative and the most pro-family platform in the history of this party."

The convention itself has often been described as having been "hijacked" by the Religious Right, referring not only to that movement's influence over the platform, but preeminently to the hardline speeches by Pat Robertson, Marilyn Quayle, and, most famously, Pat Buchanan, who declared, "There is a religious war going on in this country. It is a cultural war as critical to the kind of nation we shall be as the Cold War itself. This war is for the soul of America. And in that struggle for the soul of America, Clinton and Clinton are on the other side, and George Bush is on our side."

The frequent observation that the tone of the convention, as manifested in these speeches, cost Bush the election, is not supported by polling data. Bill Clinton's campaign advisers appear to have been on target in hammering incessantly at the blunt slogan, "It's the economy, Stupid!" The economy was flat, unemployment remained relatively high, and Bush had alienated many of his supporters by signing the 1990 budget deal that entailed reneging on his read-my-lips pledge never to raise taxes. Exit polls indicated that forty-one percent of voters claimed the state of the economy was virtually the only issue affecting their vote, and they favored Clinton by approximately two-to-one. Voters who named "family values" as of primary importance voted for Bush by a three-to-one margin, but, as Ralph Reed noted, "The problem was, there were only sixteen percent of them."

Despite such evidence, there is no question that millions of Americans, including many Republicans, found the tone of the Robertson/Quayle/Buchanan speeches troubling. But there may have been little the president could do about it. Bobbie Kilberg said, "In 1988, [delegates from the Religious Right] were mostly with the agenda, which was to nominate George Bush. In 1992, George Bush clearly had the nomination, he was president, but they were much less malleable. They were there to be counted, and to express themselves, and to have their way. They were a very, very strong force."

Kilberg felt the religious conservative contingent had been given too much freedom, and thought she knew why. "It was obvious," she said, "that the campaign [managers] viewed the religious right as a base they desperately needed and had to shore up, and they were going to make every effort to do that. There was little input from most of the senior White House staff—there were exceptions; there were people who met with them on a daily basis, but it was a very small group. Jim Baker came in too late. If Jim Baker had come into that operation in June rather than in August, I don't think you would have had a convention that looked like that. I don't think Jim Baker, in a hundred years, would have permitted Pat Buchanan to get up on that stage and make the speech he did." Unlike other speakers, Kilberg revealed, "Buchanan refused to submit his speech to any sort of clearance or review. All the other speakers, no matter how important they were, had their speech reviewed by the speechwriters of the convention team, and if they were a little off-base, or somebody thought, 'This could be inflammatory,' it was gone, and the speakers were very nice about it. Pat Buchanan refused to submit anything to the scrutiny of the convention team. And they were so frightened of the religious right, because of their perceived power, because of Buchanan's showings in New Hampshire, that they let him get onstage and say whatever the heck he wanted. And look what we got."

Morton Blackwell offered a slightly different perspective, observing,

"When you have an incumbent president running for re-election, as a practical matter, everything at the convention is in the control of that president's campaign apparatus. Who speaks, what order they speak, when they speak—all that is determined by the national campaign of the incumbent president. And it was the decision of the Bush campaign to allow the traditional-values conservatives some prime-time television. They knew what they wanted to achieve, and the truth of the matter is, the overnight tracking polls showed that they did achieve it, because Bush went up in the polls the next day, and then [again] the next day. But the biggest jump was after the night when these traditional conservative things were said."

Ralph Reed also doubted that the Robertson/Quayle/Buchanan speeches had directly cost the president many votes, but contended that the Bush administration's neglect of religious conservatives had placed it at a strategic disadvantage. With the economy in the doldrums, he explained, "the only card the Bush campaign had left to play was the social-conservative moral-issue, 'family values' card. And they played it very well. The problem was that sometimes, in order to make up for the lack of conviction, you have to say things louder than you otherwise might. If you've been neglecting your spouse for the last decade, you might feel it necessary to shower her or him with four dozen roses. But if you've been a faithful and loving [spouse] forever, a simple 'I love you' will do. Well, because of real problems with conservatives in its own party, the Bush campaign found it necessary to send the equivalent of four dozen roses, and that became known as the Houston Convention. They made sure that the message coming off that podium was to the core base of the party, which is 'pro-family,' 'pro-life' religious conservatives.

"And contrary to the conventional wisdom, I don't really think it cost them the election by alienating other voters, although clearly there's some of that. The real problem was the missed opportunity to speak to the ticket-splitting voter in the middle, which is what the convention is supposed to do. Your convention is supposed to be a four-day paid infomercial in which you're marketing your message to ticket-splitting voters. In 1980, when Ronald Reagan was nominated, they decided to hold the convention in Detroit, because they wanted to emphasize that they were going after the industrial Midwest, after blue-collar, traditionally Democratic voters. By going to the president's home town and by speaking mostly to evangelicals who were in that hall, they were trying to shore up their base when they should have been speaking to the voters beyond the hall. If [religious conservatives] made any mistake, it was simply to become identified with that process, so that we got really blamed for Houston when in fact we had very little to do with staging it and putting it together."

The Bush campaign did not restrict its bouquet-tossing to the convention. Vice President Dan Quayle addressed a Christian Coalition God and Country rally in Houston, President Bush spoke to the organization's second annual Road to Victory conference in Virginia Beach and gave the *700 Club* an exclusive interview. Bush also addressed a National Affairs Briefing sponsored by the Religious Roundtable, which had lain dormant during the Reagan years. Unlike the gathering at which Reagan had given his famous endorsement of politically active evangelicals, the hall was only half full for Bush's speech and the president was unable to strike fire as his predecessor had done. In what he apparently intended as the high point of his speech, Bush said, "I am struck by the fact that the other party took thousands of words to make up its platform and left out three simple letters, G-O-D." Unimpressed, Ralph Reed described the president's oratory as having "an awkward and disjointed quality about it that invited criticism. Religion became a 'wedge' issue that divided the electorate, and that was unfortunate."

Despite the Religious Right's lukewarm feelings toward Bush, a certain amount of backlash against the perceived extremism of the Houston convention, and the acknowledged importance of economic issues, conservative Christians once again offered strong support to Republican candidates. To make sure as many evangelicals as possible were registered to vote, Christian Coalition urged its members to see to it that voter registration materials were distributed and filled out during church services and collected right along with the offering. ("You're not organizing churches," Guy Rodgers explained, "you're organizing Christians, so you reach into a place where they naturally congregate.") While ostensibly a neutral tactic, this invariably swelled Republican ranks, since various analyses of voting data indicated that highly committed members of all religions tended to vote for the GOP. Bill Clinton and Al Gore, both Southern Baptists, drew a lower percentage of evangelical voters than Michael Dukakis had attracted in 1988.

In his look at the polling data, Ralph Reed pointed out that, although Bush suffered the worst loss of any incumbent president since William Howard Taft in 1912, "the reality is he probably would have done even worse had it not been for the support of 'pro-family' evangelicals. They turned out to the polls in the largest numbers they ever had in a presidential year—twenty-four percent of the electorate. They cast about sixty percent of their ballots for George Bush and only about twenty-eight percent for Bill Clinton; about seventeen percent went for Ross Perot. And even as George Bush was losing at the top of the ticket, the Republicans gained ten House seats. And People for the American Way [a liberal lobby founded by Norman Lear to oppose the Religious Right] estimated that up to five hundred pro-family candidates were elected at the local level—mostly school boards and state legislatures. So, even as George Bush was losing the White House, we felt our movement was very strong, very healthy, and on the rise."

Before founding Moral Majority, Inc., Jerry Falwell tested the waters of politicking with his "I Love America" rallies. These patriotic gatherings at state capitals featured music, oratory, and guest appearances by conservative notables. By 1979, Falwell was a natural target for New Right strategists seeking to bring evangelicals into the Republican party.

In its first electoral outing, the Religious Right hitched its star to candidate Ronald Reagan. Though Reagan's personal life was not as religiously oriented as Jimmy Carter's, he championed the "family values" agenda that Falwell and others espoused. But when his administration failed to follow through, the Religious Right began learning the compromises of political involvement.

The Reagan White House had a battleground between "Wall Street" Republicans, concerned mainly with economic growth, and "Main Street" conservatives, who focused on social issues. Faith Whittlesey, head of the Office of Public Liaison (seen here with Reagan), pushed to put school prayer and anti-abortion measures on Reagan's daily schedule but encountered resistance from Michael Deaver, the president's close aide and scheduler.

Religious broadcaster James Dobson dispenses daily family advice and conservative political opinions to an estimated five million radio listeners as part of his phenomenally successful Focus on the Family ministry. Only Paul Harvey and Rush Limbaugh reach a wider daily audience.

Charges of fiscal and sexual misconduct led not only to the resignation of Rev. Jim Bakker as head of the Praise the Lord (PTL) television ministry but also to intense national scrutiny of religious broadcasting across the board. Here, Bakker and his wife, Tammy Faye, pose before a replica of the United States Constitution in June 1987.

As surgeon general, Dr. C. Everett Koop alienated many among his conservative constituency by advocating condom distribution and sex education to combat the AIDS epidemic, which exploded into the public consciousness during his time in office.

In the Bedford-Stuyvesant section of Brooklyn in October 1987, AIDS activists and other protesters disrupted a rally arranged by Pat Robertson and his supporters to announce his intention to run for president in 1988.

In 1960, the opposition said this candidate wasn't fit to be president. Why? Because of his religion.

In 1988, the opposition is saying the same thing about this man.

VOTE PAT ROBERTSON FOR PRESIDENT.

Pat Robertson's second-place showing in the Iowa caucuses—behind Bob Dole but ahead of then Vice President George Bush—stunned conservative pundits and provided a major boost to Robertson's campaign. This advertisement appeared in the *Des Moines Register* on February 7, 1988, the day before Iowa's caucuses.

State Center for Health
Statistics
Dept. of Human Resources

Abortion vs **Birth**

	Abortion	Birth
1980	5079	4584
1981	5210	4505
1982	5193	4821
1983	4866	4772
		682

TOT

Ralph Reed estimates that he consulted on twenty-five congressional campaigns during his college and graduate school years. In that time, he rose to Executive Director of the College Republicans; he then left to start his own college political organization, Students for America.

Pat Robertson and Ralph Reed, shown here at the 1993 Christian Coalition Convention "Road to Victory" rally, were a formidable religious and political duo. Reed calls theirs a "very strong, collaborative relationship," adding that "[Pat] knew that if we decided to try to get something done, that I would probably be able to make that happen."

Phyllis Schlafly and Rush Limbaugh attend the Republican Coalition for Life at the 1992 Republican National Convention in Houston. Schlafly gleefully declared that the pro-life movement had revitalized the GOP and "any Republican powers-that-be are fools not to see it!"

Just before the 1992 presidential election, George Bush made a series of last-minute outreach appearances to rally the support of conservative groups. Seen here at the Christian Coalition's Road to Victory Conference in September of that year, he received a standing ovation when he told his audience, "I join with you in committing to uphold the sanctity of Life."

WANTED

WE NEED YOUR HELP TO STOP

DR. DAVID GUNN

Eufaula resident Dr. David Gunn GYN is an abortionist. His work has him in two cities doing first and second trimester abortions. His regular itinerary is as follows:

Day	Arrival Time	Location	Death Toll
Tuesday	11:00 a.m. until finished	Montgomery Womens Clinic Montgomery, Alabama	8-12 approx.
Tuesday	3:00 p.m. until finished	Beacon Clinic Montgomery, Alabama	12-18 approx.
Wednesday	9:30 a.m. until finished	Pensacola Medical Services Pensacola, Florida	8-10 approx.
Thursday	9:30 a.m. until finished	The Ladies Center Pensacola, Florida	10-13 approx.
Thursday	1:30 p.m. until finished	Pensacola Medical Services Pensacola, Florida	8-10 approx.
Friday	9:30 a.m. until finished	The Ladies Center Pensacola, Florida	10-13 approx.
Saturday	10:30 a.m. until finished	Beacon Clinic Montgomery, Alabama	15-25 apprx.
Saturday	2:30 p.m. until finished	Montgomery Womens Clinic Montgomery, Alabama	12-16 approx.

Please joins us by:

1. Prayer and fasting -- God is not willing that any should perish. Pray for Dr. Gunn's salvation.
2. Write and call him and share the gospel and your willingness to help him leave his profession.
3. Ask him to STOP DOING ABORTIONS! "Do not participate in the unfruitful deeds of darkness, but instead even expose them." Ephesians 5:11

He can be reached in the following ways:

| Montg. Women's Clinic 3866 South Court Street Montgomery, AL 36105 1-800-239-3063 annual death toll: 1,200 babies approx. | Beacon Clinic 1011 Monticello Ct. Montgomery, AL 36117 1-800-321-2181 annual death toll: 2,000 babies approx. | Pensacola Med. Srvcs. 7100 Plantation Road Unit 2 Pensacola, FL 32514 1-904-478-2477 annual death toll: 900 babies approx. | The Ladies Center 6770 N. 9th Avenue Pensacola, FL 32504 1-904-478-9460 annual death toll: 1,100 babies approx. | Home: Dr. David Gunn 10 Barbour Lane Eufaula, AL 36027 Home: 687-9088 Eufaula off: 687-2083 |

The base cost of an abortion is $250.00. Most doctors in his position earn 50% of the cost of each abortion. That would make Dr. Gunn's annual income for abortions alone at approximately $650,000 on the estimated 5,200 exterminations.

REWARD: Babies' Lives Will Be Saved If He Stops!!!!!!

Flyers like this one, with names and addresses of doctors who performed abortions, were distributed by the pro-life group Operation Rescue at rallies in 1992 and 1993. In March 1993, Dr. Gunn was murdered by a pro-life supporter. Of this killing, and others like it, Operation Rescue's leader Randall Terry noted that "the opposition wants to blame our rhetoric for a few isolated acts. I totally, utterly, and unconditionally reject that assertion."

In 1994, Randall Terry was placed under arrest in front of the White House. While legal difficulties now force him to distance himself from Operation Rescue, he continues a steady drumbeat against Clinton administration policies and has widened his agenda to oppose such diverse causes as intervention in Bosnia and gay marriage.

From an initial meeting of 71 men in 1990, Promise Keepers grew to 50,000 members by 1992 and has continued to grow exponentially (supporters are shown here at Mile High Stadium in Denver). Dissatisfied with the organization's expansion, founder Bill McCartney now focuses on racial outreach. "God won't be there if the races aren't together," he says. "White men don't know black men's pain."

CHAPTER

13

AND WHO SHALL
LEAD THEM?

BILL CLINTON'S SMASHING victory in the 1992 election may have
appeared to some as a decisive rebuttal to Ralph Reed's assertion that Pat
Robertson's defeat in 1988 had sown "the seeds of victory for religious
conservatives," but not all religious conservatives saw it that way. Guy Rodgers recalled talking to members of Christian Coalition the morning after
the election. "Politics and public policy are not about just one election," he
reassured them. "What the American people don't know is that they just
elected an openly pro-abortion, pro-gay rights liberal to the presidency for
the first time in the history of this country. Now you are going to have a
face on modern liberalism, and everybody is going to be able to see it in a
way they haven't seen it before." Former Bush aide Bobbie Kilberg agreed:
"What better way to galvanize your troops than to have Bill Clinton to fight
against? He was a new bad guy. They no longer had the bad guy of communism. The Cold War was over, the Berlin Wall was gone. They had a lot of
trouble raising money and organizing in the last two years of the Bush
administration, because there was nobody to be angry at, and you don't raise
money just by sending out 'feel-good' letters. Now they had this other big
bad guy, and the first thing he did was decide to put gays in the military. I
don't know where his head was, but what a wonderful issue to galvanize the
far right, and they were off and running."

Membership in Christian Coalition more than doubled in 1993, with
almost a million people listed as "donors and activists." Ralph Reed, like his
colleagues, gave much of the credit to the Commander-in-Chief. "The first
thing we had going for us," said Dr. Reed, wearing the mantle of political
scientist, "was Bill Clinton. I really thought Bill Clinton would come in and
govern as the 'New Democrat' he said he was. I thought he would put
forward a welfare-reform plan and a balanced-budget plan with a tax cut for

the middle class, and I thought it was entirely possible that he could be the most successful Democratic president since F.D.R. Unfortunately, first impressions matter, and Bill Clinton got off to a horrific start. He came in and immediately had gender and racial quotas in the cabinet, the snafu involving Zoë Baird, then the Lani Guinier blow-up, the two-hundred-dollar haircut at LAX, the gays-in-the-military controversy, and it just went on and on."

Even so, Reed observed, "Something else was going on that doesn't get focused on much. We decided that the social conservatives and the economic conservatives, who were social libertarians, had to find a way to agree more than they disagreed. They had to work together on things that united them. Two things happened early on that helped make that possible. The first was a special election in Georgia two or three weeks after the regular election. Paul Coverdell, the Republican, was moderately pro-choice, but he was against federal funding of abortion; he was against the Freedom of Choice Act [designed to provide federal legislative underpinning to the intent of *Roe v. Wade*] and he was conservative on everything else. We distributed over one million voter guides and phone-banked our entire file in Georgia, and Coverdell was elected as only the second Republican Senator from Georgia since Reconstruction, by fifteen thousand votes out of more than a million cast. That was the first of a string of special-election defeats for Bill Clinton and the Democrats that stretched all the way into 1994 and actually served as a foreshadowing of what was to come.

"The second thing that happened was we decided our top legislative priority for the 103rd Congress would be a tax cut for middle-class families with children. We held a news conference and announced that; then we began to meet with members of Congress and lobby them. That issue, which is now the centerpiece of the Republican economic agenda, allowed economic conservatives and religious conservatives to unite on something we both agreed on. They supported a tax cut because they were against big government and for lower taxes. We supported it because we were pro-family. We brought it to the Republican leadership. They weren't all that enthusiastic about it, but we kept pressing and kept working. The Heritage Foundation got on board, we got a bill introduced, we began to add cosponsors, and ultimately John Kasich, who was the ranking Republican on the House Budget Committee, and Newt Gingrich made it a part of the official House Republican budget. When it came time for a vote, we ginned up our phone banks, we got it on Christian radio and television, and they got more votes for a Republican budget than they had gotten in ten years—because there was family tax-relief in it. Those two things—the Coverdell election combined with the Clinton White House's missteps, and our broadening the agenda to speak to economic and tax issues—marked the critical turning points for our movement." And the strength of that movement, he asserted, was a critical factor in the sweeping Republican victories of 1994.

Christian Coalition's willingness to cooperate with those who did not subscribe to every point of their agenda pleased no one more than Paul Weyrich. Sounding like a proud godfather, Weyrich said, "I have been a firm advocate of the sort of mutual alliances that have been formed. People come into a movement for different reasons, and one of the greatest satisfactions I've had in my political life has been to introduce people who came into this movement because of right-to-work or tax or defense issues to people who came in because of value issues. I told the values people, 'Be interested in taxes; be interested in labor reform; be interested in what kind of national defense we have,' and I told the others, 'Be interested in what the [values] people are saying, because without them, you're not going to get anywhere with your issues.' That's been a true labor of love. I've had a great deal of success in getting these people to cooperate with each other."

One of Weyrich's most inventive efforts to facilitate this cooperation has been the establishment of National Empowerment Television, which bypasses conventional cable systems and beams conservative programs via satellite directly to individuals and groups who subscribe to the service. Like investment advisory services with confidential "hot-line" telephone numbers, Weyrich's NET periodically changes its satellite frequency so that only its affiliates can locate its programs. Begun in 1991 with just an occasional broadcast, NET is now a twenty-four-hour operation carrying several dozen different programs, a number of which are interactive and offer detailed advice on specific issues and legislation of interest to conservative activists. NET vice chairman Burton Pines has called the network "C-SPAN with an attitude," and Paul Weyrich has been quoted as saying, "Our objective is to wire this country. We want a C-NET affiliate not just in every Congressional district—[but] in every town or city of any size where people have the capability of gathering and taking action. . . . The only way you take Washington is by taking the countryside."

SOME LOCAL VICTORIES produced mixed results for the Religious Right, vividly demonstrating not only the movement's ability to get its way, but also, on occasion, an intolerant spirit and a narrow vision of American culture. Shortly after exiting the White House along with the rest of the Bush team, Bobbie Kilberg decided to seek her party's nomination for Lieutenant Governor in the 1993 election. Her opponent was Michael Farris, a veteran Religious Right operative who had served as executive director and general counsel of the Moral Majority in Washington state, general counsel for Concerned Women for America, and treasurer of the Draft Robertson campaign. He was best known, however, for his work in defense of conservative educational positions. During his Moral Majority days, he had sued a Spokane school district in an effort to have Gordon Parks' novel, *The Learning Tree,* removed from the curriculum on the grounds that it was anti-Christian. While working for Concerned Women for America, he had defended the so-called Nebraska Seven, a group of fathers who spent three months in jail for refusal to cooperate with state authorities investigating the Christian school their children attended. And, in a legal battle that ranged over much of 1983–1986 and was dubbed "Scopes II" by journalists, he served as lead attorney for a group of Hawkins County, Tennessee, fundamentalists who sought to ban a set of textbooks they believed would lure their children into witchcraft, false religions, and secular humanism. Farris's experience had convinced him that Christian parents might serve their children best by removing them from public schools and teaching them at home. In 1987, he became president of the Home School Legal Defense Association, and in 1993, he barnstormed Virginia attacking "Outcome Based Education," a new teaching approach that he and his conservative colleagues believed focused too much on learning how to cooperate and negotiate, and too little on basic academic skills. Clearly, he was a champion of the Religious Right.

Kilberg's experience in the White House office of public liaison had made her well aware of the Religious Right, but she failed to appreciate its growing power and dedication until the 1993 campaign and the Republican state convention. "I was running," she said, "as a mainstream Virginia Republican, which to me meant conservative on economic issues and moderate on social issues. I was running against a Religious Right activist, and I saw the power of the Religious Right. The home-school movement that Mike Farris controls—there are six thousand home-schooling families registered in the state of Virginia with Mike's group—and the Christian Coalition, those two together, have become an extraordinarily potent organizing force. They were everywhere. The organizational structure they have put into place in the Republican Party more than rivals what the Democrats had with the radical left back in the seventies and early eighties. And there is nothing in the middle of the Republican party that can compare with it.

"I think you will still find that the majority of Republican voters are in the center of the party, but it's hard to get moderate, pragmatic people to organize themselves. They're into too many other things in their lives. But people who are ideological and who believe they are directed by God to do something have an enormous force and enormous energy. [The Virginia organization] is very well disciplined and well run, and it runs with a lot of high tech. They have a phone network and a fax network and a whispering network that is not to be believed. They could start a rumor in Alexandria, in northern Virginia, at eight in the morning, and by four in the afternoon it was down there in Big Stone Gap, almost into Tennessee, and by the next day there would be letters to the editor of newspapers all over the state, condemning me for something or other."

At the convention, Kilberg's opponents reheated an old chestnut, labeling her a "Rockefeller Republican." When Barry Goldwater, who first gained fame as the antithesis of Nelson Rockefeller, endorsed her, the Farris forces denounced him as an unrepentant liberal who was showing signs of senility. Such tactics, of course, are common campaign fare, but Farris supporters went further, surrounding Kilberg delegates and shouting, "Kill baby, kill baby, kill baby," as a play on her name and an attack on her pro-choice position. "And when I was trying to speak," she recalled, "people were carrying posters of dead fetuses back and forth in front of the podium. Our video was sabotaged. And the people standing behind me—more than two-thirds of the elected legislators in Virginia and the entire leadership of the Virginia Federation of Republican Women—were pelted with ice and, evidently, other things. After that convention, Ralph Reed called to say he wanted me to know that none of his Christian Coalition delegates behave that way, because he would not tolerate it, and that this was all those home-schoolers, of which there more than four thousand at the convention. He said, 'I don't have those people whipped into shape yet. They're a little green behind the ears, but give me two years and I'll have them as a lean, mean fighting machine.' And by golly, a year later he certainly had a much more disciplined force of individuals marching under that banner."

Pat Robertson's perhaps naïve resurrection of several classic anti-Semitic themes and terms in his 1994 book, *The New World Order,* stirred reasonable fears that sinister elements of the Religious Right of the 1930s and early forties might be resurfacing. Like most observers, however, Kilberg does not regard the Religious Right as an anti-Semitic movement. Still she did occasionally encounter what she called "unintentional sensitivity." She noted that, as she traveled throughout the state during her campaign, she found that most party meetings began with a prayer, "which I don't object to, but most of the time the prayer would be in the name of Jesus Christ, yet I was there and everybody knew I was Jewish. That never happened any time the prayer was done by a minister. The ministers were always conscious I was there and always made it an ecumenical prayer. It was [usually] when a lay person was giving the prayer. But I don't think anybody meant anything by it." As for deliberate anti-Semitism, Kilberg said she had seen none "until we got to the convention, and I never saw that, but some of my delegates tell me that during my speech, more than one person up in one section of the coliseum was shouting, 'There's one that Hitler missed.' That was disturbing to me, but that's life. Some people get carried away and say things they shouldn't say or shouldn't mean. But that was a clear aberration. In Virginia, I have not experienced, in the Republican Party or the body politic at large, any anti–Semitism."

Farris defeated Kilberg but lost the general election in 1993. Though he undoubtedly benefited from a warm endorsement from Pat Robertson, who told his Virginia supporters that the contest was "a campaign for the future of the Republican Party," he later suggested that some Christian Coalition workers had hurt his cause by distributing voter guides at polling places. It is one thing, he said, to pass out such scorecards in churches, but implying that only one candidate has "the Christian answer" is out of place in the secular political arena. "I was in polling places in Richmond, Virginia," Farris said, "where one or two sweet people were handing out these scorecards on election day. I wish I had had the courage to say to them, 'Please throw those in the wastebasket,' because I was losing votes with every one that was handed out."

Despite her admiration for Reed, whom she describes as "a political genius," Bobbie Kilberg is not sure his increasingly well-disciplined troops will stay in formation on issues whose relevance is not clear to them. Reed, she recalled, "made it very clear to me at one point that I should watch and wait and listen, because the Christian Coalition was going to have a very active role in the passage of NAFTA [the North American Free Trade Agreement]. And then, NAFTA disappeared from their agenda, because his delegates didn't buy it. They kept on saying, 'What does NAFTA have to do with our issues? We are religious conservatives and we don't care about NAFTA.' Despite Ralph's polling that says Christian Coalition members are as concerned about economic issues as anybody else, I'm not sure that's true. I wish it was, because I do think economic issues are family issues, but every evidence I've seen in Virginia is that you couldn't talk to those delegates about business regulation or economic growth or jobs. The only thing they wanted to talk about was right-to-life, prayer in the schools, absolute parent control over everything in the classroom, the teaching of creationism instead of evolution, and, for some reason, the right to bear arms. Those were the issues. And if you tried to talk about business regulation, they just rolled their eyes."

A MORE PROTRACTED version of the cultural conflict Bobbie Kilberg described took place in Lake County, Florida, during the early 1990s. There, as elsewhere, Christian Coalition actively encouraged religious conservatives to become active in shaping the course of public education. "We focused heavily on school boards," Florida state director John Dowless explained. "It's a big issue with parents right now. They are concerned with what's being taught or not taught in the schools, and if their kids are safe while they're there. There's [a feeling] that the schools are more concerned with self-esteem and cultural issues—it almost seems like a political agenda. And, you know, if you capture the minds of the children, you've captured the next generation. That's why schools are a real hot-button issue with the voters, especially with parents. We found a very high demand to get more involved in that area." When Dowless visited Lake County, west of Orlando, he found that some religious conservatives had already become involved.

Pat Hart, a Baptist, had campaigned for Pat Robertson in 1988. "I was just one of the little campaign workers," she said, "handing out literature and talking to people about why I supported him and encouraging them to go to the polls and [vote for] him. It opened up a whole new world for me, seeing that ordinary people like me—a homemaker, a wife, and a mom—can have a say in what our government does." Hart subsequently got involved with Beverly LaHaye's Concerned Women for America and began to track state and national legislation pertaining to families. She also developed a habit of writing letters to the local newspaper, voicing her concern over various issues. As a result of her obvious interest and increasing public recognition, friends encouraged her to run for a school-board seat that opened up in 1990. As she thought about it, she realized that "[school-related] issues affected everyone and that, yes, I could make a difference. So I chose to run."

Hart's pledge of allegiance to a back-to-basics approach and her vow to hold the line on school taxes played well in the churches and mobile-home parks where she campaigned hardest. Though she won by only twelve votes, she regarded her victory as a mandate and embarked immediately on a vigorous campaign to rescue Lake County schools from secular humanist captivity. In one of her first acts, she proposed that a children's book, *When Itchy Witchy Sneezes,* be banned from the district's elementary schools because "it might create a tolerance for the occult in students." She next opposed an exercise in which a puppet named Duso the Dolphin invited children to imagine what it would be like to live in an undersea world. Hart feared such an exercise might put students in "an altered state." She recalled that another book contained a story of a father who made strange noises that aggravated his wife and embarrassed his children. "It seemed like it really demeaned the role of a father," she said. "Why do we want to concentrate on the negative? If ever there was a time in our country when we need to lift our daddies up, it's now."

Not long after she was elected, Pat Hart met John Dowless. He was impressed by what he had heard of her and she was attracted by what she perceived Christian Coalition could offer concerned conservatives who wanted to get involved in the public arena. "I was immediately intrigued," she said, "because I saw so many people like me, scattered throughout our community and our country, who shared the same belief system but didn't have a vehicle for learning what you do if you don't like something that's happening in your government. Christian Coalition was able to come in and say, 'This is what you do.' They are very much abreast of the issues, at the national level especially, so it helps keep the grassroots informed about what is really taking place."

Hart was eager to learn from whatever sources were available to her. To find out more about how to fight Florida's state-mandated sex-education program, she affiliated with Phyllis Schlafly's Eagle Forum, which prompted her to promote an abstinence-based program. For background on early-childhood education, she obtained materials from Dr. James Dobson's ministry, Focus on the Family. She also joined Citizens for Excellence in Education, headed by Californian Robert Simonds and devoted to such familiar goals as restoring prayer to classrooms and including creationism in the science curriculum. Simonds has been quoted as saying, "We have a plan to take our entire education system back and put it in God's hands. And the way we're going to do it is to take control of every school board in America." Though his figures are hard to document, he claimed in 1993 that his organization had helped elect more than 5,000 school-board members and expected to see that number exceed 12,500 by 1998. He also claimed that people advised by his organization already control more than 2,000 school boards.

All these organizations helped Hart shape and articulate her positions, but her impact during her first two-year term was limited, since her four colleagues on the board voted her down, four-to-one, time after time. That changed in 1992 when Mrs. Hart was not only re-elected, but was joined on the board by Claudia Ramsey and Judy Pearson, both of whom shared her distinctive views on education. All three women had been endorsed by Christian Coalition, which had abetted their cause by using one of its trademark tactics: widespread last-minute distribution of ostensibly neutral "voter guides" that purported to compare the views of the "conservative candidates" with those of the "liberal incumbents"—all of whom, in this case, regarded themselves as conservative Republicans. A sample issue gives the flavor of the handout:

Morals: A high priority should be to teach absolute values, morality and character."
 Liberal Incumbents: NO.
 Conservative Candidates: YES.

The incumbents were also depicted as favoring abortion and opposing parental input in education, charges one of the defeated candidates flatly called "a lie." However, because the handouts were distributed mainly at churches on the Sunday before the election on Tuesday, candidates who felt they had been misrepresented had insufficient time to deny the charges or explain their positions more fully.

At the first meeting of the new board, Pat Hart was elected chairwoman by a three-to-two vote, the first of many to follow over the next two years. The conservative majority had run on a platform of lower taxes, smaller classroom size, and an emphasis on academic achievement. Though all were evangelical Christians, they stressed the secular issues far more than those with a religious overtone. They had also made clear their belief that proper education stressed the inculcation of basic methods and time-honored facts, not the development of self-esteem, or sex education, or instruction in other matters they felt should be the sole prerogative of parents. They could not be accused of "stealth" techniques. They had stated plainly what they believed in, and a majority of Lake County citizens who went to the polls indicated they shared those beliefs. Still, many parents, teachers, and school administrators fervently disapproved of the new ruling majority and its conservative agenda, "labeling them as incompetent do-gooders with a religious-right agenda." Board meetings, formerly held in relative isolation, began to draw so many supporters of both factions on the board that they had to be moved from the school administration building to the multipurpose room at an elementary school. The result, according to one observer, was "an ideological logjam of shouting matches, surly crowds, conspiracy theories, the occasional arrest threat . . . and precious little actual School Board business."

Pat Hart perceptively observed that the conflict was in part a manifestation of demographic and cultural changes occurring in the area. A series of freezes had taken such a heavy toll on the citrus crop that many fruit-growers had given up and sold their land. "We're seeing Lake County change from a rural agricultural community into a bedroom community," she explained, "getting more of a metropolitan feel, as opposed to the rural feel that we are losing." John Dowless agreed, adding that "a lot of things that might go over well in Miami or New York City or some of the larger metropolitan areas don't go over well in your smaller rural areas." Adjusting to the problems of a more diverse population and some of the problems long associated with cities helped stir a longing for an earlier, simpler time. Two issues illustrate the struggle well.

In attempts to help meet the many needs of a poor rural community comprising many single-parent families and minimum-wage agricultural workers, Jack Currie, the principal of Seminole Springs elementary school, proposed a preschool program, similar to Head Start, to provide youngsters from this milieu the kind of enriched learning experience that would prepare them to succeed when they encountered the standard curriculum. The program was warmly supported by parents, teachers, and community leaders, and exemplified Currie's belief that schools should be community centers that serve a wide range of needs. The Florida Department of Education applauded Currie's plan, honoring him with an award for outstanding leadership in 1993. Pat Hart and her conservative colleagues, however, saw the program as, in the words of a reporter who followed the story closely, nothing more than "a power grab by educators to get children into the system as early as possible—the sooner to supplant the family, the better to inculcate the liberal agenda." Children, they said, belonged at home, not in the care of some government-funded organization.

A second major struggle revolved around one of the most controversial issues in contemporary education: multiculturalism. In 1992, the Florida legislature passed a statute mandating that children in public schools should be taught to appreciate diverse cultures. To Pat Hart, such a notion was fraught with peril. Multicultural education, she charged, "is absolutely eroding the beliefs and values that built our country. Our national sovereignty, our republican form of government, and our economic system are being undermined by material that says maybe capitalism is not the best way to build an economic system. So I said, 'Yes, we will abide by Florida state law. We will teach our children about other countries and other cultures; however, we're going to ensure that they understand the greatness of America.' "

Such a directive might not have generated much reaction had not Hart pushed it a giant step further. Lake County teachers, she declared, must not only give attention to America's good points, but must teach that American culture is "superior to all other cultures, past and present." Predictably, some teachers objected to a policy that, in essence, left them unable to teach their students how to cast a cool, analytical eye at their own culture, or how to deal with aspects of American history and culture that are anything but flattering: slavery and segregation, the genocide of Native Americans, the massacre at My Lai, extreme and increasing levels of inequality, and rates of crime, illiteracy, and infant mortality higher than those in almost all other industrialized nations. Hart admitted she was astonished when she heard such objections to the approach she had ordered. What disturbed her most was when students came to the podium and said, 'Mrs. Hart, America is not a good country. We were not founded on principles that are the greatest in the world.' It broke my heart that these children did not understand that they were living the freedoms they were trashing. How many other countries could they have come up and voiced their opinion like that? I guess that is what just solidified in my mind and my heart that this policy was even more necessary than I had thought."

Lake County's "Great America" program drew nationwide attention, as the major news networks flocked into central Florida to film school-board meetings and reflect on the impact Christian Coalition, Citizens for Excellence in Education, and other conservative organizations were having on America's schools. Of the many opinions offered, none seemed more on target than that of afternoon philosopher Geraldo Rivera, who noted that avoiding multiculturalism is no longer an option. "Is the 'American culture' we're talking about here the Southern Baptist culture?" he asked. "Is it the Puerto Rican culture? Is it the Hasidic Jewish culture? Is it the California surfer culture? Is it the Tex-Mex culture?" Pat Hart was stung by media charges that she and her conservative colleagues were "trying to indoctrinate, trying to brainwash our children with jingoism," but felt vindicated by local support. "There was such an outpouring of letters to our school board," she recalled. "We received over six hundred letters of support for what we were trying to do and only twenty-two that were not supportive of it."

Hart chose not to run for re-election in 1994, and a three-person contingent backed by the teachers union defeated a slate supported by Christian Coalition. Hart described the new board as "moderate to liberal" and lamented the fact that its meetings no longer draw hundreds of vitally interested citizens. "We are going back to business as usual," she said. "The good ol' boys are back in control."

BY 1994, CHRISTIAN Coalition reportedly had close to a million members and an annual budget in excess of twelve million dollars, most of it provided by regular members who contributed modest amounts each month, and Ralph Reed's name and boyish face had become increasingly familiar to most Americans who paid even minimal attention to politics. Moreover, the larger public awareness was backed up by palpable clout. A survey of political experts conducted by the nonpartisan magazine *Campaigns & Elections* reported that Christian Right forces had "dominant strength" in the Republican Party in eighteen states and "substantial" influence in thirteen others. In about half the states in each category, however, moderate Republicans were offering strong resistance. Moreover, an October 1995 survey indicated that eight in ten Republicans did not think of themselves as members of the Religious Right, and forty-nine percent believed "religious conservatives are more likely to divide than strengthen the Republican Party." When the GOP gained fifty-two House seats, eight Senate seats, eleven governorships, and 472 seats in state legislatures in the November 1994 elections, the Religious Right joined fully in the victory dance of the elephants, flush with the knowledge that 114 members of the new House and 26 Senators had either received a perfect rating on the Christian Coalition Congressional Scorecard or were freshmen elected with the group's strong approval. An additional fifty-eight members of the 104th Congress voted for Christian Coalition positions more than eighty-five percent of the time.

To let voters know exactly what they thought they had been elected to do, Newt Gingrich and his euphoric Republican colleagues drew up a Contract with America, summarizing the legislation they hoped to pass during the next session of Congress. Six of the contract's ten points called for such economic changes as a balanced budget amendment, cuts in welfare spending, and various tax credits and incentives. Others dealt with term limits, tort reform, anti-crime measures, and national defense. Almost immediately, Ralph Reed announced the Christian Coalition's approval of the Contract with America. Then, early in January, he promised the new Speaker that the coalition would spend an estimated one million dollars and use its "fax [and telephone] networks, satellite television, computerized bulletin boards, talk radio, and direct mail" to drum up support for the contract.

The Contract with America said nothing about such key Religious Right issues as abortion or school prayer, but Reed and his colleagues were willing to hold off on these issues until the new congress had a chance to settle in. Unlike their forerunners in the Reagan years, however, they were not willing to trade their support for a few photo-ops in the Oval Office or the Rose Garden, nor were they willing to wait very long. In May, Reed unveiled what he called the Contract with the American Family. Unapologetically taking advantage of the popularity and name recognition of the Contract with America, the Contract with the American Family was an attempt to build on, rather than compete with, the Republican agenda. Noting that not all the problems facing America are economic, the ten points of this contract called for a Religious Equality Amendment that would relax some of the restrictions the Supreme Court has placed on prayer and other religious expressions; abolition of the Department of Education and return of power over schools to local levels; vouchers, tax credits, or other mechanisms that would enable parents to send their children to "the public, private, or parochial school of their choice"; a Parental Rights Act that would reaffirm parents' right to direct the education, medical care, discipline, and religious upbringing of their children; reductions in the tax burden on families; further hindrances to abortions; welfare reform that would transfer many functions to private charities; increased controls on pornography; more severe penalties for criminals; and an end to public funding of the Corporation for Public Broadcasting and the National Endowments for the Humanities and the Arts. It was, to be sure, a quite conservative agenda, but it was not radical or loony, and several of its recommendations were put forth as experiments worth testing in pilot programs rather than as nonnegotiable demands. Significantly, it did not call for a Human Life Amendment outlawing virtually all abortions, and it made no mention whatever of gays and lesbians.

WHILE RALPH REED and Christian Coalition were drawing most of the public attention paid to politically involved religious conservatives, another man and another organization, Dr. James Dobson and Focus on the Family, were quietly building what may become, if it is not already, an even more powerful political and cultural influence.

Dobson grew up in Texas and Oklahoma as the son of an itinerant evangelist and small-town pastor in the deeply conservative and perfectionist Church of the Nazarene. After graduating from a Nazarene college in California, he earned a doctorate in child development at the University of Southern California, then joined the pediatric faculty of the USC medical school. While still at USC, Dobson wrote his first book, *Dare to Discipline,* which religion journalist Steve Rabey characterized as a blend of "biblical principles, Christian psychology, common sense, a nostalgia for the 1950s, and a conservative reaction to trends like the sexual revolution, youth rebellion, psychedelic experimentation, and the women's movement." The book's authoritative assurance that children needed consistent and appropriate discipline as well as love struck a warm response in a wide audience, turning it into a huge best-seller—by 1995, sales had topped three million copies.

Other books followed, including another blockbuster, *What Wives Wish Their Husbands Knew About Women,* which racked up sales of 2.3 million copies. Sensing he had uncovered a deep need, Dobson left academia in 1976 to devote full time to writing, speaking, and responding to an ever-growing volume of telephone calls and letters. The following year, he founded Focus on the Family (FOF), which in less than twenty years expanded from a rented office with a part-time secretary into a phenomenally successful and widely respected operation that takes in more than one hundred million dollars a year and employs more than twelve hundred people at a forty-seven acre complex in Colorado Springs.

The heart of Dobson's ministry is an octet of daily and weekend radio programs. The daily thirty-minute flagship program, also called *Focus on the Family,* is aired eighteen thousand times a week over four thousand facilities, reaching an aggregate audience estimated to exceed five million listeners.

Only Paul Harvey and Rush Limbaugh speak to more people on a daily basis. Few would argue with Rabey's assertion that "Focus on the Family does Christian radio better than anyone," but radio is far from the whole story. Dobson's fourteen books, not counting revised editions, have sold more than sixteen million copies, most of them in the U.S. A set of lectures, filmed in 1978 and shown in thousands of churches, has been seen by an estimated sixty million people—far more than have viewed any other evangelical film. In addition, the organization publishes ten magazines and newsletters, aimed at different audiences or focusing on different issues, with a combined circulation of nearly three million, and a weekly syndicated column, "Dr. Dobson Answers Your Questions," is published in approximately five hundred newspapers. As Bush aide Doug Wead observed, "Dobson is strong. He's very strong."

As his reputation and influence have grown, some have expected Dobson to follow Pat Robertson's lead and run for some high office. Others believe not only that his consistent disavowal of interest in public office is sincere, but that his abhorrence of compromise would likely make him ineffective and miserable in Washington. On his radio programs, Dobson comes across as a warm, caring man with deep convictions and a determination to stick by them. Those who know and work with him also describe him as having few doubts about the correctness of the positions he holds and no reluctance to communicate his sense of certainty. Gary Bauer, who got to know Dobson while working in the Reagan administration, described him as "pretty transparent, unlike many of the people I had to deal with in Washington every day. You only had to be with him for a very brief period of time to know that he believed in a certain set of values, and that you wouldn't get far with him trying to play the typical Washington games. He wanted to know what you were going to do about the stuff that mattered to him, and he wanted to know whether you would stand up and fight for those things, no matter what the consequences were."

Bauer's ties to Dobson remain particularly close. In 1980, during the White House Conference on Families, Dobson and several other evangelical leaders had met in a hotel room and decided to form an organization that would represent the interests of families to legislators and other government bodies. The result was the Family Research Council (FRC), headquartered in Washington and officially independent, but always closely associated with Focus on the Family. In 1988, when Bauer left government at the end of Reagan's second term, the two groups were formally merged, and Bauer was brought in to run FRC. In 1992, with Dobson's blessing, FRC once again became formally independent and has flourished under Bauer's direction, taking its place alongside Christian Coalition and Concerned Women for America as the "Big Three" evangelical political organizations in Washington, and its 250,000 supporters provide it with an annual budget of ten million dollars. When Jim Lehrer or Ted Koppel or one of the Sunday morning political discussion programs wants the evangelical slant on a particular issue, Bauer is fully as likely as Ralph Reed to be invited to serve as spokesman.

In addition to maintaining informal ties to Bauer and the Family Research Council, FOF has its own public policy division, which publishes the politically oriented *Citizen* magazine and faxes a two-page *Family Issues Alert* containing "up-to-the-minute news the media ignore" to nearly four thousand subscribers each week. In January 1994, Dobson joined with Bauer, Bill Bright, D. James Kennedy, NAE director Robert Dugan, and several other key evangelicals to establish the Alliance Defense Fund, a legal advocacy group whose purpose would be "to fight for believers' rights in precedent-setting cases in the nation's courtrooms." Like the Rutherford Institute, founded by John Whitehead in 1982, and the American Center for Law and Justice, founded by Pat Robertson in 1990, the Alliance Defense Fund is a conscious attempt to engage and defeat the American Civil Liberties Union and the federally funded Legal Services Corporation in what its founders regard as a deliberate, protracted campaign to expunge religion from American life.

Unlike Bauer and Reed, Dobson rarely talks to the secular media about his political views—he declined to be interviewed for this book or the television documentary series it accompanies—but he is not bashful about making them known to those he believes can affect their implementation. In March 1995, after Republican National Committee Chairman Haley Barbour declared that the party's "big tent" was large enough to include a considerable range of opinions, including those who disagreed with its platform's hard-line position on abortion, Dobson sent an eight-page letter to his 2.1 million supporters and, in a special mailing, to 112,000 clergy, 8,000 national and local politicians, and 1,500 members of the media. He informed them that "a struggle [is] under way for the soul of the party, [and] I am committed never again to cast a vote for a politician who would kill one innocent baby." Of this effort, he was quoted as saying, "If that doesn't change some hearts and minds at [the Republican National Committee], then we'll launch a second, third and fourth wave to generate support." At about the same time, Gary Bauer and Ralph Reed hinted they might align with a third party if the GOP softened its stand on abortion. Dobson's threat got the response he sought, as virtually every Republican presidential hopeful besides Steve Forbes either traveled to Colorado Springs to seek his blessing or, in the case of Bob Dole and Newt Gingrich, welcomed him warmly when he came to Washington.

In keeping with the perfectionism of his Nazarene background, which stressed the importance of striving for complete holiness and integrity, Dobson is quick to criticize, often in sharply worded letters, those he believes fall short of his own highly principled stands. For example, he apparently agreed with Paul Weyrich, Morton Blackwell, Gary Bauer, Michael Farris and other conservative luminaries when they held a press conference in November 1995 to assail General Colin Powell, who had gone on record as pro-choice on abortion, as a "risk averse" bureaucrat (Weyrich's depiction) barely indistinguishable from Bill Clinton—Bauer called the general "Clinton with [military] ribbons." More tellingly, after Ralph Reed and outspoken conservative William Bennett went on *This Week with David Brinkley* to discuss a possible Powell candidacy, Dobson fired off a five-page letter to Reed, accusing him of a serious lack of character for "[sitting] passively while Bill Bennett spoke of rewriting the pro-life plank in the GOP Platform. You uttered not a peep of protest. . . . We've come to expect our politicians to jettison their principles and compromise their ethics when the chips are down, but I was extremely disappointed to see you go along with it. . . . Is power the motivator of the great crusade? If so, it will sour and turn to bile in your mouth. . . . This posture may elevate your influence in Washington, but it is unfaithful to the principles we are duty-bound as Christians to defend." Dobson went on to say he and Bauer "had considered the need to distance ourselves from you and the Christian Coalition."

Perhaps as a measure of his lack of confidence in the integrity of politicians, evangelical and otherwise, Dobson is unwilling to count too heavily on political solutions to the problems he sees threatening America and its families. Using language increasingly common among religious conservatives, he has written, in a book coauthored with Gary Bauer:

> Nothing short of a great Civil War of Values rages today throughout North America. Two sides with vastly differing and incompatible worldviews are locked in a bitter conflict that permeates every level of society. . . . The struggle now is for the hearts and minds of the people. It is a war over ideas. And someday soon, I believe, a winner will emerge and the loser will fade from memory. For now, the outcome is much in doubt.

Dobson does not believe this "Civil War of Values" is simply the by-product of "a casual and random drift of social mores, shifting over time from one end of the political spectrum to the other." On the contrary, he contends that it is the result of "a coordinated, well thought out strategy" devised by secular humanists who, for reasons not clearly explained, seek to destroy their own civilization.

Secular humanists, particularly the more radical activists, have a specific objective in mind for the future. They hope to accomplish that goal primarily by isolating children from their parents. . . . It will then be relatively easy to "reorient" and indoctrinate the next generation of Americans. . . . Children are the key to the future. . . . [They] are the prize to the winners of the second great civil war. . . . Given that influence, the predominant value system of an entire culture can be overhauled in one generation, or certainly two.

A professional soldier on the "traditionalist" side, Dobson fights this war every day with his radio programs and publications, but he does not disdain well-trained reinforcements from other quarters. To help parents make sure their children do not become casualties in the war of ideologies, particularly as victims of professorial snipers on secular college campuses, Dobson encourages them to equip their teenagers with the whole armor of anti-humanism by sending them to a two-week summer encampment program known as Summit Ministries.

Summit, headquartered in Manitou Springs, Colorado, is run by David Noebel, a former associate of the anti-communist warhorse, Billy James Hargis, who founded the program in 1962. Noebel has directed the program since its inception and became its official head in 1974, when Hargis was forced by a sexual scandal to sever ties with his various ministries. During the 1960s, Noebel achieved some notoriety in evangelical circles for his heated assertions that rock music is one of several diabolical tools used by communists to render "a generation of American youth useless through nerve-jamming, mental deterioration and retardation." His often extreme views and long association (until 1987) with the John Birch Society have kept him at the margins of the mainstream of the Religious Right, but he has received warm endorsements from Dan Quayle, D. James Kennedy, Howard Phillips, and Oliver North, as well as Dobson.

Summit's intensive two-week program (total price, $495), explicitly accepts Francis Schaeffer's challenge to test the worldview of "Biblical Christianity" against its major competitors, which are identified as Marxism/Leninism, Secular Humanism, and something called Cosmic Humanism, which Noebel associates with pantheism and the New Age movement. Summit literature promises that, by immersing themselves in intensely conservative readings, videos, and lectures, students will be able to withstand the assaults on their faith they are sure to meet in college, in the secular media, and even in some of their churches.

Noebel readily admitted that, because the program entails two weeks of intensive study, few teenagers are particularly enthusiastic about attend-

ing, but said, "we lose hardly any after the first three or four days." Matt
Cothern was a typically reluctant Summiteer. "When I graduated from
high school," he said, "my big graduation program [wasn't] the car I was
hoping for, but a trip to Summit Ministries. I was not real happy. I had a
bad attitude and did not really participate for the first four or five days."
Finally, after his girlfriend suggested he try to make the best of the opportunity, he plunged into his studies and emerged an enthusiastic convert to the Summit approach. He spoke particularly of having been convinced that the theory of evolution could not be true. "One of the
examples they gave us," he recalled, was that accepting evolution as a
valid explanation for the marvelous complexity of biological nature is like
believing that "a hurricane could hit a scrap yard and a '94 Honda Accord would pop out and drive away on its own. It's just ridiculous.
There's just too many things that fit together too well for random
chance. I just can't believe it's anything other than God."

Cothern felt some of what he heard was difficult to accept without qualification. A musician himself, he found Noebel's theories about the Satan-
inspired nature of rock music a bit extreme. He also filtered out some of the
anti-government messages he heard at the camp, particularly those stressing
the intent and ability of the FBI, the CIA, and other government agencies to
monitor the lives of individuals. "I don't necessarily believe the government
is that bad, that it's out to get everybody," he said. "I just think it's become
a little too forceful in everyday life." Such minor quibbles aside, Cothern
became a strong advocate for the program. When he returned home, he not
only persuaded his closest friend to attend, but took the lead in raising
money to purchase Summit's *Understanding the Times* curriculum, consisting
of sixty videotapes and a host of publications. That accomplished, he recruited seventy-eight high-school students to enroll in the program, which
stretched over months of Sunday evenings.

After James Dobson's son Ryan attended a Summit encampment and
came home similarly enthusiastic, Dobson became one of Noebel's most
avid and effective supporters. A two-part program aired back-to-back on his
"Focus on the Family" radio program in 1989 immediately brought in fourteen thousand applications, raising that summer's enrollment to a thousand
students, up from three hundred the previous summer. In 1990 and 1991,
enrollments rose to twelve hundred and fifteen hundred, respectively. With
Dobson's continued help, Noebel expects to see an additional one hundred
thousand teenagers go through the video curriculum each year. "In ten
years," he pointed out, "we'll have a million kids. And next year, a conservative television [satellite] link is going to go up, so we'll be able to put
our curriculum up on the big airways. We're looking at changing this whole
culture."

. . .

ONE OF THE aspects of culture that deeply troubles most pro-family activists is an increasingly widespread view of homosexuality as normal and, even more galling, of homosexuals as people entitled to special protection against discrimination. "We have devoted a great deal of time and energy to the gay-rights issues," Gary Bauer explained, "because we see this issue as saying a great deal about the country and how we think about liberty and virtue. Most Americans believe in 'Live and let live. What your neighbor does behind closed doors is his business.' But when the gay-rights agenda goes into the public square and says, 'We want the right to teach children in school that homosexuality is no better or worse than heterosexuality,' or 'We want to be included in civil-rights laws,' so that [we will have to consider sexual orientation] much as we do now on race and gender, then we think it's imperative [to] counter that agenda."

The most notable encounter so far in this culture-splitting controversy arose in 1992 around Colorado's now-infamous Amendment 2, a referendum that nullified gay-rights ordinances in Aspen, Boulder, and Denver, and prohibited the passage of similar measures anywhere else in the state. The ordinances to which Amendment 2 responded prohibited bias in jobs or housing on the basis of sexual orientation. Not surprisingly, pressure from gay activists had been instrumental in getting these measures passed. "I think if you look what happened," Ralph Reed pointed out, "religious conservatives did not act. They reacted to a pro-active and muscular gay political movement. The referendum sponsored by religious conservatives was designed to overturn what they had already done. In most cases, it's not an issue for us, but if they push it, we will then attempt to level the playing field."

The driving force behind the campaign to secure passage of Amendment 2 was a group known as Colorado for Family Values (CFV), which grew out of a meeting David Noebel had with two other men in the basement of a church. "The homosexuals were moving from city to city," Noebel explained, "and all of a sudden we were facing them right here in Colorado Springs. We decided we'd better take a stand, because if we lost Colorado Springs, we were going to lose the whole state totally." The men formed CFV and drew up an amendment, with substantial help from the National Legal Foundation, established by Pat Robertson for just such a purpose. They then took their case to the people, particularly the people who gathered in evangelical churches. When addressing skeptical or mixed audiences, they insisted they did not want to discriminate against homosexuals, but objected to their being singled out for "special rights" or "special privileges," asserted that gay-rights ordinances meant, or would soon come to mean, that a certain proportion of a company's employees would have to be gays. It would mean that employers could be forced to provide spousal benefits for partners in a gay domestic relationship. And it would mean that people who wanted to rent out rooms in their home would not be able to refuse to rent to a gay couple, even though they considered homosexual behavior to be immoral and in direct violation of God's commandments. Will Perkins, a car dealer who often represented CFV in public appearances, liked to pose the question, "Why should homosexuals benefit from the same legal protections afforded the truly disadvantaged—minorities, women, elderly, handicapped—simply because of what they do in their bedrooms?" CFV did not advocate mistreatment, Perkins insisted; it merely wanted to deny homosexuals the benefits of special protected status.

When making presentations before evangelical churches or other audiences who needed to be mobilized to vote rather than convinced that homosexuality is a sin, CFV activists showed "The Gay Agenda," a video filled with scenes of the most outrageous segments of Gay Pride parades and other sure-to-offend behavior, and distributed brochures charging or implying that gays regularly engage in such behavior as eating feces or urinating on one another. They also displayed samples of materials from the North American Man/Boy Love Association, whose motto was said to be, "Sex by eight, or it's too late." Will Perkins felt such inflammatory tactics were necessary "to offset the claims of homosexuals that they're just like the rest of us, because they're not!"

Amendment 2 did not appear to be a popular cause. According to David Noebel, "Most of the press was against us, the [local] television was against us—the Denver television stations wouldn't accept our commercials—and the national television was against us. I think maybe we had a couple of good comments from our local newspaper, but that was about it. If it hadn't been for [University of Colorado football coach] Bill McCartney and Focus on the Family, we would have died. They helped us a whole lot." In a controversial move, the popular and successful coach called a press conference and, standing in front of a university banner and wearing a university sweater, called homosexuality "an abomination of almighty God" and urged Coloradoans to vote in favor of the Amendment. James Dobson devoted an entire broadcast to Amendment 2. "It was very soft," Noebel said. "It wasn't ranting and raving. Just 'these are the issues you need to keep in mind. We think it's important for you to hear our side too, not just the pro-homosexual side.'" Though attracting less public attention than McCartney's endorsement, Dobson probably had the greater impact. Noebel provided a perceptive insight to the political power of conservative religious broadcasters by pointing out that Dobson was "able to bypass the national and statewide media, because he's on all these independent stations. That's why he's such a powerhouse today. He is able to speak to the country [without] being filtered out by the national news media that don't care to listen to any Christian conservative point of view."

When the referendum was finally voted on in November 1992, Amendment 2 passed by a hundred thousand votes. More tellingly, it won in fifty-two of sixty-three counties. The response from liberal, often libertarian, Coloradoans was one of astonishment that such a thing could happen. Their chagrin increased as they saw their state depicted as a hotbed of bigotry and as individuals and groups canceled plans to visit or hold conventions in Colorado. Almost immediately, Aspen, Boulder, and Denver managed to get an injunction that kept their ordinances in place until the courts could render a final decision. In May 1996, by a six-to-three decision, the United States Supreme Court ruled that Amendment 2 was unconstitutional.

COLORADOANS MAY HAVE been offended at Coach Bill McCartney's outspoken support of Amendment 2, but they can hardly have been surprised, since by 1992 McCartney was already well known for his strong religious convictions. Reared a Catholic but more involved in football and alcohol than in spiritual matters, McCartney was "born again" at a meeting of Christian athletes while serving as an assistant coach at the University of Michigan in the 1980s. When he came to coach at Colorado in 1982, he quickly compiled a winning record, cleaned up the team's renegade image, and stirred minor controversy by having his players pray before practice and games and encouraging them to participate in such evangelical organizations as the Fellowship of Christian Athletes. But since it is reasonably common to overlook serious felonies committed by college athletes, particularly if they are key players, it was not difficult to forgive the CU Buffaloes for praying, even if such exercises might be ruled unconstitutional if challenged in court.

McCartney's life took a new direction in 1990. During a three-hour trip to Pueblo, where he was going to speak at a banquet, he and Dave Wardell, the state director of Fellowship of Christian Athletes, who were sponsoring the banquet, "did what two guys typically do who love Jesus and are going to be together for that long. We put some Christian music in the cassette and sang along, and then we turned that off and began to pray—about our wives and our children, and everything. And then I turned to Dave and said, 'Dave, if you could do anything with your life, money notwithstanding, what would you do?' And he quickly said, 'I would disciple men, one on one. I've got a calling to do that. I can't afford to do it, but if I could, I'd meet with them in coffee shops, an hour a week, and I'd take them into a deeper walk with Christ.' And he said to me, 'What would you do if you could do anything?' And I said, 'More than anything, I would love to see men come together in great numbers and proclaim Christ.' I had traveled around and spoken at different gatherings—when you're a man of God and you're in sports, you have a chance to do that, because pastors are always looking for someone to get everybody's attention, and that's a way to present the gospel. I had discovered that a tremendous power would be there when just men and boys would be in the crowd. The Lord put me in touch with the dynamic that existed, and his spirit would always show up on those occasions. We said, 'Couldn't we both have our dream? Couldn't we get into a job where we could disciple men and couldn't we find a way to bring men together?' "

That conversation was the beginning of a remarkable organization known as Promise Keepers. With the support and encouragement of seventy men who met with them on successive Saturdays during the summer of 1990, McCartney and Wardell went to work, and in July 1991, 4,200 men showed up at the CU basketball arena for the first official Promise Keepers rally. The next year, the number swelled to 22,500, and in 1993, 52,000 men appeared. "With that," McCartney said, "it became obvious that this thing was going to spread all over the United States, and perhaps all over the world." McCartney's claim may not be outlandish. In 1995, a total of 727,000 men attended two-day Promise Keeper rallies in thirteen cities. Twice the number of rallies were planned for the summer of 1996. In between the mass meetings Bill McCartney had envisioned, small groups of men all over America fulfilled Dave Wardell's dream of providing men with the opportunity to share intimate details of their lives with four or five close friends who are willing to hold them accountable to high standards of spiritual discipline, personal morality, and family responsibility.

Instead of becoming a rival to churches, Promise Keepers has proved to be an effective means of plugging men back into their home congregations on a higher voltage line. A huge proportion of those who attend the summer rallies arrive on church buses, accompanied by their enthusiastic pastors. In Colorado alone, the organization works with eight hundred churches. The two-day meetings, for men only—though women are permitted to work at registration tables and service booths—are filled with presentations by dynamic evangelical speakers who punctuate their talks with sports and military metaphors, and speak in stirring language of six steps to take, three stages to go through, or seven promises to keep, frequently eliciting a mass response from their audience with such exhortations as "Stand up, high-five your neighbor, and say, 'Christ is the answer!' "

Springing from McCartney's own belated realization that, despite the outward trappings of success, he had failed to give his wife the kind of loving attention she deserved and had fallen short in fulfilling his duties as a father—underscored by his daughter's bearing two out-of-wedlock children, both fathered by players on his football teams—attention to one's familial role has become one of Promise Keepers' strongest emphases.

The paradigm presented in the rallies, small meetings, and the organization's unofficial text, Seven Promises of a Promise Keeper, is that of the patriarchal family: fathers exercising spiritual and temporal authority and leadership in a compassionate, considerate manner, wives in cooperative submission to the authority God has granted their husbands, and children obedient and respectful toward their loving parents. An underlying premise is that many of the problems plaguing American families can be traced to the fact that men have become "feminized" and have abandoned or neglected the leadership roles for which God has ordained them. Tony Evans, a regular speaker at Promise Keeper rallies, has written, "I'm not talking about sexual preference. I'm trying to describe a misunderstanding of manhood that has produced a nation of 'sissified' men who abdicate their role as spiritually pure leaders, thus forcing women to fill the vacuum." Evans explicitly rejects the notion that men should try to emulate the Rambos or Wilt Chamberlains of the world, who flaunt their masculinity by destructive feats of derring-do or astronomical numbers of sexual conquests. Instead, "men [must] assume their responsibilities and take back the reins of spiritually pure leadership God intended us to hold. Otherwise, our culture is lost."

As a first step to regaining this lost authority, Evans recommends a straightforward approach:

> [S]it down with your wife and say something like this: "Honey, I've made a terrible mistake. I've given you my role. I gave up leading this family, and I forced you to take my place. Now I must reclaim that role." Don't misunderstand what I'm saying here. I'm not suggesting that you ask for your role back, I'm urging you to take it back. . . . [t]here can be no compromise here. If you're going to lead, you must lead. Be sensitive. Listen. Treat the lady gently and lovingly. But lead!

And to the women in this exchange, Evans urges:

> Give it back! For the sake of your family and the survival of our culture, let your man be a man if he's willing. Protect yourself if you must, by handing the reins back slowly; take it one step at a time. But if your husband tells you he wants to reclaim his role, let him! God never meant for you to bear the load you're carrying.

Such assumptions obviously clash with changing notions of equality between the sexes and changing roles of modern women. For that reason,

Promise Keepers has produced skepticism in feminists and others who regard such an approach as outmoded and injurious to women. McCartney is aware of that, of course, but counters by noting, "Most people who are opposed to Promise Keepers have never been there. They haven't seen what God is doing." In fact, rally speakers, including McCartney, increasingly speak of the need to see wives as equal partners. Further, though little systematic evidence has been gathered thus far, it appears that Promise Keepers has been warmly received by the women whose husbands participate. As one observer noted, "their husbands are praying with them, showing their emotions, and becoming better parents. Women are thrilled because men are keeping their promises not only to God, but to them as well."

In addition to its emphases on personal spiritual growth and responsible manhood, Promise Keepers has taken on an additional and quite formidable task: racial reconciliation. Based on his experiences while recruiting in inner cities and coaching African-American football players, McCartney seems to be genuinely convinced that "the white man has held down the man of color through oppression" and that white communities and churches have failed to recognize the pain that racism has caused to minorities. At the first Promise Keepers rally in 1991, at which all the participants were white, McCartney felt that "the Spirit of God clearly said to my spirit, 'You can fill that stadium, but if men of other races aren't there, I won't be there, either.' " Since then, black speakers have been featured and the chairman of the Promise Keepers board, Philip Porter, is an African-American pastor. Most observers regard McCartney's stance as quite genuine and believe the organization's commitment to racial understanding is a hopeful sign, despite still-modest attendance by blacks at Promise Keepers rallies.

As Promise Keepers has grown and attracted increased attention, a suspicion has arisen that it may be, or may become, another regiment in the army of the Religious Right. McCartney has steadfastly denied any such intention, but some overtly political religious conservatives acknowledge that he and his movement face hard choices. Gary Bauer observed that he thought it would be a mistake for Promise Keepers to stop speaking out against abortion or homosexuality simply because they feared being seen as a political organization. "To people who are driven by faith," he said, "those are moral issues. The fact that politicians argue about them is beside the point." Bauer has met with Promise Keepers' leaders, "to give them advice on how they can avoid inadvertently sending the wrong message when they're in Washington, but other than that we really haven't had any further dealings with them." Even so, Bauer made clear that he believed McCartney's movement has enormous potential to help effect the kinds of changes to which he is committed. "I have said publicly," he noted, "that if I had a choice between winning the presidency and having Promise Keepers sweep the country, I'd take Promise Keepers sweeping the country, because I think that would do a lot more to change America than whoever's sitting in the Oval Office."

AS RALPH REED and the Christian Coalition grow familiar and comfortable with the pragmatic measures necessary to bring about legislative changes, and as James Dobson, David Noebel, and Bill McCartney claim increasingly to be less interested in changing laws than in changing the culture, another significant segment of Religious Right figures pursues an even more ambitious agenda. Exponents of this movement, known variously as Christian Reconstructionism, Dominion Theology (as in "fill the earth and subdue it; and have dominion over . . . every living thing that moves upon the earth" [Genesis 1:28]), or Theonomy (the "rule of God"), propose to change the culture, then change the laws, and then—in the worst extreme versions—to expel, subdue, or perhaps even exterminate all those who do not share their vision. Broadly speaking, Reconstructionists believe that Christians have a mandate to rebuild, or reconstruct, all of human society, beginning with the United States and moving outward. They contend that the Bible, particularly Mosaic Law, offers the perfect blueprint for the shape a reconstructed world should take. Since its ethical principles reflect the will of an immutable God, they are applicable to all people in every era.

Reconstructionist theologians, the most notable of whom are Rousas John Rushdoony, Gary North, Gary DeMar, and Greg Bahnsen, tend to be both prolific and voluminous authors and they do not always agree among themselves, but a sampling of their views provides some sense of how a reconstructed America might look. The federal government would play no role in regulating business, public education, or welfare. Indeed, if it survived at all, its functions would likely be limited to delivering the mail and providing some measure of national defense. Some government would be visible at the level of counties, each of which would be protected by a fully armed militia, but citizens would be answerable to church authorities on most matters subject to regulation. Inheritance and gift taxes would be eliminated, income taxes would not exceed ten percent—the biblical tithe—and social security would disappear. Public schools would be abolished in favor of home-schooling arrangements, and families would operate on a strict patriarchal pattern. The only people permitted to vote would be members of "biblically correct" churches. Most notably, a theonomic order would make homosexuality, adultery, blasphemy, propagation of false doctrine, and incorrigible behavior by disobedient children subject to the death penalty, preferably administered by stoning.

A reconstructed America would have little room for Jews, Buddhists, Muslims, Hindus, atheists, or even non-Reconstructionist Christians. "The

Christian," one Reconstructionist author has asserted, "must realize that pluralism is a myth. God and His law must rule all nations. . . . At no point in Scripture do we read that God teaches, supports, or condones pluralism. . . . Clearly our founding fathers had no intention of supporting pluralism for they saw that the Bible tolerates no such view." The founding father and patriarch of Reconstructionism, R. J. Rushdoony, also regards pluralism as a heresy, since, "in the name of toleration, the believer is asked to associate on a common level of total acceptance with the atheist, the pervert, the criminal, and the adherents of other religions."

It is difficult to assess the influence of Reconstructionist thought with any accuracy. Because it is so genuinely radical, most leaders of the Religious Right are careful to distance themselves from it. At the same time, it clearly holds some appeal for many of them. One undoubtedly spoke for others when he confessed, "Though we hide their books under the bed, we read them just the same." In addition, several key leaders have acknowledged an intellectual debt to the theonomists. Jerry Falwell and D. James Kennedy have endorsed Reconstructionist books. Rushdoony has appeared on Kennedy's television program and the *700 Club* several times. Pat Robertson makes frequent use of "dominion" language; his book, *The Secret Kingdom*, has often been cited for its theonomic elements; and pluralists were made uncomfortable when, during his presidential campaign, he said he "would only bring Christians and Jews into the government," as well as when he later wrote, "There will never be world peace until God's house and God's people are given their rightful place of leadership at the top of the world." And Jay Grimstead, who leads the Coalition on Revival, which brings Reconstructionists together with more mainstream evangelicals, has said, "I don't call myself [a Reconstructionist]," but "A lot of us are coming to realize that the Bible is God's standard of morality . . . in all points of history . . . and for all societies, Christian and non-Christian alike. . . . It so happens that Rushdoony, Bahnsen, and North understood that sooner." He added, "There are a lot of us floating around in Christian leadership—James Kennedy is one of them—who don't go all the way with the theonomy thing, but who want to rebuild America based on the Bible."

Unlike most evangelicals, who expect the Second Coming to occur quite soon, Reconstructionists are postmillennialists. They expect to bring in the millennium by their own efforts and that Christ will return at the end of that glorious thousand-year period. Moreover, they do not expect that those now living will see the millennium dawn. On the contrary, they believe the transformation of society, to be accomplished by spiritual renewal and other nonviolent, majoritarian means, will require centuries to complete. Thus, when confronted with the application of the death penalty to, for example, homosexual behavior, theonomists typically hedge by noting that, by the time society is willing to allow such severe measures, fear of capital punishment and the conversion of most people will have rendered them virtually unnecessary. Even so, the obligation to Christianize the nation is already in force. If these views are infused into the mainstream of the Religious Right, with its strong strain of belief in the imminent return of Jesus, the theonomic project's timetable could be dramatically accelerated.

Among evangelical leaders who have shown a marked affinity for the Reconstructionist enterprise is Randall Terry, who has grown increasingly impatient with the conventional political tactics favored by Ralph Reed and his associates. In January 1993, Operation Rescue began holding twelve-week training sessions, which they called the Institute of Mobilized Prophetic Activated Christian Training (IMPACT). According to a newspaper account of one such institute, anti-abortion activists "came from around the country to perfect their skills at exposing and harassing women's clinic owners, doctors, maids, receptionists, volunteers, medical-waste truck drivers . . . and anyone else associated with abortion or the abortion-rights movement." IMPACT was symptomatic. Despite pledges of nonviolence, Randall Terry and others in the movement had begun to use increasingly inflammatory rhetoric. Terry had called pro-choice Supreme Court justices "enemies of Christ" and had compared them to Hitler and Stalin. At an IMPACT training session, he had said, "Intolerance is a beautiful thing. We're going to make [abortionists'] lives a living hell."

In a similar vein, both OR and Rescue America had distributed "wanted" posters for abortionists, and an IMPACT trainee had pulled alongside a doctor at a Florida fast-food restaurant and pantomimed the act of shooting him. Then, while the first IMPACT session was still in progress, the abortion wars entered a new and deadly phase. On March 10, 1993, Michael Griffin, who had participated in several Rescue America rallies, moved beyond street theater and assassinated Dr. David Gunn outside the Pensacola clinic where Gunn performed abortions.

Griffin was sentenced to life imprisonment, and many pro-life activists repudiated such acts and quickly distanced themselves from OR, Rescue America, or any other group that seemed likely to incite or condone such behavior. That summer, attendance at a series of OR-sponsored protests fell far below expectations, but Terry was not chastened. If anything, he had grown more militant. At a July rally, he urged a group of Denver Christians to become "intolerant zealots [regarding] baby killers, sodomites, condom-pushers and that pluralism nonsense." Two weeks later, he told an Indiana congregation, "I want you to just let a wave of intolerance wash over you. I want you to let a wave of hatred wash over you. Yes, hate is good."

Some people apparently took his words to heart. In July of the following year, Paul Hill, who headed a Florida organization called Defensive Action, which circulated a statement defending Griffin, and who had been a guest on James Dobson's radio program, shot and killed another abortion doctor and his driver. Fearful that Griffin and Hill might trigger other zealots to imitate them, various participants in the anti-abortion struggle met in Chicago in November 1994 to discuss the legitimacy of violence in behalf of their cause. OR leader Flip Benham suggested that violence may sometimes be justified. Another activist went further. "It isn't always wrong to kill," he said. "Violence doesn't necessarily beget violence. Sometimes it solves violence." But sometimes it doesn't. A month later, John Salvi murdered two people at an abortion clinic in Brookline, Massachusetts.

With every such tragedy, more moderate anti-abortion forces distanced themselves even further from Randall Terry, Operation Rescue, and other militant pro-life groups. Marlene Elwell, whose introduction to politics came through anti-abortion efforts, gave Terry credit for having played an important role in dramatizing the nature and scope of abortion in America, but lamented the violent turn his wing of the movement had taken. Paul Weyrich criticized Terry and OR not simply for the violence, but for the shortsightedness of their tactics. "The Christian Coalition people," he noted, "followed the advice of those of us like Morton Blackwell and myself, who said, 'Train people and deploy them effectively, if you're going to have an impact.' The Randall Terry group didn't want to hear this. They thought of everything in terms of mass rallies and confrontation, and not in terms of building an infrastructure of support that will make sure laws aren't passed that do you in. So all I can say is that one group followed our advice and one did not. You'll have to judge whether you think one group is more effective than the other."

Gary Bauer neither condemned nor condoned Terry and his colleagues. Instead, he suggested that it may be unrealistic to expect any peaceful, rational resolution of the abortion question anytime soon. "On an issue like abortion," he said, "it's very difficult to find any real common ground. I think that's one of the reasons politicians on both sides hate the issue: because it doesn't lend itself to the kind of typical Washington deal-making that we've seen over the years. The danger of [Randall Terry's] approach is that, in a culture that is hostile to his views, most Americans will read about him and what he does through a filter that will always put the worst possible spin on the point he's trying to make. So there's a fifty-fifty chance that what you end up doing is driving people away who would otherwise be inclined to make common cause with you. I think Randall Terry and all of us have to rethink our approaches constantly and make sure that we're not being counterproductive."

Os Guinness clearly preferred Christian Coalition's approach. Ralph Reed, he said, "is realizing that you have to fight in a way that is truly persuasive. The essence of a pluralistic society is that anyone can prevail if they persuade. On abortion you have a strong minority opposed to it, a strong minority in favor of it, and the broad American middle rather ambivalent. Some are confused and therefore open to the argument that is the most principled and the most persuasive. And yet, most of the anti-abortion fight has been led by evangelicals in ways that gave up on persuasion. They should have gone back to the way the early evangelicals fought for abolition, using every persuasive means they can, rooted in the whole understanding of human rights and human dignity and make a very powerful, persuasive case, just as Martin Luther King did for civil rights in the fifties and sixties."

Persuasion, of course, is not the only skill required for effective political engagement. Often just as essential is a willingness to compromise, and here evangelicals have a harder time. Though they may disagree with his tactics, most anti-abortion Christians accept Randall Terry's assertion that "abortion is murder, period. Murder is the deliberate taking of a judicially innocent life in times of peace, right? We're not talking about war. We're not talking about capital punishment. We're not talking about manslaughter, an accident. We're talking about murder." If abortion is indeed murder and fetuses are truly babies, how can pro-lifers possibly concede that a little bit of murder, or the murder of only some babies, might be acceptable? Who can imagine that a God on the pro-life side might be willing to overlook "a little bit of murder" or take no offense at the murder of babies, as long as it is not paid for with tax money and concerned parties are given ample notice that it is to occur?

GIVEN THE RELIGIOUS Right's difficulty in accepting compromises, Gary Bauer noted, "There has been a great deal of controversy about how organizations that believe in the pro-family issues ought to conduct themselves when it comes to elections in which you have a candidate who is less than ideal. I go back and forth in my own mind about whether you should accept a candidate who [disagrees with] you on several issues, because he or she is better than the opposition candidate. But when it comes to the 'right-to-life' issue, my own personal viewpoint is that this is so important that I would not recommend compromise in the political arena on it. And I think that, to the extent that candidates or organizations do compromise on that issue, they run the risk of alienating their own base and sending the message that they're really not serious about an issue like the sanctity of human life."

Bauer's attitude seemed to dominate during the run-up to the 1996 presidential campaign. James Dobson, Ralph Reed, and Bauer, speaking for his Family Research Council, all warned that any attempt to remove or water down the strong anti-abortion plank in the Republican platform or for nominee-apparent Bob Dole to choose a pro-choice running-mate—most notably, Colin Powell, who repeatedly insisted he had no interest in the vice presidential slot—would result in widespread defection from Republican ranks by evangelical voters, quite possibly in support of a third-party or independent candidate. Pat Buchanan, ever unyielding on abortion, warned that he might bolt the party—perhaps taking with him his 146 delegates—if it relaxed its stand on the issue, and Howard Phillips, now head of the U.S. Taxpayers Party and usually regarded as a Reconstructionist, let it be known that he would welcome Buchanan as his group's standard-bearer.

Reed, however, angered many in the anti-abortion movement when he came out publicly for Dole, since Dole had made it quite apparent that he not only would accept General Powell as a running-mate, but would exert considerable pressure on the ostensibly reluctant former general to recognize his duty to the party and the nation. Reed quickly tried to squelch any intimation that he had grown soft on abortion by letting the Republican Party know what he expected in return for his support. Speaking to a large gathering of the Michigan Christian Coalition but aiming his remarks at Republican leaders, Reed said, "If you want to retain the majority that you [won] in 1994, and you want to add to it in 1996, then you cannot, you should not, and you must not retreat from the pro-life and pro-family stand that have won you that majority in the first place." Reed also defended Pat Buchanan, who spoke immediately afterward, against charges by the "liberal media" that he was an extremist—even though that label had in fact been applied to Buchanan by Dole in a television advertisement.

Then, in early May, it became apparent that an intransigent stance on abortion was likely to cost Senator Dole and the entire Republican ticket critical support, particularly among women. Reed told the *New York Times* that he and Christian Coalition "favored an exception to an abortion ban only if the mother's life was endangered," and that "he would 'reluctantly' accept exceptions in cases of rape and incest if that were the only way to get an anti-abortion law passed." He also said that he would be willing to consider alternate wording of the language in the Republican Party's platform, which declares its support for a Human Life Amendment to the Constitution and for "legislation to make clear that the Fourteenth Amendment's protections [forbidding states to 'deprive any person of life, liberty, or property, without due process of law'] apply to unborn children." While acknowledging that a Human Life Amendment, presumably banning all, or virtually all, abortions, "may be one of the most remote weapons at our disposal at this time," Reed insisted that he was not softening his opposition to abortion and would consent only to some tinkering with the language of the party platform, not to any watering down of its content. In his new book, *Active Faith,* he offered—as a personal statement, not as the position of the Christian Coalition—a reworded plank regarding "the sanctity of innocent human life." It made no mention of a Constitutional amendment.

James Dobson and Pat Buchanan strongly disagreed with what they regarded as Reed's willingness to compromise on such a fundamental issue. Buchanan's sister and campaign manager, Bay, warned that if the Republicans tried to change a single word of the abortion plank at their summer convention, "they'll regret it." James Dobson concurred, declaring that Dole would be committing "political suicide" if he allowed the plank to change. Meanwhile, back at the barricades, Randall Terry hooted at the whole idea that the Republican Party could be counted on to do the Lord's work. "The platform plank," he said, "is the perennial pacifier. What has it done? Platforms don't vote. Only Senators and Representatives have the ability to vote. Bob Dole can say, 'I supported the Republican Party platform,' but when it's time to vote on Ruth Bader Ginsberg or to oppose Janet Reno, these guys cave in. So my warning to pro-lifers is 'Stop being seduced by this stupid party platform.' I'm thankful it's there in words, but darn it, I want deeds. I'd rather have silence on the platform about child-killing and have Republican Senators and Representatives who are fierce pro-lifers. Don't put bumper stickers all over your car; do something for me.

"I don't call myself a Reconstructionist," Terry said, "but I want to see the righteous lead. I [want to] see Christian statesmen who believe that the Bible is the foundation of civilization, and that the Ten Commandments must be the foundation of this republic. The real battle is over leadership: Who has the levers? And right now the bad guys have the levers, and that's why this country is going down the drain." Mocking Ralph Reed's declaration that all religious conservatives want is "a place at the table," an agitated Terry said, "I don't want a place at the table, because the table is corrupt. We don't want equal time with baby-killers and homosexual recruiters and latex losers. We don't want them to have one minute of time with our children in government schools. We're tired of their table. We want a new table, with a new set of players. I'm looking for people who will do what is right because they fear God and because they are filled with a passion for what is right. I know this: a lot of good God-fearing men believe that Biblical law must be the foundation for our civil law. And if America does not return to biblical values, we cannot survive. So for Ralph Reed or anyone else to say that the Christian community should not base its politics on theology—that really is treachery against God's law. It is troubling to me that much of the evangelical community—the so-called Religious Right—has become the mistress of the Republican party."

It has been some time since anyone expected Randall Terry to express himself in moderate, conciliatory terms, but harshly censorious language, directed at any who fail the tests of ideological purity, is becoming increasingly common in evangelical circles, a phenomenon many find disturbing. Early in 1995, the editors of *Christianity Today,* still the flagship publication of mainstream evangelicalism, asked John Woodbridge, a highly respected church historian at Trinity Evangelical Divinity School, to address this troubling tendency in an article. Woodbridge's article, "Culture War Casualties: How Warfare Rhetoric is Hurting the Work of the Church," appeared in the magazine's March 6, 1995, issue. In it, Woodbridge warned that "culture-war rhetoric leads us to distort others' positions, to see enmity in place of mere disagreement. It leaves no room for nuanced positions, or for middle ground," and thus creates divisions among Christians. In addition, he said, harsh language makes it easy for critics to stir up fears that the Religious Right is seeking to impose a theocratic regime on American society. While acknowledging that the Bible frequently uses military metaphors to speak of the godly life, he noted that intemperate language often violated not only Jesus' command to love one's enemies, but also the prohibition against bearing false witness. The essay was altogether gentle and non-censorious. In one brief paragraph, however, Woodbridge mentioned, with only the barest hint of disapproval, James Dobson's frequent use of the term, "civil war of values."

Dobson, who seems to give criticism more easily than he receives it, fired back a long and agitated defense of his use of the language of warfare, titling it, "Why I Use 'Fighting Words.' " Apparently stunned at the intensity of Dobson's article, Woodbridge wrote a conciliatory response, praising Dobson for his ministry and integrity, yet upholding his original point. Decades of the study of religious intolerance, he said, had made him keenly aware of "how precious is the gift of freedom of conscience and how unexpected and unhappy the results can be of using powerful rhetoric in a highly charged religious-political situation. . . . Not every word that can be spoken should be spoken." Elaborating on what he had written, Woodbridge said, "I wasn't trying to be a Lone Ranger on this. Many other evangelicals feel the same way." He felt hopeful, he said, that Christians and non-Christians could work together in fashioning a consensus "that may not be all that we want, but would still help bind us together as a nation, respecting [each other's] liberties. But if we traumatize other people with our rhetoric, the possibility of creating that vision becomes more elusive. That's a tremendous concern for many of us. If you stir up troops, you may get people to give you money, and that obviously helps grease your operation and keep it going, but that is a temptation that has to be resisted, because the inflammatory language can go out and cause undue damage, damage you didn't anticipate."

ASKED TO REFLECT on the progress of the Religious Right since he helped launch it in the late 1970s, Jerry Falwell asserted that, despite Moral Majority's demise, it had played a critical role. "Just as the black church never again has to be indoctrinated to get involved politically," he said, "neither does the evangelical church. I think these multiple movements out there are doing the right thing in focusing where their strengths are. Focus on the Family is working primarily through young to-middle-aged couples, millions of them. Family Research Council is connecting with the leaders in society. The Rutherford Institute and the American Center for Law and Justice are both focusing on religious-freedom issues. Christian Coalition is probably doing the best work of training and mobilizing people at the grass roots. These are all rifle approaches. Ours was a shotgun approach. We just aimed at the crowd and let 'er rip. Whatever it took to get a crowd or to get Phil Donahue or MacNeil/Lehrer or Dan Rather to have us on, we fired that gun. My thing now is to be a voice, in a statesman-like way, to continue to give direction through national television, but the infantry is marching now. The air force is not needed quite as much."

Most active participants seem full of optimism. Marlene Elwell said, "I believe we've changed the face of America and politics forever, and this movement's only going to grow as we have greater opportunity to educate the American people as to who we are and what we're doing. You are going to find a greater respect for us, because we are now part of the mainstream." Guy Rodgers sounded a similar note. "You will see a vastly different America ten years from now," he ventured. "I think you've already seen some of that play out in the 1994 election. Give it a couple more election cycles and you will see this permeate not only the national level but the state and local level as well."

Doug Wead predicted that evangelicals would not only continue to gain influence in the Republican Party, but would come to be accepted as equal partners, not just a large group whose votes needed to be courted. "The Democratic party went through the same thing a hundred years earlier," he noted, "with the influx of Catholic voters." As waves of Irish, Italian, and Polish Catholics immigrated to America, "they were resisted. They smelled of steerage and garlic, they spoke different languages, they had their own school systems, they censored books, they indexed films. And there was anti-Catholic backlash that was shameful and continued for many years. The Catholics had Father Coughlin, the equivalent of a modern-day televangelist, and they had Cardinal Spellman, who visited Franco and sent a telegram back to Roosevelt saying, 'You misunderstand this guy. He's great.' That whole thing was experienced by Democrats, but they took them in, with all their rough edges, and made them a part of Franklin Roosevelt's winning coalition, and assimilated them into their party. And today, they're leaders in the party and there's no conflict between Catholics and non-Catholics within the party. My argument is, if [Republicans] exclude evangelicals and play games with them, we prolong the process. If we bring them in, we can share the sensitivities we have for the non-evangelical electorate, and we can use their wisdom and contacts to win elections. It's not healthy in America to exclude any group of people."

Still toiling away quietly in the background, Morton Blackwell runs the Leadership Institute, a program he established in 1979 to train political activists. "From the late sixties," Grover Norquist observed, "Morton has believed in the importance of political training, and that it's more effective to train twenty-year-olds instead of sixty-year-olds, because you just bought an extra forty years there. He also believes it is easier to teach a conservative some technological proficiency than to take a technologically proficient person and teach him a world view that he doesn't have to start with. So he starts by looking for conservatives and then he asks, 'How would you like to become a more effective activist for your values and beliefs?' He teaches young conservatives how to run student newspapers, how to appear on television, how to go to work for the Executive Branch, how to be effective on Capitol Hill, how to run a campaign. He walks you through what you can do, what works and what doesn't work. At the end of Morton's training, people feel confident that they have some real skills, and that there's nobody on the other side who knows some secret handshake or judo move that will embarrass them because they don't know it. Morton Blackwell is a Johnny Appleseed of politics, spreading activists all around. And years later, you can see people who've studied under Morton Blackwell and have gone off to win elections and become Congressmen and Senators. Ralph and I have both been through Morton's schools. We've sent people to him and we've brought in people who've had his training. Both of us have taught at Morton's schools. So there's a lot of overlap."

Paul Weyrich readily acknowledged that the Christian Coalition and its allies in the evangelical camp had made themselves into a potentially important political force, but he warned against allowing the Republicans to take them for granted. "The last thing the Christian Coalition needs," he said, "is to become what blacks have become to the Democratic Party—something you trot out at election time but don't really want to deal with later on. A strategic alliance is fine, provided you don't sell your soul and remain silent when treasonous acts occur, which will happen. Getting into bed with the party too often may end up causing them to get a fatal disease. They should not be for any political party. They should be for principles, and they can support whichever party happens to adopt those principles, but not the party for the party's sake, because the party brings them nothing."

Gary Bauer agreed that it was important for the pro-family movement never to think of itself as an auxiliary to one party. Instead, he said, it is better "to elect candidates of whatever party agrees with them and then to be somewhat impatient about the candidates' fulfilling their campaign promises. There's a natural tendency by politicians to put the most difficult things on the back burner, and to do that over and over and over again, but then to come back to you thirty days before an election and tell you how desperately they need your help. I think it's important that the pro-family movement not fall prey to that sort of constant delay in the things that matter to us."

To avoid exploitation, Doug Wead suggested it might be time for evangelicals to cast an eye toward the other party, noting that, "When a party thinks you can't go anywhere else, they take you for granted. The evangelical movement will be in a much better position if it is involved in the Democratic party as well." Wead believed such a tactic should also help evangelicals secure more positions in a given administration. "If you're committed to one party," he said, "you're going to have a hard time getting positions. And if your party is not in power, you're in trouble if you want inclusion. So any movement is stronger if it's winnable by either party."

Not all evangelicals felt their concerns about the transformation of conservative Christians into a significant political involvement would be allayed if only both major parties took them more seriously. "I'm sure none of the people on the left or the right would actually say it," evangelical theologian Michael Horton observed, "but there is an assumption that God votes a certain way, that if you asked him, he would say he was either a Democrat or a Republican. The American hubris involved in this is really quite remarkable—to think that the creator of the universe thinks of himself as an American. One of the Ten Commandments is for us not to take God's name in vain. That means we are not to use his name in a way he has not authorized. We have to be careful about what we make him the patron for. We, on the left and the right, have made God something of a mascot. Instead of a transcendent God who speaks to us, he's someone who sort of blesses our agenda and sanctifies our programs. There is a real confusion of God and country in America. For example, flag-burning episodes have raised concerns about desecration of our 'sacred' flag. Referring to our national images as 'sacred' is of grave concern to many of us. This confusion of American identity with Christian identity leads not only to problems within the culture [regarding people of other faiths], but it compromises the integrity of Christianity, because Christianity is a religion based on historical events relating to the life and times of Jesus of Nazareth. It is a religion based on myths about America's destiny. The reason Jesus died on a cross was not so Republicans could sweep Congress in the 1996 elections. That is not the goal of the Kingdom of God."

RALPH REED HAS acknowledged that "even if you believe there's only one way to get to heaven, you can still believe there is probably more than one way to balance the budget." In his 1994 book, *Politically Incorrect,* he called for a revival of a "civil religion" that would give greater freedom of public expression of "common attributes of faith," but explicitly denied that America is or should become "a theocratic state or a unicultural society." In the introduction to the *Contract with the American Family,* he explicitly stated that the contract is neither a Christian agenda nor a theological statement, but a political agenda of limited scope. And in *Active Faith,* published in the summer of 1996, he wrote, "we should resist the temptation to identify our religious convictions with the platform of a party or the platitudes of favored politicians." Given a history of inconsistent statements by Pat Robertson on the validity of the separation of church and state as interpreted by the Supreme Court, and of Reed's own demonstrated ability to shade his statements to meet the expectations of his audiences, some skeptics choose to reserve judgment on the sincerity of such declarations until more time has passed. Others, aware that overt duplicity in an age of "gotcha" journalism is a perilous tactic indeed, are willing to take his statements at approximate face value and to regard his apparently diminishing bellicosity and growing appreciation of pluralism as an age-appropriate sign of maturation. They also indicate his desire and intention to be a long-term player in mainstream politics.

Numerous evangelicals have suggested that their colleagues would do well to be wary of the hubris described by Michael Horton. John Woodbridge, still persuaded that modesty and charity are valuable traits in both personal and political interaction, recalled hearing Gary Bauer indicate to Republican National Committee chair Haley Barbour that, if the party did not do certain things, evangelicals would not be on board with the party in the fall elections. "That was intriguing," Woodbridge gently observed, "because it seemed to me that not all evangelicals were necessarily behind Mr. Bauer in that threat. I think we have to be careful not to indicate that we are the only voice of evangelicalism. I appreciate Mr. Bauer, but there are many, many other folks who speak for the evangelical cause, and for him to intimate that all evangelicals are behind him and will do what he says seemed to me to be a reach. And frankly, he is not the representative of the evangelicalism that I would personally espouse." Lest his point be missed, Woodbridge added, "I believe Ralph Reed represents a position more or less like the one I've been articulating when he indicates that the goal of his organization is always to respect the beliefs of others. He is very much in favor of upholding freedoms, and I would think that position is one a lot of Americans would appreciate. With Dr. Dobson, sometimes I think critics might ask, 'Have you made it very, very clear that, if you are successful in your political aspirations, the full rights of people who don't happen to agree with you will be maintained?' I assume he would say, 'Of course, that's true.' But my impression is that it's important for him to reiterate that."

Interestingly, several thoughtful observers ventured that, if he felt able, Reed might distance himself even further from any association with theonomic language or aims. Ed Dobson said, "I think he does represent something different. I think they ought to drop the religious attachment to their organization and just admit they're a conservative political group, but since [Christian Coalition was] birthed in the environment of religious commitment, it's hard to drop that. . . . I don't see that happening." Os Guinness agreed: "I think Ralph Reed realizes both the importance of pragmatism and the need for principle and, [in light of] the excesses of the last fifteen years, he is trying to lead them in a wiser direction. But of course, he's riding a populist tiger, and he has people above who are insisting on certain things, such as the name 'Christian Coalition,' which I believe he strongly disagrees with, but cannot change. So he is a much more thoughtful leader than those who went before."

Bobbie Kilberg, with fewer worries about stepping on sensitive evangelical toes, was even more explicit. "Ralph," she said, "is a very practical politician, but in his flock he is dealing with some [people] who believe they are directed by God to do x, y, or z. And when you're directed by God to do something, it's hard to compromise. I think Ralph gets that, certainly at times from Pat Robertson, but I think he gets it from his flock, too. He would have preferred, I think, not to have made abortion a litmus test for a vice-presidential nominee. His early indications were that he could live with a nominee who may be pro-choice, as long as he was not in favor of funding and [advocated some other restrictions]. Now he says, 'You must have someone who agrees with us on every issue as the nominee.' I think he gets buffeted and can't always lead as far or in the direction he wants to. It's hard to be a practical politician in that environment, but he's done it very well."

As part of his effort to "cast a wider net," a term he likes to use, Reed has called on Christians not just to espouse their support for the nation of Israel, but also to manifest greater "sensitivity on issues of religious intolerance and anti-Semitism." And, like Bill McCartney, he has made a conscious effort to win the trust and cooperation of evangelical blacks. "There's no question," he said, "that white evangelical Protestants, especially in the South, were not only on the sidelines but were on the wrong side of the most central struggle for social justice of the twentieth century, namely the struggle for civil rights. They preached against it, they organized against it, they used their pulpits to argue that the mixing of politics and religion by black ministers like Martin Luther King was wrong. The words we used against them and the moral authority we misused against them came back to haunt us in our own trek for social justice after *Roe v. Wade*. I have always argued, and still believe, that until the pro-family, religious conservative movement becomes a truly biracial or multi-racial movement, it will not have [real] moral resonance with the American people, because we were so wrong at that time. Being wrong on issues that big, as Charles Lindbergh was about the rise of Nazism, for example, causes you to lose moral authority as a political actor, and I think we lost moral authority. What we've tried to do at the Christian Coalition, and we're not the only ones, is to get our own house in order before we tried to legislate for the rest of the society." He told of efforts to reach out to minority communities, including Hispanics and Asians as well as African Americans. "I want the Christian Coalition to be truly a rainbow coalition," he said. "I want it to be black, brown, yellow, white. I want it to bring Christians of all faith traditions, all denominations, and all races and colors together. I don't think that's going to happen over-night. It's going to take years, but we're committed to it."

Reed's rainbow already stretches beyond the borders of evangelicalism. In Michigan, state director Marlene Elwell, a Roman Catholic, has worked from the outset to keep the organization from becoming too sectarian. Convinced that many Americans are wary of a fundamentalist attitude that consigns to perdition all who disagree with its views, Elwell insisted, "That's not the center of this movement. In the Jerry Falwell days, I looked into Moral Majority. I attended a couple of their meetings. I was pursued by some of their leadership, but that was not a movement I could embrace, because there was no openness to someone of my faith. It was very narrow in its thinking. There was a lot of anger, a lot of judgment. Frankly, I found it very scary. I came away saying, 'I'm going to work real hard to make sure it doesn't go anywhere.' That was just the opposite of what I experienced with Pat Robertson." Although she notes that some members of Christian Coalition still believe she needs to leave the Catholic church in order to be "saved," she believes the organization as a whole is broader than that. As proof, she noted that she also serves on the board of the Catholic Alliance, which she identified as "an arm of Christian Coalition. We just put that together in the fall of 1995. It ties us in with the directive of the Holy Father of the Catholic Church, who directs us to become ecumenical and to join forces with one another on issues where we see wrong being done.

"My personal hope," Elwell continued, "is that we can respect each other for our disagreements with regard to our beliefs and our denominational differences, and that where we do agree, as on abortion, we can join together and become a greater force against this evil. I think the Christian Coalition has already gone a hundred miles beyond anything they'd ever dreamed of, and for the first time I'm beginning to believe these denominational differences are crumbling. I believe this movement has been given divine direction. It's providential that all these things have happened. Most of the people involved with the Christian Coalition—evangelical, Catholic, or whatever their denominational belief—are people of love, people of care and concern, people of compassion, who really have a desire to put America back on its feet in a righteous order, who truly believe that God and family are very important to the future of America. They have dreams and memories of long past. If they're too young, they remember their parents speaking of it. If they're my age, they remember the days when they could walk the streets and not worry, when people cared about one another, and when there was not all this divisiveness. There wasn't violence on TV, there weren't lyrics in music that said the opposite of everything you believe. We're wanting to go back to those days. Are we ever going to get totally back? I don't know, but I do know that a lot of people care about that. And that is really the make-up of Christian Coalition: people like that."

Without question, an alliance of evangelical Protestants and Roman Catholics could be a political force of great power, but a nostalgic longing for the 1950s will not by itself dissolve the inherent tensions common to mixed marriages. Harvard theologian Harvey Cox, an astute and often sympathetic observer of the Religious Right, noted that "certain tenets of Roman Catholic social teaching directly contradict some of the things the Christian Coalition is for. I was reminded of that very dramatically when I watched Pope John Paul II in Central Park when he was saying Mass, and seated on the stage behind him was Pat Robertson. The Pope gave an eloquent sermon, with three points: "You shouldn't slam the door on immigrants, because this is a great part of the American tradition; the U.N. is a fine hope for world peace and you have to stay in it; and you cannot destroy the welfare net for the poorest in your society." Now, here's Pat Robertson sitting behind him, bathed in the nimbus of Pope John Paul II, but whose position on all of those issues is at the opposite end of the spectrum. Robertson's book, *The New World Order,* is a cry of alarm against international organizations, including the U.N., and the people who support the Christian Coalition are often the same people who are calling for at least a temporary stoppage on all immigration and who are in the act of dismantling the welfare net. I watched the meeting of the Christian Coalition [on C-SPAN] last fall, and the most thunderous applause anybody got was for saying, 'We really have to get tough with the death penalty. We have to [use] capital punishment more and more.' If there's anything the Catholic bishops are clear about, perhaps other than abortion, it's that they are uniformly against the death penalty. You can't have it both ways. On issues like abortion, there's some common ground, no doubt about it. There'll be some support from Roman Catholics on school vouchers. But there are some real tensions there. I don't think they're going to get very far with this Catholic Alliance. I think it's a noble effort, but I think it's fated for failure."

AT SEVERAL JUNCTURES over the past two decades, intelligent and perceptive analysts of American religious and political culture have proclaimed the Religious Right to be, variously, a marginal group of culturally retarded whiners who did not understand that the battle with modernity was over and that they had lost; a juggernaut about to overwhelm and destroy American democracy; a paper tiger whose strength had been laughably overestimated; a surprisingly resilient and industrious aggregate capable of organizing themselves into an effective political force; a fanatical tribe bent on turning America into a fundamentalist dystopia; and a remarkably effective political coalition led by extraordinarily canny and pragmatic political operatives whose deepest motivations are not always easy to identify. As I trust the story told in this book and in the television series it accompanies has made reasonably clear, no portrait painted from a single angle is likely to provide a faithful likeness of this large and still evolving movement. It is complex, contradictory, and still struggling with what it wants to become and how it can remain faithful to its understanding of the will of a transcendent God while engaged in the gritty, utterly mundane give-and-take of practical politics. As has been true throughout this journey, our understanding of its variegated nature is likely to be most accurate if we do not imagine that any one voice can provide us with all we need to know, or that anything we learn about it is not subject to revision.

Ed Dobson, after serving as president of the first major Religious Right organization, Moral Majority, has dramatically altered his outlook and stance. "I am probably as committed to not being in politics," he said, "as I once was to being in. I advocate that the church and pastors stay out of politics, period, and focus on the gospel and on compassion in their own community." Dobson feels it is appropriate to encourage church members to be involved, but views his own calling an attempt to change the culture from the bottom up. "I think you do that," he explained, "by living out your faith with radical acts of compassion: by loving people who are HIV-positive, by forming coalitions across ethnic and racial boundaries, by breaking down walls of racism, by extending love and compassion to the poor, by empowering people through opportunity. I know all that sounds like a social gospel, but to me it's the gospel lived out in real life, and Jesus said, 'It is by your good works that they will glorify your Father who is in heaven.' I think we've forgotten that. It's the message of Scripture, Old and New Testaments: concern for the poor, the marginalized, the disenfranchised; loving people who are forsaken. Jesus said, 'Everybody will know you're my disciples if you have love, one for another,' not 'if you form a political organization and elect someone to the White House.' I don't think you have loved until you have loved the people who are the most difficult to love. And that's a challenge. I'm not there yet. I hope I'm on the journey. When I die and they wheel me down front for the service, if someone will get up and say, 'Dobson loved homosexuals,' or 'He loved single parents' or kids who had been abused or people on the streets—if they'll say that about me, I'll feel like I have done something in life, that maybe in a small way I've tried to live out the teachings of Jesus with authenticity.''

James Muffett, who worked for Freedom Council and Americans for Robertson, has no plans to abandon political activism, but hopes for a toning down of angry words and uncharitable behavior. "Sometimes [members of the Religious Right] convey that 'We're Christians, we read the Bible, we know the truth and you don't; therefore, we're right and you're not.' There's a self-righteous air that we have to get away from. And I see people on the other side who are more moderate or liberal, and they have an air of 'We know what's best.' There's an elitism there. I think everybody has to get rid of that and just sit down and say, 'Okay, let's talk.' I, for one, want to do that. That doesn't mean I'm not going to be political and lobby and still be involved in all of these issues, but I'm not interested in being a John the Baptist and calling for Herod's head on a platter. I think a little bit of humility, a little bit of servant-heartedness, and a faithful attitude can get you a whole lot more than trying to bust down the door with a battering ram.''

Sounding less and less like a guerrilla warrior watching his enemies being carried off in body bags, Ralph Reed echoed Dobson's and Muffett's aspirations. "There's an awful lot of talk," he observed, "about the religious conservative movement's being powerful and effective and feared, and all those things. That's not the force of this movement. Ultimately, the force of this movement, if it is a force, will be that it is decent, that it is honorable, that it is loving, that it is merciful, and that, if it ever did gain control of government, it would not try and use government to hurt those it seeks to help. That will ultimately be our message. That is the kind of apologetic I've tried to develop at the Christian Coalition, because when you are people of faith, you can't get focused on being close to power or having power, because you don't really ultimately believe that will solve the problems.''

Virgil Wood, the former Lynchburg pastor who went to jail repeatedly in the 1960s for trying to persuade a society dominated by white evangelical Christians that it needed to open its doors and its hearts to people of color, did not dismiss such talk as pious cant. Neither, however, did he accept such assurances without qualification. "There are conservatives out there," he said, "and I know some of them, who care as much as I do about economic justice and a moral foundation for the society. They are in a place they haven't been before, and they've got all this power they've never had before. At one time, they were the folks who were being [true] to their cause simply by shooting at other ideas. Now they've got to come up with ideas of their own. They've got to sit down and devise a workable set of solutions to make America good for all its citizens. The jury is still out as to whether they can measure up to that task."

UP AGAINST THE WALL

AMERICA, THOUGH NOT perfect in its record of religious tolerance, has been remarkable in its success at avoiding wars over differing faiths and, overall, at granting freedom to a wide variety of religious expressions and practices. That is a notable achievement in human history, and one of our nation's most admirable accomplishments. At present, however, the level of religious conflict appears to be rising and the historically unprecedented extent of religious freedom may be in some danger. To many, the Religious Right is an obstreperous demon that threatens to upset the valuable balance of religious and secular interests and to create a repressive theocracy that will trample on the freedoms of all who do not share its theological and political beliefs. To others, that same movement is a valiant warrior struggling to preserve religious liberty, and the last, best hope to save America's soul.

Like other major political movements, the Religious Right seeks to control, or at least to exert strong influence over the legislative, executive, and judicial branches of the United States government. In the process, some of its leaders have challenged, either explicitly or by their actions, what has come to be the operative understanding in America of the appropriate relationship between religion and government—or, in the more familiar wording, between church and state. In the legally dominant "separationist" view, the state is seen as a secular institution strictly enjoined by the Constitution and the Supreme Court neither to aid nor to hinder religion. The competing view, clung to by some since the founding of the nation and generally held by members of the Religious Right, is "accommodationist" in outlook, asserting that as long as the government acts in a nonpreferential manner, it can—and, for the good of the nation, *should*—offer support to religion. Proponents of this view typically charge that, in its zeal to avoid giving aid to religion, the Supreme Court has not only misinterpreted the Constitution, but has actually interfered with the free exercise of religion.

The Framers of the Constitution were keenly aware of the threat to unity that religion could pose, and set out to prove that a nation could exist and flourish without an established religion—a novel proposition in the eighteenth century. Throughout hundreds of years of recorded history, governments and religious institutions had struggled with each other for dominance, or at least parity, but neither had given much thought to the possibility that they might proceed independently of each other. During much of the colonial period, the governments of the individual colonies provided financial support either to a single denomination (usually the Church of England/Episcopal) or to several of the larger bodies, with Congregationalism the standard frontrunner. Those not in the favored groups typically operated under a handicap, and nonbelievers were at a distinct disadvantage. In some colonies, nonfavored groups were forbidden to evangelize, attendance at the established church was sometimes required, expressions of disrespect toward ministers were often forbidden, and blasphemy could be punished by death.

By the time of the Revolution, the quest for political liberty was often accompanied and bolstered by a desire for religious liberty. This tendency had been encouraged by the Great Awakening, the mid-eighteenth-century revival movement that had stressed a direct and individual response to the urgings of the Holy Spirit. Just as the colonists felt it intolerable to support and take direction from a government in which they had little voice, many felt it equally offensive to be compelled to support with their taxes or follow the rules of a religion to which they did not belong. When, in addition, their own religious practice was the object of repression or discrimination, those feelings could be quite intense. This yearning for freedom of religion was acknowledged and met in the framing of the Constitution.

THE FOUNDING FATHERS who played the greatest role in shaping the American understanding of the appropriate relationship between church and state were Thomas Jefferson and James Madison. With the aid of like-minded colleagues, these two close friends managed to get their path-breaking views incorporated first into the laws of Virginia and ultimately into the Constitution of the United States.

Both Madison and Jefferson, like many of the Founding Fathers, were heavily influenced by British political theorist John Locke, who believed that all humans have natural rights to life, liberty, and property. Since these rights are not granted by government, government cannot take them away—they are "unalienable." Fundamental among these liberties is freedom of conscience. While God may expect obedience to his will, no human entity can coerce or enforce that obedience. To be meaningful, it must be entirely voluntary. Government exists because naturally free people enter into a "social contract"—here the Founding Fathers drew also on the writings of the French philosopher Rousseau—in which they agree to accept certain regulations as a means of fostering communal existence and protecting these natural, inalienable rights. Because one of these rights is freedom of conscience, of which freedom of religion is a prime example, government should have no role in regulating religion. Since religious belief and practice must be voluntary, so churches must be voluntary associations, operating entirely without the support or oversight of the government. The other side of that equation is that the government must be entirely secular, neutral toward all religious bodies and views.

With these as their convictions, Madison and Jefferson set about to end the establishment of the Anglican Church in Virginia. In 1779, in response to a bill to provide tax support to a variety of religious groups, Jefferson submitted his Bill for Establishing Religious Freedom to the Virginia legislature. As is often noted, he regarded it as one of his three finest accomplishments, along with primary authorship of the Declaration of Independence and the founding of the University of Virginia. It seems fair, then, to view it as a definitive statement of his views on the matter. In the bill, Jefferson contended that, 1) The government should not compel people to support a religion in which they do not believe, and that to do so "is sinful and tyrannical"; 2) There should be no religious test for holding public office; 3) The magistrate should not enter into the field of religious opinion, but should interfere only when religions violate the public peace; 4) Religious establishment bribes (and thereby runs the risk of corrupting) religion when it offers it rewards from the public coffers.

Neither Jefferson's bill nor the one he opposed passed, but the fight was renewed in 1784, with Patrick Henry contending for multiple establishment—giving money to most or all denominations—and James Madison against. The decision was put off until 1785. In the interim, Madison composed and circulated anonymously the singularly important document, *Memorial and Remonstrance Against Religious Assessments*. "It is proper to take alarm at the first experiment on our liberties." wrote Madison, for "who does not see that the same authority which can establish Christianity in exclusion of all other religions, may establish with the same ease any particular sect of Christians, in exclusion of all other sects; . . . that the same authority which can force a citizen to contribute three pence only of his property for the support of any one establishment, may force him to conform to any other establishment in all cases whatsoever."

Madison was not concerned solely with oppression. Government support of religion, he insisted, would lead inevitably to the corruption and weakening of religion itself. Fifteen centuries of governmental entanglement with Christianity had made clear that neither institution benefited from the relationship. He noted that ecclesiastical establishments "have [in some instances] been seen to erect a spiritual tyranny on the ruins of Civil authority; in many instances they have been seen upholding the thrones of political tyranny; in no instance have they been seen the guardians of the liberties of the people. . . . A just government . . . will be best supported by . . . neither invading the equal rights of any Sect, nor suffering any Sect to invade those of another."

In a further flourish on the theme of taking alarm at "the first experiment on our liberties," Madison characterized Patrick Henry's "General Assessments" bill not only as unwise and unjust, but as "a signal of persecution" because "it degrades from the equal rank of Citizens all those whose opinions in Religion do not bend to those of the Legislative authority. Distant as it may be in its present form from the Inquisition, it differs from it only in degree. The one is the first step, the other the last in the career of intolerance." Madison insisted that this freedom of conscience also extended to unbelievers. He wrote, "While we assert for ourselves a freedom to embrace, to profess and to observe the Religion which we believe to be of divine origin, we cannot deny any equal freedom to those whose minds have not yet yielded to the evidence which has convinced us."

Sensing the tide was moving with him, Madison reintroduced Jefferson's 1779 Bill for Religious Freedom and, in January, 1786, it passed by a vote of sixty-to-twenty-seven. In an attempt to give some kind of official recognition to Christianity, some assemblymen tried to insert an acknowledgment of "Jesus Christ, the holy author of our religion." Though Jefferson himself was in Paris at the time, he followed the progress of the debate closely in correspondence with Madison, and he took pleasure in the fact that this effort "was rejected by a great majority, in proof that they meant to comprehend, within the mantle of its protection, the Jew and the Gentile, the Christian and the Mahometan, the Hindoo, the infidel of every denomination."

Virginia's resolution of the issue was neither unique nor universal. At the time of the framing of the Constitution, other states had also rejected all establishment of religion. No state any longer had a European-style establishment of a single denomination, but several provided support to multiple denominations. Still, when the time came to draw up a constitution to guide the new nation, belief that government ought to sever all official ties with religion was becoming increasingly common. This sentiment did not arise from a hostility toward religion, but from a conviction that both religion and government, as well as individuals with their unalienable rights, would best flourish under such an arrangement.

IN KEEPING WITH their determination to separate religion and government, the framers wrote a constitution that was entirely secular. Unlike the Declaration of Independence—which, it should be noted, speaks of "nature's God," rather than of a God associated with the Bible—the Constitution does not mention God, though it implicitly acknowledges Christian culture by identifying its date as "the Year of our Lord one thousand, seven hundred and eighty-seven" and by noting that Sundays are not to be counted among the ten days during which the President can veto legislation. (Article I, Section 7). The only other mention of religion in the original document, before the addition of the Bill of Rights, is found in Article VI, which states that "no religious test shall ever be required as a qualification to any office or public trust under the United States."

At the time, the constitutions of several states required that public officials be Christians, and even that they acknowledge the divine inspiration of Scripture. It is likely that many of the framers could hardly imagine that a non-Christian would be elected to office. Still, the secular nature of the Constitution was no accident, nor did it go unnoticed, and "no religious test" was well understood to extend beyond the boundaries of "general Christianity." One delegate complained "that in a Christian country, it would be at least decent to hold out some distinction between the professors of Christianity and downright infidelity or paganism." A group of Massachusetts and New Hampshire ministers complained to George Washington that no "explicit acknowledgment of THE TRUE ONLY GOD AND JESUS CHRIST who he sent" had been "inserted somewhere in the Magna Carta of our country." A North Carolina minister warned that the absence of a Christian oath would constitute "an invitation for Jews and pagans of every kind to come among us." And, during the ratification process, a New Hampshire man observed that, without a religious test, "A Turk, a Jew, a Roman Catholic, and what is worse than all, a Universalist, may be President of the United States."

For their part, the few Jews in America expressed gratitude, thanking George Washington for his part in creating a government that "enfranchised us with all the privileges and immunities of free citizens, and initiated us into the grand mass of legislative mechanism." Constitutional scholar William Lee Miller has written that "in the framing of Article VI, . . . the new nation was electing to be non-religious in its civil life."

Madison, the "Father of the Constitution," at first saw no need for amendments securing particular liberties, but Jefferson and others soon convinced him of the value of spelling out certain rights. Given Jefferson's convictions, it is hardly surprising that, when he began to draw up the list of amendments that would come to be known as the Bill of Rights, he chose religion to be the first freedom. After careful deliberation, the First Amendment was formulated to proclaim that "Congress shall make no law respecting an establishment of religion, nor prohibiting the free exercise thereof. . . ."

This monumental declaration of religious freedom was written in a spirit of neutrality, not hostility, toward religion. The new government was to be neutral among the competing religious denominations, denying to each the privilege of establishment. The Founding Fathers were cosmopolitan intellectuals devoted to the rationalism of the Enlightenment, but they were not, for the most part, humanistic atheists. On the contrary, they regarded religion and morality as indispensable to a healthy state. It should be noted that the federal Constitution did not deny the individual states the right to support a religious establishment. The First Amendment applied only to the national government, not to state governments. Indeed, when the Constitution was written in 1787, nine of the thirteen states had some form of establishment. By 1789, when the First Amendment was composed, four of those states had ended all tax support of religion, and prominent voices in the remaining states had spoken against establishment. Clearly, the tide was running in favor of severing formal ties between church and state. But the Constitution did not prohibit continuation—or initiation—of such ties. Still, those whose views prevailed did in fact believe that the state and the church should be separate at both the state and federal levels.

That this was Jefferson's intent is made clear in a letter to the Danbury (Connecticut) Baptist Association in 1802, the second year of his presidency. At that time, and indeed until 1818, Connecticut had a form of establishment under which denominations approved by a majority of the voters in a community could receive tax monies. According to the law, those who could prove they belonged to one of the nonestablished churches could be exempted from paying the church tax. But Baptists, who typically opposed all forms of establishment, did not like the system, and wrote the president to ask that he use his influence to discourage it. Though Jefferson could do little about the Connecticut law, he did take the opportunity to put his convictions on record. In his sympathetic response, he said, "I contemplate with solemn reverence that act of the whole American people which declared that their legislature should 'make no law respecting an establishment of religion, or prohibiting the free exercise thereof,' thus building *a wall of separation between Church & State.*" (Emphasis added.)

Today, supporters of strict separation of the two institutional orders point to Jefferson's famous metaphor as the shining example of the "original intent" of the founders. Those who think the framers would have been appalled at the extent to which religious content has been excluded from state-related institutions tend to dismiss the Danbury letter as nothing more than an incidental document of which entirely too much has been made. Chief Justice William Rehnquist, for example, has characterized Jefferson's comment as "a short note of courtesy" that should not be taken too seriously.

On close inspection, it appears the separationists have the correct interpretation of Jefferson's letter. Far from dashing off a perfunctory mollifying letter to a disgruntled group of sectarians, the president regarded his response to their appeal as a signal opportunity to reiterate his long-standing convictions. So concerned was he to strike just the right tone that he asked Attorney General Levi Lincoln to review what he had written. In his note to Lincoln, he observed that he liked to use such letters as a means "of sowing useful truths and principles among the people, which might germinate and become rooted among their political tenets." More specifically, he said that the Danbury letter "furnishes an occasion, too, which I have long wished to find, of saying why I do not proclaim fastings and thanksgivings, as my predecessors did." Jefferson did not imagine his letter would please everyone. "I know," he said, that "it will give offence to the New England clergy [who benefitted from establishment]; but the advocate of religious freedom is to expect neither peace nor forgiveness from them." Attorney General Lincoln excised from the original draft Jefferson's comments about fasting and thanksgiving proclamations—it would have likely cost Jefferson much-needed votes in New England—but the "wall of separation" stood, as Jefferson intended.

A more systematic thinker than Jefferson, Madison hewed an even straighter line. During his presidency (1809–1817), he issued proclamations encouraging prayer and fasting, but later set forth five reasons why he had been mistaken to do so and noted that he had always made them "merely recommendatory." Similarly, he condoned tax support of congressional chaplains, then later rejected this as "a palpable violation of . . . Constitutional principles." As for military chaplains, Madison believed they served a worthwhile purpose, but thought they should be supported by their respective denominations rather than from the public coffers. In the main, Madison was remarkably consistent. As president, he argued that ministers should not even be identified as such in the census, because he thought singling them out might constitute unlawful governmental interference in religion.

Shortly after leaving the presidency, Madison observed in a letter to a friend that the civil government performed ably without interference from the church and that "the number, the industry and the morality of the priesthood, and the devotion of the people have been manifestly increased

by the total separation of the church from the state." Madison fully recognized, of course, that he and the framers had forged a new arrangement
between church and state. He called it a "decisive test" of the new political
order. He also thought America would pass that test.

IN THE FOLLOWING decades, various attempts were made to gain some
official recognition and status for Christianity. Again and again, those efforts
failed. Still, there is little question that the dominant cultural ethos of the
nation strongly reflected that of its Protestant Christian majority. Sunday
laws and blasphemy statutes either went unchallenged or, if challenged, were
upheld by the courts. Likewise, education in the public schools had a Protestant Christian flavor, with prayer and Bible reading common in many
schools and learning materials themselves infused with Christian teaching.

Significant immigration, beginning in the 1830s and 1840s and surging
enormously after the Civil War and on into the twentieth century, changed
the ethnic and cultural make-up of the nation, and as new religions such as
Mormonism, Seventh Day Adventism, and Christian Science arose, this tacit
Protestant hegemony inevitably created friction. When, for example, Roman Catholics complained about the use of the King James Bible and the
Protestant version of the Lord's Prayer in school devotional exercises, since
both differed somewhat from their preferred versions and since the Roman
Catholic church did not encourage the reading of Scripture without clerical
guidance, they were subjected to ridicule and, occasionally, to physical
abuse. Jews raised similar complaints against the schools and also against
being forced by Sunday laws to close their businesses two days a week if they
observed their own Sabbath.

Sunday laws proved quite durable, but by the end of the nineteenth century, several states began to declare school devotional exercises unconstitutional, typically declaring that the purpose of public schools is secular education, and that forcing unwilling students, usually Catholics, to participate in
Protestant exercises subjects them to a stigma and puts them at a disadvantage
in the school. When Catholics organized private schools to protect their
religious beliefs, the states uniformly decreed that parochial schools should
not receive public funds.

Despite moving generally toward greater separation of church and state,
the individual states continued to vary considerably in their practices and
policies. It was not until 1940, in the case known as *Cantwell v. Connecticut,*
that the federal government, through the Supreme Court, formally declared
the First Amendment stipulations regarding religion to be binding on the
states. Over the next twenty-five years, the Supreme Court wrestled with
the meaning and scope of Jefferson's famous "wall of separation between

church and state" metaphor. But that process did not begin immediately. In another 1940 case, *Minersville School District v. Gobitis,* the Court ruled that schools did not have to excuse Jehovah's Witness children from reciting the Pledge of Allegiance, which violated their convictions. Feeling this decision had given them license to do so, irate citizens subjected Witnesses to widespread persecution that included humiliating and expelling children from school, burning down a house of worship, running Witness families out of town, and at least one case of castration.

Fortunately, just three years after this affront to First Amendment guarantees of freedom of conscience, the Court, whose composition and sentiment had changed somewhat, accepted a similar case, involving the refusal of Jehovah's Witness children to participate in flag-saluting exercises in West Virginia schools. This time, the court reversed its decision in *Gobitis* and upheld the right of citizens to abstain from any such practices that offended the teachings of their religion or the dictates of their conscience. That decision has been repeatedly sustained.

The cases involving Jehovah's Witnesses undergirded what has come to be called the "Free Exercise clause" of the First Amendment—"Congress shall make no law . . . prohibiting the free exercise [of religion]." In 1947, the Court heard a case that laid a firm foundation for its future decisions on the amendment's "Establishment clause"—"Congress shall make no law respecting an establishment of religion." The case, *Everson v. the Board of Education of Ewing Township, New Jersey,* involved a challenge to a policy under which the local government reimbursed parents for the cost of transporting their children to parochial schools on public buses. Writing for the majority, Justice Hugo Black said, "The 'establishment of religion' clause of the First Amendment means at least this: Neither a state nor the Federal Government can set up a church. Neither can pass laws which aid one religion, aid all religions, or prefer one religion over another. . . . No tax in any amount, large or small, can be levied to support any religious activities or institutions, whatever they may be called, or whatever form they may adopt to teach or practice religion." Black capped off this summary by asserting that, "In the words of Jefferson, the clause against establishment of religion by law was intended to erect a 'wall of separation between Church and State.'

Despite some subsequent inconsistencies, these cases enabled the Supreme Court to develop what constitutional scholars refer to as a "bright-line" or clear test on matters "respecting an establishment of religion." Basically, after the 1947 Everson decision, if religion, a religious practice, or a religious institution received any support or sponsorship from a public institution, the Court was likely to decide that the First Amendment had been violated. By far the most famous—or infamous—practices to fail the Court's "bright-line" separatist test were prayer and Bible reading in the public schools, which were deemed unacceptable in 1962 and 1963. Writing for the court in the 1963 case, *Abington v. Schempp,* Justice Tom Clark asserted that, to be valid, any enactment by a government body must have "a secular legislative purpose and a primary effect that neither advances nor inhibits religion." Afterward those two "tests" would be regularly applied in establishment cases.

In 1971, in a case called *Lemon v. Kurtzman,* a third test was added to these two. The case involved arrangements in Rhode Island and Pennsylvania whereby the state paid part of the salaries of teachers who taught "secular" subjects in parochial schools. In finding the arrangement unacceptable, the Court expressed its fear that, since most of the schools receiving the aid were Roman Catholic, the Catholic religion might be "advanced" by this practice. Ironically, scrupulous efforts by state-paid administrators of the program to make sure teachers did not introduce religious content into the classes led to the Court's main objection: that such monitoring constituted "excessive entanglement with religion" by the state. Subsequently, "excessive entanglement with religion" was added to the two earlier tests, and the three-pronged "Lemon Test" became the standard measure of establishment. If a law or practice failed any one of the three tests, it was deemed unconstitutional.

Despite the Court's search for a serviceable "bright-line test," Chief Justice Warren Burger candidly admitted in his opinion on *Lemon* that "the line of separation . . . is a blurred, indistinct, and variable barrier." And indeed, since the *Lemon* case, the Court has manifested considerable inconsistency in its decisions regarding the establishment of religion, with some going one way and some another, and a number by five-to-four decisions. As Constitutional scholar A. E. Dick Howard observed after reviewing a number of such cases, "The casual reader of opinions that draw such seemingly fine distinctions may be forgiven if he thinks that he has stumbled into the forest of Hansel and Gretel, the birds having eaten all the crumbs that mark the way out."

The Court has been more consistent, thus far, in its demand that public schools not sponsor religious observation or exercise. In 1980, it ruled that public schools could no longer display copies of the Ten Commandments openly, not only because the Commandments are inextricably associated with Judaism and Christianity, but also because commandments prohibiting the worship of other gods and the making of graven images, as well as the injunction to keep the Sabbath, conflict directly with the teachings of some religions and are regarded as irrelevant by nonbelievers. In 1985, in *Wallace v. Jaffree,* the Court once again ruled against school prayer exercises, declaring that Alabama's mandated minute of silence for prayer or meditation was unconstitutional because it was a deliberate effort to encourage religious activity. The Court's majority opinion cited more than two hundred cases that it regarded as having set abundant precedent for its decision.

Schools and school-related activities have been a major battleground for church-state issues both because they involve children, about whose welfare parents typically care deeply, and because education is mandated by the state and under continuing state supervision. Thus, according to the Supreme Court, anything involving religion within school jurisdiction inevitably involves a relationship between church and state. Another source of hot dispute has been public sponsorship of religious symbolism. In a highly publicized 1984 case, the Court narrowly (again, five to four) approved of city-sponsored manger scenes at Christmastime—but only when the crèche is part of a larger display that includes such nonreligious objects as Santa Claus, reindeer, and Christmas trees, all of which may be viewed as exemplifying "a friendly community spirit of good will in keeping with the season." Once again writing for the majority, Chief Justice Burger gave examples of "an unbroken history of official acknowledgment by all three branches of government of the role of religion in American life from at least 1789." Such a history, he concluded, should not be abrogated by "absolutist" applications of the Establishment Clause. Writing for the minority, Justice William Brennan observed that, while no great offense might be involved in such an eclectic display of a crèche, the Court's willingness to permit "official acknowledgment" of entrenched traditions might imply favoritism toward dominant religious beliefs and practices.

Critics of Supreme Court decisions on establishment cases have sometimes accused the Court of stifling free exercise of religion, which is also guaranteed by the First Amendment. They assert that those who want to exercise their religion by praying and reading the Bible are told it is against the law. In fact, the Court's position is that citizens are quite free to read the Bible and pray, but not with state sponsorship. And even in some of its most unpopular decisions, the Court has made clear its general support not only of religious freedom but of religion itself.

In the 1962 *Engel v. Vitale* decision, which banned institutionally sponsored prayer in the schools, Justice Black directly addressed the question of whether the decision "indicate[s] a hostility toward religion or toward prayer." His response was that "nothing, of course, could be more wrong. The history of man is inseparable from the history of religion." He noted that America was founded by believers who sought to worship God according to the dictates of their conscience, and that the framers of the Constitution "knew that the First Amendment, which tried to put an end to governmental control of religion and of prayer, was not written to destroy either."

Similarly, in *Abington v. Schempp*, the 1963 decision that banned school

Bible-reading exercises, Justice Tom Clark asserted that "one's education is not complete without a study of comparative religion or the history of religion and its relationship to the advancement of civilization," and that such study, along with the study of the Bible as literature and history, has a legitimate place in the public schools. "The place of religion in our society," he concluded, "is an exalted one, achieved through a long tradition of reliance on the home, the church and the inviolable citadel of the individual heart and mind. We have come to recognize through bitter experience that it is not within the power of government to invade that citadel, whether its purpose or effect be to aid or oppose, to advance or retard. In the relationship between man and religion, the State is firmly committed to a position of neutrality."

The continuing struggle between accommodationists and separationists has two foci: what the "original intent" of the framers actually was, and how much that should matter. Neither issue is capable of easy resolution. The Constitution did not descend from heaven on the back of a dove but was hammered out in numerous, often acrimonious, and, at the Constitutional Convention itself, secret meetings. Its formulation and ratification were accompanied not only by reasoned debate but also by vituperous charges and countercharges in speeches, newspapers, pamphlets, and doggerel poetry. It achieved ratification with the aid of compromise, strategic craft, and at least a measure of cynical political maneuvering. Though a great document, it was written by fallible men who disagreed with one another on key points, and it achieved passage over the strenuous objection of a sizable proportion of the population. Given that history, it is hardly surprising that earnest and honest people may disagree about the original intent of the framers of the Constitution. With respect to church and state, it appears that the most influential of the framers, with James Madison as the leading figure, were strict separationists. It is equally clear that many of their colleagues would surely have fallen into the accommodationist camp.

The second issue—whether or not "original intent" is important—is similarly problematic. Characterizing the Constitution as the Scripture of American civil religion, Sanford Levinson uses the Fundamentalist Protestant and Roman Catholic attitudes toward the Bible as models of the two major modes of interpreting the Constitution. In the Fundamentalist Protestant mode, the original document (Bible/Constitution), as originally written, is the binding authority. Moreover, every individual has the right to construe the original meaning according to his or her own best lights. In the Catholic mode, the original document is augmented and shaped by "tradition," the equally authoritative interpretation of the Supreme Court (the equivalent, in this comparison, to the Roman Catholic Magisterium). As the Protestant interpretation of Scripture resulted in an explosion of sects, each convinced of its own correctness, a strict "Protestant" interpretation of the Constitution would result in political anarchy. For that reason, most judges understandably prefer a "Catholic" approach, which allows for development and change in interpretation in response to changing social and political conditions, and which acknowledges the Supreme Court as the final arbiter of what the Constitution means today, which may differ from what it meant in 1789. Levinson calls for an intermediate approach that would allow for some change and development, but always in the light of careful and respectful attention to the original meaning.

Few would contend that the Constitution is an infallible document, written on tables of stone by the finger of God. Its acceptance of slavery should by itself disprove that. Its framers, however, understood the need for change and set forth orderly mechanisms for achieving it. Few would argue that amendments ending slavery and giving women and former slaves the vote did not improve on the original document. Similarly, amendments giving citizens the right to vote directly for their senators, limiting the number of terms a president can serve, or changing the voting age from twenty-one to eighteen were all efforts to effect improvements in an ever-evolving republic. And even amendments eighteen and twenty-one, instituting and then abolishing Prohibition, attest to the nation's ability both to undertake a major social experiment and then to declare it a failure. These changes, following rather complex and lengthy procedures, are generally accepted as valid alterations to the supreme law of the land. In marked contrast, it is troubling when major questions of constitutionality are decided by five-to-four votes, and when citizens understand that the "supreme law" can change quite suddenly with the appointment of only one or two new justices.

IN LIGHT OF the historical record and the still-unsettled nature of the debate between separationists and accommodationists, what lessons may we reasonably draw?

As a basic premise, we must remember that the Founding Fathers intended that the state be neutral toward all religions, but did not intend that religious people or their organizations be neutralized, their voices restricted to private matters only. Of course, religious people have a right to be involved in political activity, and they cannot be expected to leave their religious convictions behind when they enter the political arena. They have a right to organize themselves to work effectively for the good of their country as they understand it, and that understanding will inevitably be informed by their religious faith. Jews and Christians of every description, as well as

Buddhists and Muslims and Hindus and secular humanists, drawing on the values and beliefs of their religious or secular traditions, may all legitimately work to shape public policy, within the limits of the Constitution which has served us so admirably in avoiding society-rending religious conflict.

There are, however, real and reasonable limits to that shaping process. The most important of these is that a religious body does not have the right, simply because it may be in the majority or better organized than other groups, to bind its specifically religious doctrines on others or to require that others help pay for the propagation of those doctrines. It also makes sense to draw the line at political partisanship. If a church or other religious body enjoys immunity from taxation because it is theoretically not subject to the state, then it seems reasonable to demand that, beyond expressions of principle and policy, churches not engage in partisanship by endorsing candidates or parties, lest such activities result in the corruption of both the political and religious institutions.

Further, religious individuals and groups ought also to respect and honor the valuable principle of pluralism. This does not mean that all values are up for grabs and that no value position is to be preferred over another. Rather, it means that our society is one in which "any number can play," in the belief that a multiplicity of views contributes not to chaos, but to a rich and diverse republic. (It has also contributed mightily to a free-market environment in religion that helps account for the amazing vitality of American churches, a vitality unmatched by any other comparably modern society.) As James Madison observed more than two hundred years ago, "In a free government the security for civil rights must be the same as that for religious rights; it consists in the one case in the multiplicity of interests and in the other in the multiplicity of sects."

Political zealots sometimes seem to suggest that only one political party has a legitimate claim on the American heritage. The Founding Fathers saw that attitude as dangerous. The system of checks and balances they built into the Constitution was informed not only by the recognition that good citizens may differ over the proper course of action, but also, at least in part, by the biblical understanding of humans as fallible and prone to wrongdoing and therefore frequently in need of some healthy opposition from their fellows. Nobody, in their view, has a corner on Truth, Justice, and the American Way. Christians should recognize, in justified humility, that there is no single Christian position on many, perhaps most, social issues. Intelligent, informed, sincere Christians may honestly differ not only with unbelievers, but also among themselves and adherents of other religions, as to what God or whatever powers govern the universe think about such issues as abortion, the distribution of wealth among nations, the legitimacy of a particular political regime, or the desirability of a given weapons system.

America has been remarkably favored—blessed, if you prefer—by a wise constitutional policy of nonpreferential protection for the free and responsible exercise of religion. For the good of the entire community of Americans, religious and secular alike, we should protect that policy against encroachments from whatever quarter. Each generation must redraw the line of separation between the rights of religion and the rights of civil authority. It matters a great deal when there are flagrant violations of this boundary. We understand that. We must remind ourselves again and again that the best way to prevent such flagrant violations is to watch diligently for apparently minor ones, to "take alarm at the first experiment upon our liberties" (as Madison put it), to look out not only for the interests of our own parochial group, but for the interests of the entire community. That process often involves standing up for the rights of minorities, even though we may find them disagreeable.

In the political arena, if *they,* whoever "they" are, cheat, lie, or deceive, then *we,* whoever "we" are, have every right to complain, oppose, and expose "them." If, however, "they" play by the rules, then "we" should not cry foul when those whose views displease us organize themselves into an effective political force. Instead, we should play by the same rules and organize ourselves into an effective counterforce, to see who can persuade the most people. If we are the ones who prevail, who gain power, we should exercise it with humility and fear, recognizing always its tendency to corrupt its possessors and the causes they represent. If we feel certain we are right, we should recall that certainty can also corrupt, and that absolute certainty corrupts powerfully.

We cannot separate religion and politics. The question is how they are to be related in such a way as to maintain the pluralism that has served us so well. The core of that pluralism is not the dogma that all opinions are equally valid but the conviction that civility and the public peace are important, that respect for minorities and their opinions is a crucial element of a democratic society, and that, however persuaded I am of the rightness of my position, I may still, after all, be wrong.

AFTERWORD

A Permanent Fixture on the American Political Landscape

Since 1996, when this book and the companion PBS television documentary series first appeared, the Christian Right has undergone significant change and development. The Christian Coalition, the most notable organization at that time, is a shadow of its former self. It claims to have distributed 70 million voter guides during the 2004 campaign, but it has active organizations in only a handful of states and exhibits little grassroots clout. Pat Robertson has less obvious political power but communicates his views daily to hundreds of thousands via his *700 Club* broadcast. Jerry Falwell appears frequently on talk shows as a senior spokesman for the Religious Right but has not been able to build a worthy successor to the Moral Majority. Both Robertson and Falwell, however, continue to have an impact through the universities they founded, training young conservatives for leadership positions in the movement.

Gary Bauer remains active as head of an organization called American Values, and the Family Research Council, which he once headed, continues as an important source and distributor of thoughtful and influential conservative data and publications. Dr. James Dobson's Focus on the Family remains quite strong, but Dobson's tendency to demand perfection from those he supports limits his effectiveness in a realm in which compromise and negotiation are vital components.

When Ralph Reed resigned from the Christian Coalition in 1997 to open a political consulting firm, many observers thought his heyday was past, especially after candidates he advised made a poor showing in the 1998 elections. But Reed soon became an adviser to George W. Bush and in 2002, as head of the Georgia Republican Party organization, engineered a stunning Republican victory in which an incumbent Democratic governor and senator were defeated with the aid of a strong mobilization of Christian conservatives. After continued success in the 2004 election—he led the Bush campaign in the Southeast—Reed gave signs that he might consider running for lieutenant governor in the next election. Success in that office could plausibly lead to the governorship, a platform from which a leap to the White House is not without precedent.

Reed's transition from an explicitly Christian organizer and spokesman to a more mainstream practical political operative is mirrored in the maturing of the conservative Christian movement overall. Many who were recruited into politics by the Christian Right no longer see the need to wear that label. They are simply Republicans, now possessing far more sophistication and knowledge of how the political system works, and their influence in the party continues to grow. Pollster Andrew Kohut estimated that white evangelical Christians made up 37 percent of the Republican Party in 2004. More important, according to *Campaigns and Elections* magazine, they dominate Republican Party organizations in at least eighteen states and have substantial minority influence in at least twenty-six other state Republican organizations—all but six northeastern states and the District of Columbia.

Christian conservatives have not gotten all they seek, but their prospects for continued gain give them reason for optimism. In the Republican-majority Congress in place in January 2005, the top echelon of Republican leaders in both the House and the Senate received approval ratings of 87 percent to 100 percent on the 2004 Christian Coalition Scorecard, indicating their vote on issues of key interest to Christian conservatives; the highest score received by their Democratic counterparts was 16 percent. With few exceptions, the Scorecard assigned similar scores to Republicans and Democrats throughout both houses of Congress.

The effects of the growing cohort of legislators favorable to Christian Right positions are reflected in significant policy decisions and initiatives, both domestic and international. Christian conservatives have worked tirelessly at both state and federal levels to limit abortions by pressing for statutes that prohibit "partial birth" abortions, require minors to obtain parental consent for abortions, require doctors to tell women seeking an abortion that their unborn child would feel the pain of the procedure, and deny funding to organizations and nations that regard abortion as an acceptable part of family planning or population control. In large measure because of opposition from the Religious Right, the United States has canceled or severely reduced contributions to the UN Population Fund, jeopardizing a program that provides contraceptives to nearly 1.4 million women in 150 countries.

Pressure from Christian conservatives also led to legislation stipulating that all federal monies for sex education in U.S. schools ($167 million in 2004) go to abstinence-only programs that are forbidden to provide information about contraceptive options. In a similar spirit, Congress currently requires that one-third of all funds allocated to the global HIV/AIDS pandemic ($2.9 billion in 2004) be spent on abstinence-only programs rather than for such proven disease-reduction measures as instruction about safe sex and provision of condoms.

In keeping with other key concerns, Christian conservatives have vigorously lobbied for legislation that would impose sanctions on countries that persecute or limit the freedom of Christians to worship and evangelize. They pressured Congress to pass the International Religious Freedom Act in late 1998, creating a White House office for reporting religious persecution worldwide and allowing the president to choose from a variety of measures to punish offending countries.

In a more controversial realm, Christian conservatives constantly lobby Congress and the White House to side with Israel in its struggle with the Palestinians. The key to understanding this phenomenon is widespread— though not universal—adherence among evangelicals to dispensationalist premillennialism (see pages 7–8), a doctrinal scheme that includes belief that a complete restoration of the nation of Israel in all of "Judea and Samaria" (the West Bank) is a prerequisite to the Second Coming of Christ and the establishment of his millennial reign. While overlooking the irony that this scenario also envisions a mass conversion of Jews, Jewish leaders have welcomed the efforts of America's evangelical Christians to bolster Israel's defense against hostile neighbors. In April 1998, when Israeli Prime Minister Benjamin Netanyahu addressed a Washington audience of 3,000 people attending a Voices United for Israel conference, of whom at least two-thirds were evangelical Christians, he observed that "we have no greater friends and allies than the people sitting in this room." Underscoring the accuracy of that assessment, Jerry Falwell responded, "There are about 200,000 evangelical pastors in America, and we're asking them all, through e-mail, faxes, letters, telephone, to go into their pulpits and use their influence in support of the state of Israel and the Prime Minister."

Even more significant to evangelical Republican legions than their strength in Congress is their confidence that President George W. Bush is, like them, a Bible-believing, born-again Christian who shares virtually all their bedrock convictions. His recovery from alcohol abuse and his repentance and return to church and the Bible, a new birth midwifed at least in part by Billy Graham, provide him with venerable credentials. His decisive demarcations between good and evil and his with-us-or-against-us rhetoric echo the preaching they hear in their churches Sunday after Sunday. Add to that his professed reliance on prayer, his apparent conviction that God has expressly brought him to office to accomplish great things, and his ability to sound the notes of familiar hymns and catch the cadences of Scripture in his better speeches, and one can understand why millions of evangelical Christians have no doubt that George W. Bush is indeed "The Real Deal" and, like God, is on their side.

Coincidentally, I write these words on the day President Bush begins his second term in office, after an election in which evangelical Christians provided crucial core support. Unlike Ronald Reagan, whom they still revere but who offered only symbolic support to most of the key items on their agenda, Bush seems committed to delivering on a number of their key concerns. Appearing on the National Public Radio program *Fresh Air* on Inauguration Day, Dr. Richard Land, President of the Ethics and Religious Liberty Commission of the Southern Baptist Convention, said, "We are expecting him to keep his campaign promises. This president did not run an 'It's morning in America' campaign like Ronald Reagan did. He ran a very specific policy-oriented campaign, laid out a whole series of proposals in his acceptance speech, campaigned on those issues, and said, 'If you reelect me, I will do this and this and this.' And we expect him, and not only expect him, we are fully confident that he will. This is a conviction politician."

Though concern about terrorism, the war in Iraq, and the economy loomed largest in most voters' minds, some of Bush's strongest support came from evangelical Christians for whom abortion and homosexuality still trump other issues a fact fully exploited by Bush's campaign manager Karl Rove. They cherish his support of abstinence-only sex education and his calls for a "culture of life" that restricts not only abortions but stem-cell research as well. They applaud his call for a Defense of Marriage Amendment to the Constitution to override decisions by state legislatures or courts to permit same-sex marriage. They cheer his determination to support "faith-based" social services with state and federal funds. They also place great hope in the likelihood that he will have opportunity to appoint several justices to the Supreme Court, justices who might shift the balance in the Court sufficiently to overturn *Roe v. Wade* and remove what many on the Religious Right increasingly regard as an illegitimate wall of separation between church and state. Tearing down that wall, they believe, would preserve "under God" in the Pledge of Allegiance, permit the display of the Bible and the Ten Commandments in courthouses and other public buildings, return the practice of prayer and Bible reading to public schools, and allow churches to become more overtly involved in partisan political organization. Some even hope for official designation of America as a Christian Nation.

Whether and which such dreams will be fulfilled remains to be seen. Congressional Democrats may still be able to block the appointment of some judges whose views they regard as unacceptable. But soon after his party's gains in the November 2004 elections, Bush announced his intention to resubmit to Congress the nominations of a slate of judicial candidates whose confirmation had been rejected or held up during the previous session. Assuming he will serve a full second term, it appears likely that Bush will, by the end of that term, have appointed more federal judges than any president in American history. This will have wide-ranging and long-lasting effects.

Critics of President Bush and his close ties to the conservative Christian segment of his party may hope that his successor, even if a Republican, will espouse more moderate views. Richard Land warned that they will be disappointed. "Let me bring some really bad news to some of your listeners," he said to *Fresh Air* host Terry Gross. "The next Republican nominee for president will look an awful lot like George W. Bush, because George W. Bush is the product of long-term cultural and historic forces. . . . This debate is *over* in the Republican Party, state by state. . . . If a social moderate, [even though an] economic and foreign policy conservative, wants to run for president in 2008, fine, let them. They won't win a primary west of the Hudson."

Though not a juggernaut that can level all opposition, the Religious Right is clearly a formidable movement with a powerful set of resources. Enmeshed in webs of churches and clergy, reinforced by the intense personal networks common in congregations, and exposed repeatedly to a clear theological and political message in sermons, religious publications, direct mail, television, and talk radio, its members tend to have a missionary zeal seldom matched by those on the left and almost never by the more moderate middle. Even more important, they are determined not to give up the fight, especially since they seem to be winning more and more rounds. Speaking for the movement while still with the Christian Coalition, Ralph Reed said, "We want to be a permanent fixture on the American political landscape. We are going to stay and stay and stay. If it takes three presidents and six Congresses to pass these items, we're going to be there in the morning, we're going to be there in the evening when they turn the lights out. We will be there as long as it takes to see that these issues are addressed."

Over the past twenty-five years, since the rise of the Moral Majority, critics and other observers of the Religious Right have declared that the movement had reached its peak and gone into inevitable decline, only to be surprised by its continued gains. It is, of course, possible for a movement to overreach, to stir a backlash that will blunt its effectiveness. Some of the fierce opposition to the Bush–Cheney ticket in 2004, often self-described as "anybody but Bush," clearly signaled such a response, as do serious attempts by Democrats to rethink their message and strategies, and efforts by pundits to analyze a deepening polarization within American society. Whatever the future, it has become abundantly clear that anyone who expects to make sense of American politics, domestic or foreign, over the short or long term, must acknowledge that religious conservatives have become an enduring and important part of the social, cultural, and political landscape. I have written this book to help explain how that happened.

AS NOTED ABOVE, this book is the companion volume to a PBS television documentary series of the same name, conceived and produced by Calvin Skaggs and David Van Taylor of Lumiere Productions. The book is neither a script nor a transcript of the series but a closely coordinated and complementary product based on the same body of material. Neither the documentary nor the book takes an adversarial approach. Our mutual aim has been to represent, as accurately and fairly as we are able, the views and statements of the more than one hundred people who have graciously agreed to cooperate in this project by participating in extensive interviews.

We have chosen, in the title of these works, to speak of the movement we describe as the Religious Right. It is not a perfect term, but after much deliberation, we have used it because of its wide recognition in the general population. As the movement has gained detractors and the term becomes less neutral in connotation, some have preferred to call themselves religious or Christian conservatives. I also use these terms, but since the subjects of this study are religious people whose political views do in fact nestle safely on the right side of the political spectrum in this country, I find no serious fault with the term, nor do I mean to use it in any sense other than a descriptive one.

Because such a large portion of the book is based on original interviews, I have elected not to provide footnotes for material taken from these interviews. Unless a footnote specifically indicates otherwise, all statements by named characters in the story are taken from interviews with those individuals. A listing of interviewees is provided at the beginning of the Endnotes section.

Far more than any research project in which I have ever participated, this has truly been a collaborative process, in which all participants have shared our talents, resources, and insights. I gratefully acknowledge my debt to Cal Skaggs, President of Lumiere Productions and Executive Producer of the documentary series, and to Series Producer David Van Taylor for their trust, support, counsel, and friendship. Other members of the Lumiere staff who made invaluable contributions include Jerret Engle, Bennett Singer, LaShaune Fitch, Brad Lichtenstein, Ali Pomeroy, Lynn Mirabito, Lewanne Jones, Gretchen Schwartz, Jason Boughton, Jason Bowen, Lina Cheung, Claudia Gorelick, and David Deschamps. The Lumiere team and I were greatly assisted by advice and feedback from a distinguished advisory group that included Chip Berlet, Michael Cromartie, Frances FitzGerald, John Green, Susan Harding, George Marsden, and Leo Ribuffo.

I am, as always, deeply grateful to my literary agent, Gerard McCauley, who, with Cal Skaggs's agent, Virginia Barber, handled the contact with Broadway Books. Past and present Broadway folk due special thanks include John Sterling, Victoria Andros, Nancy Peske, Rebecca Holland, and, for the current edition, Charles Conrad.

Finally, I proclaim my love and gratitude for Patricia, whose patience, encouragement, and loving companionship no longer surprise me but remain no less a treasure.

ENDNOTES

Unless explicitly indicated, all quotations drawn from interviews conducted by the staff of Lumiere Productions or by William Martin are used without a footnote citation. Interviews with Billy Graham were conducted by William Martin in connection with his book *A Prophet with Honor: The Billy Graham Story* (New York: William Morrow, 1991). The following individuals were interviewed expressly for the book and the series of *With God on Our Side*:

Melody G. Albert
Dr. Jimmy Allen
Carl A. Anderson
Gary L. Bauer
Dr. William Billings
Morton Blackwell
Father Jon Braun
Kenneth Briggs
Dr. Harold O.J. Brown
Reverend Phil Campbell
John Carr
Sam Clark
Charles W. Colson
John Conlan
Matt Cothern
Harvey Cox
David W. Cunningham
Jerry Curry
Dr. Evelyn K. Davis
Ruth Davis
Michael Deaver
E.J. Dionne, Jr.
Dr. Edward G. Dobson
John Dowless
Dr. Donald J. Dunlap
Dr. James M. Dunn
Michael Edds
Stuart Eizenstat
Marlene D. Elwell
Dr. Jerry Falwell
Elmer Fike
Charlotte Gaylor
John Gilman
Father Peter Gillquist
William E. Godsey
Nancy Godsey
Dr. A. Pierre Guillermin
Dr. Os Guinness
Dr. Billy James Hargis
Billy James Hargis, Jr.
Senator Mark O. Hatfield
Dr. Carl F.H. Henry
Pastor Edward V. Hill
Michael S. Horton
Eleanor Howe
Cynthia Karraker Brazil
Bobbie Greene
Matthew M. Kinsolving
Dr. C. Everett Koop
Drs. Tim and Beverly LaHaye

Dr. Harold I. Leif
Reverend Jim Lewis
Kathryn Long
Dr. Robert L. Maddox
Ira Manhoff
Connaught "Connie" Marshner
Martin Mawyer
Bill McCartney
James T. McKenna
Leigh Ann Metzger
Udo W. Middelman
James Muffett
Alice W. Moore
David Noebel
Grover G. Norquist
R. Marc Nuttle
Sharon Overcast
Rebecca Owen
Pat Hart
Kathy Potera
Jody Powell
Claudia Ramsey
Dr. Ralph Reed
Jerry P. Regier
Dr. M.G. "Pat" Robertson
Reverend Haywood Robinson, Jr.
Dr. Haywood A. Robinson, III
Reverend Dr. Mary E. Robinson
James Robison
Guy Rodgers
Edith Schaeffer
Phyllis Schlafly
Ambassador Peter F. Secchia
Emmett M. Shafer
Barbara Shannon
Constance Snapp DeBord
Carolyn Sundseth
Reverend Kenneth Swanson
Randall Terry
Olivet C. Thaxton
Cal Thomas
M.W. Thornhill
Dr. Elmer Towns
James H. Townsend
David A. Walters
Douglas Wead
Richard Weinhold
Paul M. Weyrich
Dr. Mel White
Faith Whittlesey

Sally R. Williams   John D. Woodbridge
Dr. Virgil A. Wood   Lorinda Wortz

INTRODUCTION: A RIGHTEOUS EMPIRE

PAGE Portions of this chapter have been adapted, with the permission of the respective
      publishers, from the following earlier works by author William Martin: *A Prophet with
      Honor: The Billy Graham Story* (New York: William Morrow, 1991), pp. 32–52; "The
      Transformation of Fundamentalism between the World Wars," in Kenneth Keulman,
      ed., *Critical Moments in Religious History* (Macon, GA: Mercer University Press, 1993),
      pp. 141–160; and "Mass-Communications," in Charles H. Lippy and Peter W. Wil-
      liams, eds., *Encyclopedia of the American Religious Experience: Studies of Traditions and
      Movements* (New York: Charles Scribner's Sons, 1988), Vol. III, pp. 1712–1713.

   2 *For a succinct, helpful discussion of the Puritan influence:* see Kenneth D. Wald, *Religion
      and Politics in the United States* (New York: St. Martin's Press, 1987), pp. 36–48.

   2 *"The New Heaven and the New Earth":* John Cotton, quoted in Harry S. Stout, *The
      New England Soul: Preaching and Religious Culture in Colonial New England* (New York:
      Oxford University Press, 1986), p. 62.

   3 *Edwards on the Millennium:* Jonathan Edwards, *Some Thoughts Concerning the Present
      Revival* (Boston, 1742), quoted in ibid., p. 204.

   3 *Marshall, Voltaire, and Paine on religion in America:* J. Edwin Orr, *The Role of Prayer in
      Spiritual Awakening* (Los Angeles: Oxford Association for Research in Revival, n.d.),
      p. 1, quoted in Lewis Drummond, *A Fresh Look at the Life and Ministry of Charles G.
      Finney* (Minneapolis: Bethany House, 1985), p. 18.

   4 *"Nowhere else . . .":* Kenneth K. Bailey, *Southern White Protestantism in the Twentieth
      Century* (New York: Harper and Row, 1964), p. ix.

   5 *"The great business of the church . . .":* Charles Grandison Finney, "The Pernicious
      Attitude of the Church on the Reforms of the Age," Lectures on Revivals, no. 23,
      The Oberlin Evangelist, January 21, 1846, p. 11. This letter is reprinted in full in
      Donald W. Dayton, *Discovering an Evangelical Heritage* (New York: Harper and Row,
      1976), pp. 20–22.

   5 *"useful in the highest degree possible . . .":* Finney, *Lectures on Revivals of Religion*
      (Cambridge, Mass.: Belknap Press of Harvard University, 1960), p. 404.

   5 *"the millennium may come . . .":* Ibid., p. 306.

   8 *"Moody, save all you can":* D. L. Moody, *New Sermons, Addresses, and Prayers,* p. 535,
      quoted in James F. Findlay, *Dwight L. Moody: American Evangelist 1837–1899* (Chicago:
      University of Chicago Press, 1969), p. 253.

   9 *"With Christ you are saved . . . decide now":* Boston Herald, December 9, 1916, p. 3,
      quoted in William G. McLoughlin, *Modern Revivalism: Charles Grandison Finney to
      Billy Graham* (New York: Ronald Press, 1959), p. 409.

   9 *One dollar to education:* William G. McLoughlin, *Billy Sunday Was His Real Name*
      (Chicago: University of Chicago Press, 1955), p. 121, quoting *Boston Herald,* Novem-
      ber 23, 1916, p. 6.

  11 *The Fundamentals: A Testimony to the Truth,* 12 vols., ed. Amzi Clarence Dixon (1–4),
      Louis Meyer (5–10), and Reuben Archer Torrey (11–12). Originally published 1910–
      1915 in Chicago by Testimony Publishing Company as twelve booklets under the
      auspices of Moody Memorial Church and Moody Bible Institute as initiated and
      underwritten by the Stewart brothers; reorganized by Torrey, combined into four
      volumes, and reissued in 1917 in Los Angeles by the King's Business, later the Bible
      Institute of Los Angeles. Reprinted in four volumes by Baker Book House of Grand
      Rapids, Michigan, 1970. Reprinted in four volumes, with introduction by George
      Marsden, Fundamentalism in American Religion Series (New York and London:
      Garland Pub., 1988).

  11 *The war and biblical criticism associated:* "The International Jew's *perverse accomplish-
      ment* . . .":* McLoughlin, *Billy Sunday,* p. 281.

  12 Leo Ribuffo, *The Old Christian Right: The Protestant Far Right from the Great Depres-
      sion to the Cold War* (Philadelphia: Temple University Press, 1983), p. 12. I am in-
      debted to Professor Ribuffo for much of the discussion of anti-Semitism in this
      chapter.

  13 *"All the ills . . . Genesis":* Maynard Shipley, *The War on Modern Science,* 1927,
      pp. 254–255, as quoted in Richard Hofstadter, *Anti-Intellectualism in American Life*
      (New York: Vintage, 1962), p. 125.

  14 *"the issue should be decided . . .":* Quoted in ibid., p. 128.

PAGE

14 *"Why should the Bible be discarded . . .":* Quoted in Norman Furniss, *The Fundamentalist Controversy, 1918–1931* (Hamden, CT: Archon Books, 1963), p. 122.

14 *Lippmann on Bryan:* Quoted in Hofstadter, *Anti-Intellectualism,* p. 128.

14 *This sketch of the evolution controversy* is based primarily on Furniss, *Fundamentalist Controversy,* pp. 78–100, and Sidney E. Ahlstrom, *A Religious History of the American People* (New Haven: Yale University Press, 1972), pp. 909–910.

14 *Teaching of German banned:* Ribuffo, *The Old Christian Right,* p. 84.

15 *Scopes trial:* Furniss, *Fundamentalist Controversy,* pp. 90–91.

18 *Father Coughlin:* This material is adapted from William Martin, "Mass-Communications," in Charles H. Lippy and Peter W. Williams, eds., *Encyclopedia of the American Religious Experience: Studies of Traditions and Movements* Vol. III (New York: Charles Scribner's Sons, 1988), pp. 1712–1713.

20 *Winrod on FDR:* Ribuffo, *The Old Christian Right,* pp. 102–104.

20 *Winrod runs for U.S. Senate:* Ibid., pp. 119–124; *United States v. Winrod* and *United States v. McWilliams,* Ibid., p. 124, pp. 194–214.

20 *Winrod's last years:* Ibid., p. 231.

20 *Mencken on Smith's oratory:* Ibid., p. 143.

21 *"The Lunatic Fringe":* Ibid., p. 146.

22 *MLK a "revolutionist":* Neil R. McMillen, *The Citizens Council: Organized Resistance to the Second Reconstruction, 1954–1964* (Urbana: University of Illinois Press, 1971), p. 22, quoted in Ribuffo, *The Old Christian Right,* p. 234. Smith's other positions during this period, Ibid.

22 *Smith's last days:* Ibid., p. 236.

CHAPTER 1: BILLY GRAHAM—GEARED TO THE TIMES

Portions of this chapter have been adapted from William Martin, *A Prophet with Honor: The Billy Graham Story* (New York: William Morrow, 1991), with the permission of the publisher.

26 *"We punched them right between the eyes":* William G. McLoughlin, *Billy Graham: Revivalist in a Secular Age* (New York: Ronald Press, 1960), p. 38.

26 *1945 Memorial Day Rally:* "70,000 Attend Memorial Day Rally," *United Evangelical Action,* June 15, 1945; "Billy Graham Tours Country for YFC," *United Evangelical Action,* April 4, 1945; Torrey Johnson, oral history, collection 141, Billy Graham Center Archives.

27 Time *Devoted four columns:* "Youth for Christ," *Time,* February 4, 1946, pp. 46–47.

27 Christian Century *grudgingly acknowledged . . . :* Harold E. Fey, "What About 'Youth for Christ'?" *Christian Century,* LXII (June 20, 1945), p. 731.

29 *"America will stand alone":* Charlotte *Observer,* November 23, 1947.

29 *Sermon excerpts:* The quotations in these paragraphs are from Billy Graham, "We Need Revival!" *Revival in Our Time* (Wheaton: Van Kampen Press, 1950), pp. 69–80.

30 *"Oiltown U.S.A. promotion":* McLoughlin, *Billy Graham.* pp. 98–99. "Mr. Texas" appeared in 1951; "Oiltown" appeared in 1952.

30 *Washington crusade statistics:* "Rockin' the Capitol," *Time,* March 3, 1952, p. 76. "40,000 Heard Billy Graham in Drizzle on Capitol Steps," Washington *Times Herald,* February 4, 1952. Scrapbook, Billy Graham Center Archives. Also, Graham, Press Conference, National Press Club, Washington, April 24, 1986.

31 *Sen. Robertson's resolution:* AP, February 15, 1952.

31 Graham, "bloc . . . can hold the balance of power," will follow "instructions of their religious leaders": International News Service, October 17, 1951, in Collection 74, Box 1, Folder 12, Billy Graham Center Archives.

31 *Religious leaders "will use my views as a guide":* Ruth Gmeiner, "Billy Graham Making Check of Candidates' Spirituality," UP, February 2, 1952, in Collection 17, Boston Scrapbook, 1949, "Mid-Century Campaign," Billy Graham Center Archives.

31 *"I'd be elected":* AP, February 4, 1952. A slightly different account, setting this statement in the context of a conversation with a presidential candidate, presumably Estes Kefauver, was reported in the Aberdeen, Maryland, *World,* February 9, 1952. Crusades Scrapbook 1952–54, Billy Graham Center Archives.

32 *Numerous congressmen encourage Graham to run for Senate:* AP, February 19, 1950.

32 *"I will offer myself . . . sixteen million votes":* UPI, July 9, 1952. Crusades Scrapbook, 1952–54, Billy Graham Center Archives.

32 *Richardson prompts Graham to write Eisenhower:* McCall's, June 1964, p. 64; Gerald Beavan, interview, July 27, 1988.

PAGE

32   *Graham views MacArthur as promoter of Christianity: Time,* March 3, 1952, p. 76. See also, AP, February 20, 1952.

32   *U.S. needs "new foreign policy":* The Hour of Decision, November 2, 1952, quoted in McLoughlin, *Billy Graham,* p. 115.

32   *Graham's "personal survey":* "Billy Graham: Churchmen Favor Ike," Minneapolis *Morning Tribune,* October 27, 1952. Crusades Scrapbook, 1952–54, Billy Graham Center Archives.

33   *"I have been deeply impressed . . . born-again Christians":* From a sermon, "Peace in Our Time," preached early in 1953, quoted in McLoughlin, *Billy Graham,* p. 96.

33   *"God is giving us a respite": Hour of Decision,* February 8, 1953; "Sermon on the Mount," *Hour of Decision,* April 19, 1953. Both quoted in McLoughlin, *Billy Graham,* p. 117.

33   *"No union dues in the Garden of Eden":* Graham quoted in James L. McAllister, "Evangelical Faith and Billy Graham." *Social Action,* XIX (March 1953), p. 23, cited in McLoughlin, *Billy Graham,* p. 99.

33   *"Some of the finest men I know":* "Partners with God," *Hour of Decision,* 1954.

33   *"The only one I mention is communism":* Hugh Scott, "Rabbi Criticizes Evangelist Billy Graham; Southern Baptist Ministers Offer Defense," Portland *Oregonian,* February 17, 1950. Quoted again in July 25, 1950 edition.

33   *"a battle to the death":* "Satan's Religion," *Hour of Decision,* 1953.

34   *Graham on communism, Stalin in hell:* McLoughlin, *Billy Graham,* p. 139; "Are You Getting What You Want?" *Hour of Decision,* 1957; "The Home" *Hour of Decision,* 1956; Graham, "Impressions of Moscow," *Christianity Today,* July 20, 1959, pp. 14–16.

34   *"over 1100 organizations":* Graham, *America's Hour of Decision* (Wheaton: Van Kampen Press, 1951), p. 144; Communism has attracted key leaders, "Satan's Religion," *Hour of Decision,* 1953; "There Is a Cancer," *Hour of Decision* tape for July 5, 1953. All these sources are quoted in McLoughlin, *Billy Graham,* p. 112.

34   *"Then let's do it":* Hour of Decision, June 10, 1951. Quoted in McLoughlin, *Billy Graham,* p. 112.

35   *"While nobody likes a watchdog":* "Labor, Christ and the Cross," *Hour of Decision,* 1953. Later reprints of this sermon delete "the lavenders," probably in an effort not to offend homosexuals unnecessarily.

35   *"There can be no bargaining"; how to resist communism:* "Satan's Religion."

35   *U.N. weakness:* "Teach Us to Pray," *Hour of Decision,* March 1953, quoted in McLoughlin, *Billy Graham,* pp. 116f.

35   *"Communism's enemy number one":* William H. Stoneman, "Billy Graham: Communism's Public Enemy #1," *Chicago Daily News,* June 11, 1955, p. 1.

35   *McIntire's books:* were all published by his Christian Beacon Press.

35   *"the most ideal conditions":* Erling Jorstad, *The Politics of Doomsday: Fundamentalism of the Far Right* (Nashville: Abingdon Press, 1970), p. 49.

36   *"a complete and frank showdown": Christian Beacon,* November 4, 1948, p. 2. Quoted in Jorstad, *The Politics of Doomsday,* p. 50.

36   *America's "moral responsibility to strike first":* News item issued by the Religious News Service, Ibid., p. 50.

36   *"three theological factors":* Ibid., pp. 50–51.

37   *Hargis, McIntire et al. assist McCarthy:* Ibid., pp. 50–56.

39   *Edgar Bundy and Verne Kaub:* Ibid., pp. 73–79.

40   *"It is wrong to abdicate responsibility . . .":* H. J. Ockenga, quoted in David Moberg, *The Great Reversal: Evangelism Versus Social Concern* (Philadelphia: Lippincott, 1972), pp. 228–229.

40   *First Presidential Prayer Breakfast:* Donald Scott McAlpine, "Mr. Christian of Washington," *United Evangelical Action,* July 1, 1954, pp. 266–67.

41   *"high ecclesiastical circles":* Letter, Billy Graham to Nixon, September 13, 1955. Collection 74, Reel 1, National Archives Pre-presidential, Box 299. National Archives and Record Service. Unless otherwise noted, all subsequent pre-presidential correspondence between Graham and Nixon is also from this source.

41   *"Governor Dewey said . . . in the U.S.":* Letter, Graham to Nixon, October 8, 1955.

41   *Nixon "a splendid churchman":* Graham, quoted in *Newark Sunday News,* September 4, 1955, quoted in McLoughlin, *Billy Graham,* p. 118.

PAGE

42   *Graham invites Nixon to meet with key religious leaders:* Letters, Graham to Nixon, June 4 and July 14, 1956.

42   *"all in my power":* Letter, Graham to Eisenhower, August 24, 1956. Collection 74, Box 1, Folder 12, Billy Graham Center Archives.

42   *"divorce no longer seemed to disqualify":* "The Home," *Hour of Decision,* 1956.

42   *Graham's plan for Christianity Today:* "In the Beginning," interview with Billy Graham, *Christianity Today,* July 17, 1981, p. 26. Also, interview with the author.

43   *Baptist colleges should admit blacks:* John Carruth, "Billy Graham urges Negroes in colleges," Memphis *Commercial Appeal,* May 18, 1952.

43   *No segregation at the cross:* United Press story, July 9, 1952. Crusades Scrapbook, 1952–54, Billy Graham Center Archives, Wheaton, Illinois.

43   *"I believe the Lord is helping us":* Letter, Graham to Eisenhower, June 4, 1956. Collection 74, Box 1, Folder 12, Billy Graham Center Archives. Unless otherwise noted, further correspondence between Graham and Eisenhower is from this source.

43   *Life article about racial problems:* Billy Graham, "Billy Graham Makes Plea for End to Intolerance," *Life,* October 1, 1956, pp. 138–40.

44   *Graham commends Martin Luther King, Jr.,:* Stanley Rowland, Jr., "As Billy Graham Sees His Role," *The New York Times Magazine,* April 21, 1957, pp. 17, 25.

44   *Eisenhower consults Graham about sending troops:* Graham, interview, February 27, 1987.

44   *Graham holds integrated rally in Columbia, S.C.:* "Graham Sets the South an Example," *Christian Century,* November 19, 1958, p. 1326.

45   *Graham in Clinton, Tenn.:* UPI, December 15, 1958; Drew Pearson, *Diaries, 1949–1959* (New York, 1974), pp. 487–488, cited by Jerry Beryl Hopkins, "Billy Graham and the Race Problem, 1949–1969," (Ph.D. dissertation, University of Kentucky, 1986), p. 95.

CHAPTER 2: WARFARE OF THE SPIRIT

48   *Graham intercedes with Eisenhower on Nixon's behalf:* Graham interview.

48   *Graham urges Nixon to attend church:* Letter, Graham to Nixon, November 19, 1959. Collection 74, Microfilm Reel 1, from Box 299 (pre-presidential papers of Richard Nixon, National Archives and Record Service), Billy Graham Center Archives.

48   *"I don't think this is a time to experiment with novices":* This quote is a reconstruction of two reports, one in a story by Bill Lamkin, *Charlotte Observer,* May 21, 1960, and the other in an unidentified newspaper clipping dated May 21, 1960, included in file of correspondence between Graham and Nixon.

49   *Graham recommends Judd as Nixon's running mate:* Letter, Graham to Nixon, June 21, 1960. Collection 74.

49   *Correspondence between Billy Graham and Lyndon Johnson:* Graham to Johnson, August 8, 1960; Johnson to Graham, August 16, 1960. White House Central Files, Box 227a, "Billy Graham" Name File, Lyndon Johnson Library Archives.

49   *Graham urges Nixon to weave religion into addresses, mentions Martin Luther King:* Billy Graham to Richard Nixon, August 23, 1960.

49   *Billy Graham "delighted to cooperate":* Letter, Graham to Nixon, August 23, 1960.

49   *Kennedy on the president's oath of office:* Quoted in *Chronicle of the 20th Century* (Mount Kisco, NY: Chronicle Publications, 1987), p. 847.

50   *"The Roman Catholic Church will take advantage of this":* Letter, Graham to Eisenhower, August 4, 1960. Dr. Bell has made this same point in his speech, "Protestant Distinctives."

50   *Graham's statement to* Time *and* Newsweek: Statement was dated August 28, 1960. A reprint was attached to a letter from Graham to Nixon on the same date.

50   *Ockenga's sermon on religion and politics:* "Religion, Politics, and the Presidency," Sermon preached at Park Street Church, Boston, June 5, 1960. Reprinted and distributed by Christ's Mission, Sea Cliff, New York.

51   *Criswell's article,* Sword of the Lord *(August 12, 1960). pp. 1, 9:* Anti-Catholic pamphlet, *Sword of the Lord,* (October 7, 1960).

51   *McIntire's ACCC resolution: Christian Beacon,* May 5, 1960, p. 1, quoted in Jorstad, *The Politics of Doomsday,* p. 84.

52   *National Association of Evangelicals' concerns over a Catholic president:* Ford pamphlet filed in Robert Ferm Papers, Collection 19, Box 9, Folder 9, Billy Graham Center Archives; NAE "Plan of Action" located in "1960 Campaign Files," Religious Issues files of James Wine, John F. Kennedy Pre-Presidential Papers, Box 1018, Archives, John F. Kennedy Library.

52 *Christianity Today warns of Catholic oppression:* See, for example, *Christianity Today*, February 1, 1960, p. 20; June 20, 1960, p. 31; October 24, 1960, p. 25.

53 *Bell's warnings about Catholics:* Speech,"Protestant Distinctives and the American Crisis," reprint, in Ferm papers Collection 9, Box 9, Folder 8, "Materials Regarding Catholicism," Billy Graham Center Archives. The speech was apparently given at least twice, on August 21, 1960 in Montreat and on September 7, 1960 in Washington.

53 *Peale, encouraged by Graham, leads attack on Kennedy:* For a fuller account of this episode, see Carol V. R. George, *God's Salesman: Norman Vincent Peale and the Power of Positive Thinking* (New York: Oxford University Press, 1993), pp. 194–215.

53 *"detaching myself . . . stay a million miles away . . .":* Letter, Graham to Nixon, September 1, 1960.

53 *John F. Kennedy in Houston:* Videotape.

54 *"Dr. Graham hails Kennedy victory":* *New York Times*, January 17, 1961, p. 24. Collection 74, Reel 1, Billy Graham Center Archives. In the copy of this article contained in Nixon's pre-presidential papers, a Nixon staff-member had circled the headline before routing it to his boss.

55 *Photographs for personal use only:* Letter, Pierre Salinger to Jack Ledden (photographer, *Palm Beach Post-Times*), February 24, 1961. Letters, White House File, Billy Graham. John F. Kennedy Archives.

55 *"Proclaim liberty . . .":* (Leviticus 25:10).

55 *Falwell biographical material:* Jerry Falwell and Elmer Towns, *Church Aflame*, (Nashville: Impact Books, 1971), passism; Jerry Falwell, *Strength for the Journey* (New York: Simon and Schuster, 1987), passim; and Falwell interview with the author, 1976.

58 *First baptism of an African American:* There is some dispute as to precisely how that came about, but apparently none over the year it happened. Elmer Towns, a sociologically trained journalist who moved to Lynchburg in 1971 to help build a new college sponsored by the Thomas Road Baptist Church, recalls telling Falwell during that summer, "We must integrate this church if we're going to have a school that will reach the nation and reach the world." He reported that a black teenager was ready for baptism and told the pastor, "I'm nobody here. I'll baptize this black person, and if the church gets mad, you could always fire me. But if you do it and they get mad, then that has severe ramifications." Apart from the departure of one "culturally biased type of family," the baptism stirred no measurable reaction. With a laugh, Towns said, "Dr. Falwell and I have a disagreement as to who baptized the first black person at Thomas Road. He will give you the name of the man he baptized. I think that [was a few weeks later], but I shouldn't get into an argument with my boss."

66 *Further sit-ins at Patterson's and elsewhere:* Lynchburg *News* 2/14/61; 2/22/61; interviews with Thornhill and Wood. "all-out warfare." Lynchburg *News*, May 15, 1961.

68 *Falwell: "It should be considered civil wrongs":* Quoted in Mel White, *Stranger at the Gate* (New York: Simon and Schuster, 1994), p. 103.

69 *CORE demonstrators at Thomas Road:* White and O.C. Thaxton interview; quoting Lynchburg *News* article.

69 *"Like a boxer feels a bad blow":* White, *Stranger*, p. 104.

69 *Anti-King literature:* Lumiere staff interview with Elliot Schewel, Lynchburg citizen and Virginia legislator, July 27, 1995.

69 *"Ministers and Marches":* Jerry Falwell, sermon preached on Sunday evening, March 21, 1965, to a congregation of approximately one thousand, and reproduced for wide distribution.

70 *Lynchburg Christian Academy announced:* Lynchburg *News*, November 10, 1966, and April 8, 1967.

70 *Lynchburg Christian Academy to be white:* Lynchburg *News*, April 14, 1967.

72 *Growth at Thomas Road Baptist Church:* White, *Stranger*, p. 105; Falwell, *Strength*, p. 299.

CHAPTER 3: A MAN ON HORSEBACK

74 *"Let's grow up, conservatives":* Archival footage from CBS News of the Republican National Convention, September 27, 1960, in Chicago.

75 *Ike a "dedicated . . . agent":* From *The Politician,* a notorious Birch publication. Because of the furor this charge stirred, it was expunged from later editions of the book. Quoted in Erling Jorstad, *The Politics of Doomsday: Fundamentalists of the Far Right* (Nashville: Abingdon Press, 1970), p. 112. Ike: "To try . . . stupid." Mary

PAGE

Brennan, *Turning Right in the Sixties: The Conservative Capture of the GOP* (Chapel Hill: University of North Carolina Press, 1995), p. 54. Billy Graham comments: on communism, Billy Graham, "Facing the Anti-God Colossus," *Christianity Today* (December 21, 1961), pp. 6–8; on ministers, AP, July 9, 1961; on the Peace Corps, AP, August 23, 1963; on sending food to China, AP, February 13, 1961.

75 *Kennedy a perfect target:* Jorstad, *The Politics of Doomsday,* p. 83.

75 *Kennedy's speech: New York Times,* November 19, 1961, p. 54; Arthur M. Schlesinger, Jr. *A Thousand Days: John F. Kennedy in the White House* (Boston: Houghton Mifflin, 1965), p. 753; Theodore C. Sorenson, *Kennedy* (New York: Harper & Row, 1965), p. 355.

76 *Hargis: "This nation today is in the hands of a group of Harvard radicals . . .": The Weekly Crusader,* June 1, 1962, p. 2. Quoted in Jorstad, *The Politics of Doomsday,* p. 82.

76 *Subscription, income, and radio figures:* Jorstad, *The Politics of Doomsday,* pp. 83, 88. *Life Line* figures are from Brennan, *Turning Right,* p. 61.

77 *Conservative complaints about the Kennedy administration:* Jorstad, *The Politics of Doomsday,* pp. 85–87; PBS interviews with Billy James Hargis and Phyllis Schlafly.

78 *McIntire: "A Communist Kills Our President . . .": Christian Beacon,* December 26, 1963. Hargis, *The Far Left* (Tulsa: Christian Crusade Press, 1964), cited in Jorstad, *The Politics of Doomsday,* p. 90.

79 *Hargis and McIntire on segregation:* Hargis, *The Truth about Segregation,* Christian Crusade pamphlet, pp. 1–2; *Newsweek,* December 4, 1961; *Brotherhood of Man . . . a Smoke Screen,* Christian Crusade pamphlet, pp. 3–4. McIntire and ACCC, *Christian Beacon,* May 8, 1958, p. 5; and July 2, 1964, p. 3. McIntire's monthly newsletter, May 25, 1965, p. 1; McIntire, *The Rise of the Tyrant: Controlled Economy vs. Private Enterprise,* p. 205; *The Death of the Church,* pp. 71–72; *The Bible versus Civil Rights,* a McIntire pamphlet, p. 1. All quoted in Jorstad, *The Politics of Doomsday,* pp. 93–95.

79 *George Wallace commended:* Jorstad, *The Politics of Doomsday,* p. 96; original sources not cited.

79 *King "a stinking racial agitator":* Quoted by Donald Quinn, *The Oklahoma Courier,* reprinted in the U.S. Congressional Record, 87th Cong., 2nd session, 1962, 108, pt 5, 6579-80. Cited in Jorstad, *The Politics of Doomsday,* p. 97. "Jim Crow must go . . . too far and too fast." *Chicago Sun-Times,* May 31, 1962, quoted in Jerry Beryl Hopkins, "Billy Graham and the Race Problem, 1949–1969," (Ph.D. dissertation, University of Kentucky, 1986), p. 112; also, AP story, *Charlotte Observer,* July 9, 1961; Graham feels King should "put on the brakes." *New York Times,* April 18, 1963, p. 21. King's "Letter from Birmingham Jail." Graham's response to King's dream, "Graham discounts human efforts at racial harmony," *Los Angeles Times,* August 3 and 10, 1963.

80 *Goldwater with horse: Life,* November 1, 1963, cover.

80 *"bright banner . . . pale pastels":* Ronald Reagan speech, quoted by Morton Blackwell, interview.

80 *Goldwater's views, from his three popular books: The Conscience of a Conservative* (Shepherdsville, KY: Victor Publishing Co., 1960); *Why Not Victory?* (New York: McGraw-Hill, 1962), and *Where I Stand* (McGraw-Hill, 1964), passim.

81 *Rockefeller on the "radical right":* Quoted in Mary Brennan, *Turning Right,* p. 53.

81 *Schlafly's account of Republican conventions:* Phyllis Schlafly, *A Choice, Not an Echo* (Alton, Illinois: Pere Marquette Press, 1964), passim; Goldwater's reaction to Nixon's compromise, *ibid.,* p. 75. Rusher's characterization, William Rusher, *The Making of the New Majority Party* (Ottawa, Il: Green Hill Publications, 1975), p. 44; "New York City had . . ." Richard Whalen, *Taking Sides: A Personal View of America from Kennedy to Nixon to Kennedy* (Boston: Houghton-Mifflin, 1974), p. 101. Both the Rusher and Whalen quotes are from Alan Crawford, *Thunder on the Right: The "New Right" and the Politics of Resentment* (New York: Pantheon Books, 1980), p. 231.

82 *White on Goldwater:* Theodore White, *The Making of the President 1964* (New York: Atheneum, 1965), p. 295.

84 *Rockefeller speech:* Brennan, *Turning Right,* p. 77. Rockefeller drowned out. Townsend interview.

84 *Goldwater acceptance speech: New York Times,* July 17, 1964, p. 10.

84 *Reporter: "My God . . . !:* Brennan, *Turning Right,* p. 78.

84 *Goldwater on America's NATO commanders:* White, *The Making of the President 1964* p. 296.

PAGE

85 *Goldwater on bomb commercials:* Barry Goldwater, *Goldwater* (New York: Doubleday, 1988), p. 188. Goldwater's campaign manager's frustrations.: White, Ibid.

85 *Goldwater on the Civil Rights Act:* Goldwater, *Goldwater,* p. 194. Goldwater delivered the civil rights speech mentioned here on October 19, 1964.

85 *Townsend on Goldwater campaign errors:* Interview.

85 *Goldwater and Social Security:* White, *The Making of the President 1964,* p. 303. Goldwater's various campaign positions: Goldwater, *Where I Stand,* passim.

86 *Goldwater speech:* delivered October 12, 1964, at Mormon Tabernacle, Salt Lake City, Utah, ABC News video.

86 *"Choice" documentary:* Sidney Blumenthal, "The righteous empire: a short history of the end of history, and maybe even of the G.O.P." *The New Republic,* Vol. 191 (October 22, 1984), p. 18.

87 *Broder comment on Reagan's speech:* Michael Schaller, *Reckoning with Reagan* (New York: Oxford University Press, 1992), pp. 12–13.

87 *"Goldwater's campaign was hopeless . . ."* White, *The Making of the President 1964,* p. 315.

88 *Viguerie copies names:* That Viguerie copied the names of Goldwater donors is well known, though the story sometimes has Viguerie copying all the names himself, from lists at Goldwater headquarters. Morton Blackwell, who worked with Viguerie for a time, provided information regarding the GAO and the Kelly Girls.

89 *Dean Burch comments:* Brennan, *Turning Right,* p. 101. American Conservative Union formed, Ibid., p. 114.

91 *Reagan's statements: New York Times,* June 1, June 6, and August 7, 1966.

91 *Bright's condemnation of criticism:* Richard Quebedeaux, *I Found It: The Story of Bill Bright and Campus Crusade* (San Francisco: Harper and Row, 1979), p. 108.

92 Hal Lindsey with C. C. Carlson, *The Late Great Planet Earth* (Grand Rapids: Zondervan, 1970).

93 *"to confront the hotbed . . . with the gospel":* From Special Anniversary Issue of Campus Crusade magazine, *World Wide Challenge,* May/June, 1991, p. 21.

95 *Reagan's "antipathy":* Brennan, *Turning Right,* p. 125.

96 *Telegram and mail campaign:* Charlotte *News,* November 3, 1964; AP, December 23, 1964.

96 *Graham spends the weekend prior to election in the White House:* Marshall Frady, *Billy Graham: A Parable of American Righteousness* (Boston: Little, Brown, 1979), p. 266.

96 *"we're way off the main track":* Quoted in Cort R. Flint, with the staff of *Quote* magazine, *Billy Graham Speaks!: The Quotable Billy Graham* (New York: Grosset & Dunlap, 1968), pp. 105–106.

97 *Nixon in VIP section:* "The Politician's Preacher," *Time,* October 4, 1968, p. 58, and David E. Kucharsky, "Soul Search in the Steel City," *Christianity Today,* September 27, 1968, pp. 31–32.

97 *"a big segment . . . at the polls":* Charlotte *News,* September 19, 1968.

97 *Nixon claims Graham's support; Graham confirms:* Charlotte *Observer,* November 1, 1968. Campaign exploits Graham's acknowledgment. "The Preaching and the Power," *Newsweek,* July 20, 1970, p. 54.

98 *Action memo to Colson:* Memo, February 23, 1970, Log. no. 275, Folder RM 2–1 "Religious Services in White House, March 1–April 30, 1970," SF Religious Matters Box 12, White House Central Files, Nixon Presidential Materials.

98 *Guest list of corporate leaders:* Memo, Marge McFadden to Debbie Murray, October 12, 1970, Folder Religious Matters 2–1, "Religious Service in White House" SF Religious Matters Box 12, White House Central Files, Nixon Presidential Materials.

98 *"It isn't going to do us one bit of good":* Memo, H.R. Haldeman to Alex Butterfield, Folder "February," Box 196 (HRH Chronological 1971–, A–H), White House Special Files, Nixon Presidential Materials.

99 *Colson on Nixon's exploitation of religious leaders:* Colson's comments are based on a 1990 interview with the author and a 1994 interview with Lumiere Productions. Both interviews contained many quite similar observations. The first paragraph is taken entirely from the first interview; the remainder is taken from the Lumiere interview.

CHAPTER 4: THE BATTLE OF ANAHEIM

100 Allen Matusow, *The Unraveling of America: A History of Liberalism in the 1960s* (New York: Harper and Row, 1984).

PAGE

101 *Changes in sexual behavior:* John D'Emilio and Estelle B. Freedman. *Intimate Matters: A History of Sexuality in America* (New York: Harper & Row, 1988), pp. 176, 250, 266, 294.

106 *Williams on homosexuality:* Interview and Mary Breasted, *Oh Sex Education* (New York: Praeger Publishers, 1970), p. 116.

107 *"We had all our members briefed":* James Townsend, interview.

108 *"Sex knowledge test":* Breasted, *Oh Sex Education*, p. 123.

112 *National Convention on Crisis in Education:* "Saving Sex Education for the Back Seat," *Village Voice*, September 18, 1969.

112 *Cook's quotes: Oh Sex Education*, pp 124–125.

113 John Steinbacher, *The Child Seducers* (Fullerton, California: Educator Publications, Inc., 1971.)

113 The Child Seducers book and record: Described in *Oh Sex Education*, p. 145.

CHAPTER 5: CULTURE WAR

119 *Possible Birch Society support of Alice Moore's school board campaign:* James Moffett, *Storm in the Mountains* (Carbondale: Southern Illinois University Press, 1982), p. 13. Moffett's account of the events discussed in this chapter is by far the most comprehensive published record. Though he had vital personal interest in the outcome, was on the losing side (which understandably affects his perspective), and takes a position that will strike some as excessively psychological because he relies heavily on the concept of the "authoritarian personality" to describe the textbook protesters, he is generally fair and respectful toward the opposition. Anyone interested in the Kanawha County conflict or the larger issue of textbook selection and school control will benefit from reading *Storm in the Mountains*. Any quotes from Moffett not footnoted to this book are from interviews conducted by the Lumiere staff.

119 *Moore: "God's law is absolute":* Moffett, *Storm*, p. 13.

120 *Moore persuades colleagues to extend inspection:* Ibid., p. 13.

120 *The Gablers:* William Martin, "The Guardians Who Slumbereth Not," *Texas Monthly*, November 1982, pp. 144–150, 266–271.

121 *NEA: "To accuse American textbook publishers. . . .":* Ibid., p. 105.

126 *Churches and other groups take sides over textbook adoption; June School-Board meeting:* Ibid., pp. 14–16. Magic Valley Mothers Club petition, ibid., p. 15, citing Catherine Candor-Chandler, *A History of the Kanawha County Textbook Controversy, April 1974– April 1975*, Ed. D. dissertation, 1976 (Ann Arbor: University Microfilms International, 1982), p. 163. Moffett regards Candor-Chandler's dissertation as the most dependable chronological record of the dispute.

127 Christian-American Parents and Concerned Citizens protest. Moffett, *Storm*, pp 16–17.

128 *September protests and Board cave-in:* Ibid., pp. 17–18.

128 *Marvin Horan, "The common man . . . ":* Ibid., p. 22, quoting Calvin Trillin, "U.S. Journal: Kanawha County, West Virginia," *New Yorker*, September 30, 1974, p. 121.

128 *Moore is jeered, Horan perseveres:* Moffett, *Storm*, p. 18.

129 *Incidents of violence:* Ibid., pp. 21–22, citing James C. Hefley, *Textbooks on Trial* (Wheaton, Illinois: Victor Books, 1976), p. 175.

129 *Plans to bomb carloads of children:* Moffett. *Storm*, p. 20, citing Thelma R. Conley, "Scream Silently: One View of the Kanawha County Textbook Controversy," *Journal of Research and Development in Education* 9, No. 3, Spring 1976, 93–101.

129 *Moore: "I never dreamed . . . ":* Moffett, *Storm*, p. 19, citing "West Virginia Hills Echo with Anger over Textbooks," *Los Angeles Times*, September 9, 1974.

130 *Quigley's prayer:* Moffett, *Storm*, p. 19.

131 *James Lewis's article:* Ibid., p. 54, quoting Lewis, "Ugly Demons in West Virginia Textbook War," syndicated feature article, pt. 2, p. 7.

133 *Fike on 'hillbilly preachers":* Moffett, *Storm*, p. 36.

133 *Fike: "Why the hell do we have to indoctrinate . . .":* Ibid., p. 72.

133 *Fike's column on traditionalists: Moffett,* Ibid., p. 73.

134 Moffett: *Mountaineers don't like central government:* Ibid., p. 38, and Moffett interview.

134 *Journalist: "room for them in my America":* Unnamed individual in story told by James Lewis, interview.

136 *Survey results:* Moffett, *Storm*, p. 35.

136 *November school board meetings:* Ibid., pp. 22–23.

137 *Horan changes his mind and protests texts again:* Emmett Shafer interview.

137 *Hill leads protest, board members go to Washington:* Moffett, *Storm*, p. 24.

137 *Board members assaulted:* Ibid.

137 *NEA hearings and report:* NEA press release, February 6, 1975, quoted in Moffett, *Storm*, p. 42.

138 *January seminar sponsored by educational traditionalists:* Moffett, *Storm*, p. 22.

138 *KKK rally:* Ibid., p. 23, citing Candor-Chandler, *A History*, p. 177.

138 *Horan is convicted and sentenced:* "Minister Gets 3-year Term in School Bombings," *New York Times*, May 20, 1975.

139 *Competitors criticize controversial books.* Moffett, *Storm*, p. 33.

139 *1981 survey of book challenges:* Ibid., p. 188, quoting Stephen Arons, "The Crusade to Ban Books," *Saturday Review*, June 1981, p. 17.

139 *1985 USA Today report:* Moffett, *Storm*, p. 188, quoting Gregory Katz, "School Censorship Rise Cited," *USA Today*, August 18, 1985.

140 *Private schools "a time bomb":* Moffett, *Storm*, p. 211.

CHAPTER 6: BORN AGAIN

145 *Graham seeks deferments for Campus Crusade workers:* Memo, Dwight Chapin to H. R. Haldeman and John Erlichman, February 15, 1969, Folder RM 1/69-12/70, Box 1, White House Central Files, Nixon Presidential Materials (NPM), National Records and Archives Service; memo, Jay Wilkinson to Robert Ellsworth, February 22, 1969; memo, Jonathan Rose to Harry Dent, February 26, 1969; note date April 23, 1969, labeled "Two problems: Billy Graham's people want to be deferred," all in Box 63, Egil Krogh (372-OA #2982), SMOF, White House Special Files, NPM.

145 *Southern Baptists criticize Graham:* Editorial, Charlotte *Observer*, October 15, 1971.

145 *For an account of Graham's unofficial diplomatic work* regarding Chiang Kai-shek and the Republic of China, see William Martin, *A Prophet with Honor: The Billy Graham Story* (New York: William Morrow, 1991), pp. 388–39.

145 *"Graham wants to be helpful . . . can't have leak":* H. R. Haldeman, handwritten notes, February 6 and 8, 1971, HRH Box 43, Haldeman Notes, Part I, Jan–Mar 71, Folder Jan 1–Feb 15, 71. White House logs indicate that Graham had seen the president on February 1, the date of the annual National Prayer Breakfast. Master List, Contacts File by Name, p. 1413. WHCF, NPM.

146 *Graham: Nixon's "moral and ethical principles. . . .":* Martin, *Prophet*, p. 425.

146 *Nixon will be the only President we have. . . .":* Billy Graham, Thanksgiving press release, November 22, 1973, sent to Rosemary Woods by Charles Crutchfield, PPF Box 8, WHCF, NPM.

146 *Graham: "Watergate . . . has hurt America":* "Watergate," *Christianity Today*, January 4, 1974, pp. 8–10.

146 *Peale and Colson responses:* See Martin, *Prophet*, pp. 428–429.

147 *Graham: "I never saw that side of him":* Quoted in John Dart, *Los Angeles Times News Service*, Charlotte *Observer*, August 17, 1974.

147 *Graham: "I felt like a sheep led to the slaughter":* Interview with author, February 1991, Montreat, North Carolina.

151 *Carter on 700 Club:* Richard G. Hutcheson, Jr. *God in the White House* (New York: Macmillan, 1988), p. 155.

153 *Intercessors for America and Billy Graham:* Kenneth Woodward, "Politics from the Pulpit," *Newsweek*, September 6, 1976.

153 *Citizens for Carter Ad: Christianity Today*, July 1976.

154 *Michael Novak observation:* Kenneth Woodward, "Born Again," *Newsweek*, October 25, 1976.

154 *"I've got a good family":* Betty Glad, *Jimmy Carter: In Search of the Great White House* (New York: W. W. Norton, 1980), p. 346

155 *Carter speech on family:* Transcript distributed by Carter campaign.

156 Newsweek *cover story:* October 25, 1976.

157 *Bailey Smith endorses Carter:* Myra MacPherson, *Washington Post*, September 27, 1976, quoted in William R. Goodman and James J. H. Price, *Jerry Falwell: An Unauthorized Profile* (Lynchburg, VA: Paris and Associates, 1981), p. 83.

157 *"Playboy Interview: Jimmy Carter": Playboy*, November 1976. It did not help that Jody Powell was quoted as having used considerably more explicit language.

158 *Carter's pastor's comment; W. A. Criswell "highly offended":* Jules Witcover, *Marathon: The Pursuit of the Presidency, 1972–1976* (New York: Viking, 1977), p. 567.

158 *W. A. Criswell endorsement of Ford:* Ford campaign commercial.

PAGE

158   *Falwell disillusioned:* Myra McPherson, *Washington Post,* September 27, 1976, p. 1.

158   *Jim Wooten observations: Dasher: The Roots and the Rising of Jimmy Carter* (New York: Summit Books, 1978), p. 54.

162   *Pro-ERA efforts in Florida:* Anastasis Toufexis, "A Ten-year Struggle Teaches American Women the Art of Politics," *1994 Time Almanac* (CD-ROM).

162   *"from breadmakers to breadwinners":* "Unmaking an Amendment: ERA," *Time,* April 25, 1977, pp. 89–90.

164   Time *estimate of conservative delegates:* "Houston Produces New Alliances and a Drive for Grass-roots Power," *Time,* December 5, 1977, from *Time Almanac.* Also, "The Three 'Hot Button' Issues: ERA, Abortion, Lesbian Rights," Ibid.

165   *Rosalynn Carter on the ERA:* "First Ladies Out Front," *Time,* December 5, 1977, from *Time Almanac.*

165   *Lottie Beth Hobbs:* Burton Yale Pines, *Back to Basics: The Traditionalist Movement That Is Sweeping Grass-Roots America* (New York: William Morrow, 1982), p. 159.

165   *Statements at Pro-Family Rally:* "Houston produces new alliances," *Time,* December 5, 1977, from *Time Almanac.*

166   *Women on both sides repelled:* "Houston produces." Ibid.

166   *Pat Robertson: "I wouldn't let Bella Abzug . . .":* Dick Dabney, "God's Own Network: The Electronic Kingdom of Pat Robertson," *Harper's,* August 1980, pp. 33–52.

166   *Falwell on National Women's Conference:* Jerry Falwell, *Listen, America!* (Garden City: Doubleday-Galilee, 1980), p. 155.

167   *James Robison, "like a summary":* James Robison, *Attack on the Family* (Wheaton, Illinois: Tyndale House, 1980), p. 62.

CHAPTER 7: WE—SOME OF US—ARE FAMILY

172   *Falwell, "In some states . . ."* Jerry Falwell, *Listen, America!* (Garden City: Doubleday-Galilee, 1980), p. 220.

174   *Carter announces White House Conference on Families (WHCF): Listening to America's Families: Action for the 80's—The Report to the President, Congress and Families of the Nation,* (The White House Conference on Families, October 1980.)

177   *"I came to read the script":* Lumiere Background interview with a member of the National Advisory Committee.

177   *"these guys rent a bus":* Lumiere Background interview with White House Conference delegate.

177   *Carter Proclamation:* "National Family Week." *Public Papers of the Presidents of the United States: Jimmy Carter, 1979, Book II* (Washington: U.S. Government Printing Office, 1980), p. 2133.

183   *Marshner and Pratt explain walk-out:* "Band of Conservatives walk out of Conference on Families," *Washington Post,* June 7, 1980. Also, *New York Times,* June 7, 1980.

185   *Thirty gay delegates come out:* Article by Don Leavitt in *The Blade,* June 12, 1980.

186   *James Kilpatrick remarks:* James Davison Hunter, *Culture Wars* (New York: Basic Books, 1991), p. 179.

CHAPTER 8: MORAL MAJORITY

192   *"We neither asked for nor expected this much":* Lumiere interview with Harold O. J. Brown.

193   *Falwell did not preach on abortion until 1978:* Interview with Falwell associate Elmer Towns.

193   Abortion statistics—"America's Abortion Dilemma," *Newsweek,* January 14, 1985, p. 24, citing statistics from the Alan Guttmacher Institute.

194   *Koop and Schaeffer agree to collaborate:* In her book, *Tapestry* (Waco: Word Books, 1984), Edith Schaeffer supplies a slightly different version of the story. In her account, son Franky heard Koop's lecture and suggested the joint venture to his father.

196   *"Justice Black's decision: Torcaso v Watkins,"* 367 US 488, 495 (1961).

196   *To understand humanism":* "A Special Report," *Christian Harvest Times,* June 1980, p. 1.

197   *Liberty official on university goals:* Elmer Towns, interview.

197   *Schaeffer: "Why don't you use pagans?":* Mel White, interview.

198   *Homosexuality unspeakably evil:* Jerry Falwell, *Listen, America!* (Garden City: Doubleday-Galilee, 1980), pp. 181–186.

PAGE

198 *Falwell on Moscone and Milk assassinations:* Jerry Strober and Ruth Tomczak, *Jerry Falwell: Aflame for God* (Nashville: Thomas Nelson Pub., 1979).

199 *Christian Voice:* See Peggy L. Shriver, *The Bible Vote* (New York: The Pilgrim Press, 1982), pp. 13–16.

200 *Weyrich wants anti-abortion plank to attract Catholics:* Dinesh D'Souza, *Falwell, Before the Millennium* (Chicago: Regnery Gateway, 1984), pp. 109–112.

201 *Rationale and purpose of Moral Majority:* Jerry Falwell, *Listen, America!* (New York: Doubleday-Galilee, 1980), pp. 257–263.

202 *"I had the advantage . . . leanings":* Frances FitzGerald, *Cities on a Hill* (New York: Sands, 1981), p. 156.

205 *"THE TOMB OF THE UNKNOWN SODOMITE":* Moral Majority fund-raising letter, August 14, 1980.

205 *Questionnaire items:* Undated Moral Majority questionnaires.

207 *Falwell: "I don't know why . . .":* Frances FitzGerald, *Cities on a Hill* (New York: Simon & Schuster, 1986).

210 *"the Soviet Union would kill 135 million . . .":* Falwell, *Listen, America!* p. 98.

212 *Falwell doubted "Washington for Jesus" could succeed:* Edward E. Plowman, "Washington for Jesus: Revival Fervor and Political Disclaimers," *Christianity Today,* May 23, 1980, p. 46.

212 *Robertson: "partison politics is the wrong path":* "A Tide of Born-Again Politics," *Newsweek,* September 15, 1980.

213 *Erroneous estimates of audience for religious broadcasting:* William Martin, "The Birth of a Media Myth," *The Atlantic,* June 1981, pp. 7, 10, 11.

213 *1980 Republican Convention:* Frank B. Merrick, et al., "The G.O.P. Gets Its Act Together," *Time,* July 28, 1980. See also James Davison Hunter, *Culture Wars: The Struggle to Define America* (New York: Basic Books, 1991), p. 275.

214 *Library Court Group is formed:* "Conservatives join on social concerns," *New York Times,* July 30, 1980.

215 *Bailey Smith's prayer:* Quoted in Peggy L. Shriver, *The Bible Vote* (New York: Pilgrim Press, 1981), pp. 29–30, citing "Whose Prayer Does God Hear?" *Ecumenical Trends,* Graymoor Ecumenical Institute, vol. 10, no. 1, January 1981, p. 12.

218 *Blackwell: "turning point":* Sidney Blumenthal, "The Righteous Empire: A short history of the end of history and maybe even of the GOP," *The New Republic,* October 22, 1984, pp. 18–24.

218 *Ninety-minute presentation:* Dudley Clendinen, "Rev. Falwell inspires evangelical vote," *New York Times,* August 20, 1980. The presentation was entitled, "America, You're Too Young to Die."

218 *Coalition statement criticizing Moral Majority and Christian Voice:* "Religious Leaders Fault Policies of Evangelical Political Groups," *New York Times,* October 21, 1980.

219 *Falwell repudiates "Ministers vs. Marchers":* FitzGerald, *Cities,* p. 171.

220 *Falwell: "my finest hour":* FitzGerald, *Cities,* p. 189.

CHAPTER 9: PROPHETS AND ADVISERS

222 *Viguerie and Phillips complaints:* David Alpern, et al., "The Right: A House Divided?" *Newsweek,* February 2, 1981.

222 *Weyrich, "I had a conference call . . . meaningless access":* Michael Cromartie, ed., *No Longer Exiles: The Religious New Right in American Politics* (Washington: Ethics and Public Policy Center, 1993), pp. 53–54.

223 *Falwell and Deaver regarding "back door" comment:* The account is Falwell's, based on interview. Morton Blackwell confirmed the accuracy of Falwell's account during his interview.

224 *Deaver "the grand producer":* Lou Cannon, *President Reagan: The Role of a Lifetime* (New York: Simon and Schuster-Touchstone, 1991), p. 53.

226 *Reagan receives right-to-life advocates:* "The Battle Over Abortion," *Time,* April 6, 1981. *Time Almanac.*

227 *Jesse Helms on the Helms-Hyde Human Life Statute, John Willke comment:* Ibid.

228 *Moral Majority has "substantive concerns . . . answered":* UPI, July 15, 1981.

228 *Cal Thomas, "not a very good signal":* Wes Pippert, "Reagan's Supreme Court Nomination," UPI, July 25, 1981.

229 *Marshner comments on O'Connor nomination:* Time, July 20, 1981, and interview.

230 *Jepsen discovered in a brothel:* For this and a longer list of Jepsen transgressions and

improprieties, see John Hyde, "Roger on the Run," *The New Republic,* October 1, 1984, pp. 17–20.

231 *"a grocery list":* "Family Act Appears to Be Going Nowhere," Midland, Michigan, *Daily News,* October 13, 1981.

231 *Family Protection Act a "mish-mash" and "the New Right more skilled at denouncing . . .":* George J. Church, *"seeking strategy on social issues; rightists agree on policy but they differ on ways and means":* Time, September 14, 1981.

231 *Marshner describes strategy behind Family Protection Act:* "The New Right's Plan for '82," Washington, D.C. *City Paper,* November 27, 1981.

231 *Conservative Digest poll:* Reported by Ira Allen, UPI, September 22, 1981.

232 *Viguerie's open letter to Reagan: Conservative Digest,* July 1982, p. 46.

232 *Nellie Gray complaint:* Ibid., p. 18.

232 *Falwell, "absolutely imperative" and "the front burner":* Ibid., p. 19.

232 *Family Forum II.* Nicholas D. Kristof, *"New Right Meeting Grumbles about Reagan": Washington Post,* July 28, 1982, p. A5.

232 *Liberals may have overestimated clout:* Charles Austin, "Religious Right Growing Impatient with Reagan," *New York Times,* August 16, 1982, p. A13.

233 *Reagan speeches at National Prayer Breakfast and before National Religious Broadcasters:* "Polls show people care about education, moral issues," *Conservative Digest,* May 1982, p. 13.

233 *The Leadership Foundation:* Ibid., pp. 13–14. The Leadership Foundation was established by conservative radio and TV personality Martha Rountree, who also founded "Meet the Press."

234 *Ron Godwin complaints:* "Moral Majority Official Questions Reagan Stands," Lynchburg *News and Daily Advance,* August 8, 1981.

234 *Falwell visits Reagan:* "Falwell offers Reagan plan," Lynchburg *News and Daily Advance,* April 2, 1983.

234 *"keep the Religious Right in perpetual mobilization":* Sidney Blumenthal, "The Righteous Empire: A Short History of the End of History and Maybe Even of the GOP," *The New Republic,* October 22, 1984, pp. 18–24.

234 *SBC takeover by conservatives:* Sidney Blumenthal, *Pledging Allegiance: The Last Campaign of the Cold War* (New York: HarperCollins, 1990), pp. 99–100.

235 *Reagan's remarks at prayer breakfast: MacNeil/Lehrer News Hour* transcript #2334.

236 *Criswell and Robison pray at Republican National Convention:* Blumenthal, *The New Republic,* October 22, 1984, pp. 18–24.

CHAPTER 10: THE UNTOUCHABLES

240 *Waxman opposes Koop:* "Fight Over the Surgeon General," NBC News special segment, broadcast May 8, 1981.

240 *Director of Public Health opposes Koop:* John Judas, "Nice Guys: An Officer and a Gentleman," *The New Republic,* January 23, 1989.

241 *Early stages of AIDS epidemic:* C. Everett Koop, *Koop: The Memoirs of America's Family Doctor* (New York: Random House, 1991), pp. 194–195.

241 *Koop kept silent on AIDS:* Ibid., pp. 195–196. By Koop's own account, he gave an interview on AIDS to *Christianity Today* in November 1985, which would mean his period of silence lasted a few months less than five years.

242 *Koop: AIDS pitted the politics . . .":* Ibid., pp. 197–198.

242 *Pat Buchanan: "The poor homosexuals . . .":* Quoted in Lou Cannon, *President Reagan: The Role of a Lifetime* (New York: Simon and Schuster-Touchstone, 1991), p. 816.

242 *"Reporters heard Falwell call AIDS 'wrath of God' ":* Dennis Altman, *AIDS in the Mind of America* (New York: Anchor Books, 1986), p. 67.

243 *Gingrich: "AIDS . . . a great rallying cry":* "Newt Set Strategy for Religious Right—10 Years Ago," *The Freedom Writer,* February 1995, p. 1.

243 *Falwell compares AIDS to brucellosis:* Altman, *AIDS,* p. 67.

243 *American Family Association calls for quarantine:* Ibid., p. 67.

243 *Buckley recommends tattoos for AIDS victims:* William F. Buckley, Jr., "Identify All the Carriers," *New York Times,* March 18, 1986, p. A7.

243 *Mason acknowledges government consideration of quarantine:* Black, *Plague Years,* p. 216.

243 *Los Angeles Times poll.* July 20, 1988.

245 *Scott Allen comments:* ABC News interview, August 3, 1994. All Scott Allen quotes are from this interview.

PAGE

245 *Lydia's essay:* Reprinted in Jimmy Allen, *Burden of a Secret: A Story of Truth and Mercy in the Face of AIDS* (Nashville: Moorings, 1995), pp. 128–130.

246 *Jimmy Allen's comments:* From Lumiere interview and ABC News coverage of speech by Jimmy Allen, April 24, 1994, Dunwoody, Georgia.

247 *Increased anti-gay violence:* David Black, *The Plague Years* (New York: Simon and Schuster, 1985), p. 216.

247 *Nevada minister: "cut their throats":* Altman, *AIDS* (New York: Anchor Books, 1986), pp. 67–68.

248 *Dannemeyer: "Wipe them off . . .":* Koop, *Memoirs,* p. 208.

249 *Koop: "telling the truth":* Koop, *Memoirs,* p. 204.

250 Conservative Digest, National Review, *Weyrich, and Schlafly attack Koop:* John Judas, "Nice Guys: An Officer and a Gentleman," *The New Republic,* January 23, 1989, p. 21, and Koop, *Memoirs,* p. 213.

250 *Schlafly: Report "edited by the Gay Task Force":* Koop, *Memoirs,* p. 218.

251 *Schlafly "went on television . . .":* The quotation is from the Koop interview, in which he speaks of Schlafly only as "a prominent conservative woman." In *Memoirs,* p. 218, he identifies the woman as Schlafly.

251 *Schlafly: free publicity for condom manufacturers:* Cannon, *President Reagan,* p. 815.

251 *Schools using Koop's message to teach condom use:* New York Times, March 15, 1987.

251 *Koop's view of Schlafly:* Koop, *Memoirs,* p. 218.

251 *Evans and Novak "distorted the truth . . . lack of real influence":* Ibid., pp. 217–219.

251 *Buchanan shared Anderson's and Bauer's views:* Cannon, *President Reagan,* p. 816.

251 *Anderson wanted report to read "All Americans . . .":* Koop, *Memoirs,* p. 220.

252 *Bauer tells of Christmas dinner; Koop, "Reagan . . . reasoned anecdotally":* Koop, *Memoirs,* pp. 220–221.

252 *Weyrich and Schlafly engineer dinner boycott:* Koop and Schlafly PBS interviews; *The New Republic,* January 23, 1989; *New York Times,* May 1, 1987; Koop, *Memoirs,* pp. 218–219.

253 *Koop addresses National Religious Broadcasters; McAteer's response: Washington Times,* January 20, 1987.

254 *D. James Kennedy program on AIDS:* Television program, broadcast July 24, 1988. Information based on *People for the American Way Televangelist Transcripts 1988–1989,* p. 48.

254 *Bennett's views on sex education:* Koop, *Memoirs,* p. 221.

254 *Koop and Bennett disagree over AIDS testing:* David Whitman, "A Fall from Grace on the Right," *U.S. News and World Report,* May 25, 1987. Bennett believed hospital and clinic patients, immigrants, felons, and couples seeking marriage licenses should be tested.

254 *Falwell's anti-gay fund-raising letters:* Richard Cohen, "Falwell's Hate Mailing," *Washington Post,* May 1, 1987.

254 *Robertson: Quarantining not a bad idea:* Rick Pearson, Rockford, Illinois *Register-Star,* October 31, 1987.

255 *Tammy Faye Bakker: "How sad . . .":* Excerpt from *Tammy's House Party,* television program, broadcast October 15, 1985.

255 *Reagan's speech on AIDS:* Cannon, *President Reagan,* pp. 816–819. Also, Koop interview.

255 *Reagan appoints AIDS commission:* Ibid., p. 819.

256 *"advertisements for condoms":* Marie Winn, "The Legacy of Dr. Koop," *New York Times Magazine,* Part II, "Good Health Magazine," October 9, 1988, p. 30. The critic was James P. McFadden, chair of an organization called the Ad Hoc Committee in Defense of Life.

256 *Shilts praises Koop:* Randy Shilts, *And the Band Played On* (St. Martin's Press, 1987), p. 588.

CHAPTER 11: THE INVISIBLE ARMY

259 *"the Lord refused to give me the liberty":* Pat Robertson, with Jamie Buckingham, *Shout It from the Housetops* (South Plainfield, NJ: Bridge Publishing, 1972), p. 195.

259 *"partisan politics is the wrong path":* Allen Mayer, et al., "A Tide of Born-Again Politics," *Newsweek,* September 15, 1980.

259 *"Your objective . . . Mine is through spiritual means":* Duane Oldfield, *The Right and the Righteous: The Christian Right Confronts the Republican Party* (Ph.D. dissertation, University of California, Berkeley, 1991), pp. 311–312.

PAGE

259 *"We're not running ads . . ."*: California assistant state coordinator Fred Niergarth, quoted in Sara Diamond, *Spiritual Warfare: The Politics of the Christian Right* (Boston: South End Press, 1989), p. 74.

261 *Michigan caucus system:* See Jack W. Germond and Jules Witcover, *Whose Broad Stripes and Bright Stars? The Trivial Pursuit of the Presidency 1988* (New York: Warner Books, 1989), pp. 80–82.

261 *Weyrich: "I'd lead a draft movement":* Cory SerVaas and Maynard Good Stoddard, "CBN's Pat Robertson: White House Next?" *Saturday Evening Post,* March 1985, p. 51.

262 *"Pat was behaving like . . . politician":* General Jerry Currie, Interview.

262 *Marc Nuttle:* David Shribman, "Robertson's Strategist, Nuttle, Sticks to His Credo as Campaign Is Threatened by Swaggart Scandal," *The Wall Street Journal,* February 23, 1988.

263 *Doug Wead's recommendations:* Memo, "The Vice President and the Evangelicals: A Strategy," December 18, 1985. Photocopied memo furnished by Doug Wead.

265 *Freedom Council instructions:* Robert Boyd and Angelia Herrin, "Pat Robertson's Christian backers gain influence in GOP," *Miami Herald,* May 6, 1986.

266 *Freedom Council requests 25,000 petitions:* Joel Smith, "Political mission mounted," Detroit *News,* May 1, 1986.

266 *Cobo Hall gathering:* David Waymire, "TV evangelist Robertson flexes his political muscle," Muskegon, Michigan *Chronicle,* May 9, 1986.

266 *"Atwater's got great information."* Bush aide Ron Kaufman to Wead, as recalled by Wead, interview.

267 *"anecdotal evidence suggests . . .":* Paul Taylor, "Churches Were the Way to Robertson's Recruits," *Washington Post,* May 28, 1986.

267 *"When a person of Robertson's newcomer status . . . home run":* Jacob V. Lamar Jr., "Michigan's Holy Confusion," *Time,* June 9, 1986, p. 31.

267 *"The Lord has spoken here tonight":* Matt Galbraith, "Evangelist tests political waters." South Bend, Indiana, *Tribune,* April 16, 1986.

267 *"Pat, Go For It":* "Presidential Exploratory Panel Gets Approval from Robertson," *Washington Post,* August 3, 1986.

268 *Robertson and Hurricane Gloria:* Reported in, among other places, Jeffrey K. Hadden and Anson Shupe, *Televangelism: Power and Politics on God's Frontier* (New York: Henry Holt, 1988), pp. 192–193. 1995 hurricane statement heard by author.

268 *Freedom Council: "The Christians have won":* Oldfield, *The Right and the Righteous,* p. 357.

268 *"God's plan . . . establishing this" and "no coincidence":* Sidney Blumenthal, *Pledging Allegiance: The Last Campaign of the Cold War* (New York: HarperCollins, 1990), p. 103.

269 *"If God is for us . . .":* Germond and Witcover, *Whose Broad Stripes?,* p. 90.

269 *Nuttle: "a masterful job of 'spin control' ":* Quoted in Germond and Witcover, p. 91.

270 *Robertson reorganizes to meet legal requirements:* Germond and Witcover, pp. 86–89. Bush also reorganized his campaign operations to meet federal requirements.

270 *Former Freedom Council employees offered $100:* Oldfield, *The Right and the Righteous,* p. 331.

270 *Robertson seeks three million signatures:* "Three-hour Robertson telecast planned," *Washington Times,* August 20, 1986. See also Oldfield, *The Right and the Righteous,* p. 314, and Germond and Witcover, *Whose Broad Stripes?,* p. 89.

270 *Robertson made history:* Dudley Clendinen, "Robertson sets condition for making a run in 1988," *New York Times,* September 18, 1986.

270 *ACTV backed by the Reverend Sun Moon:* Carolyn Weaver, "Unholy Alliance," *Mother Jones,* January 1986, p. 14.

271 *"He's probably the best-trained . . . president":* Falwell, quoted in Oldfield, *The Right and the Righteous,* pp. 315–316.

271 *"a marriage of convenience" and "Anybody But Bush":* Germond and Witcover, *Whose Broad Stripes?,* p. 92, quoting Kemp campaign workers Saul Anuzis and Clark Durant, respectively.

271 *Robertson-Kemp forces "changed the rules" and gained control of state central committee:* Germond and Witcover, p. 93.

272 *"We don't really care . . . Christian philosophy":* Mary Matalin, quoted in Germond and Witcover, p. 95.

276 *PTL falls:* For a full account of the PTL scandal, see Charles Shepard, *Forgiven: The*

PAGE

Rise and Fall of Jim Bakker and the PTL Ministry (Atlantic Monthly Press, 1989). See also Hadden and Shupe, *Televangelism,* and Larry Martz with Ginny Carroll, *Ministry of Greed* (New York: Weidenfeld and Nicolson, 1988).

276 *March 1987 NYT poll:* Cited in Hadden and Shupe, *Televangelism,* p. 16.

276 *Robertson announces income drop and layoffs:* Ibid., p. 17.

276 *"Scandal has hit . . . like a bombshell":* Ibid., p. 17.

276 LA Times *and* USA Today *polls show Robertson hurt by scandals:* Ibid.

283 *Nuttle: "To our base . . . in the South":* Quoted in David R. Runkel, ed., *The Campaign for President: The Managers Look at '88* (Dover, MA: Auburn House, 1989), p. 69.

284 *McCloskey claims Senator Robertson kept his son from combat:* See, for example, Joe Conason, Jack Newfield, and James Ridgeway, "With Dad on His Side," *Village Voice,* September 16, 1986.

284 *Robertson's libel suit dragged on:* Sara Diamond, *Spiritual Warfare: The Politics of the Christian Right* (Boston: South End Press, 1989), p. 76.

284 *CBN funds Contras:* Sara Diamond review of David Edwin Harrell, Jr., *Pat Robertson: A Personal, Political and Religious Portrait* (San Francisco: Harper and Row, 1987), in *The Nation,* February 13, 1988. For a critical account of the activities of Robertson and other Christian conservatives with regard to politics in Central America and other locales, see Diamond, *Spiritual Warfare,* especially pages 161–229, and *The Road to Dominion: Right-Wing Movements and Political Power in the United States* (New York: The Guilford Press, 1995), pp. 237–241.

284 *Robertson's claims regarding U.S. hostages in Lebanon:* Diamond, *Spiritual Warfare,* pp. 18–19. Diamond's source for Robertson's original claim is the *Washington Post,* February 25, 1988.

291 *Robertson supporters swamp post-primary meetings:* For an account of these events, see Allen D. Hertzke, *Echoes of Discontent: Jesse Jackson, Pat Robertson, and the Resurgence of Populism* (Washington: CQ Press, 1993), pp. 160–161.

294 *Evangelicals give Bush eighty percent of their votes:* Ibid., p. 180.

295 *"tidal wave shift . . . in evangelical world":* Robertson, quoted in Wilcox, p. 145.

295 *Voting data analyzed:* John Green and Lisa Langenbach, "Hollow Core: Evangelical Clergy and the 1988 Robertson Campaign," *Polity,* Fall 1992, vol. xxv, no. 1.

296 *Vicki Kemper article:* "Looking for a Promised Land," *Sojourners,* June 1988, pp. 22 28.

CHAPTER 12: CHRISTIAN COALITION

299 *"Pat, you've got to do something":* McCormack call as recalled by Robertson.

307 *Moderate Republican commends Christian Coalition manual:* Former Bush aide Bobbie Greene Kilberg, interview.

307 *"Like Queen Esther":* See Esther 4:14.

315 *Land and Dugan comments on gays at the White House:* Frank J. Murray and George Archibald, "Bush Link to Right is Fired," *Washington Times,* August 2, 1990.

316 *Wead: Bush "a man who lives . . . family values" and "staff did not serve him well":* Quoted in Lawrence M. O'Rourke, "Dismissed: The Firing of a White House Aide Angers the Religious Right," *St. Louis Post-Dispatch,* August 16, 1990, 1A, 18A.

316 *"decision 'poorly served' the president":* Washington Times, August 2, 1990.

316 *Bauer and Grant comments on gays at White House, Wead firing:* Murray and Archibald, "Bush Link to Right."

318 *Reed: "I do guerilla warfare":* Virginian Pilot, November 9, 1991.

318 *Reed recommends substitution of sports metaphors for warfare imagery:* The Christian Coalition's "Road to Victory," a report prepared by the Interfaith Alliance Foundation and Americans United for Separation of Church and State, September, 1995, p. 7. According to this account, Reed's letter was sent in December 1992, shortly after Bill Clinton's election.

319 *"The San Diego Model":* Barry Horstman, "Crusade for Public Office in 2nd Stage," *Los Angeles Times,* March 22, 1992; Horstman, "Christian Activists Using 'Stealth' Campaign Tactics," *Los Angeles Times,* April 5, 1992.

319 *Reed disavows San Diego Model:* Interview. A similar disavowal is published in *A Campaign of Falsehoods: The Anti-Defamation League's Defamation of Religious Conservatives,* (Chesapeake, Virginia: Christian Coalition, July 28, 1994), p. 10. This report was written specifically as a response to David Cantor, *The Religious Right: The*

Assault on Tolerance & Pluralism in America (New York: Anti-Defamation League, 1994).

319 *Reed: Stealth was a factor in San Diego . . . more effective":* Quoted in Horstman, "Crusade"; Horstman, "Christian Activists."

320 *Reed denies "guerilla warfare" quoted in* Los Angeles Times: Thomas B. Edsall, "Christian Political Soldier Helps Revive Movement," *Washington Post,* September 10, 1993.

321 *"One of the things . . . impact on me":* Francis A. Schaeffer, *A Christian Manifesto* (Westchester, IL: Crossways Books, 1981).

321 Scheidler Books. Joseph M. Scheidler, *Closed: 99 Ways to Stop Abortion* (Westchester, Illinois: Crossways Books, 1985).

322 *Terry's jeremiad:* From "Operation Rescue," video produced by Operation Rescue.

323 *Judge Kelly's order:* Protesters "should say farewell . . . going to jail." John Elson, et al., "Abortion: The Feds v. a Federal Judge," *Time,* August 19, 1991, p. 22. "Nobody is above the law." ABC-TV News, Nightline, August 6, 1991.

323 *Anti-OR sentiments expressed:* ABC-TV News coverage of Operation Rescue protest in Wichita, Kansas, August 25, 1991.

323 *Terry: "Absolutely not":* Richard Lacayo Interview with Randall Terry, "Crusading Against the Pro-Choice Movement," *Time* (October 21, 1991), p. 26.

324 *Terry attempts to see President Bush:* ABC News coverage of President Bush vacationing in Kennebunkport, Maine, August 17, 1991.

325 *Church at Pierce Creek runs ad, Terry says, "tax-exempt status be damned":* Cantor, *The Religious Right,* p. 116.

325 *Reed: "the most conservative platform":* CBS News coverage of conservative press conference on GOP platform August 13, 1992.

325 *Buchanan convention speech:* CBS News coverage of Republican National Convention in Houston, Texas, August 17, 1992.

326 *Convention may not have hurt Republicans significantly:* For an example of an analysis of 1992 exit-poll data, see James L. Guth, et al., "God's Own Party: Evangelicals and Republicans in the '92 election," *Christian Century,* February 17, 1993, pp. 172–176.

328 *Bush and Quayle address Christian Coalition groups: Church and State,* October 1992.

328 *Bush's "G-O-D" and Reed's reaction:* Ralph Reed, *Politically Incorrect: The Emerging Faith Factor in American Politics* (Dallas: Word, 1994), p. 72.

328 *Voter registration in church:* Reed, on National Public Radio, September 23, 1992, quoted by Erin Saberi, "From Moral Majority to Organized Minority: Tactics of the Religious Right," *The Christian Century,* August 11, 1993, p. 782.

328 *Clyde Wilcox: Sociology of Religion,* Fall 1994, 55:3, pp. 232–261.

CHAPTER 13: AND WHO SHALL LEAD THEM?

330 *Reed: "Clinton got off to a horrific start":* Interview. Zoë Baird was Clinton's first nominee for Attorney General. She withdrew from consideration when it was revealed that she had employed illegal aliens as drivers and nannies. Lani Guinier, nominated for the post of Assistant Attorney General for civil rights issues, was forced to withdraw because of opposition to her controversial suggestions as to ways voting laws might be altered to improve the chances of electing minority candidates.

331 *Weyrich's National Empowerment Television:* David Cantor, *The Religious Right* (New York: Anti-Defamation League, 1994), p. 96.

332 *"Scopes II":* For an engaging and admirably objective account of the Hawkins County conflict, see Stephen Bates, *Battleground: One Mother's Crusade, the Religious Right, and the Struggle for Control of Our Classrooms* (New York: Poseidon Press, 1993).

333 *Anti-Semitic themes in Robertson's* The New World Order: See Michael Lind, "Reverend Robertson's Grand International Conspiracy Theory," *New York Review of Books,* February 2, 1995, pp. 21–25.

334 *Robertson letter in support of Farris:* Jill Smolowe, et al., "Crusade for the Classroom," *Time,* November 1, 1993, p. 35.

334 *Farris challenges of wisdom of distributing voter guides to general public:* Quoted in Michael Cromartie, ed., *Disciples and Democracy: Religious Conservatives and the Future of American Politics* (Grand Rapids: Wm. B. Eerdmans Publishing Co., 1994), p. 97.

335 *Hart seeks to ban Itchy Witchy and Duso the Dolphin:* Michael McLeod, "Superiority Complex," *Florida* Magazine, August 21, 1994, p. 12.

336 *Robert Simonds quotation and statistics:* David Cantor, *The Religious Right: The Assault*

on Tolerance and Pluralism in America (New York: Anti-Defamation League, 1994), p. 102.

336 *Sample from voter guide:* McLeod, "Superiority Complex," p. 13.

337 *Voters Guide assertions called "a lie":* The defeated candidate was Tim Sullivan, quoted in Elizabeth Shogren and Douglas Frantz, "School Boards Become the Religious Right's New Pulpit," *Los Angeles Times,* December 10, 1993.

337 *"incompetent do-gooders":* McLeod, "Superiority Complex," p. 10.

337 *School board meeting described:* Ibid.

338 *Currie's plan "a power grab":* Ibid., p. 11.

338 *Children belong at home:* Elizabeth Shogren and Douglas Frantz, "School Boards . . ." *Los Angeles Times,* December 10, 1993.

339 *Geraldo Rivera on multiculturalism:* McLeod, "Superiority Complex," p. 8.

339 *Assessment of Religious Right strength within Republican Party:* John Persinos, "Has the Christian Right Taken Over the Republican Party?" *Campaigns and Elections,* September, 1994, pp. 21–24. Professor John Green and his colleagues at the University of Akron offer two qualifications to these findings. First, in some states, social-issue conservatives not ordinarily viewed as part of the Christian Right contribute to this strength. Secondly, about half the states in both the "dominant strength" and "substantial influence" categories are in the South, where religious conservatives are largely unopposed. In the remaining states, mostly in the Midwest and on the West Coast, more moderate Republicans provide stiff opposition. Conversation and correspondence with John Green, May 1996.

340 *Members of 104th Congress receive high marks on Christian Coalition scorecards: The Christian Coalition's "Road to Victory"* (Washington: The Interfaith Alliance Foundation and Americans United for Separation of Church and State, September 1995), p. 31.

340 *Reed pledges support to Contract with America:* Ralph Reed, "Remarks to the Detroit Economic Club," January 17, 1995, reprinted in *Contract with the American Family, A bold plan by Christian Coalition to strengthen the family and restore common-sense values* (Nashville: Random House Moorings, 1995), p. 138.

341 *Dare to Discipline, a blend of "biblical principles . . .":* Steve Rabey, *For God, Home and Country: James Dobson's Focus on the Family,* M.A. thesis, Denver Conservative Baptist Seminary, October 1995, pp. 3–4. I gratefully acknowledge a debt to Mr. Rabey for his balanced and thoughtful treatment of Dobson and Focus on the Family. Unless otherwise noted, all statistics are from Rabey's thesis.

342 *"Focus on the Family does Christian radio better. . . .":* Rabey, Ibid., p. 101.

342 *Family Research Council Statistics:* Elizabeth Kolbest, "Bauer Power," *New York Times* News Service 1995, published on America Online.

343 *Family Issues Alert containing "up-to-the-minute news":* Undated promotional flier, code number 4PTXCI FC019, quoted by Rabey, Ibid., p. 143.

343 *Alliance Defense Fund established:* Ibid., p. 155.

343 *Dobson reacts to Barbour's comments; Bauer and Reed threaten to bolt:* Ibid., citing Rabey's article, "Focus on Family to GOP: Don't budge on abortion," Colorado Springs *Gazette Telegraph,* March 9, 1995, A1–2.

344 *Conservatives assail Colin Powell:* Richard L. Berke, "Powell Record is Criticized by Conservatives in G.O.P.," *New York Times,* November 3, 1995; Paul Taylor and Dan Balz, "Conservatives Fire Away at Powell's Possible Bid," *Washington Post,* November 3, 1995. "Clinton with ribbons" is from "Fight Over Colin Powell Splits Religious Right," *Church and State,* December 1995, pp. 14–15.

344 *Dobson's letter to Reed:* "Fight Over Colin Powell Splits Religious Right," *Church and State,* December 1995, p. 15, quoting the *Washington Post.*

344 *Dobson on the Civil War of Values:* James Dobson and Gary L. Bauer, *Children at Risk* (Dallas: Word, 1990), John Henderson, "Coach's Crusade Catches Fire," p. 22.

345 *Dobson on secular humanist objectives:* Dobson and Bauer, *Children at Risk,* p. 38.

345 *Noebel claims rock music is communist tool:* Cantor, *The Religious Right,* p. 83, quoting Noebel, *Communism, Hypnotism and the Beatles* (Tulsa: Christian Crusade, 1965). Another anti-rock book by Noebel include *Rhythm Ride in Revolution, The Marxist Minstrels, The Beatles: A study in Drugs, Sex, and Revolution,* and *The Legacy of John Lennon.*

348 *Will Perkins on Amendment 2:* Bella Stumbo, "The State of Hate: Colorado's anti-gay rights amendment," *Esquire,* September 1993, p. 73.

348 *Content of CFV presentations to evangelical churches, Perkins comment, "they're not!":* Ibid.

348 *McCartney, Homosexuality "an abomination":* **Sporting News,** November 2, 1992.

PAGE

349 *Amendment 2 carries:* Stumbo, "The State of Hate," *Esquire,* p. 73.

349 *McCartney background, team prayers:* Denver *Post,* July 24, 1994; Gannett Rochester Newspapers, December 29, 1992; Interview, the Reverend Philip Campbell.

350 *Promise Keepers statistics:* David Van Biema, with Richard Ostling, "Full of Promise," *Time,* November 6, 1995, pp. 62–63.

351 *Promise Keepers' unofficial text:* Bill Bright, Edwin Cole, Dr. James Dobson, Tony Evans, Bill McCartney, Luis Palau, Randy Phillips, and Gary Smalley, contributing authors. *Seven Promises of a Promise Keeper* (Colorado Springs: Focus on the Family Publishing, 1994).

351 *"I'm trying to describe . . . vacuum":* Tony Evans, "Spiritual Purity" in *Seven Promises,* p. 73. The Seven Promises of a Promise Keeper are:
1. Honor Jesus Christ through worship, prayer, and obedience to his Word.
2. Pursue vital relationships with a few other men, understanding that a man needs brothers to help him keep his promises.
3. Practice spiritual, moral, ethical, and sexual purity.
4. Build strong marriages and families.
5. Support the mission of the church by honoring and praying for one's pastor and by actively giving of one's time and resources.
6. Reach beyond racial and nominational barriers to demonstrate the power of biblical unity.
7. Influence the world by being obedient to the Great Commandment (Mark 12:30–31) and the Great Commission (Matthew 28:19–20).

351 *Evans on reclaiming the reins:* Ibid., pp. 79–80.

352 *"Women are thrilled":* Denver *Post,* July 17, 1993.

352 *McCartney: "the white man . . . oppression":* Ed Morrow, Denver *Post,* June 10, 1993.

352 *McCartney felt Spirit of God ". . . won't be there either":* Edward Gilbreath, "Manhood's Great Awakening," *Christianity Today,* February 6, 1995, p. 23.

354 *"pluralism is a myth":* Rob Boston, "Thy Kingdom Come," *Church & State,* September 1988, pp. 7–8, quoting an article by Reconstructionist author Byron Snapp in a 1987 issue of *The Council of Chalcedon,* a Reconstructionist journal.

354 *Rushdoony, "in the name of toleration . . .":* Rodney Clapp, "Democracy as Heresy," *Christianity Today,* February 20, 1987, p. 19, quoting a passage from R. J. Rushdoony's massive tome, *The Institutes of Biblical Law.*

354 *"Though we hide their books . . .":* Unidentified interviewee, quoted in Laurence R. Iannaccone, "The Economics of American Fundamentalists," in Martin E. Marty and R. Scott Appleby, eds., *Fundamentalisms and the State: Remaking Politics, Economics, and Militance,* Volume 3 of The Fundamentalism Project (Chicago: University of Chicago Press, 1993), p. 348.

354 *Robertson: "only bring Christians and Jews," and "There will never be world peace . . .":* *The New World Order* (Dallas: Word, 1991), pp. 218 and 227, respectively.

354 *Jay Grimstead: "I don't call myself [a Reconstructionist":* Quoted in Randy Frame, "The Theonomic Urge," *Christianity Today,* April 21, 1989, p. 39.

355 *Newspaper account of IMPACT:* Reported in *Sunshine,* the Sunday magazine of the Fort Lauderdale *Sun-Sentinel,* quoted in David Cantor, *The Religious Right,* p. 117.

355 *Terry statements on intolerance and hatred:* Ibid., p. 118.

356 *Statements on violence from Chicago meeting:* New Orleans *Times-Picayune,* November 19, 1994.

358 *Reed addresses Michigan Christian Coalition:* James Bennet, "Abortion Opponents Unite to Warn Dole on the Issue," *New York Times,* March 17, 1996.

358 *Ralph Reed considers revisions in hard-line abortion policy:* James Bennet, "Top Conservative Would Back Shift on Abortion Issue," *New York Times,* May 4, 1996, pp. 1, 9, and Bennet, "Leader of Christian Coalition Denies Shifting on Abortion," *New York Times,* May 5, 1996, pp. 1, 15. Reed's calling a Human Life Amendment a "remote weapon," quoted in the latter article, as well as the description of his proposed platform plank, are taken from his book, *Active Faith* (New York: Free Press, 1996), excerpted before publication in *Newsweek,* May 13, 1996, p. 29.

359 *Buchanan and Dobson warn against changing anti-abortion plank:* Howard Fineman, "The Fight Inside the Tent," *Newsweek,* May 13, 1996, pp. 24–25.

360 *Woodbridge: "Culture-war rhetoric leads us to distort . . ." and mention of Dobson:* John D. Woodbridge, "Culture War Casualties," *Christianity Today,* March 6, 1995, p. 22.

PAGE

360 *Dobson's response:* James Dobson, "Why I Use 'Fighting Words,'" *Christianity Today,* June 19, 1995, pp. 27–30.

360 *Woodbridge's rejoinder:* Woodbridge, "Why Words Matter," *Christianity Today,* June 19, 1995, pp. 31–32.

364 *Reed rejects theocratic language:* Reed, *Politically Incorrect,* p. 134; *Contract with the American Family,* pp. xi–xiii; *Active Faith,* excerpt published in *Newsweek,* May 12, 1996, p. 29.

365 *Reed: "sensitivity . . . anti-Semitism":* Charlie Rose Show, PBS transcript #1318.

EPILOGUE: UP AGAINST THE WALL

373 *Jefferson's Bill for Establishing Religious Freedom:* Thomas Jefferson, *Writings,* edited by Merrill D. Peterson (Library of America, 1984), pp. 346–47.

373 *Madison's "Memorial and Remonstrance against Religious Assessments":* The Papers of James Madison (Chicago: University of Chicago Press, 1973), VIII, pp. 298–304. Also available in various collections of doctrines pertaining to church-state relations.

374 *Acknowledgment of "Jesus Christ, the holy author" rejected: Writings of Thomas Jefferson,* ed. P. F. Ford (New York: G. P. Putnam's Sons, 1892), I, p. 54, quoted in Leo Pfeffer, *Church, State, and Freedom* (Boston: Beacon Press, 1967), p. 114.

375 *Reactions to absence of religious references in Constitution:* Quoted in Martin Borden, "Christ and the Constitution." *Church and State,* Vol. 10, 1987, p. 10.

375 *William Lee Miller quoted:* James E. Wood, Jr., "No Religious Test: Good Medicine for the Body Politic," *Church and State,* Vol. 10, 1987, p. 14, adapted from an editorial in *Journal of Church and State,* Vol. 29, Spring 1987, pp. 199, 206–208.

376 *Jefferson's letter to the Danbury Baptists:* For the text of the letters from the Baptists and from Jefferson, as well as other relevant materials, see Charles Haynes, *Religion in American History: what to teach and how* (Association for Supervision and Curriculum Development), 1990, pp. 39–58.

377 *Rehnquist on Jefferson's letter to the Danbury Baptists:* Mary Ann Glendon and Raul Yanes, "Structural Free Exercise," *Michigan Law Review* (Dec. 1991), Vol. 90, no. 3, p. 483.

377 *Jefferson asked Lincoln to review his letter:* Haynes, *Religion in American History,* pp. 51–52.

377 *Madison hewed a straighter line:* See Leonard W. Levy, "The Original Meaning of the Establishment Clause of the First Amendment," in James E. Wood, Jr., ed., *Religion and the State, Essays in Honor of Leo Pfeffer* (Waco: Baylor University Press, 1985), p. 55.

377 *"the number, the industry . . . church from the state":* Anson Phelps Stokes and Leo Pfeffer, *Church and State in the United States,* 1950, p. 89. Cited in Robert Boston, *Why the Religious Right Is Wrong About Separation of Church & State* (Buffalo: Prometheus Press, 1993), p. 70.

377 *Madison's response to Adams:* Norman Cousins, *In God We Trust* (New York: Harper, 1958), p. 299. Quoted in Boston, *Why the Religious Right Is Wrong,* p. 71.

379 *Persecution following Gobitis decision:* Pfeffer, *Church, State, and Freedom,* p. 638.

379 *Court accepts flag-saluting case. West Virginia State Board of Education v. Barnette,* 319 U.S. 624 (1943).

379 *Everson v. the Board of Education.* 330 U.S. I (1947).

380 *Abington School District v. Schempp,* 374 U.S. 203 (1963).

380 *"the forest of Hansel and Gretel":* A. E. Dick Howard, "The Wall of Separation: The Supreme Court as Uncertain Stonemason," in James E. Wood, Jr., ed., *Religion and the State: Essays in Honor of Leo Pfeffer* (Waco: Baylor University Press, 1985), p. 96. In making these points, Howard cites *Meek v. Pittinger,* 421 U.S. 349 (1975) as well as the other cases mentioned in this paragraph.

380 *Display of Ten Commandments prohibited: Stone v. Graham,* 499 U.S. (1980).

380 *Alabama school prayer exercise unconstitutional: Wallace v. Jaffree,* 472 U.S. (1985).

381 *Crèche display approved: Lynch v. Donnelly,* No. 82-1256, 1984. Quoted in Howard, "The Wall of Separation," p. 111.

381 *Justice Black's opinion in Engel: Engel v. Vitale,* 421 U.S. (1962), pp. 433–435.

382 *Justice Clark's remarks in Schempp: Abington Township School District v. Schempp,* 203 U.S. (1963) pp. 225–226.

383 *"Protestant" and "Catholic" attitudes toward the Constitution:* Sanford Levinson, "'The Constitution' in American Civil Religion," in Martin E. Marty, ed., *Civil Religion, Church and State.* Vol. 3 in *Modern American Protestantism and Its World, Historical*

PAGE
  Articles on Protestantism in American Religious Life (New York: K. G. Saur, 1992),
  pp. 326–354.

For permission to reprint, grateful acknowledgment is given to the following:

Mercer University Press for portions of "The Transformation of Fundamentalism Between the World Wars" by William Martin. *Critical Moments in Religious History* edited by K. Keulman. Macon: Mercer University Press, 1993. Used by permission of Mercer University Press.

William Morrow and Company for portions of *A Prophet with Honor: The Billy Graham Story* by William Martin. Copyright © 1991 by William Martin. Used by permission of William Morrow and Co., Inc.

The New York Times for quotations. Copyright © 1961, 1964, 1966, 1996 by The New York Times Co. Reprinted by permission.

Charles Scribner's Sons for portions from William Martin, "Mass Communications." Excerpted by permission of Charles Scribner's Sons, an imprint of Simon & Schuster Macmillan, from ENCYCLOPEDIA OF THE AMERICAN RELIGIOUS EXPERIENCE, Charles H. Lippey and Peter W. Williams, Editors. Vol. III, pp. 1711–1726. Copyright © 1988 Charles Scribner's Sons.

INDEX

Abington v. Schempp, 380, 381
Abortion, 182, 192–96, 200, 260, 320–25,
    355–59. *See also* Operation Rescue;
    Terry, Randall
    1992 presidential campaign and, 325
    Bush and, 264, 310, 324
    Carter's policy on, 156
    Human Life Statute (Helms-Hyde bill)
      and, 226–27
    Koop and, 238–41, 252
    Reagan administration and, 226–29
    Reed and, 356–59
Abraham, Spence, 292
Abzug, Bella, 166
Active Faith, 359, 364
ACT UP, 282, 315
Adult Bulletin, 104, 109
AIDS, 241–57
    federal government and, 249
    Jimmy Allen and, 243–47, 257
    Koop and, 241–42, 248, 249–57
    quarantine of people with, 243
    Reagan administration and, 249–56
Allen, Jimmy, 157
    AIDS and, 243–45, 246–47, 256–57
Allen, Lydia, 244, 245, 246
Allen, Matthew, 244, 245
Allen, Scott, 244, 245, 257
Allen, Skip, 244, 246
Alliance Defense Fund, 343
Amendment 2 (Colorado), 347–49
American and International Councils of
    Christian Churches (ACCC-ICCC),
    22, 35, 36, 38, 51, 79
American Center for Law and Justice, 361
American Civil Liberties Union, 14

American Coalition for Traditional Values,
    270
American Conservative Union, 89
American Council of Christian Laymen, 39
American Family Association, 243
American Family Forum, 181, 186
Americans for Freedom, 270
Americans with Disabilities Act, 315
AmWay distributors, 289
Anaheim, California, sex education in,
    102–16
Anaheim Bulletin, The, 102, 108, 113
Anderson, Carl, 239, 251, 279
Anderson, John, 214
Androcles and the Lion, story of, 125
Antichrist, 7, 20
Anti-communism, 46
  in 1960s, 75–77
  Billy Graham and, 29, 33–35, 41–42, 75
Anti-semitism, 9, 11–12, 20, 39, 215, 333,
    365
Anti-war movement, 144
Armstrong, Ben, 212
Association of Gentlemen, 4–5
Athletes in Action, 92
Atwater, Lee, 262, 267, 269, 289, 291, 311

Bahnsen, Greg, 353
Bailey, Kenneth K., 4
Baker, Howard, 222
Baker, James, 223, 224, 235, 326
Bakker, Jim, 172, 212, 275–76
Bakker, Tammy Faye, 255, 275
Balfour Declaration, 12
Baptists, 56, 151, 154. *See also* Northern

Baptists; Southern Baptist Convention
(SBC); Southern Baptists
Barbour, Haley, 343, 364
Battle for the Mind (LaHaye), 196
Bauer, Gary, 251, 252, 254, 312, 316, 342–
43, 347, 356, 357, 363, 364
Bay of Pigs invasion, 77
Becker Amendment, 78, 80
Bell, Clayton, 206
Bell, L. Nelson, 52
Bell, Terrel, 222
Benham, Philip "Flip," 322, 356
Bennett, John C., 53
Bennett, William, 254, 344
Berg, Joseph, 181
Berkeley Blitz, 93–94
Bible, the
reading in public schools, 71, 77–78, 86,
168, 192, 378–82
Revised Standard Version of, 37–38
Bible Balloon Project, 39
Bible colleges and institutes, 17–18
Bible Institute of Los Angeles (BIOLA),
17–18
Bible Presbyterian Church, 16
Biblical criticism, 6, 9, 15
Biblical inerrancy, 7–8, 126
Bill for Establishing Religious Freedom
(Jefferson), 373, 374
Billings, Bill, 173, 174, 181
Billings, Robert, 169, 171, 192, 199, 200,
222, 230
Bill of Rights, 376. *See also* First
Amendment
Black, Hugo, 19, 196, 379, 381
Black evangelicals, 59–60, 64, 67, 73, 260,
279, 318, 352, 360, 365–66
Blackmun, Harry A., 227
Blackwell, Morton, 87–88, 89, 191, 218,
221–22, 223, 225, 232–35, 300, 326–
27, 362
Blake, Eugene Carson, 49–50
Blumenthal, Sidney, 234
Bob Jones University, 169
Bond, Rich, 291
Bonhoeffer, Dietrich, 64
Boone, Pat, 293
Bork, Robert, 227
"Born-again" experience or concept, 149–
52, 263–64
Brandt, Ed, 241
Braun, Jon, 26, 27, 51, 92, 93
Brennan, William, 381
Briggs, Kenneth, 149, 151, 208, 217
Bright, Bill, 28, 45, 91–93, 146, 153, 179,
186, 191, 205, 206, 212

Broadcasters. *See* Radio programs;
Television preachers
Brock, Bill, 214
Broder, David, 87
Bronfenbrenner, Ure, 180
Brown, Harold O. J., 156, 193–94, 214,
238, 240
Brown v. the Board of Education of Topeka, 43
Bryan, William Jennings, 13–14, 15
Bryant, Anita, 166, 197
Buchanan, Bay, 359
Buchanan, Pat, 242, 251, 325, 326, 358–59
Buckley, William, 243
Bundy, Edgar C., 39, 77
Burch, Dean, 89
Burger, Warren, 380, 381
Bush, George, 234, 252–53, 261, 300
1988 presidential campaign and, 262–67,
269, 271, 277, 289–94
1992 presidential campaign and, 325–28
abortion issue and, 324
homosexuals and, 314–16
as president, 309–17
Religious Right and, 310–17, 325–28
Bush, George, Jr., 292
Bush, Neil, 290
Business and Professional People's Alliance
for Better Textbooks, 123, 133, 137–
38

Calderone, Mary, 101, 114–15
Califano, Joseph, Jr., 155
California Citizens Committee. *See* Citizens
Committee of California
California Families United, 108
Campbell, Sam, 89, 102–3, 107, 108, 115
Campus Crusade for Christ (CCC), 28, 45,
91–93, 145
Cannon, Lou, 224, 255
Cantwell v. Connecticut, 378
Capital punishment, 228, 353, 354, 357,
367
Carr, John, 174, 176, 177, 179–82, 184,
187–88
Carter, Jimmy, 148–61, 166, 169, 207, 208,
259
1976 campaign and election, 153–59
abortion policy of, 156
as born-again Christian, 149–52
Equal Rights Amendment and, 161, 189
Falwell and, 207, 211, 220
family policy of, 154–56, 177–78
Playboy interview, 157–58
White House Conference on Families
(1980) and, 155–56, 173–78, 180,
188–89

Carter, Rosalynn, 164, 165
Castro, Fidel, 76–77
Catholic Alliance, 366, 368
Center for Sex and Religion, 115
Centers for Disease Control (CDC), 241
Chancellor, John, 150
Charismatics, 258–59
Charleston Gazette, 126, 136
Chicago Evangelization Society, 8
Choice, Not an Echo, A (Schlafly), 81–82
Christian Action Coalition, 172
Christian Action Council, 156, 193–94, 238–39
Christian-American Parents, 127
Christian Anti-Communism Crusade, 39
Christian Beacon, 76, 79
Christian Broadcasting Network (CBN), 160, 269, 276, 303
Christian Century (journal), 27
Christian Coalition, 302, 303–9, 311, 312, 317–20, 328, 329, 331, 332, 334, 336, 339, 340, 361, 362, 365, 366–67
  abortion issue and, 356
Christian Crusade, 37, 76, 79
Christian Crusade, 76
Christian day schools. *See* Private Schools
Christian Echoes Ministry, 37
Christian Embassy, 191
Christian Freedom Foundation (CFF), 40–41, 179, 191
Christianity, schoolbooks and, 121, 125–26
Christianity Today (magazine), 42, 51, 52, 193, 359
Christian Manifesto, A (Schaeffer), 321
Christian Reconstructionism. *See* Reconstructionism
Christian schools. *See* Private schools
Christian Voice, 172, 210, 218, 270
Christian World Liberation Front, 94
Church and State. *See* Separation of church and state
Church League of America, 39
Citizens Committee of California, 81, 106, 112
Citizens for Carter, 153–54
Citizens for Decency through Law, 135
Citizens for Excellence in Education, 319, 336
Citizens for Religious Freedom, 52, 53
Civic League, 270
Civil Disobedience, 59, 79, 219, 323. *See also* Civil rights movement; Operation Rescue; Terry, Randall
Civil Rights Act of 1964, 68–69, 80, 85, 169

Civil rights movement, 55, 58, 60, 78–79, 202, 219, 226, 321–24, 357, 365–66
  in Lynchburg, 61–68, 72–73
Clark, Sam, 179, 182–83, 184
Clark, Tom, 380, 382
Clean Air Act, 317
Clendinen, Dudley, 270
Clinton, Bill, 324, 325, 328, 329
Coalition on Revival, 354
Cobelligerency, 197, 204
College Republicans, 300–301
Colorado, gay rights in, 347–48
Colorado for Family Values (CFV), 347, 348
Colson, Charles, 98, 99, 146, 149, 208
Committee for the Survival of a Free Congress, 171
Communism. *See* Anti-communism
Concerned Citizens (Kanawha County, West Virginia), 127, 137
Concerned Women for America, 164, 177, 178, 305, 309, 311, 331, 332, 335, 342
Condoms, AIDS and, 249–52, 255, 256
Congregationalists, 15
Congressional elections
  1986, 270
  1991, 317–18
  1994, 330–31, 339–40
Conlan, John, 153, 191, 192, 204, 209, 217, 221, 227
Connally, John, 209, 216, 217
Conservative Caucus, 192
Constitution, United States, 2, 49, 63, 78, 79, 85, 123, 147, 192, 213, 226–27, 232–34, 280, 349, 358, 372, 376, 374–78. *See also* Bill of Rights; First Amendment
  modes of interpreting, 382–83
Constitutions, state, 375
Contraceptives, 101. *See also* Condoms
Contract with America, 340
Contract with the American Family, 340–41, 364
Cook, Paul, 102, 112
Coors, Joseph, 135, 171
Cothern, Matt, 345–46
Cotton, John, 2
Coughlin, Charles, 18–19, 361
Court Street Baptist Church, 59, 61
Coverdell, Paul, 330
Cox, Harvey, 367
Crisp, Mary, 213
Criswell, W. A., 51, 158, 199, 236
Crowley, Mary, 199
Cuban missile crisis, 77

cummings, e. e., 122
Cunningham, David, 181–82, 185, 186
Currie, Jack, 337–38

Dade County, Florida, 197
Dannemeyer, William, 248
Dare to Discipline (Dobson), 341
Darrow, Clarence, 15
Davis, Angela, 144
Davis, Evelyn, 152, 188, 190
Davis, Ruth, 124, 126, 129–30, 140
Dearborn Independent, The, 12
Death penalty, 228, 353–54, 357, 367
Deaver, Michael, 208, 209, 217, 223, 224–
    25, 228
Decision (magazine), 51
Declaration of Independence, 2, 375
Defender (magazine), 19–20
Defenders of the Christian Faith, 19
Defensive Action, 355
DeMar, Gary, 353
Demarest, David, 312, 313, 316
Denton, Jeremiah, 220
DeVos, Richard, 152
Dewey, John, 195
Dexter Avenue Baptist Church, 59
Diamond Hill Baptist Church, 58
Dionne, E. J., 285, 288, 295, 309, 325
Dispensationalism (dispensationalist
    premillennialism), 7–8, 12, 36, 201
  New Evangelicals and, 40
Dixon, Amzi, 16
Dixon, Greg, 200
Dobson, Ed, 197, 200–203, 217, 219, 220,
    225–26, 229, 235, 247, 254, 278, 365
  on politics, 236, 368–69
Dobson, James, 172, 180, 184, 186, 188,
    341–46, 348–49, 356, 357–60
Dodd, Leighton, 72
Dole, Bob, 252, 277, 286, 288, 290, 343
  1996 presidential campaign and, 357, 358
Dominion Theology. *See*
    Reconstructionism
Donaldson, Sam, 154
Dornan, Robert, 135, 136, 142, 166
Dortch, Richard, 289
Dowless, John, 308–9, 334–37
Drake, Gordon, 107–08, 112
Draper, Jimmy, 206, 234
D'Souza, Dinesh, 200
Dugan, Robert, 180, 316
Dunlap, Donald, 280
Dunn, James, 51, 147, 149, 211, 216
DuPont, Pete, 252
DuVall, Jed, 129

Eagle Forum, 162, 177, 181, 317, 336
Edds, Mike, 123, 124, 126, 131–32, 138,
    141, 142–43
Edwards, Jonathan, 2, 3
Eisenhower, Dwight, 32, 33, 38, 41, 42,
    44–46, 75, 92
  Graham and, 44–45
Eizenstat, Stuart, 148, 156, 176, 193
Elwell, Marlene, 260–61, 265, 266, 272,
    277, 287, 288, 289, 292, 299, 356,
    361, 366
Engel v. Vitale, 381
English language, nonstandard, 120
Equal Rights Amendment (ERA), 161–66,
    181, 189, 196, 198, 204–05, 213–14
Establishment of religion, 373, 374, 376,
    377, 379–81
Evangelical Christians, historical
    background of, 4–6
Evans, Bob, 26
Evans, Rowland, 251
Evans, Tony, 351
Everson v. Board of Education, 379
Evolution, 6, 9, 13–14, 121, 133, 168, 196,
    217, 334, 346
  teaching of, in public schools, 13, 14

Faith Theological Seminary, 16
Falwell, Jerry, 55–58, 68–72, 158, 169, 193,
    196–99, 210, 212, 270–71, 275–76,
    293, 322, 354. *See also* Liberty
    University
  1980 election and, 220
  1988 presidential campaign and, 278
  AIDS and, 242, 243, 248, 254–55
  television audience of, 213
  Carter and, 207, 211, 220
  Christian schools and, 172. *See also*
    Lynchburg Christian Academy
  civil rights movement and, 57–58, 68–72,
    219
  direct mail and, 204–5
  Equal Rights Amendment and, 163, 166
  integration and, 57–58
  Lynchburg Christian Academy and, 70–
    72
  Moral Majority and, 200, 201–5, 218,
    219, 258, 270, 361, 366
  Sandra Day O'Connor's nomination to
    the Supreme Court and, 228
  Reagan administration and, 223, 232–35
  Robertson and, 258
  use of direct mail, 204–5
Families, White House Conference on
    (1980). *See* White House Conference
    on Families

Family Forum II, 232. *See also* American Family Forum

Family Life and Sex Education (FLSE), 103–6, 110, 111, 113

Family Life Seminars, 196

Family Protection Act, 230–31

Family Protection Report, 175

Family Research Council (FRC), 312, 342, 357, 361

Farris, Michael, 331–32, 333

Faubus, Orval, 44

Federal Council of Churches, 10, 22

Fellowship, The, 191

Fellowship of Christian Athletes, 349

Ferguson, "Ma," 14

Fike, Elmer, 123–24, 132–33, 135, 138

Finney, Charles, 4, 5, 7

First Amendment, 376, 378, 379, 381

Focus on the Family, 341–43, 348, 361

Focus on the Family (radio program), 341–42

Ford, Betty, 164

Ford, Gerald, 147, 158, 208

Ford, Henry, 12, 21

Founding Fathers, 31, 372–73, 383, 384

Free Congress Foundation, 224, 232

Freedom Council, 259–62, 265–69

Friedan, Betty, 164–65

Fuller, Charles E., 18, 56

Fuller Theological Seminary, 18

Fundamentalists, 11
  in 1920s, 13–17
  AIDS and, 242–43, 247, 254, 256
  pietism of, 201–2
  separatism of, 8, 36, 201–2, 204

Fundamentals: A Testimony to the Truth, The, 10–11

Gabler, Mel and Norma, 120–24, 135–37, 140

Gay rights, 197–98
  in Colorado, 347–48
  National Women's Conference and, 164–65
  White House Conference on Families (1980) and, 185

Gays and lesbians. *See* Homosexuals; Gay rights

George, Carol V. R., 53

Gilquist, Peter, 48, 94

Giminez, John, 212

Gingrich, Newt, 242–43, 330, 340, 343

Godsey, Bill, 57, 72, 207

Godsey, Melody, 57

Godsey, Nancy, 57, 72–73, 202, 235

Godsey, Emmitt, 57

Godwin, Ron, 234

Goldwater, Barry, 68–69, 74, 80–81, 82–88, 96, 333

Gore, Al, 328

Gospel Broadcasting Association, 18

Gothard, Bill, 180

Graham, Billy, 25–35, 39, 40, 41–42, 47, 51, 94, 193, 198, 206, 238, 263
  1952 presidential campaign and, 31–33
  1960 presidential campaign and, 48–53
  anti-communism and, 29, 33–35, 41–42, 75
  on "born-again" experience, 149
  civil rights movement and, 79–80
  Lyndon Johnson and, 95–96
  McCarthy and, 34–35, 38–39
  Nixon and, 31, 41–42, 48, 49, 95, 96–97, 145, 146–47
  organizing Christians into a political bloc opposed by, 153
  racism and, 42–44
  Watergate scandal and, 145, 146–47

Graley, Ezra, 130, 137, 140

Grant, Robert, 199, 316

Grassley, Charles, 220

Gray, Nellie, 232, 240, 252, 321

Great Awakening, 2–3, 372

Great Revival (Second Great Awakening), 3–4

Green, John, 295

Green v. Connally, 169

Griffin, Michael, 355

Grimstead, Jay, 354

Guardians of Traditional Education, 135

Guillermin, Pierre, 71

Guinness, Os, 157, 159, 356, 365

Gunn, David, 355

Guttmacher, Alan, 101

Hahn, Jessica, 275

Haldeman, H. R., 98, 145, 146

Hard Core Parental Group, 135

Hargis, Bill, 77–78

Hargis, Billy James, 37, 38, 39, 76–79, 95, 345

Harrell, David E., 212

Hart, Pat, 335–39

Hatch, Orrin, 252

Hate Crimes Bill (1990), 314–15

Hatfield, Mark, 83, 91, 98

Health, Education, and Welfare, U.S. Department of, 161

Hearst, William Randolph, 27, 29

Hefner, Christie, 315

Helms, Jesse, 172–73, 226, 227, 232, 252, 317

Henry, Carl F. H., 51–52

Henry, Patrick, 373, 374
Heritage Foundation, 135–36, 138, 141–42,
    171, 192, 214, 305, 330
Heritage USA, 275
Hill, Avis, 130, 137
Hill, E. V., 248–49
Hill, Paul, 355
Hilton, Conrad, 41
Hitler, Adolf, 20
Hobbs, Lottie Beth, 165, 166, 214
Home schooling, 139, 332
Homosexuals (homosexuality), 100–101,
    105–6, 164–66, 178, 205, 211, 347.
    See also AIDS; Gay rights; Lesbians
  Bush and, 314–16
  intolerance and violence against, 247
Hoover, Herbert, 19
Hoover, J. Edgar, 69
Horan, Marvin, 127, 128, 137, 138
Horton, Michael, 363, 364
Hour of Decision (radio program), 30
House Un-American Activities Committee
    (HUAC), 35
Howard, A. E. Dick, 380
Howe, Eleanor, 103–7, 109–10, 115–16
How Should We Then Live? (film and book),
    160, 195, 197
HUAC (House Un-American Activities
    Committee), 38
Humanism, 195. See also Secular humanism
Humanist Manifesto, 195
Human Life Amendment, 358
Human Life Statute (Helms-Hyde bill),
    226–27
Humbard, Rex, 206, 213
Hunt, H. L., 76
Hyde, Henry, 214, 226, 240

"I Love America" rallies, 203
Immigration, 6, 367
IMPACT (Institute of Mobilized Prophetic
    Activated Christian Training), 355
Improvement Association (Lynchburg), 66
Inerrancy of Scripture. See Biblical
    inerrancy
Integration. See also Civil rights movement;
    Racism; Segregation
  Falwell and, 57–58, 219
  Goldwater's view of, 85
  Graham and, 43–45
Intercessors for America, 153
Interchurch World Movement, 16
Internal Revenue Service (IRS), 78, 169,
    171–73, 192, 198, 256, 269–70, 275
  Christian schools and, 172, 173
International Christian Leadership, 40–41

International Council of Christian
    Churches (ICCC), 22
International Jew, The, 12
Iowa
  1988 presidential campaign and, 277,
    286, 288
Israel, 201, 204, 209, 263, 365
Is the School House the Proper Place to Teach
    Raw Sex? (Drake), 107–8

Jackson, Jesse, 219, 279
Jefferson, Thomas, 372–74, 376, 377, 379
Jehovah's Witnesses, 379
Jepsen, Roger, 230–31
Jesus Movement, 94
Jews, 9, 11, 215, 375, 378. See also Anti-
    semitism
John Birch Society, 75, 76, 77, 83, 107,
    114, 119, 135, 138
John Paul II, Pope, 367
Johns, Vernon, 59
Johnson, Lady Bird, 164
Johnson, Lyndon, 49, 68, 78
  1964 campaign and election, 84–85
  Graham and, 31, 95–96
Johnson, Torrey, 25
Jones, Bob, Sr., 51, 204
Jordan, Barbara, 154, 164
Jorstad, Erling, 36, 75
Judd, Walter, 48, 92

Kanawha County, West Virginia
  schoolbook controversy in, 119–43
  sex education in, 117–19
Kanawha County Coalition for Quality
    Education, 130
Kasich, John, 330
Kaub, Verne, 37, 39
Kelly, Patrick F., 323
Kemp, Jack, 252, 267, 269, 271, 272, 277,
    286, 288, 290, 310
Kemper, Vicki, 296
Kennedy, D. James, 198, 200, 209, 212,
    254, 322, 354
Kennedy, John F., 47–54, 74, 78, 80, 287
  on right-wing fringe, 75–76
Kentucky, teaching of evolution in, 14
Khrushchev, Nikita, 76
Kilberg, Bobbie Greene, 310, 312–16, 326,
    329, 331, 332, 333–34, 365
Kilpatrick, James, 186
King, Martin Luther, Jr., 22, 44, 49, 59,
    60, 64, 69, 79–80, 212, 321, 322, 357,
    366
King, Martin Luther, Sr., 154
Kinsey, Alfred, 101

Kinsolving, Matthew, 124, 127
Kissinger, Henry, 213, 214
Koop, C. Everett, 156, 193–94, 231
  abortion issue and, 238–41
  AIDS and, 241–42, 248, 249–57
  background of, 238
Koppel, Ted, 276
Korean war, 35
Krol, Cardinal, 98–99
Ku Klux Klan, 45, 138
Ku Klux Klan Act, 323, 324

Labor unions
  Graham and, 33
LaHaye, Beverly, 164, 177, 178, 184, 196,
  214, 301, 305, 311, 335
LaHaye, Tim, 184, 189–90, 191, 196, 200,
  211, 214, 242–43, 270
Lake County, Florida, public schools in,
  334–39
Lance Tarrance and Associates, 172, 192
Land, Richard, 315
Laxalt, Paul, 230
Leadership Foundation, 233
Leadership Institute, 362
Lear, Norman, 282
Leif, Harold, 102, 110, 114–15
Lemon v. Kurtzman, 380
Lesbians, 164, 165. *See also* Gay rights;
  Homosexuals
Let Our Children Pray (television special),
  233
"Letter from Birmingham Jail" (King), 79
Levinson, Sanford, 382–83
Lewis, C. S., 263
Lewis, James (Jim), 130–33, 138, 141–42
Liberty Federation, 270
Liberty Foundation, 270
Liberty University (Lynchburg Baptist
  College, Liberty Bible College), 55,
  71, 196–97, 203–4, 233–34, 248, 253,
  271
Library Court Group, 181, 214, 230
Lincoln, Abraham, 92
Lincoln, Levi, 377
Lindbergh, Charles, 366
Lindsey, Hal, 92
Lippmann, Walter, 14
Locke, John, 372
Lodge, Henry Cabot, Jr., 82
Long, Huey, 21
Luce, Henry, 30, 54
Lutherans, 15
Lynchburg, Virginia, 55, 60
  Civil rights movement in, 61–68, 72–73.

  See also Jerry Falwell; Moral Majority;
  Liberty University
Lynchburg Baptist College. *See* Liberty
  University
Lynchburg Christian Academy, 70–72
Lynchburg College, 61
Lynchburg News, 70, 71

MacArthur, Douglas, 32
McAteer, Ed, 191, 199, 200, 214, 215, 228,
  234, 253, 259
McCarthy, Joseph, 20, 21, 34–35, 37–39,
  49, 80
McCartney, Bill, 348–52
McCloskey, Paul "Pete," 284
McCormack, Billy, 299
McCormack, John, 30, 50
McDowell, Josh, 93
McGraw, Onalee, 181
Machen, J. Gresham, 16
McIntire, Carl, 16, 22, 35–40, 51, 78, 79,
  137
McKenna, James, 135, 140–41
Maddox, Robert, 151, 188–89, 211
Madison, James, 372–77, 384
Manhoff, Ira, 282–83
Mansfield, Mike, 50
Mapplethorpe, Robert, 303
March for Life, 189, 212, 232, 252
Marshall, John, 3
Marshner, Connaught "Connie," 174–77,
  180–84, 187, 192, 214, 229, 230, 231
Mason, James O., 243
Matalin, Mary, 272, 285
Matthews, J. B., 37
Matusow, Allen, 100
Mears, Henrietta, 28
Meese, Ed, 217, 223, 224, 228
Mellon, Janet, 135, 136, 138
*Memorial and Remonstrance Against Religious
  Assessments* (Madison), 373
Mencken, H. L., 15, 20–21
Methodists, 4, 15
Metzger, Leigh Ann, 316–17
Michigan, Robertson's 1988 presidential
  campaign and, 260, 261, 262, 265–93,
  295, 297
Michigan Committee for Freedom PAC,
  270, 272
Millennialism, 4, 5, 7
Miller, William Lee, 375
Minersville School District v. Gobitis, 379
"Ministers and Marchers" sermon (Falwell),
  69, 219
Moffett, James, 124–25, 128, 132, 133–34,
  136, 137, 139, 140, 141

Mondale, Walter, 155
Moody, D. L., 7, 8
Moody Bible Institute, 8, 17
Moon, Sun Myung, 270
Moore, Alice, 117–20, 122–29, 137, 140,
     141
Moral Majority, 2, 55, 200–205, 210, 218–
     19, 228–29, 232, 258, 268, 270, 282,
     296, 298, 300, 331–32, 360–61, 366,
     368
  Reagan administration and, 236
Moral Majority Report, 231
Mosaic Law, 353
Moyers, Bill, 84, 85
Muffett, James, 280, 288, 292, 297, 369
Multiculturalism, 338
  Kanawha County schoolbook controversy
     and, 130–31
Myths and legends, 126

NAACP, 59–60, 65, 66
NAFTA (North American Free Trade
     Agreement), 334
National Affairs Briefing (1980), 214–16
National Association of Broadcasters, 19
National Association of Evangelicals (NAE),
     23, 43, 51, 52
National Christian Action Coalition, 172
National Convention on the Crisis in
     Education, The, 112
National Council of Churches, 36
National Education Association, 111, 137
National Empowerment Television (NET),
     331
National Endowment for the Arts, 303
National Gay Task Force, 185
National Legal Foundation, 347
National Organization for Women (NOW),
     162, 164, 240, 282
National Parents League, 138
National Pro-Family Rally, 165
National Religious Broadcasters, 189, 233,
     262
National Women's Conference (1977),
     163–67
Nazi Germany, 20
Nebraska Seven, 332
New Christian Right. See Religious Right
New Deal, 36
New Evangelicalism, 40, 41
New Jersey
  sex education in, 114
New Right, 88, 121, 174–75, 192, 220–22,
     229, 231, 235, 258. See also Heritage
     Foundation; Phillips, Howard;
     Viguerie, Richard; Weyrich, Paul

New World Order, The (Robertson), 333,
     367
Niebuhr, Reinhold, 53, 157
Nixon, Richard, 82, 95, 151, 174
  1960 presidential campaign and, 48, 49,
     51–53, 74
  1968 presidential campaign, 95–97
  Goldwater and, 84, 86
  Graham and, 31, 41–42, 48, 49, 95, 96–
     97, 145, 146–47
  Watergate scandal and, 145–49
  White House Sunday services under, 97–
     98
Noebel, David, 345–49
Non-Christian American Parents, 127
Norquist, Grover, 300–301, 306, 362
Norris, J. Frank, 17
North, Gary, 353
North American Man/Boy Love
     Association, 348
Northern Baptist Church, 16
Novak, Michael, 154
Novak, Robert (Bob), 207, 251
Nuttle, Marc, 262, 270, 283, 287, 297

Ockenga, Harold John, 40, 50, 51
O'Connor, John Cardinal, 322
O'Connor, Sandra Day, 227–30
Old Time Gospel Hour (television program),
     197
Oliver, Revilo P., 78
Operation Rescue (OR), 320, 321–25, 355,
     356
Orange County, California, 304. See also
     Anaheim, California, sex education in
Orthodox Presbyterian Church, 16
Oswald, Lee Harvey, 78
Overcast, Sharon, 163–64, 178, 184
Owen, Rebecca, 60–66, 62
Oxnam, G. Bromley, 38, 49–50

Packer, Lori, 260, 292, 297
Paine, Thomas, 3
Parental Rights Act, 340
Parents of New York United, 135
Parochial schools, 155, 325, 340. See also
     Private schools
  aid to, 98
Patriarchalism, 161
Patterson, Paige, 207
Patterson's Drugstore, 62, 66
Paul (Apostle), 161
Pavlov's Children (film), 107
Peale, Norman Vincent, 52, 53, 54, 146
Pearson, Drew, 45
Pearson, Judy, 336

Pentecostal Christians, 172, 199, 212, 240,
    258–59, 267–68, 280, 294
People for the American Way, 282, 328
Percy, Charles, 213
Perfectionism (sanctification), 4, 343
Perkins, Will, 348
Peterson, Jay Allen, 180
Pew, J. Howard, 152
Phillips, Howard, 171, 192, 199, 200, 214,
    222, 358
Pietism, 201–2
Pines, Burton, 331
Planned Parenthood, 101
Playboy (magazine), 315
Playboy magazine, Carter interview in, 157–
    58
Pledge of Allegiance, 379
Pluralism, 384
    Reconstructionist view of, 353–54
Poe, Edgar Allan, 121–22
Political activism, 197–205, 360–70. *See also*
    Christian Coalition; Moral Majority
Porter, Philip, 352
Postmillennialism, 7, 354
Potera, Kathy, 267–68, 280–81, 292–93
Powell, Colin, 344, 358
Powell, Jody, 148, 149, 150, 178, 197, 211,
    358
Pratt, Lawrence (Larry), 135, 183, 184
Prayer and Bible reading in the public
    schools, 71, 77–78, 86, 168, 192, 232–
    33, 378–82
Premillennialism, 7–8, 12, 36, 201
Presbyterian Church, 15
Presbyterian Church in America, 16
Presbyterian Church in the U.S.A., 16
Presidential campaigns and elections
    1952, 31–33
    1960, 47–54, 74
    1964, 82–88
    1968, 95–97
    1972, 145–46
    1976, 153–59
    1980, 213–15, 219–20
    1984, 235–36
    1988, 261–98
    1992, 325–28, 329
    1996, 357
Presidential Prayer Breakfasts, 40
Private schools (Christian schools; Parochial
    schools), 98, 139, 155, 168–69, 171–
    73, 325, 340, 378
Pro-Family Coalition, 181
Prohibition, 10, 13, 383
Pro-life groups. *See* Abortion
Promise Keepers, 350–53

Protocols of the Learned Elders of Zion, 12, 20
PTL Network, 275, 276
Public Health Service, 255, 256
Public schools, 245, 274, 325, 332, 353
    Anaheim, California, 102–16
    Kanawha County, West Virginia, 119–43
    Lake County, Florida, 334–39
    prayer and Bible-reading in, 77–78, 86,
        168, 192, 232–33, 378, 380–82
    sex education in, 102–19
Puritans, 1–2

Quayle, Dan, 294, 328
Quayle, Marilyn, 325
Quigley, Charles, 130

Rabey, Steve, 341
Racism, 47, 57–73, 78–79. *See also* Civil
    rights movement; Integration;
    Segregation
    Graham and, 42–44
Rader, Paul, 11
Radio programs, 18, 76, 341–42
Rafferty, Max, 102, 112, 138
Ramsey, Claudia, 336
Randolph-Macon College, 61
Reagan, Nancy, 231
Reagan, Ronald, 207–9, 209–10, 220–37,
    300, 309, 310
    1964 presidential campaign, 87, 89
    1966 gubernatorial campaign, 89–91
    1980 presidential campaign, 213–15, 220
    abortion issue and, 226–29
    AIDS and, 255–56
    economic recovery as priority of, 222,
        225
    evangelical Christians' access to, 223–25
    evangelical Christians in administration
        of, 221–23
    Falwell and, 223, 232–35
    National Affairs Briefing (1980) and,
        214–18
    O'Connor's nomination to the Supreme
        Court and, 227–30
    school prayer and, 232–33
    social agenda and, 222–23, 231–36
Reconstructionism, 353–55
Reed, Jo Anne, 302–4
Reed, Ralph, 299–309, 318, 319, 333, 343,
    344, 364–66
    1992 presidential campaign and, 325–28
    abortion issue and, 356–59
    background of, 300–301
    Christian Coalition and, 302–9, 365, 366
    on Clinton, 329–30
    Contract with America and, 340

Regier, Jerry, 152, 179–80, 184–85, 222
Rehnquist, William, 85, 377
Religious Equality Amendment, 340
Religious freedom, 376, 377, 381
Religious radio and television programs. *See*
    Radio programs; Television preachers
Religious Roundtable, 199, 259, 270, 328
Religious tolerance (religious freedom),
    371–74
Republican party, 300, 313–14, 361–63.
    See also Presidential campaigns and
    elections
    1964 national convention, 82–84
    1980, 213–14
    1988, 261, 290–94
    1992, 325–27
    Robertson's effect on, 296, 297
Rescue America, 324–25, 355
Revivals, 2–5, 8
Ribuffo, Leo, 12, 21
Richardson, Sid, 30, 31, 32
Right On (newspaper), 94
Riley, William Bell, 11, 16, 17
Rivera, Geraldo, 339
Roberts, Oral, 213, 275
Robertson, A. Willis, 31, 258
Robertson, Pat, 151, 157, 160, 166, 172,
    206, 212, 258–62, 299, 325, 347, 354,
    364, 366, 367
    1988 presidential campaign and, 261–62,
        265–74, 276–98
    abortion issue and, 322, 324
    AIDS and, 252, 254, 282, 283
    announcement of candidacy (1980), 281–
        83
    Central American activities of, 284
    Korean war and, 284
    The New World Order, 333
    public image of, 274–75, 277–78
    Reed and, 299–303, 305
    resignation of ordination, 280–81
    Swaggart scandal and, 288–89
Robinson, Haywood, 67, 68, 69, 72, 73
Robinson, Mary, 178, 179, 190
Robison, James, 167, 198–99, 205–6, 211–
    12, 213, 220, 228, 236–37
    National Affairs Briefing (1980) and,
        214–18
Rockefeller, Nelson, 80–84, 147, 213
Rodgers, Guy, 151–52, 305–7, 310–11,
    317, 320, 328, 329, 361
Roe v. Wade, 192
Rogers, Adrian, 206, 212, 234
Roman Catholic Church
    1960 presidential campaign and, 49–53

Roman Catholics, 47, 250, 361, 366–68,
    378
    1960 presidential campaign and, 49–53
    abortion issue and, 193
    Nixon and, 98–99
Roosevelt, Franklin D., 19, 20, 36, 361
Rousseau, Jean-Jacques, 373
Rushdoony, Rousas John, 353, 354
Rusher, William, 82
Rutherford Institute, 361

Salinger, Pierre, 55
Salvi, John, 356
Sanctification. *See* Perfectionism
San Diego County, California, 318–19
Schaeffer, Francis, 156, 159–60, 194–97,
    204, 238, 239, 263, 321, 323, 345
Schaeffer, Franky, 194, 195
Scheidler, Joseph, 321
Schlafly, Phyllis, 115, 165–66, 181, 231
    AIDS and, 250–53
    A Choice, Not an Echo, 81–82
    Equal Rights Amendment and, 162–64
    Goldwater and, 81, 87, 88
Schmitz, John, 107, 113
Schoolbooks, controversy over, 119–43, 335
School prayer. *See* Prayer in public schools
Schools. *See* Private schools (Christian
    schools); Public schools
Schuller, Robert, 213, 214–15, 293
Schwarz, Fred C., 39, 81
Schweiker, Richard, 226, 239
SCLC. *See* Southern Christian Leadership
    Conference
Scopes, John T., 14–15
Secchia, Peter, 265, 271–74, 291, 297
Second Coming of Christ, 7, 8
Second Great Awakening (Great Revival),
    3–4, 5
Secular humanism, 195–97, 332, 335, 344–
    45, 383
Segregation. *See also* Civil rights movement;
    Integration
    defense or justification of, 78–79
    Goldwater's view of, 85
    Graham and, 43–45
    See also Civil rights movement
Separation of church and state, 364, 371–85
Separatism of fundamentalists, 8, 36, 201–2,
    204
Serrano, Andres, 303
700 Club, 284–85, 328
Sex education, 101, 102–16, 254, 336
    AIDS and, 250–52
    in Anaheim, California, 102–16

in Kanawha County, West Virginia, 117–19

Sex Information and Education Council of the U.S. (SIECUS), 101–2, 106, 110, 112, 113, 114

Sexual attitudes and behavior, 100–102

Shafer, Emmett "Lefty," 129, 140

Shakarian, Demos, 212

Shannon, Barbara Thomas, 60–62, 64–66, 68

Shea, George Beverly, 41

Shepard, Charles, 275

Shilts, Randy, 256

Shipley, Maynard, 15

Shuler, "Fighting Bob," 17

SIECUS. See Sex Information and Education Council of the U.S.

Simonds, Robert, 319, 336

Smathers, George, 54

Smeal, Eleanor, 164–65

Smith, Al, 20, 47

Smith, Bailey, 157, 215, 216, 234

Smith, Gerald L. K., 20–22

Smith, Mary Louise, 214

Smothers, Clay, 166

Snapp, Constance (Connie), 273, 274, 276, 278, 283, 286–87, 296

Snyder, Walter, 118, 119

Social Gospel, 6, 9–10, 12, 368

Southern Baptists, Southern Baptist Convention (SBC), 15, 43, 64, 145, 148, 149, 151, 152, 156, 157, 158, 234, 244, 295

Sparks, Jack, 94

Specter, Arlen, 281

Speaking in tongues, 258–59, 267, 279, 280–81, 295

Stanley, Charles, 189, 198, 200, 206, 212, 234

Stapleton, Ruth Carter, 150

States' rights, 79

Stealth techniques, 318, 319

Steinbacher, John, 103, 107–10, 113, 115

Stevenson, Adlai, 33

Straton, John Roach, 11

Students for America, 299, 301

Summit Ministries, 345–46

Sunday, Billy, 8–11, 13

Sunday laws, 378

Sundseth, Carolyn, 297

Sununu, John, 312, 313, 316

Supreme Court, 192. See also Warren Court; and specific decisions

Swaggart, Jimmy, 213, 289

Tarrance, Lance, 172, 192

Television preachers, 212–13, 276. See also individual preachers; national broadcasters

Terry, Randall, 320–25, 355, 356, 357, 359

Texas, textbook adoption in, 120–21

Textbooks. See Schoolbooks

Theonomy. See Reconstructionism

Thomas, Barbara. See Shannon, Barbara Thomas

Thomas, Cal, 225, 227, 228

Thomas, Clarence, 317

Thomas Road Baptist Church, 56–58, 68, 69, 70, 72

Thornburgh, Richard, 213

Thornhill, M. W., 59, 68, 72

Thurmond, Strom, 29–30

Timmerman, George Bell, 44

Towns, Elmer, 210

Townsend, James, 81, 84, 85, 89, 105, 106, 107, 109, 111–15

Tribulation period, 7

Truman, Harry S, 27, 29, 30, 31

Tucker, Jim Guy, 174, 177, 180, 183

Tustin, California, 304

Twentieth Century Reformation, 76

Understanding the Times Curriculum, 346

Underwood, Kenneth, 119, 128, 129, 132, 133, 134

Unification Church, 270

United Nations, 35, 80

United States v. Winrod, 20

University of California at Berkeley, 90, 91, 93–94

University of California at Los Angeles (UCLA), 94

USA Today, Operation Rescue ad in, 325

Venable, James, 138

Vereide, Abraham, 40

Vietnam war, 96, 144

Viguerie, Richard, 88–89, 204, 205, 222, 232, 250

Virginia. See Jerry Falwell; Pat Robertson; Lynchburg; Moral Majority; Christian Coalition
  1994 Kilberg-Farris contest in, 331–34
  religious freedom in, 372–74

Virginia Seminary, 58, 60, 61, 66

Voltaire, 3

Voluntary associations, 5

Vouchers, school, 298, 325, 340, 368

Walker, Edwin, 77

Wallace, George, 79, 95

Wallace v. Jaffree, 380

Walters, David, 272, 280, 286, 295, 297
Walton, Rus, 86, 152, 192
Wardell, Dave, 349–50
Warren, Earl, 41, 77, 78
Warren Court, 77, 101
Washington, George, 375
Washington for Jesus (1980), 212
Watergate scandal, 145–49
Watt, James, 222, 234
Waxman, Henry, 240, 256
Wead, Doug, 262–67, 269, 286, 289, 293,
     294, 311–17, 342, 361, 363
Weinhold, Dick, 303, 306
Welch, Robert, 75, 78
Welfare system, 155, 308, 329, 340, 353,
     367
Westminster Theological Seminary, 16
West Virginia, sex education in, 117–19
Weyrich, Paul, 135, 169–75, 181, 192, 199,
     200, 203, 206, 214, 218, 220, 250,
     252, 261, 293, 302, 311, 356, 362
  Christian Coalition and, 307–8, 331
  National Empowerment Television
     (NET) and, 331
  Reagan administration and, 222–24, 230,
     235
  Robertson and, 283, 284
WFAA, 198–99
Whatever Happened to the Human Race? (film
     and book), 194, 195, 239, 240, 321
White, Mel, 160, 195, 254, 255
White, Ryan, 255
White, Theodore H., 82, 84, 87
White Citizens Councils, 45
Whitefield, George, 2

White House Conference on Families
     (1980), 155–56, 173–90
  Baltimore meeting, 181–86
  definition of "family" and, 177–79
  delegates to, 175–77, 180–81
  gay rights movement and, 185
  walkout of pro-family delegates, 183–85
Whittlesey, Faith, 210, 224, 225, 235
Wichita, Kansas, Operation Rescue in,
     322–24
Wildmon, Donald, 243
Williams, Sally, 102, 103, 105, 106, 110,
     111, 113
Willke, Jack, 226
Wilson, Woodrow, 9
Winrod, Gerald, 19–20
Women, role of, 161–67, 351–52. See also
     Equal Rights Amendment (ERA)
Wood, Virgil, 58–60, 64–69, 369–70
Woodbridge, John, 360, 364–65
Wooten, Jim, 158–59
World Council of Churches, 22, 36
World's Christian Fundamentals Association
     (WCFA), 11
Wortz, Lori Packer. See Packer, Lori
Wyrtzen, Jack, 25

Youth for Christ International (YFC), 25–
     28
Youth organizations, 91. See also Campus
     Crusade for Christ; Youth for Christ

Zion, Roger, 137
Zone, Richard, 199

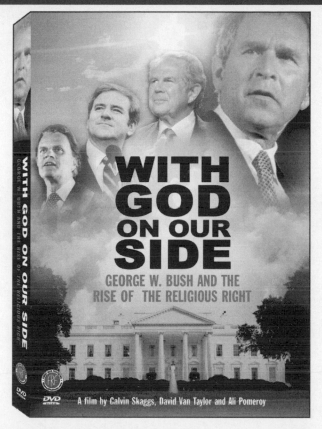